The archaeology of southern Africa

Some of the earliest human populations lived in southern Africa, and evidence from sites there has inspired key debates on human origins and on the emergence of modern humans. The sub-continent has one of the world's richest heritages of rock art, and specialists have developed innovative theories about its meaning and significance that have influenced the understanding of rock art everywhere. Passionate arguments about the hunter-gatherer way of life have centred on southern African cases, and the relationship between archaeological and anthropological data is also central to understanding the past of southern Africa's pastoralist and farmer communities. The precolonial states of the region provide some of the best-documented cases of the influence of external trade on the development of African polities. Peter Mitchell has produced the first comprehensive modern synthesis of the sub-continent's archaeology. His book offers a thorough-going overview of 3 million years of southern African history.

PETER MITCHELL is Lecturer in African Prehistory at the University of Oxford, and Tutor and Fellow in Archaeology at St Hugh's College, Oxford. He has taught previously at the University of Wales, Lampeter, and at the University of Cape Town. He has travelled widely in southern Africa and in other parts of the continent, and has undertaken two major fieldwork projects in Lesotho.

CAMBRIDGE WORLD ARCHAEOLOGY

Series editor
NORMAN YOFFEE, *University of Michigan*

Editorial board
SUSAN ALCOCK, *University of Michigan*
TOM DILLEHAY, *University of Kentucky*
STEPHEN SHENNAN, *University College, London*
CARLA SINOPOLI, *University of Michigan*

The Cambridge World Archaeology series is addressed to students and professional archaeologists, and to academics in related disciplines. Most volumes present a survey of the archaeology of a region of the world, providing an up-to-date account of research and integrating recent findings with new concerns of interpretation. While the focus is on a specific region, broader cultural trends are discussed and the implications of regional findings for cross-cultural interpretations considered. The authors also bring anthropological and historical expertise to bear on archaeological problems and show how both new data and changing intellectual trends in archaeology shape inferences about the past. More recently, the series has expanded to include thematic volumes.

Books in the series
A.F. HARDING, *European Societies in the Bronze Age*
RAYMOND ALLCHIN AND BRIDGET ALLCHIN, *The Rise of Civilization in India and Pakistan*
CLIVE GAMBLE, *The Palaeolithic Settlement of Europe*
CHARLES HIGHAM, *Archaeology of Mainland South East Asia*
SARAH MILLEDGE NELSON, *The Archaeology of Korea*
DAVID PHILLIPSON, *African Archaeology (second revised edition)*
OLIVER DICKINSON, *The Aegean Bronze Age*
KAREN OLSEN BRUHNS, *Ancient South America*
ALASDAIR WHITTLE, *Europe in the Neolithic*
CHARLES HIGHAM, *The Bronze Age of Southeast Asia*
CLIVE GAMBLE, *The Palaeolithic Societies of Europe*
DAN POTTS, *The Archaeology of Elam*
NICHOLAS DAVID AND CAROL KRAMER, *Ethnoarchaeology in Action*
CATHERINE PERLÈS, *The Early Neolithic in Greece*
JAMES WHITLEY, *The Archaeology of Ancient Greece*
PETER MITCHELL, *The Archaeology of Southern Africa*

THE ARCHAEOLOGY OF SOUTHERN AFRICA

PETER MITCHELL

University of Oxford

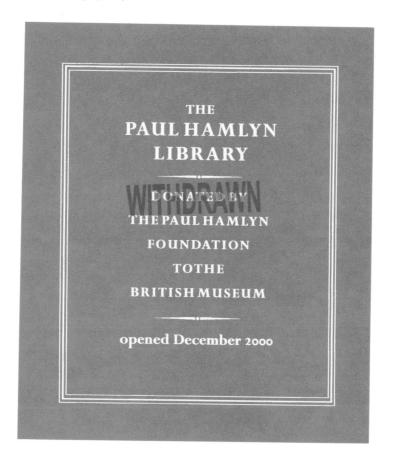

CAMBRIDGE
UNIVERSITY PRESS

PUBLISHED BY THE PRESS SYNDICATE OF THE UNIVERSITY OF CAMBRIDGE
The Pitt Building, Trumpington Street, Cambridge, United Kingdom

CAMBRIDGE UNIVERSITY PRESS
The Edinburgh Building, Cambridge CB2 2RU, UK
40 West 20th Street, New York, NY 10011-4211, USA
477 Williamstown Road, Port Melbourne, VIC 3207, Australia
Ruiz de Alarcón 13, 28014 Madrid, Spain
Dock House, The Waterfront, Cape Town 8001, South Africa

http://www.cambridge.org

First published 2002

Printed in the United Kingdom at the University Press, Cambridge

Typeface Trump Medieval 10/13pt   *System* LaTeX 2_ε [TB]

A catalogue record for this book is available from the British Library

ISBN 0 521 63307 9 hardback
ISBN 0 521 63389 3 paperback

African edition

ISBN 0 521 53382 1

CONTENTS

ILLUSTRATIONS

TABLES

ACKNOWLEDGEMENTS

As an outsider to southern Africa I have benefited enormously from the generosity and help of numerous people over the years, not least in answering questions or supplying offprints during the writing of this book. I should particularly like to thank Gabeba Abrahams-Willis, Graham Avery, Margaret Avery, Lucinda Backwell, Peter Beaumont, Jo Behrens, Johan Binneman, Charles Bollong, James Brink, Yvonne Brink, Ron Clarke, Dave Collett, Glenda Cox, Hilary Deacon (who hosted me on my first visit in 1985), Janette Deacon, Kobus Dreyer, Mandy Esterhuysen, Dave Halkett, Martin Hall, Simon Hall, Zoë Henderson, Chris Henshilwood, Tom Huffman, Gwilym Hughes, Leon Jacobson, Chopi Jerardino, Pieter Jolly, Jonathan Kaplan, John Kinahan, Jane Klose, Kathy Kuman, Julia Lee Thorp, David Lewis-Williams, Jannie Loubser, Tim Maggs, Antonia Malan, Tony Manhire, Anne Markell, Aron Mazel, Duncan Miller, Alan Morris, David Morris, Peter Nilssen, Sven Ouzman, John Parkington (to whom I owe my first teaching opportunity and a subsequent research fellowship at the University of Cape Town), Innocent Pikirayi, Ina Plug, Frans Prins, Frans Roodt, Hester Roodt, Thembi Russell, Karim Sadr, Garth Sampson, Alex Schoeman, Carmel Schrire, Judy Sealy, Paul Sinclair, Andy Smith, Ben Smith, Janette Smith, Lukas Smits, Anne Solomon, Charlotte Tagart, Mike Taylor, Taole Tesele, Anne Thackeray, Francis Thackeray, Carolyn Thorp, Maria van der Ryst, Len van Schalkwyk, Patricia Vinnicombe, John Vogel, Lyn Wadley, Lita Webley, Gavin Whitelaw, Bonny Williamson, Margot Winer, Marilee Wood, Stephan Woodborne, John Wright and Royden Yates. I have indicated in the captions to the figures those colleagues, many of them listed above, who kindly provided original illustrations or photographs, or who agreed to allow previously published material to be reused.

Some of those I have listed have also helped greatly to improve the text and minimise its errors and omissions. For shouldering this task I thank Yvonne Brink, Mandy Esterhuysen, Ray Inskeep, Kathy Kuman, Innocent Pikirayi, Andrew Reid, Karim Sadr, Garth Sampson, Judy Sealy, Ben Smith, Anne Thackeray, Francis Thackeray, Lita Webley and Gavin Whitelaw, as well as three new researchers, John Hobart, Fumiko Ohinata and Chris Wingfield, the last of whom also bravely took on producing the maps with the assistance of a grant from Oxford University's School of Archaeology. Thanks too to Dan Walsh for help with xeroxing.

Among non-archaeologists in southern Africa the help and friendship of Mark and Theresa Cotterell, Joe, Moira and Andrew Forrest, Bruce and Polly Hargreaves, Andrew and Ingrid LaTrobe, David and Corlia Richardson and Edward Roelofse were invaluable. Specifically as regards my own fieldwork in Lesotho it is a pleasure to acknowledge the support of the Lesotho Protection and Preservation Commission and its Chairwoman, Mrs N. Khitsane. I also thank David Ambrose, Lukas Smits and the chiefs and people of Ha Maimane, Ha Makotoko, Ha Mapola, Khomo-ea-Mollo, Sehonghong and Tloutle Ha Mpiti, especially Bo-Ntate T. Mapola, M. Phutsoe and J. Sengoara. Fieldwork is impossible without fieldworkers and another debt is therefore owed to all those, Basotho, South African, British and American, who have worked with me, but especially to Ruth Charles, Toby Durden, the late David Hall, Gordon Laurens, John Steinberg and Deacon Turner.

Many of the ideas reflected in this book were developed through successive years of teaching undergraduate and graduate students at the Universities of Cape Town, Lampeter and Oxford. To all of them my thanks, as well as to those British-based colleagues, particularly Larry Barham, Nick Barton, Derek Roe and Alison Roberts, who have been sources of stimulation over the years. My introduction to southern African archaeology is due to two teachers, colleagues and friends who have always provided tremendous moral and intellectual support, never once letting me lose enthusiasm for either Africa or archaeology: to Ray Inskeep and to Pat Carter my gratitude. Thanks too to my parents and brother for their constant encouragement and interest.

I should also like to thank Chris Gosden for the initial suggestion to attempt a synthesis of southern African archaeology, Jessica Kuper for her editorial support, Frances Brown for copy-editing and the rest of the CUP production staff.

Lastly, but in all ways first, my thanks to Gloria, Chiara and Cesare for continually reminding me how much more there is to life than writing or archaeology and for asking so many insightful and challenging questions. *Mille grazie.*

St Hugh's College, Oxford
November 2000

CHAPTER I

INTRODUCTION

Outside the East African Rift Valley, southern Africa has the longest record of human occupation anywhere in the world, one that reaches back over 3 million years. Spanning more than 20° of latitude from the Zambezi to Cape Agulhas, southern Africa's more than 3,000,000 km² encompass a wide range of ecological zones and a great diversity of human societies. As well as offering the opportunity to examine how the human lineage has evolved and adapted to environmental change over most of its existence, research in the sub-continent is increasingly pertinent to several major debates in contemporary archaeology. Despite having sites that are less fine grained and more difficult to date than many of those in East Africa, it has yielded by far the largest number of individual australopithecine specimens. Continuing excavation of sites in the Sterkfontein Valley promises to increase still further understanding of the evolutionary significance and adaptations of these early **hominins**. In addition, some of the oldest known fossils of anatomically modern *Homo sapiens sapiens* come from sites in present-day South Africa that also play a critical rôle in debates over the behavioural capabilities of these early modern humans. Together with still older specimens of Middle Pleistocene age, such as that from Florisbad, these sites offer crucial support to the case for a recent origin for all modern humans south of the Sahara, subsequent to *Homo*'s initial dispersal from the continent nearly 2 million years ago.

Both these issues are of global interest, but so too is the archaeology of recent southern African foragers. In the Kalahari Bushmen both prehistory and social anthropology found rôle-models for hunter-gatherer societies, as attested in numerous textbooks. However, archaeological, anthropological and historical research over the past twenty years has reappraised the extent to which ethnographically known Kalahari foragers can reasonably be employed as analogues for reconstructing past hunter-gatherer societies in southern Africa, or elsewhere. The impacts of contact with pastoralist and farming communities, in particular, have been the subject of intense discussion and research. Over the same two decades southern African archaeologists have turned to Bushman ethnography to explore the social and ideological dimensions of their data, most effectively in developing an 'insider' perspective from which to understand the region's rich rock art heritage. Combined with insights derived from neuropsychology, the shamanistic view of the art developed principally by

David Lewis-Williams, though now undergoing critique in southern Africa itself, has been widely used to investigate rock art elsewhere in the world, from Europe's Upper Palaeolithic caves and Neolithic megalithic monuments to the engravings and paintings of America's Great Basin.

Southern Africa remained exclusively a sub-continent of hunter-gatherers until little more than two millennia ago. However, the changes in social organisation and more intensive forms of landscape and resource use evident over the past 20,000 years merit more comparison with developments in other parts of the world than they have hitherto received. In particular, such comparisons can be mutually informative when made with other regions, such as Australia and much of North America, where intensifying exploitation of key animal and plant resources did *not* result in domestication and the development of indigenous forms of farming. When food-production was introduced to the sub-continent all the domesticates came from further north. Over the western third of southern Africa a pastoralist lifestyle marked by the herding of sheep and/or cattle came to dominate, while in the summer rainfall regions on the sub-continent's northern margins and across its eastern half iron-using, Bantu-speaking farmers combined livestock-rearing with the cultivation of cereals and other crops. The relationships between pastoralists, farmers and surviving hunter-gatherers and the mechanisms by which food-production spread constitute one of the most active areas of current archaeological research within southern Africa.

Less than a millennium after establishing themselves south of the Zambezi, farming communities were engaging in long-distance trade networks that linked them with the East African coast and, ultimately, the Middle East, India and China. Core–periphery models have been widely used by archaeologists since the 1980s to explore the rôle of external trade in state formation and state collapse. Despite the internationally high profile of Great Zimbabwe, southern Africa's contribution to these discussions has not been as great as it could be, and both archaeologists and (for the more recent past) historians have questioned the significance of external trade in the origins and maintenance of the Zimbabwe state, its predecessors and successors and the nineteenth-century Zulu kingdom. Perhaps less well recognised is the comparatively early date of European settlement – in the 1500s by the Portuguese and from 1652 by the Dutch. Though historical archaeology is a comparatively recent development in the sub-continent, its rapid growth should allow comparisons with other parts of the world, especially in the development of distinctive settler identities and the relations between coloniser, colonised and enslaved.

Exploring these and other developments in a way that illustrates the richness and complexity of the southern African record and its relevance for the wider global picture is one of the objectives of this book. A second is to provide an overview of southern Africa's past as reconstructed from archaeological sources for the entire 3 million years or so of hominin presence in the sub-continent.

The overall thrust of the narrative is chronological and thus, in one sense, cultural-historical. But I hope too to have covered in as balanced a way as possible the key debates within southern African archaeology, without falling into the trap of assuming that only one theoretical orientation holds a monopoly of wisdom or applicability. While I have tried to be as thorough as possible in discussing the archaeological record, in the interests of allowing the reader to investigate specific issues further I have confined references to the published literature or, where unavoidable, graduate theses. Reports from contract archaeology operations are increasingly important as sources of primary data, but they are generally much more difficult to obtain or check. For the same reason, references to works 'in press', unpublished conference papers and personal communications have also been avoided.

Several recent detailed syntheses of aspects of southern African archaeology are already in print, including books on Iron Age farming communities (M. Hall 1987), rock art (Dowson 1992; Dowson and Lewis-Williams 1994; Lewis-Williams and Dowson 1999) and Stone Age foragers and hominins (H. Deacon and Deacon 1999). All, however, like the component chapters of Klein's (1984a) synthesis of palaeoenvironmental and archaeological research, A.B. Smith's (1992a) analysis of prehistoric pastoralism, M. Hall's (1993) review of the archaeology of European settlement and even Inskeep's (1978) overview treat specific periods of southern Africa's past. Other syntheses of the Middle Stone Age (A. Thackeray 1992) and Later Stone Age (Wadley 1993; Mitchell 1997) are further restricted to those parts of the sub-continent lying south of the Limpopo, for which several regional summaries also exist, among them Voigt (1981), Parkington and Hall (1987a), Evers *et al.* (1988), Beaumont and Morris (1990), A.B. Smith and Mütti (1992), A.B. Smith (1995a) and Dreyer *et al.* (1996). Botswana (Lane *et al.* 1998) and Zimbabwe (Pwiti 1997a) have also recently been surveyed in depth. Forty years on from the last synthesis of southern Africa's past from *Australopithecus* to the modern era (J.D. Clark 1959), the time thus seems ripe for attempting another overview of the whole of the sub-continent's past.

Sources and structure

Archaeology is, of course, only one of several sources for the investigation of this past. Allied disciplines in the social and natural sciences also provide much important information. However, archaeology, with the related fields of palaeoanthropology and palaeoenvironmental research, is by far the most wide ranging in both time and space. To be sure, the sub-continent's indigenous peoples all have their own historical traditions, and these have been intensively researched to help reconstruct the precolonial past of, for example, the Shona (Beach 1980; Mudenge 1988), Xhosa (Peires 1981) and Pedi (Delius 1983). While the concentration of these sources on political or mythical events which validate present political and social arrangements means that they are often highly selective in their emphasis, combined with archaeological research they offer a much fuller picture than is possible from archaeological data alone.

Except among the Swahili settlements of the northern Mozambican coast, no southern African society used writing prior to European colonisation. The earliest documents relating to the sub-continent are thus in Arabic and reach back to the tenth century. Yet even well-informed writers, such as al-Masʿudi and Ibn Battuta, had a limited knowledge of the region, restricted almost entirely to the Indian Ocean coast. Only for the last four to five centuries are written sources more plentiful, initially mostly in Portuguese and Dutch. English and, to a lesser extent, other languages became important in the nineteenth century as European exploration and colonisation of the sub-continent's interior intensified. The writings of explorers, missionaries and government officials provide detailed accounts of the landscapes and peoples of many parts of southern Africa. With appropriate cautions, such as their competence in local vernaculars, they have been extensively used by archaeologists working on recent sites. Recent developments in the archaeology of European colonial settlement create a further locus of interaction between the archaeological record and contemporary documentary sources.

Growing partly out of the interests of colonial administrations, professional anthropological research in southern Africa has been, and is, extensive. Groups such as the Ju/'hoansi (!Kung) and G/wi Bushmen of the Kalahari have served as archetypal hunter-gatherers for generations of anthropology students. Marshall (1976), Lee (1979) and G. Silberbauer (1981) are only three of many classic texts that provide inspiration for much recent Later Stone Age archaeology, along with the incomparable archive built up from late nineteenth-century /Xam Bushman informants by Wilhelm Bleek and Lucy Lloyd. Ethnographic research among Khoe- and Bantu-speaking populations has been similarly influential in recent research on the archaeology of southern Africa's pastoralist and agropastoralist communities. As we shall see, archaeologists and historians are, however, increasingly aware that many of the uses made of anthropological research lean too heavily on widespread generalisations from a few well-known casestudies, rather than careful examination of the diverse contexts from which it is drawn (S. Hall 1990; Lane 1994/95; Webley 1997a).

Historical linguistics, especially the interconnections of the various Bantu languages spoken today in southern Africa, provides a further source for the reconstruction of the sub-continent's past. Archaeologists have sought to correlate ceramic styles with Bantu linguistic divisions (e.g. D. Phillipson 1977; Huffman 1989), but linguists have also offered detailed historical reconstructions (Ownby 1985; Ehret 1982, 1998). However, problematic assumptions about chronology, the rates at which languages change and the extent to which elements of a language's core vocabulary are, or are not, subject to borrowing from other languages (Borland 1986), as well as an apparent lack of interest in relating these speculations to the archaeological record, render many of these reconstructions suspect (M. Hall 1987; D. Phillipson 1999).

Oral traditions, written sources, anthropology and historical linguistics all provide different perspectives on the past from those recovered using archaeological methods. Where archaeology differs is in focusing on material culture (stone tools, pots, settlement plans, plant and animal remains, etc.) as the basis for reconstructing past societies. Additionally, it emphasises investigating the ecological contexts within which societies existed, understanding change over much longer timespans than those typically dealt with by historical and anthropological sources and working with individuals who are usually anonymous rather than named. Chapter 2 proceeds to examine the frameworks within which archaeologists pursue these goals in southern Africa. Relevant frameworks include contemporary and past environmental settings, the establishment of chronologies and the historical development of archaeological research as a whole.

The remainder of the book takes up the human career in southern Africa along broadly chronological lines. Chapter 3 examines the fossil and archaeological background to early hominin evolution, beginning with a focus on Plio-Pleistocene sites in South Africa's Sterkfontein Valley and moving on to discuss the lifestyles of the makers of Acheulean and early Middle Stone Age technologies. The poorer, but no less significant, fossil record from the Middle **Pleistocene** foreshadows one of the crucial themes of chapter 4, the appearance of anatomically modern humans. Some of the key fossil-bearing sites in South Africa are among those central to the related issue examined in this chapter, the extent to which the emergence of a modern skeletal morphology was coeval with that of modern behavioural capacities.

Chapter 5 then considers how southern African populations coped with the challenges and opportunities of living through the quite drastic climatic and environmental changes of the later Pleistocene and the degree to which similarities in subsistence and social behaviour can be traced between them and their Holocene successors. Chapter 6 continues this story across the Pleistocene/Holocene boundary, with one emphasis the interconnections between cultural and environmental change. Chapter 7 then reviews the archaeology of southern African foragers from the middle Holocene down to the introduction of food-production about 2000 years ago. Reflecting the shift in recent work from a predominantly ecological paradigm to one much more interested in social relations and ideology, chapter 8 breaks the chronological narrative to examine current interpretations of southern African rock art and how these have encouraged the use of Bushman ethnography to develop models of Later Stone Age social relations. The Kalahari debate touched on above demonstrates the importance of critically considering how far this dependence on recent, and exclusively southern African, hunter-gatherer ethnography can or should be pursued.

As already indicated, two basic forms of food-production were practised in southern Africa. Chapter 9 considers the introduction and impact of pastoralism across the sub-continent's western third, including the archaeological evidence for the organisation of pastoralist society and the relations between herders and foragers. Chapter 10 looks at the establishment of early farming communities in northern and eastern southern Africa, with the appropriateness of using a direct historical approach to ethnographic analogy again a major theme. In the far north of South Africa and beyond the Limpopo the last thousand years have witnessed the development of the more hierarchically organised, centralised polities of the Zimbabwe Tradition. How they formed, were maintained and collapsed is examined in chapter 11. Chapter 12 emphasises the contemporary development of farming societies further south, including the expansion of agropastoralist settlement onto the **highveld** and relations between farmers, herders and foragers on the western and southern margins of Iron Age settlement.

Chapter 13 then examines the archaeological evidence of colonial settlement and the impact that this had on indigenous populations. As well as land-based research, the growing field of maritime archaeology makes a contribution here. Southern African archaeology is itself a consequence of the colonial experience and chapter 14 thus examines the status of the discipline following recent political changes in the sub-continent. Issues such as the presentation of the past, the reburial of human remains and contract archaeology are increasingly universal ones, but this chapter concentrates on their specifically southern African dimensions. Picking up on this last point, a Glossary covers technical or vernacular terms that are not otherwise defined at their first appearance in the text.

J.D. Clark (1974) asked whether Africa played a peripheral or a paramount part in humanity's past. Affirming the second possibility, he emphasised the continent's rôle in hominin evolution, its 2.5-million-year-old archaeological record and the innovation by African populations of hafted stone tools, microlithic stone-working technologies, pottery manufacture and farming at dates easily comparable to those in other parts of the world. I hope that this book succeeds in demonstrating that in understanding and explaining all of these developments, as well as the others I have mentioned, a southern African perspective is both essential and enriching.

A note on names

More so perhaps than in many other parts of the world the appropriate nomenclature for discussing the peoples of southern Africa and their past is bedevilled by history. No one solution can be acceptable to everyone, but hopefully the terms that I have chosen to use offer least offence and greatest clarity.

Bushmen, San, BaSarwa

The vocabularies of the indigenous hunter-gatherer and herder groups of southern Africa traditionally lacked inclusive names for themselves larger than those of the linguistic unit to which they belonged. This creates a major difficulty for those who wish to talk about them. 'Bushman' first appears in written form in the late seventeenth century (as *Bosjesmans*; Wilson 1986). It came to be employed by Europeans as a generic term for people subsisting primarily from wild resources. However, it also acquired derogatory, pejorative (and, indeed, sexist) overtones, with the result that it began to be replaced in academic writings from the 1960s with the supposedly more neutral and indigenous term 'San', a Nama word for their hunter-gatherer neighbours. Unfortunately, since this literally means 'foragers', implying that those concerned are people of lower status too poor to own livestock, it too is not without problems, one of which is that many forager groups actually speak languages identical or closely related to those of southern Africa's indigenous herders! Another solution is offered by the Botswanan government's change of the Tswana term 'Sarwa' ('Bushman') to 'BaSarwa', the 'Ba' prefix placing it in the same class of nouns as people speaking Tswana and its closest relatives (Wilmsen 1989); the Sotho term 'Baroa' shows a similar predisposition. Perhaps to avoid the problems inherent in both 'Bushman' and 'San', some archaeologists now employ 'Basarwa' when describing Later Stone Age hunter-gatherers outside the confines of modern Botswana (e.g. Bollong *et al.* 1993).

Clearly, none of these terms is ideal and people of hunter-gatherer origin in the Kalahari express different preferences. While Namibia's Ju/'hoansi choose 'Bushmen' over 'San', some Botswanan groups use 'Basarwa', though 'San' and 'Khoe' also have their indigenous advocates (Lee and Hitchcock 1998). In this confused situation I use the term 'Bushman', rejecting any derogatory connotations that it may have and agreeing with Barnard (1992), who sees no reason to employ a Tswana or Nama, rather than an English, word in an international context. I follow him too in spelling the names of individual Bushman groups, but use Ju/'hoansi, their own name for themselves, for the people commonly referred to in the literature as the !Kung, a more all-embracing, linguistic term (after Biesele 1993).

Hottentot, Khoikhoi, Khoekhoen

If 'Bushman' has often been used in a derogatory sense, still more is this true of 'Hottentot'. Widely applied to all Khoisan peoples in the seventeenth and eighteenth centuries, it came to be used specifically for those following a pastoralist lifestyle early in the nineteenth century (Barnard 1992). Later rejected by scholars because of its use as a racist term of abuse, it was replaced by the words

'Khoi', 'Khoikhoi' or 'Khoikhoin', derived from the Nama word for themselves meaning 'person' or 'people'. The modern spelling, followed here, is 'Khoe' and 'Khoekhoen' for the singular and plural respectively, with 'Khoekhoe' usable as an adjective (A.B. Smith 1998). Though in most cases the languages of the Cape herders were not well recorded before they ceased to be spoken, a similar term 'Quena' was noted as the self-referential term for herders living near Cape Town in the seventeenth century (Thom 1952–58).

Khoisan

Schultze (1928) coined this as a collective designation for all southern Africa's indigenous herder and hunter-gatherer peoples. Originally intended as a biological label, it was soon also employed to reflect shared features of language and culture (Schapera 1930). An amalgam of the Nama words 'Khoe' and 'San', its literal meaning is 'person-foragers'. Though not an aboriginal term, it retains considerable popularity among scholars as a general cultural and linguistic term for both Bushmen and Khoekhoen peoples.

'Race', language and economy

The matter is not, of course, as simple as the preceding paragraphs might suggest. As will become apparent, not all Bushman groups are, or necessarily were, hunter-gatherers; some have, probably for several centuries, subsisted by other means (herding, fishing, working as clients for pastoralists and farmers), or shifted back and forth between different subsistence strategies. Furthermore, many, such as the G/wi of the Central Kalahari, speak the same Khoe language as the Khoekhoen, some of whom may have cultivated and, more certainly, temporarily or permanently reverted to a foraging lifestyle after losing their livestock. Only where historical, ethnographic and archaeological evidence is compelling do I therefore refer to Bushman and Khoekhoen communities, elsewhere preferring the more general, if sometimes ambiguous, terms 'hunter-gatherers', 'foragers', 'pastoralists' or 'herders'. In discussing the biological affinities of archaeologically known skeletal populations I follow the practice of the authors concerned (e.g. A. Morris 1992c).

Bantu languages

Bantu languages, which predominate in southern Africa today, classify nouns in different groups, using prefixes to alter the meaning of the stem term. Thus, Lesotho refers to the country of the people known as Basotho (singular Mosotho) who speak the Sesotho language. Strictly speaking, the prefixes should always be employed and the stem capitalised, e.g. BaSotho. However, since many of the Bantu-speaking peoples discussed in this book are already well known to readers of English, I employ the common English name for them, thus Zulu and not AmaZulu.

A note on orthography

Khoisan languages use a number of click sounds, tones and other vocalisations not found in English. The click sounds are represented as follows, with all but the first found in all Khoisan languages:

⊙   the bilabial click, produced by releasing air between the lips, as in a kiss. Found only in !Xõ and in extinct Southern Bushman languages;

/   the dental click, produced by a sucking motion with the tip of the tongue on the teeth, as in the English 'tisk, tisk';

≠   the alveolar click, produced by pulling the tongue sharply away from the alveolar ridge immediately behind the teeth, somewhere between / and ! in sound;

//   the lateral click, produced by placing the tip of the tongue on the roof of the mouth and releasing air on one side of the mouth between the side of the tongue and the cheek, as in urging on a horse;

!   the palatal click, produced by pulling the tip of the tongue sharply away from the front of the hard palate, something like the sound of a cork being removed from a bottle of wine.

Barnard (1992) discusses the orthography of Khoisan languages in greater detail than is possible here, except to note that most non-native speakers find it easiest to avoid pronouncing the click sounds all together. This can be done either by ignoring them completely, pronouncing the word as if they were not present, or by substituting an approximately equivalent non-click sound: p for ⊙, t for / or ≠ and k for // or !.

One final point: as a result of centuries of contact and intermarriage with Khoisan speakers some of the Bantu languages spoken in southern Africa also make use of click sounds, but here they are represented by conventional English letters – c for /, x for // and q for !. All three clicks occur in IsiXhosa, the last two in IsiZulu, SiSwati and SiNdebele and q alone in SeSotho.

CHAPTER 2

FRAMEWORKS

Any account of the past needs a set of guidelines if it is to be understandable. This chapter sketches four of these frameworks for southern Africa, beginning with some of the key geographical influences on human history in the sub-continent. Since both climate and ecology have altered considerably, often cyclically, over the last several million years, I then outline what we know of these changes. Thirdly, I review how they and the remainder of the archaeological record are dated and finally I consider the history of archaeological research in the region. Geographical definitions, like any other, can never be ideal, but when writing about Africa's past most archaeologists employ 'southern Africa' to refer to that part of the continent lying south of the Zambezi and Kunene rivers. Rivers, particularly ones so evidently crossed in the course of time, are arbitrary boundaries: witness both the southward spread of farming and the much later northward movements of *Mfecane* raiders. Some Later Stone Age industries (for example, the Pfupian of Zimbabwe) have connections with others (the Nachikufan) lying to the north, while in both the first and second millennia AD identical ceramic assemblages occur on either side of the Zambezi (for example, the Dambwa, Chinhoyi and Ingombe Ilede industries). And yet biogeographically, archaeologically and ethnographically the lands lying south of the Zambezi and Kunene are distinguishable from south-central Africa (Wellington 1955; H. Deacon and Deacon 1980; Huffman 1989), not least in being home to Africa's diverse Khoisan populations (Barnard 1992). While not ignoring developments and connections further north, this book's focus is therefore on the archaeology of the areas covered by the modern states of Botswana, Lesotho, Namibia, South Africa, Swaziland, Zimbabwe and the southern half of Mozambique (Fig. 2.1).

The physical setting

Southern Africa took on its present outline with the breakup of Gondwanaland 140–120 million years ago (mya). Shortly thereafter, volcanic activity over Lesotho and the South African interior terminated deposition of the sedimentary Karoo Sequence (Moon and Dardis 1988). Significant downwarping followed along the continent's margins and erosion initiated formation of the Great Escarpment, which separates the interior plateau from the coastal

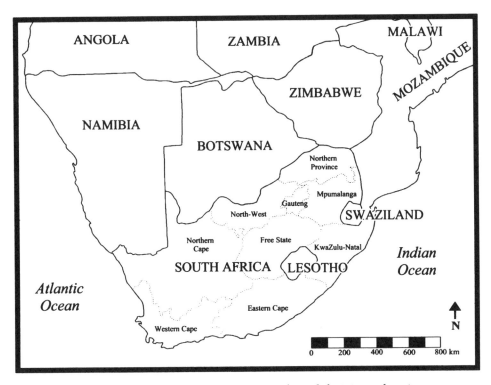

Figure 2.1   Southern Africa: contemporary political divisions showing
international boundaries and the nine provinces of South Africa.

regions. By 65 mya the sub-continent consisted of extensive plains, surrounded
to the east, south and west by a few mountain massifs, such as the Cape Fold
Mountain Belt and the Lesotho and Nyanga Highlands. Major tectonic uplift of
the eastern side of Africa occurred in the late **Pliocene** (Partridge and Maud
1987). Strongly influencing climate and concentrating precipitation on the
windward side of the uplifted areas, this may have helped create the evolutionary conditions for the differentiation of the hominin lineage (Vrba *et al.* 1995).

Today southern Africa can be divided into two main physiographic zones
(Wellington 1955), an inland plateau and the areas marginal to it (Fig. 2.2). Separating them, the Great Escarpment stretches from the highlands of Namibia
and thence inland of the Cape Fold Mountain Belt up into the Drakensberg
and Maluti Mountains and then north through Swaziland and Mpumalanga
(Fig. 2.3). Skipping the Limpopo Valley, it re-emerges as the Chimanimani
Mountains and Nyanga Highlands of eastern Zimbabwe. Only in Mozambique
and KwaZulu-Natal are the low-lying areas coastward of the Escarpment particularly extensive. The comparative shallowness of the continental shelf means
that even at the maximum Pleistocene depression of global sea-levels a large
coastal plain developed only south of the restricted area between the Cape of

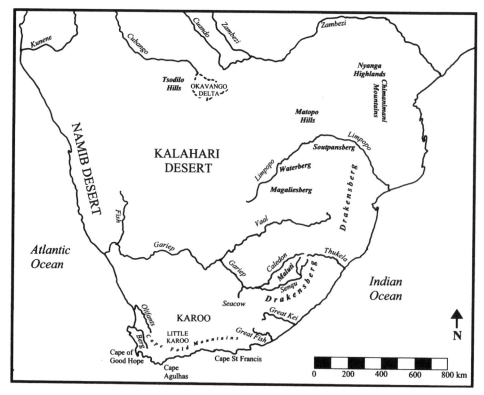

Figure 2.2   Southern Africa: main physiographic features. Rivers are italicised
in plain typeface, mountain ranges italicised in bold.

Good Hope and Cape St Francis. Inland of the Great Escarpment southern Africa
consists of an extensive plateau, dipping slightly to the north and west. In the
central interior, uplift was interrupted by downward movement, producing the
Kalahari Basin, now blanketed in aeolian sands of mostly Quaternary origin.
The Okavango Delta, in the extreme north of this basin, is the only part of
the sub-continent to experience significant tectonic activity today (Moon and
Dardis 1988).

Southern Africa is drained by few major river systems. Rising in north-
western Zambia and eastern Angola, the Zambezi, one of Africa's longest rivers,
flows east to enter the Indian Ocean halfway along the Mozambican coastline.
To the south-east, much of central Zimbabwe forms part of the catchment of the
Save, while several smaller rivers drain its eastern highlands, all flowing into
the Indian Ocean. Dividing southern Africa partly in two, the Limpopo drains
much of northern South Africa, as well as southern Botswana and Zimbabwe.
It too flows through Mozambique to enter the Indian Ocean, but is much less
impediment to movement than the Zambezi. Indeed, in drought years it may
cease to flow continuously above ground, pooling over much of its length.

Figure 2.3   The Drakensberg Escarpment at Cathedral Peak, KwaZulu-Natal, South Africa.

Conversely, as the 1999/2000 summer showed, massively destructive floods can also occur.

The second largest of southern Africa's river systems, the Gariep (formerly Orange) and Vaal Rivers flow west to empty into the Atlantic. Known locally as the Senqu, the former originates in the Lesotho Highlands. The headwaters of the Vaal lie close to the KwaZulu-Natal/Free State border in a northward extension of the Drakensberg Escarpment. A smaller river, the Caledon, drains the western edges of the Lesotho Highlands, adding significantly to the flow of the Gariep, which it joins downstream of Aliwal North. The combined river then flows north-west before merging with the Vaal, after which it turns west towards the sea. Though the Caledon pools in exceptionally dry winters, the Gariep and Vaal are both perennial.

Several smaller drainage basins occupy the area between the coast and the Great Escarpment. The Thukela, Great Kei, Great Fish, Olifants and Berg Rivers are among the most important. Further north, the many rivers draining west from the Escarpment along the Namibian coast are all seasonal. An exception is the Kunene, which drains a small area of south-western Angola. Eastern Namibia and the remainder of Botswana form an inland drainage basin in which most rivers are again highly seasonal. Rising in southern Angola, the Cubango is not, but dissipates itself into the swamplands of the Okavango

Delta. Elsewhere, although southern Africa has several coastal lakes and estuaries (*vleis*) and numerous seasonally filled depressions (*pans*), free-standing surface water is rare. Palaeoenvironmental data indicate that the current aridity ameliorated at times during the Quaternary, but water availability must have been a significant factor in the adaptations of most past inhabitants of the sub-continent.

Precipitation, rather than temperature, is thus the critical climatic factor across most of southern Africa. Two patterns stand out. First, some 90 per cent of the sub-continent experiences comparatively wet summers and dry winters. This summer rainfall pattern derives largely from oceanic air-streams entering the interior from areas of high pressure off the east coast (Wellington 1955). Only in south-western South Africa is this pattern reversed to give a winter rainfall régime. Here the dominant factor is the eastward movement of cyclones from the South Atlantic. The area between these two belts receives rainfall year round. Superimposed on these seasonal régimes is a second pattern in which precipitation declines markedly on moving away from the coast and the orographic potential of the Great Escarpment and the Cape Fold Mountain Belt. Along the Namibian and Namaqualand coasts exceptionally arid conditions are intensified by the cold water upwelling associated with the offshore Benguela Current: the name 'Skeleton Coast' reflects the lack of water in this part of the Namib Desert. Rainfall reliability shows similar trends to the overall level of precipitation, with the Karoo, Namaqualand, the Namib Desert and the Kalahari most susceptible to drought (Wellington 1955).

Because of its elevation and the influence of surrounding oceans southern Africa has a relatively mild temperature régime compared to similar latitudes elsewhere. Nevertheless, mean annual temperatures range from 20–24°C in the southern Kalahari and Mozambique to only 11–12°C in the Lesotho Highlands and the mountains of the Cape. The warm Mozambique/Agulhas Current ensures that temperatures are distinctly higher along the east coast, while the greatest diurnal temperature ranges are experienced in the Karoo, the Kalahari and the Drakensberg and Maluti Mountains. In the winter rainfall area of the Western Cape cold conditions are made more miserable by heavy rains that can persist, unrelentingly, for days at a time. Snow too can fall here on mountain tops, but lasts for more than a few days only at higher altitudes in Lesotho and along the Drakensberg Escarpment.

These climatic and topographic factors help determine the distribution of southern Africa's rich and diverse plant and animal communities. They also provide the basis for constructing an ecological framework that can structure discussions of human adaptations, at least for the recent past. Rutherford and Westfall (1988) use climatological parameters to define a series of terrestrial biomes distinguished from each other by their dominant plant life-forms. With some amendments (Butchart 1995), their classification, which is finding increasing favour with southern African archaeologists (A. Morris

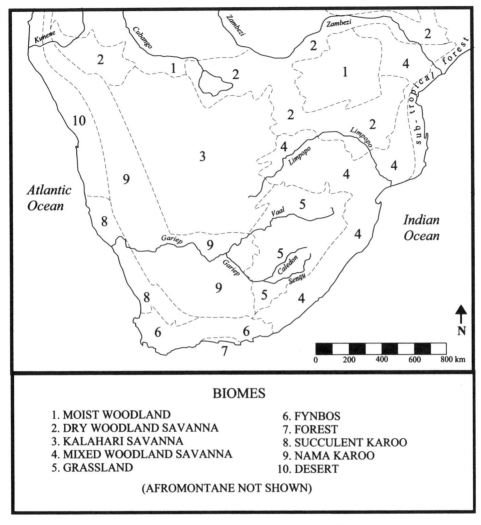

Figure 2.4   Southern Africa's biomes (redrawn after Rutherford and Westfall
1988; Butchart 1995).

1992a; H. Deacon 1993), is followed here (Fig. 2.4). It correlates reasonably well
with the ecological zones of Devred (De Vos 1975) used to structure previous
discussions of Pleistocene mammal faunas (Klein 1984b) and Later Stone Age
archaeology (Wadley 1993; Mitchell 1997).

The Moist Woodland Biome, also known as *miombo*, extends across much
of central Africa south of the tropical rainforest, including north-eastern
Namibia and Zimbabwe's central plateau. It is a wooded savanna in which
Brachystegia and *Julbernardia* often form a closed canopy (Fig. 2.5). Average
precipitation exceeds 500 mm per year and surface water is available throughout
the year. The rich and varied vegetation results in a high diversity of large

Figure 2.5   The Moist Woodland Biome. The *miombo* extends north of the
Zambezi into Zambia, where this photograph was taken (courtesy
Larry Barham).

mammals. Elephant (*Loxodonta africana*), giraffe (*Giraffa camelopardis*), blue
wildebeest (*Connochaetes taurinus*), kudu (*Tragelaphus strepsiceros*), Cape
buffalo (*Syncerus caffer*) and Burchell's zebra (*Equus burchelli*) are particularly
prominent. Fruiting trees offer the major wild plant foods, among them *Parinari*
and *Strychnos*.

To the south lies the Savanna Biome, the largest and geographically most
extensive unit of its kind in southern Africa. Rainfall is generally lower and
surface water less abundant than in the *miombo*. Grasses and shrubby trees
dominate and many plants are fire-adapted. This biome may be subdivided into
three smaller areas (Butchart 1995). In the more arid west (eastern Namibia,
much of Botswana and part of the Northern Cape) is the Kalahari Savanna, its
very open terrain covered by grassland with only scattered trees and shrubs
(Fig. 2.6). Rainfall here is below 400 mm per year, and porous, sandy soils mean
there is no permanent surface water. On its northern edge and extending east
along the Zambezi and central Limpopo valleys into western Mozambique lies a
zone of Dry Woodland, dominated by mopane trees (*Colophospermum mopane*)
and shrubs, that frequently experiences severe droughts; baobabs (*Adansonia
digitata*) are also common (Fig. 2.7). The eastern section of the Savanna Biome,
covering much of lowland Mozambique south of the Zambezi, the remainder of
the **transVaal**, the upper Limpopo Valley and most of Swaziland, forms a zone

Figure 2.6 The Kalahari Savanna Biome looking towards the Kgwebe Hills south of Maun, Botswana (courtesy Andrew Reid).

Figure 2.7 The Dry Woodland Biome, at Savuti, northern Botswana.

Figure 2.8   The Mixed Woodland Biome, Hluhluwe-Umfolozi National Park, KwaZulu-Natal, South Africa.

of Mixed Woodland (Fig. 2.8). Characterised by relatively short trees, including *Acacia*, it is often referred to as 'bushveld'. Low altitude areas of KwaZulu-Natal and the Eastern Cape also belong to this zone, but here subtropical thorn-bush and scrub forest dominate. Large mammal diversity is high throughout the Savanna Biome, which includes many well-known wildlife reserves. The species present are similar to those of the Moist Woodland Biome, with drought-adapted springbok (*Antidorcas marsupialis*) and gemsbok (*Oryx gazella*) common in the Kalahari Savanna. Plant food staples vary. Fruiting trees, such as marula (*Sclerocarya birrea*), and corms are important in the Mixed Woodland zone, other tree species (including *Ricinodendron rautanenii*, source of the celebrated mongongo nut) and legumes, as well as cucurbits, in the Kalahari Savanna.

The Grassland Biome is found on South Africa's high central plateau, extending into Lesotho and elevated inland areas of KwaZulu-Natal and the Eastern Cape. Mountainous in places, especially to the east, this is mainly a flat or rolling landscape (Fig. 2.9). Mean annual rainfall is 400–2000 mm and vegetation is heavily dominated by grasses. Nutritionally better, more palatable 'sweet' species are more common where rainfall is less than 625 mm per year, poorer-quality 'sour' species where precipitation exceeds this. Trees are rare, the grassland being maintained by factors such as frost and fire. Bulbs, tubers, corms and other geophytes are the principal wild plant foods (H. Deacon 1993).

Figure 2.9   The Grassland Biome, Soetdoring Nature Reserve, Free State, South Africa.

In precolonial times, this biome probably had the highest animal biomass of any in southern Africa. Dominant **ungulates** included black wildebeest (*Connochaetes gnou*), springbok, red hartebeest (*Alcelaphus buselaphus*), mountain reedbuck (*Redunca fulvorufula*), blesbok (*Damaliscus dorcas*) and quagga (a now extinct subspecies of Burchell's zebra).

The Nama-Karoo and Succulent Karoo Biomes can be considered together under the term 'Karoo Shrubland' (Butchart 1995). The former covers the central plateau of the Western and Northern Cape, along with the south-western Free State and much of the Namibian interior. The second largest of southern Africa's biomes, it consists of extensive plains, interspersed with **kopjes** or occasional mountains (Figs. 2.10 and 2.11). Mean annual rainfall is 100–520 mm with a summer or year-round rainfall régime. Vegetation is a grassy, dwarf shrubland tolerant of drought. The Succulent Karoo Biome lies to the west, stretching from Lüderitz as far south as Elands Bay and thence eastward to include the Little Karoo. Terrain is similar to that of the Nama-Karoo Biome, but rainfall is year-round or winter in nature, averaging 20–290 mm per year. Most water courses flow only seasonally. Plant communities include large numbers of succulent species, many endemic or nearly so (Werger 1978), and species diversity is high (Fig. 2.12). The succulents avoid drought through

Figure 2.10   Springbok in the Nama-Karoo Biome, Etosha National Park,
Namibia.

Figure 2.11   The Great Karoo between Graaff-Reinet and Aberdeen, Eastern
Cape, South Africa.

Figure 2.12   Spring in the Succulent Karoo Biome, Western Cape, South Africa.
Diepkloof Shelter is in the background.

water storage. Other taxa are also drought-tolerant or -evasive, including the
geophytes which provide many plant food staples. Dominant ungulates are the
same as in the Grassland Biome, with gemsbok and springbok particularly well
represented.

Figure 2.13   Male ostriches, a characteristic faunal element of the Desert Biome, near Sesriem, Namib-Naukluft National Park, Namibia.

The Desert Biome corresponds to the Namib Desert, one of the oldest coastal deserts in the world. Precipitation follows a summer régime, but averages only 13–70 mm per year. Partly responsible for this extreme aridity, the Benguela Current also produces fogs that are a significant source of additional moisture along the coastal belt. Vegetation is very sparse and plant diversity low (Fig. 2.13). Most plants avoid drought by lying dormant as seeds until rain falls. !Nara melons (*Acanthosicyos horrida*) and grass seeds harvested from ant nests were important wild plant staples. Large mammals are rare, with drought-adapted taxa, such as gemsbok, among the most common.

Restricted to the south-western corner of the sub-continent, the **Fynbos** Biome consists of the mountains of the Cape Fold Belt and the adjacent coastal forelands. This is a zone of winter or all-year-round rainfall, varying from 210 mm per year on its interior margins to 750 mm or more per year in favoured parts of the coast and on the windward side of mountains. With grasses rare, the dominant vegetation is a sclerophyllous shrub and heathland similar to those of the Mediterranean and California (Fig. 2.14). The biome corresponds reasonably well to the Cape Floristic Kingdom, one of six in the world, and has an exceptionally high level of species diversity and endemism among plants, insects and some larger animals (Cowling and Richardson 1995). Fires are frequent, most plants are fire-adapted and many require fire for seed germination. Hunter-gatherers may have used fire to manage the productivity of

Figure 2.14   The Fynbos Biome in winter near the Doring River, Western Cape, South Africa.

edible geophytes, which were the main wild plant staple (H. Deacon 1993). Though grazers occur, browsing species assume greater importance than elsewhere in southern Africa. They include the endemic Cape grysbok (*Raphicerus melanotis*), as well as steenbok (*R. campestris*) and common duiker (*Sylvicapra grimmia*).

Two smaller biomes complete the picture. The Forest Biome concentrates in a zone of dense, evergreen forest in the Wilderness/Knysna area of the Western Cape's south coast (Fig. 2.15). Smaller patches of montane forest are scattered along the slopes of the Great Escarpment as far as Zimbabwe, while a narrow belt of subtropical forest extends along the coast of the Savanna Biome. In almost all these areas heavy logging has greatly altered forest size and composition. Though birds are numerous, mammals are few, with some species endemic. Bushpig (*Potamochoerus porcus*) and small browsing antelope, such as blue duiker (*Philantomba monticola*) and red duiker (*Cephalophus natalensis*), are typical. Lastly, the Afromontane Biome occurs on the higher (above 2800 m above sea-level) reaches of the Drakensberg and Maluti Mountains (Fig. 2.16). Vegetation consists of sourveld grasses and heath species allied to those of the montane parts of the Fynbos Biome. Some species endemic here also occur in high-altitude areas of the Rift Valley and Ethiopia. The few large mammals include oribi (*Ourebia ourebi*) and klipspringer (*Oreotragus oreotragus*).

Figure 2.15   The Forest Biome looking east along the coast near Matjes River, Western Cape, South Africa.

Reconstructing past environments

The environments just described are, of course, subject to constant change. Some of these changes are short term and cyclical in nature. There is, for example, an eighteen-year-long cycle in total precipitation over the summer rainfall area, with nine predominantly wet years followed by nine mostly dry ones, and shorter-lived oscillations in the Karoo Shrubland and Fynbos Biomes (Tyson 1986). During the last 2000 years longer pulses of alternating warmer/wetter and cooler/drier conditions have affected the summer rainfall area (Tyson and Lindesay 1992). Over a timescale of tens or hundreds of

Figure 2.16   The Afromontane Biome, Maluti Mountains, central Lesotho.

millennia not only cyclical pulses of climatic change are detectable, linked to global patterns of glaciation and deglaciation, but also long-term directional changes. One example, with major implications for species biodiversity, was the initiation of a winter rainfall régime in the south-western Cape about 2.6 mya (Partridge 1997). Though many of the ecological changes encountered in succeeding chapters may have been gradual, their effects not obvious even within the space of several generations, this was not always the case. There is increasing evidence, much of it admittedly from better-studied higher-latitude regions in the northern hemisphere where changes may have been more intense, that some were extremely rapid, dramatically altering the environments and climates with which people had to cope (cf. Alley *et al.* 1993).

Though there is little evidence for glaciation having occurred even on the highest summits of the Drakensberg/Maluti Mountains (Grab 2000), ice ages nevertheless form the background for understanding climatic change in southern Africa over the timespan which this book considers. The basic framework derives from studies of deep-sea cores containing the stratified remains of marine micro-organisms (Foraminifera). The ratio of two oxygen isotopes (^{16}O and ^{18}O) in these fossils tracks changes in total global ice volume and, secondarily, in global temperature. Over the last 800,000 years, for example, nineteen successive **oxygen isotope stages** are recognised, each representing a warm or cold stage, the former (interglacials) designated by an odd number, the latter (glacials) by an even one, counting back from the present. Deep-sea cores are dated by a combination of radiocarbon in their upper reaches, uranium-series dating, palaeomagnetism and extrapolated sedimentation rates (Lowe and Walker 1994). They are complemented and refined by cores drilled through the Greenland and Antarctic ice caps, which give an annual record of shifts in temperature and other climatic parameters based on isotope content and physico-chemical analyses of ice and trapped dust particles. Once again, cyclical changes between colder and warmer stages are evident.

Fundamental to understanding these changes in global climate are periodic variations in the orbital geometry of the earth which affect the amount of solar radiation it receives. These Milankovitch cycles comprise a 100,000 year cycle produced by the eccentricity of the earth's orbit around the sun, a 41,000 year cycle due to changes in the tilt of its axis and a 19,000–23,000 year cycle derived from the wobble (or precession) in its spin on its axis (Imbrie and Imbrie 1979). The deep-sea and ice-core records show cycles of similar length. The connection may lie in the ways in which the Milankovitch factors influence ocean currents in a 'conveyor belt' system that can flip between glacial and interglacial modes (Broecker and Denton 1990). However, additional factors are needed to explain what triggered the onset of ice ages in the first instance. One possibility is the shift in global air circulation patterns set in motion by the tectonic uplift of the Tibetan Plateau, another changes in ocean currents brought about by the closing of the isthmus of Panama. Declines in global carbon dioxide levels, producing a reversal of the well-known 'greenhouse effect' and the cooling effects of volcanic eruptions which eject dust particles into the upper atmosphere may also be implicated. Taken together, the result has been to mark the last 2.8 million years with recurrent pulses of climate change, pulses which have become longer and more intense over the last 900,000 years (Lowe and Walker 1994).

Deep-sea cores and ice cores provide a continuous record of climatic change on a world scale. However, the southern African evidence for reconstructing past environments comes from a diverse range of terrestrial sources, in which deposition has typically been much more episodic. Correlating this evidence with the oxygen isotope framework is not straightforward. Where absolute dates are available, derived from the radiometric techniques discussed in the next section, we can be confident of the links made. The difficulty comes when stratified patterns in our terrestrial palaeoenvironmental indicators are used to infer broadbrush palaeoclimatic conditions which are then slotted into the oxygen isotope framework. The correlations made *may* be correct, but the scales of change and the sensitivities of our indicators are largely unknown and the opportunities for mismatching tremendous. However appealing as an argument for dating Middle Stone Age (MSA) cave deposits (see the critique offered by Parkington 1990a) or occupation of southern Africa's arid interior

(Sampson 1985a; Beaumont 1986), there can be no substitute for chronologies that are independent of the climatic data they seek to date (Van Andel 1989; A. Thackeray 1992). This is one of several challenges in reliably reconstructing southern Africa's past environments. Another is the paucity of long terrestrial records at single sites which extend back beyond 130,000 years ago. For these reasons I confine subsequent discussion of the available indicators and what they can tell us of past environments in the sub-continent to this period. Given the periodic nature of Quaternary climatic changes it is likely that, at least in broad terms, the picture obtained has some validity for earlier parts of the Pleistocene. Given too the rapid pace of global climatic change and its likely impact, especially through aridification, on biome diversity and extent in southern Africa (Midgley *et al.* 2000), an understanding of past ecological shifts obtained from archaeological data may prove increasingly important in predicting and managing future change.

Reconstructing **Quaternary** palaeoenvironments draws upon a wide range of specialists and data (Partridge and Maud 2000). Geomorphological evidence is important and includes the study of ancient dune systems (Lancaster 2000), alluvial sediments (Zawada 2000), periglacial landforms (Grab 2000), sea-level regressions (Illenberger and Verhagen 1990) and the isotopic composition of ancient groundwater and speleothems (Lee Thorp and Talma 2000). Sediments in rock-shelter and cave deposits are thus important (Butzer 1984a), along with those in fossil lake basins (e.g. Robbins *et al.* 1998). Coring of the Tswaing Crater near Pretoria provides one of the longest continuous sequences known for the sub-continent. Sediment analyses here define variations in rainfall that closely track the 23,000 year Milankovitch cycle of orbital precession and extend back some 200,000 years (Partridge 1999). Isotopic and colour density analyses of a stalagmite in Cold Air Cave, Makapansgat Valley, Northern Province, provide a more highly resolved sequence (in the order of five to ten years) for the last 6600 years (Lee Thorp and Talma 2000).

Biological sources of information are more widespread, not least from archaeological sites, where plant and animal remains were often introduced by people. This does, however, raise issues of cultural selection (Shackleton and Prins 1992), and the further difficulty that when people were absent so may have been many key palaeoenvironmental indicators; 'off-site' data, such as pollen analysis of spring deposits (Coetzee 1967) or **dassie** (*Procavia capensis*) middens (Scott and Bousman 1990), are thus vital in providing biologically grounded palaeoenvironmental evidence that is independent of human activity. Work in and around Boomplaas Cave in the southern Cape provides one of the most detailed records of palaeoenvironmental change over the last 80,000 years (H. Deacon *et al.* 1984). Specific indicators analysed included pollen, charcoals from people's fires (H. Deacon *et al.* 1983b; Scholtz 1986), large mammals (Klein 1978a) and variations in their size (Klein 1986a, 1991), and the ecologically more sensitive rodents and insectivores introduced by owls

(D.M. Avery 1982). These studies are complemented by oxygen isotope measurements of speleothems in the nearby Cango Caves (Talma and Vogel 1992). In other areas of the sub-continent, where climatic changes altered the spatial or altitudinal distributions of C3- and C4-plant species following different photosynthetic pathways, analysis of the stable carbon isotope composition of faunal remains and sedimentary deposits (J.C. Vogel 1983; J. Smith 1997) provides additional evidence. Tree rings can also be used where suitable species exist (M. Hall 1976; Dunwiddie and LaMarche 1980).

Even using all these datasets, further cautions are warranted. First, many palaeoenvironmental inferences are often necessarily expressed in vague, descriptive fashion, as 'cooler' or 'drier' than the present or what went before (van Andel 1989). Data from some micromammal and pollen analyses have been subjected to multivariate analyses to derive absolute measures of past temperature (J.F. Thackeray 1987, 1988a, 1990a), but these remain few. Moving beyond this to discuss, in anything remotely resembling concrete terms, the consequences of climatic change on the availability, predictability and density of food and water resources has scarcely begun. Nevertheless, much progress has been made in reconstructing Quaternary environments (J. Deacon and Lancaster 1988; Partridge and Maud 2000). This permits the thumbnail sketch of how they have altered over the past 130,000 years contained in Table 2.1, organised around successive oxygen isotope stages (OIS).

Dating

To bring order to the archaeological and palaeoenvironmental evidence for past human activity in southern Africa a sound chronology is essential (Figs. 2.17 and 2.18). The basic principles of stratigraphy and typology, developed in the nineteenth century (Trigger 1989), remain fundamental. Interestingly, the former, in the sense of long, deep sequences of superimposed occupations, is best developed for hunter-gatherer sites of the Middle and Later Stone Ages, where rock shelters often served as magnets attracting people back to the same place over and over again. Typological studies of the relationships between the design of different artefact types, by contrast, are more important for dating the archaeological materials that characterise agriculturalists. Ceramics form the chronological basis here, while they and other artefacts, such as tobacco pipes, can be used to age colonial sites.

As in other parts of the world for which written sources are few or limited in time-depth, placing chronologies derived from stratigraphic and typological inferences on an absolute footing was, before the application of radiometric dating techniques, often impossible. In rare circumstances datable connections could be made with chronologically better-known regions. Thus, finds of imported pottery and glass beads of ultimately Middle Eastern, Indian or

Table 2.1 *Southern Africa: palaeoenvironmental summary for the past*
130,000 years

Oxygen isotope stage (OIS)	Date kyr BP	Conditions
5e	127–117	Last Interglacial; temperatures slightly warmer than today, with slightly higher sea-levels and significantly more rainfall in the summer rainfall zone. Winter rainfall zone drier than today.
5d–5a	117–70	Gradually deteriorating climate with two cooler (OIS 5d and 5b) and two warmer (OIS 5c and 5a) intervals.
4	70–60	Lower Pleniglacial, a period of severely cold conditions.
3	60–25	Inter-Pleniglacial, a period of sharply oscillating conditions, but generally cooler than present. Much of southern Africa saw the wettest conditions of the past 130,000 years during parts of this timespan, e.g. in the Kalahari Savanna and Fynbos Biomes.
2	25–10	Upper Pleniglacial, the coldest period of the last glacial/interglacial cycle. Mean temperatures 5–6°C lower than today with sea-levels dropping 120 m. Generally drier than now, perhaps a quarter to a half below the modern average, except in the winter rainfall zone where increased precipitation continued. Aridity was also possibly concentrated around the Last Glacial Maximum (LGM; 18,000 BP) in the Kalahari, though active dunes are recorded both before and after this. Temperature and then rainfall increased after 15,000 BP, but amelioration was interrupted by the Younger Dryas stadial *c.* 11,000–10,000 BP. Climate became drier again in the Kalahari, Namib and southern Cape after 12,000 years ago.
1	≤10	The Holocene. Fluctuations of temperature and rainfall continued, but on a smaller, if sometimes abrupt, scale with complex patterns of change in both summer and winter rainfall zones. Temperatures generally peaked 1–2°C above today *c.* 7000 BP. Shortlived oscillations included neoglacial episodes *c.* 4200 and 3500–2300 BP, the Medieval Warm Epoch 1050–650 BP and the Little Ice Age 650–150 BP. In general terms, cooler conditions saw rainfall decrease over the summer rainfall zone and increase in the winter rainfall zone, warmer conditions the reverse. Their impact on farming settlement is discussed by Huffman (1996a) and J.C. Vogel and Fuls (1999).

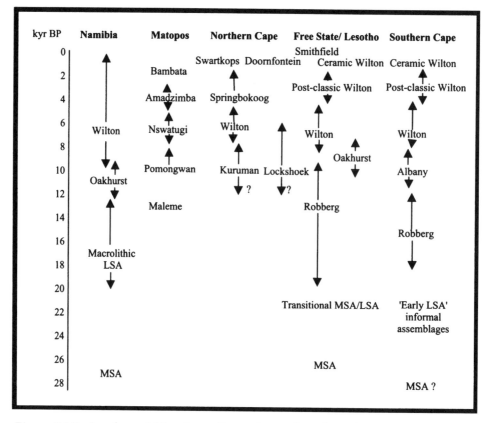

Figure 2.17   Southern Africa: Later Stone Age archaeological traditions in
Namibia, the Matopo Hills, the Northern Cape, the Free State and
Lesotho, and the southern Cape.

Chinese origin help date Great Zimbabwe to the early second millennium AD.
The same methodology allows absolute dates to be placed on associated finds
at other Later Iron Age sites, and dates the last centuries of hunter-gatherer
occupation of South Africa's Seacow Valley (Close and Sampson 1998). Written
records, along with indigenous (oral) historical traditions, provide additional
dating evidence for the recent past, as with the construction and destruction
of the Zulu king Dingane kaSenzangankhona's residence at Mgungundlovu
(Parkington and Cronin 1979) and of the Ndzundza Ndebele royal centre of
KwaMaza (Schoeman 1998a).

Without question, however, it is radiocarbon dating that has established a
sound chronological framework for the last 30,000–40,000 years. That the sub-
continent has its own radiocarbon dating facilities, notably at Pretoria, has
been, and remains, a tremendous asset. Radiocarbon dates are referred to frequently throughout this book, but their use requires some cautions. First, because all are really mean figures within a range, expressed by the accompanying

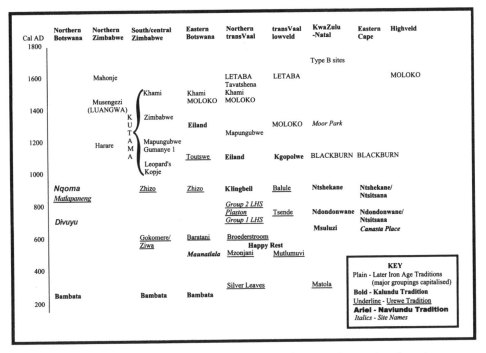

Figure 2.18 Southern Africa: major ceramic traditions of Iron Age farming communities for selected regions of the sub-continent.

standard deviation, and one sample may be contaminated by younger or older carbon, consistent patterns of dates are to be preferred to single dates. Accelerator mass spectrometer (AMS) technology, which directly dates very small samples, has, as yet, been little used. However, results from dating rock paintings in the Drakensberg and Cederberg mountains and sheep bones from presumed early pastoralist sites demonstrate its potential.

A further difficulty arises from the fact that fluctuations in the atmospheric production of the ^{14}C isotope mean that radiocarbon years do not directly equate to calendar years. Though dendrochronologically based calibration curves, corrected for the southern hemisphere, now extend back into the terminal Pleistocene (Stuiver *et al.* 1998), they have been little applied in southern Africa beyond the last two millennia (J.C. Vogel 1995; Huffman 1996a; J.C. Vogel and Fuls 1999). The effects of calibrating radiocarbon dates older than this in order to explore cultural and environmental change on a 'real' timescale have yet to be explored. For the Upper Pleistocene, calibration has been extended backwards using uranium-series dating of raised coral terraces (Bard *et al.* 1991), speleothems and lake sediments (J.C. Vogel and Kronfeld 1997; Kitagawa and van der Plicht 1998). However, all three techniques are still in the early stages of their development and detailed calibration of the period before 10,200 BP is not yet possible (van der Plicht 1999). For all these reasons, all the radiocarbon determinations used here are uncalibrated, *except* in chapters 10–13 where it becomes important to relate the events they date to others dated from historical sources. References there and elsewhere to 'centuries' or 'millennia' without further qualification refer to the Christian calendar and have been calibrated using the Pretoria calibration curve adjusted for the southern hemisphere (Talma and Vogel 1993).

Vital as it is for dating the last few tens of millennia, the radiocarbon method has two further limitations. First, it requires an organic sample, such as charcoal, bone, mollusc shell or ostrich eggshell. Happily, these are found on many archaeological sites, but where scatters of stone artefacts or potsherds lack such materials they cannot be directly dated. Typological considerations then re-emerge strongly, for example in placing the many hundred Later Stone Age Lockshoek sites of South Africa's interior into the broad bracket of 12,000–8,000 BP. Second, the amount of radiocarbon left in any sample is so low after about 40,000 years that it becomes impossible to detect. Even for the period 30,000–40,000 years ago it may be unsafe to use radiocarbon dates since the presence of even a tiny trace of modern carbon could contaminate an older than 40,000 BP (and thus infinite) sample to produce a false, but finite, age (Roberts *et al.* 1994).

Establishing a chronological framework for the remainder of the Quaternary is much more difficult. Many different techniques are used (Aitken *et al.* 1993), including, as we have seen, attempting correlations between palaeoenvironmental inferences and the global oxygen isotope record. More securely, electron spin resonance (ESR), amino-acid racemisation, uranium-series dating and luminescence dating have all been employed to anchor such key sequences as that from Klasies River. All, however, are more specific than radiocarbon in the materials to which they can be applied, while many are still under development. Cross-checking their results against one another is therefore vital. Still further back in time, the chronology of the Earlier Stone Age and of South Africa's early hominin sites rests upon palaeomagnetic measurements and the correlation of artefact typology or associated faunal remains with the radiometrically dated East African record.

History of archaeological research

The history of archaeology in southern Africa divides into five phases, broadly paralleling those noted elsewhere in the world (Trigger 1989; Robertshaw 1990). Each has its own characteristics, but the concerns of one continue into its successors: the overall effect is thus cumulative, rather than one of wholesale replacement. More comprehensive accounts are given by J. Deacon (1990a) and Gowlett (1990) for the Stone Age, A.B. Smith (1992a) for pastoralist archaeology and M. Hall (1990, 1993) for Iron Age and historical archaeology.

From the late fifteenth century the writings of European travellers and government officials include much that is useful to archaeologists, even if they often showed little interest in the history, rather than the contemporary lifeways, of the sub-continent's inhabitants. By the eighteenth century some were commenting on hunter-gatherer or pastoralist use of stone artefacts (Sparrman 1786; Patterson 1790), others on the presence of rock paintings in several parts of the sub-continent. A second phase in the development of southern African archaeology was initiated by such individuals as T.H. Bowker in the Eastern Cape (Cohen 1999), Langham Dale (1870) around Cape Town and Andrew Anderson (1887) over much of the interior, all of whom started collecting prehistoric stone tools from about 1860. Their work was broadly contemporary with, and probably influenced by, the developing acceptance of the genuineness and antiquity of stone artefacts in Europe. Many of their finds were dispatched to Britain, thus drawing them to the attention of a wider public. This simultaneously validated the artefacts and assured collectors of their significance within a broader academic community, itself concerned to use southern African data to establish the worldwide nature of the newly created Stone Age (J. Deacon 1990a). At least some Victorian scientists actively sought out southern African stone artefacts through correspondence with what was a strongly interconnected, if small, network of local antiquarians (Mitchell 1998).

By the early 1880s sufficient had been discovered for the first general syntheses of southern African archaeology to appear (Gooch 1881; Rickard 1881a, 1881b). Paralleling these developments, other scholars reported the continued use of stone artefacts (Kannemeyer 1890), collated historical information about the sub-continent's indigenous populations or commenced the copying of rock paintings (Stow 1905). The detailed testimony recorded from Bushman informants in the Drakensberg (Orpen 1874) and the Northern Cape (W. Bleek 1873, 1875; Lloyd 1889; W. Bleek and Lloyd 1911) has proven essential for understanding southern African rock art but, regrettably, little more such work was done before the extinction of southern Bushman populations at the end of the nineteenth century.

Stone tools and rock art could be linked fairly easily to surviving hunter-gatherers or their ancestors, but Europeans frequently denied that Bantu-speaking farmers had built the many abandoned stone-walled settlements on South Africa's highveld (A. Anderson 1887). A similar refusal to credit the indigenous population with the more complex ruins of the Zimbabwe Plateau initiated a century of ill-informed racist speculation, which did, however, provoke more systematic investigations. Excavations on behalf of the British Association for the Advancement of Science (BAAS) by MacIver (1906) and Caton-Thompson (1931) succeeded in demonstrating that the sites had been built by Africans early in the second millennium. The commitment to careful excavation and detailed ceramic typology lying behind these conclusions stimulated others to begin investigating the archaeology of farming communities elsewhere in the sub-continent (Laidler 1931).

A critical issue in this early phase of research was how to bring chronological order to southern Africa's past, a problem made more serious when Acheulean handaxes in stratified river gravels (Péringuey and Corstophine 1900; Fielden 1905) suggested that it might have a comparable antiquity to that of Europe. At the 1905 BAAS meeting in southern Africa Haddon (1905) advocated the development of an indigenous terminology, free from the assumptions implicit in using European terms. Initial responses saw Péringuey (1911) recognise three main 'types' in the sub-continent's Stone Age and N. Jones (1920) develop the first regional sequences for Zimbabwe and the Northern Cape. Yet both authors retained such classically European terms as 'Solutrean' and 'Mousterian', while farming communities remained in a largely undated limbo preceding the onset of European settlement (M. Hall 1990).

By 1929, when the BAAS again met in southern Africa, a more comprehensive response had been produced, at least for the Stone Age. Its development was principally the work of two men. Goodwin's (1926) studies of museum collections and the combination of his field expertise with that of van Riet Lowe led initially to a bipartite division into an Earlier Stone Age (cf. Acheulean) and a Later Stone Age (LSA). The latter was divided into two industries – Wilton and Smithfield – and a separate Middle Stone Age (MSA) was soon added (Goodwin and van Riet Lowe 1929). Excavations at Bambata Cave demonstrated the scheme's applicability north of the Limpopo (Armstrong 1931), and it was quickly taken up across sub-Saharan Africa. Much modified, it remains in use today.

Armed with Goodwin and van Riet Lowe's terminology, the third phase of archaeological research in southern Africa concentrated on establishing a cultural-historical framework for the past. An 'organic' model of culture took hold, in which the spatio-temporal patterning of different cultures was explained by geography, climate, raw material and diffusion, or migration, from further north. Rock art research followed similar lines (Burkitt 1928). Excavations on South Africa's south coast (Goodwin 1938) and in KwaZulu-Natal highlighted temporal change within industries and differential activity performance as additional influences on assemblage variability (Parkington 1984a). By 1950 a multitude of Stone Age industries had been identified, and Schofield (1948) had begun construction of pottery-based typological sequences for the Iron Age south of the Limpopo. Dart's (1925) publication of the Taung child, and Broom's (1936, 1937) discovery of further australopithecine fossils at Sterkfontein and Kromdraai, alerted archaeologists to southern Africa's potential for understanding early human origins. However, the lack of associated artefacts and continued belief in the Piltdown forgery led many to dismiss them (Gowlett 1990).

In the immediate aftermath of the Second World War radiocarbon dating offered an independent means of dating the past, new fora were created for the dissemination of archaeological research (the *South African Archaeological Bulletin* and the Pan-African Congress on Prehistory) and the number of professionally employed archaeologists began to grow (J. Deacon 1990a). In Zimbabwe this facilitated excavations at Great Zimbabwe, at Khami and in the Nyanga Highlands (K. Robinson 1959, 1961; Summers 1958, 1961) that helped launch professional Iron Age research within southern Africa. Their results and those from renewed excavations at early hominin sites in the transVaal (Gowlett 1990) were incorporated in J.D. Clark's (1959) synthesis of southern African prehistory.

By the early 1960s, however, the existing framework was under strain. The 1965 Burg-Wartenstein Conference showed many Stone Age industries to be poorly defined and in need of reassessment (Inskeep 1967). A new classificatory scheme was proposed (Bishop and Clark 1967). Sampson (1972) employed this in writing up his excavations along the Gariep, but it proved only a partial solution. Key LSA sequences at the Oakhurst (Schrire 1962) and Wilton rock-shelters were also reinvestigated. J. Deacon (1972) interpreted the latter as a single evolving artefact tradition. In contrast, radiocarbon dates suggested that, far from forming a continuous sequence, Goodwin and van Riet Lowe's (1929) Smithfield A Industry was separated from its B and C successors by several thousand years of non-occupation of South Africa's semi-arid interior (J. Deacon 1974).

These changes were one aspect of a more profound paradigm shift in southern African research encouraged by the development of processual archaeology in North America and Britain and foreshadowed by J.D. Clark's (1959) emphasis on situating the archaeological record within an ecological framework. The commitment to an agenda emphasising palaeoenvironmental reconstruction and the investigation of how people had adapted to ecological change through time and space marks the fourth phase of archaeological work in southern Africa, along with an interest in more quantitative approaches to analysing artefacts and other data (J. Deacon 1990a). In the eastern and southern Cape H. Deacon (1976, 1979) set new standards for excavation, facilitated larger projects on Quaternary palaeoenvironments and regional ecosystems (H. Deacon *et al.* 1983a, 1984) and introduced systems thinking to southern African archaeology. Successive LSA industries were modelled as homeostatic plateaux based on the interaction of climate, ecology and human subsistence strategies and technology (H. Deacon 1972). Drawing on anthropological studies of Kalahari foragers and influenced by Cambridge's palaeoeconomy school (Higgs 1972), the effects of resource availability on human behaviour were explored in many other parts of southern Africa (Carter 1978; Wadley 1979, 1984a; Cable 1984; Opperman 1987; N. Walker 1995a). The research of Parkington (1977) and his colleagues in the **farwestern Cape** has been the longest-sustained and most influential of all these projects. Now in its fourth decade, it has also stressed rock art (Yates *et al.* 1994) and helped make stable isotope analysis of human remains a powerful tool for palaeodietary research (Sealy 1989).

Archaeological studies of farming-based societies also underwent sustained growth after 1960. Several projects showed that black farming communities had been present south of the Limpopo since the first millennium AD (Mason *et al.* 1973), exploding the official *apartheid* version of history, which claimed that blacks and whites had arrived there simultaneously (Official Year Book 1974). Yet the disinclination of most archaeologists actively to engage in politics and the sheer effectiveness of racial segregation confined these results to the academy (M. Hall 1990). In Zimbabwe Iron Age archaeology was more effectively popularised by Summers (1971) and Garlake (1973a), but political pressures from the Rhodesia Front régime led to their resignations and/or exile. Despite these events, the end of the 1970s saw a sound cultural-historical framework established for the Iron Age across most of southern Africa (Maggs 1984a). Though some of the research responsible for this also examined iron technology (van der Merwe and Killick 1979), many projects emphasised past subsistence strategies, demonstrating the general prevalence of ecological thinking at this time (Mason 1972; M. Hall 1981; Voigt 1983).

Rock art research too benefited from the more systematic approaches introduced in the 1960s. A series of studies stressed accurate, quantitative recording of all the surviving images in a given area (Maggs 1967; Pager 1971; Fock 1979). Yet it quickly became apparent that this alone could not transcend the simplistic, empiricist interpretations of the past (Lewis-Williams and Loubser 1986). A critical first step was Vinnicombe's (1976) exploration of Bushman mythology. Her insights were taken further by Lewis-Williams (1981a, 1982), who used the largely unpublished Bleek/Lloyd archive to argue that the work of shamans was critical for understanding both rock art imagery and the social relations underpinning hunter-gatherer societies. Similarities with Kalahari Bushman belief systems expanded the material that could be drawn upon (Lewis-Williams and Biesele 1978), allowing the shamanistic model to be extended back into the Pleistocene and to areas away from the Drakensberg. More recently it has become apparent that shamanism does not exhaust all the levels of meaning present in the art and that alternative perspectives also merit consideration (Lewis-Williams and Dowson 1994; Lewis-Williams 1998).

In elaborating a structural-Marxist view of the socio-economic context within which rock art was produced, Lewis-Williams provoked a significant paradigm shift in LSA archaeology. Wadley's (1987) research in the Magaliesberg Mountains and that of Mazel (1989) in the Thukela Basin drew heavily on Bushman ethnography to investigate different aspects of the past from those emphasised by earlier ecological models: gift-exchange, gender relations and the social consequences of seasonal aggregation and dispersal. These ideas have been explored by several writers (e.g. G. Anderson 1996; Engela 1995), but many of their assumptions remain untested, or difficult to operationalise in the archaeological record.

The archaeology of food-producing societies has undergone comparable changes in recent decades, greatly facilitated by the institutional growth of archaeology which followed independence in Botswana, Mozambique and Zimbabwe. An initial theoretical impetus was Huffman's (1980) introduction of a more rigorous approach to ceramic typology which aimed at delineating discrete traditions, interpreted as the material correlates of specific linguistic groups. Kuper's (1980) comparative study of settlement structure among southern African Bantu-speakers allowed Huffman (1986) to distinguish two settlement patterns in the Iron Age, one characterising the state-level societies of the Zimbabwe Tradition, the second all other farming populations south of the Zambezi. Venda and Shona ethnography provided detailed interpretations of the architecture of Great Zimbabwe, Khami and similar sites (Huffman 1996b). But, just as in LSA research, these ethnographically derived models have not gone uncritiqued. Fieldwork in KwaZulu-Natal highlights important differences between the worldviews of first- and second-millennium farming communities (Maggs 1994/95; Whitelaw 1994/95). More significantly, both archaeologists (M. Hall 1987; Lane 1994/95; Mahachi and Ndoro 1997) and historians (Beach 1998) have taken issue with what they see as too selective a use of ethnographic data and too ahistorical a view of the past.

This fifth, contemporary phase of archaeological work shares with broader developments in post-processual archaeology an interest in researching issues of social relations, ideology and cosmology, but it does so enriched by the ethnographies of many of the populations whose ancestors it studies. This is so even if one future trend will probably be a greater concern for understanding the context of the anthropological data employed and renewed interest in using a wider set of ethnographic parallels than has hitherto been the case. How far it is possible to extend a research agenda emphasising social relations back beyond the commencement of the LSA is a moot point. For now research on Middle Stone Age humans continues to stress chronological, palaeoenvironmental and subsistence issues. Still more is this the case when dealing with earlier hominins, where research in the transVaal is currently undergoing a resurgence.

Another important component of current research is the investigation of interactions between societies of different social, economic, political and ideological complexion (e.g. Denbow and Wilmsen 1986; S. Hall 1994; Sampson 1995; Schrire 1995). One major aspect of this process has been the development of historical archaeology, which seeks to trace the growth of European colonial settlements and the formation of the structures of racial oppression and segregation that marked recent southern African history (M. Hall 1993; Pikirayi 1997a). A second has been systematic research into the origins and development of the pastoralist societies ancestral to the modern Khoekhoen and their relations with both foragers and farmers (A.B. Smith 1992a). The breaking down of intradisciplinary boundaries which such work demands and the stress placed on bringing archaeological, anthropological and historical evidence together in enquiring about southern Africa's past also seem likely to continue.

CHAPTER 3

ORIGINS

Hominids and hominins

The many physical and behavioural resemblances between people and Africa's great apes led Darwin (1871) to propose that the continent was the birthplace of the human lineage. Subsequent genetic studies and palaeoanthropological fieldwork have fully confirmed his hypothesis, though only in the 1920s did the first fossil evidence come to light in Zambia and South Africa. The latter find in particular, the Taung child, initiated the search for potential Plio-Pleistocene ancestors in Africa and provided the type-specimen for the genus *Australopithecus* (Dart 1925). Subsequent research has demonstrated that even if southern Africa cannot claim the finely resolved archaeological sites and detailed chronologies of the East African Rift Valley, it has an extensive hominin record of its own and archaeological assemblages that are among the oldest in the world. This chapter considers both these aspects of human origins, beginning with the classic fossil sites of the Sterkfontein Valley and its environs, Taung and Makapansgat, and moving on to discuss the less well known, but equally important, fossil and archaeological evidence of the Middle Pleistocene. Gamble (1993), Foley (1995), Vrba *et al.* (1995) and Klein (1999) discuss the issues on a more global scale than is possible here.

Discussions of human evolution continue to be framed by the classificatory terminology for living organisms devised by Linnaeus in the eighteenth century. This places *Homo sapiens* and its extinct relatives, some of them presumed to have been ancestral to modern humans, within the family Hominidae, itself grouped with the apes into the superfamily Hominoidea. Old World monkeys, New World monkeys, lemurs, bushbabies and tarsiers form the other major divisions of the order Primates. In applying this taxonomy to the fossil record several problems are apparent. First, the Linnaean scheme, formulated in a pre-Darwinian era, does not readily lend itself to discussions of evolution. Where to draw the dividing line within an evolving population is problematic and made worse where populations show considerable **sexual dimorphism**. Neither is the definition of species as reproductively isolated groups applicable in the past where such behaviour cannot be observed. Most classifications thus use morphological (i.e. skeletal) characters, even though many of the features distinguishing species from each other in the present may be differences of coloration or behaviour that do not fossilise. Palaeoanthropologists may therefore underestimate the number of fossil species: Foley (1991a), for example, suggests that for the human lineage at least a quarter of the species which probably existed 2–5 million years ago remain unknown. On the other hand, since the fossil record comprises only a tiny sample of the undoubtedly variable populations from which it derives, undue emphasis may sometimes be given to observed differences, artificially inflating the number of taxa recognised – a problem of excessive splitting, rather than lumping. For all these reasons a view of human evolution in terms of successive adaptive radiations, rather than sharply defined species or genera, may be most helpful (Foley 1992). At least six such radiations can be identified (Fig. 3.1).

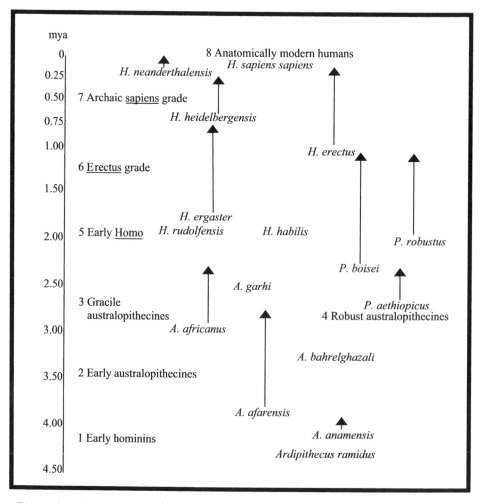

Figure 3.1   Successive radiations in hominin evolution.

A different perspective is offered by analyses of the DNA of modern humans and apes. Supporting Darwin's claim for an African origin for humanity, these studies show that humans and chimpanzees share over 98 per cent of their DNA, with gorillas only marginally less closely related (Ruvolo 1995). This kind of distance is common among very closely related species, although traditionally African apes and humans are placed in separate families. These analyses force a radical reassessment of primate taxonomy (Mann and Weiss 1996). From the standpoint of genetic or molecular systematics, chimpanzees, gorillas and humans are *all* **hominids** (Goodman 1996). The Linnaean names commonly employed by palaeontologists (Table 3.1) thus overemphasise the differences they describe and the term '**hominin**' is increasingly replacing 'hominid' when discussing humans and their immediate fossil ancestors and relatives, a usage followed here.

Comparison of blood proteins and DNA shows that chimpanzees and humans last shared a common ancestor no more than 8–6 mya (Sarich and Wilson 1967; Sibley and Ahlquist 1984). Unfortunately, no relevant fossils of this age are known, but well before 4 mya hominins had certainly evolved. The most substantial collections come from Aramis, Ethiopia, and the Lake Turkana area of northern Kenya (Fig. 3.2). Finds from the former, including a near complete skeleton, are described as *Ardipithecus ramidus* (T. White *et al.* 1994) and those from the latter as *Australopithecus anamensis* (Leakey *et al.* 1995). Dates of 4.4 and 4.2–3.9 mya respectively have been obtained for these fossils, which probably lie close to the base-line from which all other hominins evolved. Later hominins fall into two groups, conventionally treated as distinct genera, *Australopithecus* and *Homo*, though the more robustly built australopithecines from southern and eastern Africa are increasingly placed in a further genus, *Paranthropus*. In very general terms, all australopithecines, while definitely bipedal, retained features which suggest that tree-climbing was still important. Their skulls had small brains (350–530 cm^3), with relatively large, projecting faces and large cheek teeth. Members of the genus *Homo*, by contrast, exhibit trends towards increasing cranial capacity (530–1500 cm^3), stature and body weight, reduction in dentition, jaws and cranial crests, delayed maturation rates and more obligatory bipedalism (Klein 1999).

Between 3 and 4 mya the East African fossil record is represented by over 300 specimens assigned to the species *Australopithecus afarensis*, among them the famous Lucy skeleton from Hadar, Ethiopia (Johanson and Edey 1981). Several skeletal features, including curved phalanges and cranially oriented shoulder joints, indicate that *A. afarensis* spent a significant amount of time climbing trees (Klein 1999). However, other skeletal evidence and 3.7-million-year-old footprints preserved at Laetoli, Tanzania (Hay and Leakey 1982) confirm its bipedal status. Another striking feature is a variability in size that lies at the extreme range of that found among extant apes and humans (Richmond and Jungers 1995). Either this reflects a degree of sexual dimorphism inconsistent

Table 3.1 *Linnaean names of current and fossil hominins and other hominids (extant species in bold typeface)*

Linnaean name	Common name	Age	Comments
Gorilla gorilla	Western gorilla	Extant	Two subspecies recognised: *G. g. gorilla* and *G. g. diehli*
Gorilla beringei	Eastern gorilla	Extant	Probably three subspecies: *G. b beringei, G. b. graueri* and *G. b. indet.*
Pan troglodytes	Chimpanzee	Extant	Four subspecies recognised: *P. t. schweinfurthi, P. t. troglodytes, P. t. vellerosus* and *P. t. verus*
Pan paniscus	Bonobo	Extant	
Hominins			
Ardipithecus ramidus	–	4.4 mya	Known only from Ethiopia
Australopithecus anamensis	–	4.2–3.9 mya	Known only from Kenya
Australopithecus afarensis	–	3.9–2.8 mya	Known only from East Africa
Australopithecus bahrelghazali	–	3.4–3.0 mya	Known only from Chad
Australopithecus africanus	Gracile australopithecines	3.0–2.3 mya	Known only from South Africa; StW 573, a more archaic taxon than *A. africanus*, dates to 3.3 mya (R. Clarke 1999a)
Paranthropus aethiopicus	Robust australopithecines	2.7–2.3 mya	Known only from East Africa; Klein (1999) refers this taxon to *Australopithecus*
Paranthropus boisei	Robust australopithecines	2.3–1.0 mya	Known only from East Africa
Paranthropus robustus	Robust australopithecines	1.8–1.0 mya	Known only from South Africa, Howell *et al.* (1978) recognise *P. crassidens* (from Swartkrans) and *P. robustus* (from Kromdraai)
Australopithecus garhi	–	2.5 mya	Known only from Ethiopia
Homo habilis	–	1.9–1.8 mya	
Homo rudolfensis	–	1.9–1.8 mya	Specimens attributed to *Homo* from Hadar, Lake Baringo and Uraha may also belong to this taxon, extending its age range to 2.3–1.8 mya (Klein 1999)
Homo ergaster	–	1.8–0.6 mya	Known only from Africa
Homo erectus	–	1.0–0.1 mya	Reserved for East and South East Asian specimens after B. Wood (1992)
Homo heidelbergensis	–	0.6–0.2 mya	Known only from Africa and Europe
Homo neanderthalensis	Neanderthals	0.25–0.025 mya	Known only from western Eurasia
Homo sapiens sapiens	Anatomically modern humans	<0.15 mya	

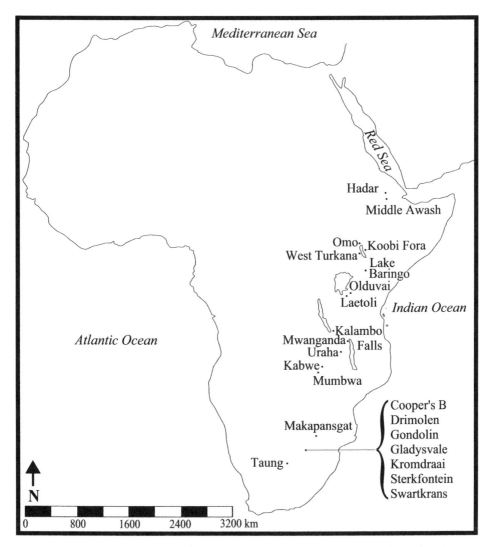

Figure 3.2   Plio-Pleistocene fossil hominin localities in East and South Africa. The locations of four Middle Pleistocene sites north of the Zambezi River – Kabwe, Kalambo Falls, Mumbwa and Mwanganda – are also shown.

with a monogamous social structure, or more than one species is present. Nevertheless, with its distinctly apelike skull and long arms, at least a part of the *A. afarensis* sample was probably ancestral to the several australopithecine taxa recognised after 3 mya (Johanson and White 1979). Identification of a mandible from Chad as similar to *A. afarensis* and its assignment to a new species, *A. bahrelghazali* (Brunet *et al.* 1996), remind us too that hominin evolution may have taken place across a much wider area of the continent, including regions where fossil preservation is much less likely. Nevertheless, the diverse landscapes and rich plant food resources of south-central Africa, extending as far as the northern transVaal, may have provided particularly favourable conditions for hominin speciation (O'Brien and Peters 1999).

Graciles, robusts and the genus *Homo*

Three South African localities have produced fossil evidence of early hominins (Fig. 3.2). Taung, in North-West Province, set the ball rolling in 1924 with the skull of an infant gracile australopithecine, the first Plio-Pleistocene hominin to be discovered (Dart 1925). Though many other fossils have come from this limestone quarry, the Taung child (Fig. 3.3) remains the only hominin discovered there. This isolation limited the impact of Dart's discovery, many anthropologists dismissing it as an ape. Crucial to changing this assessment was Robert Broom's work at three sites (Kromdraai, Sterkfontein and Swartkrans) in the Sterkfontein Valley near Johannesburg. Together they have yielded the remains of several hundred individual australopithecines, as well as a few specimens attributed to *Homo*, making them the most prolific fossil

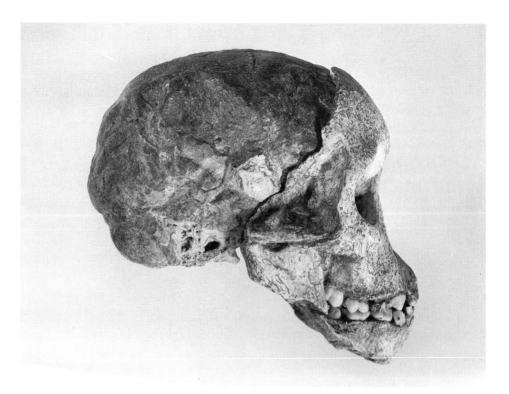

Figure 3.3   The Taung child, *Australopithecus africanus* (courtesy Department of Anatomical Sciences, University of the Witwatersrand).

Figure 3.4   Partial view of the excavation area at Sterkfontein (courtesy Ron
Clarke, Department of Anthropology and Human Genetics, Goethe
University, Frankfurt).

hominin locality anywhere in the world for the period 3.5–1.5 mya. Several
distinct geological members occur at each site, but the overwhelming majority
of the fossils come from Members 4–5 at Sterkfontein (Fig. 3.4), Members 1–3 at
Swartkrans and Member 3 in the eastern excavation area at Kromdraai Cave B
(Klein 1999). Other fossiliferous sites in the Sterkfontein area now under exploration include Drimolen, which recently yielded a surprisingly complete robust
australopithecine skull (Keyser *et al.* 2000) and two of the youngest early hominin individuals ever found (Tobias 2000); Gladysvale, which has produced a
few teeth tentatively assigned to *A. africanus* (Berger *et al.* 1993); and Cooper's B
and Gondolin, source respectively of a robust australopithecine face and of two
Paranthropus teeth (Tobias 2000). Some 300 km to the north, Makapansgat,
investigated since 1947, has contributed several more specimens older than
most of those from Sterkfontein (Klein 1999).

Southern Africa lacks directly datable volcanic ash and tephra deposits.
Determining the age of early hominin localities thus depends largely on faunal
comparisons with the better-dated East African sequence, supported by palaeomagnetic and thermoluminescence readings (Table 3.2). A further contrast is
that the most prolific sites, those in the Sterkfontein Valley and its environs,
are dolomitic limestone caves into which sediments and bones fell from the
surface. Fossils in these hardened breccia deposits typically require hammers,

Table 3.2 Dating of early hominin deposits in southern Africa

Site	Member	Faunal associations	Palaeomagnetic and radiometric readings	Fossil hominids
Cooper's B	–	– (Partridge 2000; Tobias 2000)	–	P. robustus
Drimolen	–	1.8–1.5 mya (Keyser et al. 2000)	–	P. robustus; Homo sp.
Gladysvale	–	2.5–1.7 mya (Plug and Keyser 1994)	–	A. africanus
Gondolin	–	0.9–0.6 mya (Partridge 2000)	–	–
Kromdraai	3	±2.0 mya (Vrba 1982)	Reversed polarity, 2.48–0.73 mya (D. Jones et al. 1986)	P. robustus
Makapansgat	4	≤3.0 mya (Vrba 1982; Maguire 1985)		A. africanus
	3	±3.0 mya (Vrba 1982)	±3.0 mya (McFadden and Brock 1986)	A. africanus
Sterkfontein	5	±1.9 mya (R. Clarke 1994)		P. robustus; Homo sp.
	4	2.8–2.6 mya (McKee 1993)	Normal polarity, >2.48 mya (D. Jones et al. 1986) 2.1 ± 0.5 mya (Schwarcz et al. 1994)	A. africanus
	2	3.5–3.0 mya (R. Clarke and Tobias 1995)		Australopithecus sp. indet.
Swartkrans	3	1.0–0.5/0.7 mya? (Vrba 1982)	0.9–0.6 mya	P. robustus
	2	1.8–1.5 mya (Vrba 1982)		P. robustus; H. ergaster
	1			P. robustus
Taung	–	≥2.4 (2.8?) mya (McKee 1993)	0.942 mya (J.C. Vogel and Partridge 1984)	A. africanus

chisels and even explosives as excavation tools, in marked contrast to the finer-grained lacustrine and riverine sedimentary contexts of East Africa! Brain's (1981, 1993) research suggests that some hominins were killed and eaten by leopards and their remains introduced into the deposits through carnivore activity. Taung offers a slightly different picture, as puncture marks and depression fractures on the child's skull suggest that it was carried to the site by a large raptor, such as the crowned eagle (*Stephanoaetus coronatus*; Berger and Clarke 1995), though perhaps only after having been killed by a carnivore (Hedenström 1995).

Two main kinds of hominin occur in these southern African Plio-Pleistocene deposits, the gracile and the robust australopithecines. When first discovered, separate taxa were proposed for the hominins of each site. Contemporary assessments group the Taung child, the overwhelming majority of the hominins from Member 4 at Sterkfontein, some of the Gladysvale specimens and all those from Makapansgat as *Australopithecus africanus* (Fig. 3.5). This gracile species has an age range of 3.0–2.3 mya. Though cranial capacity was perhaps only 10 per cent higher (mean 440 cm^3), several features, including a shorter, less projecting face, suggest that it was advanced over *A. afarensis* (Klein 1999). Its growth pattern, however, seems to have been closer to that of apes than of modern humans. Growth increment lines in the Taung child's teeth, for example, estimate its age at death at 2.7–3.7 years old, compared with the 5–6 years

Figure 3.5 *Australopithecus africanus* (StS 5) from Sterkfontein (courtesy Transvaal Museum).

gauged from comparing its tooth eruption sequence to that of modern humans (Bromage and Dean 1985). Limb proportions and general post-cranial anatomy indicate that *A. africanus* remained adapted for tree-climbing as well as bipedal locomotion, and may have followed an even more arboreally inclined lifestyle than *A. afarensis* (McHenry and Berger 1996).

The recent discovery at Sterkfontein of a partially reconstructable foot with an apparently splayed big toe provides additional confirmation that gracile australopithecines were facultative bipeds *and* climbers (R. Clarke and Tobias 1995). Astonishingly, the well-preserved skull and post-cranial skeleton of the same adult individual (StW 573; 'Little Foot') have since been located at the site (Fig. 3.6). Coming from Member 2, this fossil dates to 3.3 mya, making it

Figure 3.6   *Australopithecus* sp. (StW 573) from Sterkfontein recently discovered by Ron Clarke, Nkwane Molefe and Stephen Motsumi (courtesy Ron Clarke, Department of Anthropology and Human Genetics, Goethe University, Frankfurt).

Figure 3.7   *Paranthropus robustus* (SK 48) from Swartkrans (courtesy Dr G. Newlands and Transvaal Museum).

the oldest hominin known from southern Africa (Partridge *et al.* 1999). Not only is it the most complete australopithecine individual ever found, it appears not to fall within the morphological range of the younger Member 4 hominins, suggesting that it belongs to a more archaic taxon than *A. africanus* (R. Clarke 1998, 1999a). Quite clearly, the southern African fossil record holds many more surprises and looks set to continue rivalling East Africa as a key source of information on the evolutionary history of early hominins.

Unlike the gracile australopithecines, the robust branch of this hominin group (Fig. 3.7) is thus far represented in southern Africa only in the Sterkfontein Valley and its environs. Known fossils include all those from Kromdraai B, along with almost all those from Swartkrans Members 1–3 (Fig. 3.8) and a few specimens from Cooper's B, Drimolen, Gondolin and Sterkfontein Member 5 (R. Clarke 1994; Klein 1999; Keyser *et al.* 2000; Tobias 2000). Together they span a time range of perhaps 1.8–1.0 mya. Though generally considered to form a single taxon, *Australopithecus* or *Paranthropus robustus*, Howell *et al.* (1978) use differences in cranial capacity, cheek teeth size and limb robusticity to assign the much larger Swartkrans sample to *P. crassidens*. A possibly ancestral form may be subsumed within some of the *A. africanus* specimens from Sterkfontein Member 4, currently dated 2.8–2.6 mya (R. Clarke 1994). Unlike their gracile relatives, robust australopithecines are well known in East Africa. Two species are generally recognised there, *P. aethiopicus*, dating to 2.7–2.3 mya, and *P. boisei*, with dates of 2.3–1.0 mya (Klein 1999). The evolutionary

Figure 3.8   Partial view of the excavations at Swartkrans, Gauteng, South
Africa taken in 1977 (courtesy Bob Brain).

relationships of these taxa are not certain. One possibility sees *P. aethiopicus*
as ancestral to both *P. robustus* and *P. boisei*, which might then be viewed
as geographic variants of the same species (Delson 1987). Alternatively, since
A. africanus does not retain all of the primitive traits seen in *P. aethiopicus*,
the two may be ancestral to regionally separate lineages of robust australopithecines, end-products of a process of parallel evolution. Whichever view is
accepted, the robust australopithecine adaptation was clearly very successful.
What this was and how it differed from that of the gracile australopithecines
has been the subject of much research.

   In many respects, the terms 'gracile' and 'robust' are misnomers. Both differ from *A. afarensis* in much the same features, and the slightly larger brain
size of the robust australopithecines (averaging 520 cm^3; Holloway 1983) is
minimally significant. Differences in overall body size were also small. This
is best estimated at 30 and 41 kg for female and male *A. africanus* individuals and at 32 and 40 kg for females and males of *P. robustus* respectively,
no larger than modern chimpanzees (McHenry 1992). The striking difference
lies rather in the jaws and dentition. Robust australopithecines had greatly
expanded cheek teeth, thick enamel and very thick, deep mandibles, with
the massive jaw muscles needed to work them anchored on powerfully built
zygomatic arches and **sagittal crests**. This very distinctive craniofacial architecture reflects a specialisation for applying substantial force between upper

and lower cheek teeth during chewing (Rak 1983). It is this that lies at the root of most explanations of the differences between robust and gracile taxa. J. Robinson (1954) was the first to propose this 'dietary hypothesis', arguing that *P. robustus* was adapted for an exclusively vegetarian diet compared to the more omnivorous diet of *A. africanus*. More recent studies of jaw mechanics (Hylander 1988), enamel thickness (Grine and Martin 1988) and occlusal microwear (Grine 1981) also emphasise the crushing of small, hard items, most probably hard fruits, pods and nuts (Grine and Kay 1988). As well as explaining the distinctive robust australopithecine morphology, a more specialised diet could help account for their subsequent extinction (through competition with *Homo*, a dietary generalist) and apparent non-involvement in stone tool production.

Isotopic analyses suggest, however, that the dietary hypothesis is not as strong as once thought. Both the strontium/calcium and carbon isotope composition of *P. robustus* specimens from Swartkrans indicate a much greater degree of omnivory (Sillen 1992; Lee Thorp *et al.* 1994). Carbon isotopes, in particular, point to substantial consumption (30 per cent), either directly of grasses or of animals that ate grasses. Dental morphology and microwear exclude both grazing *per se* and large-scale seed consumption. Instead, scavenging of carnivore kills and direct consumption of grass-eating vertebrates and insects seem likely, supported by Aiello and Wheeler's (1995) argument that all hominins must have consumed some animal foods in order to obtain sufficient high-quality nutrients to support **encephalisation**. Though these findings encourage more subtle assessments of dietary differences between hominin taxa, they do not dispute the importance of plant food processing in the evolution of the distinctive robust australopithecine morphology. A further factor is the possibility that graciles and robusts lived in contrasting habitats where different dietary emphases would be expected. Palaeoecological reconstructions suggest that the gracile australopithecines found at Makapansgat and Sterkfontein lived in subtropical forest or forest fringe conditions (Rayner *et al.* 1993; Bamford 1999; Kuman and Clarke 2000), something clearly compatible with their retention of tree-climbing abilities, even though stable isotope analyses indicate that substantial patches of grass must also have been present (Lee Thorp and Talma 2000). *P. robustus*, on the other hand, is associated at Kromdraai and Swartkrans with more open grassland, albeit with locally wet habitats close by (Vrba 1982; Reed 1997).

Though australopithecines are by far the most common Plio-Pleistocene hominin in South Africa, *Homo* is also present at both Sterkfontein and Swartkrans. Understanding the origins of this genus is, however, better approached from the more extensive East African record. Discovered at Olduvai in 1961, *Homo habilis* for long held claim to being its oldest member (1.9–1.8 mya). Subsequent research has emphasised considerable diversity in the size and morphology of the cranial and post-cranial remains attributed to it, such that many palaeoanthropologists attribute some specimens to a separate taxon, *H. rudolfensis* (1.9–1.8 mya; B. Wood 1992). Though the latter is bigger brained and bodied, the phylogenetic status of both taxa remains uncertain; B. Wood and Collard (1999) conclude that they are better considered australopithecines on grounds of locomotion (bipedalism plus efficient arboreal activity), maturation rate (more ape-like), diet (items needing more forceful processing) and brain size (still relatively small).

Very few potential *Homo* specimens predate 1.9 mya. The best contender is the A.L. 666–1 maxilla from Hadar, Ethiopia, dating to 2.33 mya and found in association with stone artefacts (Kimbel *et al.* 1996). Approximately the same age are a partial mandible from Uraha, Malawi (Schrenk *et al.* 1993), and a temporal bone from near Lake Baringo, Kenya (Hill *et al.* 1992). These early dates are consistent with Vrba's (1992) suggestion that global climatic cooling around 2.5 million years ago provoked a burst of species turnover (extinction and evolution) among hominins, comparable to that observed among African bovids. Though other analyses only show a link to extinctions, not speciation (Foley 1994), the approximately contemporary appearance of the first stone artefacts does suggest this was a critical juncture in hominin evolution.

But to which earlier hominin population we should then look as a potential ancestor for early *Homo* remains very much in question. *A. africanus* is one possibility, implying an evolution for *Homo* in southern rather than eastern Africa, although some gracile australopithecines may have been wrongly included among the East African *H. habilis* population (R. Clarke 1999b). McHenry and Berger's (1996) analysis of hominin body proportions excludes an evolutionary progression from *A. afarensis* through *A. africanus* to *Homo*, but the potentially more archaic australopithecine remains recently found in Sterkfontein Member 2 may offer a southern African ancestry for *A. africanus* that perhaps bypassed *A. afarensis*. Alternatively, a partial cranium from Ethiopia's Middle Awash area assigned to *A. garhi* establishes the presence in East Africa of a hominin intermediate in dental and cranial features between the australopithecines and *Homo* at 2.5 mya, precisely the time required for an ancestor of the A.L. 666–1, Uraha and Lake Baringo specimens (Asfaw *et al.* 1999). Intriguingly, the same locality has yielded stone flakes and cut-marked and smashed animal bones (de Heinzelin *et al.* 1999).

Linking these early fossils to later members of the genus *Homo* remains contentious. Since the early 1950s *H. erectus* has been recognised as a widespread Lower/Middle Pleistocene taxon in Africa, China, Indonesia and perhaps Europe. More recently, many palaeoanthropologists consider that there is too much morphological variation between the Asian and African specimens for all to belong to the same species (B. Wood 1992). As a result, *H. erectus* has been reserved for fossils from the Far East, with African specimens assigned to a new species, *Homo ergaster*, though other analysts argue that there is no basis for such a separation (Bräuer and Mbua 1992). Both taxa share many anatomical features, including increases in brain and body size over earlier representatives of *Homo* and a concomitant reduction in sexual dimorphism. Other distinguishing traits include thicker cranial bones, brow ridges and a long, low skull (Klein 1999). Given the lack of convincing older hominins in Asia, *H. ergaster*, which first appears 1.8 mya, is assumed to be the African ancestor of a population that later moved into Asia, giving rise there to *H. erectus* (Swisher *et al.* 1994; Gabunia *et al.* 2000).

The southern African record for early *Homo* is much scantier than for the australopithecines. A partial cranium from Member 5 at Sterkfontein (StW 53), once assigned to *Homo habilis*, is now generally recognised as a gracile australopithecine (Rightmire 1984; R. Clarke 1999b). A somewhat better-preserved skull (SK 847; Fig. 3.9) was recovered from Swartkrans Member 1 (R. Clarke *et al.* 1970). Along with a few other fossils, all once assigned to '*Telanthropus capensis*', StW 80 from Sterkfontein (Kuman and Clarke 2000) and possibly a single *Homo* specimen from Drimolen (DNH 35; Tobias 2000) it is a rare southern African example of *Homo ergaster* dating 1.8–1.7 mya.

The well-preserved skeleton of a young male from Nariokotome, Kenya, offers our best insight into the post-cranial anatomy of this latter species (A. Walker and Leakey 1993). One of the most striking things about this individual is its large size (estimated at 1.8 m tall and weighing 68 kg had it

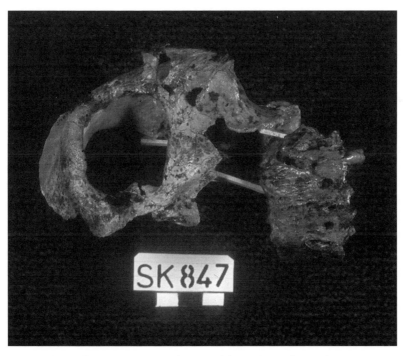

Figure 3.9   Face of *Homo ergaster* (SK 847) from Swartkrans (courtesy Transvaal Museum).

reached maturity) and tall, lean physique resembling many present-day equatorial Africans. Its narrow pelvis may have been more effectively designed for walking and running than our own and its robust, heavily muscled skeleton implies routine heavy physical exertion. Cumulatively these features suggest an adaptation quite different from those of earlier hominins, one in which improved thermo-regulation played a key rôle within an active life in dry, open savanna environments rather than more closed, wooded ones (Ruff 1991). The small size of the pelvis and adult cranial capacities of at least 850 cm³ also imply a more human-like maturation rate, coupled with a much longer period of infant dependency than inferred for the australopithecines (A. Walker and Leakey 1993); studies of tooth eruption confirm a slower growth pattern and longer lifespan relative to apes (H. Smith 1989). All these differences carry further implications for hominin behaviour, for example as regards diet quality and how mothers with young offspring acquired food (e.g. through being provisioned by other individuals). The archaeological record now increasingly offers another source of evidence for investigating such questions.

Plio-Pleistocene archaeology in southern Africa

In southern Africa definite archaeological traces of Plio-Pleistocene hominins are preserved only in and close to the Sterkfontein Valley (Kuman 1998). Though individual stone-knapping or butchery events cannot be reconstructed, dating is difficult and sites are not numerous enough to investigate how hominins exploited the wider landscape, recent work is producing a much better understanding of this earliest phase of the sub-continent's archaeological record.

Sterkfontein provides the largest Plio-Pleistocene archaeological assemblage, with over 9000 artefacts recovered from Member 5. The Oldowan assemblage from here may be the oldest cultural material yet found in southern Africa (Fig. 3.10). Faunal comparisons suggest it is 2.0–1.7 mya old, wholly consistent with dates for similar occurrences in East Africa (Kuman 1994a, 1994b). Almost all the artefacts are made in quartz, with small amounts of chert and quartzite. All three materials occur a few hundred metres away in the gravels of the Blaauwbank River. Quartz is the most easily fractured of these rocks, but Oldowan hominins could adjust their flaking technique to raw material and its size and shape (Kuman 1994b, 1996). As well as direct percussion and bipolar flaking, the principle of radial flaking was understood. Nevertheless, like Oldowan assemblages in East Africa, especially the quartz-dominated occurrences from Omo, Ethiopia (Chavaillon 1976), the industry is both simple and opportunistic, with little retouch and no flaking to predetermined patterns.

Oldowan assemblages do, indeed, show the simplest forms of stone tool working of any industry (Toth 1985). In addition to hammerstones and manuports,

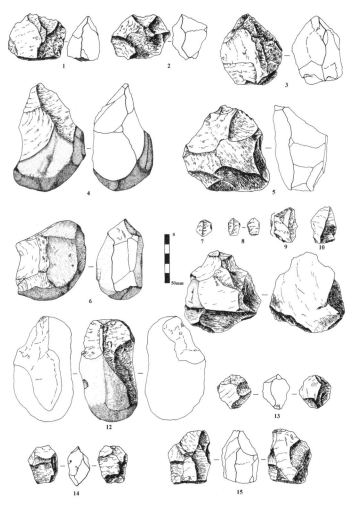

Figure 3.10   Oldowan artefacts from Sterkfontein Member 5 (courtesy Kathy
Kuman).

they comprise flakes and the cores from which these were struck. Some
flakes are variably retouched and some cores have battered or damaged edges
suggestive of use. Experiments show that variability among the core forms can
be explained by raw material, the size of the original piece of stone and the degree to which it was reduced. In conjunction with microwear studies of artefacts
from Koobi Fora, Kenya (Keeley and Toth 1981), they suggest that the flakes
were mainly the desired end-product, the core-tools often just by-products of
their manufacture. Oldowan assemblages are thus highly informal, especially
when made of quartz, which produces large amounts of chips, chunks and
small flakes. Additional criteria, such as the consistent absence of more complex artefacts and independent evidence of Plio-Pleistocene age, are necessary

to substantiate their identification as Oldowan (Kuman 1994a). It would not be surprising if contemporaneous assemblages exist elsewhere in the sub-continent (Pickford 1990), but none has yet been found in a secure chronological context.

Oldowan artefacts were probably employed for many different purposes. In East Africa (Toth and Schick 1986), but rarely at Sterkfontein (Pickering 1999), cutmarks on animal bones and experiments show that some flakes were used to remove meat from carcasses. The Koobi Fora microwear study adds scraping or sawing wood and cutting grass or reeds to this, while core-tools could have been used for heavier-duty butchery, wood-cutting tasks, or even as projectiles (Isaac 1984). Another perspective may be offered by identifications of organic residues on some Sterkfontein artefacts. Both plant and animal residues are distributed over Oldowan flakes, consistent with morphology and potential use, but are lacking from natural stones in the same deposit (Loy 1998).

Stone artefacts are also present at Kromdraai, Swartkrans and, on a very small scale, Drimolen. A few flakes and pebbles from Members 4 and 5 at Kromdraai B are contemporary with the robust australopithecine fossils (Brain 1975), while the larger assemblage from Kromdraai A postdates them (Kuman *et al.* 1997). At Swartkrans J.D. Clark (1993a) assigned artefacts from Members 1–2 to the 'Developed Oldowan', with a probable age of 1.7–1.5 mya. More recently, Field (1999) has argued that there is nothing diagnostic in the Member 1 assem-blage and that the 'Developed Oldowan' material from Member 2 should be in-cluded within the Acheulean Complex. Further north, rare flakes and cobbles in Makapansgat's Member 5, which may substantially postdate the australop-ithecine fossils from Member 3, do not unequivocally result from deliberate flaking or introduction by hominins (Maguire *et al.* 1980).

Not all the artefacts from these early assemblages are made in stone. Several polished long-bone fragments come from Drimolen, Sterkfontein Member 5 and Swartkrans Members 1–3 (Fig. 3.11). Experiments show that this polish could result from using them to dig out edible plants from rocky soil (Brain 1985) or from excavating termite mounds (Backwell and d'Errico 2000). Strontium/calcium ratios of the SK 847 specimen from Swartkrans imply a substantial intake of underground plant foods, suggesting this was an important compo-nent of the early *Homo* niche (Sillen *et al.* 1995). Though bone in Oldowan and Acheulean assemblages was never more than minimally modified, such worked fragments, combined with microwear studies, are important in indi-cating that from the very beginning of the surviving archaeological record, if not before, organic materials were also used. Perhaps Dart's (1957) claim for an **osteodontokeratic** culture preceding the use of stone is not wholly implausible, though the skeletal part frequencies in the australopithecine-bearing Member 3 at Makapansgat on which he based his argument wholly reflect pre- and post-depositional factors, not hominin choice (Brain 1981).

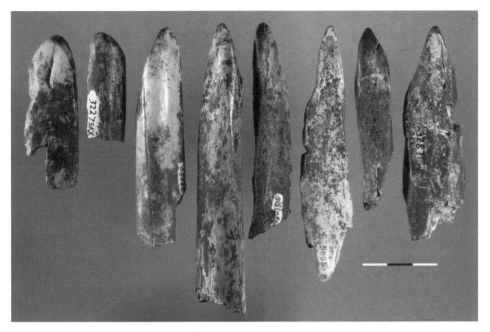

Figure 3.11 Polished bone fragments from Swartkrans Members 1–3 thought to have been used in excavating underground plant foods and/or termite nests (courtesy Francesco d'Errico and Lucinda Backwell).

Understanding how these artefacts, bone and stone, were integrated into the day-to-day behaviour of early hominins is more easily approached from the East African record. However, the largely fresh condition of the Sterkfontein Oldowan artefacts implies an origin close to the caves in which they were found. Kuman (1994b) suggests two features that might have attracted hominins to such a location: the shade provided by trees growing around the cave openings and the shelter from the elements offered by the dolomite outcrops themselves. These features could have repeatedly brought hominins back to the site, just as the availability of flakable chert may have attracted them to the MNK Factory site at Olduvai (Stiles *et al.* 1974).

By 1.5 ± 0.3 mya the Sterkfontein sequence registers the change to Acheulean technology (see below). As well as the production of bifacially worked handaxes and cleavers, Kuman (1994a) shows that the crucial factor in this was the ability to strike large (>10 cm) flakes. At Sterkfontein this permitted greater use of chert and quartzite and an expansion of raw material range to include diabase, coupled with more extensive transport of stone to the site, probably because downcutting of the Blaauwbank River had increased the distance over which raw materials had to be obtained. Kuman and Clarke (2000) estimate the age of the oldest Acheulean material at Sterkfontein to be 1.7–1.4 mya. Acheulean artefacts in Member 3 at Swartkrans are estimated to be 1.0 million years old (J.D. Clark 1993a).

Quite which hominins were responsible for the artefacts we have considered is not totally clearcut. Both *Homo ergaster* and *Paranthropus robustus* occur with Developed Oldowan tools in Members 1 and 2 at Swartkrans and *P. robustus* alone has been found with Acheulean artefacts in Member 3 (Brain 1993). A comparable picture is evident in East Africa, where both *Homo* spp. and *P. boisei* were contemporary with the Oldowan (Klein 1999). Since chimpanzees use and make tools (Wynn and McGrew 1989), including stone artefacts under experimental conditions (Toth *et al.* 1993), it seems likely that all hominins had some ability in this area. Indeed, Susman (1988) suggested that the morphology of (probably) robust australopithecine hands was well adapted to the precision gripping needed for artefact manufacture. This conclusion has, however, been criticised (Marzke 1997), and the lack of two distinct artefact traditions may argue against *Paranthropus* making stone tools, though much more recently Neanderthals and anatomically modern humans produced virtually identical lithic assemblages in the Near East and the Oldowan's informality can scarcely be definitive in this regard (Klein 1999). If a primary role for early stone artefacts was in accessing meat and bone-marrow, as experimental, cutmark and microwear evidence all suggest, this would fit a presumed greater interest in meat-eating by *Homo*, as compared with the robust australopithecines. That stone artefacts and *Homo* appear in the archaeological record at broadly the same time reinforces this view. The combination of extended tool use and greater dietary breadth with more efficient heat regulation and locomotion may have been crucial in *Homo*'s success and (through competitive exclusion) the eventual extinction of the robust australopithecines.

Regrettably, the fact that the faunas at Sterkfontein and its neighbours were almost wholly accumulated by non-hominin agencies means that southern Africa is not yet able to contribute much to these questions. Such work has, however, been carried out at finer-grained, more readily dated East African sites. Important and interrelated research themes there include the degree to which meat was important in early hominin diets, how it was obtained and whether the association of bones and stones implies the sharing of food, perhaps accompanied by a sexual division of labour and provisioning of a home-base as among recent hunter-gatherers (Isaac 1984). Contrary to the initial expectations of such a model, critical assessments of site taphonomy suggest that many associations of fauna and artefacts are not causally linked, that supposed early shelters did not exist and that scavenging of carnivore kills or naturally dying animals was probably more significant as a source of meat and bone-marrow than hunting (Klein 1999). Though the connection between meat-eating (however obtained) and food-sharing has recently been raised again (Rosa and Marshall 1996), both at the Plio-Pleistocene boundary and for long afterwards a humanlike appearance may have gone hand-in-hand with a way of life distinctly unlike that of modern people.

Acheulean assemblages and the transition to the Middle Stone Age

Probably the longest-lasting artefact tradition ever created by hominins, the Acheulean is found from Cape Town to north-western Europe and as far as India between 1.4 and 0.2 mya, with the oldest secure dates coming from Ethiopia (Asfaw *et al.* 1992). It occurs widely in southern Africa, with some sites, such as Kathu Townlands, containing tens of millions of artefacts (Beaumont 1990a). Yet despite these many sites, Inskeep's (1978) comment that the Acheulean falls within a 'prehistoric dark age' still rings true. Organic remains are only rarely preserved and dating remains extremely difficult. This was, however, probably a critical period in hominin evolution, encompassing the transition from *Homo ergaster* to archaic forms of *Homo sapiens*.

The hallmark of Acheulean technology, first recognised in southern Africa in river gravels at Stellenbosch (Péringuey and Corstophine 1900), was the production of two kinds of bifacial implements, handaxes and cleavers. These were made in a variety of rocks, depending on local availability. Sometimes cobbles served as the blanks for these artefacts as in western Eurasia, but more typically African, and an Acheulean innovation, was the use of large flakes struck from cores. Handaxes and cleavers (Fig. 3.12) occur in a variety of shapes, but the essentials are that handaxes have an elongated, pear-shaped or triangular form terminating in a point, while cleavers have a broad axe-like cutting edge. Handaxes tend to be more heavily worked since the sides of cleavers were apparently not used and their cutting edge was the natural edge of the flake on which they were made. As well as bifaces, Acheulean assemblages include cores and flakes, as in the Oldowan. Some flakes were deliberately retouched, the majority conventionally classified as scrapers.

Handaxes and cleavers give the impression of being purposefully designed. However, Meneses's (1996) study of Acheulean artefacts from southern Mozambique demonstrates that final shape depended on the dimensions of the original blank, the intensity with which edges were used, the degree to which they were resharpened and, we might add, raw material choice. The finished product may not, therefore, have been the primary objective of knapping. This must be borne in mind when assessing handaxe function, which has been widely debated. They seem to have been more than just cores, though this may have been among their functions. Experimental work indicates they are superior to retouched or unretouched flakes in almost all heavy-duty butchery situations, especially if larger mammals or longer work periods are involved (P.R. Jones 1980). Microwear analysis of two chert handaxes from Wonderwerk Cave suggests they were also used to work plant materials, such as wood and sedge

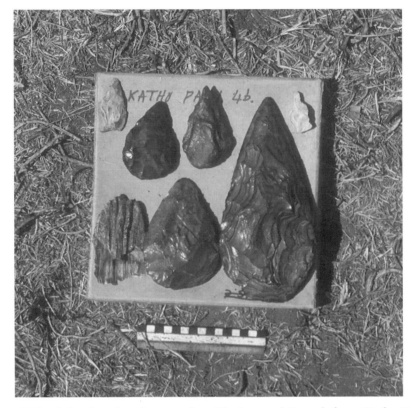

Figure 3.12   Acheulean handaxes and an *Elephas reckii* tooth from Kathu Pan
1, Northern Cape, South Africa, photographed during the
Southern African Association of Archaeologists excursion,
September 1990.

(Binneman and Beaumont 1992). Waterlogged Acheulean contexts at Amanzi
Springs (H. Deacon 1970) and Kalambo Falls (J.D. Clark 1969, 2001) have
produced examples of worked wood. A range of uses thus seems likely.

Almost all Acheulean assemblages in southern Africa come from disturbed
open-air locations. Rock-shelter occupations are generally lacking (Fig. 3.13).
The few exceptions include Cave of Hearths and Olieboompoort (Mason 1962),
Wonderwerk (Beaumont 1990b) and Montagu Cave (Keller 1973) in South
Africa and the Zimbabwean sites of Bambata and Pomongwe (Armstrong 1931;
Cooke 1963). Developing a reliable chronology is consequently difficult. Earlier
schemes relating artefacts in supposedly stratified gravel deposits along the
Vaal River have long been abandoned (Partridge and Brink 1967). An Early
Acheulean, predating 1.0 mya, is securely represented only at Sterkfontein
and Swartkrans. Handaxes in Later Acheulean assemblages do tend to show
greater numbers of flake scars and there are signs in the transVaal (Mason 1962)
and in stratified sequences from Montagu Cave (Keller 1973) and at Rooidam

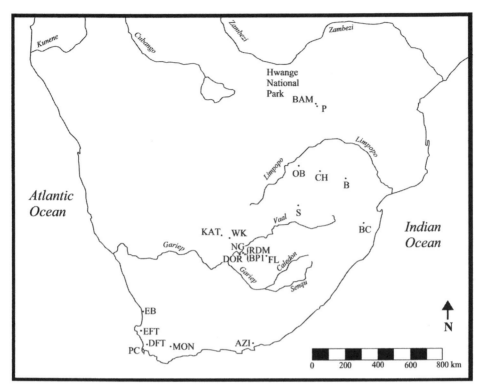

Figure 3.13   Southern Africa: Middle Pleistocene archaeological sites. Site names
are abbreviated thus: AZI Amanzi; B Bushman Rock Shelter; BAM
Bambata; BC Border Cave; BP1 Biessiesput 1; CH Cave of Hearths;
DFT Duinefontein 2; DOR Doornlaagte; EB Elands Bay Cave; EFT
Elandsfontein; FL Florisbad; KAT Kathu Pan; MON Montagu Cave;
NG Nooitgedacht; OB Olieboompoort; P Pomongwe; PC Peers
Cave; RDM Rooidam; S Sterkfontein Valley; WK Wonderwerk.

(Fock 1968) that handaxe relative breadth increased with time. However, experimental work shows that both traits are raw material dependent (P.R. Jones
1979). Typological differences between Acheulean assemblages therefore
remain indistinct.

The subsequent transition between Acheulean and Middle Stone Age (MSA)
artefact traditions is also poorly defined and dated. MSA assemblages overlie
Acheulean ones at Cave of Hearths, Olieboompoort, Wonderwerk and Montagu
Cave, but may be separated from them by a long hiatus. While the presence or
absence of large cutting tools is the only widespread marker, there can be no
expectation that ESA hominins left cleavers and handaxes wherever they went
(Volman 1984). Additionally, some Acheulean flaking techniques involved a
degree of core preparation that allowed a single large flake of predetermined
size and shape to be produced. In the Karoo this is represented by the so-called
Victoria West cores, which involved preliminary flaking of the surface from

which the desired flake was to come to a low dome, leaving the lower part of the core deep and steeply flaked. Striking the core at the right point detached a flake with the size and shape of the dome (Inskeep 1978). Both endstruck and sidestruck flakes could be produced. Comparable techniques are known from Kenya and the Sahara (J.D. Clark 1996) and indicate an origin within the Acheulean for the same **Levallois technique** used in the Middle Stone Age. Allowing a range of flake tools to be made from one core offered scope for a more task-specific toolkit and may represent a significant development in planning depth and efficient raw material use, though conjoining studies and usewear analyses in European assemblages suggest that flakes removed prior to detachment of the Levallois flake itself were often also used (Noble and Davidson 1996).

In the South African interior, assemblages incorporating these prepared core techniques with flake tools that include long, narrow flake-blades and convergent points are known as Fauresmith; associated handaxes are small and broad (Fig. 3.14). Almost all known occurrences are at open-air sites. Humphreys (1970a) suggested that the Fauresmith is merely a local variant of 'normal' Acheulean technology resulting from the use of hornfels. Assemblages made in quartzite and chert, such as that from Nooitgedacht, indicate that there is

Figure 3.14   Fauresmith artefacts from Biessiesput 1, Northern Cape, South Africa, photographed during the Southern African Association of Archaeologists excursion, September 1990.

more to the Fauresmith than this, revitalising the older view (J.D. Clark 1959) that its combination of handaxes with prepared cores and flake-blades represents a terminal phase of the local Acheulean, transitional to the Middle Stone Age (Beaumont 1990c). Amino-acid racemisation dates on ostrich eggshell from Wonderwerk suggest that the Fauresmith there is in excess of 200,000 years old (Beaumont 1990b), while a uranium-series date from the basal Fauresmith stratum at Rooidam gave a minimal age of 174 ± 25,000 BP (Szabo and Butzer 1979). An older phase of the Acheulean at Wonderwerk from which prepared core techniques are absent has a uranium-series date of >350,000 BP (Binneman and Beaumont 1992).

Further north and extending as far as Uganda, the Acheulean was followed by assemblages termed Sangoan, in which handaxes and cleavers are rare, but small scrapers and crude pick-like artefacts occur. J.D. Clark (1988) suggested that they represent an adaptation to more forested conditions, but recent fieldwork indicates that some Sangoan assemblages were deposited in semiarid, open grassland (McBrearty 1992). Making assessments more difficult, most southern African Sangoan assemblages are highly selected. In Zimbabwe supposedly late Sangoan assemblages termed Charaman (C. Cooke 1966) are said to contain fewer handaxes and picks but more retouched points, but again come from disturbed contexts. A gradual transition between Sangoan/Charaman assemblages and ensuing MSA industries is possible (Volman 1984), but the lack of well-excavated, well-dated sites remains a massive handicap (N. Walker and Thorp 1997).

Whatever its origins, Goodwin and van Riet Lowe (1929) saw the Middle Stone Age as intermediate in technology between the Acheulean and the LSA, marked by the loss of handaxes and cleavers, the use of prepared core techniques and the production of triangular flakes with convergent dorsal scars and **faceted** striking platforms. To this we can add the deliberate manufacture of elongated, more-or-less parallel-sided blades and flake-blades, sometimes struck from cores comparable to the Levallois blade cores known from the European Middle Palaeolithic (Volman 1984). Foley and Lahr (1997) view the widespread occurrence of this technology across Africa and its spread into much of Eurasia in oxygen isotope stage (OIS) 7 as part of a process of population dispersal associated on the one hand with the ancestors of later Neanderthals (in Eurasia) and on the other with those of anatomically modern humans (in Africa). They emphasise the behavioural similarities, rather than the differences, between the two, and note evidence for increases in brain size from 300,000 years ago that may have triggered more human life histories and social organisation. The corollary is that contrasts seen in the global archaeological record before and after 50,000 BP may reflect distinctive regional adaptations, instead of wholesale cognitive reorganisation within the modern human lineage, a different reading of the biological and archaeological evidence than that developed below.

Most surviving MSA occurrences date to the Last Interglacial (OIS 5) and its aftermath, continuing down to around 25,000–20,000 BP. The earliest MSA

Table 3.3 *Radiometric dates relevant to the Acheulean/Middle Stone Age transition in sub-Saharan Africa*

Site	Country	Industry	Age kyr BP	Technique[a]	Reference (Klein 1999 unless otherwise stated)
Gademotta	Ethiopia	MSA	>180	K/Ar	
Kapthurin	Kenya	Acheulean	230	K/Ar	
Malewa Gorge	Kenya	MSA	240	K/Ar	
Isimila	Tanzania	Acheulean	$260^{+70}/_{-40}$	Th/U	
Twin Rivers	Zambia	MSA	$\geq 230^{+35}/_{-28}$	Th/U	
Rooidam	South Africa	Fauresmith	$\geq 174 \pm 25$	Th/U	Szabo and Butzer (1979)
Florisbad	South Africa	MSA	279 ± 47	ESR	Kuman *et al.* (1999)
Wonderwerk	South Africa	Fauresmith	>200	AAR	Beaumont (1990b)

[a]AAR = amino-acid racemisation; ESR = electron spin resonance; K/Ar = Potassium-Argon dating; Th/U = Thorium-Uranium dating.

assemblages, on the other hand, which Volman (1984) classifies as MSA 1, are of late Middle Pleistocene age, along with the earliest MSA assemblages from eastern Africa (Table 3.3). MSA 1 assemblages have very little evidence of retouch (Fig. 3.15). Scrapers are rare, retouched points completely absent and denticulates the most common retouched form. Small, broad flakes and radial and discoid cores are other distinguishing features. These occurrences are known from only a few sites: Duinefontein 2, Peers Cave and Elands Bay Cave in the Western Cape, Florisbad in the Free State and Bushman Rock Shelter and Border Cave on South Africa's eastern extremity (Beaumont 1978; Volman 1984; Kuman *et al.* 1999). Most are rock-shelters, an important point since regular use of these fixed points in the landscape now becomes an increasingly common feature of the archaeological record. Unless this is a preservation bias, with many Acheulean rock-shelter occupations lost through cave collapse, or flushing out of deposits, this marks a significant shift in hominin behaviour. The happy consequence for archaeologists is that it facilitated the preservation of a much wider range of evidence, particularly organic materials such as bone and plant remains.

Middle Pleistocene adaptations

Investigating the subsistence strategies of Middle Pleistocene hominins is hampered by an extreme scarcity of evidence. Unlike the australopithecines, southern African fossils of early *Homo* are too few to offer scope for stable isotope studies, and barely more than a dozen sites preserve animal bones and ESA artefacts in anything like a primary context. Klein (1988) analysed the faunas from six, including Wonderwerk, Cave of Hearths, Kathu Pan and the extensive

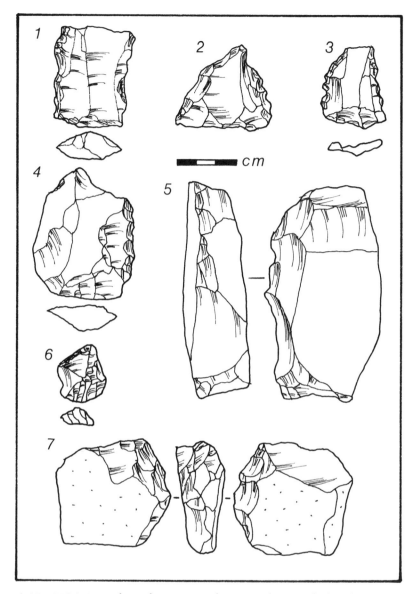

Figure 3.15   MSA 1 artefacts from Duinefontein 2 (1, 3 and 4) and Peers Cave
(2, 5–7). 1–4 denticulates; 5 and 7 slabs with heavy-duty retouch;
6 scraper (redrawn after Volman 1984: Fig. 7; courtesy Tom Volman).
1–3 and 6 are in silcrete, 4, 5 and 7 in quartzite. Stippling denotes
the position of remaining cortex.

bone scatters found in deflation hollows at Elandsfontein, Western Cape. All
reflect moister climatic conditions than exist at present, consistent with sediment analyses from other Acheulean sites, such as Doornlaagte and Rooidam
(Butzer 1984a). This could be a preservation bias if moister environments

encouraged sediment deposition and drier conditions greater erosion, but it may also indicate higher hominin populations during mesic episodes. The lack of Acheulean material in areas such as the Northern Cape under more arid conditions may indicate limited effectiveness in coping with reduced resource productivity at these times. Comparing MSA and LSA site distributions in the Fynbos Biome reinforces the suggestion that Acheulean hominins were more tightly tied to standing water, perhaps because they lacked containers with which to transport it (H. Deacon 1975), but this generalisation may not be universally true; in the Seacow Valley, for example, at the eastern edge of the Nama-Karoo Biome it is Acheulean, not MSA, sites that are less tied to water sources (Sampson 1985a). That almost all the raw materials used in Acheulean assemblages seem to have been available close to where the artefacts are found may indicate minimal interest in carrying artefacts across the landscape, perhaps with implications for planning depth. However, chert was probably moved over distances of 30–50 km in Hwange National Park, Zimbabwe (Klimowicz and Haynes 1996), while at Kathu Pan, in a rare Middle Pleistocene instance of the possible use of pigments, **haematite** and **specularite** were introduced from outcrops at least 20 km distant (Beaumont 1990a).

Addressing how Middle Pleistocene hominins obtained meat is difficult, though evidence from Germany and Britain suggests that projectile weapons extend back at least 400,000 years (Dennell 1997). Few of the bones from recent excavations at Duinefontein 2 have cutmarks, suggesting Acheulean people rarely obtained large game, whether by hunting or scavenging (Fig 3.16; Klein *et al.* 1999); Elandsfontein 'Cutting 10' with an apparently primary association of bones and Acheulean artefacts may be a rare example to the contrary (Klein 1978b; Volman 1984). Coming from cave contexts, the Wonderwerk and Cave of Hearths assemblages are potentially more useful, but assemblages are small and other bone-collectors, such as carnivores and porcupines, may have been at work (Klein 1988). While it seems reasonable to assume that Acheulean hominins were probably less successful hunters than their MSA successors, a degree of meat-eating may be indicated by the bone pathology of a 1.6 mya *Homo ergaster* individual from Koobi Fora (A. Walker *et al.* 1982), and by more certain butchery sites north of the Zambezi, like Mwanganda, Malawi (J.D. Clark and Haynes 1970). Use of plant resources is even more of an unknown quantity, though they probably formed the bulk of the hominin diet. Fruits and seeds of edible plants were preserved at Kalambo Falls (J.D. Clark 1969, 2001), but none of the plants found at Amanzi Springs belong to edible species (H. Deacon 1970). Charred or calcified grass stems and twigs found deep within Wonderwerk Cave are interpreted as remnant bedding areas (Beaumont 1990b).

One of the most important technological innovations associated with Acheulean hominins may have been the ability to control fire. Concentrations of charcoal interpreted as hearths are reported from Pomongwe (Cooke 1963), Bambata (Armstrong 1931) and Cave of Hearths (Mason 1962), but many,

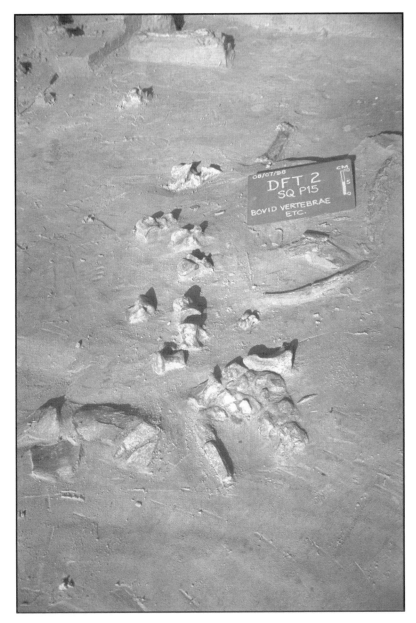

Figure 3.16   Eland bone scatter exposed in excavation at Duinefontein 2,
Western Cape, South Africa (courtesy Richard Klein).

perhaps all, may have natural origins (Volman 1984). This is certainly true
of the black staining noted by Dart (1957) at Makapansgat, which led him to
name the hominins from this site *Australopithecus prometheus* (Oakley 1954).
More convincing are the ash, charred bone and fire-shattered stone throughout
the Acheulean levels at Wonderwerk (Beaumont 1990b; Fig. 3.17). Reaching further back into the late Lower Pleistocene, 270 bone fragments from Swartkrans

Figure 3.17   Interior view of Wonderwerk Cave, Northern Cape, South Africa (courtesy Peter Beaumont).

Member 3 (1.5–1.0 mya) show darkening from carbon residues. Microscopic examination and comparison with control samples indicates they were subjected to prolonged heat of at least 315–450°C, which may be significantly higher than the temperatures likely to have been reached in any natural fire (Brain and Sillen 1988). How far such fire-management extended to making fire at will is uncertain, but by OIS 6 this seems to have been well established. Clearly defined hearths occur in MSA 1 contexts at Cave of Hearths, Border Cave and Peers Cave and are common thereafter (Volman 1984; H. Deacon 1995).

As well as extending the range of edible foods, fire must have offered added security from predators, warmth and the possibility of making fire-hardened artefacts. It may also have assisted the territorial expansion of Acheulean hominins which is evident by at least 1 mya. In southern Africa this encompassed the sub-continent's one temperate zone, the Fynbos Biome, paralleling *Homo*'s northward movement into Eurasia (Gamble 1993). Rare Acheulean artefacts also occur up to 1800 m above sea-level in the Lesotho Highlands (Carter 1978). The Acheulean's profound technological conservatism and the limitations of the archaeological record may mask the evolution of important new *social* capacities that were primarily responsible for this expansion (Gamble 1993). But this does not appear to have extended to using artefacts as symbols,

encoding information about places or people in ways that could build extensive social networks, even if Acheulean handaxes show an engagement with
concepts of symmetry and spatial measurement not apparent in the Oldowan
(Wynn 1991). There is, indeed, nothing in the Acheulean toolkit to require
that stone-working skills were learned other than by observation and imitation
(J.D. Clark 1996), nothing that *requires* language in a form that we would find
recognisable (Noble and Davidson 1996). Less effective respiratory expansion
of the Nariokotome skeleton (A. Walker and Leakey 1993) reinforces this view;
brain enlargement and asymmetry in *H. erectus*, or the presence of features
such as Broca's area, which is associated with language production in modern
humans, do not offer sound evidence to the contrary.

Middle Pleistocene hominins: the fossil record

After the riches offered by the Sterkfontein Valley and Makapansgat, southern
Africa's Middle Pleistocene fossil record is comparatively poor, though by
no means insignificant. Hominid remains are known from four sites south
of the Zambezi and from Kabwe and Mumbwa in Zambia (Rightmire 1984).
The Kabwe (Broken Hill) cranium was recovered from cave fill deposits that
also produced fragments of several other individuals and doubtfully associated Acheulean/Sangoan artefacts; faunal evidence suggests a late Middle
Pleistocene date is likely (Klein 1973). Much more certainly associated with
Acheulean artefacts are a juvenile mandible from Cave of Hearths (Tobias
1971) and an incomplete cranium and unassociated mandibular fragment from
Elandsfontein (Drennan 1953). At both sites the artefacts suggest a mid-
Quaternary age (0.5–0.2 mya), supported at Elandsfontein by Klein's (1988)
faunal analyses. Another Middle Pleistocene hominin comes from a carnivore-
accumulated assemblage at Florisbad. This partial cranium (Fig. 3.18) was found
in a spring eye that predates most, but not all, of the MSA activity at the same
site. Recent ESR determinations give it a weighted mean age of 259 ± 35,000 BP
(Grün *et al.* 1996). Finally, Gladysvale has produced some fragmentary *Homo*
remains that appear to be of Middle Pleistocene age (Tobias 2000).

This is not a large sample from which to draw conclusions, but it can be expanded by reference to other specimens from elsewhere in Africa and beyond.
The most striking thing about all four fossils is their archaic appearance. Kabwe,
in particular, has a low skull and massive brow ridges. Nevertheless, its cranial
capacity (1280 cm^3), like that of the Elandsfontein skull (1200–1250 cm^3), shows
significant advance over earlier *ergaster* grade fossils. This is reinforced by several morphological features of the Kabwe and Florisbad crania. All can be placed
within *Homo sapiens* as a distinctly archaic and African subspecies, *H. sapiens
rhodesiensis* (Rightmire 1976). Alternatively, if we reserve *H. sapiens* for individuals identical to contemporary humans, then these Middle Pleistocene
African fossils should be assigned to *Homo heidelbergensis* (Rightmire 1996),

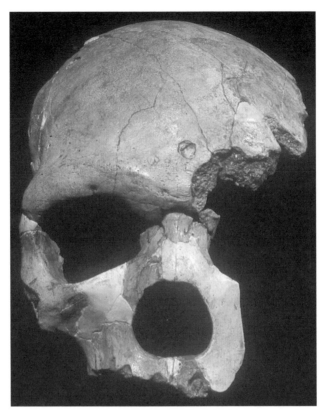

Figure 3.18   Front view of the Florisbad cranium (*Homo heidelbergensis*;
courtesy Zoe Henderson and the National Museum, Bloemfontein).

along with contemporary pre-Neanderthal populations in Europe. Whichever
position is taken, it is increasingly evident that some *sapiens*-like features
are present in African fossils of the early Middle Pleistocene. The Bodo cranium from Ethiopia, dating to 0.6 mya, demonstrates this particularly well
(J.D. Clark *et al.* 1994), and shows striking resemblances to that from Kabwe.
Other archaic *sapiens* fossils from Kenya (Bräuer *et al.* 1997), Tanzania (Hay
1987) and Namibia (Grine *et al.* 1995) support the view that the African record
documents a transition from *Homo ergaster* through increasingly *sapiens*-like
fossils to modern humans (Bräuer 1989). The Florisbad cranium, on this reading
of the evidence (R. Clarke 1985), falls closer to the modern end of this process,
which is more fully documented by anatomically modern human fossils of
Upper Pleistocene age from southern African MSA contexts. I discuss these
fossils, their significance for the argument that modern humans evolved only
in sub-Saharan Africa and the debate surrounding their behavioural competence
in the following chapter.

CHAPTER 4

MODERN HUMANS, MODERN BEHAVIOUR?

Goodwin and van Riet Lowe (1929) assumed that Middle Stone Age (MSA) artefacts were made by archaic forms of *Homo sapiens*, predecessors of the 'neoanthropic' humans responsible for the Later Stone Age. Radiocarbon dates initially supported the view that the MSA was a cultural backwater compared to the supposedly contemporary Upper Palaeolithic of Europe. That most MSA assemblages are significantly older (J.C. Vogel and Beaumont 1972) threw into sharp focus modern-looking hominin remains from Klasies River (sometimes termed Klasies River Mouth) and Border Cave. Together with other African fossils, they raised the possibility that anatomically modern humans had originated south of the Sahara before spreading to other parts of the world (Protsch 1975; Beaumont *et al.* 1978; Bräuer 1982; Stringer 1985). Subsequent studies of the DNA of modern people showed that African populations are genetically more diverse and probably older than those elsewhere (Cann *et al.* 1987). Combined, the fossil and genetic evidence underpins the so-called 'Out-of-Africa 2' model of modern human origins and the continuing debate as to whether it should be preferred to its multiregional alternative (Mellars and Stringer 1989; Mellars 1990; Aitken *et al.* 1993; Nitecki and Nitecki 1994). The related issue of the behavioural competence of MSA hominins is equally complex. Concentrating on the period 127,000–40,000 BP, this chapter examines two questions for which southern African data are crucial. How strong is the evidence for the Out-of-Africa 2 model? And how far was anatomical modernity accompanied by behaviour comparable to that observable today or in the recent past?

Theories of modern human origins

No simple definition distinguishes anatomically modern humans from earlier hominins: large brain size, gracile skeletons and faces, small teeth, chins and an absence of continuous brow ridges are among the key features (Klein 1999), though most Pleistocene people were still more robust than their Holocene successors (Foley 1991b). Two main models compete in explaining the origins of this modern morphology. The Multiregional Evolution hypothesis argues that modern humans evolved more-or-less simultaneously right across the Old World. Anatomical features distinctive of African, European, Far

Eastern and Australasian populations traceable far back into the Pleistocene would thus imply continuity within each region from its first colonisation. Continuing gene flow between regional populations is claimed to have ensured that they never diverged to the point of becoming different species. Different modern features, on the other hand, are argued to have evolved in different parts of the world, later combining through gene flow and universal selection for the modern phenotype (Frayer *et al.* 1993; Wolpoff *et al.* 1994).

For the Out-of-Africa 2 model (Stringer and Gamble 1993) gene flow and natural selection led regional hominin populations along distinct evolutionary trajectories after *Homo*'s expansion from Africa in the Lower Pleistocene (Out-of-Africa 1). Continuity between archaic and modern hominins should therefore only be apparent in Africa, making this the sole, and comparatively recent, home of modern humans before their dispersal into the rest of the world. Opinion differs as to whether and how far genetic admixture (interbreeding) with resident archaic populations occurred (cf. Bräuer 1992; Cann *et al.* 1994).

As the two hypotheses were formulated independently of the genetic evidence that now plays such an important part in the debate, it is sensible to evaluate the fossil record first. One difficulty with the multiregional model is that most of the skeletal features that it emphasises do not, in fact, show presence/absence patterns of variation within specific regions. Their frequencies vary among both fossil and modern populations (Lahr 1994). Others, which may be highly adaptive to specific environments, could have evolved in successive, but not necessarily linked, populations (Stringer and Bräuer 1994). More significantly, repeated Pleistocene environmental changes, creating barriers to interbreeding between regional populations, and the low density at which these populations must have existed, make the assumption of extensive gene flow across the whole of the Old World difficult to credit (Harpending *et al.* 1993).

Throughout human evolution, sound dating evidence is crucial to making sense of the fossil record. That anatomically modern humans were present in Israel by 100,000 BP, some 30,000 years before Neanderthals, is incompatible with them having a descendant/ancestor relationship, as is European evidence for their later overlap (Mellars 1996). Dating of key Chinese and Indonesian fossils is less certain. Many supposedly transitional specimens have only poorly constrained dates (Brown 1993), and in Java the evolved form of *Homo erectus* represented at Ngandong may be as recent as 100,000 years old (Swisher *et al.* 1996). Neither the latter (Rightmire 1987), nor comparisons with anatomically modern fossils from Australia, offer convincing support of regional population continuity from the Middle Pleistocene (Groves 1989; P. Brown 1993). The one part of the world where this does seem traceable is Africa. Finds from the continent's southern tip are particularly crucial.

MSA hominins

Six southern African sites have produced fossil remains of anatomically modern humans in MSA contexts (Fig. 4.1). Most significant is Klasies River Main Site, a complex of interconnected shelters on South Africa's Indian Ocean coast (Fig. 4.2). Singer and Wymer's (1982) initial investigation of its 20 m thick deposits provided an outline depositional history, chronology and cultural stratigraphy, plus important information on subsistence. Subsequent smaller, but more highly resolved, excavations by H. Deacon (1995) offer greater detail on

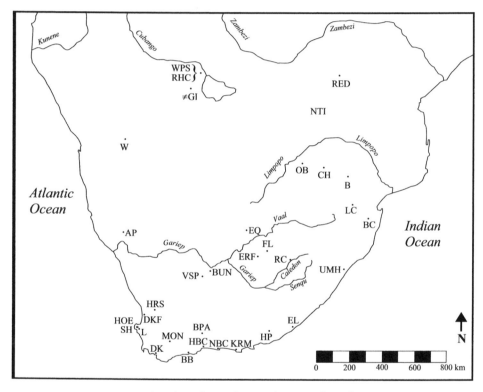

Figure 4.1   Location of archaeological sites discussed in chapter 4. Site names abbreviated thus: AP Apollo 11 Cave; B Bushman Rock Shelter; BB Blombos; BC Border Cave; BPA Boomplaas; BUN Bundu Pan; CH Cave of Hearths; DK Die Kelders; DKF Diepkloof; EL East London; EQ Equus Cave; ERF Erfkroon; FL Florisbad; GI ≠Gi; HBC Herolds Bay Cave; HOE Hoedjiespunt; HP Howieson's Poort typesite; HRS Hollow Rock Shelter; KRM Klasies River Main Site; L Langebaan; LC Lion Cavern; MON Montagu Cave; NBC Nelson Bay Cave; NTI Nswatugi; OB Olieboompoort; RC Rose Cottage Cave; RED Redcliff; RHC Rhino Cave; SH Sea Harvest Midden; UMH Umhlatuzana; VSP Vorentoe se Pan; W Windhoek; WPS White Paintings Shelter.

Figure 4.2   Klasies River Main Site, Eastern Cape, South Africa. Cave 1 is in the
central foreground with Cave 2 above. Cave 1A is to the left and
Cave 1B extends up the slope on the right and beyond the
photograph.

the site's dating and palaeoenvironmental context and the behaviour of its occupants. Both projects recovered the fragmentary remains of several individuals, including mandibles, teeth, cranial fragments and isolated post-cranial
bones. Individual finds occur later in the Klasies sequence, but most are tightly
dated, using the uranium-series, ESR and amino-acid racemisation techniques,
to around 90,000 BP (H. Deacon and Schuurman 1992). Two upper jaw fragments come from an older occupation about 120,000 years ago (H. Deacon
1995). There is no sign that the Klasies hominins were buried. Instead, their
condition, including the fact that some exhibit cutmarks, impact marks and evidence of burning comparable to the rest of the site's fauna, raises the possibility
that they reflect episodes of cannibalism (T. White 1987).

Metrical and morphological data suggest that the Klasies fossils, especially
the teeth, mandibles and facial elements, fall within the range of variation
typical of modern humans (Rightmire and Deacon 1991; Bräuer et al. 1992).
Nevertheless, some specimens seem surprisingly robust or archaic, a conclusion supported by analysis of a partly preserved ulna, one of the most complete
post-cranial bones from the site (Churchill et al. 1996). However, a mosaic evolutionary pattern, with cranial and post-cranial elements evolving at different
rates, would not be surprising. A similar explanation may account for some of

the dimorphism present in the teeth, skull and jaws. Rightmire and Deacon (1991) also suggest that more gracile specimens may be female, more robust ones male, with body size differences caused by differential access to protein-rich foods. Overall, an assessment placing the Klasies fossils early in a process of gracilisation leading to the modern skeletal morphology seems warranted (H. Deacon 1995).

Border Cave (Fig. 4.3) is the other key site to have yielded anatomically modern human remains and MSA artefacts. Here, however, both age and provenance are strongly contested. BC1, a partial adult cranium, and BC2, a partial adult mandible, were found during removal of cave deposits for fertiliser. Other post-cranial fragments found out of context in more recent excavations may originally have been associated with BC1 (A. Morris 1992a). BC3, an infant skeleton found in a clearly defined grave in 1941, and BC5, a mostly intact adult mandible found in 1974, were recovered in archaeological excavations (Beaumont *et al.* 1978). However, bone diagenesis shows that these specimens are both intrusive and that the only ones of demonstrably great age are two isolated ulna and humerus fragments (Sillen and Morris 1996). While this reduces Border Cave's relevance to debates on modern human origins, it remains important for understanding MSA cultural stratigraphy, environments and subsistence patterns.

Further fragmentary human remains come from Equus Cave, a hyena lair that has produced eleven teeth and a partial mandible (Grine and Klein 1985). Its date of > 40,000 BP depends on geological inferences and pollen analysis, rather than association with *in situ* MSA assemblages (cf. A. Morris 1992a). Another hyena lair, Sea Harvest on the Atlantic seaboard, has yielded a further tooth and a phalanx (Grine and Klein 1993). Excavations of MSA levels at Die Kelders (Fig. 4.4) on the southern Cape coast retrieved several more isolated teeth, which share most of their attributes with modern southern African populations, including some not found in modern Eurasian samples (Grine *et al.* 1991; Grine 1998). Further east along the same coast MSA deposits at Blombos Cave dating *c.* 100,000 BP have also produced isolated teeth that fall within the modern southern African range (Grine *et al.* 2000). Two sets of footprints in coastal aeolianite deposits complete the MSA fossil record from southern Africa. Thermoluminescence and uranium-series dating place the older set at East London in the late Middle Pleistocene and the younger ones at Langebaan in the immediate aftermath of the Last Interglacial (H. Deacon 1966; Roberts and Berger 1997; J.C. Vogel *et al.* 1999).

Few and incomplete as they are, these fossils suggest that anatomically modern people were present in southern Africa at least 120,000 years ago (A. Thackeray 1992). The well-dated Klasies River specimens are particularly significant in this respect. Further north, MSA-associated or early Upper Pleistocene human remains are known from several regions of Africa, as well as Israel (Table 4.1). All exhibit modern, or near modern, craniofacial features.

Figure 4.3   Border Cave, KwaZulu-Natal, South Africa (courtesy Peter
Beaumont). The photograph shows the steep west-facing scarp
of the Lebombo Mountains with the Ngwavuma River and
Swaziland's lowveld in the distance. Border Cave itself
is in the centre at far right; the fence along the dripline is
faintly visible.

Figure 4.4   Die Kelders, Western Cape, South Africa (courtesy Ray Inskeep).

Their early dates and the existence of Middle Pleistocene African fossils transitional between *Homo ergaster* and *H. sapiens*, including the Florisbad, Kabwe and Elandsfontein specimens mentioned in chapter 3, suggest a continuity in regional populations difficult to maintain for other regions of the Old World. Though widely dispersed, these specimens thus support the Out-of-Africa 2 model of modern human origins. Genetic studies of modern populations reinforce this conclusion.

All in the genes?

Studies of enzyme and blood group polymorphisms suggested a recent origin for the modern human genome (Nei and Roychoudhury 1974) before Cann *et al.*'s (1987) work on mitochondrial DNA (mtDNA) impacted on the Out-of-Africa/Multiregional debate. While almost all DNA occurs in the cell nucleus, a small amount (<0.001 per cent) is found in mitochondria, the organelles within each cell where respiration takes place. MtDNA evolves rapidly and, because it is only inherited maternally, does not undergo recombination during reproduction. As a result, it retains a record of an individual's evolutionary history; surname inheritance provides a good analogy. Cann *et al.* (1987) showed that Africans exhibit greater genetic diversity than other populations. The most parsimonious set of linkages between populations identified two lineages, separating most Africans from some Africans plus everyone else. They interpreted

Table 4.1 *Early anatomically modern human fossils from Africa and the Near East with absolute dates in excess of 40,000 BP*

Site	Country[a]	Estimated age kya BP	Principal dating techniques used[b]	Reference (Klein 1999 unless otherwise stated)
es Skhul	Israel	90	ESR, TL	
Jebel Qafzeh	Israel	100–90	ESR, TL	
Taramsa	Egypt	55	OSL	Vermeersch *et al.* 1998
Omo-Kibish I	Ethiopia	130	Th/U[c]	
Mumba	Tanzania	130–109	Th/U	
Blombos	South Africa	≥103	ESR, TL	J.C. Vogel *et al.* 1999; Grine *et al.* 2000
Border Cave	South Africa	90–50	AAR, ESR, bone diagenesis	
Die Kelders	South Africa	60–80	ESR, luminescence	Feathers and Bush 2000; Schwarcz and Rink 2000
Equus Cave	South Africa	71–>27	Geology, pollen, radiocarbon	Grine and Klein 1985
Hoedjies Punt	South Africa	71–300	Th/U, geology, fauna	
Klasies River	South Africa	110 and 90	ESR, Th/U	
Sea Harvest	South Africa	127–40	Geology, radiocarbon	

[a]Specimens from Dar es Soltan 2 and Zouhrah, Morocco, and Haua Fteah, Libya, may date to OIS 3–5 on the basis of their artefact associations, but no absolute dates are available.
[b]AAR amino-acid racemisation; ESR electron spin resonance; OSL optically stimulated luminescence; Th/U Thorium-Uranium dating; TL thermoluminescence.
[c]Considerable doubt exists over the stratigraphic associations of this fossil.

these findings as meaning that all present-day humans descend from a single African population, calculating that the common ancestor (dubbed Eve because of mtDNA's maternal transmission) lived 290,000–140,000 years ago.

Criticisms of this work have been numerous and often well founded. Its dependence on African-Americans for its 'African' sample was soon improved upon by Vigilant *et al.*'s (1991) larger study, which again showed an African/non-African split. However, both analyses are statistically flawed. Numerous trees, only some rooting in Africa, can be generated from the same data. There are no statistical grounds for preferring one to another (Hedges *et al.* 1992). Furthermore, tracing the ancestry of one set of genes does not give a complete picture of an individual's genome. This may have multiple origins, depending on the person's ancestry. Gene trees, in other words, are not population trees (Templeton 1993). Placing an age on the common ancestor at the apex of a genetic tree is also problematic. Cann *et al.* (1987) used archaeological evidence for the colonisation of Australia, New Guinea and the Americas to calibrate the rate at which genetic mutations in mtDNA accrue, dates that have now been pushed back. More refined techniques calibrate human mtDNA evolution against the degree of divergence between chimpanzee and human mtDNA (Vigilant *et al.* 1991).

Notwithstanding these critiques and others, such as the likelihood that if Africa supported a larger population then Africans would show greater genetic variation (Relethford and Harpending 1995), numerous other analyses reinforce two of the key conclusions reached by these initial studies. First, sub-Saharan Africans have greater mtDNA diversity than other populations and exhibit a significant degree of genetic distance from them (Merriweather *et al.* 1991). These conclusions are matched by studies of nuclear DNA, which is inherited from both parents (Wainscoat *et al.* 1989; Mountain *et al.* 1993; Tishkoff *et al.* 1996), the genes inherited paternally on the Y-chromosome (Hammer 1995; Whitfield *et al.* 1995), and dental morphology (Irish 1998). Second, humans as a whole show remarkably little mtDNA diversity compared to chimpanzees and gorillas (Cann *et al.* 1994; Horai *et al.* 1995). Together, these findings imply that modern humans have a very recent and African genetic origin.

But dating this remains difficult. Depending on assumptions about mutation rates, the extent to which the genes studied are subject to selection and the calibration used, dates of between 1,000,000 and 112,000 years are obtainable. While the more recent support the Out-of-Africa 2 model, the older ones might just fit *Homo*'s Lower Pleistocene expansion into Eurasia. In this context, the dating of *H. erectus* fossils in Java and Georgia to 1.8–1.7 mya (Swisher *et al.* 1994; Gabunia *et al.* 2000), if confirmed, is important. Given the Multiregional model's need to maintain gene flow across the Old World throughout human evolution, these dates, if correct, make any match with the genetic evidence other than that implied by Out-of-Africa 2 difficult to sustain. For western Eurasia, analysis of mtDNA retrieved from a Neanderthal skeleton in Germany may strengthen this conclusion. Though only about 50,000 years old, its estimated divergence from the modern human line is set 600,000 years ago, using chimpanzee DNA for calibration (Krings *et al.* 1997). Interbreeding between an expanding modern population and archaic hominins in Eurasia is not excluded, but the overall thrust of these analyses is that it must have been extremely limited. Recent estimates of the origin of mtDNA diversity in modern humans reinforce the case for this having been relatively recent. Results from what are known as coalescence times (Ruvolo 1996), and other studies examining stretches of DNA that evolve especially rapidly (microsatellites – Goldstein *et al.* 1995), or are resistant to mutational change (*Alu* sequences – Erlich *et al.* 1995), average at 100,000–200,000 years.

DNA analyses using techniques known as mismatch and intermatch distributions offer one further crucial insight into human history. It seems likely that a major population expansion, of the kind required by the Out-of-Africa 2 model, took place about 60,000–70,000 years ago (Gibbons 1995). Preceding this came a population bottleneck when human numbers were reduced to only a few thousand adults. This too seems difficult to reconcile with a multiregional model of modern human origins, and invites the question as to what caused the crash. Its broad correlation with the explosion of the Sumatran super-volcano Mount Toba around 71,000 BP, which produced the coldest, driest millennium of the Late Pleistocene, offers a highly plausible explanation (Ambrose 1998a). Followed soon after by the onset of OIS 4, these climatic changes perhaps helped cold-adapted Neanderthals replace anatomically modern humans in southwest Asia (Bar-Yosef 1994). Only when they ameliorated may modern humans have expanded north into Eurasia, though early dates for the colonisation of Australasia (Stringer 1999) hint at an earlier eastward dispersal across the southern end of the Red Sea, Arabia and the Gulf.

MSA stone tool assemblages 127,000–50,000 BP

Fossil and genetic evidence points to sub-Saharan Africa as the continent on which modern humans evolved. Whether the emergence of behavioural patterns recognisably the same as those of recent and contemporary humans coincided with or followed this is the subject of continuing debate, one to which southern African evidence increasingly contributes. Before examining these data I first review the MSA record before 40,000 BP, a period when there is little recognisable sign of behavioural modernity elsewhere in the world (Klein 1995).

Middle Stone Age assemblages, as we have seen, probably originated close to 200,000 years ago, but only in and from the Last Interglacial (OIS 5) are they common on the southern African landscape. Well-dated, long-sequence sites are few. The cultural stratigraphy from Klasies River (Singer and Wymer 1982; H. Deacon and Geleijnse 1988; A. Thackeray 1989; H. Deacon 1995) remains crucial. It is supported by observations from other South African sites, especially Boomplaas (H. Deacon 1995), Border Cave (Beaumont 1978; Beaumont *et al.* 1978), Die Kelders (Grine *et al.* 1991; G. Avery *et al.* 1997; A. Thackeray 2000), Blombos (Henshilwood and Sealy 1997), Florisbad (Kuman *et al.* 1999), Rose Cottage Cave (Harper 1997) and Umhlatuzana (Kaplan 1990). Apollo 11 Cave (Wendt 1972) provides the key Namibian sequence (Vogelsang 1996), with several other sites in Lesotho (Carter 1969, 1978; Carter *et al.* 1988). Swaziland, Mozambique and Botswana provide few observations, Zimbabwe a picture more confused than clear (N. Walker 1995a; Larsson 1996). Beyond the radiocarbon barrier, MSA chronology remains dependent upon interweaving the several radiometric techniques mentioned in chapter 2, along with amino-acid racemisation and inferences drawn from palaeoenvironmental data correlated with the global oxygen isotope curve. Emergence of a securely dated framework is further hindered by the limited technological and typological patterning evident in MSA assemblages (A. Thackeray 1992).

As discussed above, Volman's (1984) fourfold scheme offers the best subdivision of southern African MSA lithic assemblages, replacing the variants and industries of earlier authors (Goodwin and van Riet Lowe 1929; Sampson 1974). Detailed inter-site comparisons of morphological variability remain few outside the southern Cape (Volman 1981), constrained by the low proportion of formally retouched artefacts in most assemblages. Emphasising otherwise largely unexamined aspects of stone tool production, such as core reduction techniques and patterns of utilisation, might thus be worth exploring in future classificatory exercises. Table 4.2 outlines Volman's groupings with suggested ages based on the few absolute dates available.

Within the MSA 2 (Fig. 4.5), older (MSA 2a) and younger (MSA 2b) assemblages can be distinguished. Retouched pieces are more common and varied in the latter, though this seems reversed in Namibia (Vogelsang 1996). Large, partially backed flake-blades occur in eastern southern Africa (Cave of Hearths, Border Cave), and some MSA 2b occurrences also include rare small **backed** and/or truncated forms similar to those of the succeeding Howieson's Poort (Volman 1984). Stillbay material from the southern Cape demonstrates a sophisticated competence in pressure-flaking silcrete and other materials (Henshilwood and Sealy 1997). In Zimbabwe the Bambatan Industry includes **scrapers**, **denticulates** and unifacial and bifacial **points**, but no clear trends in raw material or artefact typology are apparent at Redcliff, the only long-sequence MSA site with a collection available for study (Cooke 1978a).

Succeeding the MSA 2, the Howieson's Poort is the best-known and most puzzling component of the southern African Middle Stone Age (Fig. 4.6). Enhanced use of fine-grained rocks and the production of numerous backed pieces recall both LSA microlithic industries and the Eurasian Upper Palaeolithic, exciting interest for what the Howieson's Poort may say about the behavioural competence of its makers and of MSA people as a whole (H. Deacon 1989; Ambrose and

Table 4.2a *The successive subdivisions of the southern African Middle Stone Age (after Volman 1984)*

Division	OIS	Date kyr BP	Core-reduction	Flakes/blades	Retouched artefacts
MSA 3	3–2	60–21	Varied	Highly varied, chief characteristic its post-Howieson's Poort age	Highly varied, but with fewer backed pieces than the Howieson's Poort
Howieson's Poort	5a/4	80–60	Punch technique used for blade production; greater use of fine-grained rocks	Generally smaller, broader and with fewer faceted butts than before or later	Backed tools relatively common, including segments, most often in fine-grained rocks; also scrapers, points
MSA 2	5e–5b	127–80	Prepared cores more common	Many flake-blades, decreasing in length with time	More common: denticulates; points (unifacial and bifacial); scrapers; backing rare
MSA 1	6	200–127	Many radial and disc cores	Small, broad, few have faceted butts	Rare; points absent, scrapers few

Table 4.2b *Absolute dates for the southern African Middle Stone Age before 40,000 BP (excluding radiocarbon determinations)*

Division	Site	Context	Technique[a]	Age kyr BP	Reference
HP	Border Cave	3BS, 3WA and 1RGBS	AAR	106 ± 11 to 69 ± 7	G. Miller *et al.* 1993
			ESR	75 ± 5 to 45 ± 5	Grün *et al.* 1990a
	Die Kelders (HP affiliation unclear)	Layers 4–15	ESR, TL	80–60	G. Avery *et al.* 1997; Feathers and Bush 2000; Schwarcz and Rink 2000
	Diepkloof	Orange Black Series	TL	70.6 ± 8.1	Parkington 1999
				70.9 ± 8.9	
			AMS	>40	
	Klasies River Main Site	Upper Member	ESR	60–40	Grün *et al.* 1990b
			PAL	±70	H. Deacon 1989
MSA 2	Blombos	Uppermost MSA occupation	TL	103 ± 9.8	J.C. Vogel *et al.* 1999
	Border Cave	4BS, 4WA and 5BS	AAR	≥106 ± 11	G. Miller *et al.* 1993
			ESR	141 ± 14 to 62 ± 6	Grün *et al.* 1990a
	Florisbad	Unit F	ESR	121 ± 6	Grün *et al.* 1996
		Units G–M	ESR	157 ± 21	
	Klasies River Main Site	SAS Member	AAR	90–110	Bada and Deems 1975
		SAS Member	ESR	94 ± 10, 88 ± 8	Grün *et al.* 1990b
		LBS Member	OIA	OIS 5e	Shackleton 1982
		LBS Member	Th/U	<110	H. Deacon *et al.* 1988
MSA 1	Florisbad	Units N–P	ESR	≤279 ± 47	Grün *et al.* 1996

[a] AAR amino-acid racemisation; AMS radiocarbon accelerator; ESR electron spin resonance; OIA oxygen isotope analysis; PAL palaeoenvironmental data; Th/U Thorium-Uranium dating; TL thermoluminescence.

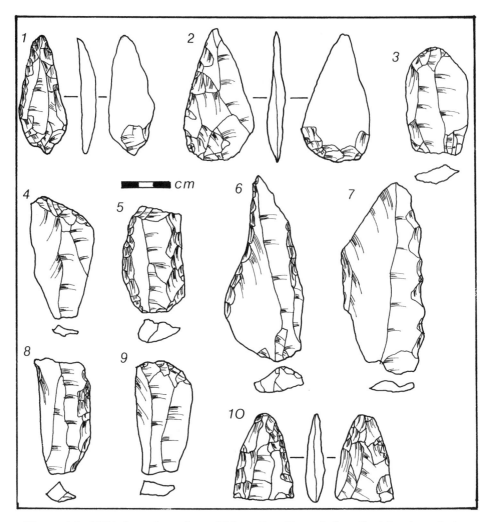

Figure 4.5   MSA 2 artefacts from Nelson Bay Cave. 1–2 unifacial points; 3–4
and 9 scrapers; 5–6 and 8 'sidescrapers' or knives; 7 denticulate; 10
bifacial point fragment (redrawn after Volman 1978: Figs. 16, 17, 22,
23; courtesy Tom Volman). All in quartzite.

Lorenz 1990). These similarities led to its previous classification as transitional
between MSA and LSA technologies under the heading 'Second Intermediate'
(J.D. Clark 1959). Associated radiocarbon dates probably reflect sample contam-
ination (J. Deacon 1995), though Parkington (1990a) suggested that some may be
credible, raising the possibility that not all Howieson's Poort occurrences form
part of the same phenomenon. However, this view is not widely shared and the
consensus of radiometric dates from Border Cave, Die Kelders, Diepkloof and
Klasies River (Table 4.2) is that the Howieson's Poort falls within the period
80,000–60,000 BP. A more precise age of c. 70,000 BP may be indicated by

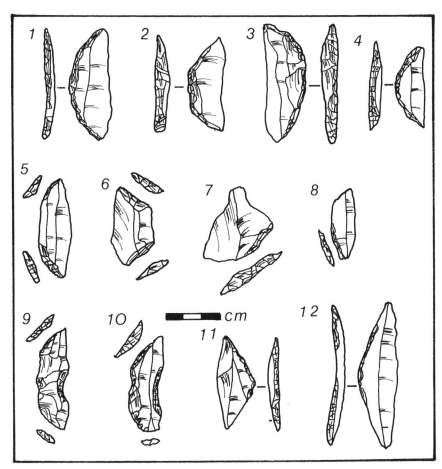

Figure 4.6   Howieson's Poort artefacts from Nelson Bay Cave. 1–4 segments;
5–6 trapezoids; 7–8 truncated pieces; 9 trapezoid with notch
(silcrete); 10 strangulated and backed piece (silcrete); 11–12 triangles
(redrawn after Volman 1978: Figs. 27, 28, 30, 32; courtesy Tom
Volman). All in quartzite unless otherwise stated.

palaeoenvironmental data from Klasies River (Klein 1976; D.M. Avery 1987a;
J.F. Thackeray 1988b; H. Deacon 1989), but alternative matches with the global
oxygen isotope curve are not impossible (Van Andel 1989; Parkington 1990a).

Post-Howieson's Poort MSA assemblages (MSA 3) exhibit considerable variation in typology and stone-working techniques, opening up the possibility of
regionally diverse trajectories between MSA and LSA stone-working traditions
(Fig. 4.7; chapter 5). At Boomplaas, for example, larger flake-blades characterise
the uppermost part of the MSA 3 sequence (Volman 1984), while at Border Cave
blades became shorter and squatter with time (Beaumont *et al.* 1978). Other
contrasts affect retouched artefacts. Scrapers dominate MSA 3 assemblages at

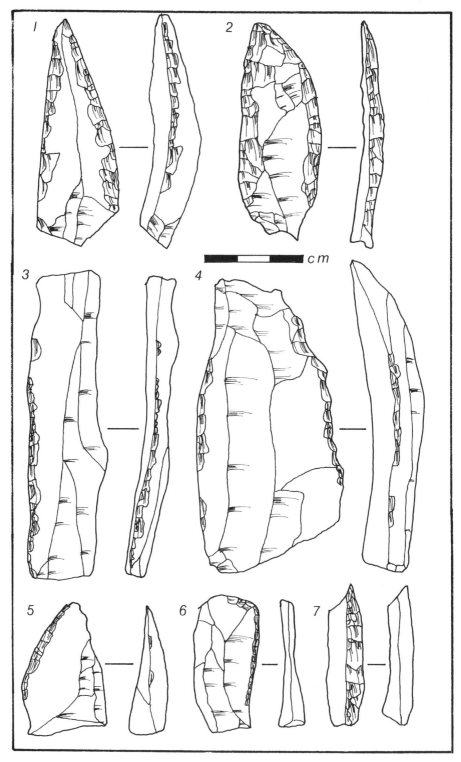

Figure 4.7 Post-Howiesons Poort (MSA 3) artefacts from Sehonghong. 1 point
(hornfels); 2 unifacial point; 3 knife (hornfels); 4 denticulate
(hornfels); 5 scraper; 6 knife; 7 backed blade. All in opaline unless
otherwise stated.

Rose Cottage Cave, which has one of the longest sequences with material of this age (Harper 1997), but at Umhlatuzana unifacial and bifacial points are the most common formal tools (Kaplan 1990). How to make sense of this inter-site variability and integrate excavated sequences with open-air sites that, in almost all cases, lack any dating framework at all are among the principal challenges of MSA studies.

Artefact patterning in space and time

With chronology poorly developed, studies of artefact patterning necessarily emphasise within-site comparisons. At issue here, as in Europe's Middle Palaeolithic (Mellars 1996), is the degree to which formal artefacts of standardised design can be recognised and time-restricted 'stylistic' changes in artefact popularity identified. Their presence would support claims for recognisably modern behaviour among southern Africa's MSA inhabitants before 40,000 BP. The Howieson's Poort is particularly important here since it seems so distinctive and is recognisable across a much wider area than other MSA variants. Nevertheless, studies at Klasies River (A. Thackeray 1989; Wurz 1999), Border Cave (Beaumont *et al.* 1978), Rose Cottage Cave (Harper 1997) and Umhlatuzana (Kaplan 1990) make plain that it cannot be separated from the rest of the MSA stone-working tradition, notwithstanding its greater use of backed tools and changes in artefact size and raw material usage. Continuities in flake-blade production there and at Rose Cottage show this clearly. The Howieson's Poort is by no means the only time-restricted patterning evident in the MSA. At Klasies, for example, increasingly standardised small triangular convergent flake-blades concentrate at the top of the SAS Member and long, thin flake-blades with bruised platforms earlier on at the base of the LBS Member (A. Thackeray 1989).

Such time-restricted patterning has been used to argue that MSA people employed the stylistic attributes of stone artefacts to convey information about their makers' identity just as material culture is used by all modern societies. The case has been most strongly developed for the Howieson's Poort at Klasies River (H. Deacon 1989, 1995; Wurz 1999). The argument is grounded in the similarity between Howieson's Poort backed artefacts and mid-Holocene backed microliths assumed to have been used to arm hunting weapons, as well as in the preferential selection of non-local (more valuable?) raw materials, rather than local quartzite, for their manufacture. Recent Bushman hunters exchanged arrows among themselves and these arrows also helped define linguistic boundaries between Bushman groups (Wiessner 1983). Howieson's Poort backed artefacts, which were probably also hafted, could have functioned similarly. Dating them to the colder, drier conditions of OIS 4 provides an environmental context for their innovation, with subsequent climatic amelioration removing selection for the same level of symbolic behaviour and provoking a return to more 'typical' MSA technologies. The implication is that the makers of Howieson's Poort artefacts responded to ecological stress and structured inter-group social relations in ways similar to those of recent hunter-gatherers (H. Deacon 1989).

This is an attractive proposition, but far from proven. The analogy with mid-Holocene **backed microliths** is weak, since microwear and experimental work suggest that Wilton segments were used as knife components, not weapon armatures (Wadley and Binneman 1995). Direct evidence for the function of Howieson's Poort backed artefacts is simply lacking (Wurz 1999). What makes rocks 'non-local' is also unclear. Different patterns of movement and changes in how sites and their surroundings were used could have altered the procurement strategies of their inhabitants, particularly if they brought some component of their assemblages with them ready made. Additionally, some of the silcrete and hornfels used at Klasies may have been transported close to the site by rivers (A. Thackeray 1989). Finally, the degree of standardisation evident among Howieson's Poort backed artefacts can be overstated, although Wurz (1999) indicates that at least for some metric parameters those from Klasies River show a comparable degree of variation to their LSA homologues.

Except in the Howieson's Poort and Stillbay Industries, retouch is a rare and minimal feature of MSA assemblages (A. Thackeray 1989, 2000). Considerable morphological variability is also evident among artefacts classified as scrapers, points and **knives** at Rose Cottage Cave (Wadley and Harper 1989). Other than at Klasies River (Wurz 1999), few MSA assemblages have yet been systematically investigated from the standpoint of reconstructing the **chaînes opératoires** leading to their production, but such variability in size, shape, and extent and position of retouch recalls studies of Middle Palaeolithic toolkits which emphasise the important part played by differential reduction and use in final artefact form (Mellars 1996). Discounting this kind of situational variability is necessary before invoking more complex explanations to account for time-restricted patterning in MSA assemblages.

The other, and as yet unexplained, way in which Howieson's Poort assemblages stand out within the overall MSA sequence lies in their extensive spatial distribution. Known from across South Africa (J. Deacon 1995), Lesotho (Carter 1978; Mitchell and Steinberg 1992) and Namibia (Vogelsang 1996), they may also occur in Zimbabwe. There the Bambatan Industry was followed by the Tshangulan, but the latter term has been applied to at least two distinct industries, a situation complicated by stratigraphic anomalies and coarse excavation techniques (Larsson 1996; N. Walker and Thorp 1997). Large segments at Nswatugi suggest an affiliation of at least some 'Tshangulan' material to the Howieson's Poort (N. Walker 1995a).

Detailed connections between southern African MSA assemblages and those north of the Zambezi are more difficult to trace. The Howieson's Poort, for example, seems to be very much a southern African phenomenon, with a distribution recalling those of several LSA industries (H. Deacon and Deacon 1999) and southern Africa's distinctively naturalistic rock art (D. Phillipson 1977). The northern limits of all correspond closely to the southern limit of the Miombo Biome (H. Deacon 1993). Conversely, the foliate points and core-axes distinctive of the Congo Basin's Lupemban Complex are with very few exceptions (Mason 1962; MacCalman and Viereck 1967; Humphreys 1974) unknown in southern Africa. Persistence of this regional distinctiveness over the last 70,000 years or more *could* imply a long-lasting isolation of southern African populations with implications for the evolution of the Khoisan phenotype (H. Deacon 1989), though backed artefacts also occur in chronologically diverse MSA contexts north of the Zambezi (Mehlman 1991). The potentially long-standing distinctiveness of the Khoisan among a generalised African population is hinted at by some genetic studies (Nurse *et al.* 1985; Wainscoat *et al.* 1989).

Not by stone alone – bone tools and composite artefacts in the MSA

Though detailed edge-wear and residue studies of stone tools have yet to be undertaken, evidence also exists for the use of organic materials in MSA technology. Wood itself is only represented by a possible throwing stick from Florisbad (J.D. Clark 1955), but hafting of stone tools may have been a crucial technological innovation of MSA people. Microwear studies of Middle Palaeolithic stone artefacts from western Eurasia (Mellars 1996) show that it was widely employed by both Neanderthals and modern humans alike. In southern Africa it is indicated as early as the MSA 2 when tanged artefacts and others with extensive proximal retouch suggest modification to fit into a handle. The unifacial and bifacial points which appear from the same time are also best interpreted as having been held in a haft, retained in place by lashing or the use of **mastic** (Fig. 4.8). Size considerations make it probable that the backed pieces typical of the Howieson's Poort were also hafted, but direct evidence of the use of mastic is limited to a single utilised blade from MSA 3 levels at Apollo 11 Cave (Wendt 1972).

All the hafts used by MSA people were probably of wood; neither bone handles nor specialised stone tools for their production have been recovered. Excavations of MSA 2 (Stillbay) levels at Blombos (Fig. 4.9) have, however, produced over twenty items of worked bone, including 'awls', a possible peg and two ground and polished bone points, one with minute indentations at its snapped end perhaps caused by tight binding to a haft (Henshilwood and Sealy 1997; Fig. 4.10). Carbon and nitrogen analyses group them with the site's MSA faunal remains, confirming their age, now put at ≥ 100,000 BP (J.C. Vogel *et al.* 1999). Barbed and unbarbed bone points are also known from apparently MSA contexts at Semliki in eastern Congo bracketed between 174,000 ± 800 and 82,000 ± 8000 BP (Brooks *et al.* 1995; Yellen *et al.* 1995). The Semliki specimens closely resemble similar artefacts from the same area of terminal Pleistocene/Holocene

Figure 4.8 Pressure-flaked Stillbay points from Blombos Cave (courtesy Chris Henshilwood).

Figure 4.9 Blombos Cave, Western Cape, South Africa (courtesy Chris Henshilwood).

Figure 4.10   Bone artefacts from Blombos Cave, Western Cape, South Africa (courtesy Chris Henshilwood).

age, but may be wrongly dated (Feathers 1996). Otherwise, they and the Blombos finds suggest that bone tools similar to those made by LSA people also formed part of MSA toolkits. They also lend credibility to earlier finds of bone points at Kabwe (J.D. Clark *et al.* 1950) and Klasies River (Singer and Wymer 1982) and to ground warthog and bushpig tusk 'daggers' of MSA 3 age at Border Cave (Beaumont *et al.* 1978).

Modern behaviour: a question of subsistence?

Obtaining food dominates discussions of MSA behavioural competence, with much of the debate centred around Klasies River and other Cape coastal sites. Plant remains, though, are virtually absent from the record, carbonised seeds at Border Cave (Beaumont 1978), Bushman Rock Shelter (Plug 1981a) and Umhlatuzana (Kaplan 1990) being possibly intrusive. Grindstones, only rarely ochre-stained, do occur, most frequently in the Savanna Biome where seeds and nuts would have been dominant staples (Volman 1984). At Klasies River Main Site carbonised lenses in Howieson's Poort levels resemble the humified, burnt residues of geophytes on Holocene sites in the Eastern Cape, indicating exploitation of this resource (H. Deacon 1989). Their sustained use may have required controlled burning of the landscape. The abundance of hearths in MSA contexts renders this feasible, though palaeoenvironmental support for changes in the intensity and frequency of fires is so far lacking. If MSA people, at least in the Fynbos Biome, did rely on carbohydrate-rich plant foods, supplemented by game and, in places, shellfish, their subsistence strategies may have been much the same as those of LSA foragers in the same environment. MSA and LSA assemblages occur at many of the same sites, including those within the Cape Fold Belt Mountains, supporting this argument and contrasting with Acheulean site distributions in the same biome (H. Deacon 1995).

With plant residues so rare, research emphasises animal food waste. Notwithstanding (or because of?) the relative poverty of its terrestrial ecosystem, the Fynbos Biome preserves some of the oldest evidence for marine resource exploitation anywhere in the world. Extensive MSA shell middens, all of broadly Last Interglacial age, accumulated at Klasies River, Die Kelders, Herolds Bay (J. Brink and Deacon 1982) and open-air sites such as Sea Harvest and Hoedjies Punt (Volman 1978; Parkington 1999). The intensity of exploitation may, however, have been less than at LSA middens, where the mean size of species such as limpets (*Patella* spp.) is noticeably smaller (Klein 1989); the same kind of evidence also indicates less intensive MSA exploitation of tortoises (Klein and Cruz-Uribe 1983).

As well as shellfish, MSA coastal sites document the procurement of several other marine animals. Cape fur seals (*Arctocephalus pusillus*) occur at both Klasies River and Die Kelders. Analysis of age distributions suggests that MSA people took more adult and subadult animals and fewer 9- to 11-month-old individuals than Holocene people in the Cape (Klein and Cruz-Uribe 1996). Since yearling seals wash up along the coast in large numbers when forced from breeding sites by adults, perhaps only LSA people homed in on this seasonal abundance to time coastal visits accordingly. Fish and flying birds are virtually absent from some coastal MSA sites, again unlike later Holocene LSA faunas from the same areas. At Klasies River, for example, only small fish occur, concentrating in non-occupation levels consistent with an introduction by roosting seabirds (H. Deacon 1989). However, excavations at Blombos require a revision of previous wisdom on this point. Here three species (*Cymatoceps nasutus, Galeichthyes (Aries) feliceps, Liza richardsonii*) seem too big to have been brought to the site in bird stomachs, implying they were caught by people, perhaps using spears or harpoons tipped with the bone points described above (Henshilwood and Sealy 1997). Inland, freshwater fishing is indicated by catfish and **cichlid** bones in basal layers at White Paintings Shelter in the north-western Kalahari (Robbins *et al.* 1994).

How should we interpret these contrasts between MSA and LSA faunas? On one view MSA people either did not see some resources (flying birds; fish?) as food, did not practise the same kind of seasonal mobility (perhaps living on the coast year-round) and exploited resources less efficiently (Klein and Cruz-Uribe 1996). Alternatively, the observed differences could reflect lower MSA population densities, different (but not necessarily less 'efficient') patterns of seasonal movement, a lack of appropriate technology (e.g. the bow and arrow for taking flying birds) and a reduced need for bird bone as a raw material (H. Deacon 1989; A. Thackeray 1992). Existing evidence supports both arguments, and the Blombos fish caution against assuming that a complete picture of marine resource exploitation is yet available.

Large mammals comprise the remainder of the MSA faunal record and have provoked the most intense discussion, with Klasies River again centrestage. One analytical strategy emphasises comparisons between MSA faunas there and at Die Kelders of Last Interglacial (OIS 5) age and Holocene LSA faunas in the Fynbos Biome. The idea is to control for environmental differences by contrasting assemblages accumulated under broadly similar conditions. Any differences may thus be behaviourally significant. LSA people seem to have taken animals roughly proportional to their historically observed frequencies, but MSA faunas emphasise species such as eland (*Taurotragus oryx*; Fig. 4.11), said to be comparatively docile and easy to hunt. More dangerous taxa, such as Cape buffalo and bushpig, are rare (Klein 1975, 1976; Klein and Cruz-Uribe 1996). The implication is that MSA people found it more difficult to hunt dangerous animals, perhaps because they lacked access to the traps and bows used by their LSA successors.

Klein (1978c, 1981) also uses reconstructed mortality profiles of MSA bovids to investigate differences in hunting strategy. Established by measuring dental

Figure 4.11   Eland (*Taurotragus oryx*) photographed in Etosha National Park, Namibia.

crown heights calibrated against modern specimens of known age, they show that, for the most part, MSA people focused on old and very young individuals, those most vulnerable to predation because of age, inexperience or disease. This is true, for example, of Cape buffalo at Klasies River, among which very young animals are abundant, perhaps even reflecting targeting of mothers giving birth (Klein 1976). Eland, on the other hand, exhibit a catastrophic mortality profile comparable to the age structure of living herds. This implies that MSA hunters took whole groups, possibly exploiting this species' susceptibility to flight and to being driven (Estes 1992). Such hunting is unlikely to have been frequent, however, or it would have impacted heavily on total eland numbers. Furthermore, since eland were uncommon in the Fynbos Biome in the recent past and there is no reason to think that a different situation prevailed in OIS 5, their higher frequencies in MSA contexts suggest that other animals were encountered even more rarely (Klein and Cruz-Uribe 1996).

Klein's arguments can be summarised as indicating that MSA people were less competent hunters than their LSA successors. A much more limited view of their abilities was taken by Binford (1984), who argued that the Klasies people acquired most of their meat from scavenging, with only limited hunting of the smallest antelope, that they did not share food and that the site itself was used only sporadically for 'snacking' rather than as a home-base. These conclusions derive from his taphonomic study of the fauna from Singer and Wymer's (1982) excavation, which emphasised skeletal part frequencies and evidence for hominin and carnivore damage to the bones interpreted by reference to actualistic studies of modern hunters and predators. Critiques have been numerous. Not all the Klasies fauna was accumulated by people (J.F. Thackeray 1990b), some of the excavated bones were discarded on-site as unidentifiable (Turner 1989) and the vast amounts of shellfish brought back to the site over several kilometres argue overwhelmingly for food-sharing (H. Deacon 1985). Most discussion turns on the scavenging/hunting question. Similar body part representations, emphasising feet and skull bones over upper limbs, are common at many later sites where hunting or culling domestic herds was clearly practised (Klein 1989). Differential preservation (in part because of processing of long bones for marrow) and transportation (the **'schlepp effect'**) may account for the skeletal frequencies which Binford observed, coupled with the exclusion from most archaeozoological analyses of supposedly unidentifiable long bone shaft fragments (Bartram and Marean 1999). In addition, eland mortality profiles strongly imply hunting of adult animals (Klein 1989).

Additional perspectives are afforded by Milo's (1998) more recent study of bone damage signatures at Klasies River. This indicates active predation on all sizes of bovids, including even giant buffalo (*Pelorovis antiquus*), a vertebra of which has the tip of a stone point embedded within it. This is as direct a piece of evidence for hunting as one could find. Thrusting or throwing spears, perhaps already using poison (J.D. Clark 1993b), would make sense of some of

Figure 4.12   Partial view of the excavation area at Florisbad, Free State, South
Africa.

the evidence for the hafting of MSA artefacts discussed above, as would planting
spears in pit-traps, which implies knowledge of animal movements and use of a
variety of strategies to take large game. Milo further concludes that eland were
butchered in a more systematic 'production line' manner than other animals,
consistent with Klein's suggestion that they were killed in groups, rather than
as individuals.

Dating to the Last Interglacial, Florisbad (Fig. 4.12) is one of the few inland
or open-air locations to inform on MSA subsistence. J. Brink's (1987) analysis
shows that people targeted bovids weighing less than 100 kg and preferentially
took prime-adult blesbok and bastard hartebeest (*Damaliscus* spp.). Finds concentrate around several spring eyes, suggesting that hunters ambushed animals
coming to drink, butchering them nearby. Hippo bones in the same occupation
may, however, represent scavenging of animals dying naturally (Kuman *et al.*
1999). Preliminary observations from other open-air Free State locations, including Erfkroon, suggest a different land-use pattern along river margins, with
a much more diverse fauna that includes several large ungulate taxa (J. Brink
and Henderson 2001; Churchill *et al.* 2000). In the northern Kalahari, ≠Gi
tells a similar story. Here excavation of a MSA occupation probably dating to
OIS 4/5 documents procurement of several large and/or dangerous animals,
including warthog (*Phacochoerus aethiopicus*), zebra, giant buffalo and Cape
horse (*Equus capensis*), again perhaps using ambush hunting as a technique

(Helgren and Brooks 1983). Both sites, along with Border Cave (Klein 1977), Klasies River and others in Namibia (J.F. Thackeray 1979; Cruz-Uribe and Klein 1983), support the case for MSA people hunting a range of animals. No doubt like recent foragers they scavenged those that died naturally or were killed by predators, but they were far from the subhumans pictured by Binford (1984). Studies of Middle Palaeolithic faunas in western Eurasia concur in showing that both Neanderthals and early modern humans practised a mix of hunting and scavenging strategies (Mellars 1996).

Of necessity, MSA subsistence studies emphasise those few sites with adequate faunal preservation. However, their rarity means that they have generally to be considered in isolation from the settlement-subsistence systems of which they formed part. Larger-scale investigations that consider the distribution of MSA sites across the landscape are therefore important. In the Fynbos Biome, as we have seen, MSA and LSA sites occupy similar locations, distinct from the more water-focused situations preferred by Acheulean hominins. In the Nama-Karoo Biome, sites of the Orangian Industry in the Seacow Valley concentrate more around riverbanks than in the Acheulean, perhaps denoting a different mobility pattern (Sampson 1985a). Pan-centred MSA settlement is also indicated further west in Bushmanland, where Bundu preserves a range of large mammal bones in association with MSA artefacts (Fig. 4.13; Beaumont *et al.* 1995). In both areas MSA occupation may have been largely

Figure 4.13   Bundu Pan, Northern Cape, South Africa.

restricted to wetter episodes (Sampson 1985a; Beaumont 1986). The makers of MSA 2 and Howieson's Poort artefacts also sustained more intensive occupation of higher altitude (≥ 1800 m above sea-level) parts of Lesotho than their Acheulean predecessors (Carter 1978). However, contrasts with LSA settlement signatures (Bousman 1988; Mitchell 1996a) are difficult to assess without better chronologies and more information on subsistence and palaeoenvironmental context.

Further insights come from considering evidence for the long-range movement of items found at MSA sites. Most impressive are a few fragments of marine shell from MSA 2b deposits at Apollo 11 (Fig. 4.14), over 100 km from the Atlantic Ocean (Wendt 1972), and a single unperforated *Burnupena africana* shell found in sediments yielding MSA 1 artefacts at Vorentoe se Pan, near Vanwyksvlei, Northern Cape, over 400 km from the Atlantic (Beaumont *et al.* 1995). Elsewhere claims have been made that some Howieson's Poort assemblages show enhanced use of non-local rocks, with Border Cave, where chalcedony was obtained from over 40 km away (Beaumont 1978), the most convincing example since raw material sources are less tightly identified or within a few kilometres at Klasies River (A. Thackeray 1989), Nelson Bay Cave (Volman 1981) and Rose Cottage Cave (Harper 1997); preferential use of 'non-local' materials for making retouched artefacts is also claimed at MSA sites

Figure 4.14   View out from Apollo 11 Cave, Namibia (courtesy David Coulson, Trust for African Rock Art, Robert Estall Agency).

in the Tsodilo Hills, Botswana (Robbins and Murphy 1998). Expansion of local foraging ranges and/or development of inter-group alliances to cope with reduced resource abundance and predictability during OIS 4/5a remain to be demonstrated as a general pattern.

Art, ritual and the use of living space

The stone tools and animal bones that comprise most of the archaeological record often prove ambiguous or uninformative when comparing the behaviour of MSA people with that of their LSA successors. We can also look for evidence that MSA people before 40,000 BP produced art, decorated their bodies, engaged in ritual activities or modified the space in which they lived.

Other than the tools discussed earlier, worked bone is limited to rare notched or incised fragments at Apollo 11, Klasies River, Blombos and Border Cave. All except the latter (MSA 3) come from MSA 2 contexts (Volman 1984; Henshilwood and Sealy 1997). How far these items, or notched or incised pieces of ochre from the Howieson's Poort type-site (Volman 1984), Wonderwerk (Fig. 4.15) and Hollow Rock Shelter in the Cedarberg Mountains (Evans 1994), document a notational system is doubtful, though the suggestion has been made

Figure 4.15   Incised and ground fragment of haematite from Howieson's Poort levels at Wonderwerk Cave, Northern Cape, South Africa (courtesy Peter Beaumont).

(Beaumont 1978). Similar finds in Europe's Middle Palaeolithic are explained in functional terms (Chase and Dibble 1987). Evidence for jewellery or ritual is also weak. Ostrich eggshell beads at Boomplaas (H. Deacon 1995) and Bushman Rock Shelter (Plug 1981a) are probably out of their original (LSA?) contexts, and the instrusive nature of the infant skeleton from Border Cave removes from consideration the only burial with claims to a MSA association and its perforated *Conus* shell ornament (Sillen and Morris 1996). Arguments that cannibalistic activity at Klasies River necessarily carried ritual implications that speak to modern cognitive capacities (H. Deacon 1995) need substantiation.

More persuasive evidence of ritual activity or bodily decoration might be the widespread presence of red ochre at MSA sites, the sharp jump in its use in the MSA 2 and signs of colour selection (Knight *et al.* 1995; Watts 1998). Sometimes, as at Klasies River (A. Thackeray 1989) and Olieboompoort (Mason 1962), ochre pieces were apparently used as crayons. Mining of specular haematite was underway at Lion Cavern, Swaziland by at least 40,000 and perhaps as early as 110,000 BP (Beaumont 1973) and specularite occurs in MSA levels at Rhino Cave in the Tsodilo Hills (Robbins *et al.* 1996a). Presumably these pigments were used in body decoration, but decoration of artefacts, hide-working and use in barrier creams are also possible. For rock art, however, there is no evidence older than 27,000 BP, although incised ostrich eggshell fragments occur in Howieson's Poort contexts at Apollo 11 Cave (Wendt 1976) and Diepkloof, where two pieces are AMS-dated to > 40,000 BP (Parkington 1999).

Few sites have sufficient spatio-temporal resolution to allow investigations of how MSA people organised their living space. At Florisbad, where over 450 m^2 have been excavated, individual stone-working and butchery events are identifiable, but show little sign of being spatially structured in a distinctively modern manner (Kuman *et al.* 1999), though distinct carcass-processing and consumption areas seem identifiable (Fig 4.16; J. Brink and Henderson 2001). At Klasies River Main Site the limited area left for Deacon's fine-scale excavations greatly reduced the opportunities for investigating spatial patterning. However, the MSA 2 occupation of Shelter 1B provides evidence of consistency in hearth positioning and discrete dumping of shellfish (Henderson 1992), the latter paralleled in Shelter 1C (H. Deacon 1995). Whether this reflects more than purely functional considerations relating to the removal of waste and reuse of hearths in a context of repeated/lengthy occupation is a moot point.

Evidence that early modern people in southern Africa modified their living sites in any other way is limited. Enigmatic artificial stone accumulations *may* occur in MSA 2 levels at Apollo 11 (Wendt 1976) and Montagu Cave (Keller 1973), and groups of stone balls, some of them worked but of unknown purpose, come from spring deposits at Windhoek (with a MSA point) and Esere, Namibia (Fock 1954; J.D. Clark 1982). More convincing are the stone-lined hearths and posthole-supported windbreaks excavated at Mumbwa, Zambia, which offer the best evidence of their kind south of the Sahara (Barham 1996).

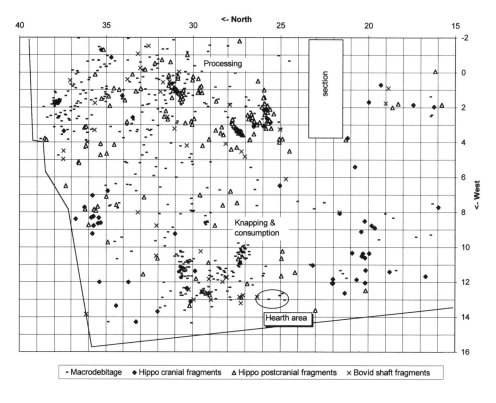

Figure 4.16   Spatial patterning at Florisbad, Free State, South Africa (courtesy Zoe Henderson).

Defining modernity

This chapter has examined three datasets relating to distinct, though interrelated, aspects of modernity. Genetic evidence points to a recent African origin for the genome shared by modern human populations, with most estimates placing this within the range 250,000–100,000 BP. Khoisan populations may have diverged from other African groups by 150,000 years ago and contain a surprisingly high degree of genetic diversity, perhaps indicating that the modern genome evolved in the southern part of the continent. Africa (with Israel) also has the oldest well-dated anatomically modern human fossils anywhere in the world, with Klasies River offering crucial support to this position. Neither in the Far East nor, more certainly, in Europe is evidence of continuity between archaic Middle Pleistocene hominins and anatomically modern humans as sustainable. Together, fossil and genetic research thus support the argument that modern humans originated in Africa late in the Middle Pleistocene. That some DNA studies suggest that the common ancestor of modern humans lived 100,000 or more years before the earliest known anatomically modern specimens is not a problem for the Out-of-Africa 2 model. The ancestor of the present-day human mtDNA genome, or any particular set of nuclear DNA genes, need not have been anatomically modern (Stoneking *et al.* 1993). An even longer timelag may be expected before major change is evident in the archaeological record, since much human behaviour is socially constructed and transmitted, not genetically programmed (Gamble 1993).

If there is no reason why genetic, anatomical and behavioural modernity should all have developed at the same time, why did at least the first two have an African origin? Foley (1989) notes that while major environmental shifts cyclically affected all continents during the Pleistocene, south-east Asia was ecologically more stable and higher latitudes in Eurasia witnessed more severe, rapid changes. Local evolution and eventual speciation are likelier in tropical savanna settings with more mosaic spatio-temporal patterning of resources. Africa, on this model, witnessed sufficient, but not too much, environmental change. But what, in particular, led to the evolution of the modern human morphology is unclear. The possibility, supported by the Klasies fossils, that craniofacial change came first in a process of mosaic evolution suggests that the ancestors of modern humans initially reduced reliance on their jaws, perhaps for tools as well as for food-processing (Klein 1999). Only later may behavioural changes have reduced selection for robust post-cranial skeletons.

Accepting that anatomically modern humans originated in Africa, how can we summarise the archaeological evidence for their behaviour? The criteria used to evaluate behavioural 'modernity' (Table 4.3) are judged Eurocentric by some (H. Deacon 1995), though many are also applicable elsewhere in the Old World, not just in Europe's Upper Palaeolithic (e.g. Morse 1993). Other potential biases are less easy to correct. One danger is to view cultural change through the Upper Pleistocene as directional and progressive (given that we benefit from the hindsight of knowing that ultimately behaviourally/anatomically modern humans – ourselves – survived and flourished where other hominins did not). A second is the tendency when evaluating a very sparse, poorly dated southern African record to lump everything together, emphasising the few well-excavated sequences with good organic preservation and ignoring potentially profound variability across time and space.

Evidence for symbolic activity on the part of MSA people has long been considered weak during the time-frame covered by this chapter. Ochre was used, but arguments that this necessarily implies the development of ritual and group identities within the context of structuring female reproductive strategies (Knight *et al.* 1995; Power and Watts 1996) seem strained. Perhaps more

Table 4.3 *Archaeological criteria commonly accepted as evidence of modern behaviour (after Mellars 1989; Klein 1995)*

More diverse, specialised and standardised artefact types, including construction
    of composite artefacts involving several raw materials or multi-insert forms
More rapid and tightly patterned assemblage variability over time and across space
Production of formal artefacts from bone, antler and ivory
Unequivocal evidence for art, including personal ornaments
Modification of living space, e.g. through construction of pavements, walls,
    elaborate hearths and spatial segregation of activities
Regular long-distance (>50 km) transport of stone raw materials and other
    items (e.g. shells for jewellery)
Unequivocal evidence for ritual behaviour, including deposition of grave goods
    in burials
Colonisation of major new environments (Siberia, Australasia) and more sustained
    settlement of high-latitude/high-altitude/desert areas previously abandoned
    under full glacial conditions
Evidence of fishing, more specialised hunting and food storage
Population densities more comparable to those of modern foragers in similar
    environments

---

tellingly, there is no evidence for burial, personal ornaments or art, except in the form of rare incised fragments of ochre and ostrich eggshell. Blombos and other sites do suggest that (some) MSA people made bone tools and Mumbwa offers evidence that they (sometimes) modified their living space. Given the small number of carefully and extensively excavated MSA sites with good organic preservation, we must ask if such evidence is rare because of sample error. If not, then future research must address the social and ecological circumstances under which such innovations developed and whether when similar circumstances developed again, or elsewhere, similar or different responses were evoked. Alternatively, perhaps MSA societies structured themselves on a scale that precluded widespread diffusion of innovations (Yellen 1998). Despite enhanced use of more distant lithic raw materials in some Howieson's Poort assemblages, the scale on which they moved is no different from that seen at the same time in Europe (Mellars 1996), and much less impressive than in the Upper Palaeolithic (Gamble 1986), even though seashells were occasionally transported over longer distances. The Howieson's Poort may, like MSA industries in East Africa (J.D. Clark 1988), show a distinct regional distribution, but smaller-scale spatial patterning suggestive of the use of stone artefacts to transmit information about group affiliation is lacking. Or is this once again because we have too few well-dug sites and little way of integrating open-air occurrences with excavated assemblages? Hints of temporal patterning in the Klasies sequence and of standardisation in the manufacture of Howieson's Poort and Stillbay artefacts suggest that at least some MSA sequences exhibit tight chronological patterning of the kind known in the LSA.

Thus while MSA people hafted stone tools, hunted a wide range of animals (sometimes co-operatively), fished and collected geophytes and shellfish, evidence for art, jewellery, bone tool manufacture, exchange and tightly restricted artefact patterning is more limited or ambiguous. New research at Blombos, Diepkloof, Klasies River, Mumbwa and elsewhere is challenging the view that the anatomically modern people whose remains we have considered in this chapter displayed significantly less complex kinds of behaviour than humans living after 40,000/50,000 years ago, but far too little high-quality research has yet been undertaken to determine the spatio-temporal scale over which this challenge can be sustained, still less to offer explanations for it. While significant contrasts *may* exist between MSA and Acheulean behaviour, there are also strong similarities between the pre 40,000/50,000 BP MSA record in southern Africa and that produced by Middle Palaeolithic populations in Eurasia (Table 4.4). But Diepkloof and Blombos to one side, the absence of art and jewellery still seems crucial in suggesting important, perhaps profound, differences between anatomically modern humans either side of 40,000/50,000 BP.

If so, is it to this time-frame that we should look for the emergence of humans who were cognitively, as well as anatomically, like ourselves, and was this the competitive edge that then allowed them to colonise the rest of the Old World? Precisely when and where such a transition took place is unknown. East Africa is one possibility, given the increased artefact standardisation and ostrich eggshell beads evident at Enkapune ya Muto, Kenya, from 45,000 BP (Ambrose 1998b). Expansion from here would be consistent with dates for the earliest Upper Palaeolithic industries in the Levant (46,000 BP; Bar-Yosef *et al.* 1996) and south-eastern Europe (43,000 BP; Mellars 1996), as well as with the oldest securely dated ostrich eggshell beads from southern Africa (38,000 BP at Border Cave; chapter 5). On the other hand, a surprisingly early ochre-stained burial from Australia dating 62,000 BP, the oldest sure evidence for its colonisation (Stringer 1999), suggests that southern and south-western Asia must also be considered.

Explaining how and why the modern capacity for culture manifested itself is yet more difficult. Purely technological innovations, for example in stone-working or food extraction, seem insufficient. To account for what Pfeiffer (1982) terms the Creative Explosion, something more fundamental is needed. Neurological changes, perhaps permitting a fully modern language facility, could prove the answer, but are impossible to test. There is, however, no reason why acquisition of a modern skeleton should have meant the simultaneous acquisition of the modern mind, and little evidence thus far for anatomically modern humans behaving differently from archaic hominins elsewhere before 40,000/50,000 BP. If the final stages in language development involved adding the ability to talk about events removed from speaker and listener in both space and time (Bickerton 1981), then this could provide a context for beginning to use material culture to transmit information and negotiate relationships

Table 4.4 *Comparison of evidence for the behaviour of MSA people in southern Africa before 40,000/50,000 BP with Acheulean hominins and with contemporary populations in western Eurasia (after H. Deacon 1995; Klein 1995; Mellars 1996; Stringer 1999; this chapter)*

	Southern Africa		Western Eurasia
	Acheulean	MSA	Middle Palaeolithic
Hunting	Hominin involvement in faunal assemblages uncertain	Hunting of all size classes, but generally avoiding most dangerous taxa; driving of eland	Hunting of all size classes; some specialisation evident; probable use of game-drives, e.g. for killing mammoth
Use of marine resources	None	Shellfish, seals, penguins, fish	Shellfish
Use of landscape	Restricted	More like LSA, using geophytes; fire-management?	Different mobility patterns suggested for Neanderthals and modern humans in Near East
Temporally restricted patterning of stone artefacts	None	Yes, but perhaps over a longer time-frame than in the LSA	Yes, but over a longer time-frame than in the Upper Palaeolithic
Regional industries	None	Howieson's Poort; possibly Stillbay	Yes, suggestive of different technological traditions, but imposition of style on artefacts seems doubtful
Hafting/composite tools	None	Yes	Yes
Formally shaped bone tools	None	Present, but rare	None

Long-distance movement of stone, etc.	None	≥40 km in some Howieson's Poort assemblages; seashells >100 km	Limited compared to Upper Palaeolithic; most lithics from <5 km, rare retouched tools/primary blanks from up to 100 km
Hearth construction	Use of fire; no repeated use of hearths	Like LSA; stonelined examples at Mumbwa	Generally open; rare stone-lined examples known
Site modification	None	Limited beyond purely functional considerations; but cf. Mumbwa	Minimal by contrast to Upper Palaeolithic; rare evidence for stone paving, pits, postholes
Art	None	Engraved ostrich eggshell – Diepkloof; Apollo 11 Cave?	None
Personal ornaments	None	None	None
Use of ochre	Very rare or wholly absent	Frequent	Frequent
Burial	None	None	Yes; some burials of modern humans in the Near East have deliberate grave goods; NB one from Australia is ochre-stained

between individuals and groups. The origins of art, style and language may thus have been tightly interconnected (Noble and Davidson 1996), the result an all-or-nothing one dramatically transforming the organisation and scale of human society. Expansion of modern humans beyond Africa and the Near East and their colonisation of major new environments (Australasia, Siberia, Europe) followed (Gamble 1993).

If so, then in southern Africa the transition from Middle Stone Age to Later Stone Age stone-working traditions discussed in chapter 5 was much less significant than the local emplacement of modern cognitive abilities. This emphasises the importance of developing research programmes that target the vastly understudied millennia either side of 40,000/50,000 BP. One crucial question must be the extent to which MSA 3 assemblages exhibit more restricted spatiotemporal patterning than their predecessors or show significant increases in the movements of raw materials. Obtaining comparable, but firmly dated, evidence for Howieson's Poort and Stillbay assemblages may also help determine whether they represent a 'flash in the pan', or the southern African beginnings of the more fundamental rearrangement of human behaviour evident worldwide after 40,000/50,000 BP.

CHAPTER 5

LIVING THROUGH THE
LATE PLEISTOCENE

The last 40,000 years of the Pleistocene witnessed two major changes in the
southern African archaeological record: the replacement of Middle Stone Age
stone-working traditions by Later Stone Age (LSA) microlithic technologies
and the first unambiguous, widespread signs of symbolic activity in the form
of art and jewellery. Other artefacts used by recent southern African hunter-
gatherers also now appear for the first time (tortoise-shell bowls, bored stone
digging-stick weights) or occur more regularly (bone points). The relationships
between these changes define one major research theme for late Pleistocene
archaeology. As described in chapter 2, while oxygen isotope stage 3 (60,000–
25,000 BP) was, in many parts of the sub-continent, the wettest period of the
last 125,000 years, it was followed by the maximum of the Last Glaciation.
This was a time of significantly greater cold and, for much of southern Africa,
of intensified aridity before generally moister, milder conditions returned after
16,000 BP. How people coped with these long-term trends and the smaller-scale
climatic fluctuations superimposed on them forms a second research interest.
A related issue is the extent to which late Pleistocene LSA populations practised
subsistence-settlement strategies and forms of social relations quite different
from those of their Holocene successors. Though the sub-continent has few
sites occupied throughout the period with which this chapter deals, and even
fewer with good preservation of plant and animal remains (J. Deacon 1990b:
173), the southern African record also invites comparison with other parts of
the world, such as western Eurasia and Australasia.

Population and climate

Greater chronological resolution, facilitated by the applicability of radiocarbon dating, makes it possible to assess human responses to climatic change
much more readily than in earlier periods. H. Deacon and Thackeray (1984)
use temporal patterning in radiocarbon dates to measure the distribution and
density of human populations. Disconformities in several southern Cape rock-
shelter sequences suggest that a long time elapsed here between MSA and LSA
occupations, backing the proposition that most MSA assemblages may be of
Last Interglacial age. After this human numbers are thought to have declined
markedly for the rest of the Pleistocene, picking up only from 15,000 BP as

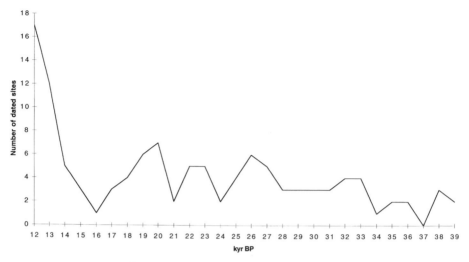

Figure 5.1   Temporal patterning in southern African radiocarbon
determinations from archaeological sites, 39,000–12,000 BP.

climate ameliorated and ecological productivity increased following the Last
Glacial Maximum (LGM) at 18,000 years ago. Though the scale, duration and
impact on people of milder interstadial events, especially during OIS 3, remain
uncertain, this picture has come to be widely accepted.

Figure 5.1 summarises southern African radiocarbon determinations for the
period 39,000–12,000 BP. Given the problems attending its use in the Pleistocene (van der Plicht 1999), no attempt has been made to explore the impact calibration may have on these data. With this caveat, Figure 5.1 generally
supports the link between presumed environmental productivity and archaeological site numbers. However, conditions were clearly not uniformly disad-
vantageous to human settlement, either in time or space, during the period
leading up to the LGM. For example, the intense MSA occupation of the c.
32,000-year-old BP Member at Boomplaas in the southern Cape, which is associated with a warmer interval inferred from both charcoal and micromammalian data (H. Deacon 1995), is also evident in Lesotho (Carter 1978), the
Caledon Valley (Wadley 1997a), southern Namibia (Wendt 1972, 1976) and
the southern Kalahari (Beaumont 1990a). The same event, Europe's Denekamp
Interstadial, was also marked by a major increase in site numbers in western
Eurasia and North Africa, good evidence for the global impact of Quaternary
climate change on the size and distribution of human populations (Van Andel
1998).

Other 'higher energy' signatures in site numbers are evident on three further occasions before the Last Glacial Maximum. Dating 28,000–26,500 BP,
23,500–22,500 BP and 21,000–19,500 BP, all are most visible in the same areas

as the 32,000 BP pulse. Particularly striking are several sites in Namibia and Botswana, where geomorphological data suggest that conditions were markedly wetter at various times after 40,000 years ago (J. Deacon and Lancaster 1988; Thomas and Shaw 1991). Both the radiocarbon dates graphed in Figure 5.1 and the accumulating palaeoclimatic evidence for at least episodically wetter conditions during OIS 3 in the Kalahari, transVaal, and southern and farwestern Cape suggest that claims for major aridity-induced reductions in southern African populations during the Interpleniglacial have been overstated (cf. Klein 1999).

A major downturn in population size and distribution, perhaps even producing localised extinctions, does, however, appear to have followed LGM itself. Only eight sites in South Africa/Lesotho are radiocarbon dated to the four millennia 19,000–15,000 BP and only at Nelson Bay Cave, Boomplaas (J. Deacon 1984a) and Sehonghong (Mitchell 1995) was occupation more than ephemeral. North of the Limpopo and Gariep, dates in the same time range are confined to between 19,000 and 18,000 BP and exist only for Apollo 11 (Wendt 1976), Duncombe Farm (N. Walker and Wadley 1984) and Depression Cave (Robbins 1990). When site numbers again picked up they initially concentrated in these same areas, but their rise was slow until 13,500 BP. Thereafter sites were also reoccupied, or occupied for the first time, in other areas: the Northern Cape, Zimbabwe's Matopo Hills, Swaziland, Mpumalanga and the Namib Desert. This patterning appears to indicate resettlement of parts of the interior from which populations were absent under stadial conditions. Its dating broadly tracks the progress of climatic amelioration, undergoing a sharp, though temporary, reverse during the Younger Dryas stadial.

What accounts for the repeated concentration of later Pleistocene sites in the same parts of the sub-continent? Differential research may be a contributory factor, but only to a limited extent. In the extremely well-surveyed Seacow Valley, for example, no open-air sites attributable to the Robberg Industry (see below) have been found (Sampson 1985a). Nor is the pulsing of rock-shelter occupations simply an artefact of radiocarbon dating. Instead, strong similarities in the dates of occupation pulses as far apart as Mpumalanga, Lesotho and the farwestern Cape implicate processes, presumably climatic, operating on a sub-continental scale (Parkington 1990b). One possibility is to look at what these areas may have had in common. In contrast to the interior plateau, areas in and coastward of the Great Escarpment, including the Caledon Valley, display a combination of higher and more reliable (orographic) rainfall, more broken topography and greater ecological diversity (J. Deacon 1984a; Mitchell 1990). These features may have been particularly desirable as cold and aridity reduced ecological productivity over much of the sub-continent, but even in some of these areas occupation may have concentrated in short-lived interstadial episodes. In the Drakensberg/Maluti Mountains, for example, this

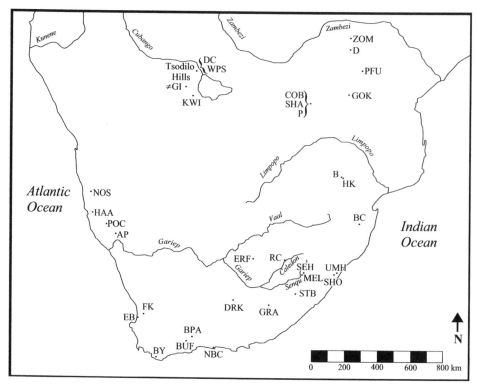

Figure 5.2   Location of archaeological sites discussed in chapter 5. Site names
abbreviated thus: AP Apollo 11 Cave; B Bushman Rock Shelter; BC
Border Cave; BPA Boomplaas; BUF Buffelskloof; BY Byneskranskop;
COB Cave of Bees; D Duncombe Farm; DC Depression Cave; DRK
Driekoppen; EB Elands Bay Cave; FK Faraoskop; Gi ≠Gi; GOK
Gokomere East; GRA Grassridge; HAA Haalenberg; HK
Heuningneskrans; KWI Kwihabe; MEL Melikane; NBC Nelson Bay
Cave; NOS Nos; P Pomongwe; PFU Pfupi; POC Pockenbank 1; RC
Rose Cottage Cave; SEH Sehonghong; SHA Shashabugwa; SHO
Shongweni; STB Strathalan B; UMH Umhlatuzana; WPS White
Paintings Shelter; ZOM Zombepata.

is indicated by the pulsing of occupation at Sehonghong (Mitchell 1996b) and
the abandonment of both Melikane (Carter 1978) and Strathalan B (Opperman
1996a) just before the LGM.

   An alternative view suggests that the surviving evidence of human occupation of the Cape Fold Mountain Belt and other Escarpment areas may be
no more than the 'tip of the iceberg' of populations concentrated elsewhere
(Fig. 5.2). This is most likely to have been on the continental shelf, though
during OIS 3 and the terminal Pleistocene higher effective rainfall over the
interior plateau, where rock-shelters are few and most open-air sites undated,
has suggested this as another (more important?) location (Parkington 1990b).

Along the now drowned Pleistocene coastline, marine resources and more equable temperatures probably mitigated the impact of the Pleniglacial. Furthermore, much of the Agulhas Shelf was probably covered by grassland, which supported extensive herds of grazing animals (J. Deacon 1984a). Van Andel's (1989) reconstruction of the impact of global sea-level changes suggests that a wide coastal plain existed only at times of maximum depression (say, 25,000–12,000 BP). Here then Parkington's 'iceberg hypothesis' may only be applicable during OIS 2. If the continental shelf was a core area for southern African populations at this time, then having access to but part of the late Pleistocene settlement pattern means that we may misconstrue the full range and diversity of people's activities. More complete reconstructions may be possible where coastal plain loss was negligible, or irrelevant, as in KwaZulu-Natal, Mpumalanga and areas north of the Limpopo.

Other explanations for the site concentrations lying behind Fig. 5.1 must include the likelihood that some areas experienced wetter conditions than present during at least part of OIS 3; in the farwestern Cape they persisted until the very end of the Pleistocene (Cartwright and Parkington 1997). In the northern Kalahari too, aridity, though marked at the Last Glacial Maximum, may have been more time-restricted than south of the Limpopo (Thomas and Shaw 1991). Both here and in southern Namibia an average 6°C Glacial Maximum temperature depression will also have rendered rainfall more effective by reducing evaporation. Nevertheless, population may still have concentrated in those areas (around the Tsodilo Hills and the Fish River, for example) where water and therefore food could most reliably be obtained.

Our discussion thus far takes the data represented in Figure 5.1 as a reasonable approximation to the overall density and distribution of late Pleistocene populations. It may be, however, that these parameters are being seriously underestimated. To begin with, some sequences have been only infrequently dated, if at all. At both Grassridge (Opperman 1989) and Boomplaas (H. Deacon 1995), for example, substantial MSA occupations *postdate* the single radiocarbon determinations available for inclusion in the graph. Second, in Botswana and Namibia, where palaeoclimatic data suggest wetter conditions prevailed for much of the later Pleistocene, many more sites can be expected once fieldwork extends beyond the limited areas yet investigated. Third, it remains difficult to place undated open-air sites within the overall cultural-stratigraphic framework. This problem particularly affects MSA 3 assemblages which are, as we have seen, highly variable in content. In the Seacow Valley, for instance, on the eastern edge of the Nama-Karoo Biome, two industries (cf. Florisbad and Zeekoegat) may postdate OIS 5, representing short-lived occupations during late Pleistocene interstadials (Sampson 1985a). Their exact chronological placement and status (in the case of the cf. Florisbad, which could represent a mixture of MSA and LSA material) remain uncertain, but MSA occupation of the valley late in OIS 3 is attested at Driekoppen (Wallsmith 1990). Parkington's (1990a) suggestion that some occurrences assigned to the Howieson's Poort might belong in OIS 3 would have a similar, but more widespread, effect.

Three further caveats are more generally relevant to all attempts to use radiocarbon dates as proxy palaeodemographic data. Climatic factors, such as rainfall, are only one among several (technology, social alliances, previous settlement histories, perceived alternatives) influencing decisions to occupy, or abandon, parts of a landscape. We are also still a long way from being able accurately to transform palaeoclimatic evidence into statements about resource productivity, availability and reliability. Late Pleistocene wet conditions in the Caledon Valley, for example, may have facilitated expansion of sour grasslands, which are nutritious only for a short time early in the growing season (Wadley 1996a). Lastly, Brooks and Robertshaw (1990) point out that changes in site numbers or the density of occupation within stratigraphic sequences may reflect changes in how people organised their settlement and subsistence strategies, not increases or decreases in population *per se*. Changes in archaeological visibility may thus be an artefact of how the archaeological record was formed, not of human presence/absence. The recolonisation of the southern African interior in the terminal Pleistocene is one situation where this caution may be appropriate.

The Middle to Later Stone Age transition

The ebbs and flows of regional populations just considered might, if better defined, help in understanding one of the critical changes in the late Pleistocene archaeological record, the transition from Middle Stone Age to Later Stone Age stone-working traditions. Suggestions that the LSA was introduced to southern Africa by modern humans entering from the north (Goodwin and van Riet Lowe 1929; J.D. Clark 1959) are ironic in the light of subsequent research, but how and why the transition took place and what its significance may have been remain poorly understood. Reasons include a lack of clarity on how assemblages are to be defined, limited publication of some of the sequences at which chronologically early LSA occurrences have been identified, and the overall scarcity of late Pleistocene sites (Wadley 1991). In addition to addressing some of these problems, recent work makes clear that the MSA/LSA transition cannot be directly compared with the processes by which Upper Palaeolithic industries replaced Middle Palaeolithic ones in western Eurasia.

As the application of radiocarbon dating pushed back LSA and MSA chronologies, Beaumont and Vogel (1972) introduced the term 'Early Later Stone Age' (ELSA) for LSA occurrences of Pleistocene age. Six criteria were advanced for their recognition: the presence of unretouched bladelets; the lack of prepared core technology; an abundance of worked-out **bipolar cores** (*pièces esquillées*, *outils écaillés* or core-reduced pieces); a dominance of scrapers among formally retouched tools, which should also include backed artefacts; the presence of bone implements and ostrich eggshell beads. Identification of the bladelet-rich microlithic Robberg Industry in the Fynbos Biome and elsewhere (Klein 1974; J. Deacon 1984a) helped restrict usage of the term ELSA to microlithic assemblages of broadly pre-20,000 BP age from which bladelets are effectively absent (Table 5.1). By far the most important of these comes from layers 1WA and 1BS.LR at Border Cave. Firmly dated by multiple radiocarbon determinations to about 38,000 BP (Beaumont 1978; J.C. Vogel *et al.* 1986), it is predominantly made in opalines and quartz, flaked using a bipolar technique that produced large numbers of *pièces esquillées*. Bladelets and formal tools, however, are extremely rare and backed microliths completely absent. Also present are **bored stones**, ground bone points, bushpig and warthog tusk 'daggers' and ostrich eggshell beads, the latter making their first securely dated appearance in the southern African record. On the basis of the dates for this assemblage, the transition between MSA and LSA stone-working traditions was placed still earlier between 40,000 and 60,000 years ago (Beaumont *et al.* 1978).

A major difficulty for such an early date for the MSA/LSA transition has been the recognition that MSA assemblages continued until much more recently in many parts of southern Africa. MSA occurrences dating to 40,000–20,000 BP are known from southern Namibia, the Cape Fold Belt, the north-eastern Karoo, the Drakensberg/Maluti Mountains, KwaZulu-Natal, Swaziland and the eastern Free State (Beaumont and Boshier 1972; Wendt 1972, 1976; H. Deacon 1976, 1995; Carter 1978; Freundlich *et al.* 1980; Price-Williams 1981; J.C. Vogel and Visser 1981; Cooke 1984; J.C. Vogel *et al.* 1986; Carter *et al.* 1988; Opperman 1989, 1992, 1996a; Kaplan 1990; Wallsmith 1990; G. Miller *et al.* 1993; Mitchell 1994; Wadley 1997a). While some determinations have been questioned, such as those run on calcretes for open-air colluvium-associated MSA sites in Swaziland (Price-Williams and Watson 1982; cf. Butzer 1984b), the overall pattern is robust and clear. The problem is how to reconcile this widespread evidence for MSA persistence with the ELSA assemblages from Border Cave and elsewhere.

A partial answer comes from Wadley's (1997a) re-excavation of Rose Cottage Cave, which demonstrates that there is *no* ELSA assemblage at this site. Instead, the sequence shows a transitional assemblage with both MSA and LSA features sandwiched between the latest MSA occupation and the earliest Robberg-like occurrence. The dating and status of most other ELSA occurrences are also open to doubt (Table 5.1). Border Cave stands alone in having a firmly dated ELSA assemblage, but even its associations can be questioned. About 10 per cent of the flakes from the 1WA/1BS.LR layers do, in fact, have faceted platforms, and rare radial prepared cores are present, both more typically MSA features (Beaumont 1978). In addition, of Beaumont and Vogel's (1972) six criteria, only the high frequency of *pièces esquillées* is sustainable, and this surely reflects no more than the necessity of using bipolar reduction to cope with the small size of

Table 5.1 *Pleistocene assemblages classified as Early Later Stone Age (ELSA)*

Site	Layer(s)	Age (kyr BP)	Reference	Comments
Boomplaas	LP, LPC	21	H. Deacon 1995	Quartz-dominated, informal, microlithic assemblage with very few bladelets or bladelet cores (Mitchell 1988); now assigned to the Robberg Industry (H. Deacon 1995)
Border Cave	1WA, 1BS.LR	±38	Beaumont 1978; Beaumont et al. 1978	May be more of a MSA/LSA transitional assemblage (Mitchell 1988; Barham 1989a), or a situational response to changes in raw material usage; bone points present, also the earliest securely dated ostrich eggshell beads in southern Africa
Cave James	MM	>29	Wadley 1987, 1988	A possibly transitional MSA/LSA assemblage underlies the ELSA levels
Heuningneskrans	3b–3h	24.7–12.6	Beaumont 1981	Few bladelets in 3f–3h, though bladelet cores are relatively common; site was excavated in spits that may have crosscut the natural stratigraphy; the lower part of the sequence dated only by a single amino-acid racemisation date to 31,000 BP with occupation estimated to have started, from extrapolation of rate of sediment accumulation, c. 32,000 BP; radiocarbon dates indicate the site was probably unoccupied 19,300–13,100 BP
Jubilee Shelter	A–BC	Undated	Wadley 1987, 1988	A possibly transitional MSA/LSA assemblage underlies the ELSA levels
Kathu Pan 5	Stratum 2b	32.1–19.8	Beaumont 1990a	No details published; quartz microlithic assemblage with large convex scrapers and ostrich eggshell beads (P. Beaumont, pers. comm. cited in Wadley 1993)
Rose Cottage	–	40–≥29	Beaumont 1978	Wadley's (1991, 1997) re-excavation shows that MSA assemblages persist down to 26,000 BP and are followed ±20,000 BP by an occurrence transitional between MSA and LSA technologies; no ELSA assemblage present at this site
Shongweni South	Lower	23–11.9	Davies 1975	Clearly two distinct occupations are present, separated by a long interval; a parallel, but unpublished, sequence of Pleistocene occupation appears to occur nearby at Shongweni North (J.C. Vogel et al. 1986)

the **opaline** and quartz nodules that were, for whatever reason, the dominant raw materials employed. Beyond such situational explanations, designating the 1WA/1BS.LR assemblages as transitional between MSA and LSA stone-working traditions might be more appropriate (Mitchell 1988; Barham 1989a). It seems, in fact, that the term ELSA has become a catch-all category for assemblages, many of them poorly defined, united only by their informality and an emphasis on quartz, typically reduced by bipolar flaking. Confusion would be reduced if it were abandoned (Wadley 1991) and more attention paid to developing an understanding of the MSA/LSA transition that takes account of regional differences (A. Clark 1997a).

Border Cave highlights the problem of looking at the MSA/LSA transition from the perspective of single sites, especially since people must have used multiple locations at which they employed different kinds of raw materials to make different kinds of assemblages for different purposes. Only where several carefully excavated sites of broadly the same age exist close together will it be possible to address this problem satisfactorily. Though still on too large a scale to reflect the movements of any one human group, south-eastern southern Africa is slowly beginning to accumulate such a series of sites. Rose Cottage Cave and Sehonghong, for example, have closely parallel sequences in which MSA occurrences extend down to 26,000 BP. Lacking prepared cores, these have knife-dominated formal tool assemblages. Around 20,000 BP they were succeeded by others combining a formal tool component of MSA knives, scrapers and rare points with increased use of fine-grained opalines and the production of unstandardised small flakes and rare **bladelets** (Fig. 5.3; Mitchell 1994; A. Clark 1997a). Bladelet-rich microlithic assemblages from which MSA formal tools are absent followed rapidly in the Sehonghong sequence (Mitchell 1995).

Both Rose Cottage (Fig. 5.4) and Sehonghong also demonstrate that long-term trends towards greater use of fine-grained rocks, employment of bipolar flaking and the production of smaller flakes and blades, sometimes of bladelet dimensions (<25 mm length), reach back well *beyond* 30,000 years ago (Carter *et al.* 1988; A. Clark 1997b; Harper 1997). This supports Parkington's (1990a) suggestion that in some parts of southern Africa the Howieson's Poort might be better viewed as initiating long-term trends that culminated in a fully microlithic LSA technology rather than as a 'one-off' within the overall MSA sequence. Kaplan (1990) makes the same point at Umhlatuzana. Here, after 35,000 BP, bladelet production gradually increased, prepared core technology, including the use of platform faceting, disappeared and MSA formal tools, in this case mostly unifacial, bifacial and hollow-based points, persisted. Unfortunately, the fact that some of the deposits at this shelter have slipped vertically relative to others raises doubts over the accuracy of this interpretation.

Other sequences, such as the flake-blade dominated MSA assemblages from Strathalan B at the south-eastern edge of the Grassland Biome (Opperman and Heydenrych 1990; Opperman 1992, 1996a) and Boomplaas in the Cape Fold Belt

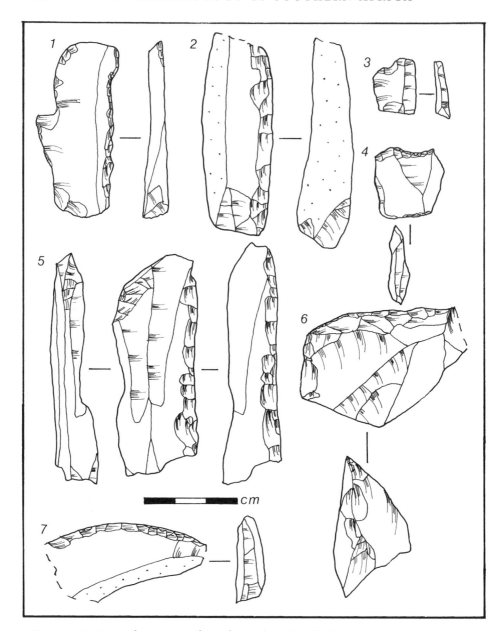

Figure 5.3   Formal stone artefacts from the MSA/LSA transitional assemblages
at Sehonghong. 1–2 Knives; 3–4 truncated flakes; 5 knife (hornfels);
6 scraper (tuff); 7 scraper (hornfels). All in opaline unless otherwise
stated. Stippling denotes the position of remaining cortex.

(H. Deacon 1995), show no sign of this 'creeping microlithisation'. At the latter
the appearance of a microlithic technology around 21,000 BP thus appears more
sudden than at Rose Cottage, Sehonghong or Umhlatuzana. However, further
understanding of the MSA/LSA transition in the Fynbos Biome is made difficult

Figure 5.4   Excavation underway at Rose Cottage Cave, Free State, South Africa.

by the breaks in occupation evident at many of the region's rock-shelters (H. Deacon and Brooker 1976). To the west of Boomplaas, Buffelskloof was occupied *c.* 22,500 BP, but this occurrence, which lacks MSA artefacts, was not separated in excavation from an overlying terminal Pleistocene assemblage (Opperman 1978).

North of the Gariep and Limpopo the situation is similarly complex. MSA 3 assemblages in Namibia placed less emphasis on flake-blade production than their predecessors (Vogelsang 1996) before being replaced by informal, non-microlithic assemblages 27,000–20,000 BP (Wendt 1972, 1976; J.C. Vogel and Visser 1981). In north-western Botswana's Tsodilo Hills a microlithic technology involving some element of bladelet production was already in place before the Last Glacial Maximum (Robbins 1990). Further south at ≠Gi this may extend back to 33,000 BP (Helgren and Brooks 1983; Brooks *et al.* 1990). Connections with earlier MSA assemblages remain unknown, but AMS dating confirms manufacture of OES beads and containers by 32,000–25,000 BP (Robbins 1999). In Zimbabwe the situation remains obscured by inadequately defined stratigraphies, poor excavation techniques and confusions over nomenclature (Larsson 1996). Investigating the MSA/LSA transition here will require much more basic fieldwork. However, the Matopo Hills, which have seen the greatest concentration of Stone Age research, may prove unsuitable for this: MSA occupation may have continued at Pomongwe and Shashabugwa until at least 35,000 BP, but the area seems then to have been unoccupied until well after the LGM (N. Walker 1995a).

Making sense of these data is difficult, perhaps premature. Having discarded the term ELSA, the problem of explaining how and why MSA lithic technologies were replaced remains. Beyond the scarcity of well-excavated, long-sequence sites, other difficulties are of archaeologists' own making. For example, if MSA and LSA technologies are considered so distinct that wholly different typologies are required for their analysis (J. Deacon 1984b: 226), then it becomes next to impossible to deal with assemblages that are transitional between them (Mitchell 1994). When different stratigraphic units are combined for purposes of comparison, this too artificially inflates differences at the expense of obscuring potentially more gradual change (Kaplan 1990). The very fact that we inherit a stadial terminology which combines technology ('Stone') and time ('Age') also de-emphasises the search for transitions and their explanation. More informative might be a redirection of research towards examining how the organisational properties of cultural systems changed over the course of the late Pleistocene. Freed from a typological straitjacket, we could consider changes in raw material usage and procurement, patterns of retouch, utilisation, reuse and breakage, strategies of core reduction and, moving beyond lithic technology, methods of meat procurement and processing, the use of space within sites and the placement of sites in the landscape. Such an approach would help contextualise changes in stone tool technology, which has to be a precondition for their explanation.

In line with broader developments in LSA research, analyses of the Rose Cottage and Umhlatuzana sequences thus suggest that still undefined social variables might explain the shifts in technology marking the MSA/LSA transition (Kaplan 1990; A. Clark 1997a). Summarising the changes in lithic assemblages discussed above, Table 5.2 none the less emphasises that the transition must have carried behavioural implications for how people made and used stone artefacts; alterations in their stylistic preferences are insufficient. One focus ought to be the advantages offered by microlithisation: expanding the range and size of raw materials that could be worked, coupled with the possibility of using multiple microlithic inserts to make more complex composite artefacts, suitable for a wide range of extractive and maintenance tasks (D. Clarke 1976; Robertshaw 1988). These features may have been desirable throughout the later Pleistocene, accounting for the long-term trends evident at Rose Cottage, Sehonghong and Umhlatuzana. But the growing number of dates placing the MSA/LSA transition early in OIS 2 do not exclude the possibility that, at least in some regions, coping with declining environmental productivity immediately before the Last Glacial Maximum was instrumental in the final, widespread adoption of microlithic technology (Mitchell 1988).

Looking beyond the Zambezi, comparable developments are evident in central and eastern Africa. In Zambia transitional MSA/LSA assemblages at Kalemba and Leopard's Hill dating *c.* 22,000 BP preceded the LSA Nachikufan I Industry, which is characterised by production of backed blades and points

Table 5.2 *Principal changes in stone artefact assemblages accompanying the MSA/LSA transition*

1. Disappearance of most kinds of MSA formal tools (knives, unifacial points, bifacial points) and changes in the size and design of others (scrapers).
2. Downsizing of assemblages to emphasise the production of small flakes and, increasingly after 20,000 BP, standardised but unretouched bladelets. This is accompanied by the disappearance of unmodified and utilised flake-blades.
3. Changes in core-reduction technology (disappearance, where still used, of Levallois and radial prepared cores and platform faceting of flakes; enhanced use of bipolar flaking).
4. Shifts in raw material usage in most sequences towards greater use of finer-grained rock types and/or raw materials occurring in smaller preforms (e.g. opalines, quartz, silcrete).

(S. Miller 1969; D. Phillipson 1976; Musonda 1984). But in East Africa the exceptionally well-dated sequence from Enkapune ya Muto registers this switch ≥46,000 BP, consistent with recently obtained dates for other sites in the region (Ambrose 1998b). Such a widespread replacement of MSA technology seems to demand a major technological innovation, perhaps the introduction of the bow and arrow (H. Deacon 1995). Bone points interpreted as arrow armatures do indeed occur more regularly in southern African sites from 21,000 years ago (J. Deacon 1984b), but this leaves the switch to microlithic technologies, as opposed to the disappearance of some MSA elements, unexplained. Earlier suggestions that backed microliths were themselves innovated as arrow armatures for hunting solitary game in wooded environments (D. Phillipson 1976) are unsupported by palaeoenvironmental or subsistence data (Brooks and Robertshaw 1990). They also leave unexplained the disappearance of MSA technology south of the Zambezi, where backed microliths are extremely uncommon in Pleistocene LSA assemblages. Emphasising the greater flexibility offered toolmakers by microlithic assemblages may ultimately prove more helpful.

Pleistocene Later Stone Age assemblages

It may already be apparent that no single lithic industry succeeded the MSA across the whole of southern Africa. This might, indeed, be predicted, given the diversity of the MSA 3 and of late Pleistocene environmental change. At least four different traditions can be identified. South of the Limpopo, the earliest microlithic assemblages known from Elands Bay Cave (Parkington 1990b), Boomplaas Members LP/LPC (H. Deacon 1995), Shongweni (Davies 1975) and Heuningneskrans (Beaumont 1981) date to 25,000–20,000 BP. All are quartz-dominated, are extensively worked using a bipolar technique and have few formal tools or bladelets; a possibly similar occurrence made in opalines is dated 20,000 BP at Melikane in the Lesotho Highlands (Carter 1978). These assemblages are followed by the Robberg Industry, first identified at Rose Cottage Cave, but named from Nelson Bay Cave on South Africa's Robberg Peninsula (Klein 1974). Most Robberg assemblages postdate the Last Glacial Maximum (Wadley 1993), but they are known around 18,000 BP at Boomplaas, Nelson Bay Cave (J. Deacon 1984b), Heuningneskrans (Beaumont 1981) and perhaps Elands Bay Cave (Parkington 1992). Re-excavation of Sehonghong places the earliest Robberg assemblage there immediately following the MSA/LSA transition c. 20,000 BP (Mitchell 1995), and at Boomplaas the aforementioned LP/LPC occurrences are now referred to it (H. Deacon 1995). At the other end of the Pleistocene, the timespan of the Robberg is also being extended. Instead of being superseded everywhere around 12,000 BP as previously thought, evidence is emerging that in south-eastern southern Africa it persisted down to the beginning of the Holocene (Opperman 1987; Barham 1989b; Kaplan 1990; Mitchell 1995; Wadley 1997a).

Robberg assemblages are found across a broad swathe of southern Africa, in and coastward of the Great Escarpment, extending after the LGM to the Caledon Valley (Wadley 1996a) and perhaps the extreme southern margins of the Kalahari (Beaumont 1990b). They resemble pre-20,000 BP microlithic occurrences in having few retouched tools (typically less than 1 per cent of all flaked stone artefacts) and emphasising fine-grained rocks. Scrapers are the most common formal tools, but they and the few backed microliths and adzes found are less standardised in size or shape than in the Holocene (J. Deacon 1984a; Wadley 1993). Umhlatuzana is unique in featuring several unifacial points, similar to earlier MSA examples at the same site (Kaplan 1990), but this again raises the concern that the occurrences here are mixed.

What distinguishes Robberg assemblages above all else is their systematic production, using a punch technique (H. Deacon 1995), of standardised bladelet blanks from highly distinctive forms of bladelet core (Fig. 5.5). Where quartz was a favoured raw material, as in the farwestern and southern Cape and at Heuningneskrans, cores are often, though not always, bipolar; worked-out examples are common. Some (termed flat and small bladelet cores) were probably wrapped in leather or fibre when struck to facilitate bladelet production (J. Deacon 1984a). Bipolar flaking is much less evident where quartz was rarely used. In Lesotho, the eastern Free State and the northern Eastern Cape opalines, easier to flake and probably occurring in larger nodules, were the preferred raw material. Here bladelets were often produced by a technique reminiscent of Upper Palaeolithic blade technology in which cores were first carefully prepared before flaking was initiated by removing a crested blade (*lame à crête*); both these wedge-shaped (high-backed) cores and the bipolar flat bladelet cores were also sometimes used in working skins or plant materials (Binneman 1982; Williamson 1997). Other geographical differences among Robberg assemblages are difficult to define.

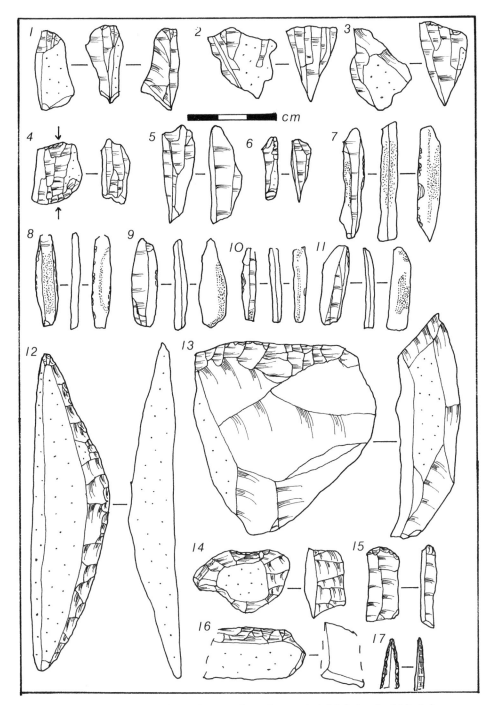

Figure 5.5 Robberg artefacts from Sehonghong. 1–3 high-backed bladelet cores;
4 core-reduced piece; 5–6 flat bladelet cores; 7–11 unmodified
bladelets; 12 naturally backed knife (hornfels); 13 scraper (hornfels);
14–15 scrapers; 16 adze; 17 backed point. All in opaline unless
otherwise stated. Dense stippling on bladelets indicates the position
of mastic, less dense stippling on other artefacts remaining cortex.

Despite a timespan of perhaps 10,000 years, temporal differences are also vague. The clearest is the presence of rare **naturally backed knives**, typically made in hornfels, in some late Robberg assemblages (Mitchell 1988, 1995). Changes in raw material usage, formal tool frequencies or the details of bladelet core reduction may all be site-specific.

Bladelets are such a distinctive feature of the Robberg that they constitute the real 'formal', i.e. deliberately designed, component of the industry, but only a small proportion show evidence of retouch or utilisation. At Rose Cottage this is normally on the ventral surface. At Sehonghong the same is true for those bladelets dating 12,500–12,000 BP, but not for those predating the LGM, which may have been employed in a different way. Their small size leaves no doubt that all must have been hafted when in use. This is confirmed by microwear and organic residue analyses, and by traces of mastic on some specimens from Sehonghong (Binneman 1997a; Binneman and Mitchell 1997; Williamson 1997). Identified uses include cutting and whittling hide, soft plant materials (wood, reed, sedge), bone and freshwater mussel shell. Almost all the bladelets examined in these analyses were hafted parallel to their mount, probably sequentially to form an extended cutting edge reminiscent of the *taap*-sawknives of Aboriginal Australia (Mulvaney 1969). Earlier suggestions (H. Deacon 1983; Parkington 1984a; Mitchell 1988) that they might also have been employed as barbs on projectile weapons remain unsupported, although the use of parallel-mounted microliths in slotted spear and arrow shafts is known in both North America (West 1981) and Europe (J.G.D. Clark 1975).

Studies of how lithic technologies were organised in other parts of the world give further insights into the structure of Robberg assemblages. Not only does the decision to produce bladelets, rather than blanks of another form, maximise the length of cutting edge obtainable (Hayden 1989), but their standardisation lends itself to making different kinds of artefacts from the same basic lithic component. Robberg bladelets are also good examples of what Bleed (1986) terms maintainable and reliable design technologies: quick and easy to repair and replace, but also, where employed in series in composite tools, still usable should one or two microlithic inserts be lost. Their lightness and that of the cores from which they were struck would also have made them eminently transportable for use away from home or raw material sources; a group of bladelets found close together at Boomplaas may have been kept in a bag (H. Deacon 1983). Overall, the impression is that the Robberg emphasis on systematic bladelet production offered access to a wide range of raw materials, economies in their use and versatility in artefact production and maintenance, all ways in which people could employ technology to minimise the risks of failure associated with toolstone procurement and implement use.

Robberg bladelets were presumably always hafted in wooden handles since, even where faunal preservation is good, bone hafts are unknown. Bone points

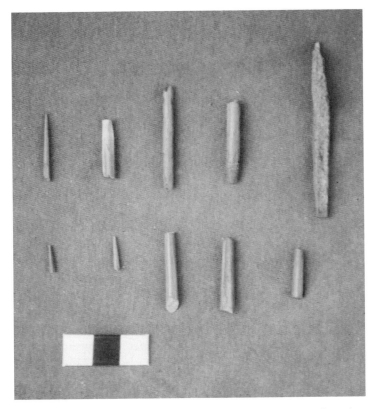

Figure 5.6   Bone artefacts from the Robberg assemblages at Sehonghong.
            The top row shows, from left to right: the tip of a point; two
            mid-sections, both with facets remaining; the butt of a possible
            point; a multiply faceted, whittled shaft fragment. The lower row
            shows two point tips and three mid-sections. All save the whittled
            shaft fragment have been ground and polished.

are reported, however, from Boomplaas, Nelson Bay Cave and Sehonghong
(J. Deacon 1984a; Mitchell 1995), some closely resembling the points and
linkshafts used as arrow components in the Holocene (Fig. 5.6). Flaked bone
artefacts and polished pig tusk fragments are also known from several sites
(Wadley 1993). Containers are represented by a partial tortoise-shell bowl from
Boomplaas and fragments of ostrich eggshell flasks there and at Byneskranskop
(Schweitzer and Wilson 1982; J. Deacon 1984a). Such artefacts, as well as items
of jewellery discussed below, are not as frequent as in the Holocene. This may
sometimes be due to differential preservation (J. Deacon 1984a: Fig. 103), but
more profound social differences between Pleistocene and Holocene populations have also been postulated.

   North of the Limpopo and Gariep at least three further Pleistocene LSA industries have been recognised. In Namibia post-MSA non-microlithic assemblages

have few, if any, bladelets. Formal tools, which mostly comprise scrapers, are also rare (Wendt 1972, 1976), while a substantial heavy-duty tool component is present at the Oryx kill-site in the central Namib, dating 12,800 ± 140 BP (Pta-2596; Shackley 1985). Assemblages from Nos, Pockenbank 1 and Apollo 11 fall both before and after the Last Glacial Maximum, but have not been published in detail, while dates in OIS 3 at Pockenbank 1 and Haalenberg are for others even less well defined (J.C. Vogel and Visser 1981). Ostrich eggshell containers and beads occur at both Apollo 11 and Pockenbank 1, bone tools also at the former (Wendt 1972, 1976).

Across the continent in Zimbabwe a small bladelet-rich assemblage at Duncombe Farm, Mashonaland, dated 18,970 ± 275 BP (SR-243) recalls the Robberg Industry further south. However, its backed bladelets also suggest similarities with Zambia's Nachikufan I Industry (N. Walker and Wadley 1984) and Pleistocene LSA occurrences in East Africa (Brooks and Robertshaw 1990). Zombepata (Cooke 1971), Pfupi (K. Robinson 1952) and Gokomere East Cave (N. Walker 1993) may also have late Pleistocene LSA occupations, but assemblages are either mixed or very small. In south-western Zimbabwe the Matopo Hills were reoccupied only from 13,000 BP, initially by makers of the Maleme Industry. Found at Pomongwe and Cave of Bees, this is a microlithic scraper-dominated industry with some MSA traits, specifically rare small triangular points and prepared cores (N. Walker 1995a). Ostrich eggshell beads and a few bone artefacts are also present. However, both sites may have disturbed stratigraphies in the relevant layers and the number of potentially diagnostic MSA artefacts is tiny (N. Walker 1995a). The Maleme may thus represent yet another set of mixed assemblages rather than the persistence of MSA technology after the LGM.

The possibility that MSA toolmaking traditions continued anywhere in southern Africa after 20,000 BP is also rendered less likely by the emerging Pleistocene record from northern Botswana. Here, as we have already seen, bladelet production extends back into OIS 3. In the Tsodilo Hills a microlithic industry featuring at least some bladelets continued after the LGM (Robbins 1990), and at White Paintings Shelter (Fig. 5.7) was accompanied by a sophisticated bone technology. Fragments of barbed bone points recall others found in Holocene deposits at the same site (Robbins *et al.* 1994), as well as late Pleistocene and Holocene examples from eastern Africa (Yellen 1998). The associated fauna suggests their use in spearing fish. Bladelet technology was also employed 200 km to the south at Kwihabe between 12,450 and 11,240 BP, though excavation here has been limited in scale and carried out in arbitrary levels (Robbins *et al.* 1996b).

Dating and definition of all these assemblages stand in need of refinement, but it is tempting to suggest that the apparently distinct technological traditions reported from south of the Limpopo (the Robberg), southern Namibia,

Figure 5.7   White Paintings Shelter, Tsodilo Hills, Botswana (courtesy Larry Robbins).

northern Botswana and perhaps Mashonaland equate to relatively isolated populations, centred where conditions for human settlement were most favourable over the Last Glacial Maximum. The underlying reasons for this were explored at the beginning of this chapter, and for the period 25,000–12,000 BP the now drowned continental shelves may have offered a further desirable refugium. The implications of these patterns for southern Africa's biological and linguistic history still need to be explored. One possibility arises from Westphal's (1963) studies of Bushman languages which suggest that those spoken until recently south of the Limpopo and Gariep (Fig. 5.8) were distinct at language family level from those of various Botswanan and Namibian groups that are themselves genetically closely interrelated (Nurse *et al.* 1985). Is it possible that this distinction could reach back to the apparent confinement of Robberg assemblages south of the same rivers (Fig. 5.9)?

Late Pleistocene adaptations

Southern African archaeology has long shown an interest in comparing Pleistocene and Holocene LSA settlement-subsistence strategies. An early and influential argument contrasted large, mobile, non-territorial Pleistocene

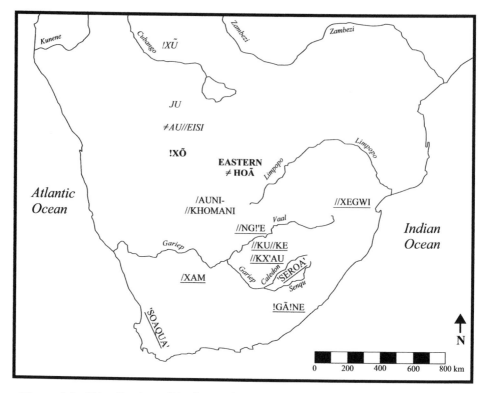

Figure 5.8   Distribution of Bushman languages (after Westphal 1963; Traill
1996). Those languages that are now extinct are underlined.
Languages in plain typeface belong to the !Wi family of Southern
Khoisan, within which /Xam may be a separate grouping. Languages
in bold belong to other families within Southern Khoisan.
Languages in italics are !Kung and belong to Northern Khoisan.

groups who hunted migratory grazers with smaller, more sedentary Holocene
communities whose subsistence needs were met from plants, shellfish and territorial browsing antelope (H. Deacon 1972). Recent work, however, suggests
that the importance of plant foods in late Pleistocene subsistence has been un-
derplayed. On a general theoretical level this can be argued from the physiologi-
cal difficulties of living on a protein-rich diet without consuming carbohydrates
or fat (low on almost all African ungulates; Speth 1987) and from global comparative data on the links between subsistence and environmental productivity
as measured by Binford's (1980) use of an index of effective temperature, a proxy
indicator for length of growing season (Bousman 1991). Supporting empirical
evidence comes from the extensive humified carbon-rich horizons in the CL
Member (14,200–12,000 BP) at Boomplaas, which appear to derive from *in situ*
disintegration of plant food residues (H. Deacon 1995), as well as from the

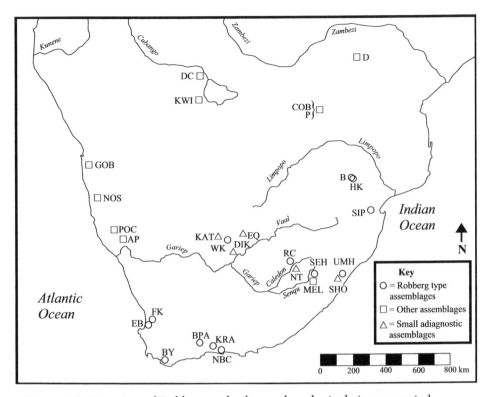

Figure 5.9   Location of Robberg and other archaeological sites occupied
c. 20,000–12,000 BP (*pace* Figs. 22–3, Partridge and Maud 2000).
Sites with Robberg or Robberg-like assemblages are shown by
circles, other sites by squares. Site names abbreviated thus: AP
Apollo 11 Cave; B Bushman Rock Shelter; BPA Boomplaas; BY
Byneskranskop; COB Cave of Bees; D Duncombe Farm; DC
Depression Cave; DIK Dikbosch; EB Elands Bay Cave; EQ Equus
Cave; FK Faraoskop; GOB Gobabeb; HK Heuningneskrans; KAT
Kathu Pan; KRA Kangkara; KWI Kwihabe; MEL Melikane; NBC
Nelson Bay Cave; NOS Nos; NT Ntloana Tsoana; P Pomongwe;
POC Pockenbank 1; RC Rose Cottage Cave; SEH Sehonghong; SHO
Shongweni; SIP Siphiso; UMH Umhlatuzana; WK Wonderwerk.

wide range of plant food remains known from several sites (Table 5.3). Many
late Pleistocene communities may have been just as 'patch-bound' to specific
parts of the landscape as their Holocene successors (H. Deacon 1993), though
undoubtedly integrating specific plant and animal resources into subsistence
strategies in individual ways. Exploitation of underground plant foods may have
been facilitated by the innovation of bored stone digging-stick weights at some
time in the late Upper Pleistocene (N. Walker 1990); however, examples from
Border Cave (Beaumont 1978) and Zombepata (Cooke 1971) seem too small to

Table 5.3 *Edible plants known from late Pleistocene contexts in southern Africa, 40,000–12,000 BP*

Biome and site	Date BP	Taxa	Reference
Fynbos Biome			
Byneskranskop	≤12,700	*Chrysanthemoides monilifera*	Schweitzer and Wilson 1982
Grassland Biome			
Sehonghong	12,500–12,000	*Euclea* sp., *Rhus* sp.	Mitchell 1995
Strathalan B	29,000–22,000	*Tritonia-Freezia* sp., *Watsonia* sp.	Opperman 1992, 1996a; Opperman and Heydenrych 1990
Mixed Woodland Biome			
Border Cave	38,000	*Bridelia micrantha, Diospyros dichrophylla, Encephalartos lebomboensis, E. vollosus, Encephalartos* spp., *Harpephyllum caffrum, Pappea capensis, Strychnos spinosa, Vangueria infausta, Ziziphus mucronata*	Beaumont 1978
Umhlatuzana	37,000–13,000	*Berchemia discolor, Curtisia dentata, Grewia occidentalis, Harpephyllum caffrum, Kedrotis* sp., *Pavetta* sp.,	Kaplan 1990
Moist Woodland Biome			
Cave of Bees	13,000–12,000	*Sclerocarya birrea, Ziziphus mucronata*	N. Walker 1995a
Pomongwe	13,000–12,000	*Cordia grandicalyx, Grewia monticolor, Sclerocarya birrea, Solanum nigrum, Vangueria randii, Ziziphus mucronata*	N. Walker 1995a

have been used in this way. Digging-sticks themselves have not yet been found; direct evidence of the use of wooden artefacts is limited to two needle-like objects from Strathalan B (Opperman 1992). Grindstones are, however, now more common than before, especially in the Grassland Biome where geophytes may have been a key resource (Mitchell 1995; Wadley 1996a): since few are ochre-stained the assumption is that most were used in processing plant foods.

Better preserved than plants, faunal remains suggest that any idea of a single late Pleistocene economy is unrealistic. At Heuningneskrans, for instance, both Holocene and late Pleistocene faunas are dominated by small and medium-sized ungulates, perhaps reflecting greater environmental stability on the eastern slopes of the Great Escarpment (Klein 1984c). If so, then human populations may also have been better able to maintain themselves in these mixed woodland habitats than elsewhere. Opperman's (1987, 1996a) research suggests that, in the northern Eastern Cape too, late Pleistocene (here pre-LGM) and early Holocene faunal exploitation was similar, in this case in emphasising **alcelaphines**. In the Fynbos Biome, on the other hand, both large-mammal faunas and other palaeoenvironmental indicators argue for grassland expansion during the late Pleistocene. Grazing animals were probably more prominent than in historical times, as witnessed by the dominance of alcelaphines and equids, including several now extinct hyperspecialised grazers, at Boomplaas and Nelson Bay Cave (J. Deacon 1984b). However, many of these large animals were probably not migratory, and the idea of human groups attempting to follow migrating herds should be rejected (Fig. 5.10; H. Deacon 1995). Additional variability in how animals and plants were exploited, as yet little explored, can be expected from the quite different palaeoenvironmental conditions reported at many sites before, at and after the Last Glacial Maximum (e.g. Boomplaas; H. Deacon *et al.* 1984), as well as where the same species were hunted in such different landscapes as the southern Cape or the Drakensberg/Maluti Mountains. Here what is striking is the wide variety of game – equids, alcelaphines, eland, springbok and territorial smaller antelope, such as common duiker and steenbok – taken at Sehonghong both just before the LGM and between 12,500 and 12,000 BP.

A final dimension of late Pleistocene subsistence remains difficult to investigate. Though the evidence of much older MSA, as well as younger LSA, sites suggests that marine foods must also have been exploited, changes in sea-level and occupation hiatuses at several coastal rock-shelters during OIS 3 mean that there is virtually no proof of this before 12,000 BP. On the other hand, freshwater fish were certainly taken in both the north-western Kalahari (Robbins *et al.* 1994) and the Lesotho Highlands (Mitchell 1995). In the former area this supports the case for significantly wetter than present conditions both before and after the Last Glacial Maximum (Brook *et al.* 1992).

Figure 5.10   Burchell's zebra (*Equus burchelli*) photographed in Etosha National
Park, Namibia. This is one of several large grazers common in
Pleistocene LSA faunal assemblages in the Fynbos Biome of the
Western Cape.

Continuities in time and space

If Pleistocene LSA populations were not as big-game focused as earlier interpretations suggested, the impression of greater mobility over the landscape
is still conveyed by the rarity of their sites, which are often several hundred
kilometres apart. This pattern may, of course, represent the 'iceberg effect'
that we considered earlier, with the surviving sample of sites no more than
a fraction of the original settlement pattern (Parkington 1990b). Rock-shelter
collapse or failure to extend excavations to bedrock may also sometimes be an
issue, and in the Caledon Valley (Mitchell 1993a; Wadley 1997a), the farwestern Cape (Parkington 1990b; Manhire 1993) and Mpumalanga (Beaumont 1981;
Wadley 1987) pairs of Robberg sites are known within 40 km of each other.
But the scarcity of open-air sites is still striking: claims from Swaziland (Price-
Williams and Barham 1982) and the Northern Cape (Beaumont 1986) have not
been confirmed, though a more likely candidate has recently been identified
at Erfkroon, Free State (Churchill *et al.* 2000). Since it seems improbable that
Pleistocene LSA people did not leave other artefacts in the open air, we are perhaps looking at a complex situation in which open-air site visibility in some
areas is now poor (the Fynbos and Mixed Woodland Biomes, for example) and
the relevant open-air assemblages either small and/or sufficiently nondescript,

where they lack enough bladelets and bladelet cores, to be differentiated from those of Holocene people.

One consequence of significantly greater late Pleistocene settlement mobility, if it was practised, might be the enhanced presence of exotic raw materials in stone tool assemblages (Ambrose and Lorenz 1990). Boomplaas provides the only instance of this for the Last Glacial Maximum itself. The 18,000 BP Robberg occupation here made extensive use of silcrete, which does not occur within the local Cango Valley; perhaps significantly, this occupation is represented in the site's stratigraphy by massive leached ash lenses which may result from large-scale meat-drying operations, not by humified plant residues as in the overlying CL Member where **toolstone** is almost wholly local in origin (H. Deacon 1983, 1995). At Nelson Bay Cave silcrete occurs at more than a trace level only in layer YSL, which immediately postdates the LGM, in this case perhaps derived from a now drowned source on the continental shelf (J. Deacon 1984b); other non-quartzite raw materials probably came from beyond the Robberg Peninsula, but remain unsourced (Inskeep 1987). At most other sites data are unavailable, or indicate that fine-grained rocks moved over only a few kilometres (e.g. at Rose Cottage Cave; Wadley 1996a). The strongest evidence for greater mobility comes from Depression Cave, where some of the chert used to make bladelets travelled 100 km to reach the site (Robbins 1990), and Elands Bay Cave, where much of the hornfels used after 13,600 BP was probably derived from a comparable distance on the plateau side of the Cape Fold Belt (Parkington *et al.* 1987).

Seashells found at inland sites provide additional evidence for items moving over the late Pleistocene landscape (Table 5.4). Examples are known from several regions, but it is the few ornaments from Sehonghong which

Table 5.4 *Movement of marine shell and marine shell ornaments in the late Pleistocene, 20,000–12,000 BP*

Site	Marine shell finds	Estimated straightline distance to the LGM coast	Reference
Apollo 11 Cave	1 pendant; 'some fragments'	140 km	Wendt 1972, 1976
Boomplaas	10 *Donax serra* fragments; 5 *Patella* sp. fragments	130 km	J. Deacon 1984a
Faraoskop	16 *Choromytilus meridionalis* fragments; 9 *D. serra* fragments; 1 *Patella* sp. fragment	75 km	Manhire 1993
Pockenbank 1	'some fragments'	170 km	Wendt 1972
Sehonghong	4 *Nassarius kraussianus* beads; 1 *Nerita* sp. pendant	200 km	Mitchell 1995
Umhlatuzana	1 *Tricolia capensis* bead	50 km	Kaplan 1990

document movement over the longest distance. Interestingly, a vervet monkey (*Chlorocebus aethiops*) shoulder blade was also found in the pre-LGM Robberg assemblage at this site. Given this species' ecological preferences (Estes 1992), it too was presumably introduced from a lower-lying area closer to the coast. Though sparse, these data offer some support to the case for greater human mobility, or the alternative possibility that people developed geographically more extensive exchange and alliance networks as means of coping with more unproductive, less reliable environments (Ambrose and Lorenz 1990). Long-ranging contacts between late Pleistocene populations are also indicated by the general uniformity of Robberg technology right across South Africa/Lesotho/Swaziland, as well as by the virtually identical deeply incised spiral ornamentation of bone beads from Robberg contexts at Boomplaas and Nelson Bay Cave (J. Deacon 1984a) and a slightly later occurrence at Bushman Rock Shelter (Plug 1982). However, the scale and intensity with which items of jewellery moved across southern Africa do appear to have increased significantly after 12,000 BP.

The marine shell and bone ornaments, ostrich eggshell beads, ostrich eggshell and tortoise-shell containers, bone points and bored stones found in late Pleistocene assemblages establish continuities in material culture with more recent archaeologically and ethnographically known hunter-gatherers in southern Africa, as well as the presence of forms of behaviour, including art, which can, without hesitation, be termed 'modern' (J. Deacon 1984b). The contrast with MSA assemblages predating 40,000/50,000 BP is marked. The most visually impressive example of this continuity and contrast comes from Apollo 11 Cave, where seven painted, and apparently deliberately broken, slabs of rock are associated with a terminal MSA occupation dating *c.* 27,000 BP (Fig 5.11; Wendt 1976). As well as depictions of a rhinoceros, an antelope and a zebra-like creature, one image shows a quasi-feline creature with human legs. Large felines and part-human/part-animal beings are regular features of much more recent southern African rock art, in which they may represent the actions and powers of shamans (Lewis-Williams and Dowson 1999), but we should not forget that images can remain constant while undergoing radical changes of meaning.

The innovation of art in the late Pleistocene may have helped to facilitate the flow of information between individuals and groups, thus acting as another means of coping with harsher environmental conditions (N. Walker 1990). In this respect, art and the long-distance movement of exotic rocks and seashells could have played similar rôles in structuring inter- and intra-group relations. However, it is noteworthy that other evidence for art (except for rare engraved fragments of ostrich eggshell) is completely lacking in the southern African record until the very end of the Pleistocene (N. Walker 1987; Wadley 1993). The significance of art and jewellery may rather lie in indicating that items of

Figure 5.11 Painted slab from Apollo 11 Cave, Namibia, showing a feline with human-like legs (courtesy David Coulson, Trust for African Rock Art, Robert Estall Agency). The legs may have been added after the original ones had faded and the image as a whole may relate to beliefs about shamans' ability to become large cats while in trance (Lewis-Williams 1984).

material culture were being actively designed and manipulated to convey meaning about personal and group identities and relations with the natural (and spiritual) world. Though deployed only sporadically between 40,000 and 12,000 BP, and perhaps even long before, such symbolising becomes evident at broadly the same date in southern Africa as in other parts of the Old World (Klein 1995). The Apollo 11 paintings (27,000 BP) and ostrich eggshell beads from Border Cave (38,000 BP) are particularly important in showing that these uses of material culture preceded and transcended the MSA/LSA transition. In this respect, as well as in the absence of any change in hominin type, events in southern Africa were thus quite different from western Eurasia's more widely discussed and better-documented Middle/Upper Palaeolithic transition. Indeed, globally there is no necessary match at all between lithic technology and late Pleistocene evidence for new cognitive skills (Foley and Lahr 1997).

One of the areas considered in chapter 4 as potentially informative on the behavioural competence of MSA hominins has yet to be considered, the internal organisation of space on archaeological sites. Strathalan B, a difficult-to-reach rock-shelter in the Drakensberg Mountains of the Eastern Cape, has already been mentioned. As well as preserving evidence for geophyte exploitation and the use of wooden artefacts, its several MSA occupations, separated from each other by sterile sands, offer a fine-grained record of human activity, uncovered by spatially extensive excavations and point-plotting of finds. Hearths and discrete grass bedding patches occur in several of the horizons, the latter against the shelter wall and somewhat protected by a large rock (Opperman and Heydenrych 1990; Fig. 5.12). Though the hearth/bedding patch pattern recalls Holocene site organisation (Liengme 1987), there seems nothing to indicate that activities were structured spatially beyond what might be predicted from simple physics (sleeping between the shelter wall and the hearths) and comfort (concentrating bone waste and stone artefacts around the hearths, not the sleeping areas).

At Rose Cottage Cave, however, the other late Pleistocene site to have been excavated on a sufficiently large scale, spatial contrasts have been noted between MSA and LSA horizons. Here the Robberg occupation in layer DB (13,600–12,700 BP) focused around two sets of hearths, each associated with extensive stone-knapping. Ochre and grindstones cluster distinctly from these and from each other, while bone waste concentrates around the western set of hearths (Wadley 1996a). Spatial patterning in the underlying transitional MSA/LSA level G is more diffuse and less structured (Wadley 1997a). However, the spread of dates and high density of artefacts in DB indicate that this layer represents an accumulation of repeated occupations. Coupled with uncertainty over whether taphonomic processes were comparable in both layers, this suggests that the observed contrasts may not be quite as straightforward as they seem, nor necessarily a signal of more significant behavioural differences between populations either side of 20,000 BP. Spatial data thus remain as ambiguous a source of evidence for comparing MSA and LSA occupations within the temporal confines of this chapter as they do still earlier in the Upper Pleistocene.

The global impact of late Pleistocene climatic changes also invites comparison between the southern African record reviewed here and those of other parts of the world. Coping with environmental shifts and the challenges of regional abandonment and recolonisation, for example, are themes of worldwide relevance around the Last Glacial Maximum (Gamble and Soffer 1990).

Figure 5.12   Spatial patterning in terminal MSA levels at Strathalan B Cave, Eastern Cape, South Africa, showing the layout of grass bedding patches and the hearth on occupation floor BPL dated *c.* 24,000–21,000 BP (after Opperman and Heydenrych 1990: Fig. 4; courtesy South African Archaeological Society).

Both here and through the late Pleistocene as a whole, however, there is a risk that northern hemisphere agendas, developed in the historically better-investigated regions of central and western Europe, create expectations or pre-conceptions about the significance of developments in southern Africa. As Wobst (1990) indicates on a global scale and H. Deacon (1995) specifically for southern Africa, low-latitude populations do not show the same complexity of art, jewellery, ritual or technology (artefacts, clothing, shelter) that charac-terises many Upper Palaeolithic Eurasian groups and, perhaps, high-latitude communities in the southern hemisphere (R. Jones 1990). The reason is surely not that lower-latitude populations were cognitively unable to undertake the kinds of behaviours implied by these artefacts, but that they chose to deploy them rarely, if at all. They were not, as Wobst (1990: 325) puts it, situationally appropriate, in (large?) part because environmental conditions did not demand such high-cost responses, or, it might be added, narrower, single-species focused hunting strategies. More conservative, but arguably more stable, adaptations could thus maintain themselves (Gamble and Soffer 1990: 18). Their success is evident from the persistence of archaeologically visible populations across so much of southern Africa during the late Pleistocene, a persistence presumably facilitated by the symbolic use of material culture after 40,000/50,000 BP and, secondarily, by the innovation of new kinds of stone and organic artefacts that cumulatively help to define and identify Later Stone Age assemblages.

CHAPTER 6

FROM THE PLEISTOCENE INTO THE HOLOCENE: SOCIAL AND ECOLOGICAL MODELS OF CULTURAL CHANGE

Comparative studies of cultural change across the millennia spanning the Pleistocene/Holocene boundary (conventionally set at 10,000 BP) isolate several themes (Straus *et al.* 1996). Set against major shifts in precipitation, temperature and the distribution and availability of plant and animal resources, they include the colonisation and migration of human populations, technological innovation, the elaboration of exchange networks and new subsistence strategies. Ecological changes in southern Africa may not have been as dramatic as those affecting formerly glaciated and periglacial higher latitudes nor the previously hyperarid Sahara, but they are none the less detectable. Major shifts in the intensity and seasonality of rainfall and the make-up of plant and animal communities, including the extinction of several large ungulates, can all be identified. So too can the disappearance of late Pleistocene microlithic technologies, an expansion of interaction networks in the form of the non-microlithic Oakhurst Complex and the latter's eventual replacement by the microlithic Wilton Industry. Superimposed on these were changes in how people exploited southern African landscapes and the resources that they offered and, perhaps, the innovation of new patterns of social relations. The connections between all these changes over the period 12,000–8,000 BP form a major theme of LSA research and the principal concern of this chapter (Fig. 6.1).

Environmental background

Postglacial warming commenced earlier in the southern than the northern hemisphere, but observations from several areas suggest that relatively cool conditions prevailed as late as 10,000 BP (Scott 1982; Scholtz 1986; Tusenius 1989). Quantifying these observations is difficult: factor analysis of micromammalian species at Byneskranskop suggests that maximum temperatures were reached only after 8000 BP (J.F. Thackeray 1987). Important as temperature amelioration was, particularly at higher altitudes and in arid areas, where it will have increased loss of surface water by evaporation, shifts in rainfall were more significant. Observations at Elands Bay Cave suggest that the winter rainfall zone experienced relatively moist conditions 12,000–8,000 BP (Klein 1991; Cartwright and Parkington 1997). To the east, expansion of the winter rainfall

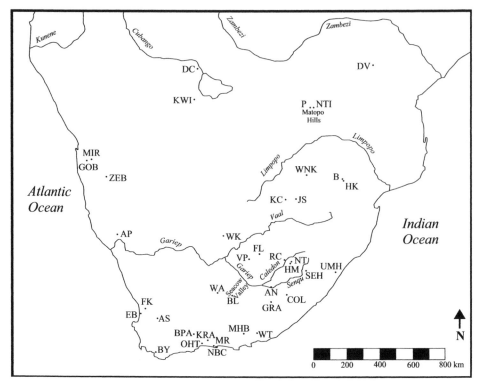

Figure 6.1   Location of archaeological sites discussed in chapter 6. Site names
are abbreviated thus: AP Apollo 11 Cave; AS Aspoort; AN Aliwal
North; B Bushman Rock Shelter; BL Blydefontein; BPA Boomplaas;
BY Byneskranskop; COL Colwinton; DC Depression Cave; DV
Diana's Vow; FK Faraoskop; FL Florisbad; GOB Gobabeb; GRA
Grassridge; HK Heuningneskrans; HM Ha Makotoko; JS Jubilee
Shelter; KC Kruger Cave; KRA Kangkara; KWI Kwihabe; MHB
Melkhoutboom; MIR Mirabib; MR Matjes River; NBC Nelson Bay
Cave; NT Ntloana Tsoana; NTI Nswatugi; OHT Oakhurst;
P Pomongwe; RC Rose Cottage Cave; SEH Sehonghong; UMH
Umhlatuzana; VP Voigtspost 1; WA Wilde Als Put 2; WK
Wonderwerk; WNK Wonderkrater; WT Wilton Large Rock Shelter;
ZEB Zebrarivier.

régime is indicated rather earlier at Boomplaas 14,000–12,000 BP, but from
10,000 years ago there was a shift to a drier climate, with rainfall increasingly
concentrated in summer (H. Deacon *et al.* 1984; Scholtz 1986).

Changes in rainfall seasonality and intensity picked up in the summer rainfall zone have yet to be worked into a coherent narrative. In the Caledon
Valley cool, possibly moist, conditions prevailed around 12,000 BP (Esterhuysen
1996), but by 11,000 years ago a trend towards less precipitation, more strongly

concentrated in summer, has been identified (Scott 1989). Alpine heathland taxa progressively disappeared from charcoal assemblages at Rose Cottage Cave, but several biological indicators register a significantly cooler and drier episode there and in western Lesotho *c.* 8600–8100 BP (Plug and Engela 1992; Esterhuysen 1996; Esterhuysen and Mitchell 1997; J. Smith 1997). Drier early Holocene conditions are also evident in the transVaal (Partridge *et al.* 1990), with bushveld replacing more open grassland in the Wonderkrater pollen sequence after 9500 BP (Scott 1982) and at Jubilee Shelter by 8500 BP (Dowson 1988a). However, this was not a uniform process across the whole summer rainfall area. In Swaziland, for example, Prior and Price-Williams (1985) report wetter conditions through the early Holocene.

Further north increased rainfall is suggested by diatoms in deposits at Nswatugi, Matopo Hills, *c.* 10,265 BP (N. Walker 1995a). More widespread is the evidence of high lake and *pan* levels in the Kalahari until 11,000 BP, though drier conditions prevailed both there and in the Namib by 10,000 years ago (J. Deacon and Lancaster 1988); near Kwihabe, north-western Botswana, aridity intensified as early as 11,500 BP, after several millennia of substantially moister than present conditions (Robbins *et al.* 1996b). Increases in precipitation of 10–20 per cent over modern figures are, however, indicated across the Kalahari and the Namibian interior by 7000 years ago (Partridge 1997).

The overall picture of environmental change afforded by these observations is highly discontinuous, in time as well as in space. One of the few studies providing a sequence of more closely dated climatic fluctuations is Coetzee's (1967) analysis of pollen from spring deposits at Aliwal North. Here, on the southern edge of the Grassland Biome, several short-lived oscillations between grassland (implying cooler, moister conditions) and more karroid (thus drier, warmer conditions) plant communities are evident from ≥12,600–9600 BP. Coetzee correlated the second of these karroid episodes (11,650–11,250 BP) with northern Europe's Allerød Interstadial, one of the few attempts at placing the southern African record within the broader global context of terminal Pleistocene/early Holocene climatic fluctuations. More recently, and paralleling its recognition in several other parts of the world, evidence has emerged that the significantly colder stadial episode known as the Younger Dryas can also be identified in southern Africa, for example in oxygen isotope analysis of seashells in sites along the Cape coast (Cohen *et al.* 1992), in the micromammalian record at Elands Bay Cave (D.M. Avery 2000) and in the Wonderkrater pollen sequence (J.F. Thackeray 1990a). As research proceeds, it may become possible to detect this and other short-lived climatic fluctuations within the southern African record, bringing a greater degree of coherence to the present broad-brush picture.

It is the present Fynbos Biome that exhibits the greatest differences between late Pleistocene and Holocene environments. Here warmer temperatures and increased rainfall facilitated the replacement of open grassland by more closed habitats, a process documented by changes in the composition of archaeological faunas across the region (Klein 1978a). In broad terms, smaller, browsing antelope replaced large, gregarious grazers as the dominant ungulate taxa. Within this, shifts in the relative proportions of grysbok to steenbok at Elands Bay Cave suggest more subtle changes in the mix of browse plants were also at work (Klein and Cruz-Uribe 1987).

In the Fynbos Biome at least four ungulate taxa became extinct by 9500 BP (Klein 1980): giant buffalo, Cape horse, giant hartebeest (*Megalotragus priscus*) and southern springbok (*Antidorcas australis*). However, these extinctions were not restricted to the southern and south-western Cape. In fact, the most recent record for both Cape horse and giant hartebeest comes from Wonderwerk, Northern Cape (10,000 and 7500 BP respectively; J.F. Thackeray 1984). A further variety of springbok (*Antidorcas bondi*), which is found everywhere but the Fynbos Biome, is last known of at Kruger Cave, Gauteng, *c.* 7600 BP (Brown and Verhagen 1985). These data suggest that extinction was a regionally variable phenomenon, by no means solely linked to changes in plant communities in the Fynbos Biome. As elsewhere in the world (Martin and Klein 1984), increased hunting has been suggested as one explanation, but this argument is based solely on presumed contrasts between MSA and LSA hunting efficiency (Klein 1984d). Faunal assemblages are too small and scattered in time and space to allow more sensitive breakdowns of this dichotomy. Solid evidence for associated changes in hunting technology or for people preferentially targeting these particular taxa is also lacking.

We thus have to allow for environmental change having been more important than previously thought. All those species that became extinct were, in fact, the most specialised grazers of their kind. If, as Klein (1980) suggests, some (such as Cape horse, giant hartebeest and Bond's springbok) were interlinked within grazing successions, then population decline or extinction of just one could have precipitated a domino effect among the others. Hunting may have been secondary to this. However, the completeness of some of the 'extinctions' has also been queried, with Churcher and Richardson (1978) suggesting that the Cape horse survives as the present Grevy's zebra (*Equus grevyi*) of East Africa. Peters *et al.* (1994) similarly argue that *Pelorovis antiquus* should be considered no more than a chronospecies of the modern Cape buffalo; changes in **agonistic behaviour** may have provoked the shift from one form to the other.

One further aspect of palaeoenvironmental change remains to be considered, changes in sea-level, one result of which was to drown previously exposed areas of the continental shelf. Off the southern and south-western Cape this process was effectively complete by 9000 BP (Van Andel 1989), taking with it large areas of grassland and perhaps contributing, on a regional level, to some of the extinctions just discussed. The detailed impact of sea-level changes on both coastal configuration and the availability of marine, littoral and estuarine resources has been particularly well studied at Elands Bay Cave, where successive changes in site catchment are documented (Parkington 1988). A change with more than local significance is the switch in emphasis from collecting limpets to black mussels (*Choromytilus meridionalis*) around 10,000 BP, which suggests that the upwelling of cold water associated with the Benguela Current was reinitiated around that time (Parkington 1986). Around the same time the replacement of black mussels by thermophilous brown mussels (*Perna perna*) in the Nelson Bay Cave sequence suggests a strengthening of the warm water Agulhas Current (Klein 1972).

Artefact assemblages

Three technological traditions are generally recognised in southern Africa between 12,000 and 7000 BP. As we saw in chapter 5, there is increasing evidence that early microlithic assemblages closely linked to the Robberg Industry of the southern Cape continued to be made in south-eastern southern Africa after 12,000 BP. The most recently obtained and compelling example comes from Rose Cottage Cave, where the Robberg assemblage from level LB is dated 9560 ± 70 BP (Pta-7275; Wadley 1997a). Explaining why Robberg technology should have survived in this part of the sub-continent much later than in the Fynbos Biome adds another dimension to discussions of cultural and environmental change across the Pleistocene/Holocene boundary.

Spanning most of the period we are considering are what J. Deacon (1984b) terms terminal Pleistocene/early Holocene non-microlithic assemblages, otherwise more formally designated as the Oakhurst Complex (Sampson 1974; Wadley 2000). Broadly equivalent to Goodwin and van Riet Lowe's (1929) Smithfield A, they share a general preference for using more coarsely grained rocks and/or rocks occurring as larger preforms. Flakes and scrapers tend to be longer and broader than before or later, flakes were often sidestruck and cores typically casual, irregular affairs. One of the most striking features of Oakhurst occurrences compared to their Robberg predecessors is the rarity of bladelet production. Formally retouched artefacts are also few. They include large D-shaped scrapers and a range of sidescrapers (Fig. 6.2), along with what Parkington (1984a) terms naturally backed knives. Overall the impression is one of considerable expediency in stone artefact manufacture, though after 9500 BP formal tools become more frequent in some areas. Later Oakhurst assemblages in the southern Cape (J. Deacon 1984b) feature, for example, distinctive end-retouched scrapers with **adze**-like retouch along their lateral margins that Bousman (1991) suggests may have been used in a range of extractive and maintenance tasks. Found also in the Drakensberg/Maluti Mountains (Cable *et al.* 1980; Opperman 1987; Mitchell 1996d), they are less common further west at sites like Byneskranskop (Schweitzer and Wilson 1982). A further important feature of some Oakhurst assemblages, such as that from Byneskranskop and those from Bushman Rock Shelter (Plug 1982) and Nelson Bay Cave

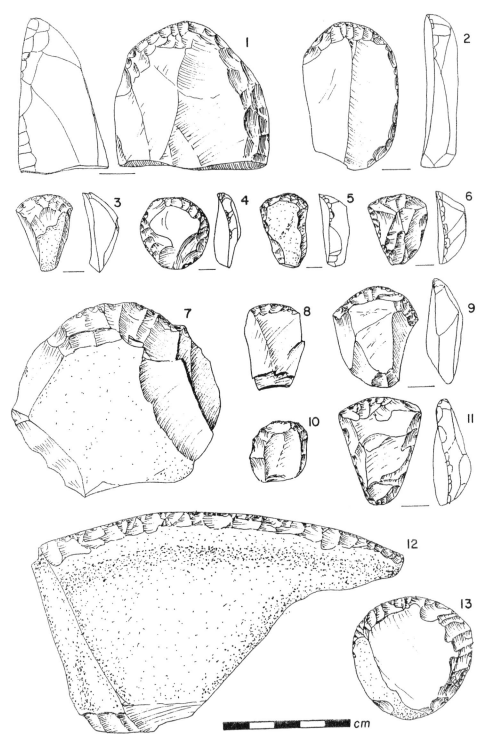

Figure 6.2 Oakhurst artefacts. All are scrapers, though 12 resembles a naturally backed knife. 5, 6 and 11 have adze-like lateral retouch (after J. Deacon 1984a: Fig. 157; courtesy Janette Deacon).

(J. Deacon 1984b), is the presence of a greater variety and number of bone and shell artefacts than before.

First appearing just before 12,000 BP, Oakhurst assemblages persisted south of the Limpopo into the eighth millennium BP. Several regional industries have been defined: the Albany in the Cape Fold Mountain Belt and its coastal fore-lands (J. Deacon 1984b), the Kuruman in the Northern Cape (Humphreys and Thackeray 1983) and the Lockshoek in the Karoo and Free State (Sampson 1974). Parkington (1984a) suggested that the presence of naturally backed knives in both Lockshoek and some Robberg assemblages implies that the two were made by the same population, the differences between them due to situational vari-ability in the availability of raw materials (hornfels in the interior, mostly quartz along the Atlantic coast). Radiocarbon dates for Lockshoek assemblages remain rare. Those from Blydefontein (8541 ± 417 BP, SMU-1823; Bousman 1989) and Voigtspost 1 (6350 ± 75 BP, Pta-1520; Horowitz *et al.* 1978) are both quite late, as is one for an Oakhurst assemblage obtained from presumably as-sociated ostrich eggshell at Wilde Als Put 2 (5464 ± 170 BP, Pta-4223; Beaumont and Vogel 1989); an earlier determination from Florisbad dates the peat horizon within which Lockshoek artefacts were found (Kuman and Clarke 1986). Direct support for placing the Lockshoek within the broad period 12,000–8,000 BP is therefore weak, though the absence of distinctively Lockshoek occurrences in Lesotho, where hornfels is abundant, militates against Parkington's sugges-tion. So too does the clear replacement of Robberg by Oakhurst assemblages in southern Cape sites such as Boomplaas and Nelson Bay Cave.

Another variant of the Oakhurst Complex has been identified in Zimbabwe's Matopo Hills. Termed Pomongwan (N. Walker 1995a) and featuring scrapers, rare backed tools and bone matting needles, it suggests that, unlike before 12,000 BP, areas to the north and south of the Limpopo now formed part of the same interaction network. Elsewhere connections are more difficult to define. Northern and central Zimbabwe, in particular, remain greatly under-researched, though we know that the Oakhurst Complex is not found north of the Zambezi, where microlithic Nachikufan assemblages continued to be made. In the northern Kalahari observations are also few, but bladelet technology con-tinued in use in north-western Botswana where terminal Pleistocene assem-blages from Depression Cave and Kwihabe have very few formal tools (Robbins 1990; Robbins *et al.* 1996b). In southern Namibia the informal macrolithic occurrences recognised from around 20,000 BP continued into the terminal Pleistocene at Apollo 11 (Wendt 1976), Zebrarivier and Gobabeb (J.C. Vogel and Visser 1981) and perhaps into the early Holocene in the central Namib (Shackley 1984). Within a cultural-historical paradigm this might suggest that it is to Namibia that we should look for the innovation of the large scrapers that help typify the Oakhurst (N. Walker 1995a: 253). Whether scraper size should be seen as a culturally diagnostic trait is, however, to be doubted; other expla-nations for the replacement of Robberg by Oakhurst assemblages are possible.

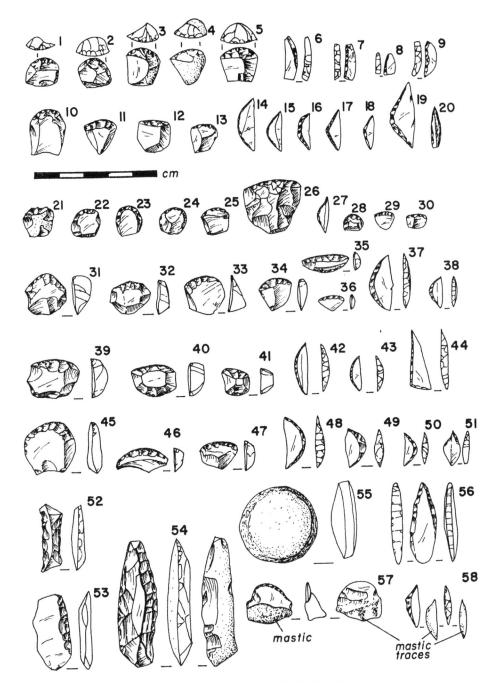

Figure 6.3 Wilton artefacts. 1–5, 10–13, 21–6, 28–36, 39–42, 45–7 scrapers;
57 scraper with mastic; 6–9, 14–20, 27, 37, 38, 42–4, 48–50 backed
microliths; 58 backed microlith with mastic; 51, 56 borers;
52–4 adzes; 55 milled edge pebble (after J. Deacon 1984a: Fig. 158;
courtesy Janette Deacon).

The third set of occurrences with which we must deal are described as Holocene microlithic assemblages (J. Deacon 1984b) or the Wilton Complex (Sampson 1974). In general terms they feature increased use of finer-grained rocks, a marked increase in formal tool frequencies, systematic production of both small, standardised, often thumbnail-shaped scrapers and backed microliths (segments, backed points and bladelets, etc.) and a still greater variety of bone, wood and shell artefacts (Fig. 6.3). In their lithic raw material preference and the smaller size of flakes and formal tools they show similarities to the Robberg, but the latter's bladelet emphasis is lacking and backed microliths and scrapers were typically formed on flake, not bladelet, blanks. Wilton assemblages are found across southern Africa, but before 8000 years ago occur only to the north of the Limpopo and Gariep. This suggests a north-to-south diffusion of microlithic technology, with Diana's Vow, Zimbabwe (10,650 ± 80 BP, Pta-1857; Cooke 1979) and Apollo 11 (9430 ± 80 BP, Kn-I-610; Wendt 1976) among the earliest occurrences. South of the Limpopo a further diffusionary movement is evident from east to west within the Cape Fold Belt (H. Deacon 1976), though the 'late' (c. 6300 BP) appearance of segment and small scraper-dominated assemblages at Grassridge and Colwinton in the northern Eastern Cape (Opperman 1987) indicates that still other anomalies to these generalisations exist. Shifts in scraper morphology and the relative frequencies of different kinds of backed microlith define successive phases within the Wilton tradition south of the Limpopo (J. Deacon 1972; Sampson 1974) and in Zimbabwe (N. Walker 1995a). Following an Early phase, high numbers of segments at 7000–4000 years ago characterise Classic Wilton assemblages. Thereafter the Post-classic Wilton sees greater use of backed bladelets and points and, in many areas, a proliferation of adzes prior to the introduction of ceramics c. 2000 BP. Few distinct regional industries have, however, been identified before 5000 years ago.

Finding food

The availability of plant and animal resources must have altered considerably through the Pleistocene/Holocene transition. For reasons of preservation, faunal remains continue to dominate our understanding of subsistence strategies, but the period after 12,000 BP does provide increasing evidence for the use of plant foods. Some of the best comes from Bushman Rock Shelter (Plug 1981a), Heuningneskrans (Beaumont 1981), Kruger Cave (Mason 1988) and Umhlatuzana (Kaplan 1990), at all of which a variety of fruiting species were used. Given that all save Kruger Cave lie in the Savanna Biome this is to be expected, but the Bushman Rock sequence also suggests that people shifted their diet between collecting marula fruits and nuts and *Hypoxis* corms depending on whether climate was warmer or colder (Wadley 1987). In the Namib, people collected *!nara* melon seeds (Fig. 6.4) at Zebrarivier and Mirabib (Wendt 1976;

Figure 6.4   *!Nara* melons (*Acanthosicyos horrida*), an important plant food
resource in the Desert Biome (courtesy John Kinahan).

Sandelowsky 1977), a major staple of recent foragers in this area. Across the
continent, N. Walker's (1995a) excavations in the Matopo Hills suggest that
marula (Fig. 6.5) was systematically collected and processed throughout the
period 12,000–8,000 BP, with up to 400,000 fruits per cubic metre estimated
for some stratigraphic units at Pomongwe. Though other fruits (e.g. *Strychnos*
and *Grewia* spp.) were also collected, along with underground plant foods such
as *Cyperus*, they were clearly of secondary significance. Evidence is therefore
emerging that by the Pleistocene/Holocene transition, if not long before, people were exploiting a wide range of plants, with fruits and nuts dominant
in savanna vegetations. What remains obscure is the extent to which geophytes were used in the Grassland or Fynbos Biomes. Though expected to have
been staples in both regions (H. Deacon 1995), direct evidence is lacking before 8000 BP, despite their later importance. Where plants are preserved, as at
Byneskranskop (Schweitzer and Wilson 1982), fruiting species are once again
most evident.

We have already seen that the Pleistocene/Holocene transition witnessed
changes in the composition of archaeological faunas across the Fynbos Biome.
This appears to have been comparatively rapid at some sites (Boomplaas; Klein
1978a), but at others (Melkhoutboom (H. Deacon 1976) and Byneskranskop
(Schweitzer and Wilson 1982)) browsers only became dominant from 6000 BP.
The shift to a diet in which meat was increasingly derived from hunting, trapping and snaring small antelope may thus have been a regionally variable

Figure 6.5   Marula trees and fruit (*Sclerocarya birrea*), an important plant food
resource in the Savanna and Moist Woodland Biomes (courtesy Lyn
Wadley).

phenomenon. It can be identified in the Caledon Valley (Plug and Engela
1992) and the Matopos (N. Walker 1995a), though in Mpumalanga (Plug 1981a;
Klein 1984c) late Pleistocene hunting practices had not focused so heavily on
large grazers. One area where it does not seem to have occurred at this time
is the northern Eastern Cape where the shift to small ungulates was a late
Holocene phenomenon (Opperman 1987).

Increased exploitation of animal resources that are more predictable, occur
in large numbers, reproduce rapidly but are found in small package sizes is
another feature of the Pleistocene/Holocene transition in some areas. This is
most marked along the coast, where such resources include shellfish, fish,
rock lobster and seabirds. How far the evidence for intensive shellfish gathering that becomes widespread in several Cape coastal sites from 11,000 years
ago reflects coastline regression as opposed to shifts in subsistence is uncertain. Changing sea-levels, water temperatures, salinity and current strengths
may all have affected resource densities (Van Andel 1989) and it cannot be
assumed that they were as available in the late Pleistocene as in the recent
past. Indeed, the Elands Bay Cave (Fig. 6.6) sequence suggests that exploitation of some resources was strongly focused temporally. Rock lobsters (*Jasus
lalandii*), for instance, were collected in large numbers only during an apparently brief episode almost exactly 10,000 years ago, one that may reflect a

Figure 6.6   Elands Bay Cave, Western Cape, South Africa. The Atlantic
Ocean is visible at the far right.

mass stranding of these animals when low oxygen levels drove them onshore
(Parkington 1992). Slightly higher up in the same sequence, whelks (*Burnupena*
sp.) are superabundant in the molluscan fauna, as they are too at Nelson Bay
Cave almost 1000 km to the east at approximately the same time (*c*. 9600 BP;
J. Deacon 1984a). Once again, a specific palaeoenvironmental event may have
been involved. Elands Bay Cave also registers greatly intensified exploitation
of terrestrial small-package resources 11,000–9000 BP, notably ostrich eggs and
tortoises, 'pavements' of which were observed in excavation there (Parkington
1990b) and around 9800 BP at Byneskranskop (Schweitzer and Wilson 1982).
The concatenation of these resource changes plays an important part in explaining the connection between environmental and cultural changes at this

site across the Pleistocene/Holocene boundary. They were not, however, limited to South Africa's Atlantic coast. Increased capture of both dassies and rodents is suggested, for example, in the Matopo Hills in the early Holocene (N. Walker 1995a).

Explaining change

Orchestrating changes in environment, artefact assemblages and subsistence strategies into a coherent whole has been a major theme of LSA archaeology since the 1970s. H. Deacon's (1972) distinction between Pleistocene and Holocene adaptations emphasised the shift towards a postglacial pattern in which groups were smaller, more territorial and increasingly focused on less mobile resources (plants and small game). Cultural change was subsequently conceptualised using terms derived from systems thinking, with the three successive industries recognised in the Eastern Cape (Robberg, Albany, Wilton) described as homeostatic plateaux within which changes were comparatively minor and self-regulating. Briefer periods of more rapid positive feedback brought about change from one plateau to the next (H. Deacon 1976). This emphasis on linking technology, subsistence, social organisation and environment was a milestone in the development of an ecological approach in southern African archaeology, but the anomalous position of the Albany Industry (Oakhurst Complex) within an essentially dichotomous model was quickly recognised (Parkington 1980b). As with other systems models there was also a temptation to view change as solely initiated by environmental factors.

Closer examination of three southern Cape sequences (Boomplaas, Kangkara and Nelson Bay Cave) suggested that the replacement of Robberg technology by the Albany Industry exhibits a pronounced lag (of the order of 2000 years) relative to the onset of climatic amelioration (J. Deacon 1984a). Such lags, which may even interact with each other to produce what Parkington (1987) terms a 'megalag', are also a consequence of having to detect climatic change through proxy measurements, rather than directly. Inevitably, they constitute a significant problem to understanding connections between human behaviour and environmental change (Wobst 1990). Borrowing ideas about the 'deep structure' of a culture developed by Deetz (1977) in his study of colonial New England, Deacon therefore argues against any directly functional explanation. Instead, she suggests, shifts in stone tool assemblages (such as scraper and flake size) may indicate the 'social stress' people experienced when adapting to changing environmental conditions. The shift from a late Pleistocene economy geared to hunting large game to one in which smaller antelope and other resources became increasingly important provides the articulation between human behaviour and environmental change (J. Deacon 1984a). That most stone tools were probably never employed directly to extract food from the environment adds to the attractiveness of this argument (Isaac 1980), while the recognition that not all changes may have been provoked by the same stimuli is also useful. However, as Sampson (1985b) and others point out, neither this model nor that advanced earlier by H. Deacon (1976) fully takes on board the highly *discontinuous* nature of our stratigraphic sequences in which some distinctions between industries are drawn along these time-gaps. This automatically enhances contrasts between compared assemblages, which are also inflated when many smaller stratigraphic units are sunk together to create large enough samples (of artefacts, fauna, etc.) for analysis. Punctuated, rather than gradual, change is the result (Kaplan 1990). Independently assessing what is meant by 'stress' is also problematic.

While J. Deacon's model explored links between cultural and environmental change in the southern Cape, many of these processes had a much broader geographical span. Even if valid in the Fynbos Biome, other explanations might be needed where bladelet-dominated technologies were replaced in the absence of significant faunal change, such as Mpumalanga, the Lesotho Highlands and the northern Eastern Cape. Furthermore, it seems *prima facie* unlikely that the wholesale disappearance of toolkit components (unmodified bladelets and bladelet cores) that had been widely used for millennia could have occurred without at least some technological or economic cause and/or consequences. Could therefore the introduction of the bow and arrow account for both the disappearance of bladelet technology and the proliferation of bone points that mark some sites from about 12,000 BP (Mitchell 1988)? In the absence of evidence regarding bone point function or changes in hunting success as inferred from faunal analyses, this argument remains circumstantial and leaves unexplained other changes in stone tool assemblages (e.g. those affecting raw material choice), as well as the increasing evidence for regional variation in the date at which bladelet technology went out of use. Nevertheless, in so far as artefacts were used for particular purposes, those ends must have either changed or been met in other ways by the makers of Oakhurst assemblages. Purely 'social' factors, especially where left unspecified, seem insufficient.

More helpful may be the model developed by Ambrose and Lorenz (1990), which places the Robberg/Albany transition in the southern Cape within a broader theoretical and comparative framework that relates the organisation of technology, subsistence-settlement patterns and exchange to ecological variability. Arguing that shifts in raw material usage between the two industries indicate a breakdown of non-local lithic procurement systems as mobility and exchange decreased in response to increasingly plentiful and secure resources at the Pleistocene/Holocene boundary, they propose that locally available, often coarser-grained rocks were increasingly used instead, thus accounting for other observed changes in assemblage character, such as flake and scraper size. Some of their predictions, such as more local lithic procurement by Oakhurst foragers, do seem to be borne out, for example at Nelson Bay Cave, at Blydefontein and in the Caledon Valley. However, detailed sourcing data are still sparse in most of the sub-continent, while in some areas (e.g. Lesotho; Mitchell 1995) Oakhurst-like assemblages replaced Robberg-like ones without corresponding changes in toolstone use. Nevertheless, the connections which this model develops between palaeoenvironmental change, resource structure, technology, mobility and social organisation establish a productive research agenda, not least for explaining why bladelet-rich microlithic assemblages persisted much longer in south-eastern southern Africa than further west or north.

A different perspective comes from John Parkington's work (1980a, 1986, 1987, 1988, 1990b, 1992) at Elands Bay Cave. Eschewing cultural labels in favour of a more narrative approach, Parkington (1993) views interlocking shifts in artefact and faunal assemblages as documenting how people rescheduled their use of this site between 13,000 and 7800 years ago. Change is seen as more ongoing and less punctuated than in the Deacon models, with the key concept that of 'place', defined as the set of opportunities that a location affords and thus the probability that particular activities will take place there (Parkington 1980b). Seen in this light, Elands Bay Cave at the beginning of the terminal Pleistocene seems to have been used on a short-term expedient basis, perhaps as a largely male-occupied hunting station. Over the period 12,000–10,000 BP increased artefact densities, including those associated ethnographically with women (grindstones, evidence of ostrich eggshell bead manufacture) or suggestive of other kinds of on-site tool manufacture and repair (bonework), as well as gathered foods and burials, all attest to people using the site for longer periods and/or in a more regular way. Though larger numbers of grindstones may indicate increased collection of plant foods after 11,000 years ago, much more strongly evident is a massive focus on slow or immobile sources of protein. We have already seen that shellfish, tortoises, ostrich eggs and rock lobster were among the resources now targeted, but the numbers of newborn individuals of two small antelope species, steenbok and grysbok, increased dramatically at this time (Parkington 1988). It seems unlikely that the interconnectedness of these changes is only the result of coastal advance or increased attention to these resources. Wider organisational changes are implied, minimally at the level of the site's position within a regional settlement system as its catchment changed from riverine through estuarine to coastal (Parkington 1988; Poggenpoel 1987). However, these changes do not neatly fit within a Robberg/Albany/Wilton succession, nor do they necessarily lead into later Holocene patterns. Indeed, a shift back towards shorter visits, probably using many more sites within a seasonal round, occurred after 9000 BP (Parkington 1998). Successive, short-term adaptations to immediate problems seem like the rule here, though high frequencies of tortoise bone and ostrich eggshell in terminal Pleistocene deposits at Faraoskop, 30 km north-east of Elands Bay Cave, suggest that at least some problems, or their solutions, were not site-specific (Manhire 1993).

Changes in place deserve greater attention than they have received hitherto outside the farwestern Cape, and Parkington (1987) has raised the possibility that sites along South Africa's southern coast, such as Nelson Bay Cave, underwent comparable organisational adjustments. Yet 'place' alone will not suffice as an explanation where similar technological or social processes are observable across the whole of southern Africa. Allowance has to be made too for variation in resource opportunities, environmental constraints and social histories across the sub-continent. As is increasingly widely recognised, we need to distinguish changes and variables of local or regional importance from those that are sub-continental in scale and seek explanations that take such differences into account, with the expectation that different explanatory processes may be most in evidence and of greatest utility at different spatio-temporal scales (Bailey 1983; Knapp 1992). J. Deacon's (1984a) distinction between innovative changes (the appearance of new artefacts) and post-innovative changes (shifts in artefact size, frequency and shape), with only the former expected to have direct functional links, expresses a related concern. For the Pleistocene/Holocene transition, if the *details* of the Elands Bay Cave sequence come from one end of this spectrum of change, then similarities in the trajectories in mean ostrich eggshell bead size registered there and at Sehonghong, over 1200 km away (Fig. 6.7), represent the other, along with

Figure 6.7   Sehonghong Shelter, Lesotho. Sehonghong itself is in the foreground to the right of the Sehonghong River, photographed in early summer.

the sub-continental 'explosion' in evidence for personal jewellery *c.* 12,000 BP discussed below.

Recognition of these points also emphasises the value of continuing to search for high-resolution phenomena within the archaeological record, 'events' that can most closely approximate the decisions of individuals within actual social and environmental contexts. Once again, Elands Bay Cave illustrates what is possible where stratigraphic divisions are sufficiently fine-grained and archaeologists are prepared to work with small sample sizes. Parkington (1992) notes, for example, that 88 per cent of all its bone 'fish gorges', slivers of bone pointed at both ends thought to have been used for fishing, date 9600–8640 BP. This suggests a short-lived technological innovation also shared with Byneskranskop and Nelson Bay Cave ± 10,000 years ago (Schweitzer and Wilson 1982; J. Deacon 1984a). That over 80 per cent of the white mussel (*Donax serra*) shell scrapers in the Elands Bay Cave sequence concentrate between 8860 and 7910 BP, on the other hand, may represent a site-specific manufacturing/use/discard phenomenon, as these artefacts continued to be used until the end of the LSA elsewhere in the Western Cape.

All these remarks apply equally to attempts to explain why Oakhurst assemblages were themselves replaced in the early/middle Holocene by those classified as Wilton. Indeed, it is, perhaps, the regular appearance of much higher numbers of formal tools that marks the real 'break' in the LSA stone-working tradition, not the disappearance of Pleistocene bladelet technology or shifts in raw material usage between some Robberg and Oakhurst assemblages. The apparent north–south diffusion of the Wilton microlithic tradition raises the possibility of connections between Zimbabwe, where it first appears, and areas beyond the Zambezi, where backed microlith-producing Nachikufan industries continued uninterrupted from the late Pleistocene into the Holocene. However, these connections have not been investigated and do not by themselves offer an explanation. Humphreys and Thackeray (1983) suggest that the replacement of Oakhurst by Wilton assemblages in their Northern Cape research area coincided with a shift from drier to wetter conditions, but comment that Wilton microlithic technology may have been more effective in *all* environments since it involved a wider range of specialised tools. In the Caledon Valley, on the other hand, segments and thumbnail scrapers first appeared in a cooler and much drier phase *c.* 7200 BP, which also saw people economise their use of stone (for example, through greater use of bipolar flaking) and broaden their diet. Specific artefact functions remain uncertain, but changes in hafting technology, the employment of more carefully made, standardised tools and perhaps the innovation of more specialised scrapers may all be implicated in the adoption of the new tools (Mitchell 2000). It seems likely that archaeologists will eventually find that Wilton technology was adopted for a variety of local reasons, only some of them relatable to ecological pressures.

Demography and settlement

Population movements and the necessity of adapting to different environments as parts of southern Africa were recolonised after the Last Glacial Maximum are among the factors that need incorporating into the models just discussed. Site visibility is much greater after 13,000 BP than before and plotting the number of radiocarbon determinations against time reveals some interesting fluctuations across the Pleistocene/Holocene boundary. The most striking are the falls in total site numbers recorded 12,000–10,500 BP and again after 8500 BP (Fig. 6.8). The first coincides in part with the Younger Dryas, which probably produced more arid conditions in many parts of southern Africa, while the second saw a shift to lower precipitation across much of the summer rainfall zone: the Mixed Woodland Biome, in particular, has fewer sites at this time. Though site numbers are too few to discuss the comparative advantages and disadvantages of particular regions in more detail, some patterns stand out. Long-term research in the Thukela Basin of KwaZulu-Natal has, for example, failed to locate any evidence of pre-10,000 BP rock-shelter occupations (Mazel 1989), while other areas, such as South Africa's arid north-west, remained unoccupied until much later (Webley 1992a).

We remain ignorant of many of the ecological constraints operating on key plant and animal staples and still have too impressionistic a view of climatic change. But in general terms what we are probably seeing is a combination of population increase and infilling of a wider range of environments as biotic diversity increased and climate ameliorated. The many open-air Lockshoek sites

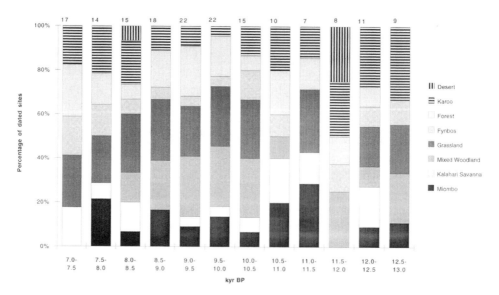

Figure 6.8   Patterning by biome in southern African radiocarbon
            determinations from archaeological sites, 12,000–8000 BP.

in the Karoo, compared to the complete absence of ones referable to the Robberg Industry, speak to this, as Sampson's (1985a) survey of almost 1000 km² of the Seacow Valley illustrates in detail. Here marked differences in landscape use between Lockshoek people and their Wilton successors have also been identified. The latter were less closely tied to spring eyes, perhaps indicating a greater use of ostrich eggshell water containers, and favoured locations with commanding views. Further north, early Holocene occupation of the Caledon Valley was more focused on a few large rock-shelters, like Rose Cottage Cave, than after 5000 BP (Mitchell 2000).

Elands Bay Cave and Faraoskop remain the only two sites known from the Verlorenvlei/Lamberts Bay area 13,000–8000 years ago. If this is not a reflection of limited sampling of deposits at other sites, it suggests that the late Pleistocene emphasis on a few selected rock-shelters continued there too (Parkington *et al.* 1987; Manhire 1993). Increased frequencies of hornfels in the Elands Bay Cave sequence also suggest connections between the coast and areas east of the Cape Fold Belt Mountains since this material was probably derived from dolerite dykes in the Karoo, rather than from eroded pieces carried downstream towards the sea (Parkington *et al.* 1987). Naturally backed knives may be another marker of this connection (Parkington 1990b), as may high (coastal plain derived?) silcrete frequencies in undated, basal levels at Aspoort on the Karoo side of the mountains (A.B. Smith and Ripp 1978).

One implication of increasing population densities brought out by Ambrose and Lorenz (1990) in their discussion of the Robberg/Oakhurst transition is that it may have become easier for people to find marriage partners within more circumscribed areas. This presumably had consequences for rates of gene flow within and between regional populations, though human remains are not sufficiently common to allow this proposition to be directly evaluated. In addition, however, people may have begun to make more use of material culture as a way of differentiating themselves from neighbours and asserting claims to particular sets of resources or parts of the landscape. In general terms, these connections are much easier to trace in the later Holocene, but some patterns are also emerging across the Pleistocene/Holocene boundary. Alliance networks between different hunter-gatherer groups can be investigated by considering evidence for the movement of items across the landscape. South-eastern southern Africa is one area favourable for this kind of study, as not only were marine and estuarine shells conveyed inland but ostriches appear to have been absent from most of it. Ostrich eggshell beads and pieces there were therefore probably also transported by people. A variable geology adds scope for tracing the movement of rocks used to make stone tools (Fig. 6.9).

Seashell ornaments (such as *Nassarius kraussianus* beads) continued to be introduced to the Lesotho Highlands in the early Holocene, but also reached western Lesotho, which may have been one source of the finished ostrich eggshell beads found at Sehonghong (Mitchell 1996c). Both the northern Eastern

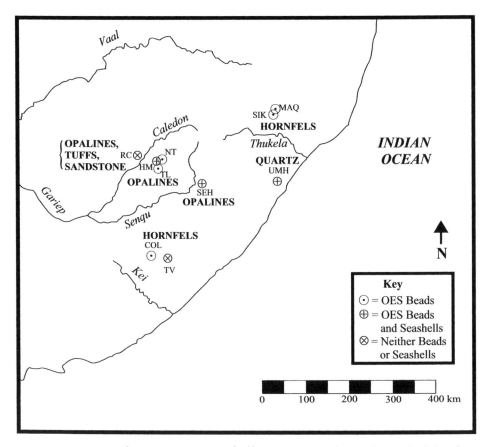

Figure 6.9   Spatial patterning in seashell ornament and ostrich eggshell bead
occurrence in south-eastern southern Africa 12,000–8000 BP. Site
names abbreviated thus: COL Colwinton; HM Ha Makotoko;
MAQ Maqonqo; NT Ntloana Tsoana; RC Rose Cottage Cave; SEH
Sehonghong; SIK Sikhanyisweni; TL Tloutle; TV Te Vrede; UMH
Umhlatuzana. Dominant lithic raw materials appear in capitals.

Cape and the eastern Free State have few ostrich eggshell beads and lack these
connections with the Indian Ocean coast, near which ostrich eggshell beads
occur in early Holocene deposits at Umhlatuzana (Kaplan 1990). After sharing
a common preference in the late Pleistocene for using opalines to make stone
tools, early Holocene assemblages are also more diverse, despite the continued
availability of this rock type. In both highland and lowland Lesotho opalines
remained the dominant raw material right across the Pleistocene/Holocene
boundary, but in the northern Eastern Cape hornfels was at least as important
after 10,000 BP (Opperman 1987) and at Rose Cottage coarser-grained tuffa-
ceous rocks and sandstone were used intensively from 9500 years ago (Wadley
1997a). The degree of coherence visible in this patterning suggests that these

three areas came to form fairly self-contained zones of social interaction after a late Pleistocene situation in which this was probably not the case.

Complicating this interpretation, however, is the presence of a Robberg-like assemblage at Rose Cottage Cave as late as 9500 BP (Wadley 1996a, 1997a), while 40 km to the east terminal Pleistocene/earliest Holocene assemblages from Ntloana Tsoana and Ha Makotoko are non-microlithic and almost lacking in formal tools (Mitchell 1993b). Here, in miniature, we confront the problem raised by Parkington (1984a) when discussing possible links between Robberg and Lockshoek assemblages: how can we recognise as the product of the same group of people artefacts that they may have produced using different raw materials or made for quite different purposes? There seems no way of resolving this problem in the Caledon Valley on current evidence, but the mid-tenth millennium BP does mark a breakpoint in the archaeological record on both sides of the river. Thereafter Oakhurst-like assemblages in which scrapers bearing adze-like retouch are frequent occur both at Rose Cottage (Wadley 2000) and in western Lesotho (Mitchell 2000).

Changes in social relations

South-eastern southern Africa is one of the few parts of the sub-continent in which evidence for the long-distance movement of potential exchange items has been examined in depth. However, the possibility that the Pleistocene/ Holocene transition witnessed a major increase in exchange within the context of a broader shift in the organisation of southern African societies has been repeatedly discussed. The key ideas here derive from Lyn Wadley's (1987) identification of gift-exchange, such as the **hxaro** practised by modern Ju/'hoansi Bushmen (Wiessner 1977, 1982), as a central pillar structuring hunter-gatherer social relations. The small number of bone points (= arrows?) and ostrich eggshell beads (both popular contemporary *hxaro* gifts) in the earliest LSA assemblages may mean that gift-exchange was only weakly developed during the late Pleistocene (Wadley 1987, 1993; J. Deacon 1990b). Increased numbers of both items (Fig. 6.10) after 12,000 years ago, on the other hand, could indicate that it then became more common, perhaps because exchange ties helped people pool information and spread economic risks as they expanded territorially and recolonised the southern African interior (cf. Gamble 1982). Wadley (1987) also argues that seasonal aggregation and dispersal and the different social rôles that people adopt at these times are another fundamental feature of Bushman social relations, but once again it is difficult convincingly to identify aggregation and dispersal in the Robberg, at least using the criteria which appear to work for the Holocene (Table 8.1). The appearance of a wider variety of sites, including open-air ones, and more smaller rock-shelters might therefore also document social relations closer to those of modern Bushmen after 12,000 BP (Wadley 1998).

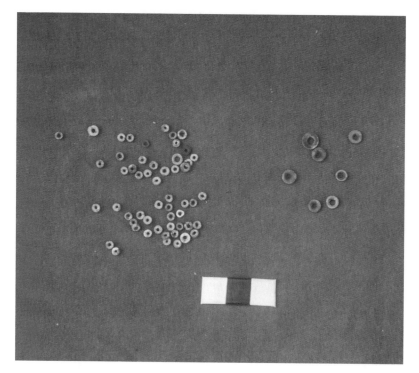

Figure 6.10   Ostrich eggshell beads from Sehonghong, Lesotho. Those on the
right are of a size typical of assemblages dating to within the last
2000 years. Those on the left are of mid-Holocene age.

Bows and arrows have already been mentioned several times. The sad reality
is that we have no real idea when this important technology was developed.
Since bone artefacts cannot always be unequivocally identified as arrowpoints
or **linkshafts** the oldest firm evidence is that of a broken arrowshaft from
Melkhoutboom (H. Deacon 1976) and a partial bowstave from Gwisho, Zambia
(Fagan and van Noten 1971). Thus while H. Deacon (1995) takes the bone points
from Pleistocene LSA assemblages mentioned in chapter 5 to indicate that
the bow and arrow were innovated at the start of the LSA, J. Deacon (1984b),
Mitchell (1988) and Wadley (1998) emphasise their increased numbers 12,000–
10,000 BP to indicate a much later introduction or popularisation. Parkington
(1998), on the other hand, opts for a date around 9000 years ago because not
a single point or linkshaft of later Holocene form occurs in the extensive terminal Pleistocene worked bone assemblage from Elands Bay Cave. Resolving
this question is relevant to more than merely issues of hunting technology and
subsistence competence because hunting with bow and poisoned arrow is in-
timately bound up with ethnographically documented Bushman beliefs about
sex, gender and even the parallel drawn between the behaviour of dying eland
and that of shamans entering trance (chapter 8). As Parkington (1998: 34) points

out, without this technology such links could not have existed, at least in their ethnographically known form, implying major differences in social relations and ideology between Pleistocene and Holocene populations. The organisation of hunting may also have been very different before the bow and arrow became available since without it people may have had to hunt large game using traps or in groups with spears. To ensure sufficient labour, women may have played an active part in hunting, contrary to recent Bushman practice, with effects not only on gender rôles (Wadley 1998) but also on the ideology of meat ownership and food-sharing (Vinnicombe 1972).

Unfortunately, art, which could offer another means of assessing arguments for or against continuity in social structure or ideology, is virtually lacking for the Pleistocene/Holocene transition. A single engraved dolomite slab from Wonderwerk shows a mammal of some kind, associated with a date of 10,200 ± 90 BP (Pta-2786; A. Thackeray *et al.* 1981), while painted spalls occur in terminal Pleistocene/early Holocene deposits in the Matopo Hills (N. Walker 1987). Otherwise we are restricted to geometrically incised ostrich eggshell fragments, which have a much wider occurrence (Schweitzer and Wilson 1982; J. Deacon 1984a; Beaumont 1990b).

Burials are also too few to offer much insight, though the very fact that they now begin to appear may be significant. Other than at Elands Bay Cave (A. Morris 1992c) and in the Matopo Hills, where cremation and deliberate dismemberment are attested (N. Walker 1994a), all come from rock-shelters in the southern Cape coastal forelands. This regional concentration continued into the middle and later Holocene (Inskeep 1986) and may indicate the early build-up in this area of dense populations interested in asserting resource-claims to the landscape. Grave goods are extremely rare in all early Holocene burials, though red ochre is associated with some of those at Oakhurst (Goodwin 1938) and Matjes River (Döckel 1998). Covering the body with stones is also reported there, Nswatugi (N. Walker 1994a) and at Wilton Large Rock Shelter (J. Deacon 1972).

Direct and indirect evidence for exchange thus offer the greatest potential, at present, for examining changes in LSA social relations across the Pleistocene/Holocene boundary. Inferences drawn from the presence of bone points and ostrich eggshell beads depend solely upon ethnographic analogy for their plausibility, as direct evidence of their long-distance movement is lacking. South-eastern southern Africa is something of an exception to this generalisation, but inland movement of marine shells is also attested in southern Namibia (Wendt 1972) and in the southern and Eastern Cape (J. Deacon 1972, 1984a; H. Deacon 1976; Opperman 1978). This increased interest in moving items of decoration around the landscape offers a further perspective on the shift from Robberg to Oakhurst stone-working traditions. I suggested earlier that the combination of reliable and maintainable design strategies within Robberg technology offered people a technological means of minimising risks associated with failure to find sufficient social and economic resources for ensuring their survival. Perhaps the greater evidence for exchange indicates that social solutions to these problems became increasingly important from 12,000 BP. Increasing ecological productivity and population densities may have made reliance on inter-group alliances a more dependable strategy of risk-management (cf. Barut Kusimba 1999 for East Africa). Technological alternatives, especially those requiring considerable skill, such as bladelet production (Hayden 1989), would have been progressively downplayed. Much along the lines outlined by Torrence (1989) when contrasting the lithic technologies and exchange patterns of Mesolithic and Neolithic Europe, stone artefact assemblages thus became marked by greater expediency of artefact manufacture and use, effecting the change from those archaeologists term 'Robberg' to those termed 'Oakhurst'. As with other explanations of the connections between cultural and environmental change across the Pleistocene/Holocene boundary, this idea too both accommodates and expects that these changes were regionally time-transgressive.

CHAPTER 7

HUNTING, GATHERING AND INTENSIFYING: HOLOCENE FORAGERS IN SOUTHERN AFRICA

By 6000 years ago Wilton microlithic technologies were in use across southern Africa by people whose lifeways are better known than those of their predecessors. Here I explore this evidence down to 2000 BP, using the ecological framework discussed in chapter 2. Several themes stand out. One is the extent to which seasonal patterns of mobility are discernible, another, following Janette Deacon's (1974) suggestion that aridity constrained settlement of the interior during the middle Holocene, the impact of climatic changes on regional settlement history. Others include shifts in exchange networks, growing regionalisation of material culture, changes in landscape use, heightened use of foods occurring in small 'package' sizes and the development of more formal means of disposing of the dead. Frequently discussed jointly as evidence of social and economic intensification, these issues raise the question of just how 'complex' later Holocene southern African hunter-gatherer societies were becoming.

The Moist Woodland Biome

The key archaeological evidence for this biome (Fig. 7.1) comes from the Matopo Hills, where Holocene adaptations focused on a narrow gathering niche stressing marula (Fig. 7.2; N. Walker 1995a). With a protein/energy-rich nut and fruits that drop to the ground to ripen, marula has an edible food productivity of 190 kg/ha, far exceeding other plants and capable of supplying an adult's daily calorific needs from just three hours' labour. However, late spring/early summer would have been a potentially critical time for obtaining food. Excavations at Pomongwe and Bambata document exploitation of other species which helped to bridge this gap, including *Ximenia*, *Cordia* and, from 4800 BP, *Annona* and *Ficus capensis*. Geophytes, however, were ignored and adzes for making and resharpening digging sticks are correspondingly rare. After 4800 BP storage of plant foods is also indicated. Several dozen pits at Pomongwe and Bambata contain plants, especially marula, which can be eaten throughout the year, while one held unidentified caterpillars, raising the possibility that larvae were also dried for future use; a thriving trade in *mopane* caterpillars (*Gonimbrasia belina*) continues today. The main archaeologically identifiable source of animal protein, however, was small game,

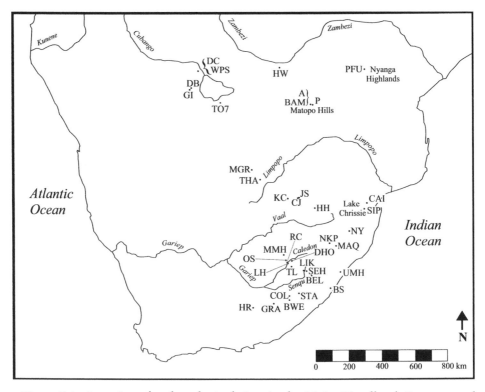

Figure 7.1 Location of archaeological sites in the Moist Woodland, Savanna and
Grassland Biomes discussed in chapter 7. Site names abbreviated
thus: A Amadzimba; BAM Bambata; BEL Belleview; BS Borchers
Shelter; BWE Bonawe; CAI Caimane 1; CJ Cave James; COL
Colwinton; DB Dobe; DC Depression Cave; DHO De Hoop; GI ≠Gi;
GRA Grassridge; HH Hope Hill; HR Highlands Rockshelter; HW
Hwange National Park; JS Jubilee Shelter; KC Kruger Cave; LH
Leliehoek; LIK Likoaeng; MAQ Maqonqo; MGR Magagarape; MMH
Mauermanshoek; NKP Nkupe; NY Nyonyane; OS Orange Springs;
P Pomongwe; PFU Pfupi; RC Rose Cottage Cave; SEH Sehonghong;
SIP Siphiso; STA Strathalan A; THA Thamaga; TL Tloutle; TO7
Toteng 7; UMH Umhlatuzana; WPS White Paintings Shelter.

Figure 7.2 Matopo Hills, Zimbabwe (courtesy Innocent Pikirayi).

notably dassie and small bovids suitable for trapping, since the Matopos' hilly terrain and dense vegetation do not support dense herds of larger antelope.

A paucity of palaeoenvironmental evidence hampers understanding of changing settlement-subsistence patterns in the Matopos, but one noteworthy observation is that only from 6000 BP were both large and much smaller rock-shelters occupied. Perhaps more regular patterns of dispersal and aggregation were now initiated within more reduced home ranges. The earliest backed microlithic assemblages, the Nswatugi Industry, were followed *c.* 4800 BP by others in which chalcedony, derived from beyond the Matopos, was more commonly employed. Other innovations in this Amadzimba Industry included new kinds of ornaments, ostrich eggshell containers with neatly bored apertures and bone linkshafts suggesting hunting with poisoned arrows designed to detach themselves into the animal. Extended aggregations may be indicated by more intensive occupation at Bambata, Amadzimba and Pomongwe, supported in part by stored food, while painted spalls in mid-Holocene deposits suggest that rock art was produced and, with associated rituals, played a part in structuring social relations. Unfortunately, the lack of excavated assemblages dating 3800–2200 BP leaves us ignorant of the centuries immediately preceding the local appearance of pottery and domesticates.

Elsewhere far less is known of Zimbabwe's Holocene prehistory. Numerous microlithic surface assemblages in Hwange National Park are undated (Klimowicz and Haynes 1996), as are those from excavations at Pfupi and nearby shelters in Mashonaland. Recent assessments conclude that supposedly distinctive features (bored stones, backed scrapers and ground stone axes) also occur in south-western Zimbabwe (N. Walker and Thorp 1997). Different kinds of axe are, however, found in Mashonaland/Nyanga and Matabeleland. Their functions probably included bark removal, and there are good correlations between their occurrence and areas with more closed vegetation receiving >600 mm rainfall per year in which traditional clothing was made of bark cloth rather than leather (H. Deacon and Deacon 1980; N. Walker 1980). Plentiful adzes and **spokeshaves** in some apparently late Holocene occurrences in Mashonaland (Cooke 1978b) and the Nyanga Highlands (Martin 1938; K. Robinson 1958) hint at extensive wood-working, but considerable inter-site variability exists. Much more fieldwork is needed to make sense of these isolated reports.

The Savanna Biomes

Southern Africa's various savanna regions have a markedly patchy Holocene record. Despite its size, few sites are known from all but the southern margin of Botswana's Kalahari. Excavations at open-air sites near Dobe revealed two later Holocene occupation pulses, at 3650–3200 BP and after 2260 BP, both probably linked to brief wetter episodes (Yellen and Brooks 1989). Bone was not preserved, but lithic occurrences were rich in segments, particularly steep and biconvexly retouched 'double segments'. More appropriately termed 'backed scrapers', these artefacts occur over most of Botswana and Namibia, though they are absent from Zimbabwe and the Shashe–Limpopo Basin (N. Walker 1995b). Patterning in their distribution and that of other formal stone tool types, as well as Botswana's rock art, may prove to relate to the long-term distributional history of different Bushman populations (N. Walker 1994b, 1995b).

Several localities on the northern edge of the Dry Woodland Biome have produced evidence of intensive exploitation of aquatic resources during the Holocene. They include White Paintings Shelter in the Tsodilo Hills, with its numerous barbed bone points probably used to catch catfish and other species in seasonal spawning runs (Fig. 7.3; Robbins *et al.* 1994), and Toteng 7 on the southern margin of the Okavango Delta, where fishing intensified after 3200 BP as lower lake levels provided better possibilities for catching fish in shallower waters (Robbins *et al.* 1998). Aquatic resource exploitation at these sites and other open-air later Holocene sites along the Botleli River (Denbow 1986) may have allowed more sedentary lifestyles that subsequently encouraged the acquisition of domestic sheep. However, other resources were also exploited. At White Paintings Shelter people hunted lechwe (*Kobus leche*), common reedbuck

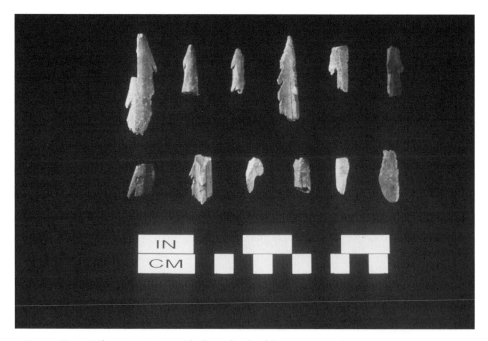

Figure 7.3   White Paintings Shelter: barbed bone points (courtesy Larry Robbins).

(*Redunca arundinum*) and bushpig, further evidence for mid-Holocene wetter conditions since none occur there today. Nearby Depression Cave was occupied in both the early and later Holocene, but here steenbok comprise almost the entire fauna; fish are absent. Isolated mongongo shell fragments reach back to 7100 BP, and the microlithic Wilton-like assemblage includes hammerstones and anvils for opening them similar to those used recently (Robbins 1990). ≠Gi, though dating to within the second millennium AD, documents yet another subsistence strategy, the use of pits as hunting blinds for taking large game (Helgren and Brooks 1983). Occupation of other parts of the Dry Woodland Biome, including the Zambezi Valley, eastern Botswana and Zimbabwe's southern lowveld, is little attested prior to farming, implying they were extremely marginal for hunter-gatherers.

Offering strong support to J. Deacon's argument that mid-Holocene aridity discouraged settlement of South Africa's interior, occupation of the Mixed Woodland areas of the transVaal was long undemonstrated before 1000 BP. Wadley's (1987) research in the Magaliesberg has helped reassess this conclusion. Dates in the sixth and seventh millennia BP from Jubilee Shelter are supported by others from Cave James (Wadley 1988) and Kruger Cave (Mason 1988), the latter lying within the Grassland Biome. Both Jubilee and Cave James were also used intensively after 4000 BP. Despite their closeness and broad contemporaneity, their artefact assemblages are quite distinct. These differences were instrumental in Wadley's (1987) development of an influential model (see also chapter 8), which explores how contrasts in the social and economic consequences of seasonal patterns of group aggregation and dispersal manifest themselves archaeologically. Using expectations generated from Kalahari Bushman ethnography, Jubilee Shelter (Fig. 7.4) is identified as a mid-Holocene aggregation centre from its many curated, standardised formal tools, exotic toolstone and extensive debris from the manufacture of ostrich eggshell beads and bone points, both potential *hxaro* items. Cave James, on the other hand, has an expedient lithic assemblage with few formal tools or potential *hxaro* items and a predominantly local raw material signature. As expected if they were occupied at different times of the year, the two sites also have different seasonality and subsistence profiles: at Cave James there is little evidence for hunting, birds, rodents and small bovids were probably snared and only summer fruits were found, while Jubilee has only winter fruits and a fauna featuring both large and small bovids (Wadley 1987).

Kalahari ethnography also suggests that gender roles are more strongly defined in aggregation phases. One way of identifying this archaeologically may be to look for spatial patterning in activity location. In Jubilee Shelter's mid-Holocene levels beads and bead-making debris concentrate to the left of a hearth and bone tool debris to its right, both observations made facing inwards from the dripline. Wadley (1987) suggests this indicates a formal female/male seating arrangement, based on the gender associations of bead and arrow

Figure 7.4   Excavations in progress at Jubilee Shelter, North-West Province, South Africa (courtesy Lyn Wadley).

manufacture among the Ju/'hoansi and a male-right/female-left symbolism common among Bushmen. Items interpreted as a shaman's toolkit – quartz crystals, ochre and MSA artefacts – were found near the same hearth. Such indications of ritual activity, perhaps further demonstrated by the presence of several decorated bone artefacts, are also expected of situations in which people aggregate together. That only one such hearth arrangement was observed and Ju/'hoansi practice is for men and women to work in separate areas, not at the same hearth, raises doubts over the detail of some of these interpretations (N. Walker 1995a), but does not gainsay the many other contrasts between Jubilee and Cave James, nor the potential of aggregation/dispersal for understanding inter-assemblage variability. Looking beyond the Magaliesberg, the comparative richness of Wilton material culture at Jubilee and in other parts of southern Africa may reflect intensification of ritual activity and exchange as means of coping with the risks imposed by drier mid-Holocene climates (Wadley 1987).

More evidence of mid/later Holocene occupation will probably emerge as research proceeds north of the Vaal. In south-eastern Botswana, Thamaga (Robbins 1986) and Magagarape (N. Walker 1995b) are among the observations that suggest this. One difficulty may be that people preferred open-air locations to rock-shelters. In Mpumalanga, for example, the basal layer at the open-air site of Honingklip I dates to 4870 ± 70 BP (Pta-5049). A scraper/segment-dominated Wilton assemblage accompanies a diverse fauna dominated by small and medium-sized bovids (Korsman and Plug 1994). //Xegwi Bushmen survived until recently close to Lake Chrissie (Potgieter 1955), but little further work has been undertaken in this area. The Holocene LSA of Mozambique, where research has emphasised the archaeology of farming communities, is also little known, though microlithic scraper-dominated assemblages from Caimane I in the far south contrast strongly with backed blade/scraper-rich occurrences reported north of the Zambezi (Sinclair *et al.* 1993a). In Swaziland people making Wilton artefacts visited Siphiso Shelter (Fig. 7.5) 7500–6500 BP and Nyonyane after 3300 BP, but drought may have curtailed human settlement during the

Figure 7.5   Excavations in progress at Siphiso Shelter, Swaziland (courtesy
Larry Barham).

intervening millennia (Barham 1989b, 1989c). Assemblages with many adzes and some bored stones suggest geophyte exploitation, but there is only minimal evidence for small-scale seasonal movements between dispersal phase rock-shelters and possibly contemporary, but undated, extensive open-air (summer aggregation?) sites (Barham 1989a). Though published in far less detail, sites in north-west Swaziland (Grassland Biome) have dates suggesting occupation was less erratic there than at lower elevations (Stuiver 1969; J.C. Vogel *et al.* 1986).

Undoubtedly the most extensive observations in the Mixed Woodland Biome come from the Thukela Basin of KwaZulu-Natal. Early Holocene occupation centred on the Eastern Biggarsberg, with settlement expanding from there after 7000 BP (Mazel 1989, 1996). Tracing the development of alliance networks between hunter-gatherer groups has been a key feature of Aron Mazel's research here (Fig. 7.6). Essential for both biological and social reproduction, these networks manifested themselves archaeologically, so he argues, through exchange and the elaboration of distinctive kinds of material culture, as the Bleek/Lloyd records suggest was the case among /Xam Bushmen in the Northern Cape (J. Deacon 1986). A single alliance network may have spanned the Basin before 4000 BP, and with far more ostrich eggshell and seashell ornaments than other

Figure 7.6   Nkupe Shelter, KwaZulu-Natal, South Africa (courtesy Aron Mazel).

sites Maqonqo may have been particularly important within this (Mazel 1996). Its abandonment coincided with the emergence of three, perhaps four, smaller social regions, each associated with a distinct set of assemblages. Backed microlithic assemblages at sites in the Ndaka social region, for example, are dominated by segments, those in the Toleni region by backed points and blades (though segments still occur), and those in the Injasuthi region by backed points and blades without segments.

Mazel (1986, 1988, 1989) argues that exploitation of plant foods (both seeds and geophytes), fish and small game intensified significantly from 4000 BP within a context of regional population growth. Increased numbers of adzes (for digging-stick manufacture and repair) and grindstones in post-4000 BP assemblages further suggest enhanced plant food exploitation. Gender relations may also have altered, enabling women to increase their status after an initial occupation phase in which hunting (and thus men) are claimed to have predominated (Mazel 1989). Although both the possibility that these changes reflect differential survival of plant and animal remains and the appropriateness of the gender rôles attributed to men and women need to be considered more thoroughly (Wadley 1989), one interesting aspect of Mazel's general interpretation is the differential use of lithic raw materials north of the Thukela. Here exotic opalines were preferentially employed for items associated with men in Kalahari Bushman ethnography (scrapers for hide-working, backed microliths as arrow armatures). Adzes, on the other hand, which may have had stronger female associations, were made from locally available (less prestigious?) hornfels.

South of the Thukela, observations are fewer (Davies 1975; Kaplan 1990), and they are virtually absent all together from the former Transkei (but cf. Laidler 1934, 1936). The lack of detailed information on the now largely destroyed shell middens of the South Coast is particularly distressing. Cable's (1984) remains the one extensive project undertaken in southern KwaZulu-Natal, motivated by the desire to test a model of seasonal movement across the landscape originally developed by Carter (1970). This envisaged people spending summers along the Drakensberg Escarpment (because of better grazing for game and a proliferation of geophytic foodplants) before moving downslope to winter in the Natal Midlands. Cable postulated that winter movements reached the coast, noting pronounced contrasts between coastal and highland artefact assemblages. The former have few adzes, bored stones and bone points, whereas all are common in the latter, where geophyte collection and arrow-hunting may have concentrated. However, only the most ephemeral sites exist in the Midlands and it remains difficult to see why people should have moved away from the coast in summer, although connections between shore and interior are documented by seashell ornaments at Sehonghong in the Lesotho Highlands; rare ostrich eggshell beads at Borchers Shelter and Umhlatuzana may have moved coastward in return (Mitchell 1996b).

The Grassland Biome

Eastern Lesotho was among the first areas in this biome to witness significant LSA research. Initial observations suggested that it saw little occupation 10,000–2000 years ago, though scraper-dominated Wilton-like assemblages extend back beyond 3300 BP at Belleview (Carter 1978). Renewed excavations at Sehonghong supported this picture, demonstrating only two occupation pulses between 9500 and 1700 BP, of which only the younger (*c.* 6000 BP) yielded a Wilton assemblage (Mitchell 1996d). Work only a few kilometres away at Likoaeng (Fig. 7.7) shows that the area's settlement history has, in fact, been more complex. There a series of well-stratified occupations built up against, and perhaps in the lower levels within, a now-buried rock-shelter between 3100 years ago and the local introduction of ceramics *c.* 1800 BP. Excellent faunal preservation documents growing interest in exploiting local fish resources, which may have been processed for removal elsewhere (Mitchell and Charles 2000).

Across the Maluti Mountains, Tloutle has a well-defined mid-Holocene sequence in which segments first appear 7200 BP, but only become frequent after 6900 BP (Mitchell 1993b); only two other sites date 7000–2000 BP (Mitchell *et al.* 1994). This dearth of evidence contrasts with the situation in the eastern Free State. At Rose Cottage Cave middle Holocene assemblages belong, like

Figure 7.7   Likoaeng, Lesotho, looking north across the excavation area and out into the Senqu (Orange) Valley.

their contemporaries at Tloutle, to the Classic phase of the Wilton Industry. Following a long break in use, occupation resumed around 2200 BP; this Post-classic Wilton occurrence is particularly rich in bone artefacts and ostrich eggshell beads and containers, some with geometric engravings (Wadley 1997a). Nearby, Leliehoek (Esterhuysen *et al.* 1994) shows that the reorganisation of settlement patterns which excluded Rose Cottage did not involve wholesale abandonment of the area. An isolated burial from near Ladybrand (A. Morris 1992a) and excavations at Orange Springs, De Hoop and Mauermanshoek (Wadley 1995) also attest to continuing hunter-gatherer presence. On the Grassland Biome's northern periphery Hope Hill, occupied either side of 4400 BP, is the only dated site beyond the Vaal (Wadley and Turner 1987). Its small, informal artefact assemblage recalls Cave James, as well as several other undated occurrences in the southern transVaal. With a fauna emphasising large mammals, especially alcelaphines, and several bone points/linkshafts, it was probably used as a hunting camp by people who made many of their artefacts on fine-grained rocks from over 25 km away.

Mid/later Holocene faunas at these sites were diverse, but had stronger components of small and small–medium bovids than their Pleistocene predecessors (Plug and Engela 1992; Plug 1993a). Evidence for plant exploitation is rare, but at Sehonghong both geophytes (*Cyperus usitatus, Moraea tritia, Watsonia,* etc.) and fruits were recovered from the mid/late Holocene levels (Carter *et al.* 1988). South of the Gariep, Highlands Rock Shelter adds yet other geophytes, especially *Bulbine alooides* and *Freezia corymbosa*. Upper grindstones that are morphologically different from those typical of Cape Fold Belt sites may also indicate a greater interest in wild grass exploitation, while faunal resources emphasised ground game, small bovids, ostrich eggs and freshwater mussels (H. Deacon 1976).

In the south-eastern part of the Grassland Biome, on the other hand, subsistence strategies in which large grazers were the most important meat source persisted longer (Opperman 1987). Alcelaphines, zebra and bluebuck (*Hippotragus leucophaeus*) dominate mid-Holocene faunas at Grassridge and Colwinton, with grey rhebuck (*Pelea capreolus*) and eland more common after 3000 BP when moister conditions facilitated the growth of shrubs at the expense of grasses (Tusenius 1989). Arguing for more restricted seasonal movements than did Cable further north, Opperman (1987) emphasises the close proximity of patches of sourveld (grazable only in summer) and mixed grassveld (grazable all year round), the former lying above, the latter below the Drakensberg Escarpment. With game moving over short distances and along predictable paths up and down mountain valleys, sites in mixed grassveld areas, such as Bonawe, may have been specialist hunting camps. Its third-millennium BP occupation has much higher bone and lower artefact densities than other sites, but high frequencies of bone points and scrapers. By this time, however, if not before, subsistence strategies had also broadened. The contemporary site of

Strathalan A has a fauna of dassie, klipspringer and grey rhebuck, and evidence for the collection of *Watsonia* bulbs, some found chewed or with their stems knotted together; three whole digging-sticks were probably used in gathering them (Opperman 1996b).

The Fynbos and Forest Biomes

Of all southern Africa's biomes, it is those in and seaward of the Cape Fold Mountains that offer the richest Holocene LSA record (Fig. 7.8). Dry microenvironments at many sites offer excellent organic preservation, facilitating subsistence analyses and offering important insights into LSA material culture. Examples include digging-sticks (Augussie; Binneman 1994a), leather clothing, firesticks and netting (e.g. Melkhoutboom; H. Deacon 1976) and stone-tipped (Adam's Kranz Cave; Binneman 1994b) and fletched (Faraoskop; Manhire 1993) arrows (Fig. 7.9).

Wilton Large Rock Shelter, typesite of the Wilton industry (J. Deacon 1972), and Melkhoutboom (H. Deacon 1976) are among the key sequences in the eastern part of the Fynbos Biome. Along with Uniondale (Fig. 7.10; Leslie 1989), they fall within what seems to have been a core demographic area in the eastern Cape Fold Belt. Only from 5500 BP, however, did people settle the inland margins of this range, perhaps because of long-term population growth further south (Derricourt 1977; S. Hall 1990). Both north and south of the mountains, silcrete was increasingly preferred for making retouched artefacts around 5000 BP. This was so even where highly suitable local rocks were obtainable or, as at Uniondale, other exotic rocks had previously been employed. This 'silcrete plateau' may represent the development of a regional style marker to structure interaction among a spatially and numerically expanding population (S. Hall 1990). Subsequent coping strategies seem to have involved increased exchange, perhaps to spread risks among exchange partners by strengthening social ties, and greater identification with specific places on the landscape. Burials, which I discuss below, may be one sign of this. Another is the development of more distinctive artefact assemblages. **Kasouga flakes**, for instance, have a restricted range centred on Uniondale and the adjacent coast 4500–2000 BP, and stemmed bone points, edge-nicked *Turbo* shell pendants, shale **'palettes'** and the use of warthog tusks and bovid metapodials in burials may prove to be other local style markers (Leslie 1989; S. Hall 1990).

Comparable patterning is observable along and inland of the Tsitsikamma Coast, where quite different microlithic (Wilton) and macrolithic (Kabeljous) assemblages occur after 4700 BP. The latter are highly informal, except for grooved stone sinkers, bored stones, grindstones and large quartzite segments, an artefact type found along the coast from Klasies River to the Great Fish River. Binneman (1996a) interprets this diversity in terms of two distinct

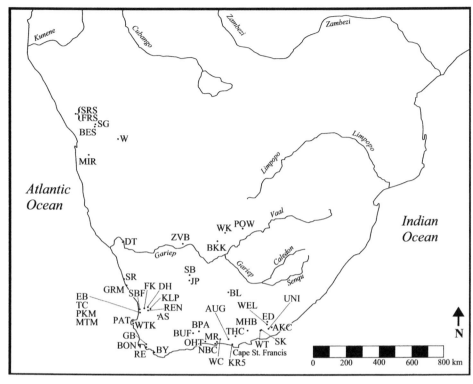

Figure 7.8   Location of archaeological sites in the Fynbos, Forest, Karoo and
Desert Biomes discussed in chapter 7. Site names abbreviated thus:
AKC Adam's Kranz Cave; AS Aspoort; AUG Augussie; BES Big
Elephant Shelter; BKK Blinkklipkop; BL Blydefontein; BON
Bonteberg; BPA Boomplaas; BUF Buffelskloof; BY Byneskranskop;
DH De Hangen; DT Die Toon; EB Elands Bay Cave; ED Edgehill; FK
Faraoskop; FRS Falls Rock Shelter; GB Gordon's Bay; GRM
Groenriviermond; JP Jagt Pan; KLP Klipfonteinrand; KR5 Klasies
River Cave 5; MHB Melkhoutboom; MIR Mirabib; MR Matjes River;
MTM Mike Taylor's Midden; NBC Nelson Bay Cave; OHT
Oakhurst; PAT Paternoster; PKM Pancho's Kitchen Midden; POW
Powerhouse Cave; RE Rooiels; REN Renbaan; SB Springbokoog 1;
SBF Steenbokfontein; SG Striped Giraffe Shelter; SK Spitzkop; SR
Spoegrivier; SRS Snake Rock Shelter; TC Tortoise Cave; THC The
Havens Cave; UNI Uniondale; W Windhoek; WC Whitcher's Cave;
WEL Welgeluk; WK Wonderwerk; WT Wilton Large Rock Shelter;
WTK Witklip; ZVB Zoovoorbij.

populations, who in part structured their interactions by making quite different kinds of artefacts: Wilton assemblages result from visits to the coast
by people based in the Cape Fold Belt where similar occurrences are found,
while the Kabeljous Industry was produced by groups permanently settled along

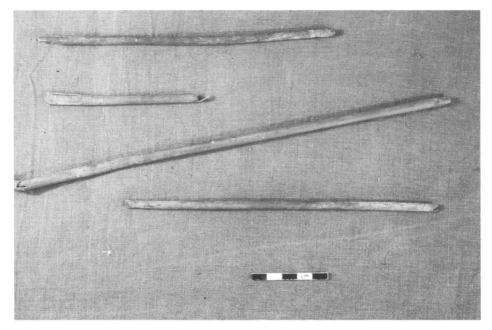

Figure 7.9   Wooden arrows from Faraoskop, Western Cape, South Africa
(courtesy Tony Manhire). Some of those found retain their original
fletching.

Figure 7.10   Uniondale, Eastern Cape, South Africa (courtesy Mary Leslie).

the shore. At Klasies River Cave 5 both populations are thought to have used the site 4200–3000 BP, though not necessarily simultaneously (Henderson and Binneman 1997).

Holocene hunter-gatherer subsistence strategies in the Eastern Cape focused on geophytes as a dependable carbohydrate source, supplemented by small bovids as the major supply of protein. The Melkhoutboom and Wilton sequences suggest that the latter superseded larger game coincident with the onset of the Wilton Industry. Particularly important were *Raphicerus* and bushbuck (*Tragelaphus scriptus*), nocturnal animals whose predictable movements render them susceptible to snaring, though at Edgehill (S. Hall 1990) and Uniondale proximity to savanna-like habitats facilitated hunting of Cape buffalo. Seashell ornaments at inland sites indicate coastal contacts, but the Eastern Cape's relatively aseasonal climate may have weighed against fixed patterns of seasonal movement (H. Deacon 1976; S. Hall 1990). Exploitation of marine resources seems, in fact, only to have gathered momentum after 6000 BP, with the best-known shell middens those near Cape St. Francis and Klasies River (Singer and Wymer 1982; Binneman 1996a). Those associated with Wilton assemblages have high frequencies of limpets, while Kabeljous assemblages are dominated by brown and white mussels.

Though geophytes were clearly the dietary mainstay, eaten roasted whole or ground and cooked into 'cakes' (J. Deacon 1984b), the specific plants used vary between sites. At Melkhoutboom, for example, *Watsonia* is most common. They are collectable throughout the year, but older corms have poor palatability, making spring, summer and autumn the most abundant seasons for both it and other important taxa, such as *Moraea* spp., *Hypoxis argentea* and *Freezia corymbosa*. On the Cape Fold Belt's drier northern margins, where *Watsonia* is less common, post-2000 BP finds at Welgeluk suggest that *Moraea* spp. and *Tritonia/Freezia* were more important, along with tubers of *Dioscorea* (S. Hall 1990). However, seeds are far more frequent than remains of these underground plants and also occur before 2000 BP. Among them *Grewia occidentalis* and *Olea africana* are well-known edible fruits, while charred remains of *Podocarpus* and *Diospyros* suggest that their palatability was enhanced by roasting.

Intensified exploitation of aseasonal food resources becomes more strongly evident after 4000 BP, probably as a further means of resolving the problems posed by increasingly smaller, more stationary home ranges. In the Koonap Valley, people focused on tortoises, crustacea, fish and mussels, the latter two resources particularly important as sources of fat and protein in otherwise lean winter months (S. Hall 1988, 1990). Shell middens occur at several places along the Great Fish River (Hewitt 1921) and use of freshwater mussels (*Unio caffer*) also intensified at Uniondale and elsewhere in the late Holocene (Leslie 1989). An additional means of prolonging access to resources was through storage. Pits, sometimes, as at Melkhoutboom, grass-lined and stone-capped

Figure 7.11   Entrance to Nelson Bay Cave, Western Cape, South Africa.

(H. Deacon 1976), characterise several sites after 4000 BP. They contain seeds of *Pappea capensis* and other species that yield cosmetic oils (H. Deacon 1976; S. Hall 1990); perhaps significantly, the former's fruits are also edible (Fox and Norwood Young 1982).

Many of the processes just discussed are also evident in the southern Cape. Here well-known sites like Oakhurst (Goodwin 1938), Matjes River (Döckel 1998) and Nelson Bay Cave (J. Deacon 1984a; Inskeep 1987) lie within the Forest Biome. Though large game was comparatively rare, the nearby coast offered plentiful shellfish, fish, birds and mammals (Inskeep 1987). Nelson Bay Cave (Fig. 7.11), the area's most comprehensively investigated site, documents exploitation of all these resources, though preserving only scanty remains of the geophytes (including *Watsonia*) and fruits that were also eaten. As further east, limpets and mussels dominated shellfish collection, while fish were taken by angling, netting and spearing. Small bovids, dassies and seals (the age of which suggests they were hunted as well as scavenged) dominate the mammals (Klein 1972; Inskeep 1987). Here too patterning in the associated artefacts has been interpreted in ethnic terms. Alongside a macrolithic quartzite industry, viewed as the product of year-round residents of the coast and derived from the pre-6000 BP Albany Industry, typically 'Wilton' segments and small scrapers made from non-local quartz and chalcedony may represent the coastward movement of groups otherwise based in the Cape Fold Belt. Interlinked changes in the cultural sequence *c.* 3300 BP suggest that these visits ceased around that time (Inskeep 1987). Since no spatially or temporally discrete local and intrusive assemblages were identified, this interpretation may not be as convincing here as on the Tsitsikamma Coast, but the richness of the Forest Biome's resources suggests its inhabitants are unlikely to have had to move far. Indeed, stable isotope analyses of human skeletons from the southern Cape suggest marked differences in the balance of marine and terrestrial food intake over even short distances. At Whitcher's Cave, for instance, only 14 km from the sea, results reflect almost wholly terrestrial diets, while the very different isotope signatures of skeletons from Matjes River and Nelson Bay Cave must imply quite different subsistence strategies either side of the Keurbooms River. Increased diversity in body size and a decline in mean body size 3300–2000 BP may also speak to differentiating lifeways and, in some cases, poorer nutrition as people settled into increasingly smaller territories (Sealy and Pfeiffer 2000).

The many burials recovered from the southern Cape support this, since repeated placement of the dead at specific sites may have asserted claims to particular sections of an increasingly crowded landscape. In the eastern Cape Fold Belt, indeed, some sites may have functioned specifically as cemeteries, among them Spitzkop and Welgeluk (Fig. 7.12), where site use began by placing

Figure 7.12 Welgeluk, Eastern Cape, South Africa: burials 1, 2 and 3 (courtesy Simon Hall). All three are adult individuals, the first two probably male. Individual 2 was accompanied by a freshwater turtle carapace, ochre, an ochre-stained grindstone and several silcrete artefacts (S. Hall and Binneman 1987).

several individuals beneath stone cairns on the shelter floor before 4500 BP (S. Hall and Binneman 1987; S. Hall 1990). Here and further west at Nelson Bay Cave, Matjes River and Oakhurst, as well as at The Havens and Klasies River Cave 5, many burials were accompanied by rich jewellery and other grave goods (Inskeep 1986; S. Hall and Binneman 1987). At least some probably had specific symbolic connotations: Bushman ethnographies suggest that grindstones and bored stones helped communication with the dead, while tortoise carapaces and ostrich eggshell containers may have contained **buchu** or water for 'cooling' dangerous supernatural potency (Wadley 1997c).

That the richest graves are often of children may reflect the Ju/'hoansi practice of grandparents passing *hxaro* goods to grandchildren not yet able to exchange them on (S. Hall and Binneman 1987). Where exchange ties were valued as means of structuring inter-group relations, deposition of *hxaro* items in graves would also have taken them out of circulation, thus encouraging continued exchange. However, the possibility that this patterning reflects development of less egalitarian forms of social organisation in which status was partly ascribed cannot be wholly dismissed (S. Hall 1990). Burials were fewer and generally less complex after 3500 BP, suggesting further changes in social organisation and how affiliations to the landscape were expressed. Rock art may have been one means of doing this, since painted stones, some carrying images with clear shamanistic connotations, cluster within the last 4000 years. They were probably used in a range of contexts, including burials (Lewis-Williams 1984; Binneman and Hall 1993; Binneman 1999).

Inland two sites are prominent in the southern Cape. Boomplaas was occupied around 6400 BP and again towards 2000 years ago. The former occupation (Member BLA) is associated with two large (2 by 1 m) charcoal beds in the site's centre, which may result from meat-drying activities. The later BLD Member saw over forty-five lined storage pits dug across the shelter's interior, several used to store *Pappea capensis*. A few painted stones were recovered from some of these pits. Paint stains on the sediment below one suggest it was placed on the ground while still wet; its ostrich image was evidently not meant to be seen (H. Deacon 1995). Another significant find is a rare example of a still-hafted scraper (H. Deacon and Deacon 1980). Coastal connections, presumably through exchange networks, are indicated here and at Buffelskloof by fragments of seashell and seashell ornaments. At both sites subsistence focused on geophytes (*Hypoxis, Moraea* spp., *Watsonia*), small and small–medium bovids and ground game (Klein 1978a; Opperman 1978).

The western part of the Fynbos Biome has also seen considerable Holocene research. Byneskranskop is interesting for its relatively late (6500/6000 BP) adoption of segments and switch from large grazers to small/small–medium browsers (Schweitzer and Wilson 1982). Mid/late Holocene subsistence also focused heavily on fish and shellfish, especially alikreukel (*Turbo sarmaticus*), along with a diverse range of fruits (*Diospyros* spp., *Euclea racemosa* and

Nylandtia spinosa) and geophytes (*Hexaglottis longifolia*). Increased frequencies of adzes after 3500 BP may indirectly suggest greater underground plant food exploitation from this time. Similarly diverse subsistence patterns, using both littoral and terrestrial resources, are indicated elsewhere in the southwestern Cape, including Rooiels (A.B. Smith 1981), Gordon's Bay (van Noten 1974), Bonteberg (Maggs and Speed 1967) and further up the Atlantic coast at Paternoster (Robertshaw 1977). Lithic assemblages at these sites are typically small and informal, perhaps reflecting the (limited?) activities carried out at the seashore: at Witklip, 10 km from the sea on the Vredenburg Peninsula, silcrete scrapers and adzes are relatively common, even though shellfish and *Donax* scrapers document repeated visits to the sea (A.B. Smith *et al.* 1991).

Still further north, the area from Elands Bay (itself at the southern edge of the Succulent Karoo Biome) east into the Cedarberg has been intensively investigated. Following the early Holocene occupation of Elands Bay Cave discussed in chapter 6, the Verlorenvlei's mouth apparently remained unused 7900–4300 BP (Parkington *et al.* 1987), perhaps because of the negative effect of the mid-Holocene marine transgression on coastal/estuarine productivity (D. Miller *et al.* 1993). This abandonment was, however, a local phenomenon and Steenbokfontein (Jerardino and Yates 1996) demonstrates middle Holocene occupation a little further north. When the Verlorenvlei area was resettled after 4300 BP the initial focus was on rock-shelters, such as Tortoise Cave and Elands Bay Cave (Parkington *et al.* 1987; Robey 1987; Jerardino 1995). Diets incorporated a broad mix of shellfish, marine and estuarine fish (Poggenpoel 1987), scavenged and possibly hunted seabirds (G. Avery 1987), small bovids and ground game (Klein and Cruz-Uribe 1987). Similarities in formal tool assemblages with the 4300–3600 BP layers at Tortoise Cave suggest that otherwise undatable artefact occurrences on deflation hollow sites further inland were probably also used at this time. There is no solid basis, however, for believing that they continued in use thereafter (Jerardino 1996). Indeed, the rarity of backed pieces after 4000 BP at Faraoskop could make them at least that old (Manhire 1993). Dominated by scrapers and backed microliths, most occur close to major water courses in areas of higher nutrient potential that probably attracted more large game (Moll 1987). Many also have abundant lower grindstones and may have been base camps from which people visited the coast (Manhire 1987).

After 3500 BP group mobility became more circumscribed, to judge from reduced frequencies of non-local silcrete at Tortoise Cave (Jerardino 1996). Steenbokfontein, in particular, shows greatly intensified use of small package resources (tortoises, shellfish and small bovids) compared to the period 6100–4000 BP when tortoises and molluscs are comparatively rare and large game more common (Jerardino and Yates 1996). Around 3000 BP the onset of cooler, wetter conditions greatly improved the productivity of both terrestrial (higher rainfall) and marine (colder seas) resources, encouraging abandonment of almost all rock-shelters and a dramatic move to large open-air sites.

Figure 7.13   Mike Taylor's Midden, Western Cape, South Africa, viewed from Elands Bay Cave (courtesy Antonieta Jerardino).

Consisting almost exclusively of black mussels, which may have been preferred because they grow fast, reproduce young and are highly productive (Jerardino 1996), these 'megamiddens' (Fig. 7.13) attest to massive intensification of shell-fish collection. Henshilwood *et al.* (1994), in fact, propose that they result from repeated processing and drying of mussels so that their flesh, which remains edible for some months, could be transported elsewhere. However, virtually *no* inland sites date to this period and excavations at Mike Taylor's Midden (MTM) and elsewhere suggest that the enormous (10,000–20,000 m³) quantities of shell swamp other categories of evidence, masking significant inter-site variability (Jerardino and Yates 1997). Although the possibility of lateral shifts in activity location makes interpretation difficult, megamiddens demonstrably witnessed stone artefact production and processing of a wide range of foods, including fish, seabirds and mammals. They may have been associated with base camps located on their peripheries or at nearby rock-shelters such as Pancho's Kitchen Midden (Jerardino 1998).

Steenbokfontein (Fig. 7.14) is the only rock-shelter with substantial occupation evidence at this time. Prominent on the landscape and centrally located among the megamiddens, it may have been an aggregation focus for an otherwise dispersed population. Modifications of its interior by digging out two large basins within the deposit at 3500 and 2700 BP perhaps helped invest it with a new identity (Jerardino and Yates 1996). Around 2400 BP, however, visits

Figure 7.14   Steenbokfontein, Western Cape, South Africa (courtesy Antonieta Jerardino). The rock-shelter is visible at the right of the kopje.

became shorter and it may have ceased to be an aggregation focus, going out of use some two centuries later. Also about 2200 BP, Elands Bay Cave began to be revisited, MTM was used less intensively and short-lived camps were made along the dune cordon further south. Important shifts in site use, settlement pattern and social organisation were thus clearly underway before the introduction of sheep and pottery some 2000 years ago (Jerardino 1996).

Earlier discussions of subsistence and settlement in this part of southern Africa posited seasonal movements between coast and interior in a model originally developed using seasonal indicators such as macroplants, birds, dassies and seals from Elands Bay Cave and the post-2000 BP inland site of De Hangen. Backed by ecological factors emphasising the coast's more moderate winters, the greater availability of standing water inland in summer and the recurrence in the same season of plankton blooms ('red tides') that render filter-feeding shellfish such as black mussels toxic, these indicators suggested people lived inland in summer and at the coast in winter (Parkington 1972, 1977). As faunal data at Elands Bay Cave showed different patterns of site use in the early Holocene and other strategies were identified after the introduction of domestic livestock, the seasonal mobility model became restricted to the period 4300–2000 BP. However, though seashells do occur in the interior (e.g. Klipfonteinrand 1; A. Thackeray 1977), very few inland rock-shelters in the south-western Cape have dates of 3000–2000 BP, and most are within

30 km of the sea (Jerardino 1996). Settlement pattern data thus strongly suggest that farwestern Cape populations were overwhelmingly coastally orientated during the period of megamidden accumulation.

Stable carbon isotope analysis of human skeletons provides independent support for this re-evaluation of seasonal mobility, since coastal and terrestrial resources have quite distinct isotope signatures. The few early/middle Holocene skeletons, all from the coast, have widely varying $\partial^{13}C$ values. The much larger 4000–2000 BP sample includes many from the coast with signatures implying close on 100 per cent marine diets, as well as a few inland burials with strongly terrestrial signatures (Sealy and van der Merwe 1986, 1988; Sealy *et al.* 1992, 2000). These results suggest marked differences in diet and landscape use between coastal and inland populations, with men having greater access to marine foods than women, but they have not gone uncontested, even though the region's isotope ecology has remained virtually stable over the last several thousand years (Lee Thorp and Talma 2000). One difficulty is that the technique may emphasise protein (from marine animals) at the expense of other dietary components (terrestrial plants; Parkington 1991; cf. Sealy and van der Merwe 1992). An exclusively marine diet is also implausible nutritionally because of the risks posed by excess protein intake (Noli and Avery 1988). Plants, whether from close to the coast or further inland, must therefore have been consumed,[1] though fat in shellfish and marine mammals could also have offset the dangers of protein poisoning (Jerardino 1996). A further stable carbon isotope study using bone apatite from the same skeletons as those previously studied confirms that at 3000–2000 BP people consumed fats/carbohydrates of both marine and terrestrial origin, as well as substantial amounts of marine protein (Lee Thorp *et al.* 1989). Experiments inspired by seventeenth-century European accounts show that seal meat and blubber remain edible for several weeks if buried in beach sand (A.B. Smith *et al.* 1992); whales could have been treated similarly (Jerardino and Parkington 1993). Such stores, along with dried mussel meat, probably helped people remain more sedentary, countering the effects on shellfish availability of red tides and winter storms.

Far fewer sites have been investigated in the farwestern Cape's interior. Klipfonteinrand 1 (A. Thackeray 1977) and 2 (Nackerdien 1989) and Renbaan (Kaplan 1987) are among those with occupation during the mid-Holocene hiatus at Elands Bay Cave. Their faunas emphasise small bovids and ground game, and lithic assemblages show widespread increases in adze frequency after 3500 BP that suggest intensive geophyte exploitation. Also documented on or near the coast (Manhire 1993; Jerardino 1995, 1996; Jerardino and Yates 1996), this phenomenon clearly predates the introduction of domestic livestock (*pace* Parkington *et al.* 1986), adding strength to Lee Thorp *et al.*'s (1989) argument for

---

[1] Seaweeds are another possible (marine) carbohydrate source, but are only minimally attested in the archaeological record (e.g. Jerardino and Yates 1996). Ethnographically recorded uses are as storage containers for whale oil and blubber (Budack 1977).

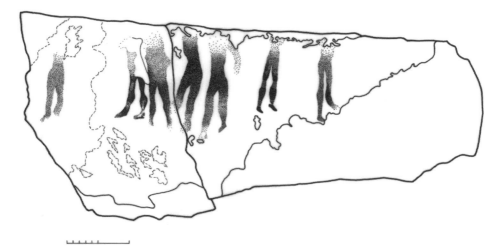

Figure 7.15   Refitted painted slab from Steenbokfontein, Western Cape, South
Africa (courtesy Antonieta Jerardino). All figures were painted red
except that the second figure from left has a white cloak and the
ankles and knees of the second figure from the right have rows of
white lines and dots. The dashed line shows the densest smear of
red paint. Radiocarbon dates from samples immediately above and
among the slabs provide a minimal age of *c.* 3600 BP (Jerardino and
Swanepoel 1999).

terrestrial carbohydrate use. Many adzes were made on recycled MSA silcrete
flakes, suggesting limited access to outcrops and thus more restricted home
ranges. Though people may have been becoming more sedentary, intensification of exchange and burials accompanied by grave goods are less evident than in
the southern and eastern Cape (Inskeep 1986). Faraoskop, where at least twelve
individuals were buried *c.* 2100 BP, is unique as a cemetery, and for its possibly contemporary cache of potential exchange items (ostrich eggshell beads,
shell ornaments, ochre, arrowshafts; Manhire 1993). Rock art, which a buried
slab from Steenbokfontein (Fig. 7.15) confirms was already being produced
>3500 BP (Jerardino and Swanepoel 1999), may have offered another means
of laying claim to the landscape and is much more prolific than in the southern
Cape.

The Karoo and Desert Biomes

Parkington's research area spans the transition between Fynbos and Succulent
Karoo Biomes. Aspoort remains the only excavated site on the Cedarberg's eastern margins, but poor preservation constrains what it can tell us (A.B. Smith
and Ripp 1978). Further north there is no sign of LSA presence in Namaqualand
until after 3800 BP. Both Spoegrivier (J.C. Vogel *et al.* 1997) and Die Toon

(Webley *et al.* 1993) contain deposits reaching back to this time, with settlement encouraged by wetter conditions than presently prevail. Rare burials are also known (A. Morris 1992b); that from Groenriviermond is remarkable because microfauna in its stomach cavity confirm that rodents sometimes formed part of LSA diets (Jerardino *et al.* 1992). Within the much larger Nama-Karoo Biome, several areas are comparatively well researched. In the Seacow Valley, for example, several hundred Wilton sites are known (Sampson 1985a). Bousman's (1991) re-excavation of Blydefontein extends and improves upon the chronology obtained by Sampson (1974) in the area of the Gariep Dam, where sustained occupation is evident after 4500 BP. He shows how range size gradually decreased, based on declining use of opalines derived from the Gariep's gravels, while people redesigned the morphology of their projectile armatures and how they were repaired and maintained to cope with fluctuating resource levels.

Both the eastern Karoo and much of the Northern Cape have been characterised as comparatively 'unstructured' environments in which markedly seasonal resource patterning is absent. As a result of spatio-temporally more unpredictable rainfall and a less varied topography, hunter-gatherers living in these areas may not have followed regular seasonal rounds (Humphreys 1987). North of the Gariep/Vaal confluence and extending up into the southern margins of the Kalahari, occupation is well attested through the middle and later Holocene. Wonderwerk is the key long-sequence site, with Wilton assemblages first reported *c.* 8500 BP. As elsewhere, successive phases are recognisable from scraper morphology, backed microlith frequencies and changes in raw material usage. In common with other Holocene microlithic assemblages, fine-grained materials (here chert and quartz) were preferentially used for curated formal tools, coarser rocks (such as banded ironstone) for presumably more expedient artefacts. These observations can be matched at other sites nearby (Humphreys and Thackeray 1983), but Wonderwerk stands out for the wealth of its material culture, which Wadley (1989) considers may mark it out as an aggregation focus. Unusual finds include stone rings, chert pendants and several engraved stones, most with grids and lines, but one showing the hindquarters of a zebra (A. Thackeray *et al.* 1981; Fig. 7.16). Faunal preservation is generally poor, but sufficient to show people exploited large–medium grazers (especially alcelaphines, zebra and springbok), along with ground game (dassie, hare, porcupine, tortoise) and smaller bovids (Humphreys and Thackeray 1983).

In Bushmanland, where surface water is extremely limited, occupation concentrated in two brief pulses, 2600–2300 and 4500–4300 BP. Both episodes are attributed to the Springbokoog Industry, distinguished by a marked emphasis on backed blades compared with assemblages further south and east (Beaumont *et al.* 1995). Still earlier occupation is hinted at by hundreds of fine-line engravings at Jagt Pan and other sites which show savanna species (giraffe, impala, roan/sable antelope, wildebeest and zebra) that may reflect southward movement of the Savanna Biome during the middle Holocene (Beaumont and

Figure 7.16 Engraved slab with an abstract fine-line design from Wonderwerk
Cave, Northern Cape, South Africa (courtesy Peter Beaumont). The
slab comes from a layer dated *c.* 2500 BP.

Vogel 1989). More securely dated (to 4400 BP) is a cluster of over eighty fine-
line engravings at Springbokoog 1, found associated with three small stone circles. This locality repeatedly attracted engravers' attention and other sites are
associated with the post-2100 BP Swartkops Industry (D. Morris 1988). Given
Bushmanland's general aridity, most occupation was probably along the Gariep.
However, there is little sign of this, except at Zoovoorbij near Upington where
a stratigraphically consistent series of late Holocene dates is associated with an
unfortunately disturbed deposit (A.B. Smith 1995b). The site is of interest as it is
next to one of two sources of specularite in the Northern Cape. Neither here nor
at Blinkklipkop (A. Thackeray *et al.* 1983) does evidence of mining reach back
beyond 2000 BP, but specularite certainly moved over distances of > 100 km to
reach sites like Powerhouse Cave (D. Morris 1990a) and Wonderwerk (Humphreys and Thackeray 1983) before then.

The Karoo Biomes extend north across the Gariep. Several research projects
have been undertaken there and within the Desert Biome inland of the Atlantic
coast. Wendt's (1975) conclusion that people were absent from southern
Namibia between 5100 and 2300 BP still holds (J. Kinahan 1991). Early Holocene
conditions, on the other hand, were more favourable than at present (Brain and
Brain 1977), and at Mirabib, in the heart of the desert, fruits and protein/fat-rich
seeds of the *!nara* melon probably played a key rôle in people's diets; marine

shells document contacts with, if not movement to, the coast (Sandelowsky 1977). Lithic assemblages here and at other southern Namibian sites, such as Apollo 11 (Wendt 1972), are typically scraper-dominated. Associated backed pieces include both segments and backed scrapers, the latter a relatively common component of the Namibian Holocene LSA. Quite different, but perhaps activity-specific, crude quartz artefacts occur with a butchered elephant at Windhoek Zoo (MacCalman 1965).

In northern Namibia a quite different settlement pattern prevailed, perhaps because inselbergs can better trap rain and offer altitudinal variations in resource availability (Parkington and Hall 1987b). Several sites occur in the Erongo Mountains, though none reaches back beyond 6000 BP (Wadley 1979). One of the best known, Big Elephant Shelter (Fig. 7.17) shows people principally taking both small bovids (steenbok and klipspringer) and ground game, a mix widely reported from Namibian sites (J.F. Thackeray 1979; Cruz-Uribe and Klein 1983). A range of plants was also used, notably *Cyperus fulgens*, which occurs in high-density stands and is edible from March to November. Wadley (1979, 1984b) suggests that people geared their lifestyle to this resource, though seasonality evidence indicates the site was visited on and off throughout the year. Indeed, the area's highly unpredictable rainfall would have made nonsense of any fixed pattern of seasonal movements (Jacobson 1984). Moving back into the Desert Biome, the Dâures (Brandberg) massif is rich in rock art (Pager 1989)

Figure 7.17   Interior view of Big Elephant Shelter, Erongo Mountains, Namibia (courtesy Lyn Wadley).

Figure 7.18   View of the Hungorob Gorge, Dâures massif (Brandberg), Namibia, a major concentration of rock art and focus of several LSA excavation programmes (courtesy John Kinahan).

and has several sites occupied, probably sporadically, from 6500 BP (J.C. Vogel and Marais 1971; Jacobson and Vogel 1975; Fig. 7.18). Among them are Falls Rock and Snake Rock Shelters, where people took dassie, klipspringer and rock hare (*Pronolagus randensis*), making microlithic assemblages in which backed microliths are at least as common as scrapers. Falls Rock also yielded intriguing hints of ritual activity in the form of pierced insect cocoons (dancing rattles?) and an ochre-smeared, polished hunting dog (*Lycaon pictus*) cranium found with ochre-stained ostrich feathers (J. Kinahan 1991). These two sites do not display evidence of coastal contact prior to the introduction of pottery, but fragments of marine shell occur as far inland as Big Elephant and Striped Giraffe Shelters in the Erongo, more than 150 km from the Atlantic (Wadley 1979). Reconnaissance of the shoreline, however, has identified only one site predating 2000 BP, a shell midden at the mouth of the Uniab River (J.C. Vogel and Visser 1981).

Intensification and complexity: integrating the record

Having surveyed the various biomes of southern Africa for the period 7000–2000 BP, in this section I draw together the evidence for socio-economic change in the Holocene LSA and ask why no indigenous system of food-production developed in the sub-continent. The Cape Fold Belt, KwaZulu-Natal and Matopos offer the richest material for discussion, but some trends, such as re-occupation of previously marginal environments and increased site densities in areas with more continuous settlement histories, are replicated elsewhere. As a starting point, it is now evident that the scale, duration and presumed impact on human settlement of mid-Holocene aridity have been overemphasised. Though discontinuities in occupation remain evident, a more complex situation has emerged. Settlement is now well attested in the Magaliesberg, Caledon Valley and Northern Cape. Even on the eastern margins of the Karoo the argu-ment that all Wilton assemblages must postdate 4500 BP depends heavily on the 8500–4200 BP break in the Blydefontein sequence (Bousman 1991). Nevertheless, the consistently higher numbers of dated sites in the Fynbos, Forest and Grassland Biomes probably reflect the richness of their geophyte resource base (H. Deacon 1993), as well as the enhanced ecological diversity and more stable precipitation on which I have commented previously. Further north, similar comments probably apply to the success of marula collection in the Matopos, though the lack of sites in the transVaal section of the Mixed Woodland Biome remains puzzling; a preference for open-air settlement may, as we have seen, go some way to explaining this.

Throughout the sub-continent, except perhaps in the south-eastern part of the Grassland Biome (Opperman 1987), middle/later Holocene adaptations fo-cused on smaller, more territorial game and plant resources. However, in the Cape Fold Belt and Thukela Basin, where the later Holocene record most con-vincingly documents rising populations and their expansion into new habitats, there is also evidence of increasing interest in aseasonal resources or ones that, though coming in small packages, were predictable, productive but low in risk. Geophytes, fish, shellfish and tortoises were among these resources, and this shift in subsistence strategies seems easiest to explain if people were increas-ingly choosing, or being compelled, to curtail their movements and adopt more sedentary lifestyles within more circumscribed ranges. Storing food was an-other strategy enabling people to cope with these problems, whether in pits (the Matopos, eastern Cape Fold Belt, Boomplaas) or by drying mussels and burying sea mammal meat (the farwestern Cape). Other solutions were more strictly social, involving increased exchange, manipulation of material cul-ture to structure intra-group relations, and the assertion of claims to the land-scape by reference to the dead (formal burial in the Forest and Fynbos Biomes) or supernaturally charged imagery (rock art in the Matopos and farwestern Cape). Interestingly, these developments are not evident on anything near the same scale elsewhere in southern Africa, although many previously marginal envi-ronments were reoccupied after 4500 BP. Examples include the eastern Karoo (Sampson 1972, 1985a; Bousman 1991) and the Drakensberg/Maluti Mountains (Cable et al. 1980; Opperman 1987; Mazel 1990; Mitchell and Charles 2000). However, in Bushmanland reoccupation remained episodic, contingent upon exceptionally favourable conditions (Beaumont *et al.* 1995), while southern Namibia and Zimbabwe's **lowveld** appear to have been completely unoccupied for much of the Holocene.

What makes the Cape Fold Belt stand out in its elaboration of material culture and burials when compared with so many other parts of southern Africa during the second half of the Holocene? Ecological diversity may be one factor, with the narrow coastal plain between George and Cape St Francis compressing varied coastal and inland habitats into a small zone that experiences less markedly seasonal rainfall than neighbouring areas (S. Hall and Binneman 1987). Many sites here have basal LSA occupations of ± 15,000–12,000 BP, and more sustained demographic growth may have promoted increasing organisational complexity and exercised density-dependent effects on adjacent areas. A related factor may have been the importance accorded geophytes since their productivity can be managed by fire: burns increase flowering (and thus reproduction) rates of *Watsonia pyramidata*, for example, by 800 per cent (H. Deacon 1976). Such 'firestick-farming' may have become important as Holocene population densities rose, and it would be interesting to know if the geophytes on which people concentrated in the southern and eastern Cape (*Hypoxis, Moraea, Watsonia*) are more susceptible to such manipulation than those that were important in the farwestern Cape, where fruits were more significant (Liengme 1987) and the elaboration of material culture, burial rites and storage more recent.

In many respects these developments match those observed in other parts of the world, where discussions of intensification have focused both on improvements in the efficiency with which resources are extracted and on overall increases in production, though the two need not be synonymous. Common archaeological indicators of these processes include many of the phenomena we have just discussed, although opinion varies as to the degree to which population growth is an independent variable in bringing them about (Price and Brown 1985). In the Thukela Basin, Mazel (1989) stresses gender conflict (women opting to contribute more to the diet) as an additional factor, while in the eastern Cape Fold Belt a broader range of social and economic strategies for minimising subsistence risks is emphasised, the outcome of which was increasingly defined and contracted territories and alliance networks (S. Hall 1990). Jerardino's (1996) analysis of the farwestern Cape also incorporates a diversity of factors, including significant changes in resource productivity, to explain the coastally orientated societies of the megamidden period. Common to all of these studies, and implicit in the Matopo Hills (N. Walker 1995a), is the development of societies with economies increasingly characterised by delayed, rather than immediate, returns from labour investments (Woodburn 1982). Storage of food and an emphasis on resources with rapid rates of regeneration were key here and may have begun to undermine the egalitarianism that food-sharing had supported (S. Hall 1990; Jerardino 1996).

Why though did such systems not lead to an indigenous development of food-production or more obviously hierarchical societies? Answering this question, H. Deacon (1972) suggested that the non-gregarious small antelope and geophytes that formed the basis of many Holocene subsistence strategies had limited potential for agricultural experimentation. More recent work pinpoints how difficult this would have been. Both Rowley-Conwy (1986) and Diamond (1997) draw attention to the very narrow evolutionary pathways along which animal domestication has taken place. African antelopes live either in pairs, or in herds in which males separate into individual, defended breeding territories at some time of the year (Estes 1992). Permanently maintained dominance hierarchies are a feature only of eland and Cape buffalo. The former is comparatively docile and can be readily driven, though recent domestication efforts have been hindered by the ease with which it clears fences, but the latter is widely regarded as highly unpredictable and dangerous; African equids may also have been too aggressive for successful domestication (Diamond 1997). Though suids might seem to offer more scope, in both Eurasia and Melanesia their rearing was linked to village life (for scraps) and the production of domesticated carbohydrate (for extra food). This in turn invites a consideration of the agricultural potential of southern African plant foods. Though no detailed study has been undertaken, several negative factors are associated with southern Africa's key plant food staples: the long maturation periods and possibly high processing costs of the nut- and fruit-bearing trees of the Savanna and Miombo Biomes; the low productivity (except where fire-managed) of geophytes elsewhere; and the possibly low protein/carbohydrate content of local cereals (little used, except as famine foods or when taken from ant nests, even where they were exploited; H. Deacon 1993).

In sum, southern African plants and animals may have had little potential for domestication. Firestick-farming of geophytes could increase their productivity and visibility, but has limited scope. Though probably important in the developing cultural complexity evident in the southern and eastern Cape from the sixth millennium BP, the lack of higher-yielding cereals, roots and tubers may have imposed an ecological ceiling on the extent to which processes of socio-economic intensification could 'take-off' compared to other Mediterranean environments, such as California and the Levant. Elsewhere there seems to have been even less ecological potential for movement towards delayed returns systems. These arguments are deliberately deterministic to emphasise that the behavioural and genetic plasticities of plant and animal species must be considered in explaining why indigenous systems of food-production did not develop in southern Africa. But this cannot, of course, be the whole story, as social relations are also critical in explaining agricultural origins (Hayden 1990). Nevertheless, although later Holocene populations in several parts of southern Africa did undergo processes of social and economic transformation, key critical thresholds may not have been passed, or passable. Intensifying resource use, greater sedentism, developing new means of affiliation to particular local land-scapes, elaboration of exchange networks and regionalisation of artefact styles are all present to a greater or lesser degree in at least four areas: the Matopos, the Thukela Basin and the Forest and Fynbos Biomes of the Cape. But, perhaps like the situation along Europe's Atlantic and Baltic coasts (Zvelebil 1986), further developments were truncated, in this case around 2000 BP by the southward movement of domestic livestock and plants ultimately originating north of the Equator. How these resources were introduced and the respective rôles in this of local hunter-gatherers and incoming communities are among the themes of the ensuing chapters.

CHAPTER 8

HISTORY FROM THE ROCKS, ETHNOGRAPHY FROM THE DESERT

Rock art is one of the most visible and informative components of southern Africa's archaeological record. Long viewed through narrowly Eurocentric eyes, exploration of Bushman ethnography has revolutionised its understanding, bringing about a wider paradigm shift in Stone Age research as a whole. This chapter discusses these developments, both as they affect rock art and as they influence archaeological discussions of social aggregation and dispersal, exchange and gender relations. Paralleling these changes, historical and anthropological research in the Kalahari questions how far we can use Bushman ethnography to write accounts of the Later Stone Age as Khoisan history. Along with a critical consideration of the empirical basis of recent applications of social theory to LSA research, this forms the second principal theme of this chapter.

The art and its dating

Well over 10,000 rock art sites occur south of the Zambezi (H. Deacon and Deacon 1999: 163), most still unrecorded in detail (Fig. 8.1). The overwhelming majority are the work of hunter-gatherers, though both engravings (Beaumont and Vogel 1989; Maggs 1995) and paintings (Prins and Hall 1994; Manhire 1998) were also made by pastoralists and agropastoralists. Additionally, Bushman rock art retains a spiritual or magical significance among many Bantu-speaking peoples today (How 1962; Loubser and Dowson 1987; Ouzman 1995a). The distinction between engravings and paintings is arbitrarily grounded in technique. Both forms of LSA art drew upon a common stock of motifs. Derived from widely shared beliefs, these include a restricted range of naturalistically portrayed animals, geometric imagery, particular human body postures and non-realistic features on both human and animal images (Dowson 1992; Lewis-Williams and Dowson 1999).

Ideas of separate painting and engraving 'races' having long been abandoned, their distinction depends largely on the availability of rock-shelter walls on which paintings could be executed, as opposed to the freestanding boulders used for engravings. Thus, paintings concentrate in the Drakensberg/Maluti Mountains, the eastern Free State, the Cape Fold Belt, Matopos, Tsodilo Hills, Namibia's inselbergs and the Waterberg Plateau and Soutpansberg Mountains

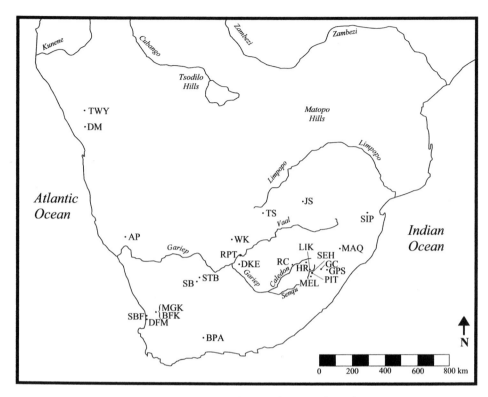

Figure 8.1 Location of archaeological sites discussed in chapter 8. Site names
abbreviated thus: AP Apollo 11 Cave; BFK Brakfontein se Kloof; BPA
Boomplaas; DFM Dunefield Midden; DKE Driekopseiland; DM
Dâures massif; GC Giant's Castle; GPS Game Pass Shelter; HR
Hololo River; JS Jubilee Shelter; LIK Likoaeng; MAQ Maqonqo; MEL
Melikane; MGK Matjiesgoedkloof; PIT Pitsaneng; RC Rose Cottage
Cave; RPT Rooipoort; SB Springbokoog; SBF Steenbokfontein; SEH
Sehonghong; SIP Siphiso; STB Strandberg; TS Thaba Sione; TWY
Twyfelfontein; WK Wonderwerk.

of South Africa's Northern Province. Engravings, on the other hand, occur
principally in the Karoo, western Free State and North-West Province. Areas
of overlap, as at Twyfelfontein, Namibia (Fig. 8.2), are rare, as are situations
where both art forms occur at the same site (e.g. Eastwood and Blundell 1999).
The Kalahari, where exposed rock of any kind is uncommon, has little art
at all.

Both engravings and paintings were produced well into the nineteenth century. Dia!kwain, a /Xam Bushman from the Northern Cape, stated in the
1870s that his father(s) had executed 'chippings' of gemsbok, ostrich and zebra
(J. Deacon 1988). About the same time Hahn (1879) recorded paintings being
made in Namibia. Across the sub-continent, horses, the second most frequent

Figure 8.2   Rock engravings of gemsbok and zebra, Twyfelfontein, Namibia.

animal painted in the Drakensberg/Maluti Mountains, must all have been produced in the middle 1800s (Vinnicombe 1976). Though disintegration and destruction of Bushman communities was well advanced by the 1870s, the painting tradition may have survived until the 1920s in rain-making rituals for Mpondomise agropastoralists into which some Bushmen assimilated (Prins 1990). The overall antiquity of the tradition and the dating of individual scenes or images are far more difficult to establish. Both Lewis-Williams (1993) and Ouzman (1996a) contend that these difficulties are unimportant, denouncing the 'chronocentric' bias of most LSA research and arguing for rock art, and the social and ideological relations of which it speaks, to be placed at the discipline's core. However, since the rest of the archaeological record is dated (or at least datable) relating rock art to it and it to the art requires that the latter also be contextualised in space and time. Avoiding or sidestepping this challenge runs the risk of producing an unvarying, ahistorical synchronic interpretation of the *whole* archaeological record (Parkington 1998). Before discussing past and present interpretations of southern Africa's paintings and engravings, a few words on their dating thus seem appropriate.

   Little of the surviving rock art is firmly dated to before 2000 BP, though the collapsed slab from Steenbokfontein (Jerardino and Swanepoel 1999) supports arguments that most fine-line paintings in the farwestern Cape predate the introduction of domestic livestock (Yates *et al.* 1994). Similarly, in the Matopo Hills the scarcity of LSA occupation during the last two millennia suggests that

Figure 8.3   Rock paintings, some of them of kudu, Matopo Hills, Zimbabwe.

their prolific paintings (Fig. 8.3) are at least this old; painted spalls occur, as we have seen, in several early/mid-Holocene deposits (N. Walker 1987), while one from a layer 3100 old at a site in Namibia's Dâures massif refits to a painting still preserved on the shelter's ceiling (Pager 1989). Middle and late Holocene painted stones from the southern Cape also form part of the same iconographic tradition as the far more numerous parietal images and include depictions with clear shamanistic associations, and the same may be true of the terminal Middle Stone Age paintings from Apollo 11 Cave (Lewis-Williams 1984). But so long as content remains our major chronological tool, it can only readily be brought into association with other forms of archaeological evidence where representations of domestic livestock, black people and Europeans provide clues to its age (Manhire *et al.* 1986; C. Campbell 1987; Dowson 1994, 1995; S. Hall 1994; Loubser and Laurens 1994). Back beyond 2000 BP, or where such 'contact' imagery is lacking or cannot be securely associated with other images, dating remains uncertain.

Direct dating of painted images surviving on rock-shelter walls remains largely unexplored. Denninger's (1971) attempt to date individual images directly by measuring the amino-acid composition of the binding agents used in them encountered considerable scepticism because of difficulties with the technique (A. Thackeray 1983). Potentially much more successful is AMS radiocarbon dating. Dependent on the presence in the paint of organics, such as charcoal or blood, or on the presence of organic matter in films above and/or below individual images, the few results published so far all fall within the past 600 years (van der Merwe *et al.* 1987; Mazel and Watchman 1997). However, the costs of this technique, the fact that blood and charcoal were not universally employed as pigment constituents and the sheer volume of the surviving art mean that direct dating can provide but one element in the construction of a firm chronology. Detailed stylistic and microstratigraphic analyses remain necessary (e.g. Loubser 1993a; Loubser and Laurens 1994). Those of Russell (2000) at Main Caves North, Giant's Castle, KwaZulu-Natal lend support to the broader stylistic sequences developed for other areas of the Drakensberg/Maluti Mountains by Pager (1971) and Vinnicombe (1976).

Research on rock engravings has often been the poor relation to work on paintings, but their chronology is better established (Fig. 8.4). This has been most extensively researched in the Northern Cape, where superpositioning, patination and radiocarbon dates for associated artefact assemblages (D. Morris 1988; Beaumont and Vogel 1989), the mobiliary engravings found in stratified, datable contexts at Wonderwerk (A. Thackeray *et al.* 1981), geoarchaeological considerations (Butzer *et al.* 1979) and cation-ratio dating (Whitley and Annegarn 1994) provide a more detailed temporal framework. Fine-line engravings were produced throughout the Holocene, but pecked and scraped

Figure 8.4   Rock-engravings of eland and other figures, Springbokoog, Northern Cape, South Africa. Taole Tesele, Archaeologist of the Lesotho Highlands Water Project, is in the rear of the photograph.

Figure 8.5   Rock engraving of nested, geometric lines, Rooipoort, Northern Cape, South Africa.

engravings are almost wholly under 2000 years old. Supporting these conclusions, domestic animals are most common among the pecked engravings, as are the geometric patterns, interpreted as images hallucinated in trance, from Driekopseiland, Rooipoort (Fig. 8.5) and elsewhere (Beaumont and Vogel 1989).

Interpreting the art

Europeans first wrote about southern African rock art in the eighteenth century (Barrow 1801; Morais 1984), but systematic recording began in the late 1800s with the work of Stow (1930) in the eastern Free State and of Hutchinson (Ward and Maggs 1994) and Tylor (Ward 1997) in the Drakensberg. Though paintings were still being produced at this time, virtually no first-hand information on what they meant to their makers was obtained. Comments by Qing, the Bushman guide of Orpen (1874), a British colonial officer, on paintings in Lesotho's highlands and by /Xam Bushmen shown copies of these and of others made by Stow (1930) are the few exceptions. Instead, and rejecting Wilhelm Bleek's prescient comment *à propos* Orpen's research that Bushman beliefs were vital for understanding the art, both paintings and engravings were long viewed from narrowly empiricist, Eurocentric perspectives (Lewis-Williams and Loubser 1986). Dismissed as 'art for art's sake' or a simple, narrative record of hunter-gatherer life, seen at best as evidence for hunting magic, rock art research was confined within a typological framework emphasising style and superpositioning as means of bringing spatio-temporal order to the data (Burkitt 1928). Breuil's (1948) predilections for finding any number of individuals from the civilisations of the Ancient Near East did little to further matters.

Systematic regional quantitative studies that began in the 1960s laid the basis for a more productive approach (Maggs 1967; Pager 1971), though without ending in some quarters, notably Cologne University's project in the Dâures massif, Namibia, the tendency towards empiricist, rather than ethnographically grounded, interpretation (Pager 1989, 1993, 1995; cf. Lewis-Williams 1990; J. Kinahan 2000). Vinnicombe's (1976) work in the Drakensberg/Maluti Mountains, in particular, showed that the art was highly selective in content. Eland, for example, the most common species depicted in her study area, were singled out for more elaborate treatment by way of size, colour and technique. Other animals, such as black wildebeest, which were no less present historically or in the archaeozoological record, are virtually missing. In trying to explain such patterning, Vinnicombe (1972, 1976) and Lewis-Williams (1972, 1974, 1981a) began to explore Bushman ethnography, a move which provided the crucial breakthrough towards an 'insider' perspective on the art, contextualising it within Bushman religious thought and practice.

Today, the shamanistic interpretation developed by Lewis-Williams forms the starting point for most analyses of the rock art produced by LSA people in southern Africa. Interpretation is grounded upon a series of ethnographic studies. Qing's account of paintings from Melikane, Sehonghong and Pitsaneng in Lesotho (Orpen 1874) is one of these. It provides an account of paintings which refer, through a series of metaphors, to the experiences of medicine people in trance and to beliefs about rain-making (Lewis-Williams 1981a). At the same time, Wilhelm Bleek and Lucy Lloyd were beginning a long-term project in Cape Town with several /Xam Bushmen from the Northern Cape. The latter and their families collectively contributed over 11,000 pages of text in interviews with Bleek and Lloyd, who recorded their words verbatim in /Xam and English (J. Deacon and Dowson 1996). Much of this material, which offers a unique insight into the worldview of southern African Bushmen in the nineteenth century (Hewitt 1986), remains unpublished (but see W. Bleek 1873, 1875; W. Bleek and Lloyd 1911; D. Bleek 1931, 1932a, 1932b, 1932c, 1933a, 1933b, 1935, 1936a, 1936b, 1956). Importantly, however, both the /Xam and Qing (who spoke a distinct, though ultimately related, language) shared numerous ideas and, in the /Xam case, details of ritual practices with Kalahari Bushmen. Correspondences in, for example, beliefs about the abilities of medicine people (Lewis-Williams 1992) or observances connected with eland hunting (Lewis-Williams and Biesele 1978) allow Kalahari ethnography to be employed in interpreting rock art, even though no Kalahari Bushman group

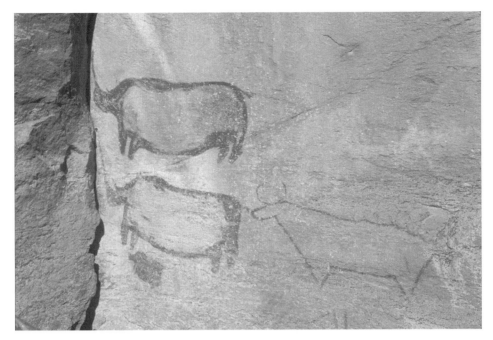

Figure 8.6   Rock paintings of rhinoceros and cattle, Tsodilo Hills, Botswana (courtesy Pierre de Maret).

retains a painting or engraving tradition and some Ju/'hoansi living near the Tsodilo Hills (Fig. 8.6) attribute this area's many paintings to God (A. Campbell *et al.* 1994). Two final sources further corroborate these ethnographies. From the Eastern Cape we have statements from Bushman descendants whose close relatives practised as rain-makers among local Bantu-speaking communities well into the twentieth century (Jolly 1986; Lewis-Williams 1986a; Prins 1990; Jolly and Prins 1994), while Hoff (1997, 1998) records beliefs about creatures associated with water and rain-making from people of /Xam ancestry in the Northern Cape.

Shamans

As originally developed, the shamanistic hypothesis concentrated on the abilities of medicine people to enter altered states of consciousness (trance) and then cure the sick, control the movements of game animals, make rain and go on out-of-body travel, the latter often in the form of lions (Lewis-Williams 1981a, 1985). Individuals can do these things because they are able to harness supernatural power, known to the Ju/'hoansi as *n/um* and among the /Xam as *!gi:*, *//ke:n* and, in its most intense form, */ko:öde* (Lewis-Williams 1981b). The /Xam distinguished four different kinds of *!gi:ten*, or 'possessors of potency', though the categories may have overlapped: those who made rain, those who controlled the game, those who sent sickness and those who cured people of it. The Ju/'hoansi use only a single term: *n/um k"au* ('owner of potency'). All are referred to as '**shamans**' in the southern African literature (Lewis-Williams 1992). Katz (1982) shows that up to half of all Ju/'hoansi men and a third of all women practise as shamans at some point in their lives. The most frequent context for this is a communal curing or healing dance in which women clap and sing special 'medicine songs', thereby activating the *n/um* that resides in the shamans who dance about them; intense concentration, hyper-ventilation and the rhythmic movement of the dance assist in this process. Hallucinogenic drugs seem not to be used today, but novice shamans may smoke ***dagga*** to help them relax (Katz 1982). Other narcotics are known to the Ju/'hoansi (Dobkin de Rios 1986) and some may have been employed in ritual contexts by the /Xam (J. Deacon 1994) and other southern Bushmen (Prins 1990).

With experienced shamans *n/um* 'boils up' inside them, catapulting them into trance. Typically, the shaman collapses, recounting his experiences in the spirit world on regaining consciousness. Either then or while still in trance he cures all those present, but especially the sick, by laying on hands and rubbing his sweat and nasal blood onto their bodies. The shaman then draws sickness (conceived of as visible-only-to-shamans 'arrows of sickness') into his own body, expelling it from a 'hole' (the *n//au* spot) at the base of his neck. This account, drawn from Katz's (1982) study of trance and healing among the Ju/'hoansi, is closely paralleled in the Bleek/Lloyd records (Lewis-Williams 1992) and an earlier description from western Lesotho (Arbousset and Daumas 1968). Furthermore, the dance, the behaviour (real and, to a western mind, 'unreal') of the shamans and their experiences in the other world are frequently represented directly, or through metaphor, in the art (Lewis-Williams and Dowson 1999). It is the great diversity of imagery explicable in this way (Fig. 8.7), including many otherwise 'bizarre' features, that makes a shamanistic understanding of the art so powerful.

Among both twentieth-century Kalahari Bushmen and their nineteenth-century predecessors further south, 'death' and 'being spoilt' are metaphors for the experience of trance. The similarities between this and prolonged stays underwater provide a third, with all three captured in Qing's statement to Orpen (1874: 2) about one of the many scenes at Melikane (Figs. 8.8 and 8.9): 'They were men who had died and now lived in rivers, and were spoilt at the same time as the elands and by the dances of which you have seen paintings.' Eland are a particularly strong and widespread metaphor, with a close relationship perceived between the behaviour of a dying eland and that of a shaman entering trance: both tremble, collapse, sweat heavily and may bleed from the nose (Lewis-Williams 1981a). The many **therianthropic** figures found in the art in the Drakensberg (Fig. 8.10) probably recall the ability of shamans to use the power of such animals, who, according to Qing, were the first and most prized of God's

Figure 8.7   Painting of a man carrying bow, quiver and flywhisk, Brakfontein se Kloof, Western Cape, South Africa.

creations. But the significance of eland goes far beyond this. Their presence in hunters' first-kill rites, girls' puberty rites and marriage among the Ju/'hoansi illustrates how much such symbols and their images resonate with multiple rather than single meanings (Lewis-Williams 1998). Though by far the most

Figure 8.8   Melikane Shelter, Lesotho. Jannie Loubser is visible at the left of the
entrance to the shelter tracing some of its rock paintings.

common animal depicted in several areas of southern Africa, other taxa may
have shared their rôle as sources of potency and *animals de passage* (Guenther
1991): hartebeest and kudu (Lewis-Williams and Dowson 1999), elephant
(Maggs and Sealy 1983) and rhinoceros (Ouzman 1996a); some recent groups
certainly privileged gemsbok or other animals over eland (Maingard 1937).
Interestingly, differential potency may relate to choice of pigment. In the farwestern Cape, for example, most eland are painted red and very few in black
(Yates and Manhire 1991). Correspondingly, among the Ju/'hoansi the most po-
tent game species, including eland, are classified as 'red meat animals', those
with least potency 'black meat animals' (Biesele 1975). Wildebeest, a black
meat animal, is, as we have already seen, very rarely painted (Vinnicombe 1976;
Loubser and Brink 1992).

   Shamans' actions reproduce the social values and ensure the physical well-
being of Bushman society. Out-of-body travel, for example, allows shamans
to visit neighbouring camps, reporting about the actions of kin and recalling them to people's mind, while trance dances are both a central religious
ceremony and a means of easing tensions between individuals, binding them
together as a community (Lewis-Williams 1981a, 1982). Bringing game animals
within reach of hunters is another important shamanistic activity, but even
more vital, and well attested in the /Xam ethnography because //Kabbo, one
of Bleek and Lloyd's principal informants, was himself a shaman of the rain

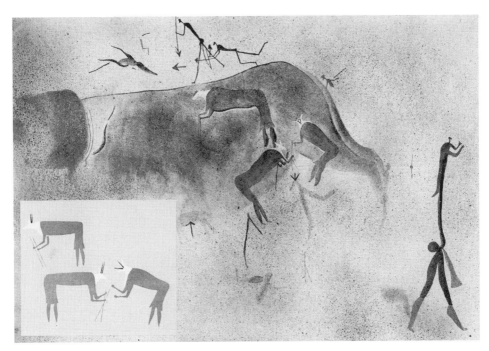

Figure 8.9   The three therianthropic figures at Melikane, Lesotho, as recorded
by Orpen (1874) superimposed on a recent tracing of the more
complex panel of which they form part by Patricia Vinnicombe
(1976: Fig. 223). Interpreted by Lewis-Williams (1981a) as trancing
medicine people, they have also been considered to reflect the
adoption by Bushmen of the dress and behaviour of Nguni- and
Sotho-speaking ritual functionaries (Jolly 1995), or to depict
mythological beings or the spirits of the dead (Solomon 1997). The
original Vinnicombe tracing forms part of the collections of the
Natal Museum, Pietermaritzburg (courtesy Patricia Vinnicombe and
the Natal Museum).

(J. Deacon 1996a), is rain-making (Dowson 1999). Rain was conceptualised as
an animal which shamans were said to kill to produce rain. This event probably took place in trance, or in dreams (Lewis-Williams 1987), rather than 'reality', though wounded and exhausted eland may sometimes have been used
(Lewis-Williams 1981a). Other animals associated with rain and contributing
to the often amorphous quadrupedal images by which rain-animals are depicted
(Fig. 8.11) include rhinoceros (Ouzman 1996a), elephant (Maggs and Sealy 1983)
and cattle (Lewis-Williams 1981a). Two such animals form the focus of the rain-
making scene recorded at Sehonghong and interpreted by Qing and Dia!kwain
(Orpen 1874).

In elaborating the shamanistic interpretation a key development has been the
incorporation of insights derived from experimental neuro-psychology. Many
of the otherwise inexplicable geometric shapes and patterns seen in the art

Figure 8.10   Complex panel of paintings from Game Pass Shelter, Kamberg, KwaZulu-Natal, South Africa, showing a dying eland stumbling to the ground with hair erect. To its right and holding its tail a therianthropic human figure has its legs crossed in imitation of the eland. Other cloaked and therianthropic figures occur further to the right (Lewis-Williams 1981a).

(especially the engravings; Dowson 1992, but see also A. Campbell *et al.* 1994) can be identified as entoptics, images produced by the human central nervous system during the initial stage of experiencing altered states of consciousness (Lewis-Williams and Dowson 1999; Fig. 8.12). Their biological, rather than cultural, origin suggests that where they occur in other rock art traditions this too may relate to the visions seen by individuals in such altered states (Lewis-Williams and Dowson 1988, 1993; Whitley 1992). Construing entoptic images into ones culturally relevant to an individual's own experience and their combination with those images are features of deeper stages of trance. They too can be identified in the art, along with some of the physical sensations reported by people in altered states of consciousness, such as bodily elongation and having more than the normal number of limbs (Lewis-Williams and Dowson 1999).

'Images of power'

None of this implies that images were produced during trance itself. Shamans' lack of physical control at this time makes this unlikely. However, people may

Figure 8.11   Painting of a rain-animal and associated figures, Matjiesgoedkloof, Western Cape, South Africa.

Figure 8.12   Painted entoptic image, Brakfontein se Kloof, Western Cape, South Africa.

have re-experienced visions as 'flashbacks' for several months (Lewis-Williams and Loubser 1986), perhaps facilitated by seeing previously painted or engraved images. This raises the question of why the art was produced at all, since among contemporary Bushman peoples shamanism and trance plainly exist in its absence. Some insight comes from reports obtained from 'M', the daughter of a Bushman rain-maker among the Mpondomise of the Eastern Cape (Jolly 1986; Jolly and Prins 1994), and from Mapote, an elderly Sotho man who had painted with Bushman relatives and was questioned in the 1930s (How 1962). Both commented that fresh eland blood was a constituent of the paint used by Bushmen. Given the significance accorded the eland this implies (and 'M' specifically stated; Jolly 1986: 6) that the paint itself was imbued with potency. Far from being mere representations, painted images may have focused and fixed supernatural power, creating expectations for those entering trance and a permanent record of their visions (Lewis-Williams and Dowson 1994). Directing attention to the particular social conditions in which this may have been desirable, this also leads us to consider who painted and engraved. Here the ethnography is very sparse. Comments recorded by V. Ellenberger (1953) and Jolly and Prins (1994) suggest that only men painted, consistent with the heavy preponderance of male to female images in the art, but Lloyd (1889) recorded a /Xam myth in which women did so. Whether only shamans were artists is unknown, though the high quality of most images suggests that painting and engraving were the work of the few rather than the many (Lewis-Williams 1995; cf. Garlake 1995). A statement made by Qing (Orpen 1874) and references by some /Xam informants to 'Brinkkop men', who may have been particularly associated with rain-making (J. Deacon 1986), suggest that ritual knowledge was more exclusive among nineteenth-century Southern Bushmen than recently in the Kalahari.

That people interacted with the images after their initial production is increasingly apparent. 'M' demonstrated how they danced before paintings and claimed that people could also draw power from them through physical contact (Jolly and Prins 1994). Smoothing of areas of pigment and smearing of paint over images point to similar beliefs in the farwestern Cape, where, as in the Drakensberg (Vinnicombe 1976), deliberate repainting of images is also known (Yates and Manhire 1991). Engravings were also refurbished (D. Morris 1988), while at Thaba Sione rhinoceros figures were repeatedly struck, probably in rain-making rituals (Ouzman 1996a; Fig. 8.13). The widespread superpositioning of images also suggests repeated contact with, and reuse of, their power. One additional factor here returns us to the neuro-psychological model referred to earlier. Worldwide, many peoples describe entry into the deepest stage of altered states of consciousness in terms of entering a hole in the ground, while Western experimental subjects refer to 'tunnels' or 'vortices' (Lewis-Williams and Dowson 1988). A not uncommon feature of the

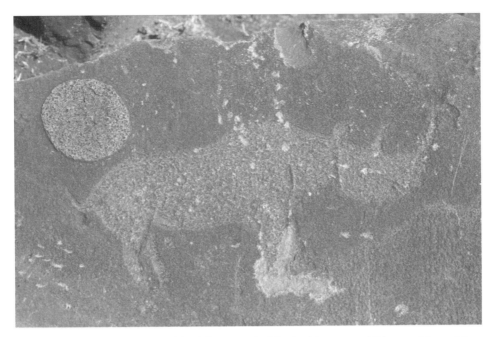

Figure 8.13   Pecked and rubbed figures of a black rhinoceros (*Diceros bicornis*), Thaba Sione, North West Province, South Africa (courtesy Sven Ouzman).

art is the depiction of animals or people disappearing into or emerging from unconformities in the surface of the rockface (Lewis-Williams and Dowson 1990; Fig. 8.14). This suggests that shelter walls and boulders were more than a *tabula rasa* onto which images were placed. They may have played an active rôle in constituting their meaning, providing the interface between this world and the spirit world into which shamans moved and from which they drew power (Lewis-Williams 1995, 1998).

Recognition of the importance of the physicality of the surfaces on which images were created goes hand-in-hand with appreciating the significance of rock art sites as arenas for ritual performance and of considering sites as integral wholes, not just collections of images (Ouzman 1997a; Solomon 1997). One particularly striking example comes from Sehonghong, where the rain-animals copied by Orpen move to the left away from a slight fissure in the rockface through which water seeps after even a slight shower – making rain where the animals have already walked, as it were (Fig. 8.15). A related concern is the placement of the art within the wider landscape. For the /Xam, some landscape features personified myths that explained their form (J. Deacon 1988, 1997). The Strandberg, for example, a mountain in the Northern Cape (Fig. 8.16), was believed to be the body of the *Agama* Lizard (W. Bleek and Lloyd 1911), a

Figure 8.14   Painting of a reptilian figure emerging from within the rock, Hololo
River, Lesotho. In front are two human figures, one supporting a
second who is bent forward at the waist as if entering trance. This
panel is discussed in more detail by Lewis-Williams and Dowson
(1990).

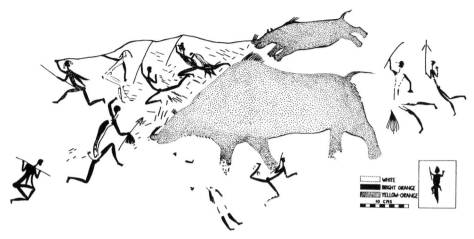

Figure 8.15   Tracing of the rain-animal scene at Sehonghong, Lesotho (courtesy
Patricia Vinnicombe). This is only part of a much larger panel that
extends upward some 2 m from the rock-shelter floor. First recorded
by Orpen (1874), it was interpreted by both Qing and Dia!kwain as
depicting the capture and control of two rain-animals.

Figure 8.16   Strandberg, Northern Cape, South Africa, seen from Springbokoog.
For details of its probable significance as a rain-making site see
J. Deacon (1988).

forecaster of rain (D. Bleek 1933a); rock engravings, many of elephant which would have moved south of the Gariep towards the Strandberg only after good rains, cluster on its slopes. It seems very likely that other paintings and engravings were also placed deliberately at spiritually significant locations in the landscape, a point further explored by J. Kinahan (1999), who shows that both natural features of the rockface and site position were taken into account in locating paintings associated with rain-making in Namibia.

Extending the paradigm: recent trends in rock art research

A necessary step in developing the shamanistic interpretation was the demonstration that it held true beyond the Drakensberg paintings that provided its initial support. Huffman (1983), Maggs and Sealy (1983), Yates *et al.* (1985) and S. Hall (1986) showed its applicability to the rock art of Zimbabwe and the Western and Eastern Cape. Dowson (1992) did the same for engravings, and Lewis-Williams (1986b) argued, perhaps less successfully (Lim 1992), for its extension to rock paintings in Tanzania. The model was also projected backward in time by identifying features diagnostic of trancing shamans on Holocene painted stones from the southern Cape. In the same paper Lewis-Williams (1984) suggested that feline and therianthropic figures depicted on the Apollo 11 rock art, and geometric (entoptic?) figures on engraved stones from Wonderwerk, indicated long-term continuity in Bushman ideology back into the Pleistocene. More recently, it has become evident that greater attention must be paid to spatial and temporal variability within the art (Skotnes 1994). Indeed, Lewis-Williams and Dowson (1994) have themselves critiqued the enthusiasm with which similarities between the beliefs and ritual practices of different Bushman groups led to initial emphasis on a 'pan-San cognitive system' (McCall 1970) at the expense of investigating such differences. One area in which significant change may have taken place is the rise of specialist shamans from the general healing tradition. Chapters 9 and 12 look at this topic and its representation in the art, in relation to the origins of pastoralist societies in the Central Namib (J. Kinahan 1991) and among nineteenth-century hunter-gatherers in the Drakensberg/Maluti Mountains (C. Campbell 1987; Dowson 1994, 1995). The same chapters, along with chapter 13, also consider the impact of interaction with herders, farmers and European settlers on the production and content of hunter-gatherer rock art (e.g. Loubser and Laurens 1994; S. Hall 1994; Yates *et al.* 1994).

Recent work emphasises that shamanism does not exhaust all levels of meaning in the art and that images had multiple resonances for those producing and viewing them (Lewis-Williams 1998). This recognition also marks a shift in emphasis from the meaning of what people painted and engraved to *why* they did so. Thus, Garlake (1995) notes that in Zimbabwe there are few explicit trance dance scenes and little imagery relating directly to shamans. Trance dances

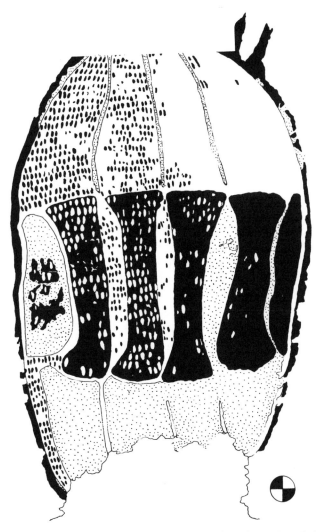

Figure 8.17   Tracing of a painting of oval designs ('formlings') with lines of large
white dots on shaped cores and small dark dots on their ends and
between them (after Garlake 1990: Fig 4; courtesy South African
Archaeological Society). These designs may be representations of
the supernatural potency tapped by medicine people (Garlake 1990,
1995).

may, perhaps, be metaphorically represented in depictions of hunting large
game (elephant, rhinoceros, buffalo), but the principal concern of painters seems
to have been the representation of potency of different kinds rather than hallucinatory experiences (Fig. 8.17). Though Garlake draws a distinction between
his approach and that of Lewis-Williams, there is clearly a degree of overlap
between them. Other workers have emphasised points of difference, one of

the earliest being the illustration in the farwestern Cape of aspects of material culture (triple-curved bows) and subsistence strategies (hunting medium-sized antelope using nets) that are poorly, if at all, known from Bushman ethnography (Manhire *et al.* 1985; Parkington 1989). Some of these paintings have since been examined from a compositional standpoint to investigate how people may have understood space and time relations and how social distinctions (such as those between initiated and uninitiated men) may have been drawn, irrespective of the merits or applicability of a shamanistic model (Parkington *et al.* 1996).

In keeping with growing archaeological interest in gender relations (Wadley 1997b; Kent 1998), another issue to receive attention is their (mis)representation in the art. Here Solomon (1992) paved the way, establishing the centrality of gender in Bushman thought. As well as proposing that gender structures much of the art, detailed analysis of motifs known as 'mythic women' (Fig. 8.18) suggests that some paintings are specifically linked to female initiation rites (Solomon 1994). Building on these insights, Parkington (1989) notes the frequently heavy overrepresentation of male figures, activities and equipment, arguing that painting enhanced male dominance in the ritual sphere. However, in some areas, such as the Shashe–Limpopo Basin, women are more often depicted than men (Eastwood and Blundell 1999), and such arguments risk underestimating the importance of female shamans in the present (Katz 1982) and among the /Xam (Hewitt 1986), creating a false male/female dichotomy

Figure 8.18   Painting of a 'mythic woman' figure from the Drakensberg Escarpment, KwaZulu-Natal, South Africa (courtesy Anne Solomon). Painted using the shaded polychrome technique, the figure has distinctly splayed legs, a markedly swollen torso and no head.

(Stevenson 1995). Lenssen-Erz's (1997) suggestion that a third gender, neither male nor female, is present in Namibian paintings adds to the need for caution here, but Parkington's (1996) argument that prepastoralist paintings in the farwestern Cape mediated opposite (male/female) sexual spheres centred around hunting and sex retains a bipolar view of gender, focusing on beliefs termed ***n!ao*** among the Ju/'hoansi.

Bushman mythology also deserves further attention, in particular beliefs about the creation, the dead and the afterlife. Solomon (1994, 1997, 2000) argues that much of what has been identified as shamanistic activity may, instead, relate to the actions of the spirits of the dead (cf. Lewis-Williams 1996, 1998). Though some studies reveal significant contrasts in content between rock art and Bushman folklore (J. Deacon 1994; Guenther 1994; Parkington 1999), Solomon (1999) argues that Qing's accounts to Orpen refer more directly (and consistently) to the temporal trajectory of Bushman mythology than to the activities of shamans. If correct, a fundamental reappraisal of the shamanistic model may be called for, though the comprehensiveness with which this accounts for so much of the art and the close parallels between southern and Kalahari Bushman beliefs leave most contemporary research still grounded in the framework developed by Lewis-Williams and his associates.

Understanding LSA social relations

Controlling game movements, making rain, curing people of sickness and visiting other camps during out-of-body journeys, shamans occupy a pivotal rôle in the socio-economic reproduction of Bushman societies. Rock art probably played a key part in this process in many areas of southern African during the LSA. In elaborating these arguments, Lewis-Williams (1982) developed the first explicitly theoretical analysis of LSA social organisation, precipitating a major shift in emphasis away from the previous ecological paradigm (J. Deacon 1990a). Instead, structural-Marxist ideas came to the fore, with social relations (especially, but not exclusively, kinship) the principal motor for societal change. Along with aggregation and dispersal, gift-exchange, gender relations and the identification of alliance networks in material culture have all emerged as important areas of study. We looked at some of these studies in chapter 7 and will encounter others later on. Here I consider the general outlines of their arguments and their critique.

Seasonal patterns of aggregation and dispersal characterise most ethnographically known hunter-gatherers (Kelly 1995) and are widely postulated in the southern African LSA. Though such models are driven by ecological factors and maximising assumptions about carrying capacity, Carter (1970) also suggested that summer aggregations of people in the Lesotho Highlands were associated with increased ceremonial activity and rock art production. His argument foreshadowed the use of Bushman ethnography to model the different activities

Table 8.1 *Wadley's (1987) criteria for the recognition of aggregation and dispersal sites*

Evidence	Aggregation phase site	Dispersal phase site
Stone artefacts	Curated, standardised Many formal tools	Expedient Few formal tools
Lithic raw materials	May include relatively high numbers of exotics	Predominantly local
Spatial patterning	Formal, gender-associated division of space	Absent
Hxaro objects	Manufacturing debris from making ostrich eggshell beads and bone points; finished examples of the same	Very rare or absent
Ritual activity	Portable art objects; rock art; decorated bonework and ostrich eggshell; shamanistic paraphernalia (e.g. quartz crystals, MSA tools); ochre	Very rare or absent
Meat procurement	Fauna includes a wide range of ungulates, many of them hunted	Little evidence for hunting; concentration on snaring small antelope and taking ground game
Seasonality	Variable, but different from dispersal phase sites	Variable, but different from aggregation phase sites

and social structures of dispersal and aggregation phases. Following the anthropological lead of Mauss and Beuchat (1906), Wadley (1987) termed these two phases the 'private' and 'public' phases of social life. Each is associated with different patterns of ritual activity, exchange, visiting and gender relations, all with implications for the archaeological record (Table 8.1). In the aggregation phase, for example, not only are Ju/'hoansi gender roles more marked, but people visit more often to exchange gifts and information, see relatives and arrange marriages. Larger numbers of people living together also encourage more frequent trance dances (in part to ease the accompanying social tensions) and, in the past, facilitated communal male initiation ceremonies (Lee 1979). However, the particular season in which aggregation and dispersal occur cannot be predicted from ecological data. Among the Ju/'hoansi, for example, aggregation takes place in the dry season around the remaining waterholes (Lee 1979), while in the drier Central Kalahari the G/wi can only do this at the height of the summer rains (G. Silberbauer 1981).

As we have seen, Wadley (1987) uses her model to explore changes in social relations over time. Though aggregation and dispersal sites cannot (yet) be identified for the Robberg and it is difficult to do so even in the Oakhurst, in her Magaliesberg research area the model seems convincing in the mid-Holocene. It has also proven a popular research tool further afield (Barham 1989b; J. Kinahan 1991; N. Walker 1995a). One of its most successful applications is also an excellent example of the integration of rock art and 'dirt archaeology'. At Rose Cottage Cave Ouzman and Wadley (1997) support its identification as an aggregation site through a combination of excavated evidence from the late Holocene levels with an analysis of the site's paintings. The large quantity of bone waste and wide range of hunted game present (Plug and Engela 1992), signs of on-site bead making and the formal structuring of space in levels Mn and A are among the data that suggest this. They are reinforced by paintings which show a lioness among a herd of eland, alluding to the threat of evil and disruption inherent in large gatherings of people, and another panel depicting the medicine dance through which social harmony is maintained.

The delayed, reciprocal system of gift-exchange known as *hxaro* is one of the defining attributes of aggregation phase sites according to Ju/'hoansi ethnography (Yellen 1977). In the case of Rose Cottage Cave, long-distance connections are indicated by a marine mollusc of Indian Ocean origin and paintings of mormyrid fish native to northern KwaZulu-Natal and areas still further north (Ouzman and Wadley 1997; Fig. 8.19). Of particular interest for archaeologists has been Wiessner's (1982) demonstration that people intensify exchange in droughts, concentrating *hxaro* ties with areas with the richest and most

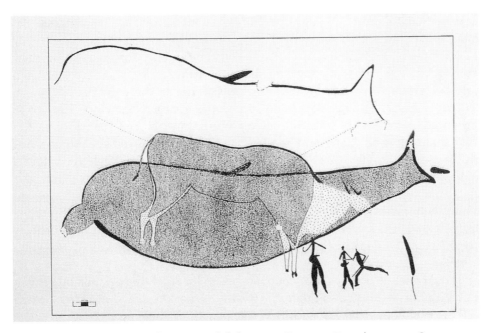

Figure 8.19   Paintings of mormyrid fish, Rose Cottage Cave (courtesy Sven Ouzman; see Ouzman 1995b, 1997a; Ouzman and Wadley 1997).

complementary resources to their own. Exchange thus both insures against ecological disaster and distributes information about people and resources over distances of 200 km or more. *Hxaro* partnerships are also intensified when parents seek husbands or wives for their children (Wiessner 1982), producing an overlap between the spatial geometry of Ju/'hoansi exchange and marriage partners (Mazel 1989). We have already seen that bone points and backed microliths (both interpreted as weapon armatures) and ostrich eggshell beads are frequently cited as evidence for the exchange of arrows and ostrich eggshell beadwork, the two favoured Ju/'hoansi *hxaro* gifts. Chapters 6 and 7 also showed how archaeologists have used the intensification of exchange in resource-poor conditions to explain the rich material culture of many Wilton assemblages during mid-Holocene drier episodes (Wadley 1987, 1989), the apparent proliferation of exchange when colonising new areas at the Pleistocene/Holocene boundary (Mazel 1989; Mitchell 2000) and rich child burials in the southern Cape (S. Hall and Binneman 1987). Exchange also plays a major rôle in analyses of the spatial patterning of material culture which seek to establish the extent of LSA interaction networks, notably in the Thukela Basin (Mazel 1989).

Since these models situate the engine of social change in the relations between people, rather than between people and environment, individuals and groups of people need to be identifiable in the archaeological record. Parkington (1998) considers three areas in which these identities may be resolved: rock art, burials and artefacts. As we have already seen, a concern with how men and women are shown in paintings and engravings is one of several recent developments in rock art research. The acquisition of imagery in trance and by other means, the manufacture of paint, the production of images and their subsequent use must all have offered opportunities for people to manipulate the production and consumption of rock art to their own ends (Lewis-Williams 1995). Though we do not know the contexts in which they were produced, some highly specific rock art motifs may be the visions of particular shamans. One example is the fantasy animals engraved at Springbokoog (J. Deacon 1994; Fig. 8.20). Two others, both unique, are the engraving of a bisexual eland from the Magaliesberg and a painting of two crabs from the north-eastern Free State (Dowson 1988b). Detailed stylistic analyses may eventually help identify other images produced by individual artists, such as the cross-legged figures, images of men fishing from 'boats' and plumed dancers recorded in the Drakensberg/Maluti Mountains (Vinnicombe 1976; Solomon 1996).

Burials provide perhaps the best opportunity for resolving person and gender, but with the obvious caveat that it is the living, not the dead, who bury. Sexing of LSA skeletons from the southern Cape suggests that most of the artefacts found with them are associated ethnographically with women (e.g. grindstones, bored stones). The possibility that men and women were not differentiated after

Figure 8.20   Engravings of a fantasy animal and human figure, Springbokoog, Northern Cape, South Africa.

death, and that the dead may even have formed a third gender (Wadley 1997c), recalls Lenssen-Erz's (1997) study of Namibian rock paintings. Though sex and gender cannot be directly equated, stable isotope and physical anthropological analyses have, as we have seen, developed into a powerful tool for investigating dietary differences between men and women in the south-western Cape (Sealy and van der Merwe 1988; Lee Thorp *et al.* 1989; Sealy *et al.* 1992). Despite the importance of gender in understanding aggregation/dispersal, *hxaro* (in which men and women both participate) and the spatial patterning of archaeological sites, resolving individual identities from artefactual data is arguably the most difficult strategy of all. Mazel's (1989) argument that Thukela Basin women strove consciously to contribute more to the diet in the later Holocene in a power struggle with men, for example, depends on a series of assumptions about stone artefact use and plant food preservation that require critical appraisal.

Social relations: a critical view of the evidence

Much of what has so far been presented in the application of social theory models to the LSA record has been described as tantalising speculation by Barham (1992: 50). Exciting as the expansion of research into these new fields has been, operationalising the models advanced has not kept pace with theoretical developments (N. Walker 1995a: 217). Nor, for the most part, has it been undertaken on the archaeology of the Kalahari peoples from whom the models are largely derived (N. Walker 1995b). This is perhaps most evident with Mazel's (1989) identification of distinct social regions in the Thukela Basin, which tended, at least until the excavation of Maqonqo (Mazel 1996), to treat all sites as if they were equal, ignoring the likelihood that cultural systems are differentially organised and that people used different sites for different purposes or the same site for different purposes at different times (Parkington 1980b). Wadley's (1989) critique of the Thukela Basin data picks up on precisely this point to reinterpret them in terms of her own aggregation/dispersal model. Yet labelling sites as *either* aggregation *or* dispersal phase sites also compresses variability into a bipolar opposition that may blind us to other differences: what of look-out stations or locations at which people obtained stone, pigment or other materials, carried out rituals or ambushed game?

Both in creating 'social regions' and in designating sites as aggregation or dispersal phase locales, archaeologists face the problem of how to assign meaning to the things they excavate. Thukela Basin alliance networks, for example, are partly defined on the basis of different proportions of backed microlith and different kinds of scraper backing (Mazel 1989). But we remain unsure about why backed microliths were made and how they were used. Were they arrow armatures (J. Deacon 1992; H. Deacon 1995), or, as microwear and residue analyses suggest (Wadley and Binneman 1995; Williamson 1997), elements of composite, multi-purpose cutting tools? How do we know that different forms of backing on scrapers signalled social identity, instead of reflecting differences in hafting, use or resharpening (Barham 1992)? And why, if these alliance networks were distinctive in their material culture, are so few artefact types exclusive to just one region (Table 8.2)? A key issue here is that we have very little ethnography from southern Africa relating to stone tool use (Rudner 1979). Identifications of function are therefore based largely on Binneman's (1982) microwear analyses of artefacts from Boomplaas, which supported traditional correlations of scrapers with hide-working and adzes with wood-working. As with other microwear and edge-damage studies (L. Phillipson and Phillipson 1970), many so-called 'unmodified' or 'waste' artefacts were probably also used, though without requiring formal retouch. Recent residue analyses suggest that determining artefact function is even less straightforward than previously thought; scrapers at Rose Cottage Cave, for example, show signs of having been employed to work plant materials while adzes bear animal traces (Williamson 1996, 1997). Much more basic, perhaps necessarily site-specific, work is clearly needed.

Difficulties in knowing the uses to which artefacts were put are as nothing compared to assigning them to men or women. Ethnographic studies of

Table 8.2 *Criteria employed to identify 'social regions' in the Thukela Basin of KwaZulu-Natal, 4000–2000 BP (after Mazel 1989, 1990, 1993)*

Evidence	Ndaka region	Toleni region	Injasuthi region
Lithic raw materials	Opaline dominated	Hornfels dominated	Hornfels dominated
Segments	Dominant	None	Virtually absent
Backed points/blades	Rare	Dominant	Dominant
Size of backed microlith sample (after Mazel 1989: Fig. 25)	10	60	54
Dominant kind of backing on scrapers	Type 2	Type 1	Type 3
Ground stone items	Rare	Relatively common	Absent
Worked bone artefacts	Relatively common	Relatively common	Rare
Mini bone points	Present	Absent	Very rare
Bone fishhooks	Present	Absent	Absent
Ochre utilisation	Present	Common	Rare
Ostrich eggshell pieces	Present	Common	Absent
Ostrich eggshell beads	Present	Present (with local bead-making)	Rare
Site numbers (after Mazel 1989)	2	2	2

Bushman peoples such as the Ju/'hoansi (Lee 1979) suggest a marked separation of craft activities between men (who hunt, make leather goods and produce hunting weaponry) and women (who gather most plant foods, collect firewood and water, and have primary responsibility for cooking and childcare). If stone artefacts' functions can be correctly identified and if these gender associations held in the past then it becomes possible to engender a much wider set of LSA material culture. Mazel's (1989) argument that increasing frequencies of adzes and plant food residues in Thukela Basin sites demonstrate a greater female contribution to subsistence after 4000 BP is underpinned by equating adzes with wood-working, wood-working with the manufacture and resharpening of digging-sticks, and digging-sticks with plant food exploitation. Yet we also know that adzes were sometimes used for working bone and that other, less formal stone tools could be used to work wood (Binneman 1982; Binneman and Deacon 1986), while digging-sticks were used for other purposes and by men (Ouzman 1997b). If Mazel's argument is less than conclusive, it has at least had the benefit of making archaeologists think of women, and not just

Figure 8.21   Painting of a line of women carrying digging-sticks weighted with bored stones, Brakfontein se Kloof, Western Cape, South Africa.

men, as stone tool makers. Though this has the backing of scarce ethnographic observations (Dunn 1930) and folklore (Orpen 1874; W. Bleek and Lloyd 1911), Wadley (1989) points out that Ju/'hoansi men make all women's tools, as well as their clothing and bags. Even with bored stones, an item for which female manufacture is quite strongly attested, Ouzman (1997b) shows that both men and women were recorded using them as digging-stick weights and that rock art, far from depicting them as an exclusively female item, employed them in gender-ambiguous ways (Fig. 8.21).

If it is by no means straightforward to identify artefacts as male or female in their associations, claims that others, such as quartz crystals, are *necessarily* to be interpreted as shamanistic paraphernalia and thus support identifying sites as aggregation centres are equally questionable. Here the only actual evidence is Wadley's (1987: 6) citation of Eliade's (1964) claim that they are universally recognised as possessing magical qualities, though other uses (e.g. as cores) are possible (Barham 1992; Wadley 1992). Identifications of aggregation and dispersal phase sites using other criteria may also be problematic. If, for example, the worked bone (1) and ostrich eggshell bead (60) frequencies from Siphiso, Swaziland, are too few to warrant aggregation status, but those from the classic Wilton levels at Jubilee Shelter are more compelling (649 and 376 respectively; Wadley 1992, *pace* Barham 1992), what are we to make of the frequencies of these items reported from sites in the Matopos, which can be of a similar order of magnitude or greater still (N. Walker 1995a)? Numbers alone may mean little, but size, nature and duration of occupation all need disentangling. Jerardino (1995) suggests how this might be done by using parameters such as area of settlement, rate of deposition of domestic debris and rate of deposition of artefacts whose presence may relate to longer visits (such as ostrich eggshell beads, which take a long time to make). Together, these provide a sounder approach than relative density values which ignore differences in matrix composition, such as those produced by differential shellfish collection.

Identifying artefacts as prehistoric exchange items also requires greater attention, not least because it may be impossible to distinguish exchange from direct procurement (Merrick and Brown 1984). *Hxaro*-based interpretations have generally avoided both this question and the issue of whether, beyond formal analogies with Ju/'hoansi practice, there is any reason to believe that ostrich eggshell beads and supposed arrow armatures are exotic to the sites at which they are found. This is all the more pressing since using these artefacts as *hxaro* items is additional to their other functions: their frequency may thus not be related to *hxaro* at all (N. Walker 1995a). As Bushman ethnography shows, other exchange mechanisms are well established, and some peoples, such as the !Xō (Barnard 1992), do not practise delayed, reciprocal exchange of the *hxaro* kind at all, perhaps because their harsher environment makes investment in such a system unfeasible as an insurance against ecological risk (N. Walker 1995a: 210). In sum, exchange needs to be better argued and does not have to take the form of *hxaro*, nor be inextricably linked to a particular set of kinship-based social relations. Regional patterning of material culture may more reliably inform on past interaction networks where we can be certain that particular items are exotic to the locations at which they are found, such as with seashell ornaments and ostrich eggshell beads in much of south-eastern southern Africa (Mazel 1996; Mitchell 1996c).

A final consideration is the degree of resolution attainable in the archaeological record. Rock-shelters act as 'magnets', attracting people (not least excavating archaeologists!) back to the same place on the landscape time and again. Even the most carefully excavated rock-shelter deposits are thus likely to be palimpsests of successive occupations within which individual 'layers' probably represent several actual visits, not just one. Add to this the possibilities for objects moving laterally and vertically through often soft deposits (Richardson 1992) and only in rare circumstances are rock-shelters likely to preserve the highly resolved spatial information that allows individual occupations to be distinguished. How then can we determine whether a site swapped between aggregation and dispersal phase status, and maybe back again, within the timeframes that archaeologists can excavate and date (Barham 1992)? Large-scale excavation of short-lived occupation horizons may better resolve spatial and temporal patterning to the degree needed to investigate social processes such as food-sharing and the use and organisation of space. But few such sites have been dug. The success of Parkington *et al.*'s (1992) work at the late Holocene open-air site of Dunefield Midden establishes the scale of the challenge and potential of searching for sites that combine excellent organic preservation with finely resolved stratigraphy; Likoaeng in Lesotho's highlands (Mitchell and Charles 2000) indicates they are not only to be found at coastal locations.

As the critiques I have discussed show, enthusiasm for developing new approaches to LSA archaeology may, at least temporarily, have outpaced defining clear-cut connections between the arguments made and the empirical data said to support them. Reinforcing the importance of rock art as both the springboard from which such approaches were developed and as probably the most informative 'artefact' for understanding LSA social relations and ideology, it is precisely those studies which deliberately combine art and excavated evidence that have been most successful (Yates *et al.* 1994; Ouzman and Wadley 1997). The critical importance of being able to date paintings and engravings is clear, along with the innovative and challenging questions that ethnographically informed approaches to the LSA record pose. Overshadowing all of the issues discussed thus far, however, and critical for everything reviewed in this chapter, is the still larger one of the dependability of the ethnography that archaeologists employ.

Ethnography only from the desert?

While Wadley (1987: iv) has described Bushman ethnography as a Rosetta Stone for deciphering past hunter-gatherer social relations, Barham (1992: 45) emphasises the lack of an unbroken ethnographic record connecting historically studied Bushman groups with LSA people. What we do have are ethnohistoric accounts by European colonial officials, explorers, missionaries and others, extending back almost to the beginning of Dutch settlement at the Cape of Good Hope. No single review of these sources exists, but comments by Burchell (1967), C. Andersson (1968), J. Chapman (1971) and many others form the background to the more systematic work of W. Bleek and Lloyd (J. Deacon and Dowson 1996), D. Bleek (1928) and Potgieter (1955) in the late nineteenth/early twentieth centuries. Collectively, their research enabled Schapera (1930) to produce the first synthesis of Khoisan ethnography. But sustained, long-term anthropological studies of Kalahari hunter-gatherers only began in the 1950s, commencing with those of the Marshall (1976) family among !Kung-speakers in the Nyae-Nyae area of Namibia; 1963–64 saw Richard Lee (1979) initiate fieldwork among other Ju/'hoansi across the border in the Dobe area of Botswana, a project that foreshadowed many others across the Kalahari (Fig. 8.22; Hudelson 1995; Lane 1998a).

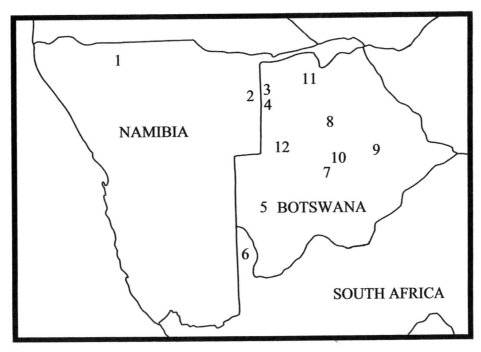

Figure 8.22   Location of principal anthropological research projects among
Kalahari Bushmen. 1 Hai//om: T. Widlok; 2 Nyae-Nyae Ju/'hoansi:
L. Marshall; 3 Dobe Ju/'hoansi: M. Biesele, P. Draper, N. Howell,
R. Katz, R. Lee, M. Shostak, J. Yellen; 4 Ju/'hoansi: P. Wiessner,
E. Wilmsen; 5 !Xõ: H. Heinz; 6 /'Auni-≠Khomani: H. Steyn; 7 G/wi
and G//ana: C. Noailles, M. Osaki, G. Silberbauer, K. Sugawara,
J. Tanaka; 8 Eastern Khoe-speakers (River Bushmen): E. Cashdan; 9
Eastern Khoe-speakers: R. Hitchcock; 10 Central Kahalari Game
Reserve groups: S. Kent, H. Vierich; 11 Northern Khoe-speakers:
C. Cowley, H. Heinz, O. Köhler; 12 Nharo: A. Barnard, M.
Guenther, H. Steyn.

I draw attention to the range of ethnographic research carried out among
southern African hunter-gatherers for three reasons. First, Kalahari hunter-
gatherers, and especially the !Kung-speaking Ju/'hoansi of Dobe and Nyae-
Nyae, have become world-famous exemplars of egalitarian hunter-gatherers.
Second, as must already be apparent, southern African archaeologists, whether
working with rock art and/or with excavated materials, have concentrated on
only a few of these communities, notably the Ju/'hoansi and the now extinct
/Xam. Other groups have elicited much less interest. Lastly, historical and archaeological research has brought much of the Kalahari ethnography and, by
implication, that of groups who lived still further south into question. LSA
stone artefacts at Iron Age village sites and Iron Age pottery and domestic

animal bones in otherwise wholly Stone Age contexts indicate two millennia of interaction between farmers and foragers in north-western Botswana (Denbow 1986). Their implication and that of the acquisition of domestic livestock by the ancestors of the historic Khoekhoen of the Cape and Namibia is that the 'hunter-gatherer' groups whom anthropologists observed were far from pristine (Schrire 1980). Instead, many of their supposedly distinctive features may reflect a position as a marginalised, oppressed class on the edges of more dominant societies (Wilmsen 1989). Historical sources confirm that nineteenth-century Bushmen participated in long-distance trading networks (Gordon 1984), but Wilmsen and Denbow (1990) also suggest that the ethnographically attested subsistence economies are the result of impoverishment following the collapse of a European-focused commercial hunting system in the 1890s.

A long and bitter debate has ensued in response to these views, echoed elsewhere in Africa (Woodburn 1988) and further afield. A particular focus has been the work of Lee (1979) and some of his associates, who, it is claimed (Schrire 1980; Wilmsen and Denbow 1990), deliberately downplayed and ignored Ju/'hoansi enmeshment in the wider pastoralist, agropastoralist and capitalist societies of the Kalahari and southern Africa in order to present them as analogues for understanding human cultural evolution. Many of the specific historical details used by Lee's 'revisionist' critics to substantiate Ju/'hoansi involvement in nineteenth-century commercial trade have proven erroneous (Lee and Guenther 1991), but what also emerges from this vitriolic debate is a widespread recognition that many, perhaps all, Kalahari Bushmen did have contacts of some kind with food-producing communities over the last 2000 years (Solway and Lee 1990).

However, it is by no means clear that contact *per se* should, as the revisionists appear to suggest, produce relations of dominance and subordination. The diversity of social organisation and economic strategies articulating recent Bushman societies with their neighbours shows that, in the 1970s at any rate, they included farm labourers, squatters and herdsmen (Guenther 1996), with some of these relationships centuries old (Vierich and Hitchcock 1996). But other societies remained autonomous, dependent on gathering and hunting wild resources (G. Silberbauer 1981). Ignoring the cultural diversity of Kalahari hunter-gatherers contributes to the view that contact with pastoralists and agropastoralists necessarily curtailed their autonomy and denies them a history prior to those interactions (G. Silberbauer 1991). To the contrary, the long-standing presence of food-producers in many parts of the Kalahari did not produce universal dependence, or result in the loss of distinctive hunter-gatherer languages, kinship systems, cosmologies, technologies and social systems emphasising sharing, reciprocity and egalitarian gender-relations (Kent 1992). Sadr's (1998) review of the archaeological evidence cited to support the incorporation of Bushmen as an underclass of clients within agropastoralist societies further demonstrates that the significance accorded the few potsherds, metal objects and livestock bones from otherwise LSA contexts in the Kalahari has been greatly overplayed (*pace* Denbow 1986, 1990; Wilmsen 1989). The conclusions to which more than a decade of discussion points are twofold. On the one hand interactions between hunter-gatherers and other groups form a vital subject of anthropological enquiry and the specific historical contexts of the ethnographic record have always to be borne in mind (Shott 1992). On the other, while there is no intrinsic barrier to employing Khoisan ethnography in LSA research, archaeology can also critically investigate the time-depth and associations of ethnographically documented patterns of behaviour.

Equally, with its concentration on the Ju/'hoansi, G/wi and /Xam as rôle models for LSA peoples, archaeological research does not adequately reflect the great diversity among surviving Bushman groups, or the linguistic, and probable cultural, variability among now extinct communities south of the Limpopo (Traill 1996). The message this holds for archaeologists is that the time is overdue to begin the 'de-!Kunging' of the Later Stone Age (Parkington 1984b). Rock art research is the area in which this process has progressed most. Jolly (1996a), in particular, has stressed the interaction between Bushmen living in the Drakensberg/Maluti Mountains and neighbouring Nguni- and Sotho-speaking farmers in the later second millennium. He argues that many of the ideas present in this area's paintings show the influence of the latter, including some of the scenes described by Qing (Jolly 1995). Linguistic parallels also suggest a sharing of beliefs between Nguni-speakers and Bushmen in south-eastern southern Africa (J.F. Thackeray 1994), though in both cases the direction of influence is assumed, rather than proven. Both Hammond-Tooke (1998) and Prins (1996), for example, argue for the adoption of features of the Bushman trance dance in the training of Nguni diviners. Nevertheless, this debate, along with exploration of shared beliefs between Khoekhoe and Bushman groups (Barnard 1992; Prins and Rousseau 1992), parallels with the rain-making and divining practices of Sotho-Tswana speakers (Schapera 1971; Tesele 1994) and sub-continent-wide beliefs about watersnakes and rain-making (Schmidt 1979; Dowson 1999) all expand the range of ethnographic evidence on which rock art researchers can draw.

The conclusion of this chapter is thus that while physical and genetic similarities are strong, and continuities in material culture between LSA people and Bushmen societies of the ethnographic present far-ranging and often profound (H. Deacon and Deacon 1999), they can also limit our reconstructions of the past and may even suggest that Bushman societies never changed. The archaeological record puts the lie to this, but simultaneously should encourage exploration of a much wider sample of societies than the purely southern African hunter-gatherer ones LSA archaeologists have hitherto used (S. Hall 1990). The quite extensive social and economic changes that took place in several areas of the sub-continent in the second half of the Holocene, as well as the relationships that hunter-gatherers developed with pastoralists, farmers and

European colonists, demonstrate the need for such a broader comparative approach. As recently argued by Maggs (1994/95) and Lane (1994/95), Iron Age archaeology faces a similar dilemma, poised between an almost embarrassingly rich ethnography and the attractions of a direct historical approach on the one hand and a tendency to produce ahistorical, structuralist interpretations that take insufficient account of variability within the archaeological and ethnographic records on the other. The creative tension between these poles lies at the heart of much southern African archaeological research.

CHAPTER 9

TAKING STOCK: THE INTRODUCTION AND IMPACT OF PASTORALISM

Arriving off southern Africa's coasts in the late 1400s, Europeans encountered Khoekhoe pastoralists whose extensive herds proved an important incentive for subsequent colonisation. The Khoekhoen, who combined herding with hunting and gathering, practised one of two forms of food-production to develop in southern Africa. The other, represented by mixed farming communities, is examined in chapters 10–12. Here I concentrate on three interrelated questions: archaeology's contribution to understanding livestock-keeping societies and their adaptations; the degree to which the origins of the historically known Khoekhoen can be correlated with the spread of livestock and pottery; and the relations between herders and people without domestic livestock. Changes in hunter-gatherer lifeways are a connected theme. The chronological remit for these discussions extends from shortly before 2000 BP up to the beginnings of Dutch colonial settlement in the seventeenth century (Fig. 9.1).

Pottery, livestock and people: single or multiple sources?

Throughout the western half of southern Africa, livestock bones in Stone Age contexts typically occur with pottery. The broad coincidence in the timing of these innovations and their association with the historic Khoekhoen, who used pots in cooking and for rendering fat, encourages common explanations for their origin and spread. Cooke (1965) proposed a movement west across northern Botswana and thence south through Namibia and into the Cape, based on the distribution of paintings of sheep and putative shepherds in Zimbabwe and the ecological improbability of movement through the central Kalahari (Fig. 9.2). His model echoes that inferred from oral traditions by Stow (1905), though without East Africa as an ultimate source.

Westphal's (1963) analysis of Khoisan languages showed that those spoken by the Khoekhoen (now represented principally by Nama) form part of the same family (Tshu-Khwe) as others spoken by Kalahari hunter-gatherers like the G/wi and Nharo (Fig. 9.3). This southern African origin for the Khoekhoen is supported by similarities in the structure of their kinship systems with those of hunter-gatherers (Barnard 1992), genetics (Nurse *et al.* 1985) and shared beliefs connected with procreation, trance and rain-making (Solomon 1989; Prins and Rousseau 1992; Hoff 1997). Westphal concluded that the Khoe language

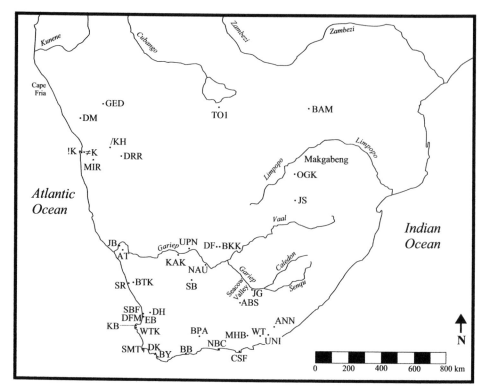

Figure 9.1   Location of archaeological sites discussed in chapter 9. Site names abbreviated thus: ABS Abbots Shelter; ANN Ann Shaw; AT /Ai tomas; BAM Bambata; BB Blombos; BKK Blinkklipkop; BPA Boomplaas; BTK Bethelsklip; BY Byneskranskop; DF Doornfontein; DFM Dunefield Midden; DH De Hangen; DK Die Kelders; DM Dâures massif; DRR Drierivier; EB Elands Bay Cave; GED Geduld; JB Jakkalsberg; JG Jouberts Gif; JS Jubilee Shelter; !K !Khuiseb Delta; ≠K ≠Khîsa-//gubus; KAK Kakamas; KB Kasteelberg; /KH /Khomas; MHB Melkhoutboom; MIR Mirabib; NAU Nauga; NBC Nelson Bay Cave; OGK Ongelukskraal; SB Springbokoog 11; SBF Steenbokfontein; SMT Smitswinkelbaai; SR Spoegrivier; TO1 Toteng 1; UNI Uniondale; UPN Upington; WT Wilton Large Rockshelter; WTK Witklip.

diverged from the broader Tshu-Khwe group somewhere in northern Botswana, a process that **glottochronology** places around 2000 years ago (Ehret 1982). Employing these observations, Elphick (1985) proposed that the Khoekhoen acquired livestock from Bantu-speaking Iron Age neighbours to their north, migrating outward as their own population and that of their herds grew. He sees the principal movement as along the Botswanan/Zimbabwean border and thence south towards the Gariep/Vaal confluence. At this point some groups moved downstream to enter Namibia from the south and Namaqualand from

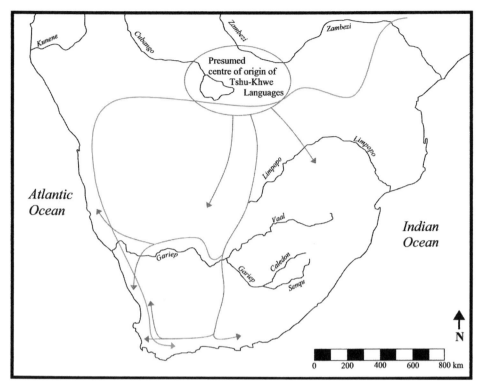

Figure 9.2   Possible southward movements of the Khoekhoen (redrawn after
Stow 1905 and C. Cooke 1965 – dotted line; Elphick 1985 – black
lines).

the north. Others turned south through the eastern Karoo to cross the Cape
Fold Belt and spread east and west along the coastal plain.

Cultural differences between the historic Cape Khoekhoen and Nama-
speakers, and early Dutch reports that people in the south-western Cape
recognised the kinship seniority of those living further east, support Elphick's
model. The homogeneity of known Khoe dialects (Westphal 1963) certainly
suggests that their speakers expanded rapidly, but without necessarily making
the Khoekhoen responsible for the spread of pottery and/or sheep (J. Deacon
1984b; Jacobson 1989; Wilson 1989). That Khoekhoe is but one of two main
branches of Westphal's Tshu-Khwe language family and many Khoe-speaking
hunter-gatherers have traditions of formerly owning livestock remind us too
that Khoekhoe expansion was but one component of a broader dispersal of
Tshu-Khwe speakers. Perhaps partly documented by an explosion of sites
across much of Botswana within the last 2000 years, another possible consequence could have been the displacement of the Ju/'hoansi away from the
Okavango and into the areas where they are found today (N. Walker 1995b).

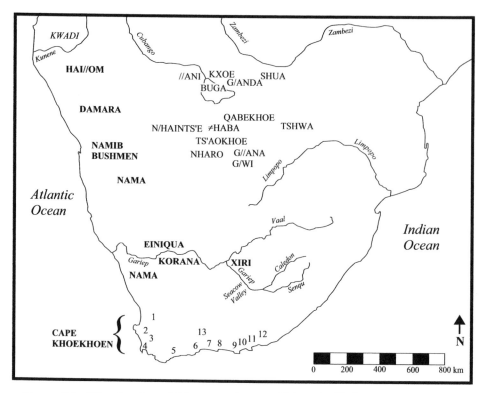

Figure 9.3   Distribution of Khoe-speakers and historically known Cape
Khoekhoe groups (after Barnard 1992; Vossen 1998). Khoekhoe
languages are shown in bold with known seventeenth-century Cape
Khoekhoe tribes numbered as follows: 1 Guriqua; 2 Cochoqua;
3 Goringhaiqua; 4 'Peninsulars'; 5 Chainoqua; 6 Hessequa; 7
Gouriqua; 8 Attaqua; 9 Gamtoos; 10 Damasqua; 11 Hoengeyqua;
12 Gonaqua; 13 Inqua. Note that an unknown Khoekhoe group was
also present in the upper Seacow Valley until the mid-eighteenth
century and that the Damara, Hai//om and Namib Bushmen were
ethnically distinct from the Khoekhoen. Non-Khoekhoe languages
fall into four groups, all shown in plain typeface: Central Khoe
(G//ana, G/wi and ≠Haba); Eastern Khoe (Shua and Tshwa, both
with several subdivisions); Northern Khoe (//Ani, Buga, G/anda and
Kxoe); and Western Khoe (N/haints'e, Nharo, Qabekhoe and
Ts'aokhoe). Kwadi (shown in italics) forms a third division, separate
from both Khoekhoe and non-Khoekhoe languages.

As a result of these considerations, most archaeological assessments concentrate on documenting the movement of pottery and livestock as things-
in-themselves, with sheep the first domesticate to appear in the archaeological
record. But sheep bones are small, and accelerator dating shows that many from
supposedly earlier contexts are considerably younger than the layers in which

they were found (Inskeep 1987; Sealy and Yates 1994, 1996). Only two sites have yielded AMS determinations preceding 1600 BP. Blombos near Mossel Bay is one, with dates of 1960 ± 50 BP (OxA-4543) and 1880 ± 55 BP (OxA-4544; Henshilwood 1996), and Spoegrivier, Namaqualand, another (2105 ± 65 BP, OxA-3862; Sealy and Yates 1994). Few sheep bones have yet been directly dated from further north (Sadr 1998); potentially early remains from South Africa's interior are only a few centuries old (Sealy and Yates 1994, 1996). Though limited, this evidence tends towards Cooke's model, rather than that of Elphick. Short-lived windows of ecological opportunity, such as that which brought cooler, wetter conditions to the Namaqualand coast and Namibia *c.* 2000 BP (D.M. Avery 1992; Scott 1996), may have been instrumental in facilitating the dispersal of sheep (and/or their owners) along southern Africa's western flanks.

Goats and cattle seem to have been later introductions. Osteological separation of sheep from goats is not always easy. Unreported historically from the south-western Cape, goats may have been more important in drier areas further north (Klein 1986b). Present at Bethelsklip, Namaqualand, in a sequence spanning the last millennium (Webley 1986), they are known in farming contexts in the eastern half of southern Africa from 1400 BP (Voigt 1986). The historic record shows that cattle were generally more important than sheep to the Khoekhoen, though both were used in rituals. Cattle were also ridden[1] and used as pack-animals in addition to providing dairy products and meat (Elphick 1985). However, their archaeological presence is more ephemeral. One reason is that their bones can be difficult to separate from those of Cape buffalo or eland, another that they may have been less frequently killed and eaten (Klein 1986b). Their oldest appearance in a LSA context is at Kasteelberg after 1300 BP (Klein and Cruz-Uribe 1989), though they too are known before this on Iron Age sites (Plug 1996a). Dogs, the last of the four domesticates with Khoekhoe associations, are also osteologically problematic, in this case because of confusion with jackals. The oldest known example in a LSA context comes from a 1150 BP shell midden near Cape St. Francis (Voigt 1983), consistent with dates for others from Kasteelberg B and chew marks on bones there and elsewhere in the south-western Cape (Cruz-Uribe and Klein 1994). Introduced no earlier than, and perhaps alongside, domestic livestock, dogs also became an important hunting aid for hunter-gatherers (Lee 1979).

Since none of these animals is indigenous to southern Africa, a northern source for them and the technologies needed for their management seems certain. Both **caprines** and cattle were kept by Stone Age people in East Africa from before 3000 BP. Though their sites are not known south of the Serengeti (Bower 1991), two aspects of material culture hint at connections with southern

---

[1] The earliest archaeological evidence for ox-riding comes from Kasteelberg, where a modified *Raphicerus* septum with traces of wear from a rope was recovered from a layer dating *c.* 900 BP (A.B. Smith 1993a).

Africa. Lugged and/or spouted ceramics, for example, are a distinctive feature of both Khoekhoe pottery (Rudner 1968) and sites in Kenya dating 2400–1700 BP (A.B. Smith 1992a). Stone bowls, common in East African Pastoral Neolithic contexts, are also recorded sporadically from Zambia (J.D. Clark 1964), Namibia (MacCalman 1962), Botswana (Fock 1960) and the Northern Cape (D. Morris 1991). Tempting as these similarities are, however, they may only be coincidental. Southern African stone bowls lack firm archaeological contexts, while lugs and spouts are functional, not just stylistic, attributes (Sadr 1998).

Other connections with East Africa have been sought using historical linguistics. Ehret (1973) suggested that Khoe terms for several domesticates (cow, goat, ram, etc.) were borrowed from speakers of Central Sudanic languages. More recently, describing these connections as flawed, he has identified parallels with speakers of Eastern Sahelian languages, another East African focused group (Ehret 1998). The prior presence of Khoekhoen in the Limpopo Valley inferred from supposed loanwords in several south-eastern Bantu languages (Ehret 1982) may be supported by paintings of fat-tailed sheep both there and around Makgabeng (Eastwood and Fish 1996). However, many of these claims are based solely on roots identified in hypothesised ancestral language forms, details of whose reconstruction remain unpublished (Borland 1986); they are not universally accepted, and are positively wrong in suggesting that Bantu-speakers acquired cattle from a Khoekhoe source (Peires 1981; Argyle 1994/95).

In the absence of sound evidence to the contrary, it seems probable that the ancestors of the livestock kept by the Khoekhoen were obtained from pioneering mixed farming communities. The limited work undertaken immediately north of the Zambezi and Kunene poses a real handicap, but if radiocarbon dates from Salumano A and Situmpa are acceptable, farmers making Iron Age ceramics were present in southern Zambia c. 2300 BP (D. Phillipson 1989). Assuming that they kept at least caprines, they may have been the source of the sheep found in LSA contexts further south. Animal diseases linked to the presence of large wildebeest and buffalo populations in the region stretching from south-eastern Angola across Zambia, Botswana and Zimbabwe into the Limpopo Valley may have precluded the southward movement of cattle at a similarly early date (Gifford-Gonzalez 2000). Both they and goats were probably obtained from other (and diverse?) farming communities more recently. Phylogenetic studies of surviving indigenous breeds (and archaeological samples?) could assist in delineating more precisely the origins of all three livestock species (J. Kinahan 1994/95).

The position with ceramics is less clear. Several sites in the south-western Cape have yielded pottery dating to the first few centuries AD. Both Die Kelders (Schweitzer 1979) and Blombos (Henshilwood 1996) place its appearance around 2000 BP, and the latter site suggests that at least in the southern Cape the long-perceived connection between the introductions of sheep and pottery holds true. Elsewhere sheep appear to be several centuries older than the first ceramics at Spoegrivier (J.C. Vogel *et al.* 1997), while in Namibia, like at Die Kelders, pottery substantially predates sheep in the Falls Rock and Snake Rock sequences (J. Kinahan 1991). However, considerable inter-site variability may be present since sheep were definitely present at Mirabib by 1550 BP (hair in a dung layer; Sandelowsky *et al.* 1979), and further north Geduld has a slightly older dung layer, with pottery present from *c.* 2000 BP (A.B. Smith and Jacobson 1995). Except in the lowest levels at Die Kelders, where some sherds are thick, fired at low temperatures and tempered with shale/siltstone (Schweitzer 1979), all these ceramics are generally well fired and thin-walled. The same is true of the undecorated pottery from Uniondale (Leslie 1989) and sites in and close to the Drakensberg from 2000 BP (Mazel 1992a). Inskeep (1978) wondered if pottery was independently developed in southern Africa, but its quality is such that it does not appear 'early' or ex-perimental, though once the basic facts of shaping and firing clay have been mastered there is no reason to expect pottery to be crude or simple (Close 1995). More convincingly, perhaps, its closeness in age to the southward expans-ion of pottery-using farming communities argues against separate invention, even if close similarities cannot be identified; recent Ju/'hoansi acquisition of Mbukushu farmer pottery highlights the degree of selection that may have been involved, at least as regards vessel form and function (J. Kinahan 1986).

The one exception to this generalisation concerns Bambata ware (Fig. 9.4), known from several sites in Botswana and Zimbabwe and associated with sheep bones and a date of 2150 BP at the eponymous rock-shelter in the Matopos (N. Walker 1983; Reid *et al.* 1998). Sherds from Jubilee Shelter (Wadley 1987), and Ongelukskraal (van der Ryst 1998) form a southernmost outlier for its distribution, occurring there, as in the Matopos and Kalahari, in otherwise exclusively LSA contexts, perhaps obtained through long-distance exchange networks. Huffman (1989) argues, however, that its decorative motifs place it within the Kalundu Tradition of the Early Iron Age (chapter 10) and that the pottery at Bambata itself derives from a younger occupation. Far from having herder associations, Bambata ware may thus represent an early phase in the agriculturalist settlement of southern Africa. Two sites at Toteng, northern Botswana, dating *c.* 1800 BP, may be the villages of such farmers (Huffman 1994), but the lack of structures and evidence for metalworking, coupled with the many stone tools found and issues of stratigraphic disturbance, make this an uncertain claim (Reid *et al.* 1998). Much more work needs to be done on the Bambata phenomenon and it may be that many different societies or adapta-tions are associated with it.

The rapidity with which ceramics appeared across southern Africa ahead of farming settlement might suggest that they were spread by a migrating pop-ulation, though their simultaneous occurrence in areas where herders never

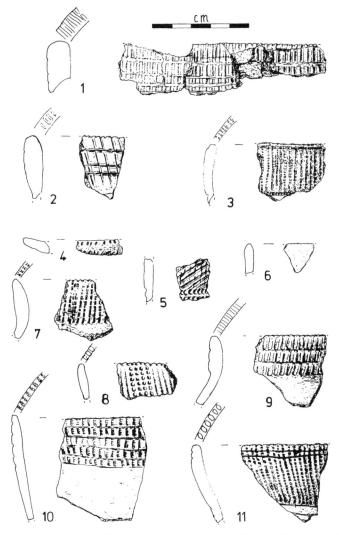

Figure 9.4   Bambata ware from south-western Zimbabwe (after N. Walker 1983:
Fig. 2; courtesy South African Archaeological Society). 1–8 Bambata;
9 Maleme Dam Shelter IV; 10 Broadlees Cave; 11 another shelter
near Bambata.

penetrated immediately raises one caution. Another results from the fact that
there is no independent measure of how 'fast' innovations spread as a result
of migration or diffusion, a problem that pertains equally to explaining the
movement of sheep. If the two formed part of a 'package' introduced by immi-
grant Khoekhoen then they might be expected regularly to co-occur, which they
do not always do. Equally, a stylistic 'chain' might be predicted to link ceramic
assemblages in Namibia and the Cape with those in northern Botswana.
Unfortunately, only Geduld, Kasteelberg and Toteng have sufficiently

well-dated decorated sherds to permit such a comparison; radical differences in vessel shape, rim profile and decoration argue against a close common origin (Sadr 1998).

Another perspective on whether sheep (and pottery?) were spread by a migrating (Khoekhoe?) population comes from considering the ease with which hunter-gatherers might adopt herding. A.B. Smith (1990) argues strongly that this is a difficult shift to undertake, since the accumulation of livestock runs counter to a foraging sharing/egalitarian ethic. The private ownership of stock and their use for storing food and as sources of status, wealth and patronage all require fundamental change in how social relations are organised. This may have happened where hunter-gatherers were incorporated into the lower levels of more strongly hierarchical, food-producing societies. While eroding egalitarianism and overcoming the ideological barriers identified, the new stockowners would have been too weakly stratified for the process to repeat itself. Further movement of livestock would thus have been through their physical expansion, not via the diffusion of domesticates to other hunter-gatherers. Whether the barriers to livestock acquisition are so high may be doubted, given the ease with which nineteenth-century Bushmen acquired horses (Wright 1971) or the 1960s Dobe Ju/'hoansi added goats to a still generalised and wild-food dominated subsistence strategy (Yellen 1984). The argument loses even more force if some later Holocene hunter-gatherers were already shifting to more delayed-returns socio-economic systems.

As we saw in chapter 7, aquatic resources may have allowed some northern Kalahari hunter-gatherers to become more sedentary well before 2000 BP, perhaps encouraging other changes in social and economic organisation (Denbow 1986). The megamidden phenomenon of the farwestern Cape is another case in point. If the period after 2400 BP saw changes in group organisation and settlement pattern, perhaps to cope with deteriorating environmental conditions (Jerardino 1996), then incorporating pottery and sheep may have been attractive. Ceramics could have offered new means of storing and cooking food, sheep new ways of accumulating wealth and prestige and of minimising subsistence risks (Yellen 1984), especially in offering additional sources of protein, fat and lactose for the survival and healthy development of children (Gifford-Gonzalez 2000). Precisely these arguments have been advanced for the spread of sheep and pottery among Impressed Ware Neolithic communities of the environmentally not dissimilar western Mediterranean (Lewthwaite 1986; Barnett 1995), a comparison that awaits further investigation.

The variability in how hunter-gatherers use and perceive sharing and the flexibility and diversity evident in the Bushman ethnographic record make comparable points. At least some local take-up of livestock-rearing by hunter-gatherers beyond the initial area within which the animals were acquired may have been possible. J. Kinahan (1991) offers an interesting scenario for how this might have happened in the central Namib. Elaborately painted polychrome

Figure 9.5 Possible shamanistic figures in the rock art of Snake Rock Shelter, Dâures massif, Namibia (courtesy John Kinahan).

male figures unassociated with dancing or clapping individuals are superimposed on more communal trancing monochrome scenes at Snake Rock and elsewhere in the Dâures massif (Fig. 9.5). Identified as specialist shamans, perhaps these individuals were able to corner access to livestock obtained through exchange, using them to support and develop their power in the economic and political, not just religious, spheres. Being undated, however, these paintings are not readily linkable to the excavated record; the reliability of the ethnography supporting this view of shamans' activities is also contested (A.B. Smith *et al.* 1996; Jacobson 1997; cf. J. Kinahan 1995, 1996a).

Quite how sheep and pottery were dispersed across southern Africa's western half thus remains deeply uncertain, and demands much more basic fieldwork, especially in the north of the sub-continent (cf. Vogelsang 1998). As we shall see, quite distinctive hunter-gatherer communities appear to have survived well into the colonial era, some 1600 years after the initial appearance of sheep. While this suggests that domesticates were introduced to these areas by people whose origins lay elsewhere, to assume that these were the Khoekhoen may be erroneous. Pierced lugs, a hallmark of the characteristically pointed-based pots historically attested among the Khoekhoen, are widely distributed across the areas where they are known to have lived (Rudner 1979; Sadr 1998). However, none is reliably dated before 1200 BP, and in the Kasteelberg B sequence in the south-western Cape their arrival correlates with other changes in pottery form and style, lithic raw materials, artefact frequencies, fauna and local settlement pattern. This extremely limited evidence raises the question whether Khoekhoe arrival in south-western southern Africa was substantially more recent than that of sheep and pottery (Sadr 1998). At the very least, some of the historically attested features of Khoekhoe society were probably not present at the initial introduction of livestock (Jacobson 1989; Henshilwood 1996).

The archaeology of livestock-keeping

If understanding the origins of sheep, pottery and the Khoekhoen is difficult, getting to grips with the organisation and development of herding societies from purely archaeological data is even more so; interpretations rely heavily on historical sources (Boonzaier *et al.* 1996). The reasons may lie in herder settlement and subsistence patterns, since mobility was essential in order to secure adequate pasture and water, traditional mat-covered houses (*matjieshuise*) leave virtually no trace (Fig. 9.6) and rock-shelters may have been used less frequently than by hunter-gatherers. Coupled with the destructive impact of farming and urbanisation in areas of the Cape with the best grazing, the result is that little sign of their presence is identifiable, even where large numbers of herders are attested historically (Hart 1987). Kasteelberg (Fig. 9.7), on the Vredenburg Peninsula, is the prime exception (A.B. Smith 1992b). In more arid areas, such as the central Namib and the Karoo, the use of stone for building has left numerous kraals as evidence of livestock management, but such open-air sites rarely preserve organic remains (Sampson 1985a; J. Kinahan 1991).

Faunal assemblages containing livestock also occur in rock-shelters, where dung deposits sometimes indicate their use as temporary stock-posts.

Figure 9.6   *Matjieshuis* in modern Namaqualand (courtesy Andy Smith).

Figure 9.7   General view of the excavation area at Kasteelberg B, Western Cape, South Africa.

Boomplaas provides the best example (H. Deacon *et al.* 1978), but it is frequently a contentious issue whether livestock remains in these contexts derive from herders or from hunter-gatherers who had obtained animals through exchange or theft, or as a supplement to wild resources. I return to the difficulties that this raises in the concluding section of this chapter when considering the debate over the archaeological recognition of herder and hunter-gatherer societies in the south-western Cape. For the moment, note that I use the term 'herder' as a shorthand to refer to people keeping livestock and 'pastoralist' for those whose entire way of life, social and ritual, as well as economic, is geared to their herds. While the historic sources show that the Khoekhoen were clearly pastoralists, the presence of livestock bones in archaeological contexts does not necessarily support the same inference.

The Kasteelberg complex provides the key archaeological evidence for pre-historic livestock-keeping in the south-western Cape. Several sites have been excavated. All but KBC, a small rock-shelter, are open-air middens in which cultural material partially fills broad depressions on the *kopje*'s sides. KBB provides the largest samples, dating 1300–880 BP (A.B. Smith 1992b). Higher up the hill most of the occupation at KBA is older, extending back to 1800 BP, while KBD and a ceramic-yielding occupation at KBC fall towards the end and beginning of the KBB sequence. Seriation of diagnostic sherds divides the ceramics into four phases (Fig. 9.8). The two oldest comprise relatively small vessels, some with spouts, distinguished by an initial preference for incised lip and neck designs (SPINC), subsequently superseded by shell-edge stamping (COMB). They were followed after 1100 BP by larger, undecorated, spoutless pots, some with pierced lugs (LUND); necks were generally decorated with horizontal incisions after 700 BP (LINC; names after Sadr and Sampson 1999). Comparable ceramics, of the kind Rudner (1968) dubbed 'Cape Coastal Ware', occur at other *kopjes* close to Kasteelberg, and more rarely in rock-shelter contexts at Witklip and Elands Bay Cave (Sadr and Smith 1991).

At both KBA and KBB, formal stone tools are rare and backed pieces completely absent in assemblages dominated by expedient flaking of quartz. However, grindstones, some ochre-stained, are relatively common, especially after 900 BP; distinctive, boat-shaped grinding grooves in the *kopje*'s bedrock may be of the same age (Fig. 9.9). This emphasis on ochre processing is one indicator that Kasteelberg was a focus for ritual activity. Others are the presence of several partial mongoose skeletons – reflecting a custom whereby women wore mongoose skin when slaughtering animals (A.B. Smith and Pheiffer 1992) – and of the remains of a lamb originally buried in an ochre-wrapped skin (A.B. Smith 1992b). Though the KBA/KBB lithics are informal, a feature thought diagnostic of pastoralist sites (A.B. Smith *et al.* 1991), a sophisticated range of bone tools was recovered, including awls, spatulae, arrowpoints and linkshafts indistinguishable from those observed ethnographically (A.B. Smith and Poggenpoel 1988).

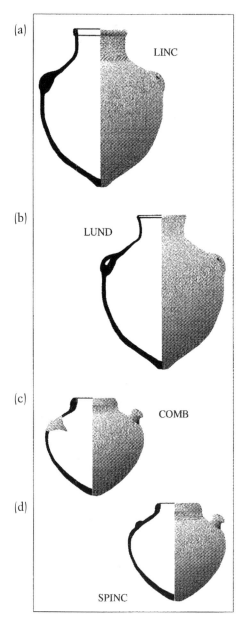

Figure 9.8   The sequence of Khoekhoe ceramic phases identified in the Western Cape (Sadr and Smith 1991; courtesy Garth Sampson): (a) Spouted ware – incised; (b) Spouted ware – impressed; (c) Lugged ware – undecorated; (d) Lugged ware – incised.

The Dutch recorded that Khoekhoen living in the Vredenburg area kept extensive cattle herds, but the prehistoric Kasteelberg fauna does not reflect this. Instead, sheep and Cape fur seals dominate at KBA and KBB, the latter *increasing* in importance with time (Klein and Cruz-Uribe 1989). The principal reason

Figure 9.9   Grinding grooves in the bedrock at Kasteelberg B, Western Cape, South Africa.

lies in the attractions that Kasteelberg offered for combining adequate shelter for livestock with exploitation of seals and shellfish at the coast 10 km away; whales stranded by a localised anomaly in the earth's magnetic field in nearby St. Helena Bay offered an additional resource (A.B. Smith 1993b). Analysis of organic residues adhering to potsherds shows that marine mammal fat was rendered in them, probably for both food and body grease (Patrick *et al.* 1985); as we saw in chapter 7, the meat of these animals can be stored in beach sand for several weeks.

Mortality profiles of the sheep and seals recovered indicate that KBA and KBB were probably occupied on a seasonal basis. Visits increasingly focused on late winter/early spring, taking advantage of the peak availability of newly weaned, washed-up seals (Klein and Cruz-Uribe 1989). We know that in the seventeenth century the Khoekhoen abandoned the Vredenburg Peninsula in summer as pasture became scarce, moving inland towards the Berg River and the higher-quality grazing of the Swartland. Further south towards Table Bay a different pattern is documented, with occasional summer rains allowing coastal visits prior to moving inland in winter. Guarding against overgrazing and the onset of stock diseases caused by trace element deprivation, such transhumance was probably encouraged as cattle numbers increased, since sheep alone could have remained on the Vredenburg Peninsula for much of the summer (A.B. Smith 1992a). Dutch records indicate that cattle were kept in far higher numbers than is evident archaeologically (Elphick 1985). This increase probably encouraged development of more complex, hierarchical pastoralist communities, marked by strongly defined patron–client relations and increased raiding (A.B. Smith 1987).

Along with the Kasteelberg complex, Boomplaas is one of the earliest and least equivocal herder sites. Multiple burnt dung horizons in the DGL Member attest to its having been a sheep kraal 1500–1700 BP. Perhaps surprisingly, large stone-packed hearths on compact dung floors indicate that people lived inside the site with their animals (H. Deacon *et al.* 1978). The rarity of wild game in this part of the sequence may suggest that Boomplaas's occupants engaged in intensive sheep raising (von den Driesch and Deacon 1985).

Boomplaas lies on the southern margins of the Karoo. On its eastern flanks, herding appears to have been introduced slightly later. The oldest pottery in the Seacow Valley (Fig. 9.10) dates to the mid-first millennium AD, providing a further argument against Elphick's model for Khoekhoe dispersal (Sampson and Vogel 1995). Overall, the same vessel types are evident as in the south-western Cape, and the same four-phase ceramic sequence probably holds true (Sadr and Sampson 1999); grass-tempered ceramics, historically associated with local hunter-gatherers, appear to have been introduced at the same time and may reflect their take-up of basic pot-making technology as a result of contact with newly arrived herders (Bollong *et al.* 1997; Sampson and Sadr 1999).

Figure 9.10   The eastern part of the Seacow Valley taken from Blydefontein Shelter, Northern Cape, South Africa (courtesy Britt Bousman).

Herder settlement spread across the valley from north-west to south-east, but remained restricted to its upper reaches, where several hundred stone kraals occur, organised around contiguous waterholes in groups approximately the same size as modern sheep farms (Sampson 1996). Diagnostically Khoekhoe sherds occur both at the kraals and in rock-shelters, from which goats, cattle but principally sheep have been recovered, along with wild animals (Plug *et al.* 1994). Whether the shelters were occupied by herders and/or the hunter-gatherers who retained control of the lower valley is unclear (Sampson 1996). Herding and Khoekhoe pottery went unreported in this area by Europeans after 1770. Rock-shelter sequences confirm their disappearance by that date, perhaps because of drought during the Little Ice Age (Bollong and Sampson 1996; Sampson 1996).

At the opposite side of the Karoo Biome, Namaqualand's location makes it a key area for understanding how livestock spread through southern Africa. Little used before the late Holocene, population increased once herding became possible (Webley 1992a). Spoegrivier's sequence (Fig. 9.11) spans the period 2400–1400 BP, yielding a small, increasingly informal lithic assemblage along with generally fine-grained, quartz-tempered ceramics, only a few of them decorated (Webley 1992b; J.C. Vogel *et al.* 1997). A rough sandstone scraper from one of the upper units resembles *//khom* stones still used by Nama-speakers to work skins (Webley 1990). Excellent plant preservation included fragments of *Scirpus* spp.,

Figure 9.11   Spoegrivier, Northern Cape, South Africa (courtesy Andy Smith).

the reed used to make the mats for *matjieshuise*. Located near the sea, people exploited both shellfish (overwhelmingly limpets) and rock lobster, while seals, which dominate the mammalian fauna, were taken locally by Nama-speakers in the nineteenth century (Alexander 1967). Increasing summer aridity and the demands of cattle for better grazing and more reliable water may have led to Spoegrivier's abandonment after 1400 BP. Ethnoarchaeological observations further east suggest that people probably then aggregated around permanent waterholes in summer before dispersing into smaller groups for winter (Webley 1986).

More detailed insights come from Jakkalsberg on the southern bank of the Gariep (Webley 1997b). Here two open-air sites were briefly occupied 1400–1300 BP; a child's burial is of uncertain age. Only a quarter of the area has been sampled, but the close proximity of hearths at site A gainsays the use of *matjieshuise*. At both sites lithic assemblages were small and informal. Several hundred potsherds share a similar thickness and temper, but differ in decoration and vessel form: at the younger site A, decoration consists almost wholly of parallel incised lines and lugs are common, while at site B, spouts occur and decoration is more varied, including punctate impressions also known from /Ai tomas further to the south-east (Webley 1992a); the shell-edge stamping found at Kasteelberg is absent. Other contrasts lie in ostrich eggshell bead manufacture (more common at site B) and bone tool working (more evident at site A), but the most striking is site B's abundant red ochre, including plugs of ochre mixed with fat and ash and ochre-stained stone artefacts, bones, and ostrich eggshell and tortoise shell containers. An ochre-stained pelvis of a young male caprine recalls the recent Khoekhoe practice of hanging the ochre/fat-stained pelvis of a slaughtered sheep or goat within the hut used in girls' initiation ceremonies (Engelbrecht 1936). Webley (1997a) interprets these differences to suggest that site B was a focus for such rituals. The sheep, the strong association between red ochre and female fertility among recent Nama and the possibility that circular motifs (cf. the punctate-impressed pottery) are similarly linked are central to her argument. Less certainly, site A's incised ceramics and a zigzag-decorated bone linkshaft may bear designs associated with men.

Though small, the Jakkalsberg fauna is dominated by sheep, with game of little importance (J. Brink and Webley 1996). Fish were also extensively exploited, as more recently (100–200 BP) further downstream (Robertshaw 1979), probably by targeting late summer spawning runs; carbonised *Euclea* fruits support the case for summer occupation at Jakkalsberg. Limited grazing may have made this a time for dispersal into smaller family units along the Gariep, with winter pasture in the foothills of the hinterland permitting seasonal aggregations (Webley 1997b).

Considerably further upstream, the Gariep supported a large pastoralist population at European contact, especially near Kakamas and Upington, where

Figure 9.12 Burial from Omdraai Grave 1, Kakamas, Northern Cape, South Africa (courtesy Alan Morris).

burial cairns are well known (Fig. 9.12). Dating to the eighteenth/early nineteenth centuries, they contain few items, though ochre and specularite were commonly placed over the body. Osteological analysis suggests that the buried individuals belonged to a population engaging in extensive gene flow with more strongly negroid groups, identified as Tswana-speakers from whom specularite and iron were obtained (A. Morris 1992d). Interestingly, ethnohistoric accounts also indicate that the Gariep Khoekhoen grew and possibly traded *dagga*, as well as keeping livestock (Mossop 1935; Raper and Boucher 1988). Few potential settlement sites have been excavated – most are probably lost to intensive farming. However, several sites along the river and close to major watersources nearby have produced assemblages termed Doornfontein. Thin-walled ceramics featuring lugs, spouts and decorated necks or rims, as well as highly informal stone artefacts and grinding grooves at some sites, recall the Kasteelberg complex and are probably the archaeological signature of herders in the Northern Cape (Beaumont *et al.* 1995).

In Namibia, home to the largest surviving Khoekhoe population, the Nama, Geduld (A.B. Smith and Jacobson 1995) and Falls Rock and Snake Rock (J. Kinahan 1991) span the introduction of domestic livestock. At all three, considerable continuities are evident in stone artefact production. The earliest pottery, which is thin walled and well fired, emphasises the use of burnished vertical lines as decoration; incised motifs became more common with time. Since many vessels are represented by only a few sherds, J. Kinahan (1991) suggests that their value was symbolic and that they were introduced from elsewhere; but perhaps broken pottery was simply disposed of outside the shelters. Sheep occur at Geduld and dung both there and at Falls Rock, but clearly identifiable remains of domesticates are rare in faunas that emphasise wild bovids, hare and dassie. This raises the important and unresolved question of how far such sites are attributable to pastoralists or hunter-gatherers, an issue affecting all the areas I discuss.

Both Geduld and Falls Rock went out of use by 700 BP. During the second millennium numerous stone huts and enclosures superseded rock-shelters as choice settlement sites in the Hungorob area of the Dâures massif (Fig. 9.13). Similar sites occur elsewhere in northern Namibia west of the 200 mm isohyet and north to Cape Fria (Noli and Avery 1987). Some may be associated with the Dama people (Carr *et al.* 1978; Jacobson 1997). The Hungorob sites, dating 450–150 BP, comprise stone huts with hearths and sometimes side lobes possibly used for keeping small stock. Other, more simply constructed houses contain pestles, a contrast that J. Kinahan (1991) interprets in gender terms. These sites, typically with a single large quern in the centre for grinding seeds taken from harvester ant nests, occur on terraces in the lower part of the Hungorob Ravine, a marginal grazing area perhaps used for summer aggregations in a transhumant cycle. Stone huts and enclosures in the perennial pastures of the upper ravine may represent more dispersed dry season settlement; both kinds of site yield ceramics featuring pierced lugs and impressed decoration (J. Kinahan 1991).

The !Khuiseb Delta offers another perspective on herder adaptations in the central Namib. Here shell middens, which emphasise white mussels and include seal bones (Jacobson and Vogel 1977), were a post-pottery development, focused on the most reliable springs. J. Kinahan (1991) suggests that, initially,

Figure 9.13   Stone huts in the Hungorob Ravine, Dâures massif, Namibia
(courtesy John Kinahan).

globular, narrow-mouthed, pointed-based ceramics, decorated by incision and
fitted with lugs, were used for storage. During the second millennium AD
wider-mouthed pots with simple incised or impressed decoration have thick
soot encrustations suggestive of cooking, perhaps to prepare storable concentrate from *!nara* melons. Bone knives of a kind employed ethnographically
to cut melons also occur and the area's recent Khoekhoe inhabitants used
both *!nara* and marine foods as staples (Budack 1977). Excavations at ≠Khîsa-
//gubus, an eighteenth-century site, confirm exploitation of seabirds, cetaceans,
seals and, overwhelmingly, fish. Cattle and small stock are rare, but were
probably herded further inland on the Namib plains; isotopic analysis of burials suggests that meat, mostly from sheep, was more important than milk
(J. Kinahan 1991).

Survival in these arid areas must have depended on inter-group alliances, as
well as mobility. Seal phalanges from Geduld (270 km inland) and marine shells
there, at Falls Rock, Mirabib (Sandelowsky 1977) and elsewhere (Wendt 1972)
demonstrate contacts between coast and interior. Portable valuables may have
been exchanged for livestock in times of drought. Glass beads formed part of
this system after their introduction by Europeans, but indigenously produced
copper beads were also important. Both at /Khomas (J. Kinahan and Vogel 1982)
and at Drierivier (D. Miller and Sandelowsky 1999) an innovative and unique
smelting technique in which furnaces and *tuyères* were made from stone was
employed to produce such items.

South of the Gariep, individuals wearing copper beads were encountered as early as 1497 and metal was highly sought after from Europeans thereafter (Elphick 1985). Early accounts of the Little Namaqua, in particular, emphasise that they used copper and iron jewellery and iron spearheads and arrowheads. The iron was probably acquired from Tswana-speaking farmers, but they were smelting copper themselves in the mid-eighteenth century (Goodwin 1956). Excavated finds confirm access to both metals before European contact, though only iron has been recovered in Namaqualand itself, notably at Jakkalsberg where a range of artefacts occurs, made using techniques comparable to those employed by contemporary Iron Age metallurgists in northern Botswana (D. Miller and Webley 1994). Other finds include copper beads from Boomplaas (H. Deacon *et al.* 1978), Bambata (N. Walker 1983), Numas Entrance in the Dâures massif (MacCalman 1965) and Byneskranskop (Schweitzer and Wilson 1982), and iron fragments from the Northern Cape (Beaumont and Vogel 1989; D. Morris and Beaumont 1991). An iron adze from Geduld associated with dates of 2000–1800 BP may be the oldest signal of such contacts (A.B. Smith and Jacobson 1995).

Pastoralists, hunter-gatherers and hunter-herders

Some 2000 years ago, all southern Africa's inhabitants depended on various combinations of hunting, gathering and fishing for their livelihood. Across the western half of the sub-continent many, by the seventeenth century, kept extensive herds of livestock that contributed heavily to people's diets and played a central rôle in their social relations and ritual life. Whether, and how, distinct populations of hunter-gatherers survived alongside these pastoralists is hotly debated, with clear resonances of the issues examined in chapter 8. On one reading of the historical sources, drought, sickness and raiding made pastoralist economies sufficiently fragile that individuals could easily lose their stock, falling back on theft, hunting and gathering, or service to wealthier people to recoup their losses (Schrire 1980; Elphick 1985). Dutch accounts of people without livestock, often termed 'Soaqua' or 'Sonqua', therefore refer not to surviving hunter-gatherers, but to the poorer sections of a hierarchical society. Communities and individuals cycled continually within a single socio-economic system.

Alternative interpretations identify distinct pastoralist and hunter-gatherer populations in the seventeenth-century south-western Cape. While some Soaqua kept livestock (Elphick 1985), others lived entirely from wild resources, though occasionally trading or working with, or robbing, pastoralists (Parkington 1984b). Some spoke a language completely different from Khoe. Furthermore, they were typically encountered towards the Cape Fold Mountains, suggesting a marginalisation that was physical, as well as social. When observed near the coast this was in summer, when pastoralists may have moved

Table 9.1 *Distinguishing criteria for the recognition of pastoralist and hunter-gatherer sites in the south-western Cape (after A.B. Smith et al. 1991)*

Criterion	Pastoralist sites, e.g. Kasteelberg B	Hunter-gatherer sites, e.g. Witklip
Formal stone tools	Few	Relatively frequent
Use of fine-grained rocks	Rare	Common
Grindstones	Common	Few
Ceramics	Common; $>700/m^3$	Few; $\leq 10/m^3$
Donax shell scrapers	Absent	Present
Ostrich eggshell beads	Large ≥ 4.5 mm	Small ≤ 5 mm, though becoming larger after 1400 BP
Wild bovids	Infrequent	Common
Sheep	Frequent	Rare
Seals	Frequent	Rare

inland (A.B. Smith 1987). Skeletal evidence provides some support for historic accounts that herders were significantly taller than people without livestock, presumably because of differences in diet quality or genetic origin (P. Smith *et al.* 1992; Wilson and Lundy 1994).

If distinct hunter-gatherer and pastoralist populations did persist in the south-western Cape until the advent of Europeans they should be recognisable archaeologically. Post-2000 BP sites on the Vredenburg Peninsula fall within two groups, one typified by Kasteelberg A and B, the other by KBC and the nearby Witklip rock-shelter sequence, which both precedes and continues after the introduction of livestock and pottery (Table 9.1). Differences in stone tools, ceramic densities, ostrich eggshell bead size and fauna suggest that the former are the residues of pastoralists, the latter of hunter-gatherers (A.B. Smith *et al.* 1991). Most sites in this area fall readily within these groups, and the apparent absence of pastoralist sites from the mountains fits the historic record well, though attention needs also to be given to situational variability in the makeup of the excavated assemblages, since neither pastoralists nor hunter-gatherers will have undertaken identical activities at every site (Schrire and Deacon 1989; Schrire 1992a). At Jakkalsberg, for instance, though sheep and an informal lithic assemblage comfortably fit Smith *et al.*'s criteria of a pastoralist site, ostrich eggshell bead size and ceramic density do not (Webley 1997b). Similar points apply to the late Holocene levels at Die Kelders (Wilson 1996), though the emphasis on seals and sheep at Smitswinkelbaai on the Cape Peninsula 1400–1100 BP in an assemblage with pottery, well-made bone artefacts and virtually no formal stone tools plausibly identifies this as another herder site (Poggenpoel and Robertshaw 1981).

Change over time must also be considered. We have already seen that the later introduction of cattle encouraged development of more complex, hierarchical societies, and the cyclical pattern Elphick describes was probably exacerbated by European demands for livestock (Boonzaier *et al.* 1996). Still more far reaching is the contention that dichotomising the archaeological record between pastoralists and hunter-gatherers obscures the possibility that many LSA sites with livestock belonged to hunter-herders, such as those studied by Ikeya (1993) in the central Kalahari, who keep goats, but derive most meat from game, around which rituals revolve. Sadr (1998) argues, though without detailed discussion of the many taphonomic issues involved, that KBA and Jakkalsberg are the only LSA sites with livestock-dominated faunas and thus alone merit attribution to pastoralists in the sense of people who depended on their herds ritually, socially and for food. He further suggests that such sheep-based pastoralism might have developed independently in the Cape from a delayed-returns hunting-gathering base, using sheep diffusing south among hunter-herder communities. If correct, the overall chronology for the Kasteelberg complex would suggest that this phenomenon was short-lived, implying once again that subsequent Khoekhoe pastoralism was a later development. As J. Kinahan (1994/95) points out, however, defining pastoralist sites has to take account of the practical arrangements of livestock management, which include the probability of herders or pastoralists leaving behind archaeological residues from which livestock are wholly absent; simple numbers of sheep or cattle bones are thus going to be a very unsure guide to economic, let alone cultural, attribution.

Variability in the mean size of ostrich eggshell beads emerges as an important element in many of these debates. First noted by Jacobson (1987), there seems to be a clear pattern for bead size to increase during the first and second millennia AD. Why is unclear, though it may relate to changing preferences in how beads were used and displayed, for example on clothing. Such preferences were perhaps related to group identity. Beads worn by recent Kalahari Bushmen are, for example, substantially smaller than those traded to farmers (P. Wiessner, cited by Jacobson 1987). Though variation between *archaeological* assemblages is often small (J. Kinahan 1996a), differences in bead size in the south-western and farwestern Cape offer some of the strongest support for interpreting inter-site variability there in terms of two distinct populations. From historic accounts we know that using cowhide/sheepskin clothing, smearing themselves with butter and wearing the intestines of slaughtered livestock were other means by which pastoralists distinguished themselves visibly (and olfactorily) from people without domestic animals (H. Deacon and Deacon 1999).

The introduction of livestock and subsequent development of a pastoralist lifestyle impacted profoundly on the settlement pattern, subsistence and material culture of hunter-gatherers. In the south-western and farwestern Cape, for example, access to the coast and coastal plain probably became increasingly

Figure 9.14   Dunefield Midden, Western Cape, South Africa, showing excavations in progress in December 1992.

difficult as herder numbers grew and livestock competed with wild game in higher nutrient areas. Reductions in mean tortoise size suggest that even these animals came under more sustained predation (Klein and Cruz-Uribe 1987). Hunter-gatherers probably found themselves forced into more marginal parts of the landscape, with the mountains and the drier Elands/Lamberts Bay area serving as refugia (Parkington and Hall 1987b). While Elands Bay Cave came back into use and megamiddens were completely abandoned, Dunefield Midden (Fig. 9.14) is one of several new campsites close to the shore (Parkington *et al.* 1992). The bulk of this site represents a single occupation event *c.* 650 BP, the initial impetus perhaps provided by a successful eland kill, reflected in the lithic assemblage's emphasis on backed microlith production. Shellfish (especially limpets), rock lobster, seals, tortoises and steenbok are the most common taxa, whale barnacles document access to beached whales (Jerardino and Parkington 1993), chewed seal bones the presence of dogs (Cruz-Uribe and Klein 1994) and rare sheep bones connections with stock-keepers. The finely resolved stratigraphy allows detailed exploration of spatial patterning in the arrangement of hearths, shell dumps and meat-roasting pits, while refitting offers scope for investigating meat-sharing.

Inland site locations stress relatively small rock-shelters in broken terrain and on heathlands unattractive to livestock. A shared feature is a central ashy area surrounded by grass bedding with well-preserved food remains and organic artefacts. First recognised at De Hangen (Parkington and Poggenpoel 1971) and identified widely in the mountains and on the coastal plain (Yates *et al.* 1994), this represents a distinctive arrangement of communal space, though one with pre-2000 BP roots. The same kind of pottery occurs on coastal sites and in the mountains. Termed the De Hangen Style (Sadr and Smith 1991) or lugged incised ware (LINC; Sadr and Sampson 1999), its defining characteristics include broader rims and more plentiful decoration that combines incisions and single punctations (Fig. 9.15). Subsistence strategies emphasised ground game, small bovids and geophytes in a pattern that shows continuities with the period preceding the introduction of livestock. High frequencies of adzes support intensive plant-food gathering and they were often made on recycled MSA tools, sometimes acquired by excavating underlying deposits (Parkington and Poggenpoel 1987). Stable carbon isotope readings from skeletons in the Olifants

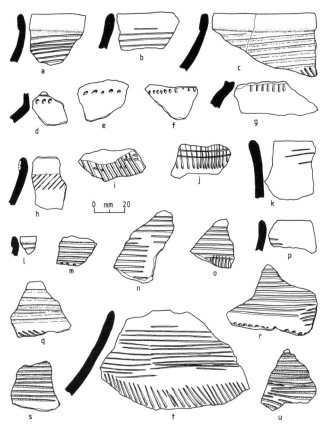

Figure 9.15   De Hangen Style pottery (after Sadr and Smith 1991: Fig. 6; courtesy South African Archaeological Society).

Valley suggest some marine input into a largely terrestrial diet, while coastal burials reveal significantly greater use of terrestrial resources after 2000 BP than before, and very little difference between men and women (Sealy and van der Merwe 1988; Lee Thorp *et al.* 1989). The integration of marine and land-based foods and gendered access to them were thus probably reworked, though there is, not surprisingly, no isotopic evidence for distinct pastoralist and hunter-gatherer populations. While regular seasonal movements may not have taken place, seashell ornaments and artefacts do document contacts between the interior and the coast.

The painted slab from Steenbokfontein (Jerardino and Swanepoel 1999) demonstrates that rock paintings do not, as once thought (Parkington *et al.* 1986), indicate an intensification of ritual to cope with the stresses brought about by supposed pastoralist intrusion. Instead, the fine-line painting tradition probably disappeared in pre-colonial times. Both the complete lack of cattle imagery and low incidence of sheep paintings suggest this (Yates *et al.* 1994; Fig. 9.16). Since the latter are almost wholly restricted to the mountains (Manhire *et al.* 1986; cf. Jerardino 1999), the fine-line tradition may have ended first along the coast, where the introduction of livestock had greatest impact. However, rock art production did not end completely. Handprints, which are widespread, sometimes decorated and often numerous, signal a change in

Figure 9.16 Painting of fat-tailed sheep, Boskloof, Western Cape, South Africa (courtesy Tony Manhire).

Figure 9.17   Painted handprints, all in red, Matjiesgoedkloof, Western Cape, South Africa.

content and technique (Fig. 9.17). Though tending to occur where few or no fine-line images are present, superimpositions invariably indicate that they are more recent. This and their rarity in the mountains may imply that at least some were made by pastoralists (van Rijssen 1984), possibly in female puberty rituals (G. Anderson 1997). Perhaps supporting this, measurements indicate most were made by sub-adults, probably as a group activity rather than alone (Manhire 1998). Some handprints may relate to colonial-era paintings (Yates *et al.* 1993), but the lack of Dutch references suggests that little rock art was being produced by the seventeenth century.

In the southern and eastern Cape Fold Belt, Boomplaas is the one site most certainly attributable to herders. Stone-packed hearths of the kind reported there are common near Cape St. Francis and shell middens with pottery are also widespread. Given the informality of many pre-2000 BP lithic assemblages, whether either can definitively be assigned to herders rather than hunter-gatherers is moot, and at least some of these hearths are more than 2000 years old (Robertshaw 1979). Tidal fish-traps, some still operable, have stronger herder links (G. Avery 1975). At Nelson Bay Cave, where sheep and potsherds occur in minimal numbers, Inskeep (1987) suggests that increased seal procurement after 2000 BP was directed at obtaining skins and meat for exchange with herders. Inland and further east, sites document a subsistence pattern still focused on geophytes, small bovids and storage of *Pappea capensis*

(Binneman 1997b). One widespread phenomenon was the extension of gathering to include a particular geophyte, *Cyperus usitatus*, perhaps a response to disrupted access to other resources, such as freshwater mussels and fish, as well as toolstone (H. Deacon 1976; S. Hall 1990). That Wilton and Melkhoutboom have quite ephemeral post-2000 BP occupations suggests that regional demographic shifts also occurred, perhaps partly towards food-producers, who in the eastern Cape Fold Belt included Iron Age farmers; the Koonap Valley may have been one area where these relationships developed (S. Hall 1990). The ceramics appearing there and at Uniondale (Leslie 1989) *c.* 1900 BP once again fall within Rudner's Cape Coastal Ware. Subsequent to 500 BP where grass-tempered sherds occur in terminal LSA contexts at Wilton (J. Deacon 1974) and Uniondale (Leslie 1989), a different rim-necked tradition reflects the emergence of mixed Khoekhoe/Xhosa groups, the Gonaqua and Gqunukhwebe; stable carbon isotope analyses of Gonaqua skeletons suggest they eventually adopted cereal agriculture too (F. Silberbauer 1979). Rock art displays related changes: sheep paintings occur mostly on the coastal forelands, implying continued hunter-gatherer presence south of the Winterberg until then, while cattle images are found only in the mountains, where ceramics are less evident (S. Hall 1994; Robertshaw 1984). Further east near the limit of Khoekhoe expansion, burials of cattle and people and finds of thin-walled, ochre-burnished pottery with lugs date to younger than 900 BP near Middledrift, though placenames and reports of Cape Coastal pottery suggest a Khoe presence as far as the Mpame area (Derricourt 1977; Feely 1987).

As well as documenting pastoralist settlement, the Seacow Valley offers by far the best evidence of terminal Holocene hunter-gatherers in the Karoo Biome, built from intensive survey (Sampson 1985a) and excavation of rock-shelters with poorly developed stratigraphies, overcome by using close vertical and horizontal controls (Sampson *et al.* 1989). As well as the quartz-tempered Khoekhoe ceramics previously mentioned, grass-fibre-tempered bowls decorated with stamp-impressed motifs and mainly used for cooking are found (Fig. 9.18). Associated in the ethnohistoric record with hunter-gatherers, they are widely distributed across the Karoo and southern Free State. Different clays were used for their manufacture, shale-derived for the Khoekhoe pots, dolerite-derived for the grass-tempered wares (Bollong *et al.* 1997); size and shape attributes are also quite distinct (Sampson and Sadr 1999). Stratigraphic evidence and direct dating (Bollong *et al.* 1993; Sampson and Vogel 1995; Bollong and Sampson 1996; Sampson *et al.* 1997) define a stylistic sequence for the grass-tempered ceramics, though attempts at reconstructing the social geography of its makers have proven difficult (Sampson 1988). Rock-shelter use intensified during warmer, wetter episodes *c.* 1100, 800 and, most notably, 400 BP, suggesting that population levels closely tracked climatic change (Bousman 1991; Sampson and Plug 1993). Drought conditions after the last of these episodes saw hunter-gatherers intensify collection of ostrich eggs as a substitute for

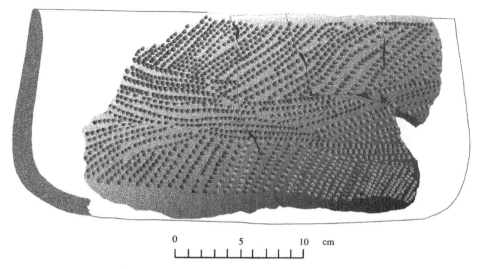

Figure 9.18   Smithfield pot from Jouberts Gif, Northern Cape, South Africa
(courtesy Garth Sampson).

declining game numbers (Sampson 1994). Earlier, however, with springbok
occurring in plague proportions in the Karoo in some years, Abbots Shelter
was used as a location for hunting them on their migratory treks (Plug
1993b).

Artefact assemblages in both the Seacow Valley and further north along the
middle Gariep have been assigned to two successive industries, the Ceramic
Wilton and the Smithfield (Sampson 1974, 1985a). It seems increasingly likely
that differences between them do not warrant such separation: the Smithfield's
characteristically long endscrapers may reflect the use of hornfels, rather than
opalines, as raw material (Humphreys 1979; Bousman 1991). In addition, backed
microliths, originally not thought of as part of the Smithfield tradition, were
still made into the late eighteenth century (Close and Sampson 1998), though
bone points were also widely used as arrow armatures. Highly distinctive
pressure-flaked projectile points and backed microliths indicate connections
with hunter-gatherers elsewhere in the southern African interior (chapter 10);
rare iron items and glass beads document contacts with Sotho-speaking farmers
(Sampson 1970).

Pressure-flaked arrowheads are also known from the Northern Cape, where
both hunter-gatherers and pastoralists engaged in exchange with agropastoralists. Red ochre from a mine at Nauga and specularite, mostly obtained
from quarries near Postmasburg, were particularly desired and widely traded.
Excavations indicate that mining was underway at Blinkklipkop (Fig. 9.19)
and Doornfontein before 1200 BP (Humphreys and Thackeray 1983) and at
Nauga before 1650 BP (D. Morris 1990c). Doornfontein assemblages thought

Figure 9.19   Blinkklipkop specularite mine, Northern Cape, South Africa. The human figures in the centre give some indication of the size of this mine.

to be the work of herders concentrate, as we have seen, close to the Gariep. Hunter-gatherers, who were probably forced into more arid areas away from the rivers, are represented by Swartkops assemblages, which reflect the addition of coarse, undecorated, often grass-tempered ceramics and rare iron objects to the preceramic backed blade dominated Springbokoog Industry (Beaumont *et al.* 1995). The Swartkops Industry can, in its terminal phase, be associated with the historic /Xam Bushmen, as well as with scraped rock engravings (J. Deacon 1986; Beaumont and Vogel 1989). At Springbokoog 11, thirteen portable engraved stones were arranged in two arcs and the high number of engravings in the general locality suggest this was an aggregation focus (D. Morris and Beaumont 1994), although /Xam extended families lived in fairly small territories (±600 km^2) and did not practise seasonal movements (J. Deacon 1986). Extending to rock art, where pecked engravings are probably the work of Khoekhoen, differences in settlement signature, ceramics and lithics between Doornfontein and Swartkops assemblages recall the contrasts between herder and hunter-gatherer sites in the south-western Cape. Occupation here was, however, much more directly affected by climatic variables: though some reach back to 1800 BP, two-thirds of dated Swartkops sites cluster after 500 BP, when cooler, wetter conditions prevailed

(Beaumont *et al.* 1995). Further east, occupation was probably also intermittent on the Ghaap Plateau, but lithic assemblages here are scraper, not backed blade, dominated (Humphreys and Thackeray 1983; Beaumont and Vogel 1989). Throughout the Northern Cape, as in the other areas discussed, the advent and expansion of European settlement had catastrophic effects on hunter-gatherers and herders alike.

CHAPTER 10

EARLY FARMING COMMUNITIES

For close on two millennia people combining cereal agriculture with stock-keeping have occupied most of southern Africa's summer rainfall zone. The rapid spread of farming, distinctive ceramics and metallurgy is generally understood as the expansion of a Bantu-speaking population. This chapter examines the evidence for this proposition, reviews what we know of these early farming communities and considers relationships between them and hunter-gatherers, before returning to how farming itself may have spread (Fig. 10.1). Traditional terminology refers to southern African farming communities as 'Iron Age', an explicit borrowing from European prehistory (Summers 1950). Though I have sometimes used this term for clarity, it seems increasingly less useful because of the emphasis placed on iron-working at the expense of other technologies, the inadequacy of stadial terms for exploring complex linguistic, economic, technological and social interactions, and its perceived insensitivity to the descendants of the communities themselves (Parkington and Hall 1987b; Maggs 1992a). Dropping it may enable us to develop more flexible and creative approaches to the archaeological record. Helpful alternatives include agropastoralists, agriculturists (Maggs and Whitelaw 1991) and early and late farming communities (Pwiti 1996a). In terms of the older literature, however, this chapter examines 'Early Iron Age' groups and principally the first millennium AD.

Origins

Exploiting both animals and indigenous cereal and root crops, by 3000 BP African societies practised diverse forms of food-production north of the Congo Basin and Serengeti. Further south, the perceived homogeneity of the material culture of the earliest agricultural groups and the fact that this was introduced rapidly and without local precursors have led archaeologists to conclude that it must reflect the physical movement of substantial numbers of people. That these assemblages occur in areas now populated by speakers of Bantu languages, which themselves demonstrably have a recent common origin, provide the basis for linking the two expansions. Farming and the presumed advantages of iron tools for land clearance and cultivation are thought to have fuelled population growth (Oliver 1966).

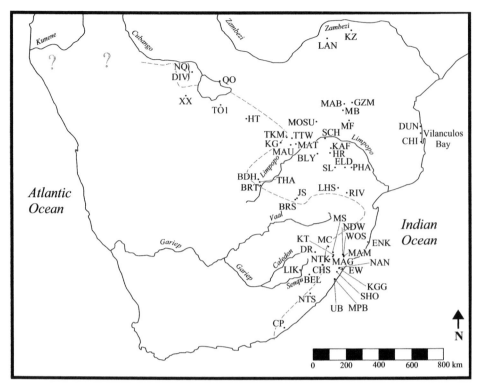

Figure 10.1   Location of archaeological sites discussed in chapter 10. Site names abbreviated thus: BDH Broadhurst; BEL Belleview; BLY Beauley; BRS Broederstroom; BRT Baratani; CHI Chibuene; CHS Collingham Shelter; CP Canasta Place; DIV Divuyu; DR Driel; DUN Dundo; ELD Eiland; ENK Enkwazini; EW Emberton Way; GZM Great Zimbabwe; HR Happy Rest; HT Hippo Tooth; JS Jubilee Shelter; KAF Klein Afrika; KG Kgaswe; KGG KwaGandaganda; KT KwaThwaleyakhe; KZ Kadzi; LAN Lanlory; LHS Lydenburg Heads Site; LIK Likoaeng; MAB Mabveni; MAG Magogo; MAM Mamba; MAT Matlapaneng; MAU Maunatlala; MB Mount Buhwa; MC Msuluzi Confluence; MF Mwenezi Farm; MOSU Mosu I; MPB Mpambanyoni; MS Mbabane Shelter; NAN Nanda; NDW Ndondonwane; NQ Nqoma; NTK Ntshekane; NTS Ntsitsana; PHA Phalaborwa; QO Qogana; RIV Riverside; SCH Schroda; SHO Shongweni; SL Silver Leaves; THA Thamaga; TKM Taukome; TO1 Toteng 1 and 3; TTW Toutswe; UB Umbeli Belli; WOS Wosi; XX /Xai/Xai. The dashed line indicates the approximate limit of Early Iron Age agropastoralist settlement.

Linguists identify the Cameroon/Nigeria border as the centre of origin for Bantu languages (Dalby 1975). Tracing relationships between them is not simple. Many classifications emphasise statistical comparison of selected vocabulary samplings (lexicostatistics), typically of words thought most resistant to change. The more laborious comparative method, which works out regular sound correspondences between languages to see if they are related, has been much less widely undertaken. Nurse (1994/95) makes the further point that many analyses use only one approach, cautioning against exclusive dependence on lexicostatistics and the pitfalls of its derivative, glottochronology. The tendency of many analysts to work with models resembling family trees in which each language has only a single ancestor, thus concealing multiple influences on its origin, is also unrealistic (Vansina 1995).

The one generally accepted division within Bantu is that between Western and Eastern languages, although debate persists on allocating some languages to one or other group (Nurse 1994/95). Vansina's (1984) reconstructions indicate that Proto-Western Bantu speakers fished, hunted, kept goats and cultivated yams and oil palm without, at first, using iron. Archaeologically, they may be represented by sites in Gabon and Congo-Brazzaville dating 3000–2300 BP (de Maret 1986; Denbow 1986). Connections between these sites and later farming communities to the south are elusive, partly because increasing aridity constrained expansion of root-crop based economies into Angola (Vansina 1994/95). Ceramics from two rather later sites in Congo-Kinshasa, Madingo-Kayes and Naviundu (Ancieux de Faveaux and de Maret 1984) may provide a link. Pottery from both emphasises comb-stamping and broad grooves organised in bands of intertwined lines and other motifs. Later facies of this Naviundu Tradition (Huffman 1989) occur in southern Zambia, north-western Botswana, including the important sites of Nqoma and Divuyu (Denbow 1990; Fig. 10.2), and northern Namibia (Sandelowsky 1979), where they may represent the arrival of the ancestral Herero language-cluster (Wilmsen 1989: 70). Others appear ancestral to the Luangwa pottery still made by Western Bantu-speakers in Zambia (Huffman 1989).

While ancestral Western Bantu-speakers moved south along the Atlantic coast and inland up rivers draining into it, Proto-Eastern Bantu speakers are thought to have spread along the rainforest's northern edge, towards the Great Lakes (Fig. 10.3). This makes ecological sense, as linguistic reconstructions suggest they became acquainted there with cereals, cattle and sheep, as well as goats (Vansina 1984; Schoenbrun 1998). Urewe ceramics occur in East Africa's Interlacustrine area from 2500 BP, frequently associated with iron-smelting debris. Though settlements have yet to be excavated and wild resources probably remained important, Urewe finds concentrate on prime agricultural land, and pollen sequences demonstrate land-clearance (Reid 1994/95). The chronological primacy of Urewe ware and its proximity to areas in which cattle, sheep and perhaps cereals had been used for several centuries make it the earliest known component of the Chifumbaze Complex, which groups together almost all the Early Iron Age assemblages of eastern, south-central and southern Africa (D. Phillipson 1993). Similarities in ceramic design traceable through

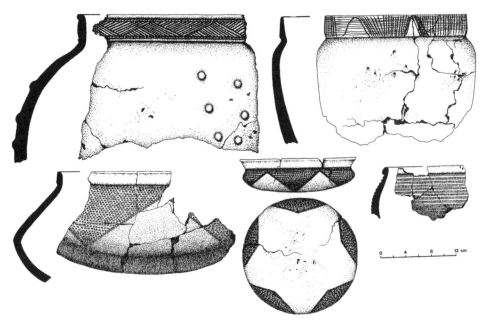

Figure 10.2   Naviundu Tradition ceramics from burial 3 at Nqoma, Botswana
(after Denbow 1990: Fig 14; courtesy Jim Denbow).

to recent pottery traditions provide an association between Chifumbaze and
Eastern Bantu-speakers (Huffman 1989).

Pottery typology: necessary evil or useful tool?

Ceramic typology is central to current discussions of the expansion of iron-
using farmers across southern Africa. The most widely used approach is that of
Huffman (1980), who employs multidimensional analysis of three variables –
vessel profile, decoration layout and motif – to reconstruct different ceramic
types. The method reliably separates the ceramics of known contemporary
groups, unlike others emphasising vessel shape and decoration technique. Since
ceramic design is part of a much larger code and overlaps considerably with
designs employed in other media, such as beadwork (Evers 1988), it may identify groups of people among whom these codes were shared, learned and transmitted. Huffman (1989) argues that since large zones of ceramic uniformity are
often punctuated by short distances over which style changes substantially,
these changes in non-verbal communication may also mirror patterning in ver-
bal communication (i.e. language). If this is correct, ceramics can thus be used
to trace the movements of people, though not necessarily of specific social or
political groupings. Counter-examples certainly exist to this equation (Collett

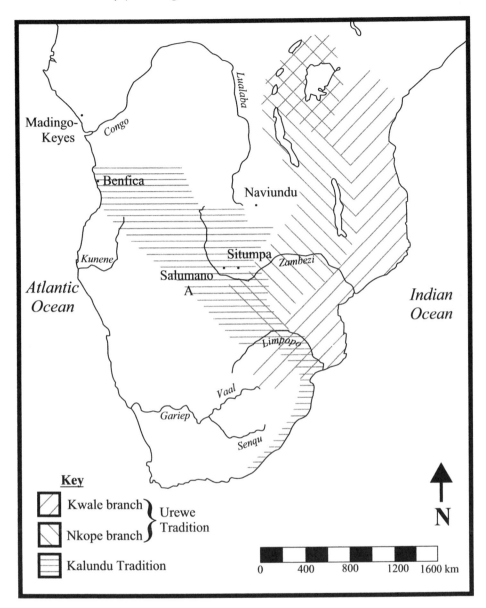

Figure 10.3   Outline of main movements in the southward expansion of farming
communities beyond the Equator. The locations are also shown of
sites lying north of the Zambezi River which are mentioned in the
text.

1987; M. Hall 1987; Vansina 1995) and I pick up on some of the difficulties
with this approach below. However, since Huffman's stance currently dominates research into early farming communities in southern Africa the ensuing
discussion follows his framework and is partly summarised in Fig. 2.18.

Within the Chifumbaze Complex a broad distinction exists between different sets of assemblages, though Collett (1988) expresses reservations as to whether all form part of the same tradition. One, D. Phillipson's (1977) 'eastern stream', essentially coincides with Huffman's (1989) Urewe Tradition. Two divisions are discernible. Assemblages belonging to the Kwale branch extend along the coast from Kenya to KwaZulu-Natal. Inland, and reaching from southern Tanzania through Malawi and eastern Zambia into Zimbabwe, others are grouped as the Nkope branch. Stretching from Angola through western Zambia, Botswana and Zimbabwe into South Africa a third series of assemblages form the Kalundu Tradition.

The Urewe Tradition

Details of the ceramics characterising these divisions and their constituent units can be found in the relevant site reports. For our purposes, only the most common features require emphasis. In southern Africa, recent work distinguishes two phases of the Kwale branch. The earliest, termed 'Silver Leaves', occurs near Maputo (Morais 1988; Sinclair *et al.* 1993a) and inland in Swaziland (Price-Williams 1980), Zimbabwe (Huffman 1978a) and South Africa's Northern Province (Klapwijk 1974); sites are associated with arable soils and iron ore deposits. Dating 250–430, Silver Leaves ceramics have high proportions of fluted rims on bowls and bevelled rims on jars (Klapwijk and Huffman 1996). A later expression of this Kwale branch, termed Mzonjani, occurs at Silver Leaves and Eiland, Northern Province, but most sites, including Mzonjani itself, occur in the coastal belt of KwaZulu-Natal. Dating 420–580, ceramics lack bevels and flutes, but display continuity in profile and design layout (Fig. 10.4). Since the Silver Leaves phase is only slightly younger than the Kwale type-site in Kenya, this implies very rapid movement along the coast, perhaps partly by boat (Klapwijk 1974), with only occasional moves inland. Subsequently people making Mzonjani-derived ceramics settled more widely in the interior, including the well-known site of Broederstroom near Pretoria, which dates 550–650 (Mason 1986; Huffman 1993, 1998); several sites in south-eastern Botswana, such as Baratani, appear to be a related expression of the same ceramic tradition there (A. Campbell *et al.* 1996).

Assemblages attributable to the Nkope branch of Urewe appear south of the Zambezi from the fifth century, with Kadzi a very early site (Pwiti 1996a). Ziwa represents an early phase in eastern Zimbabwe, with Gokomere (Fig. 10.5) deriving jointly from it and from Bambata pottery (Huffman 1994); it is found both in Zimbabwe and in central Mozambique (Sinclair *et al.* 1993a). A subsequent phase is represented by Zhizo in western Zimbabwe and the Shashe–Limpopo Basin and by Taukome in eastern Botswana (Huffman 1974; Denbow 1986); related sites occur in Kruger National Park (Meyer 1988a). Dating from the

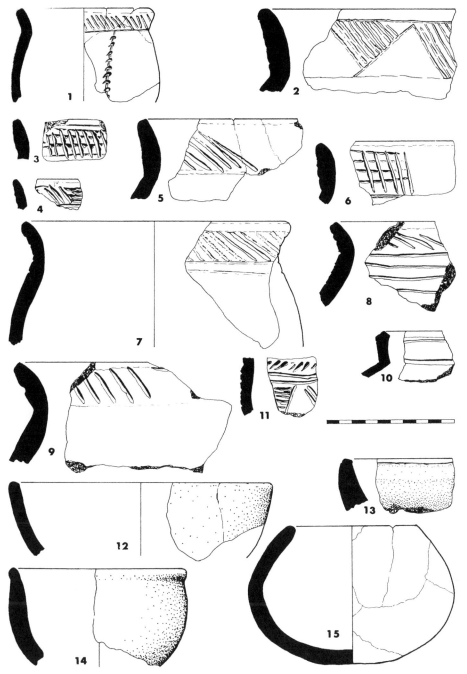

Figure 10.4   Mzonjani ceramics (after Maggs 1980b: Fig. 5; courtesy Natal Museum).

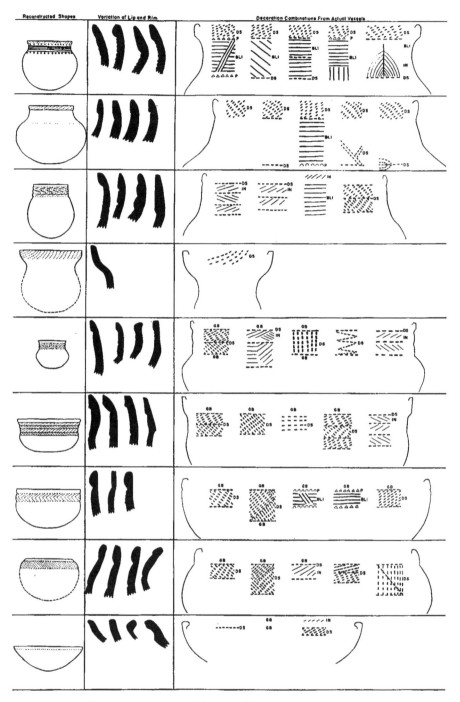

Figure 10.5 Gokomere ceramics (after Huffman 1970: Fig. 8; courtesy Tom Huffman). Key features of Gokomere pottery include an emphasis on comb-stamping, especially on rim bands, with broadline incisions on the neck (J.O. Vogel 1978).

seventh to tenth centuries, Zhizo is ancestral to the Toutswe tradition which persisted in eastern Botswana into the thirteenth century and saw important developments in socio-political complexity (chapter 11). While this discussion has concentrated on southern Africa, it is important to stress that the Zambezi was far from a barrier to people living along it. Dambwa pottery in northern Botswana and Chinhoyi ceramics in north-central Zimbabwe both have close counterparts across the river in Zambia (Huffman 1979; J.O. Vogel 1984; Denbow 1986).

The Kalundu Tradition

In south-eastern southern Africa Maggs (1984a) and Morais (1988) argue that Silver Leaves/Mzonjani assemblages, which they refer to as 'Matola', were ancestral to later ceramic occurrences. However, other analyses suggest they are not closely related to the Msuluzi assemblages that postdate 650, but derive from earlier components of Huffman's Kalundu Tradition further north, such as Happy Rest (Whitelaw 1996). As discussed previously, Bambata ware may be an early expression of this tradition, with Toteng 1 and 3 possible village sites (Huffman 1994; Reid *et al.* 1998). Though few and accompanied by younger Silver Leaves or Gokomere pottery, Bambata sherds from Mount Buhwa, Mabveni and Great Zimbabwe may also come from village settlements. Elsewhere Bambata pottery occurs as a potentially exchanged item in apparently hunter-gatherer contexts. Interestingly, however, some of its decoration combinations can be matched at Benfica, Angola (Dos Santos and Ervedosa 1970), which has third-century dates almost identical to those from Toteng.

Such a north-western derivation for Kalundu, which leaves unexplained how it first got to Angola, rests upon very isolated observations that lack extensive settlement excavations or evidence for subsistence and iron-working. Indeed, Denbow's (1990) suggestion that many features of the Benfica ceramics align them with those from Madingo-Kayes would place them within the Naviundu Tradition. This could provide a geographically more plausible picture, leaving Kalundu origins to southern Zambia, where, as we have seen, dates from Salumano A and Situmpa *may* indicate an Iron Age presence in the terminal centuries BC (D. Phillipson 1989). Connections between Angola and the Chifumbaze Complex are, however, suggested by the fact that terms for cereal agriculture and cattle-keeping in Angola's Western Bantu languages are all of Eastern Bantu origin, supporting a scenario in which these domesticates replaced earlier root-crop based economies (Vansina 1994/95). Huffman's reconstructions require this to have happened much earlier, but cattle were present near Luanda by the ninth century (Lanfranchi and Clist 1991).

While Kalundu's origins need further research, its subsequent development is becoming clearer. A post-Bambata phase is represented by fifth- to

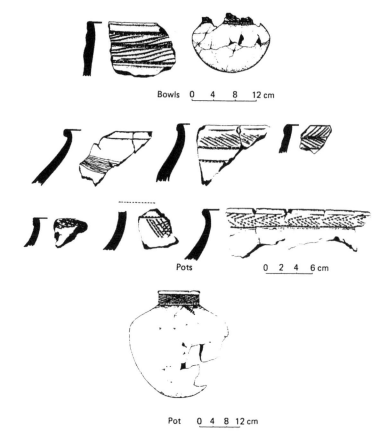

Figure 10.6   Happy Rest phase ceramics from Maunatlala, Botswana (after Denbow 1986: Fig. 2; courtesy Jim Denbow).

seventh-century sites like Happy Rest, Klein Afrika and Maunatlala in the far northern transVaal/eastern Botswana (Prinsloo 1974, 1989; Denbow 1986; Fig. 10.6). Later phases are represented at the Lydenburg Heads site (LHS; Whitelaw 1996) and by the succession of Msuluzi, Ndondonwane and Ntshekane phases in KwaZulu-Natal with dates from the seventh to tenth centuries (Fig. 10.7). The last two phases also occur further south in the Eastern Cape (Prins and Grainger 1993; Nogwaza 1994; Binneman 1996b).

In the transVaal, later Kalundu phases include Klingbeil (Evers 1980) and Eiland (Evers 1975, 1981). Klingbeil, of tenth-century date, is known principally from Northern Province. Eiland's wider distribution extends south to the Magaliesberg and from Kruger National Park westward into southeastern Botswana and also east into Mozambique (Duarte 1976); Kgopolwe is a lowveld variant in Mpumalanga, and Mutamba another north and south of the Soutpansberg (Loubser 1991a). Throughout this area Eiland is the last

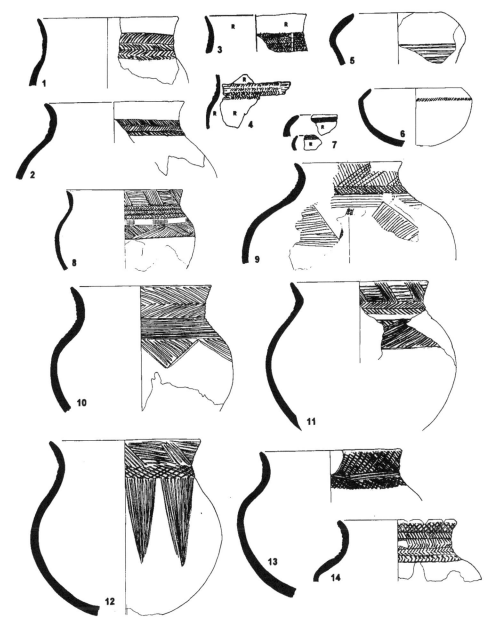

Figure 10.7   Msuluzi and Ndondonwane phase ceramics from sites in
KwaZulu-Natal (after Whitelaw 1996: Fig. 4; courtesy South African
Archaeological Society). The pottery illustrated is taken from
Magogo (Maggs and Ward 1984), Msuluzi Confluence (Maggs 1980a)
and Ndondonwane (Maggs 1984b; Loubser 1993b).

expression of the Chifumbaze Complex, dating to the eleventh/twelfth centuries. Broadhurst and other sites indicate a still later survival in Botswana, perhaps facilitated by wealth in cattle if we are to judge from the size of their byres and the many glass beads with a child burial at Moritsane (Denbow 1981, 1986; Fig. 10.8). Still later, and dating to the seventeenth century, Eiland-derived ceramics are known from sites in Botswana historically associated with the Kgalakgadi people (A. Campbell *et al.* 1991).

Arguments over individual assemblages continue to revise this picture, but three general points are important. First, some sites, like KwaGandaganda (Whitelaw 1994a), were occupied for many generations, while several (e.g. Eiland, Silver Leaves and LHS: Evers 1981; Klapwijk and Evers 1987; Whitelaw 1996) have multiple occupations. Without carefully excavated, large ceramic assemblages (and many of them from the same area) there is a danger of drawing chronological and typological inferences from mixed samples (Maggs 1984a). Secondly, Huffman's (1989) argument that ceramic style correlates with distinct groups of people sharing a common cultural code tends to encourage a migrationist view of cultural change. Though this cannot simply be dismissed out of prejudice (Sutton 1994/95), in each case archaeologists must also consider alternative explanations for change and variability in material culture and show why such movements should have occurred. Equally, relationships between putative earlier and later settlers need to be examined, as in Mpumalanga where a late variant of the Urewe Tradition survived into the seventh/eighth centuries, well after Kalundu ceramics appeared elsewhere south of the Limpopo (Whitelaw 1996).

More fundamentally, we must recognise that although ceramic typologies provide a useful, and indeed necessary, tool for our research, they remain an archaeological construct, just like any other spatio-temporal grouping of material remains (Hodder 1978). The current emphasis on them in studies of southern African farming communities is by no means mirrored in other parts of the world and risks drawing attention away from more broadly anthropological and historical concerns towards a Childe-like equation of pots and people (M. Hall 1983). One practical difficulty is the emphasis that Huffman's multidimensional analysis places on decoration layout and motif. While some characterisations may thus be based on quite small samples, undecorated ceramics, which may nevertheless have been very important functionally, tend not to be considered further. One way round this is suggested by Pikirayi's (1997a) observation that in Zimbabwe several studies, including physicochemical analyses and experimental work, have been undertaken to investigate production technology, function and exchange. Though expensive and time-consuming, they do provide the basis for alternative classificatory systems (e.g. Sinclair 1987). Future research on southern African farming communities may increasingly depart from the analytical procedures used to create the entities discussed above.

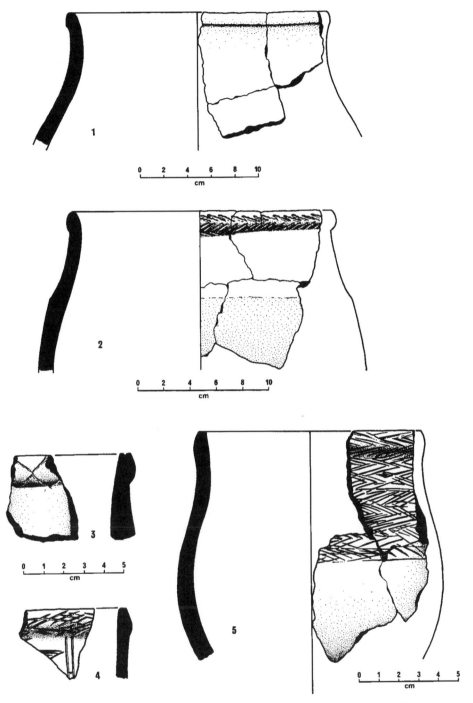

Figure 10.8   Eiland phase ceramics from Broadhurst, Botswana (after Denbow 1981: Fig. 3; courtesy South African Archaeological Society).

Subsistence ecology

With ceramic typologies arguably consuming too much archaeological energy, one underresearched area is the subsistence base of early farmers. Its animal component is fairly well understood, but this is less true of domestic and wild plant foods, partly because flotation remains too rarely used and seed taphonomy poorly understood (Jonsson 1998). Nevertheless, pearl millet (*Pennisetum americanum*), finger millet (*Eleusine coracana*) and the normally higher-yielding sorghum (*Sorghum bicolor*) were clearly the principal crops (Fig. 10.9). Grindstones in many areas typically have long narrow grooves suitable for processing small, relatively soft millet grains (Maggs and Ward 1984; Fig. 10.10). Pulses (Bambara groundnuts, *Voandzeia subterranea*, and cowpeas, *Vigna sinensis*) and cucurbits were also grown (Table 10.1). Where grown together, the cereals need ≥350 mm rainfall during the growing season, an annual rainfall of ≥500 mm and nocturnal temperatures of ≥15°C (Huffman 1996a). These requirements limited where early farmers could settle to the Miombo and Savanna Biomes. Excluded from much of the sub-continent's western half by aridity and confined in the south during the first millennium to bushveld areas of the transVaal, declining summer rainfall restricted them to a diminishing belt close to the coast and north of 33.5°S (Maggs 1994/95); sites such as Canasta Place mark the southernmost limit of Chifumbaze settlement (Nogwaza 1994).

Figure 10.9   Women threshing sorghum (*Sorghum bicolor*), Buhera District, Zimbabwe (courtesy Anders Lindahl).

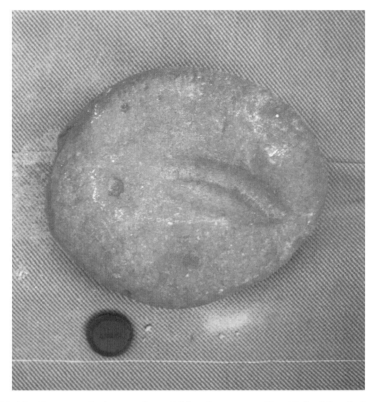

Figure 10.10   Lower grindstone from Ndondonwane, KwaZulu-Natal, South
Africa. The narrow groove is typical of Chifumbaze Complex
grindstones in South Africa and was particularly suitable for
grinding sorghum and pearl millet seeds.

Village locations show a keen preference for fertile alluvial and colluvial soils, typically close to water and with ready access to wood for building and fuel (Huffman 1979; Meyer 1984; Maggs 1994/95; Pwiti 1996a; J. van Schalkwyk 1998). In KwaZulu-Natal, Mzonjani sites lie almost wholly within 6 km of the shore, a pattern once interpreted as reflecting slash-and-burn cultivation of coastal forests and the desirability of shellfish as a protein source, given an apparent absence of evidence for livestock (M. Hall 1981). But taphonomic factors discussed below may account for this, while proximity to iron ore sources and higher coastal rainfall also demonstrably influenced Mzonjani site locations (Whitelaw and Moon 1996). Altered patterns of iron-production and less arid summers subsequently facilitated movement further inland by makers of Msu-luzi pottery (Whitelaw and Moon 1996).

Other areas in which early farming communities established themselves are today unsuitable for cereal cultivation so their presence most probably reflects wetter conditions. One such region in the ninth to thirteenth centuries seems

Table 10.1 *Domesticated plants known from early farming contexts of the first millennium*

Site	Locality	Species	Reference
Kadzi	Northern Zimbabwe	Finger millet	Pwiti 1996a
Kgaswe	Eastern Botswana	Pearl millet, sorghum	Kiyaga-Mulindwa 1993
Lanlory	Northern Zimbabwe	Cowpeas	Huffman 1979
Leopard's Kopje	Matabeleland	Bambara groundnuts, cowpeas, sorghum	Huffman 1974
Magogo	Thukela Basin	Cucurbits, finger millet, pearl millet, sorghum	Maggs and Ward 1984
Matlapaneng	Okavango Delta	Cowpeas, cucurbits, pearl millet, sorghum	Denbow 1986
Maunatlala	Eastern Botswana	Cucurbits	Denbow 1986
Ndondonwane	Thukela Basin	Pearl millet	Maggs 1984b
Nqoma	Tsodilo Hills	Cucurbits (?), pearl millet, sorghum	Denbow 1986
Schroda	Shashe–Limpopo Basin	Sorghum	Hanisch 1981
Shongweni	KwaZulu-Natal	Finger millet, pearl millet	Davies 1975; cf. M. Hall and Vogel 1980
Silver Leaves	Northern Province	Pearl millet	Klapwijk 1974

to have been the Shashe–Limpopo Basin, where Zhizo settlements and the later Mapungubwe polity depended on cultivation, as well as herding (Huffman 1996a). Direct evidence includes numerous grainbin foundations and finds of sorghum at Schroda (Hanisch 1981), though Mwenezi Farm documents intensive harvesting of wild grasses (Jonsson 1998). For the same period, xylem analysis of charcoals suggests that drier conditions in south-eastern southern Africa impacted heavily on Ndondonwane/Ntshekane site numbers (Prins 1994/95).

As among recent southern African populations (Quin 1959; Scudder 1962), wild plant foods were doubtless important alongside cultivated ones. Marula exploitation is well attested in Zimbabwe (Jonsson 1998) and Botswana, mongongo in the Tsodilo Hills (Denbow 1986) and marula and other species at Ndondonwane (Maggs 1984b). Shellfish were certainly significant in the diets of many coastal farmers. Brown mussels (*Perna perna*), which are numerous, energy rich and easy to collect, were overwhelmingly preferred, but without impacting on their viability (M. Hall 1981; Horwitz *et al.* 1991). With Mzonjani settlements located near the coast, surviving shell middens in KwaZulu-Natal probably represent specialist visits to the shore by later farmers living further inland, perhaps on a seasonal basis as recently in Mozambique (Earthy 1933); quartz inclusions in pottery at Emberton Way suggest such visits came from 20–40 km away (Horwitz *et al.* 1991) and sites like KwaGandaganda (Whitelaw 1994a) may represent the inland aspect of this cycle.

In most faunal assemblages domesticates – principally cattle, sheep and goats – are more common than game (Plug 1996a). Identifying breeds is difficult, but humped, as well as humpless, cattle may have been present by 1000 (Voigt 1983). Chickens were also kept (Plug 1993c), while dogs first appear in the seventh century (Plug 1996a). Identifications of domestic pig at Ndondonwane (Voigt and von den Driesch 1984) remain unconfirmed. Caprines (mostly sheep rather than goats) were generally more numerous into the eighth century, when they increasingly cede primacy to cattle (Plug and Voigt 1985). However, this pattern, which may represent eating rather than stockholding patterns, is not invariable, and cattle may be more common on several older sites in Zambia (Plug 1981b). Though M. Hall (1986, 1988) argues that cattle are absent from Silver Leaves/Mzonjani sites, this is not always so (Plug 1989). The presence of sheep, and of grazing as well as browsing antelope, indicates that more open savanna woodlands suitable for cattle must have been present.

Huffman (1990a) has suggested that low cattle numbers in archaeozoological assemblages reflect poor preservation, ritual destruction of bones and differential slaughter rather than the reality of past stockholding patterns. He argues that phytolith analysis of animal byres and dung-lined pits confirms that bone counts alone are unreliable. At Broederstroom, for example, though the cattle:sheep ratio is reported as 1:42, several cattle byres have been identified in this way (Huffman 1993). However, the methodology used in these phytolith analyses remains unpublished in detail and few Iron Age faunas, including those from Broederstroom, have yet been examined from a taphonomic perspective. Reaching a clear conclusion from these arguments is difficult, and perhaps no general pattern exists. While cattle seem to have become more numerically and perhaps culturally important after 700 in some areas, notably the eastern Kalahari (Denbow 1986), contrasting patterns of livestock utilisation are also evident within the same ecological zone. At Msuluzi Confluence (Voigt 1980) and Wosi (Voigt and Peters 1994), for example, surprisingly high numbers of young caprines were slaughtered, but at Ntshekane most were mature (Maggs and Michael 1976).

Hunting played a variable part in subsistence strategies, and meat may also have been obtained from hunter-gatherers. At Kadzi hunting appears to have been particularly important, focusing on buffalo and impala, and stock-keeping may have been curtailed by tsetse fly infestation and other livestock diseases

(Plug 1997). Kruger National Park, where agricultural potential was limited, is another area where cattle and sheep were apparently few in number. Here impala (*Aepyceros melampus*), Cape buffalo, Burchell's zebra and blue wildebeest were preferred prey. Their mortality profiles suggest communal hunting with pit-traps or corrals (Plug 1989). Fish and freshwater shellfish were also sometimes eaten (Plug 1989, 1993c).

The extent to which early farming communities impacted on their environment varied. In the former Transkei they occupied much of the lower-altitude wooded areas, largely ignoring higher-elevation grasslands, which must therefore be natural, not anthropogenic, in origin (Feely 1987). On the other hand, the presence of nyala (*Tragelaphus angasii*) in several Thukela Basin faunas and its absence there today document progressive clearance of dense riverine woodlands (Maggs 1994/95). That some sites were occupied for several generations must have placed heavy demands on local ecologies, especially as regards wood for building purposes and fuel. At Ntsitsana the later appearance of cattle coincided with a decline in woody species and the presence of the pioneer weed *Urochloa*, suggesting ecological degradation through clearance of forest patches (Prins 1994/95). Elsewhere, as in south-western Zambia, settlements may have shifted more frequently in cycles of slash-and-burn cultivation as soil fertility declined (J.O. Vogel 1984).

Metal-working and other technologies

Despite the importance accorded iron agricultural tools in explaining the spread of farming and frequent finds of production debris (furnace fragments, tuyères, slag), metal objects are rare. Divuyu and Nqoma in Botswana's Tsodilo Hills offer the largest and best-preserved samples of both iron and copper artefacts (D. Miller 1996). There and at KwaGandaganda (D. Miller and Whitelaw 1994) and Broederstroom (Friede 1977), iron was produced as inhomogeneous iron-steel blooms. Techniques were simple, with no sign of casting, wire-drawing or hot working other than cyclical **annealing**. Smelting used simple bowl furnaces (D. Miller and van der Merwe 1994), though one Zimbabwean natural draught furnace may be of first-millennium date (Prendergast 1975). Jewellery (bangles, beads, pendants, etc.) constitutes by far the largest number of finds, but arrows, adzes, chisels, points and spatulae are also known (Figs. 10.11 and 10.12). This may suggest recycling until fragments were too small to be welded together for reuse (D. Miller 1996), possibly implying that production was neither straightforward nor easy. However, the emphasis on jewellery, especially in the much larger Nqoma assemblage, may reflect its use as a means of differentiating between those with and without ready access to metal, especially given the fact that all the metal at both Tsodilo Hills sites was introduced, as ore or in finished form, over some considerable distance (Denbow 1999).

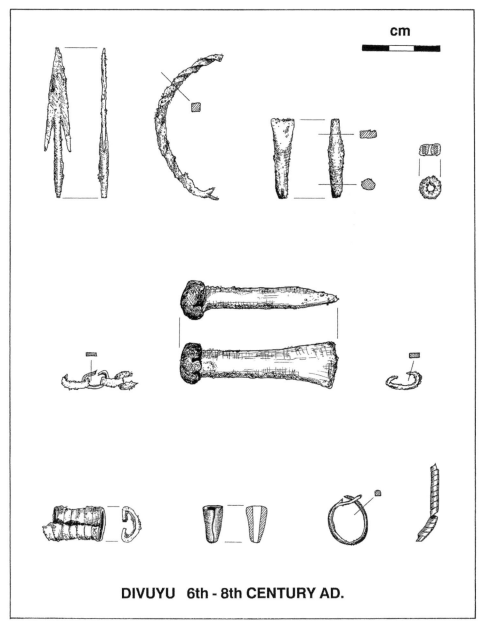

DIVUYU   6th - 8th CENTURY AD.

Figure 10.11   Metal artefacts from Divuyu, Botswana (courtesy Duncan Miller
and Philip Barrett). All in iron unless otherwise indicated. First
row: arrowhead; bangle; bar; bead. Second row: chain (one link, in
copper); chisel; clip. Third row: fused clips; conical tube (in copper);
earring (in copper); helix (in copper).

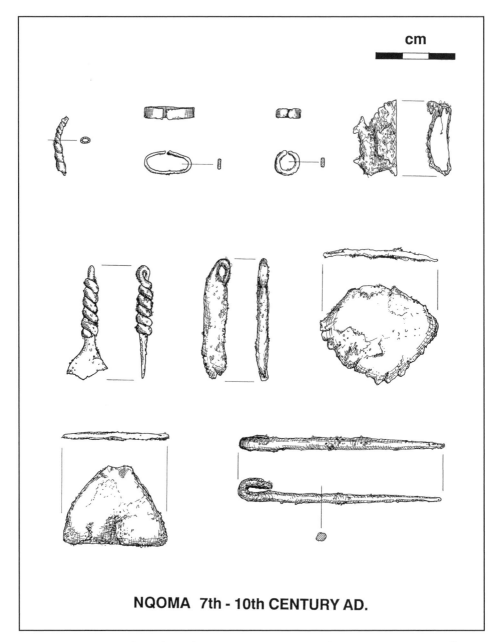

Figure 10.12 Metal artefacts from Nqoma, Botswana (courtesy Duncan Miller and Philip Barrett). All in iron. First row: helix; link; link; lump. Second row: pendant; pendant; plate. Third row: plate; point.

Smelting and forging slags are often difficult to distinguish, but forging evidently took place in the central areas of many settlements. Contrary to the practice of recent southern African Bantu-speakers (Huffman 1990a), smelting may also have been undertaken on some sites. Though assessments are complicated by deliberate dismantling of some furnaces prior to deposition of the debris else-where (Maggs 1980a), possible furnace bowls occur at Ndondonwane (Loubser 1993b), Magogo (Maggs and Ward 1984) and Beauley (J. van Schalkwyk 1998). More compellingly, slag analyses show that smelting took place near the central cattle byre at KwaGandaganda, suggesting that any anti-social qualities were dealt with differrently or did not exist (D. Miller and Whitelaw 1994). A pos-sible compromise situation is indicated at Ndondonwane, where pre-smelting operations such as ore crushing and charcoal preparation took place on the site's periphery (L. van Schalkwyk *et al.* 1997).

Iron ore is widely distributed in southern Africa, but some sites clearly pro-duced more than others. At Msuluzi Confluence this may have been for trade with hunter-gatherers (Maggs 1980a), but at Mamba I (L. van Schalkwyk 1994a) it forms part of a pattern in which many settlements ceased to produce their own iron towards the end of the first millennium (Prins and Grainger 1993; L. van Schalkywk 1994/95). Copper was also used for jewellery. Beads at Kwa-Gandaganda (D. Miller and Whitelaw 1994) and Broederstroom (Friede 1977) may derive from Phalaborwa, where mines were exploited from the eighth cen-tury (van der Merwe and Scully 1971). Salt was also probably widely traded. Spring sources in Mpumalanga were exploited in the first millennium (Evers 1975, 1981) and ceramic strainers from Divuyu were perhaps used to recover salt from saline ash (Wilmsen 1989). How these and other exchangeable items participated in the development of social complexity is among the topics addressed below.

Settlement organisation and worldview

Many early farming villages have been located during building operations and/or are heavily eroded; pits, middens and grainbin foundations are the principal surviving features (Evers 1977; Maggs 1980a; Mason 1986; Huffman 1993; J. van Schalkwyk 1998). Houses were made using ***daga*** plaster on a pole framework. Floors were sometimes specially constructed with gravel porches (Hanisch 1981), or built of *daga* (Mason 1986; Huffman 1993; Loubser 1993b; Fig. 10.13), with fireplaces central or built into the floor and offset to one side. Fundamental to understanding the internal structure of these villages and their inhabitants' worldview is a model of settlement organisation derived from Ku-per's (1980) study of modern South African homesteads (Fig. 10.14). Its basis is the recognition that cattle are an integrating feature of social life, owned by men who use them in political relationships, sacrifice to ancestors and bridewealth payments. Settlements are organised around a central byre in which cattle are kept. The community's leading man lives at its apex, opposite the entrance, with wives and junior relatives lower down and further away to left and right. Important individuals, normally men, are buried below or close to the byre (often in a sitting position), grain is stored there in dung-lined pits (under the protection of ancestral spirits) and men congregate nearby for discussion, court

Figure 10.13 *Daga* floor of a house, Ndondonwane, KwaZulu-Natal, South Africa. Pottery and grindstones are visible on the floor.

judgements and other activities. This Central Cattle Pattern (CCP; Fig. 10.15), organising settlement space through the oppositions of male:female, public:domestic, top:bottom and right:left, characterises southern Africa's patrilineal Eastern Bantu-speaking inhabitants today (Huffman 1990a).

Figure 10.14   Modern Zulu homestead, Thukela Basin, KwaZulu-Natal, South
Africa, showing the central position of the cattle byre and the
arrangement of houses around this.

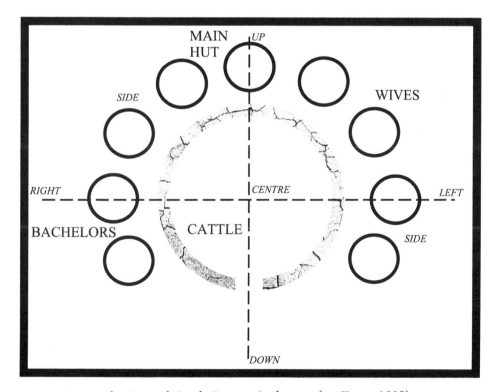

Figure 10.15   The Central Cattle Pattern (redrawn after Kuper 1980).

The CCP is traceable archaeologically at settlements in South Africa attributable on ceramic grounds to Sotho/Tswana-speakers (Evers 1984). It is also identifiable at Toutswe sites in Botswana (Denbow 1986) and on a range of first-millennium settlements, with Kgaswe, also in Botswana, one of the most convincing. There pole-and-*daga* houses are grouped around a central cattle byre containing some male burials; other men, along with women, were buried beyond this, among the houses (Denbow 1999). Broederstroom (Huffman 1990a) and Happy Rest (Prinsloo 1989; Steyn *et al.* 1994) have also produced burials from within cattle enclosures, with one at each site accompanied by items such as cowrie shells of Indian Ocean origin and ivory ornaments that are ethnographically associated with high-status individuals.

Broederstroom, Kgaswe, KwaGandaganda, Nanda and Ndondonwane (Denbow 1999) are among the few first-millennium villages excavated on a sufficiently large scale to offer a reasonably coherent picture of total settlement organisation, but only Ndondonwane has a short-lived, single ceramic phase occupation (L. van Schalkwyk *et al.* 1997; Fig. 10.16). Here iron-working areas and hearths possibly used for cooking meat occur close to the byre; most associated ceramics seem to be eating and drinking vessels. The byre was probably surrounded by a fence, against which dismantled furnace fragments, ash, ceramic sculptures and ivory-working debris were dumped (Loubser 1993b).

Figure 10.16   Ndondonwane, KwaZulu-Natal, South Africa, showing excavations in progress in the central cattle byre.

Though the sculptures probably operated in a more communal, public domain, the other activities are all consistent with this having been a male focus, as predicted by the CCP. Nevertheless, identifying the CCP from only some of its features runs the risk of ignoring potentially informative variability in settlement organisation, such as the apparently peripheral location of the cattle byre at Ntsitsana (Prins and Grainger 1993). Since this is among the criticisms advanced against the dominance of the CCP in current interpretations, it is important to examine these in detail and to consider intriguing evidence of differences between recent Nguni and Sotho/Tswana ethnography and the archaeological record of the first millennium.

Though cattle numbers may be dramatically underrepresented in archaeological faunal assemblages, even a single cow implies the presence of a total breeding population of 100 animals or more (Huffman 1998). Yet the social significance of cattle, as of anything else, is not solely, or even principally, determined by their numbers. Arguments (M. Hall 1986, 1988) that take at face value the archaeozoological scarcity of cattle before the late first millennium to propose that they could not be used in bridewealth and political transactions therefore miss the point. Loss of thousands of cattle to rinderpest did not prevent early twentieth-century Shona people in Zimbabwe from exchanging cattle for wives, although it did affect the average number of animals used (Holleman 1952).

The further suggestion that early farmers in south-eastern southern Africa could not have kept cattle because insufficient open vegetation existed prior to widespread land clearance is also flawed, as we saw above. Identification using phytolith analysis of a cattle byre and dung-lined pits at Riverside, a sixth-century site in Mpumalanga's lowlands, may support this (Huffman 1998). Its ceramics are transitional between designs used at Broederstroom and on older Mzonjani sites. This, and the attribution of Broederstroom itself to the Urewe Tradition's Kwale branch (Klapwijk and Huffman 1996), could imply that Mzonjani/Silver Leaves settlements were also associated with cattle-keeping and the CCP. However, poor faunal preservation, the limited size of the excavations and the presence of three different occupation phases leave this question unanswered. Also unresolved are two other issues: were cattle-keeping and the CCP original features of the Kalundu Tradition, or something acquired from earlier Urewe settlers after Kalundu people moved into the subcontinent (Huffman 1998)? And were Divuyu and Nqoma, with their Naviundu Tradition ceramics, organised spatially along the very different pattern characteristic of Western Bantu speakers (Huffman 1989)? Preliminary comments as to the presence of both male and female burials in middens on site peripheries and the lack of central cattle enclosures suggest that this may have been so (Denbow 1999).

More important still are broader theoretical challenges to the CCP's dominance in current Iron Age research. Lane (1994/95), for example, emphasises the importance of considering the specific historical context of the anthropological evidence from which it derives. He also questions how basic structural relationships between its constituent elements could have been maintained over almost 2000 years, given that farmers interacted considerably with both pastoralists and hunter-gatherers, as well as among themselves. He further notes that evidence for quite marked changes in the spatial structure of settlements over recent centuries (M. Hall 1984; chapter 12) opens up the possibility of similar changes over a longer timescale. Lastly, by stressing a fixed and idealised representation of space, the CCP adopts a passive view of how material culture operates within living societies at the expense of considering variability in settlement organisation and worldview (for an early contrary standpoint in Iron Age research see Davison 1988). All these points establish research agendas for the future, and Huffman (1997a) stresses that the CCP, while a normative model of past cognitive structures emphasising the general rather than the particular, does not foreclose on the latter's investigation. Instead, the question may rather be one of analytical scale. Nevertheless, recent excavations suggest that while the CCP was a key structuring principle of early farming communities in much of southern Africa, important differences with later practice and belief can also be identified.

Among the datasets encouraging this feeling are fragmentary ceramic figurines and mask fragments from several sites. The most spectacular examples, reassembled from finds made at LHS, had clearly been placed in pits, perhaps for storage or disposal (Fig. 10.17). The smaller masks were probably fixed to posts when in use, but at least two more elaborately decorated examples could have been worn. Ivory and bone lozenges may have been used in their decoration, and traces of specularite and white paint indicate they were also coloured to offset the red of the fired clay (Inskeep and Maggs 1975). Whitelaw's (1996) reassessment of the site's ceramics suggests that bands of hatching on the lower part of the heads indicate a ninth/tenth-century age, younger than previously reported radiocarbon determinations and broadly the same age as similar elements of ceramic sculpture (large eyes, horns, crocodile-like jaws) from Ndondonwane (Maggs 1984b; Loubser 1993b). This site and several others have also produced animal and human figurines, of which those from Schroda are best known (Hanisch 1981).

Though not produced by Nguni- or most Sotho/Tswana-speakers today, such figurines occur on sites of the Zimbabwe Tradition and were made until recently by Shona, Venda and north-east Sotho groups. Loubser (1993b) notes that both the Venda and the north-east Sotho use figurines and masks in male and female initiation ceremonies normally carried out near the assembly areas and cattle byres of rulers. The coincidence with the location of such finds at Ndondonwane is striking. Similarities also exist between features of modern reed and grass masks and the crocodile sculptures there.

The faces of the Lydenburg heads carry scarification marks (Evers 1982) that are also present on human figurines from Magogo (Maggs and Ward 1984) and

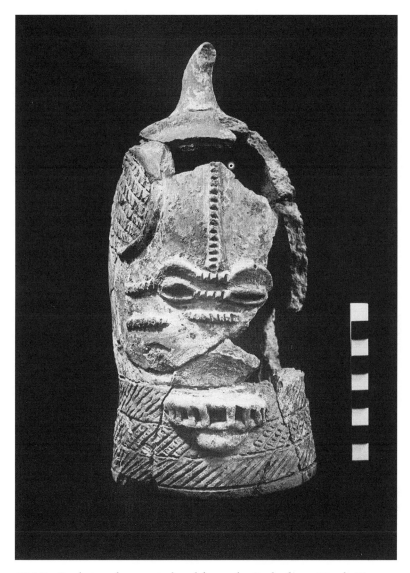

Figure 10.17   Sculptured ceramic head from the Lydenburg Heads Site, Mpumalanga, South Africa (courtesy Ray Inskeep).

Schroda (Hanisch 1981). Jewellery is also widely attested, principally as ostrich eggshell and giant landsnail (*Metachatina*) shell beads (Ward and Maggs 1988) and drilled canine teeth; at Nanda, cowries with chipped edges could have been sewn on to clothing (Whitelaw 1993). Another form of bodily modification (dental alteration) is again indicated by the Lydenburg heads (A. Morris 1993). Filing and/or removal during life of the upper and/or lower incisors of both men and women is well documented at several Chifumbaze sites (Fig. 10.18; Huffman 1990a). Ritual disposal of the removed teeth to keep them away

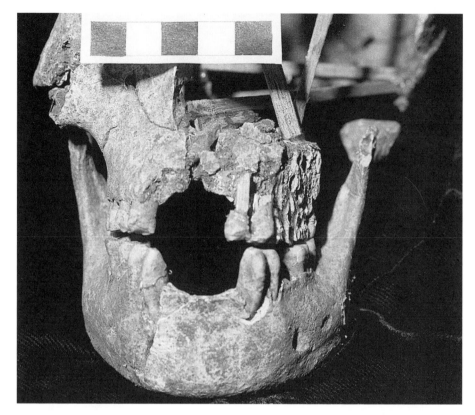

Figure 10.18   Human cranium from Nanda, KwaZulu-Natal, South Africa, showing modification of anterior teeth by removal of the four lower and two central upper incisors. One of the remaining incisors and the two upper canines have been deliberately chipped (courtesy Alan Morris and Natal Museum; A. Morris 1993).

from witches may be attested by six incisors found in a Broederstroom cattle byre (Mason 1981). No longer carried out by Eastern Bantu-speaking peoples in southern Africa, dental modification is common among Western Bantu-speakers in northern Namibia (van Reenen 1987). Though not universal among Chifumbaze skeletons and perhaps applied to a select group (Huffman 1990a), its frequency indicates another major difference with the ethnography of contemporary Nguni, Shona and Sotho/Tswana peoples, as well as supporting suggestions that the Lydenburg and Ndondonwane masks were used in initiation ceremonies.

A third ritual practice widespread on southern African Chifumbaze sites is the placement in pits of various objects, including pots from which the bottoms had been deliberately removed. Such pits (Fig. 10.19) frequently occur in residential areas away from cattle byres, suggesting, if we follow the CCP, that they were not used to store grain. Whitelaw (1993) uses ethnographic data

Figure 10.19 Pit with deliberate deposition of cattle bones at its base,
Ndondonwane, KwaZulu-Natal, South Africa.

to argue that finds of bottomless pots reflect their use in ceremonies marking
girls' initiation, with the pots and other items (broken sherds and grindstones)
carefully disposed of afterwards to avoid the attentions of witches or to remove
potentially polluting items by burying them. That these finds tend to occur
near houses suggests that these rites took place at the family, rather than the
community, level. The identification of pots and people is further supported
by similarities in fabric between masks and pottery at LHS (Inskeep and Maggs
1975) and the repetition of design motifs between the two media there (Evers
1982) and at Ndondonwane (Loubser 1993b).

Other differences between early farming communities and recent Nguni- and
Sotho/Tswana-speaking peoples include the possibly higher status accorded
women (witness the central cattle byre burial of a woman at Nanda (Whitelaw
1993) and possibly that of another, in an upright posture, at Broederstroom
(Mason 1981; Huffman 1990a)), the possibility that iron was smelted within settlements, not in the bush, and differences in site location strategy, grindstone
shape and pit form (Maggs 1984c). Along with the initiation practices discussed

above and the much larger settlement sizes reported in KwaZulu-Natal (Maggs 1984a), these features collectively point to important differences between first-millennium and recent South African agriculturalists across many areas of social life. While the CCP may be present, these differences gain added significance because of linguistic and archaeological arguments that Nguni- and Sotho/Tswana-speakers first settled south of the Limpopo only after 1000 (chapter 12).

The emergence of socio-political complexity

Suggestions that early farming communities and contemporary hunter-gatherers shared much the same mode of production (Mason 1986; M. Hall 1988) become difficult to support in the face of accumulating evidence for widespread livestock rearing, cultivation and grain storage among the former (Huffman 1990a). Not only do domestic animals and crops imply private property, long-term storage of cereals suggests this must have been controlled within families, or perhaps centrally within villages. On the other hand, early farming communities did not remain static, even though cattle were probably socially and ideologically important throughout the first millennium. Currently this is best seen in the development of complex exchange networks in south-eastern southern Africa, the Shashe–Limpopo Basin and the Kalahari, though rare stonewalled sites associated with Eiland ceramics on the Pietersburg Plateau hint that other areas also experienced increasing competition and complexity (Loubser 1994).

Trading connections between southern African communities and traders operating along East Africa's coast and within the developing commercial networks of the Near East and Indian Ocean are increasingly well attested. On the Mozambique coast, Dundo and Chibuene (Fig. 10.20) have produced glass beads and Middle Eastern pottery of mid/late first-millennium age. An Omani green glazed ware fragment at Chibuene suggests that contacts reach back beyond AD 500 (Sinclair *et al.* 1993a). A ninth-century glazed Islamic sherd and a glass bead from KwaGandaganda may indicate their later extension as far south as Durban (Whitelaw 1994a). More prosaically, widespread contacts across south-eastern southern Africa are demonstrated by marine shells at inland sites (Maggs 1984b; Maggs and Ward 1984; Whitelaw 1993, 1994a; Voigt and Peters 1994; L. van Schalkwyk 1994a) and further glass beads in Kruger Park (Meyer 1988a). Unless introduced to southern Africa from the north, the house rat (*Rattus rattus*), now known from several first-millennium sites, may also reflect overseas trade links with the east coast (Plug and Voigt 1985). As mentioned earlier, copper beads from KwaGandaganda imply connections with the transVaal (D. Miller and Whitelaw 1994), while ostrich eggshell beads suggest exchanges with hunter-gatherers.

Such exotic items concentrate, particularly in the later first millennium, on larger sites like KwaGandaganda, Wosi and Ndondonwane, where initiation

Figure 10.20   General view of the coast at Chibuene, Mozambique (courtesy Paul Sinclair).

schools involving the masks and figurines discussed above may also have been held (Loubser 1993b; Whitelaw 1994/95). Several craft activities appear to have been restricted to these sites, among them the working of elephant and hippopotamus tusks into bracelets (Voigt and von den Driesch 1984; Voigt and Peters 1994; Whitelaw 1994a) and the manufacture of talc schist beads, pendants and cosmetic powder (L. van Schalkwyk 1994b). Such specialisation presumably facilitated the expansion of trade and the possibilities for individuals or groups to benefit from this at the expense of others, including opportunities for accumulating larger herds of cattle. As a result some sites developed into centres of political power, dominating less fortunate, more peripheral settlements (L. van Schalkwyk 1994/95). The large size and rapid accumulation of assembly-area middens at KwaGandaganda and elsewhere attest to their preeminence at an early date, in this case the seventh/early eighth centuries; finds of ivory, a symbol of high status, may be particularly significant (Whitelaw 1994/95).

Writing *c.* 915, al-Masʿudi recorded ivory as a principal export of the land of Zanj (roughly the East African littoral; Freeman-Grenville 1962). As yet only hinted at for south-eastern southern Africa, the likelihood that ivory commanded the interest of merchants moving up and down the coast is better attested from the Shashe–Limpopo Basin, a prime habitat for elephants. Here Schroda, the largest-known Zhizo site, has produced many hundred glass beads and cowrie shells, as well as massive evidence for ivory-working (Hanisch 1981). The unusually high proportion of carnivores in the fauna may indicate that hunters sought animal skins as an additional trade item, as al-Masʿudi also reports (Voigt 1983). A cache of ivory bangles from a Zhizo context at Mosu I on the edge of the Makgadikgadi Pans suggests that such objects were also obtained over distances in excess of 300 km (Reid and Segobye 2000). The development of more complex political structures in this area, which culminated in the emergence of the Mapungubwe polity (chapter 11), may not, however, have depended solely upon external trade. This is because the Shashe–Limpopo Basin's *mopane* veld vegetation, though fragile, has a high grazing potential, allowing large livestock herds to be built up under favourable climatic circumstances from 850 to 1270 (Huffman 1996a). Across the Kalahari's eastern edge, indeed, markedly more pastoral societies also developed after 700, culminating in the Toutswe Tradition (Denbow 1986), examined in chapter 11.

A third area where more complex economic structures developed in the late first millennium is around the Tsodilo Hills (Fig. 10.21), where Divuyu and Nqoma successively formed part of a larger regional exchange network spanning the sixth to twelfth centuries. River mussel shells, freshwater fish and bones of water-dwelling antelope, such as lechwe, demonstrate links with the Okavango Delta. Qogana, which lies within the Delta and has produced Gokomere-Dambwa type pottery, evidence of pole-and-*daga* houses and a faunal assemblage wholly made up of wild species, may have been one source for

Figure 10.21   View of the Female Hill at the Tsodilo Hills, Botswana, from the top of the Male Hill (courtesy Larry Robbins). Divuyu is located on the top of the Female Hill, Nqoma 2 km further south on a lower plateau of the same hill.

these animals (G. Turner 1987; Denbow 1990). Moving further afield, small numbers of seashells at Divuyu and of cowries, *Conus* shells and glass beads at Nqoma imply connections with the Atlantic and Indian Ocean coasts respectively. The copper and iron used to produce the many metal items recovered must also have been imported, iron from the Delta or beyond, copper from at least 200 km away (D. Miller 1996). Nqoma probably came to dominate this exchange system as it has far more exotic items than any other northern Kalahari site. Matlapaneng, for instance, though further east and the same size, has many fewer glass beads and seashells. Its Gokomere-Dambwa ceramics and apparent lack of fish (G. Turner 1987), despite a Delta-edge location, also suggest a cultural affiliation different from the Tsodilo Hills sites (Denbow 1990).

Compared to Divuyu, Nqoma's fauna has much higher percentages of both cattle and wild game (as opposed to sheep/goat); stone tools, though still few in number, are also more common. Denbow (1990) interprets these differences to mean that many of Nqoma's cattle were acquired through exchange from further east. Some of these animals could then have moved north to livestock-poor areas in Angola and Congo-Kinshasa from which copper was probably obtained. The many wild animals hunted imply that skins were also traded, while ivory was certainly worked on-site. Other archaeologically invisible potential exchange items include salt, dyes, rhinoceros horn, feathers and aromatic woods (Wilmsen 1989). Nqoma may have flourished through a strategic middleman position in this network (Denbow 1990) and its own control of pigments from mica schist and specularite mines in the Tsodilo Hills themselves (Robbins *et al.* 1993; Fig. 10.22).

As part of the 'Kalahari debate' examined in chapter 8, much attention has focused on the rôle of hunter-gatherers in these exchange networks as suppliers of raw materials and labour. On one view the stone tools and higher wild game frequencies at Nqoma suggest they were attracted into the broader political system centred there, while increased evidence for hide-scraping in first-millennium LSA levels at Depression Cave and White Paintings Shelter, also in the Tsodilo Hills, may again reflect production for exchange (Denbow 1990, 1999). Sherds of charcoal-tempered pottery and bones of domestic animals at small sites with LSA stone artefacts, such as /Xai/Xai and Matlapaneng 2, are cited as additional evidence for the incorporation and subordination of hunter-gatherers by agropastoralists, though most are undated (Wilmsen and Denbow 1990). Chifumbaze Complex pottery and livestock remains from Hippo Tooth and Thamaga may indicate similar processes elsewhere in the Kalahari (Denbow 1986).

Attractive as these arguments are, their empirical basis is weak. Sadr (1998) shows that the absolute numbers of metal and pottery items found in LSA contexts are exceptionally low; most potsherds are small and unconjoinable, suggesting scavenging from abandoned farming villages rather than exchange. Livestock bones in LSA contexts are also sparse, while the supposed 'cattle'

Figure 10.22   Interior view of specularite mine, Tsodilo Hills, Botswana (courtesy Larry Robbins).

remains at /Xai/Xai consist of a single, undated mandible fragment that, in the absence of full publication and clear identification, may belong to a Cape buffalo (Yellen and Brooks 1989). Nor is there reason to think that wild game was not hunted, or that stone tools were made, by farmers just as much as by foragers (e.g. at Qogana, deep within the Okavango Delta). In short, there is little hard evidence for encapsulation of Kalahari hunter-gatherers on the scale Wilmsen and Denbow (1990) propose.

Farmers and hunter-gatherers

But since farming did not expand *in vacuo*, relations between farmers and hunter-gatherers constitute an important research concern across the sub-continent. The Thukela Basin is one of the best areas for looking at this question. Evidence of contact in hunter-gatherer contexts includes Msuluzi ceramics and iron ore at Mbabane Shelter (Mazel 1986), broken talc schist bowls and spatulae from Driel (Maggs and Ward 1980) and Ntshekane sherds and a set of eight modified bovid tali probably used for divination at KwaThwaleyakhe that resemble others from Wosi and Mamba (Mazel 1993; Plug 1993d). Such contacts extended to the Lesotho border and beyond, as witness iron from Belleview (Carter and Vogel 1974) and a Msuluzi/Ndondonwane sherd from Likoaeng (Mitchell and Charles 2000). As already discussed, farmers probably produced iron to trade with hunter-gatherers (Maggs 1980a). Reduced adze frequencies in the uppermost deposits at several Thukela Basin sites may reflect their substitution by iron wood-working tools (Mazel 1984).

Although more open to debate, flaked stone tools, bone points and linkshafts, and ostrich eggshell (OES) beads at farming settlements may document items moving in the other direction. Stone artefacts, a common feature of many early farming sites (Prins and Grainger 1993; L. van Schalkwyk 1994b; Binneman 1996b), are generally interpreted as evidence of contact with hunter-gatherers, but clearcut stratigraphic associations are frequently missing and systematic comparison with contemporary rock-shelter assemblages remains to be undertaken. At Msuluzi Confluence and Nanda, scrapers, not necessarily of LSA type, overwhelmingly dominate the formal tool component, perhaps reflecting the substitution of iron for stone in other tasks, such as wood-working or projectile weaponry (Maggs 1980a; Whitelaw 1993). However, we must be careful about assuming that such artefacts had tight links to ethnicity or mode of production, since stone flakes were used by recent Xhosa communities (Shaw and van Warmelo 1974) and iron production may have been a costly enterprise. Similar cautions hold with interpreting the bone tools from farming sites such as Ndondonwane (Maggs 1984b). With OES beads we may be on safer ground, since both unfinished beads and pieces for their manufacture are rare or absent at farming sites, and ostriches are unlikely to have occurred in the lower-lying thornveld areas of KwaZulu-Natal to which Chifumbaze farmers were restricted (Mazel 1989). Interestingly, beads with wear patterns indicating they were stitched onto fabric or strung on headbands occur only within the last 2000 years (Maggs and Ward 1980), while increases in mean bead size suggest other changes in ornamentation and social signalling coincided with the beginning of agropastoralist settlement.

Interpreting these data, Mazel (1989) argues that, rather than being subordinated, hunter-gatherers established close and equitable exchange ties with farmers. As well as the items already mentioned, farmers may have provided cereals, milk and perhaps livestock, with hunter-gatherers offering skins, hunted meat, ochre and honey. Additionally, farmers probably simultaneously respected hunter-gatherers as ritual owners of the land and desired their labour. That these alliances included intermarriage is suggested by genetic analyses of contemporary Bantu-speaking peoples in south-eastern southern Africa and the many Khoisan-derived click sounds in the Nguni languages (Mazel 1989). However, neither dataset comes with a chronology and Nguni itself may be a second-millennium introduction to the region (Huffman 1989). Similarly unclear is whether Bushman beliefs in Nguni divination practices (Hammond-Tooke 1998) and Tswana rain-making ideas (Ouzman 1995a) derive from the first millennium or more recent interaction.

It seems plausible that such relationships allowed hunter-gatherers to survive in the interstices of farming settlement for some time, as well as beyond the farming frontier. Parkington and Hall (1987b) suggested that sites along the eastern seaboard with extensive shell middens, Chifumbaze pottery and faunas dominated by wild species could reflect this situation. Emberton Way (Horwitz *et al.* 1991) shows this is unlikely to be true of sites like Mpambanyoni (Robey 1980) and Enkwazini (M. Hall 1980a), but it may account for others, such as Umbeli Belli (Cable 1984), though equally we cannot exclude farmers making use of rock-shelters themselves. Wadley's (1996b) research in the Magaliesberg suggests how links between farmers and foragers may have affected the social reproduction of hunter-gatherer society. Here declines in ostrich eggshell bead, bone point and formal stone tool frequencies imply that Jubilee Shelter ceased to function as an aggregation centre by the eighth century. Broederstroom, less than 10 km away, may have taken over this rôle, providing a range of attractive products and a context for intermarriage and assimilation. Supporting evidence includes the many scrapers, bored stones, OES beads, grooved stones, bone points and game species found there (Mason 1986). Hunter-gatherer gender rôles may also have altered. Mazel (1989) speculates that men probably had the major part in exchange ties with farmers as suppliers of bush products and labour, and cites observations of modern Ju/'hoansi to suggest that new beadwork styles could have been a female response to decreasing status.

Hunter-gatherers probably found it easier to develop exchange relationships with farmers than with pastoralists because of the availability of cultivated grains and iron and reduced conflicts over pasture and wild foods (Parkington and Hall 1987b). Such ties probably encouraged their relocation into areas more suitable for contact, or from which exchangeable products could be obtained. Evidence for LSA settlement of both the central Thukela Basin and the Drakensberg/Maluti Mountains is greater in the last 2000 years than before (Mazel 1989, 1993; Mitchell 1996c). More spectacularly, all known Holocene LSA sites in Zimbabwe's lowveld and the central and western Kalahari postdate 2000 BP (Denbow 1986; N. Walker 1995a), though the fact that many hunter-gatherers here speak Khoe raises the question whether we are witnessing the spread of pastoralists turned foragers.

Hunter-gatherers also frequently altered or expanded their own exchange networks. Signs include the appearance across Lesotho and South Africa's interior around 2000 years ago of distinctive pressure-flaked backed microliths and bifacial arrowheads, the latter possibly stone **skeuomorphs** of iron originals (J.D. Clark 1959). Perhaps exchanged, like arrows among modern Kalahari Bushmen, both kinds of artefact may connote affiliation to particular sociolinguistic groups (Humphreys 1984, 1991). Their distribution (Fig. 10.23) fits patterning in marine shell and OES jewellery to indicate that people living in Lesotho's highlands now interacted more strongly to the west than to the south or east (Mitchell 1996c). Further north, reorientation of hunter-gatherer

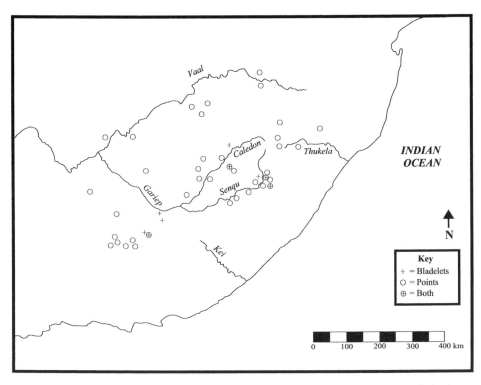

Figure 10.23   Distribution of pressure-flaked arrowheads and pressure-flaked
backed microliths in South Africa and Lesotho.

exchange networks is indicated by the disappearance of OES beads from rock-shelters inland of Durban and greatly expanded movement of seashells and OES throughout the Thukela Basin. Perhaps hunter-gatherers in these areas increasingly focused exchange links on farmers, rather than their inland counterparts. Changes in the seasonality and activity profile of Belleview demonstrate this shift in focus at the level of the individual site (Carter 1978). Other data, such as bone fish hooks (Fig. 10.24), rock paintings of mormyrid fish that live only as far south as the Phongolo River (Ouzman 1995b), and bones of red and blue duikers, both coastal forest species, not infrequently found far inland (Plug 1990, 1992, 1999), remind us of the need to envisage multiple contexts of interaction with varying spatio-temporal boundaries.

One such context that cries out for research is the appearance of pottery in LSA assemblages across much of south-eastern southern Africa around 2000 years ago. Mazel's (1992a) review confirms that these typically grit-tempered ceramics are quite different from any known from Chifumbaze sites: much thinner, undecorated, without pronounced necks, and presumably therefore used in quite different social and functional settings. At many sites

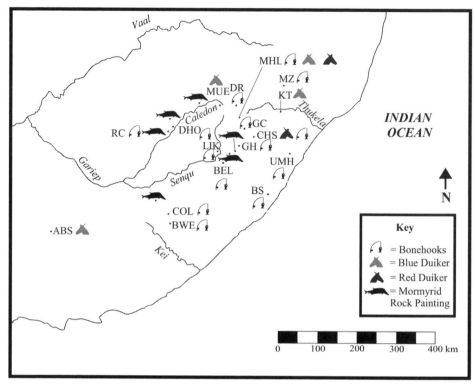

Figure 10.24 Distribution of bone fish hooks, rock paintings of mormyrid fish
and finds of red duiker (*Cephalophus natalensis*) and blue duiker
(*Philantomba monticola*) in inland locations in south-eastern
southern Africa. Site names abbreviated thus: ABS Abbots Shelter;
BEL Belleview; BS Borchers Shelter; BWE Bonawe; CHS
Collingham Shelter; COL Colwinton; DHO De Hoop; DR Driel;
GC Giant's Castle; GH Good Hope; KT KwaThwaleyakhe; LIK
Likoaeng; MHL Mhlwazini; MUE Muela; MZ Mzinyashana; RC
Rose Cottage Cave; UMH Umhlatuzana.

their dating remains imprecise, but at Collingham Shelter (Fig. 10.25), where
copper and iron beads may be associated (Mazel 1992b), they seem securely
dated to 1880–1770 BP. Older than any farming settlement south of the
Limpopo, we have to wonder about the origins of this pottery. Could it represent a continuation north-eastward of the early ceramics known from the
Cape, rather than acquisition of ceramic technology ahead of, but from, expanding Kwale farmers? Or does it reflect an otherwise unattested penetration of the
still largely unresearched central/southern transVaal by farmers or pastoralists
(Maggs 1984a)? Whatever its origins, pottery probably expanded the range of
foods (especially shellfish and plants) that could be eaten and increased nutri-
tional gains by boiling meat, as well as offering new means of storage (Mazel

Figure 10.25 Possible remains of a leather bag from between the top of Layer TBS and the collapsed ceiling of Collingham Shelter, KwaZulu-Natal, South Africa (courtesy Aron Mazel). A charcoal sample from TBS is dated 1260 ± 50 BP (Pta-5408; Mazel 1992b).

1989; Gifford-Gonzalez 2000). Its spread across KwaZulu-Natal, Lesotho and adjacent areas (Klatzow 1994) testifies to the ease with which hunter-gatherer alliance networks could transmit innovations.

The spread of farming

The spread of farming into southern Africa was clearly an uneven process, with several main movements apparent. To explain these we should look not only to demographic expansion, but also to the assimilation of hunter-gatherers into farming communities (Vansina 1995). Another, less frequently discussed, possibility would see some hunter-gatherers, perhaps already practising delayed-returns economies in favourable (coastal?) areas, adopting farming themselves. A phenomenon well known in other parts of the world, such as Europe's western and northern fringes (Zvelebil 1986), this could be looked for in southern Africa, especially along the Indian Ocean coast and perhaps in Zimbabwe, from much of which hunter-gatherers appear to have quickly disappeared (N. Walker and Thorp 1997). Social and technological factors inherent in the farming economy may also be implicated. Frequent settlement shifts, perhaps of some distance, may have coped with declining soil fertility and recurrent droughts (P. Jones 1984). Nor should we forget the rôle of community fission as a dispute-resolution mechanism (Vansina 1995). Finally, recall the clear preferences for particular settlement locations shown by early farmers. 'Hopping' from one favourable location to another, with intervening areas settled only much later, may contribute to a sense of very rapid movement, as in Kwale expansion along Africa's east coast. Rather than adventurous pioneers, such a pattern implies a conservative colonisation strategy, as among central Europe's early Neolithic LBK farmers. That ceramic designs are widely shared at a scale far greater than any conceivable political or socio-linguistic entity among many Chifumbaze groups provides another striking parallel. For both, the need for exogamy among extensive, low-density populations and subscription to widely held norms that permitted resource-sharing in times of subsistence crisis may be responsible (M. Hall 1988; Bogucki 1995).

Where does all this leave the notion of a 'package' linking farming, iron-working and the expansion of Bantu-speaking, negroid people? Further north the same cultigens and animals were once raised by stone-using communities, some of them probably speakers of Bantu languages, but south of the Zambezi and Kunene mixed farming seems always to have been associated with iron technology. Racial and linguistic affinities are much more difficult to establish. Human skeletons are few, both from farming contexts and from earlier or contemporary hunter-gatherer ones across the eastern half of southern Africa (A. Morris 1992b). Some individuals at Chifumbaze sites are clearly negroid (De Villiers 1970; Huffman 1979; Steyn *et al.* 1994), but others have stronger Khoisan features, possibly reflecting intermarriage with, or assimilation of, hunter-gatherers (Mason 1986; A. Morris 1993). Sometimes too such assimilation may have been a two-way process. On the sub-continent's western side, where farming is ecologically more marginal, the Dama of north-central Namibia, Kwadi of southern Angola and 'River Bushmen' of northern Botswana are physically negroid, but speak Khoe languages (Barnard 1992). Their combination of herding, and sometimes cultivation, with hunting, gathering and fishing attests to the complexity of the interactions from which they derive and the difficulties of maintaining hard-and-fast terminological distinctions when looking at southern Africa's past; so too the Dama's rôle as specialist black-smiths and makers of stone pipes, and the River Bushmen's specialisation as traders (Cashdan 1987).

Currently widely employed pottery typologies imply that makers of similar ceramics shared a common language (Huffman 1980; Evers 1988), but specific correlations are difficult to establish. For the first millennium Huffman (1989) argues that only Naviundu ceramics were the work of Western Bantu-speakers, while Kalundu and Urewe pottery were made by Eastern Bantu-speakers. In both cases he traces typological links to contemporary peoples who speak languages belonging to these two groups. Closer ties between linguistic and archaeological evidence are harder to find. Vansina's (1995) lexicostatistical argument for an Eastern Bantu dispersal from the equatorial rainforest south to the middle Zambezi and only then towards the Great Lakes is at variance with both the archaeology of the rainforest zone (Eggert 1994/95) and that of the Chifumbaze Complex. Ehret's (1998) reconstruction of the expansion of successive branches of Eastern Bantu offers a different picture, but only partly engages with archaeological evidence. In sum, archaeologists and linguists ought, at least for the first millennium, to get their own houses in order before seeking overly detailed correlations with each other's data. As the following two chapters show, a direct historical approach may make such correlations easier to sustain for the last thousand years.

CHAPTER 11

THE ZIMBABWE TRADITION

The glass beads and Middle Eastern ceramics that occur at some southern African sites during the late first millennium mark the beginnings of the region's incorporation into the expanding economic system that, partly tied together by maritime trading links across the Indian Ocean, increasingly united Africa, Asia and Europe long before Da Gama or Columbus. Parts of southern Africa, especially the Zimbabwe Plateau, became important suppliers of gold, ivory and other commodities, gaining in return exotic items that could not be made locally, or only at considerable cost. The elaboration of these connections and the transformation of earlier, less elaborately organised communities into the class-divided polities of Mapungubwe, Great Zimbabwe and the latter's successors (Mutapa, Torwa and various Venda entities) is the central theme of this chapter (Fig. 11.1). A related concern is again how far we can use the ethnography of contemporary southern African peoples as a guide to understanding the past. While mindful of the potential for comparative studies of the socio-political impacts of trade and imported prestige goods, a further important theme has to be the significance of local processes for the changes we observe.

Bambandyanalo to Mapungubwe: the emergence of the state in the Shashe–Limpopo Basin

By the late first millennium, ivory and skins were already being exported overseas, with sites like Chibuene interfacing between interior and transoceanic traders. The many hundred glass beads from Schroda leave no doubt that the Shashe–Limpopo Basin was a major player in these networks. Subsequent developments focused on the Greefswald farm, a few kilometres south of the Shashe–Limpopo confluence. Occupation initially centred at Bambandyanalo, often called K2 because its deep occupation deposits recalled to Gardner (1963), an early excavator, tell-like sites termed *kom* in North Africa (Fig. 11.2). Despite the poor quality of pre-1971 excavations, work by Eloff and Meyer (1981) and Meyer (1998) now gives a reasonably firm understanding of the sequence here and at Mapungubwe, to which occupation subsequently shifted.

At Bambandyanalo the main midden, dating 1030–1220, stands out above the surrounding occupation area, reaching more than 6 m deep in places. Covering more than 8 ha and possibly housing as many as 2000 people, the settlement

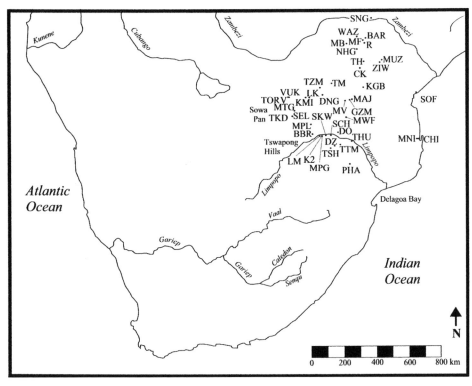

Figure 11.1   Location of archaeological sites discussed in chapter 11. Site
names abbreviated thus: BAR Baranda; BBR Bobonong Road;
CHI Chibuene; CK Castle Kopje; DNG Danangombe (Dhlo-Dhlo);
DO Dombozanga; DZ Dzata; GZM Great Zimbabwe; II Ingombe
Ilede; K2 Bambandyanalo (K2); KGB Kagumbudzi; KMI Khami;
LK Leopard's Kopje; LM Little Muck; MAJ Majiri; MB Mbagazewa;
MF Mount Fura; MNI Manyikeni; MPG Mapungubwe; MPL Mapela;
MTG Matanga; MV Montevideo Ranch; MUZ Muozi; NHG
Nhunguza; PHA Phalaborwa; R Ruanga; SCH Schroda; SEL Selolwe;
SKW Skutwater; SNG Songo; SOF Sofala; TH Tsindi; THU
Thulamela; TKD Thakadu; TM Tebekwe Mine; TOR Toranju; TSH
Tshirululuni; TTM Tshitakatsha-Makolani; TZM Thaba
Zikamambo; V Vumba; VUK Vukwe; WAZ Wazi; ZIW Ziwa.

consisted of pole-and-*daga* houses with gravel floors focused around and to
the west of a large byre, which does not (*pace* Huffman 1996b) appear to have
occupied the central position predicted by the Central Cattle Pattern (Meyer
1998). Whether this is ideologically significant or a reflection of local topography is unclear. The midden, the size of which may indicate the status of the
settlement's ruler, engulfed the byre around 1060–1080, presumably necessitating relocation of the cattle previously kept there to an as yet unidentified
location on the site's periphery. For Huffman (1996b) the reorganisation of space

Figure 11.2   General view of the excavation area at Bambandyanalo, Northern
Province, South Africa (courtesy Fumiko Ohinata).

and worldview that this implies suggests profound social changes even before
Bambandyanalo's abandonment in the early thirteenth century, when the focus
of occupation moved to Mapungubwe Hill 1 km away (Fig. 11.3). Though only
occupied for a few decades c. 1220–1290 a deep succession of gravel floors and
house debris rapidly accumulated on the Hill and on a flat, raised area at its
southern base (the 'Southern Terrace').

Huffman (1996b) suggests that the suddenness with which Mapungubwe was
occupied may imply a deliberate decision to give spatial expression to a new
social order in which leaders now physically removed themselves from ordinary
people by moving onto more inaccessible, higher elevations behind the stone
walls demarcating élite residential areas. Where these ideas came from and how
and why they were accepted remain to be established. That they were speaks
to considerable centralisation of power and perhaps the elaboration of new
ways of linking leaders and subjects. Detailed publication of the Mapungubwe
excavations now points to limited occupation of both Mapungubwe Hill and
the Southern Terrace having taken place 1100–1220, the possibility that the
Hill itself only became a major occupation focus after 1250 and a similar date
for at least some of the stone walls, as well as several widespread burning
episodes at the site before and after this (Meyer 1998). How these patterns can
best be explained remains open to discussion, but they presumably speak to a
potentially complex series of social and political events.

Figure 11.3   Mapungubwe Hill, Northern Province, South Africa (courtesy
Fumiko Ohinata).

Over 100 burials add another dimension to this story. Most of those from
Bambandyanalo come from the main midden close to the byre and show little
differentiation, though some had copper ornaments and/or iron artefacts associated with them (Meyer 1998). All those from Mapungubwe were discovered in one area during early excavations (Fouché 1937). Numerous items of
gold demonstrate the high status of three of them. As well as beads, wire
bracelets and foil objects, one man was buried with a rhinoceros, bowl and
sceptre, all made of sheet gold attached to wooden cores with gold tacks (Oddy
1984; Fig. 11.4); the other two gold-accompanied individuals, one male and
one female, and perhaps this one too, were buried in a high-status seated
position (Huffman 1996a). Probably contemporary, though placed within the
Bambandyanalo midden, another rich burial, that of a child, was accompanied
by several hundred glass beads, including seven large turquoise examples of
probable Chinese origin otherwise known only as isolated finds (Steyn *et al.*
1999; M. Wood 2000).

Stable isotope analyses hint that not all individuals from the Shashe–
Limpopo Basin ate the same diets, raising the possibility that differences may
correlate with status (Lee Thorp *et al.* 1993). Wetter than present conditions permitted much larger human populations, who supported themselves by cereal
and legume cultivation, supplemented by gathering wild fruits (Huffman 1996a;
Meyer 1998). Domestic livestock, especially cattle, produced most of the meat

Figure 11.4   The gold rhinoceros, bowl and sceptre from a male burial on
              Mapungubwe Hill, Northern Province, South Africa (courtesy
              University of Pretoria).

eaten. Perhaps foreshadowing the later situation on the Zimbabwe Plateau, caprines may have been more important for those living on Mapungubwe's Southern Terrace than on the Hill above (Voigt 1983). The social significance of cattle is reinforced by their importance among the many human and animal ceramic figurines recovered and by six 'beast burials' from Bambandyanalo. Perhaps sacrificed, these cattle were covered by deliberately smashed pottery and buried with a range of special items (Voigt 1983). The possibility should be entertained that they relate to the byre going out of use and were undertaken to mark this or symbolically to continue its functions.

Originally thought of as a provincial offshoot of Great Zimbabwe because of erroneous radiocarbon dates, Mapungubwe may in fact have been the earliest state in southern Africa. The differences in residential areas, burial treatment and diet just mentioned certainly support the notion that Mapungubwe society may have been divided into distinct, socially unequal groups. Differential access to cattle and trade goods, to which I return below, implies this too, as well as the possibility that the élite sought to monopolise strategic resources. However, it might be wrong to paint a picture based too heavily on western models of the evolution of the state with a clearly defined class structure at the expense of considering more communal forms of authority, and other defining elements of the state such as the organised use of force to enforce control, and permanently specialised govermental institutions remain out of focus. Centralised political organisation may, however, perhaps be inferred from Huffman's (1986) comparative analysis of site size which establishes Mapungubwe's regional pre-eminence over a five-level settlement hierarchy spanning some 30,000 km². Sites like Mapela (Garlake 1968) and Little Muck, though varying in size, combined hilltop locations with stone walling, extensive terrracing to create house platforms and the use of solid *daga* houses at their cores contrasted with pole-and-*daga* houses on their peripheries. Other sites, interpreted as commoner settlements, lacked these features, remained organised according to the CCP and have few glass beads; Skutwater (van Ewyk 1987) and Bobonong Road (J. Kinahan and Kinahan 1998) are examples. The wider extent of Mapungubwe's influence is shown by the occurrence of its ceramics as far as Great Zimbabwe and Toutswe, and also on hilltop locations immediately north of the Soutpansberg, where sites with Eiland-derived Mutamba ceramics may have been culturally distinct, commoner settlements (Loubser 1991a). The strength of Mapungubwe's long-distance connections is even better shown by rare Chinese pottery (Meyer and Esterhuizen 1994), numerous cowries and other Indian Ocean seashells, and the literally tens of thousands of glass beads at both Greefswald sites, over 26,000 with just one of the gold-accompanied burials alone (Voigt 1983; Saitowitz 1996; Meyer 1998). This concentration of finds is unparalleled at any contemporary site in southern Africa.

What provided the basis for these developments? Continuing on from the pattern evidenced by Schroda and reflected in the writings of al-Masʿudi, Bambandyanalo has produced good evidence of ivory procurement targeted at making bracelets in a standardised, readily tradable form. The many bone points (some designed to hold an iron tip) and linkshafts from both Greefswald sites may also be the work of specialist artisans (Voigt 1983). Textile production, however, is attested only at Mapungubwe, where spindle whorls document the spinning and manufacture of cotton cloth, using cotton plants (*Gossypium* spp.) originally introduced from across the Indian Ocean (Huffman 1971a). Despite this, textiles remained an important trade item as labour costs and the pre-sixteenth-century lack of dyes made imports more attractive (Beach 1994).

The absence of ivory-working debris at Mapungubwe suggests that ivory was no longer a major trade item in the thirteenth century, though numerous carnivore bones may indicate that skins were exported (Voigt 1983) and ivory in both worked and unworked forms does occur at contemporary Toutswe sites (Plug 1996b). Gold was probably now more important. Along with Thaba Zikamambo (K. Robinson 1966), Mapungubwe is the oldest southern African site to have produced gold objects, and its distinctive pottery occurs in the fills of several Zimbabwean gold mines (Summers 1969); alluvial sources nearby may also have been exploited. Iron from Botswana's Tswapong Hills may have been another export (Kiyaga-Mulindwa 1993); the Muslim writer Abuʾl-Fida records both metals as key products of 'Sofala', a general term for the Mozambican coast and its hinterland (Freeman-Grenville 1962). Specific foreign trading partners are difficult to identify. Claims for an Egyptian origin (Saitowitz *et al.* 1995) may be misplaced, and many of Bambandyanalo's beads may have an ultimately Indian origin, with some coming from south-east Asia. Kilwa, the major Swahili town on the Tanzanian coast, was the likely distribution point from which they

Figure 11.5   Oblate-shaped and 'Garden Roller' glass beads, Mapungubwe,
Northern Province, South Africa (courtesy Marilee Wood).

moved south (M. Wood 2000). Less certainly, the oblate-shaped beads that dominate Mapungubwe's bead assemblage may also have Indian origins (Fig. 11.5), but are unknown on East African coastal sites. Interestingly, where comparisons can be made, the Shashe–Limpopo beads seem distinctly smaller than those from East Africa, a preference probably connected to their employment in beadwork on skin or cloth (M. Wood 2000).

The anthropological concept of a prestige goods economy (Friedman and Rowlands 1978) helps explain what may have been going on in the Shashe–Limpopo Basin in the early second millennium. The exotic origins of glass beads and imported cloth must have made them highly desirable. While cattle were a 'democratic resource' since livestock herds can, in principle, if not in practice, be built up or acquired by anyone (M. Hall 1987: 89), beads and cloth were rare and not subject to natural increase. They thus provided a means for leaders to transcend the existing mode of production. Susceptible to signifying high status simply because they were exotic, they could be redistributed to juniors in return for their loyalty, expressed partly by payment of appropriate tribute, such as ivory or gold, itself needed to keep the inward flow of beads and cloth moving. Glass beads could be made even rarer, and more impressive, by melting them down and recasting them into the larger 'Garden Roller' beads made at Bambandyanalo using a unique single-use pottery mould technique (Loubser 1991a; M. Wood 2000). Cattle, as a more traditional expression of wealth and status, probably also flowed towards the Greefswald sites by way of tribute, court fines and perhaps bridewealth payments, if emerging élites foreshadowed later Pedi practice and gave royal brides to junior lineages; Loubser (1991a) raises just this possibility to explain the small quantities of Mapungubwe ceramics south of the Soutpansberg and of Eiland-like pottery on Mapungubwe sites to the north. What we do not yet see, however, is much evidence for people resisting these developments, though the hilltop locations of some sites, especially those of the Toutswe Tradition, may reflect defensive considerations. Denbow (1984, 1986) argues that political centralisation here was more exclusively based on accumulating cattle. Other ways in which élites may have established themselves could have included trading ivory towards Bambandyanalo/Mapungubwe, or exchanging cattle for agricultural produce (M. Hall 1987), though evidence for both is scarce and the lack of wheeled vehicles must have constrained the transport of bulk goods.

Largely neglected hitherto, hunter-gatherers probably played an important rôle in this evolving politico-economic system as suppliers of bush products, including ivory. Certainly, the first and early second millennia saw a marked increase in forager visibility in the Limpopo Valley and Zimbabwe's lowveld. The large number of scrapers at sites like Dombozanga (Cooke and Simons 1969) may reflect intensive skin preparation for example, with iron a valued item obtained in exchange (N. Walker and Thorp 1997). The many bone points from both Greefswald sites, but especially the 1250–1290 levels at Mapungubwe, could also point to a forager presence there (Meyer 1998), though perhaps this is to overemphasise their supposed 'ethnic' connotations. Similar problems arise in knowing whether the stone tools reported from some Toutswe sites (see below) reflect mining and trade with hunter-gatherers, ethnically and technologically mixed communities, or the use of stone by poorer, iron-deficient farming communities (Denbow 1999).

Beyond the Shashe–Limpopo Basin: Toutswe, Leopard's Kopje and the Shona expansion

Emphasising the dangers and difficulties of establishing a rigid divide between first- and second-millennium farming communities in many areas, the Toutswe Tradition bridges the centuries either side of AD 1000 in eastern Botswana. Both its ceramics, and even more so those of its earliest phase (Taukome), are similar to Zhizo pottery, although Toutswe itself is broadly contemporary with Bambandyanalo and Mapungubwe. Over three-quarters of Toutswe sites possess extensive accumulations of vitrified dung, often visible from the air because they support dense stands of *Cenchrus ciliaris* grass. As Denbow (1999) indicates, this probably implies a major increase in the numerical importance of cattle, in part perhaps due to more favourable climatic conditions either

Figure 11.6   View of Toutswemogala from another Toutswe Tradition site, Thatswane, which is visible in the foreground partly covered by *Cenchrus ciliaris* grass (courtesy Andrew Reid).

side of AD 1000. A three-tier settlement hierarchy can be identified. The three largest sites, such as Toutswemogala, cover some 50,000 m^2 and were located on hilltops, perhaps for defence (Fig. 11.6); each may represent a local paramountcy (Denbow 1984, 1986, 1999). Cattle and caprines dominate both their faunas and those of smaller Class 2 sites, such as Taukome, which are also on *kopjes*. Occupying the basal level in this system, Class 3 sites like Kgaswe with little or no dung, few livestock and locations more suitable for agriculture probably specialised in cereal production and were occupied for decades, rather than centuries. More recent research identifies specialist iron-working and pottery-making sites as other elements of economic differentiation (Kiyaga-Mulindwa 1993; Segobye 1994). The region's lack of gold sources and the scarcity of ivory artefacts and glass beads relative to Mapungubwe sites further east suggest that socio-political complexity here was based more on competitive accumulation of wealth in and power over cattle than on access to imported items (Denbow 1986). Glass beads and cowrie shells do none the less occur, and at Bosutswe are joined by the bones of fish, crocodile, hippopotamus and water-loving antelope which must have derived from over 200 km away; fragments of a bowl similar to those made at Nqoma suggest connections as far as the Tsodilo Hills (Denbow 1999). These long-distance links into and across the Kalahari withered in the twelfth and thirteenth centuries, and the lack of vitrified dung middens in

Mapungubwe levels at sites such as Bosutswe imply changes in the organisation of herding and, perhaps, the basis of élite power.

While Zhizo ceramic traditions clearly survived in modified form among Toutswe communities, the pottery found across the Shashe–Limpopo Basin after 1000 forms a southern variant of the Leopard's Kopje Tradition also represented further north in Zimbabwe. Overlying earlier Zhizo occupations at Leopard's Kopje itself, Schroda and elsewhere (Huffman 1971b, 2000), Leopard's Kopje pottery differs from it in motif layout, decoration technique and vessel form (Fig. 11.7); 'beast burials' and clay figurines of cattle and women are other innovations. Huffman (1974, 1978b, 1984a) argues that these ceramics

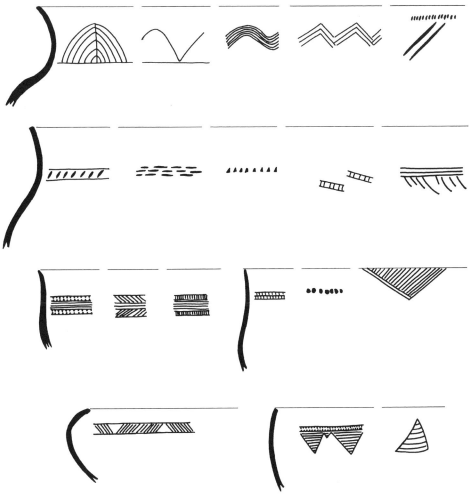

Figure 11.7 Leopard's Kopje pottery (after Huffman 1989: Fig. 7; courtesy Tom Huffman).

cannot be derived from Zhizo, but instead developed from Klingbeil pottery in the northern transVaal. This may not, however, be the whole story and van Waarden (1998) notes similarities between Leopard's Kopje and Taukome pottery; contrasts between Zhizo and Leopard's Kopje may, in other words, have been overstated. Indeed, finds of both kinds of pottery at some sites hint that their makers overlapped temporally (M. Hall and Vogel 1980), with one possibility being that Zhizo-makers came to occupy a subordinate position in an ethnically mixed society.

Huffman (1978b) places Leopard's Kopje within the Kutama Tradition, with the succession Mambo–Woolandale north of the Matopo Hills paralleling the sequence Bambandyanalo–Mapungubwe further south. Compared to the Shashe–Limpopo Basin, areas to the north remain underresearched. Van Waarden (1998) speculates as to the existence of a gold-producing chiefdom, perhaps centred around one of several stonewalled thirteenth-century sites in eastern Botswana, such as Selolwe (A. Campbell 1991), but Huffman (1986) notes that Woolandale pottery incorporates ceramic elements invented at Mapungubwe, which he reads as evidence for a regionally subordinate status for its makers. Gumanye is another Kutama component, with most sites small villages on defensible hilltops, as at Great Zimbabwe, where occupation dates to 1150–1220 (Huffman and Vogel 1991). If we accept the equation of distinctive pottery assemblages with different ethnic groups and continuities between Leopard's Kopje and the pottery historically made by the Shona, then Gumanye reflects the northward expansion of Shona-speakers, perhaps attracted by the wish to gain control over trade with the east coast (Huffman 1986).

In northern Zimbabwe, Shona settlement may have been a significantly later process, linked to the expansion of the Great Zimbabwe polity and its successors. Harare pottery is best known from burials in rock-shelters and open air locations close to Zimbabwe's capital. Dating from the twelfth to fifteenth centuries, the grave rite included occasional deposition of iron, copper and shell ornaments and glass beads (Matenga 1993). Huffman (1978b) originally included Harare within the Kutama Tradition, but both ceramics and funeral practice are similar to those of the Musengezi Tradition of northern Mashonaland, which definitely lies outside it (Fig. 11.8). Principally decorated using fibre-wrapped bead impressions, rather than Chifumbaze Complex comb-stamping techniques, Musengezi pottery dates from the thirteenth to sixteenth centuries. It represents a local development, the new technique reflecting the arrival of beads as exotic trade items (Pikirayi 1996). Sites like Wazi (Soper and Pwiti 1988) show no stratigraphic break from underlying Gokomere-derived Maxton occupations and the wrapped fibre technique is common to both traditions.

Musengezi pottery is found both on settlements like Ruanga (Garlake 1973b) and in cave/rock-shelter burials accompanied by glass beads, copper items and

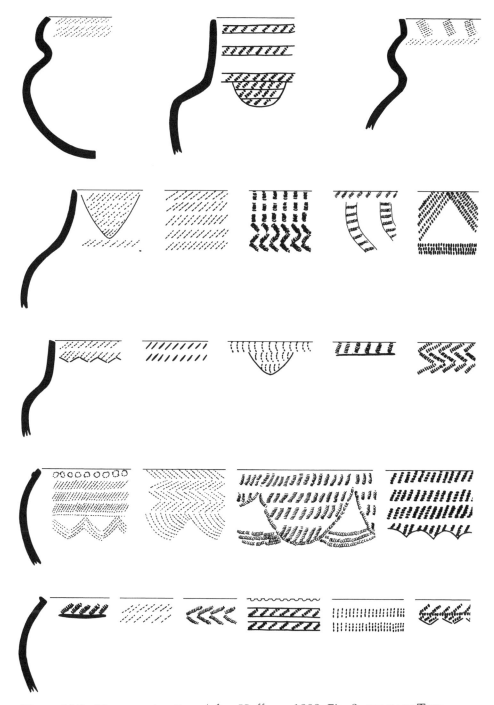

Figure 11.8   Musengezi pottery (after Huffman 1989: Fig. 9; courtesy Tom
Huffman).

bark matting, as at Mbagazewa (Crawford 1967). Both pottery (drinking beakers and shallow bowls with fine comb-stamping and graphite colouring) and cross-shaped copper ingots with characteristically trapezoidal cross-sections and raised rims resemble those at the Ingombe Ilede cemetery on the Zambian side of the Zambezi and at Ingombe Ilede Tradition sites in the Hurungwe/Makonde areas of Zimbabwe (Garlake 1970; Pikirayi 1996). Both Musengezi and Ingombe Ilede ceramics have affinities to the broader Luangwa Tradition, which may represent a major movement of matrilineal, Western Bantu-speakers into Zambia in the early second millennium (Huffman 1989). Consistent with the suggestion that Musengezi and Ingombe Ilede are of non-Shona origin, Portuguese documents identify the latter with the VaMbara, renowned copperworkers who, significantly, did not speak Shona prior to their conquest by the Mutapa state. Oral traditions suggest that this was true of both areas. Features typical of Western Bantu societies, such as matrilineality and bride service rather than bridewealth payments, still survive in the area where Musengezi sites are found. Interestingly, although it is by no means exclusive to them alone, the Western Bantu-speaking Valley Tonga of the Zambezi floodplain still practise filing and ablation of the incisors as found on the skeletons from Mbagazewa (Garlake 1973b).

Great Zimbabwe: the site

Today the drought-prone Greefswald area receives under 350 mm of rainfall a year, making cereal cultivation virtually impossible. The shift to drier conditions in the late 1200s across the Shashe–Limpopo Basin and the eastern Kalahari may have been pivotal in the breakup of the Mapungubwe polity, the collapse of the Toutswe Tradition and the emergence of Great Zimbabwe as its successor (Huffman 1996a). Though depopulation of the Greefswald area may not have been quite as comprehensive as previously thought, and Mapungubwe-type ceramics appear to occur on neighbouring sites until c. 1400 (Meyer 1998), lying on the escarpment Great Zimbabwe and its contemporaries were certainly better situated for such rain as did fall.

Probably the best-known archaeological site in southern Africa and at about 720 ha one of the largest, Great Zimbabwe (Fig. 11.9), was 'discovered' by Europeans in 1871 (Mauch 1969). It was then pillaged (there are no other words) in poorly controlled excavations that sought to prove its connection with ancient Arabians or Phoenicians (Bent 1892; R. Hall 1905). Uncompromisingly rejecting such exotic influences, systematic archaeological research has been constrained by this early destruction of evidence and has stressed the stone enclosures and their contents (MacIver 1906; Caton-Thompson 1931; Summers et al. 1961; Garlake 1973a; Huffman 1977; Collett et al. 1992). Huffman's (1986, 1997a) excavations in surrounding areas probably inhabited by commoners produced appropriately 'ordinary' artefacts – pottery, grindstones, hoes, metal

Figure 11.9   General view of Great Zimbabwe, Zimbabwe, showing the Great
Enclosure, Valley Enclosures and *dare* or open court area. The
photograph is taken from the Hill Complex.

bangles and some glass beads – giving a total population estimate for the site of
18,000. The stonewalled enclosures, on the other hand, both here and at comparable sites have virtually no grindstones and a very restricted ceramic range
(Fig. 11.10): a few beer storage vessels and numerous drinking pots, almost all
graphite-burnished, sometimes with a single band of incised decoration on the
body. The absence of pots for cooking food or carrying water implies that these
activities were carried out elsewhere and not by those inhabiting the enclosures
(Garlake 1973a).

Great Zimbabwe can be divided into several zones focused around a hill and
the valley below (Fig. 11.11). Perimeter walls at the Hill's base extended into
the Valley, separating those living on its terraced slopes and in the Valley from
commoners below and to the west. The Hill itself (Fig. 11.12) features a complex
of enclosures formed by stone walls over and between granite boulders; 3–5 m
of deposit were originally present within the Western Enclosure, the walls of
which were capped with soapstone monoliths. Houses here and elsewhere in
élite areas were built of solid *daga*. Seven of the famous soapstone birds come
from the Hill, six from the Eastern Enclosure, one from the Western (Fig. 11.13).
Representing generalised raptors with quasi-human attributes, they may have
been ancestral or divine messengers, or even specific royal forebears (Huffman
1996b).

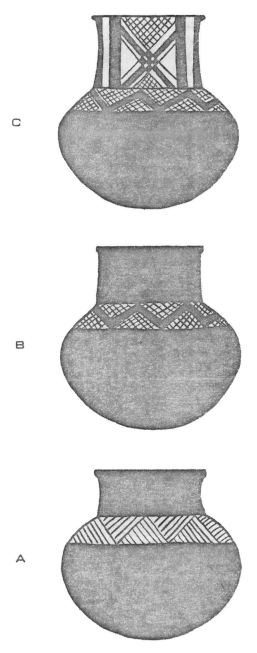

Figure 11.10   Zimbabwe Tradition pottery (after Huffman 1972: Fig. 1; courtesy
Tom Huffman). A Great Zimbabwe Period III; B Great Zimbabwe
Period IV; C Khami phase band-and-panel decorated ware.

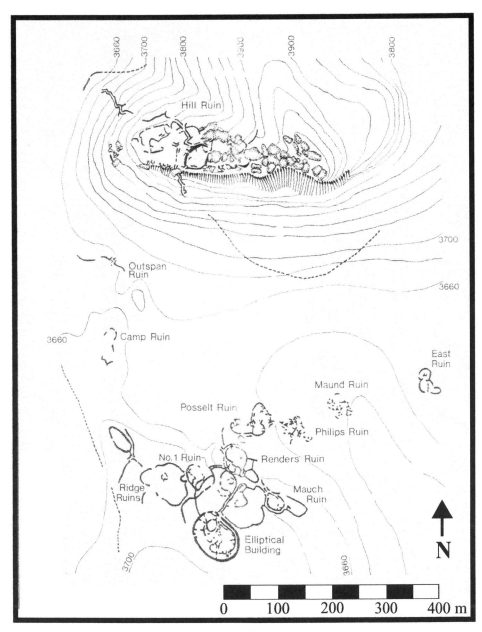

Figure 11.11   Plan of Great Zimbabwe, Zimbabwe (redrawn after Garlake 1973).

The Valley itself houses several more enclosures, linked by stone passages and walkways into a larger complex radiating out from Enclosure 1 ('Renders Ruin'). Most contain doorways and walls bearing grooves that Huffman (1996b) interprets as female symbols (*mihombwe*). The Great Enclosure stands close-by

Figure 11.12   Entrance to the Western Enclosure of the Hill Complex, Great Zimbabwe, Zimbabwe.

(Fig. 11.14). Its size can be gauged from its diameter (89 m), perimeter (244 m) and volume (over 5000 m^3 of stone; Garlake 1973a). Internal features include a platform found with clay (cattle) and soapstone (human) figurines, a cairn littered with cattle bones and charcoal, and two solid stone towers that resemble Shona grainbins. Lacking residential debris, Great Zimbabwe's main public area lay between the Hill and the Great Enclosure.

All the walls at Great Zimbabwe, as at similar sites, were designed to demarcate areas of space, not for defence or as load-bearing elements in their own right. Three main different styles can be defined, all made with one or two carefully selected outer faces infilled with less regular, but still coursed core material; their relative chronology is evident from how they intersect (Summers *et al.* 1961; P. Walker 1993). P walls have irregular blocks laid to give false courses that dip and swoop; frequently used in retaining or terracing structures, almost all are among boulders and stand on bedrock. Q walls use regularly shaped blocks in true courses, are mainly freestanding and mostly have trenched foundations. R walls too are mostly freestanding, under 2 m high and made from irregular blocks simply piled and wedged together. P walling predates Q, with R walls used in lower-status areas, as in the Nemanwa Enclosure on the site's periphery, which Huffman (1996b) suggests was used by a provincial leader when resident at Great Zimbabwe. Experiments suggest that the blocks, which are of local granite, were produced using both fire-setting and percussion.

Figure 11.13 Soapstone carving of a bird from the Hill Complex, Great
Zimbabwe, Zimbabwe.

Radiocarbon dating and exotic imports provide the basis of Great Zimbabwe's
chronology (Huffman and Vogel 1991 *pace* Chipunza 1997). Phase III, when
stone wall construction commenced, is contemporary with Mapungubwe, dating 1220–75. It witnessed construction of solid *daga* houses, the introduction of
new ceramics different from those of the preceding Gumanye occupants and the
building of the P-style south wall on the Hill. Dates from middens and wooden
lintels in the Great Enclosure and house floors on the Hill bracket Phase IV
at 1275–1550. An initial transitional period is marked by well-burnished recurved and straightnecked jars and the construction of both P and R walls.

Figure 11.14   The conical tower in the Great Enclosure, Great Zimbabwe, Zimbabwe. Huffman (1996b) suggests that its formal resemblance to a granary, location within the Great Enclosure and original surmounting by a check pattern of walling identify it as symbolising senior male status.

The site's apogee followed 1300–1450, at the start of which both Q walling and graphite-burnished Zimbabwe-type pottery were innovated. The site remained occupied for about a century thereafter, perhaps on a reduced scale and with walls now built only in Q and R styles. Blue-on-white Chinese porcelain from some Valley enclosures documents occupation into the 1500s, when de Barros describes it as a 'fortress' (Collett *et al.* 1992). Later activity included sacrifices to the Shona god Mwari, which were carried out on the Hill until the 1830s, but local histories reach back only into the seventeenth century.

The Shona term '*zimbabwe*' (plural *madzimbabwe*), often glossed as 'venerated houses' or 'houses of stone', more properly refers to a ruler's court, grave or house; sixteenth-century Portuguese authors record its use for all royal residences. In successive papers Huffman (1984b, 1984c, 1986, 1996b) has argued that such sites give concrete expression to a pattern of sacred leadership in which rulers were secluded on hilltops with their ritual sister and a few officials, surrounded and protected by concentric circles of courtiers, wives, nobles and commoners. Supporting the existence of an emerging class structure, the ruling élite was probably endogamous and had preferential or exclusive access to both imports and more basic items, such as cattle. First emerging at Mapungubwe, associated features of this Zimbabwe Tradition include breaking the Central Cattle Pattern's link between byre and court, the creation of two courts, one public for settling commoner disputes, the other private for intra-élite disputes, élite burials on hilltops rather than in cattle byres and the use of stone walls to demarcate élite residences. The ethnography employed to construct this model is fourfold: Portuguese references to the sixteenth/seventeenth-century Mutapa state; Shona ethnography collected in the early 1900s that may reach back to the sixteenth century, though not to Great Zimbabwe itself; modern Shona informants said to understand the organisational principles involved, even though sacred kingship and its associated class structure disappeared in the early 1800s; and ethnographic accounts of the Venda of north-eastern South Africa, who retained these features much longer.

Following the main elements of Huffman's model, the hilltop associations of kingship identify the Hill as the palace of Great Zimbabwe's ruler and his ritual sister; a bronze hoe and spear may have been part of the king's regalia, while features of a *daga* house in the Western Enclosure suggest it belonged to his diviner. The large boulders, rock-shelter and covered passage of the Eastern Enclosure identify this as a ritual centre, especially for rain-making; finds are non-domestic, including the majority of the soapstone birds and several soapstone bowls probably used in sacrifices. The open area between the Hill and the Great Enclosure may have served as the main court, with many of the Valley Enclosures belonging to royal wives (recall Huffman's interpretation of the grooves). Identifying Enclosure 1 ('Renders Ruin') as the residence of the king's main wife is supported by its 'treasure', since she is the person who should have controlled this. Finds include glazed Persian bowls, Chinese

celadon and stoneware, Near Eastern glass, coral, several kilograms of brass wire and cowries, tens of thousands of glass beads, over 200 kg of iron wire, hoes, axes and chisels, ivory, three iron gongs and their strikers and other gold and copper objects (Garlake 1973a).

Earlier interpretations of the Great Enclosure (Garlake 1982) suggested it was the king's palace. Huffman (1996b) contends, however, that it was used for premarital initiation ceremonies for both young men and women, similar to *domba* among modern Venda. This accounts for its size, its location close to the putative home of the main royal wife (Enclosure 1), and the range of figurines and metal-working debris reported from it since both are used in *domba* today. *Domba*'s significance, both for Venda and, if Huffman is correct, at Great Zimbabwe extends far beyond initiation: bringing together noble and commoner children, it unites the population, inculcates ideology and provides a labour force for rulers' fields and building projects. Its organisation by royal wives and the king's ritual sister explains its location close to the wives' compound. Linked to this, Huffman (1996b) analyses geometric designs on Shona divining dice and Venda drums and doors to suggest that the herringbone decoration along the top of the Great Enclosure's outer wall (Fig. 11.15) denotes senior female status. Other patterns signify other statuses, such as that of the king.

Figure 11.15   Herringbone decoration along the top of the outer wall of the Great Enclosure, Great Zimbabwe, Zimbabwe. This patterning is identified by Huffman (1996b) as standing for senior female status.

Criticisms of Huffman's model, of which I have only skimmed the surface here, are many. Beach (1998) argues that his use of ethnographic and historical data is inadequate, either applied to an ethnographic 'present' spanning several centuries, or presented with insufficient information on his choice of contemporary informants and the circumstances in which they were interviewed. The latter point, in particular, seems well made. More generally, criticisms emphasise that the search for an underlying cognitive structure characterising all élite sites of the Zimbabwe Tradition ignores the possibility that multiple symbolic systems were in use, suppresses inter-site variability and has difficulty in allowing for change over time (Beach *et al.* 1997). The applicability of Venda ethnography is particularly contentious, especially as regards the suggestion that Shona practised *domba*, something unreported in recent ethnography, Portuguese documents or their own oral traditions (Blacking 1985). Since Venda language and culture draw on Sotho, as well as Shona, sources, the possibility cannot be excluded that *domba* reflects the influence of the former, who have similar initiation schools, rather than the latter, who today do not (Beach 1998).

Huffman's (1997b) response stresses the overall importance of the Shona component to Venda material culture, language and origins and the fact that they organised their royal settlements in ways similar to those found at Great Zimbabwe and other Zimbabwe Tradition sites (Huffman and Hanisch 1987). Reiterating this conclusion, Loubser (1991a, 1998) points to other specific continuities, for example in using ceramic and stone figurines and building stone towers in royal settlements. We may also accept that alternative symbolic systems would have been subordinated to those of the élite, though surely competing with them, and perhaps in ways that had material consequences. Furthermore, Huffman (1996b) himself argues for several important changes of belief and practice during the second millennium, including the abandonment of circumcision schools (itself a controversial suggestion; Beach *et al.* 1997) and the (nineteenth-century?) emergence of spirit mediums possessed by royal ancestors. Nevertheless, while accepting the validity of multiple construction phases at Great Zimbabwe, Huffman argues that all conform to his overall scheme, even though the demonstration of functional continuity in specific areas must necessarily rest upon very limited excavated evidence. The contrary view, put by Collett *et al.* (1992), is that a complex architectural history makes it unlikely that the meanings of particular spaces will have remained static over several generations and that some supposedly symbolic elements, such as *mihombwe*, belong only to the site's latter phases.

Debate continues, but Huffman's interpretation is by far the most ambitious and comprehensive effort at understanding Great Zimbabwe and similar settlements. Nevertheless, it may not be unfair to agree with Soper (1997) that, partly because of the limited degree of excavation yet undertaken, the data and interpretations offered remain too enmeshed and dependent on extended chains of inference to carry total conviction. What they do do, however, is to set an agenda for future studies of Zimbabwe Tradition sites.

Great Zimbabwe: the wider context

Great Zimbabwe is far from unique and can only be understood in a context broader than that of a single site. Huffman's emphasis on the cognitive structures shared across the whole Zimbabwe Tradition is one means of doing this. Another is to focus on those sites, with or without stone walling, that formed part of the same political and economic system. Whether this constituted a single polity is unknown. The historically documented situation from the sixteenth century onward, when Khami, however large and complex, was merely one of several states in and eastward of the Zimbabwe Plateau (Beach 1994), suggests that it may not have been, and Garlake (1978) argues for ten competing territories. Huffman (1986), however, points out that some sites use walling styles first invented at Great Zimbabwe and that the latter's ceramics are intrusive into other areas. He discerns a hierarchy of six distinct settlement levels, the bottom two commoner agricultural sites organised around the Central Cattle Pattern with little or no walling, such as Montevideo (Sinclair 1984). The next three levels have increasingly large walled areas, all probably dependent on Great Zimbabwe since one of the largest, Majiri (6800 m^2), is only 22 km distant. Great Zimbabwe, with a walled area of 25,000 m^2, most of the known gold objects and some 90 per cent of all imported ceramics from the period 1275–1500 is far and away at the top of this hierarchy. By implication, its ruler may have controlled most of the Zimbabwe Plateau and adjacent areas, making this the largest indigenous polity to emerge in southern Africa (Huffman 1986), even if its extent fluctuated over time for specific political and economic reasons now lost to archaeology (cf. Beach 1998).

Excavations at some of the broadly contemporary *madzimbabwe* help flesh out our knowledge of the Great Zimbabwe polity (Fig. 11.16). Both Tsindi (Rudd 1984) and Nhunguza (Garlake 1973b), for example, saw construction of Q walling and solid *daga* houses. Nhunguza, which is smaller, has sufficient Q walling to enclose housing for just one extended family. Inside was a three-roomed solid *daga* structure, its roof supported by a ring of posts outside the wall; internal *daga* platforms may have been for storage and/or display of ceremonial items. The enclosure's small size and highly restricted ceramic range, again emphasising beer-drinking, imply the existence of commoner dwellings nearby, but these were not investigated. Other sites, like Ruanga and Wazi, suggest the implantation of stonewalled *zimbabwe* sites on earlier Musengezi occupations, again with commoner settlements of pole-and-*daga* houses beyond (Garlake 1973b; Sinclair *et al.* 1993b).

Expansion beyond the Zimbabwe Plateau is also indicated. In the eastern Kalahari, *madzimbabwe* extend from Sowa Pan to the Lotsane River (Denbow

Figure 11.16   House platform under excavation at Kagumbudzi *zimbabwe*,
south-eastern Zimbabwe (courtesy Anders Lindahl).

1986). Though most belong to the later Khami state, both its interests and those
of Great Zimbabwe may have focused on exploiting local resources: copper
at Thakadu (Huffman *et al.* 1995), iron in the Tswapong Hills and salt from
the Makgadikgadi Pans. There sites like Toranju, traditionally associated with
Khoe-speakers, have produced stone artefacts, along with glass and copper beads

Figure 11.17   Stone walling at Thulamela, Northern Province, South Africa
(courtesy Fumiko Ohinata).

and cowrie shells that speak to long-distance connections; published details
are few, but they may document incorporation of foragers and herders into
the politico-economic systems centred at the *madzimbabwe* (Denbow 1986).
Further east, sites like Matanga, a late fourteenth/early fifteenth-century cattle
post, probably represent the area's commoner population, descended from the
makers of Leopard's Kopje pottery (van Waarden 1987).

South of the Limpopo and north of the Soutpansberg, Mapungubwe-derived
communities survived into the fourteenth century contemporary with the establishment of Sotho-speaking makers of early Moloko pottery (Loubser 1991a;
chapter 12). Numerous Zimbabwe Tradition sites belong to the ensuing Khami
phase, the early ones perhaps linked to penetration by the Great Zimbabwe
state itself. In the far north of Kruger National Park, Thulamela (Fig. 11.17)
was a major settlement covering 9 ha, its walls built in the fourteenth and
mid-fifteenth centuries; glass beads, seashell ornaments, gold and ivory imply
contacts with the east coast (Küsel 1992; Steyn *et al.* 1998). Two élite burials, both within stone enclosures, further document its importance. That of a
woman dates to the sixteenth century, the other of a man to the fifteenth.
He was buried in a grave pit below and inside a solid *daga* structure, apparently after the body itself had decomposed, a practice recorded for senior
Venda chiefs (Stayt 1931). Both were accompanied by jewellery of gold and

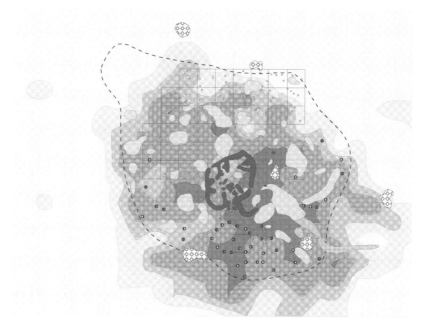

Figure 11.18   Plan of Manyikeni *zimbabwe,* Mozambique, showing stone walls (solid black), houses and middens (circles) and variation in soil phosphate levels (stippling). Grid squares were excavated and the dotted line shows the distribution of surface ceramics (courtesy Paul Sinclair).

other materials, the man also with further objects with specifically royal associations, such as a double iron gong and lion teeth. A similar grave, which may be of a woman, is known from Castle Kopje, Zimbabwe (N. Walker 1991), this time in the hilltop location expected of the Zimbabwe Tradition's élite.

To the east of the Plateau, Manyikeni's position over 400 km south-east of the nearest *zimbabwe* and 50 km from both Vilanculos Bay and the older, but still occupied, settlement at Chibuene suggests that it was an important site (Garlake 1976; Fig. 11.18). A single elliptical enclosure made of local limestone, a more intractable material than the granite used on the Plateau, resembles the P walling at Great Zimbabwe. Inside, at least some buildings were of solid *daga;* as at Ruanga and Nhunguza a commoner settlement lay outside. Pottery also resembles that of the Zimbabwe Tradition rather than anything found elsewhere in Mozambique. Oral traditions refer to dissident royals from Great Zimbabwe establishing themselves locally in the 1400s and the Portuguese observed several Shona states dominating the indigenous Tonga population (A.K. Smith 1973). However, since Manyikeni was first occupied in the thirteenth century, perhaps Shona expansion began then in order to establish closer control over links with the trans-Indian Ocean trade. Manyikeni's own participation in this is evident from several hundred glass beads and two pieces of blue-on-white Chinese porcelain. Other attractions perhaps included a location on a major tsetse-free route linking Great Zimbabwe to the sea, the local availability of ivory and salt from coastal *pans* and an ideal position for cereal cultivation relative to local rainfall patterns (Barker 1978). However, unless cattle, the main domestic animal, were wholly imported, they must have been moved seasonally further inland to avoid trypanosomiasis, seasonal drought and poor winter grazing.

Turning to the coast itself, Chibuene too was occupied from the thirteenth century, perhaps after a hiatus. Its ceramics resemble those from Manyikeni, as well as pottery elsewhere in the Bazaruto archipelago (Sinclair *et al.* 1993b). However, archaeological evidence for the development of coastal urban communities is limited. The modern town of Sofala may have seen occupation before 1500, but this is unclear (Dickinson 1975). Sancul Tradition pottery, with its characteristic raised appliqué wheel-made vessels, occurs here and as far south as the Save River; its distribution *may* relate to that of KiSwahili-speakers. North of the Zambezi, coastal settlements with stone walls and coral buildings certainly reach back to the tenth century and presumably form part of the general development of Swahili urban life along East Africa's littoral (Duarte 1993; Sinclair *et al.* 1993b; Duarte and Meneses 1996). Portuguese sources indicate that both north and south of the Zambezi such towns were substantially Muslim by 1500 (Newitt 1978).

Great Zimbabwe: creating and maintaining the state

Several explanations have been offered for the rise of the Great Zimbabwe state or states, none wholly satisfactory. Garlake (1978), for example, identified control over transhumant pastoralism as an important economic activity, suggesting that sites cluster along the edge of the Zimbabwe Plateau, an optimal location for herding within seasonally tsetse-infested low-lying areas in winter and on the tsetse-free plateau in summer. The strong emphasis on cattle at Great Zimbabwe, Manyikeni and other sites could support this model, though Garlake does not sufficiently consider that this was an élite phenomenon. Sinclair (1987) too identifies correlations with areas offering good pasturage, though significantly Great Zimbabwe itself and many contemporary sites lie in those areas of the Plateau agriculturally most productive under Little Ice Age conditions (Huffman 1996a). Site catchment analyses confirm that proximity to prime arable land was important at the level of specific settlements (Sinclair *et al.* 1993b; Pwiti 1997b), while palaeobotanical samples indicate cultivation of sorghum, pearl millet, finger millet and Bambara groundnuts, along with collection of various wild grasses (Jonsson 1998). Controlling access to agriculturally productive areas may have been an important means by which élites dominated the rest of the population (Sinclair 1984).

It should come as little surprise that a successful agropastoral economy underpinned Great Zimbabwe. Of greater interest is the significance of other 'indigenous' resources, such as metal, cattle and intra-African trade, relative to exchange links with the Indian Ocean coast. Analysing the use of metals at Great Zimbabwe, Herbert (1996) suggests that, whatever gold's significance as an internationally tradable commodity, within the Zimbabwe Tradition it was an 'add-on' decorative item, perhaps even restricted to the period of Great Zimbabwe's ascendancy; though found in élite burials, it is not employed in Shona ritual objects today. Bronze had similarly limited uses, again principally as wire, nails and sheathing. Tin for its manufacture was probably obtained from the transVaal, where the Rooiberg Mountains were extensively mined during the second millennium.

One resource with which the Great Zimbabwe area certainly is well endowed is iron ore; it witnessed extensive iron production during the nineteenth century (Herbert 1996). As well as iron's obvious technological importance, two lines of enquiry suggest that it had a much wider significance. First, sixteenth-century Portuguese sources, Holleman (1952) for early twentieth-century Shona, and Stayt (1931) for the Venda document the use of iron hoes as bridewealth, especially by commoners. Wingfield (2000) goes on to argue that the ease with which they could be converted into weapons or ritual items for ancestors and their necessity for the agricultural bulk of the population gave them a universal exchange value, as opposed to the more limited circulation of the cloth, gold and beads on which attention has traditionally fixed. The mass of iron objects found in Renders Ruin thus takes on a new significance. Second, Dewey (1991) notes that the iron staffs, spears, knives and axes used in Shona ritual contexts today descend from forms used at Great Zimbabwe, while iron as a material subject to multiple transformations of colour and form is also integrated with Shona systems of symbolic classification (Wingfield 2000).

Controlling iron production may thus have been important for rulers. Significantly, Herbert (1996) argues that reports of slag and/or furnace remains at Great Zimbabwe cannot be dismissed. Though iron-smelting in a royal/domestic context seems contrary to recent Shona practice, there is, as we have seen, evidence for this in first-millennium Chifumbaze sites that may have been occupied by ancestral Shona-speakers or their close relatives. We should not therefore ignore the possibility that iron-working was brought within the ambit of élite power. Indeed, the iron gongs from Great Zimbabwe, which as symbols of royal status are more typical of second-millennium southern Congo-Kinshasa and Zambia, suggest this. Alternatively, their production, along with that of wire, hoes and other artefacts, may have been undertaken for exchange with communities along the Zambezi, such as that represented at Ingombe Ilede (Fagan 1969).

Cross-shaped copper ingots and copper wire of the kind found here also occur at other *madzimbabwe*, supporting a two-way exchange in these metals; salt is another possible import from the Zambezi Valley or the Sowa Pan onto the Plateau (Garlake 1973a; M. Hall 1987).

Faunal analyses indicate that access to cattle was another component of élite power. This is unsurprising, given their significance as symbols of wealth and vehicles for communicating with ancestors, but in the Zimbabwe Tradition this may have taken on a new form without ethnohistoric parallels. Assemblages from Great Zimbabwe's Hill Complex appear to demonstrate preferential (some 75 per cent) consumption of young cattle aged under 30 months, with only marginal use of caprines or game (Brain 1974; Barker 1988; Thorp 1995; Reid 1996). Elsewhere at Great Zimbabwe and at other *madzimbabwe* moderate numbers of young cattle (in the order of 40 per cent) may reflect a normal offtake strategy. A possible third pattern, featuring very few immature adult cattle, may be represented at two commoner sites, including Montevideo, but assemblages are small and not analysed in detail. Sinclair (1984) has argued that these data suggest that conspicuously consuming prime beef may have been another means by which the élite demonstrated their separation from, and power over, the rest of the population. Appealing as this argument is, it is difficult to be categorical. Reid (1996) points out that the Hill Complex sample from Great Zimbabwe has no detailed provenance and could reflect more than one pattern of slaughter and consumption. The emphasis he notes on old juvenile/young adult animals at Great Zimbabwe, Toutswe and the Greefswald sites may equally speak to the importance attached to provisioning these larger sites, and particularly royal entourages, with a regular supply of meat. This may, as Sinclair (1984) argues, have derived in part from tribute from rural peasant communities, and Venda ethnography suggests élites sought to monopolise cattle ownership (Stayt 1931; Loubser 1991a).

I have left until last the connections between Great Zimbabwe and the east coast. Beach (1994) emphasises that the Zimbabwe Plateau was the only area in eastern or southern Africa to combine ivory with gold, so giving greatest returns for the limited amount of capital available first to Swahili and later to Portuguese traders. Copper from northern Zimbabwe and transVaal tin may have been other exports, with cloth, beads and exotic ceramics remaining the main imports. Writing in the mid-fourteenth century, ibn Battuta remarked that gold came to Sofala from 'Yufi', a month's journey inland (Gibbs 1962). Despite confusion with West African gold sources, 'Yufi' must refer to the Zimbabwe Plateau. From Sofala, which seems to have been under its control, gold moved north to Kilwa, at this time the largest and most important Swahili town. With rare neatness, Great Zimbabwe has produced a copper coin bearing the name of the sultan of Kilwa whom ibn Battuta visited, Abu al-Mawahib al-Hasan ibn Sulaiman (Huffman 1972). As Europeans too began to mint gold coins on a large scale, increased world demand in the late thirteenth and early fourteenth centuries probably paved the way for the prominence of both Kilwa and Great Zimbabwe, as expressed by their growing size and expansive building projects (Huffman 1996b; Sutton 1998). Kilwa, like other Swahili towns, maintained wide-ranging contacts across the Indian Ocean, extending to the Middle East, India and even China. All the Indo-Pacific glass beads found on the Zimbabwe Plateau, for example, though made in India, seem to have entered southern Africa via Kilwa (M. Wood 2000). However, while the two were at least partly interdependent, and Great Zimbabwe's relative closeness to gold sources and the coast may help explain how it eclipsed Mapungubwe, no evidence has come to light to suggest that it too declined in the late 1300s; perhaps other Swahili towns stepped into the breach. Alternatively, having partly developed on the back of international trade, perhaps the state's infrastructure was sufficiently consolidated to survive such downturns unaffected, using cattle husbandry, craft production and intra-African exchange networks as other sources of élite power (M. Hall 1987).

Focusing on gold and ivory as exports suggests that Great Zimbabwe and other southern African polities were subject to the exploitation of outside powers, caught in a core–periphery relationship (Wallerstein 1974; Champion 1989) from which they could not extricate themselves as they began a still continuing process by which Africa exported non-renewable raw materials without building up its own economic strength. But this may be to misunderstand what was taking place. Direct evidence of gold production is scarce because many ancient sites have been obliterated by modern mining (Swan 1994). However, both mining and alluvial panning were probably the labour-intensive work of peasant farmers (especially women) in the agricultural off-season (Phimister 1976). Gold, and perhaps other exports, were thus economically marginal activities (M. Hall 1987: 102), an African equivalent of the mass-produced glass beads and cloth for which they were principally exchanged. Finds of crucibles and gold-working tools at *madzimbabwe* do suggest, however, that goldsmiths operated under élite control (N. Walker 1991). Manufacture of copper ornaments, Great Zimbabwe's distinctive graphite-burnished pottery (Garlake 1982) and the soapstone dishes and monoliths almost exclusively found there may also have been court crafts, producing further items susceptible to redistribution as valued gifts to subordinates, alongside imported goods.

Whatever the benefits that junior rulers and their dependants obtained from participating in the system focused on Great Zimbabwe, coercion, of one kind or another, was presumably also important in maintaining élite power; in more recent centuries both the Mutapa and Rozvi states retained small professional armies (Beach 1994). Religious power can be exaggerated, but the associations between kings and their ancestors, especially in securing rain, may well have been significant, as illustrated by Great Zimbabwe's Eastern Enclosure (Huffman 1996b) and the internal partitioning of the Nhunguza *zimbabwe* (Garlake 1973b).

Such issues of power and ideology are certainly present in all the explanations we have considered. Perhaps Blanton *et al.*'s (1996) distinction between exclusionary and corporate power strategies in discussing early Mesoamerican states may prove helpful in understanding state formation processes within the Zimbabwe Tradition. Were, for example, exclusionary strategies pursued more strongly early on at Bambandyanalo, with the main emphasis one of limiting access to foreign goods, for example through making the 'Garden Roller' beads? If so, did corporate ones, emphasizing the sacred rôle of the king in interceding through his ancestors to ensure rain and prosperity, become more important when élites segregated themselves behind stonewalled enclosures and on hilltops at Mapungubwe and Great Zimbabwe? Could this contrast also connect, as in Mesoamerica, with differences in agricultural productivity, exclusionary strategies being more important in ecologically marginal areas (the Shashe–Limpopo Basin) than in those with greater farming potential (the Zimbabwe Plateau)? To turn to another issue, how far can we find evidence for élites developing an international style that would have reconfirmed their legitimacy *vis-à-vis* other élites? Did the exotic ceramics and iron gongs at Great Zimbabwe (Garlake 1973a) help do this by making reference to élite practices on the Swahili coast on the one hand, and in the Zambian/Katangan Copperbelt on the other? Extending this idea further, could such competitive emulation have played a part in the spread of the Zimbabwe Tradition and the incorporation/subordination of other communities into it, as local Gumanye, Harare and Musengezi élites found new ways of extending their power? And how far were these populations sources of innovation within the Zimbabwe Tradition and/or of worldviews that competed with it? As an alternative to viewing the expansion of the Kutama and Zimbabwe Traditions in ethnic or cultural-historical terms, such an extension to southern Africa of Renfrew and Cherry's (1986) ideas of peer-polity interaction demands further investigation.

These tentatively advanced thoughts underline the importance of considering the Zimbabwe Tradition in a wider context than has generally been the case. Issues of core–periphery relationships and the development and transformation of prestige-goods economies are universal (Champion 1989; Wolf 1982). As just one example,[1] what might come from a comparative analysis of the interactions between the East African coast and the southern African interior during the first and second millennia AD on the one hand, and between western Temperate Europe's interior and the expanding economies and states of the

---

[1] Cahokia, the major Mississippian centre in the American Midwest that is virtually contemporary with Bambandyanalo and Mapungubwe, offers another comparison, here focusing on how massive monumental construction and attendant social hierarchies could develop in the absence of external trade with already established states or extensive territorial control (Pauketat and Emerson 1997).

Classical World in the first millennium BC on the other (Cunliffe 1997)? While *Fürstensitzen* and *oppida* were surely not a direct analogue of *madzimbabwe*, perhaps archaeologists working in both areas have something to learn from such a study, not least an improved understanding of how complex systems form and collapse.

Power, indeed, is never wholly secure, especially where exercised without the benefit of transportation aids (boats, horses, wheeled vehicles, etc.) over an area as large as that probably controlled by Great Zimbabwe. Destruction episodes at some *madzimbabwe* may document violent resistance to authority (Monro and Spies 1975). Certainly on the larger geopolitical scale, tensions between those ruling Great Zimbabwe and provincial élites must always have existed as they competed for access to desirable, highly valued imports and the items that could be exchanged for them. Such factors, along with the ever-present vulnerability of both the arable and pastoral components of the subsistence base to drought and disease (Barker 1988), may provide the most plausible backdrop to explaining why Great Zimbabwe declined as a major centre after 1450. Additional reasons may include changing patterns of international trade and the long-term ecological impact of a dense population on the availability of fuel and arable land (Sinclair 1984), but the former is difficult to substantiate and post-1420 climate amelioration should have made agricultural production easier (Huffman 1997b). Whatever the precise causes, Great Zimbabwe's dominance broke down by the late 1400s, with several successor states emerging.

The later phases of the Zimbabwe Tradition and other developments on the Zimbabwe Plateau

When the Portuguese penetrated Africa's interior in the early sixteenth century the first major kingdom encountered was that of the Mutapa focused in northeastern Zimbabwe. Though documents and oral histories cannot be closely integrated before 1629 (Beach 1994), the Mutapa state was already established in the late 1400s and had reached the coast north of the Zambezi's mouth *c.* 1550. A stone platform capped with *daga* houses at Songo may be a newly constructed regional centre related to this expansion (Macamo and Duarte 1996). Soon after, however, élite use of stone architecture ceased and rulers' capitals were surrounded by wooden stockades. Portuguese interest centred on controlling trade in gold and ivory, with small trading communities established in the 1540s and the first (unsuccessful) attempts at conquest following in 1569. After internal wars, the Portuguese were able to impose a treaty of vassalship in 1629, but this was not permanent. Reorganised in the late 1660s, the Mutapa state shifted its focus down into the Zambezi Valley, surviving there into the late nineteenth century (Beach 1994).

Figure 11.19   Baranda, north-eastern Zimbabwe. Surface survey underway prior to excavation (courtesy Innocent Pikirayi).

Despite earlier claims to the contrary, the Mutapa polity cannot be directly linked via oral traditions to the Great Zimbabwe state (Beach 1994). Huffman (1986) suggests that it controlled an area of some 30,000 km^2 at its peak, but wrongly identifies Mount Fura as its capital (Pikirayi 1993). Nearby, the latter's fieldwork located several unwalled sites with graphite-burnished pottery similar to that of Great Zimbabwe's Phase IV. Baranda is the most extensively investigated (Fig. 11.19), but the bulk of its evidence relates only to the sixteenth/seventeenth centuries when it served as a trading centre, first for Swahili merchants and then for the Portuguese, who probably knew it as Massapa and built a fort and church in the early 1600s. Pole-and-*daga* houses are arranged around open spaces, some of which may have been markets. Quantities of slag and iron implements suggest a substantial local iron industry. Imports include glass beads, glass, and Near Eastern, Oriental and Iberian glazed wares. I consider other archaeological evidence of Portuguese activity in chapter 13.

In the same general area as Baranda are numerous hilltop sites with roughly circular, coarse stone enclosures. Many are equipped with 'loopholes', though their low level and restricted view suggest they were unsuitable for firearm use (Fig. 11.20). Imported beads or ceramics are few and the carinated pottery is quite distinct from the graphite-burnished wares mentioned earlier; architectural tradition and layout are also wholly different from the Zimbabwe

Figure 11.20   Part of the walling of a 'loopholed' enclosure at Muchekayawa,
north-eastern Zimbabwe (courtesy Innocent Pikirayi). The
'loophole' is to the right of the measuring staff.

Tradition. Dubbed the Mahonje Tradition (Pikirayi 1993), they may represent the indigenous population of north-eastern Zimbabwe subsequent to the
implantation of ruling lineages associated with the Mutapa state (Soper 1994).
Their seventeenth-century appearance may also be a reaction to generalised
insecurity as this broke down and relocated into the Zambezi Valley (Pikirayi
1997a).

   Oral traditions permit reconstructions of the histories of various Shona dy-
nasties in northern and central Zimbabwe, but these have not been looked at
archaeologically (Beach 1980, 1994). Suggestions that some developments, such
as that of the Duma confederacy, represent moves away from centralised state
power and involvement with external trade are particularly interesting. So too
is the possibility that the Tsindi *zimbabwe* retained a ritual significance into
the 1830s (Rudd 1984); extensive eighteenth/nineteenth-century cairnfields in
the same general area have also been investigated (Matenga 1994).

   By far the most distinctive development of the period following Great
Zimbabwe's decline was in the Nyanga Highlands and the adjacent lowland area
near Ziwa. Spreading over some 5000 km^2 are extensive areas of agricultural terracing and associated settlements (Fig. 11.21). Following several earlier studies
(e.g. Summers 1958), this area has recently been systematically examined by
a joint team from the British Institute in Eastern Africa and the University of

Figure 11.21   Agricultural terracing, Nyanga Highlands, Zimbabwe.

Zimbabwe (Soper 1996). The terracing and associated cultivation ridges appear designed to conserve and concentrate soil, clear land for agricultural use and in some cases facilitate drainage. This was also achieved by digging ditches in *vleis* and on valley sides to allow water to seep into the soil, while removing any excess. Water furrows, so far found only in highland grassland areas, may have brought water into fields, but there is no definite sign of irrigation. Instead, most, perhaps all, brought water to groups of pit structures for household, livestock and garden use. Excavations at Ziwa demonstrate cultivation of Bambara groundnuts, cowpeas, sorghum, pearl millet, finger millet and cucurbits; maize occurs only in the most recent contexts (Summers 1958).

Settlements are of several kinds. Over 1400 pit structures are distributed in upland areas within and beyond the main terraced areas, singly or in groups of up to thirty (Fig. 11.22). Two to three metres deep, the pits, neatly faced with stone and set within stone-revetted platforms on which sit house floors and other structures, give protection from the wind. Floors are paved or on bedrock, with a drain on the lower side and a tunnel entrance passage on the upper. Similarities in settlement architecture and ceramics suggest close links between upland and lowland communities (Soper 1996). Cattle were, indeed, the dominant livestock species, but the highly standardised tunnels and passages are too small for modern animals. Instead, faunal analyses confirm oral traditions of a dwarf breed, no more than 1 m high at the shoulder (Plug *et al.* 1997). Caprines, on the other hand, were probably kept inside houses, which commonly have a central

Figure 11.22   Pit structure and reconstructed houses, Nyanga Highlands,
Zimbabwe.

partition dividing human and animal habitation areas. Kraaling livestock in
pits suggests that people used the manure, but it is unclear whether animals
were penned in them permanently or only at night, which would have provided
sufficient fertiliser only for gardens. Limited manuring, or a limited fertility
span for the terraced areas, would account both for the extent of the terracing
and numbers of pit enclosures as a whole (Soper 1996) and for the otherwise
surprisingly low human and cattle populations Beach (1996) estimates from
historical data.

The Nyanga complex was probably initiated around 1500, after the initial
severe phase of the Little Ice Age (Soper 1996). So-called 'forts' with substantial walls 2 m high and thick appear defensive in nature and have at
least one lintelled entrance, evidence for some kind of barrier and frequently
rough banquettes, parapets and 'loopholes' (Fig. 11.23). Several sites beyond
the Nyangombe River include numerous house floors, but others seem to have
been temporary refuges, devoid of permanent occupation. The larger examples
suggest minor social ranking and at Muozi one exceptionally large house featuring numerous grindstones, monoliths, iron objects and complete pots may
have belonged to a prominent rain-maker, perhaps explaining the numerous
glass and copper beads from the associated village (Plug *et al.* 1997). Except for
such beads, the area seems to have been effectively outside trading connections
with the east coast.

Figure 11.23   Part of the stone walling at Chawonera 'fort', Nyanga Highlands,
Zimbabwe.

Its greater accessibility to the Portuguese makes Mutapa the historically best
known of Great Zimbabwe's successors, but archaeological research has been
much fuller to the south and south-west. Here Khami was the capital of the
Torwa state from the fifteenth to seventeenth centuries, before being succeeded
by Danangombe (Dhlo-Dhlo) after the Rozvi conquest of the 1680/90s. The tradition of using stone walling to demarcate élite areas survived in this area
into the 1800s, allowing Huffman (1996b) to argue that the cognitive model
of settlement architecture and worldview he discerns can also be applied to
Great Zimbabwe and its contemporaries. Covering some 40 ha, Khami itself
lies to the west of Bulawayo (Fig. 11.24). Its distinctive building form combines stonewalled house platforms with low, free-standing walls, often decorated with chequer and herringbone designs (of the kind seen in Fig. 11.25) that
identify royal and other statuses. Why such designs should have been so greatly
elaborated remains unknown, and both Khami (K. Robinson 1959) and Danangombe (Caton-Thompson 1931) experienced complex architectural histories,
again necessitating caution in applying a single structuralist interpretation.

    Compared with earlier Great Zimbabwe-phase sites, steep hilltops were now
less commonly used, with terracing giving stepped profiles to lower hills, perhaps in continuity from Mapungubwe and Mapela. Up to 100 Khami-phase
sites, accompanied by distinctive bichrome band-and-panel decorated pottery,
occur across western Zimbabwe and the north-eastern and central eastern areas

Figure 11.24   Hill Ruin, Khami, Zimbabwe (courtesy Tom Huffman).

Figure 11.25   Decorative stone walling, Danangombe, Zimbabwe (courtesy Tom Huffman).

of Botswana, where gold, copper, salt, ivory and skins may all have been important resources. As at Great Zimbabwe, excavations have emphasised élite areas, with three ceramic birds from Vukwe a unique parallel to Great Zimbabwe's soapstone birds (van Waarden 1998). Vumba is a rare example of a commoner settlement, organised according to the CCP (van Waarden 1991). At Khami itself the Hill Ruin has several features identifying it as the palace. They include an underground room, perhaps the equivalent of the rock-shelter in Great Zimbabwe's Eastern Enclosure, equipped with a toolkit of ivory divining dice and other objects for the king's diviner; cloth-wrapped bronze and iron weaponry probably represents the relics of dead kings (Huffman 1996b). Other areas probably housed the king's servants and his ritual sister. Cattle were the main domestic animal, but a wide range of carnivores and other species having associations with Shona diviners was also recovered (Thorp 1984).

The Torwa state remained largely beyond Portuguese reach, though the latter intervened in a civil war in the 1640s. Glass beads and imported ceramics from Khami and elsewhere attest to continuing trade contacts (K. Robinson 1959), as may the presence at Khami of two crops of non-African origin, peanuts (*Arachis hypogaea*) and castor oil (*Ricinus communis*; Jonsson 1998); a sixteenth-century date from the Tebekwe mine near Gweru provides one of the few definite data for precolonial gold exploitation (Swan 1994). Some time between 1683 and 1696 Torwa was conquered by Changamire Dombo, who had already expelled the Portuguese from the Plateau and was leader of a lineage previously subordinate to the Mutapa ruler; some members of the Torwa élite moved northwest into the Hwange area, establishing the Nambya dynasty and building *madzimbabwe* into the eighteenth century (Beach 1980). Changamire's followers, the Rozvi, intermarried with the Torwa ruling class, adopted their Kalanga variant of Shona and continued to use many of the same sites, as well as the same ceramics. Six rulers then reigned from Danangombe, still trading with the Portuguese through African intermediaries (Beach 1994). Moving north as part of the domino effect of the *Mfecane*, several Ngoni groups converged on the Rozvi state in the early 1830s. It collapsed shortly after Danangombe itself fell and the last Changamire died, paving the way for the Ndebele conquest of south-western Zimbabwe in 1838.

South of the Limpopo, Thulamela was probably associated with Torwa in some fashion until its own demise in the mid-1600s (M. Steyn *et al.* 1998), but much further work remains to be undertaken both at the site itself and in its hinterland. At Thulamela and elsewhere in South Africa's Northern Province extensive archaeological research combines with Venda oral traditions to document the expansion of ruling lineages derived from the Torwa and Rozvi states (Huffman and Hanisch 1987; Loubser 1991a). Sites like Tshitaka-tsha-Makolani occur in elevated locations, use regularly coursed walls and have Khami-phase pottery, rare ivory and copper prestige items, and rarer imported beads and ceramics. These sites, dating from the fourteenth century, are termed by Loubser (1991a) the Zimbabwe Pattern; they are remembered as having been occupied by groups whose origins lay north of the Limpopo. Following an earlier period when Khami and Moloko ceramics largely excluded each other spatially, a new tradition termed Tavatshena developed, combining both kinds of motifs (Fig. 11.26). This provides ceramic support

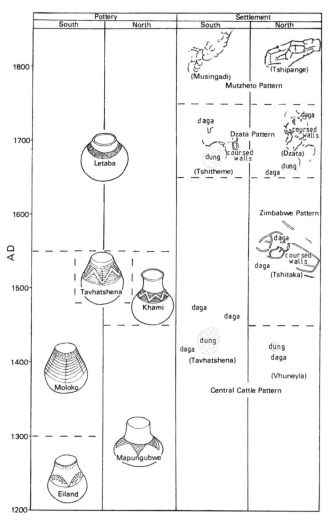

Figure 11.26   Ceramic and settlement sequences in the Soutpansberg area, Northern Province, South Africa. Settlements are not drawn to scale and Central Cattle Pattern settlements occur throughout the period illustrated (after Loubser 1989: Fig. 4; courtesy South African Archaeological Society).

for the interaction of Sotho- and Shona-speakers evident in Vhavenda's mixed linguistic origins; a third element may come from an earlier form of Shona spoken by the makers of the Mapungubwe ceramics still made locally into the fourteenth century. Developing first in the late 1400s and replacing all other styles by 1550, Letaba pottery drew on all these earlier traditions. Normally spherical, pots are graphite-burnished with incised cross-hatching or counter-hatched triangles on the shoulder. Letaba ceramics are widespread across Mpumalanga, Northern Province, southern Zimbabwe and south-western Mozambique.

Torwa's southward expansion may have been to acquire new copper, gold and ivory sources for trade with the east coast and to control flourishing local exchange networks in metals, salt and cereals. Portuguese writers record copper arriving on the coast in the late 1400s (Loubser 1991a) and Tavatshena ceramics occur at Phalaborwa, a major copper-producing site in Mpumalanga's lowveld. Singo royal lineages in Venda today claim to have been the first to introduce political centralisation to primitive 'Ngona' predecessors, misrepresenting history through myth to validate their ascendancy (Loubser, 1990, 1991a). The archaeological record of the Zimbabwe Pattern demonstrates such claims are untrue. Instead, the Singo, whose traditions document a Rozvi origin c. 1680–1700, are associated with the later Dzata Pattern, characterised by short sections of semi-coursed and longer sections of roughly stacked walls. Such sites occur both north and south of the Soutpansberg. Dzata, the largest at 50 ha, was briefly capital of a united Singo state in the early 1700s (Fig. 11.27). Uniquely for sites of this age, excavations produced Khami pottery in the basal levels, reflecting a trans-Limpopo origin. Other finds included ivory divining dice similar to those from Khami (Huffman 1996a) and copper ornaments. Dutch and Portuguese accounts show that these, along with copper ingots, were restricted to powerful chiefs who controlled the production and export of copper and tin. Though cattle do not display the same dominance of young individuals as at Great Zimbabwe, the many wild animals, overrepresentation of choice hindlegs and scarcity of caprines all suggest preferential élite access at both Dzata and Tshirululuni, a later Mutzheto Pattern capital (de Wet-Bronner 1995a, 1995b).

The Singo state split c. 1750, perhaps linked to the change in the main centre of east coast trade from central Mozambique towards Delagoa Bay (Loubser 1991a). As this process developed, further stonewalled sites were built. Sites of the Mutzheto Pattern used uncoursed, terrraced walls and were sited defensively on hilltops across the northern and eastern transVaal. Walls demarcating the main residential area were arranged in interlocking terraced enclosures with the main byre in front and below. Commoners lived below, separated by an upper space from the royal area. This altered during the *Mfecane* as commoners clustered at the bottom of royal settlements, cattle and warriors were

Figure 11.27   Royal audience chamber, Dzata, Northern Province, South Africa (courtesy Tom Huffman).

housed near the court, and chiefs moved to the very back of the royal area (Huffman 1988). During the twentieth century, weakening royal authority and forced resettlement saw sites become smaller and more open, with commoners moving away from royal centres (Loubser 1991a).

Letaba pottery is made today not only by Venda-speakers, but also by several transVaal groups who live in areas where Venda was previously spoken (van Wyk 1969) and were formerly under their influence: Tsonga, Ndebele, Phalaborwa and Lovedu. That Shona-derived communities had greater prestige is further indicated by the adoption of Shona ritual practices and forms of wall-building south of the Soutpansberg, the northward movement of some ceramics, and oral histories documenting a parallel movement of women in marriage (Jacobson *et al.* 1991; Loubser 1991a). Such processes are most apparent among the Lovedu, whose ruling lineage asserts Rozvi descent (Krige and Krige 1943), something supported by similarities between glass beads kept by them and others from Danangombe (Davison and Clark 1976).

One further aspect of these interactions deserves mention since the so-called 'late white' finger paintings of the northern transVaal occur in areas occupied by Venda or Venda-influenced North Sotho-speakers. Broadly similar paintings, some replastered until recently (Cooke 1964), reach north into Zimbabwe and central/east Africa, where they are generally associated with matrilineal or

Figure 11.28   'Late white' finger paintings, Makgabeng area, Northern Province, South Africa, showing ox wagons and saurian motifs (after Prins and Hall 1994: Fig. 4; Pager 1975).

bilateral societies; interestingly, Venda, like Shona, give rulers' sisters important power and also permit women to officiate in ceremonies for ancestors (Prins and Hall 1994). Many motifs, which include schematised humans, animals and abstract images, relate to Venda and North Sotho beliefs about fertility, initiation and reproduction (Fig. 11.28); white is strongly and positively linked to fertility, virility and ancestors, for example, making it a highly suitable choice for such paintings. Another category comprises saurian images. In the Makgabeng area both monitor lizards and finger paintings are instrumental in rain-making ceremonies; stone cairns, grindstones and pottery at other painted sites in the Waterberg document similar actions (Aukema 1989). The emphasis on lizards recalls more widespread Southern Bantu and Khoisan beliefs connecting snakes to rain and water, as well as to Venda associations of crocodiles with fertility, rain-making and kingship. The title of

Huffman's (1996b) book on the cognitive structures underlying the Zimbabwe Tradition, *Snakes and Crocodiles*, perfectly illustrates this point. Crocodile initiation masks, as we saw in chapter 10, are still used by some North Sotho-speakers and were, of course, employed by first-millennium Chifumbaze communities in the transVaal and KwaZulu-Natal. The issues of continuity and change between early and later farming communities at which these paintings and practices hint are ones I examine in greater detail in the next chapter.

LATER FARMING COMMUNITIES IN SOUTHERNMOST AFRICA

Later farming communities in the more southerly parts of southern Africa did not experience the same transformations during the second millennium as those participating in the Zimbabwe Tradition. This is not to say that similarities, if at a less complex scale, cannot also be traced, for example in increasing specialisation of production and exchange, the development of more nucleated settlement patterns and growing political centralisation. Together, they form the background to the cataclysmic events of the late eighteenth/early nineteenth centuries termed by Nguni-speakers the *Mfecane* or, by Sotho/Tswana-speakers, *Lifaqane* or *Difaqane*. As well as having generally lower levels of socio-political complexity prior to this, southernmost Africa shares a certain unity because the archaeology of its later farming communities is clearly that of the ancestors of its present day Sotho/Tswana- and Nguni-speaking inhabitants (Fig. 12.1). Accounting for the appearance of these groups in the archaeological record, their differences from the archaeology of earlier farming communities and the expansion of agropastoralist settlement into the Grassland Biome are among this chapter's other key themes (Fig. 12.2).

The beginning of the Later Iron Age south of the Limpopo

Chapter 10 showed that several features of the settlement pattern and organisation, and ritual practices, of South African Chifumbaze Complex communities differed from those recorded ethnographically among Sotho/Tswana and Nguni peoples (Maggs 1994/95) and that the latter's ceramics cannot be derived from the pottery of the Kalundu Tradition (Huffman 1989). Even at Phalaborwa, sometimes still cited as a contrary case (Ehret 1998: 228), detailed analysis shows no stylistic continuity between the Eiland-like Kgopolwe ceramics of the eleventh to thirteenth centuries and the Moloko pottery that appears in the late thirteenth century (Evers and van der Merwe 1987). Slightly later Moloko pottery (Fig. 12.3) is found in the Limpopo Valley at Icon (Hanisch 1979), on the transVaal plateau at Olifantspoort (Mason 1986) and in south-eastern Botswana (van Waarden 1998). Clearly ancestral (though not entirely so) to the ceramics of modern Sotho/Tswana-speakers, it appears to exhibit a pronounced stylistic break from those at first-millennium sites like Broederstroom (Evers 1983 *pace* Mason 1983). Principal decorative components include bands of hatching

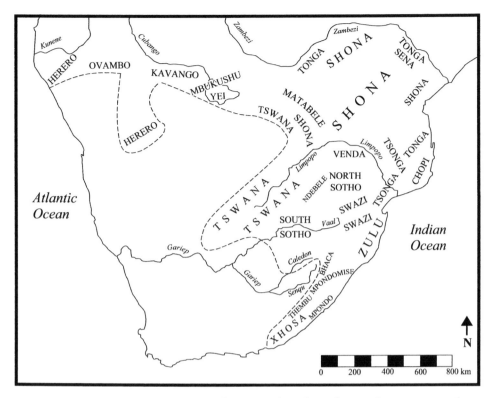

Figure 12.1   Location of Bantu-speaking peoples of southern Africa *c.*1850. The dashed line indicates the approximate limit of Later Iron Age agropastoralist settlement.

or multiple incision spaced down the vessel, with the untextured bands often coloured red or black (Evers 1981).

From about 1100 a second tradition, known as Blackburn, appears along South Africa's eastern seaboard. Blackburn itself produced mostly undecorated pottery (Davies 1971), while the Mpambanyoni assemblage further south includes examples with rim-notching, incised lines and the use of burnished ochre slip (Robey 1980). Both excavations were limited in scope, and subsistence data reflect (perhaps unfairly) massive exploitation of shellfish, especially brown mussels, and some fishing and hunting; there is no firm evidence for farming and extremely little sign of iron production. Nkanya (Feely 1987) and Mpame (Cronin 1982) repeat this story in similar hilltop locations above lagoons along the Transkei coast. As yet, no contemporary farming sites are known further inland in KwaZulu-Natal or the Eastern Cape.

Huffman (1989) argues that similarities between Blackburn and early Moloko wares imply a related, albeit not identical, origin and if this does not lie in southern Africa's own Kalundu Tradition then we must look further north towards

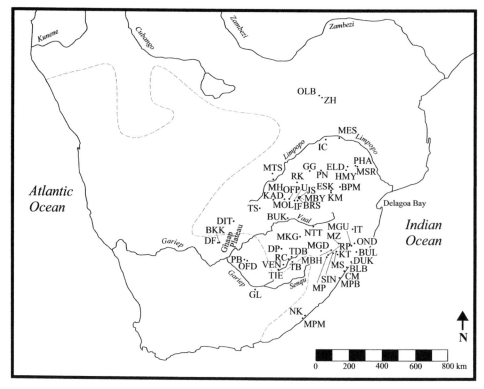

Figure 12.2   Location of archaeological sites discussed in chapter 12. Site
names abbreviated thus: BKK Blinkklipkop; BLB Blackburn;
BPM Boomplaas; BRS Broederstroom; BUK Buffelshoek; BUL
KwaBulawayo; CM Cato Manor; DF Doornfontein; DIT Dithakong;
DP Doornpoort 2826BD10; DUK Dukuza; ELD Eiland; ESK
Esikhunjini; GG Goergap; GL Glen Elliott; HMY Harmony;
IC Icon; IF Ifafi; IT Itala; JS Jubilee Shelter; KAD Kaditshwene;
KM KwaMaza; KT KwaThwaleyakhe; MBH Mabhjia; MBY
Mabyanamatshwaana; MES Messina; MGD Mgoduyanuka; MGU
Mgungundlovu; MH Modipe Hill; MKG Makgwareng; MOL
Molokwane; MP Moor Park; MPB Mpambanyoni; MPM Mpame; MS
Mbabane Shelter; MSR Masorini; MTS Matsieng; MZ Mzinyashana;
NK Nkanya; NTT Ntsuanatsatsi and OU1; OFD OFD1; OFP
Olifantspoort; OLB Old Bulawayo; OND Ondini; PB Pramberg; PHA
Phalaborwa; PN Planknek; RC Rose Cottage Cave; RK Rooikrans;
RP Rongpoort; SIN eSinhlonhlweni; TB Thaba Bosiu; TDB
Tandjesberg; TIE Tienfontein 2; TS Thaba Sione; U Uitkomst Cave;
VEN Ventershoek; ZH Zhizo Hill.

East Africa. Here both the Chifumbaze Complex assemblage from Kalambo
Falls in eastern Zambia and the 'middle component' from the Ivuna saltworks
site, Tanzania, contain a range of ceramic attributes important in Blackburn;
beehive grass huts like those made by the Nguni are also known from the Ivuna

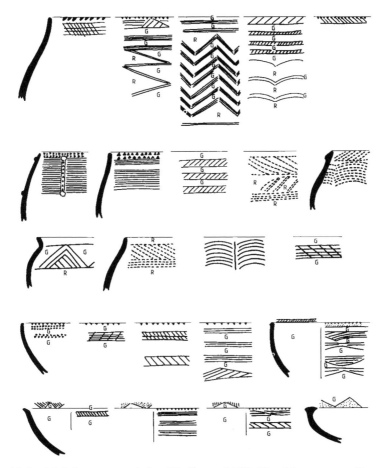

Figure 12.3   Moloko pottery (after Huffman 1989: Fig. 11; courtesy Tom
Huffman). G denotes graphite burnish and R red ochre burnish.

area. Linguistic analyses strengthen these arguments. The closest relatives of
Nguni and Sotho/Tswana occur today in East Africa among a cluster of Eastern
Bantu languages that includes Swahili and Chaga and is marked by the innovative use of a suffix *(i)ni* to denote location. Significantly, Shona, whose speakers Huffman (1989) derives from the makers of Kalundu Tradition Klingbeil
pottery, is excluded from this grouping (Huffman and Herbert 1994/95). The
possibility that many Chifumbaze communities south of the Limpopo spoke
an early version of a language that eventually developed into Shona, only for this
to be superseded in the second millennium by those spoken there today, is supported by Ownby's (1985) identification of Sala loanwords in modern Nguni.
The implication is that Sala (a 'sister' of 'proto-Shona') had a long-standing
presence in south-eastern southern Africa and that its speakers formed a major
element in the ancestry of the Nguni.

This is one of the few suggestions of contact between Sotho/Tswana- and Nguni-speakers on the one hand and the farming communities who, if Huffman is correct, were already long established south of the Limpopo. Both ethnographic and archaeological data demonstrate that the Sotho/Tswana and Nguni are patrilineal and organise their settlements according to the Central Cattle Pattern (Kuper 1980; Evers 1984), implying a degree of continuity and shared worldview with earlier Chifumbaze communities. But how the two interacted remains desperately underresearched. Could, for example, differential patterns of genetic and cultural assimilation account for some of the differences of language, kinship systems and ritual practice between Sotho/Tswana and Nguni populations (cf. Hammond-Tooke 1993)? Other important issues also need to be resolved. Why should ancestral Sotho/Tswana and Nguni groups have left their putative East African homeland in the first place? What were the circumstances by which they ended up in South Africa and where is the evidence for their movement through the intervening area? Must wholesale changes in ceramic design necessarily imply population movement rather than altered social circumstances that made elaborate decoration no longer appropriate (M. Hall 1987)? And do Moloko and Blackburn exhaust the sources for later Sotho/Tswana and Nguni pottery (and populations), leaving no scope for input from earlier southern African farming communities or their ceramics? Given that, for reasons as yet unknown, sites dating 900–1300 are very few in Mpumalanga or south-eastern southern Africa (J.C. Vogel and Fuls 1999), further fieldwork must be a *sine qua non* for addressing these points.

The expansion of farming settlement

If early Moloko or Blackburn settlements are scarce, from about 1300 there is increasing evidence for the beginning of agropastoralist expansion considerably beyond the area settled by earlier farmers and it is to this time that the genealogies of several groups, such as the Mpondo, Rolong and Thembu, reach back (Wilson and Thompson 1969). Among the first signs of this expansion is the appearance of sites like Moor Park (Davies 1974) in the grasslands of KwaZulu-Natal's interior. Adding to the natural defensiveness of hilltop or spur locations, rough stone walling enclosed areas of several hectares that have produced evidence of cattle-keeping and sorghum cultivation. Cattle figurines further attest to the importance of livestock, while bowls, jars and globular pots are mostly undecorated, with tapered rims. Interestingly in the light of the preceding discussion, Davies reported rectangular houses at Moor Park, a rare occurrence south of Tanzania, but this has yet to be confirmed at other sites. Further movement into the Grassland Biome seems to have been tightly linked to a warmer, wetter climate when more regular summer rains provided favourable conditions for cereal cultivation (Huffman 1996b). A recent assessment of relevant radiocarbon dates suggests that this expansion, which led to farming communities spreading into higher-lying areas of Transkei and southern Gauteng and across the Vaal into the Free State and western Lesotho, may have occurred as late as 1640 (J.C. Vogel and Fuls 1999). Having quickly reached the viable limits for sorghum and pearl millet growth at the modern 550–600 mm isohyet/1500 m contour, settlement contracted slightly during an ensuing colder phase that lasted into the late eighteenth century (Maggs 1976). To the north-west, place-name evidence suggests that Tswana settlement once reached as far as Postmasburg, which today receives only 250 mm of rain a year, but drier conditions and Korana expansion (chapter 13) pushed them back towards Kuruman and Taung before 1800 (Humphreys 1988).

Successful settlement of the Grassland Biome demanded several technological modifications. Livestock-rearing was of major importance, as reflected in cattle figurines and the size of livestock enclosures; a greater emphasis on cattle-keeping may have helped protect against food shortages, as well as offering increased scope for accumulating wealth and creating clientship obligations through their loan to others (M. Hall 1987). Outnumbering caprines, cattle contributed the overwhelming bulk of the meat supply, though communal hunting of alcelaphines and zebra is also well attested (Maggs 1976, 1982a; Dreyer 1992a). Carbonised remains of sorghum, cowpeas, tsamma melons and (from the eighteenth century) maize attest to cultivation (Maggs 1976, 1982a; M. Hall and Maggs 1979). Stable isotope analyses of human skeletons suggest that people living in the Grassland Biome depended more heavily on animal products relative to plants than in the Mixed Woodland Savanna further north, but also point to considerable inter-site variability in both areas, with some individuals eating a surprisingly high intake of wild plant foods (Lee Thorp *et al.* 1993).

With firewood limited in pure grassland areas, people used cattle dung for fuel, so that byres typically have lower floor levels than the area surrounding them. The lack of firewood to make charcoal also constrained metal production; there is no evidence for indigenous iron-smelting anywhere in the Free State. Metal artefacts are rare on all excavated sites and alternative materials were frequently employed, for example ceramic spoons as substitutes for wooden ones and bone scrapers for hide-working (Maggs 1976). A further critical feature was the regular employment of stone rather than wood in architecture, something that has greatly facilitated the discovery and identification of settlements, not least using air photographs. In one of the first detailed studies Maggs (1976) described four basic settlement types, all characterised by the use of semiweathered dolerite to produce a hard, binding *daga* for making house floors and a wall-building tradition that employed larger, more regular stones for the inner and outer faces and smaller rubble for the infill. As with the more dispersed homesteads of KwaZulu-Natal and the Eastern Cape, sites tend to be in locally elevated situations, reflecting a deep-seated Nguni and Sotho preference for benign higher places rather than supernaturally dangerous riverside locations, yet another contrast to the first millennium (Maggs 1976).

OU 1

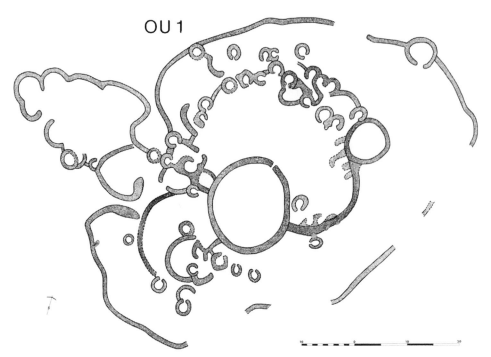

Figure 12.4   Plan of the Type N site at OU1, Ntsuanatsatsi, Free State, South
Africa (after Maggs 1976: Fig. 39; courtesy Tim Maggs and Natal
Museum).

Type N, the oldest of the highveld settlement forms, is concentrated in the
north-eastern Free State and across the Vaal in Mpumalanga. It may reach back
to the fifteenth century, though this is by no means certain (J.C. Vogel and
Fuls 1999). Sites consist of a group of primary livestock enclosures arranged in
a ring linked by secondary walling to form a large secondary enclosure and
surrounded by an outer wall; houses were of reed and *daga* construction outside
the ring (Fig. 12.4). The much more common Type V sites occur over a wider
area of the eastern Free State, distributed with access to the best arable and
grazing lands. Settlements have enclosures of various sizes arranged in a rough
circle and joined by connecting walls to form a single, large enclosure. Lacking
the outer walling and funnel-shaped entrances of Type N and sometimes featuring corbelled stone houses, they show signs of internal wealth differences
in that not all constituent units are of the same size (Fig. 12.5). Some clearly
had many hundred inhabitants, but there is nothing to indicate that any had
urban functions (*pace* M. Hall's (1987) description of them as 'towns'). Type
V sites date to the seventeenth to early nineteenth centuries. Possibly related
settlements in the Caledon Valley have a much simplified layout in which the
linking up of primary enclosures into a ring and their careful positioning around
a central area no longer applied; they may partly reflect the initial settlement

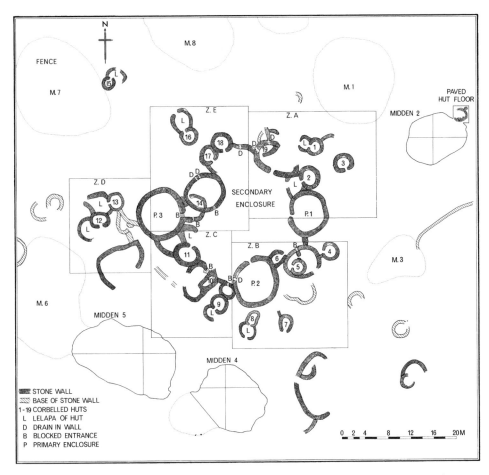

Figure 12.5   Plan of the Type V site at OO1, Makgwareng, Free State, South
Africa (after Maggs 1976: Fig. 13; courtesy Tim Maggs and Natal
Museum).

here of Nguni-speaking Zizi groups from across the Drakensberg. Finally, Type
Z sites are characterised by several large primary enclosures sometimes linked
by secondary walling. The very distinctive houses were of cone-on-cylinder construction, with stone-walled semi-circular courtyards to the front and rear giving a bilobal shape; sliding doors were a frequent feature (Maggs 1993; Fig. 12.6).
Dating again from the seventeenth century onward, they occur in the north-
western Free State, especially along the Sand and Vals rivers, but are also
widespread in the western transVaal. Associated ceramics also differ: comb-
stamping, often combined with ochre burnish, is the most prominent decorative technique found at Type N sites, finger decoration and comb-stamping on
pottery from Type V sites (Fig. 12.7) and those in the Caledon Valley, and stylus
decoration and horizontal bands of parallel grooves on the more standardised
Type Z ceramics (Maggs 1975, 1976).

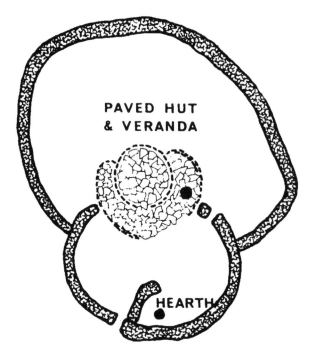

Figure 12.6   Plan of a bilobal dwelling from the Type Z site at OXF1,
Free State, South Africa (after Maggs 1995: Fig. 11; courtesy
South African Archaeological Society).

Similarities in architecture and ceramics, coupled with detailed study
of Sotho/Tswana oral histories, permit correlations between these various
settlement types and historically known groups. Type Z, for example, is clearly
the work of ancestral Tswana people, especially the Tlhaping, Rolong and
Kubung, a Rolong offshoot who arrived on the southern highveld c. 1650 (Maggs
1975, 1976). Of the various Sotho lineages the oldest are the Fokeng, whose
traditions locate their origin at a place called Ntsuanatsatsi where people first
emerged into this world from a bed of reeds (Ashton 1952). Lying only a short distance from OU1, an excavated Type N site, Ntsuanatsatsi is in the north-eastern
Free State in the centre of the Type N distribution. Other Sotho lineages trace
their origins to the headwaters of the Limpopo from south-eastern Botswana
through the Magaliesberg to Pretoria. From here the Kwena moved into the
Ntsuanatsatsi area before dispersing down the Caledon Valley in the wake of
more widespread southward movements by the Fokeng. The other main Sotho
groups, the Kgatla (especially the Tlokwa) and Taung, are associated historically
with several of the Type V sites. Overall there is a reasonably close match between the broad groups identified in the archaeological record and those known
ethnohistorically, with the distinctiveness of Type Z sites from those of Types
N and V suggesting that elements of the Sotho/Tswana dichotomy may be
several centuries old, not just a creation of the colonial period (Maggs 1976).

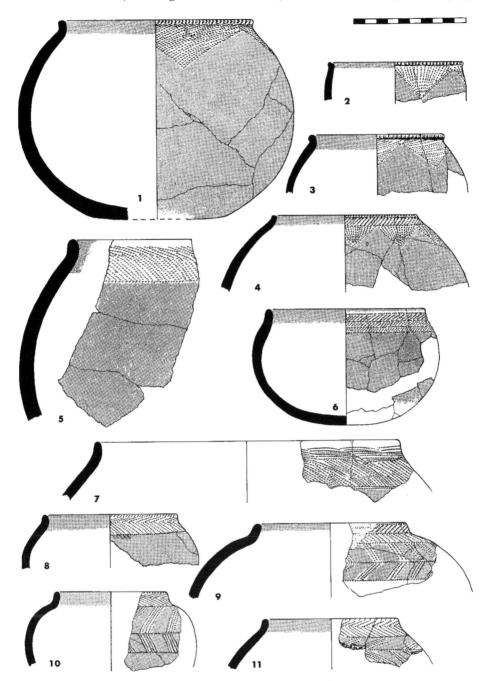

Figure 12.7   Examples of comb-stamped pottery from the Type V site at OO1,
Makgwareng, Free State, South Africa (after Maggs 1976: Fig. 26;
courtesy Tim Maggs and Natal Museum).

Research elsewhere adds to the range of settlement types known from the Grassland Biome. Both Type N ('Group I') sites of early seventeenth-century date and Type Z ('Group II') sites of the late seventeenth/early eighteenth centuries extend from the north-west Free State across the Vaal River (D. White 1977; Taylor 1979). 'Group III' sites, such as Buffelshoek (Loubser 1985), show the influence of Type Z on Type N; their ceramics also have features in common with both. Other sites in the north-eastern Free State also challenge the neatness of Magg's (1976) original distinctions by combining Type Z bilobal houses with an otherwise Type V settlement pattern (Dreyer 1999). Stone enclosures from the Qwaqwa area are again arranged differently and may belong to another Sotho group, the Kgolokwe, whose traditions locate them here c. 1700–1850 (Dreyer 1992b). Other less standardised settlements occur near Winburg. With several smaller stone structures clustered around one or more central cattle byres they recall the pattern found in the Caledon Valley. Features such as beehive-shaped reed/grass houses with central fire bowls resemble Nguni practice and may suggest a partially trans-Drakensberg origin for their builders, though the combination on pottery of comb-stamping, finger-pinching and ochre burnish resembles that found on the Type V and Caledon Valley sites (Dreyer 1992a).

Numerous stonewalled sites are also reported in southern Mpumalanga and on Swaziland's highveld, where Swazi traditions suggest earlier settlement by Sotho-speakers (Price-Williams 1980), but it is the Babanango Plateau of KwaZulu-Natal that stands out as one of the most intensively investigated areas of farming settlement outside the Free State (M. Hall 1981). Though nowhere near on the same scale as some Sotho/Tswana settlements, locational analysis and relative dating evidence suggest that the Type B sites of this area do cluster more markedly than is typical of the contemporary Nguni dispersed settlement pattern (M. Hall and Maggs 1979; M. Hall and Mack 1983). Each consists of a ring of primary enclosures opening into a larger secondary one that forms its core. Lowering of the floor level to remove dung for fuel and house floors shows that animals were kept in the primary enclosures. Houses were probably of thatched beehive construction, as at Mgoduyanuka near Bergville (Maggs 1982a), where the primary enclosures are not linked and many are actually earthworks faced with stone. Pottery consists mainly of bowls and bag-shaped pots with little decoration other than frequent red ochre burnish and occasional applied bosses.

In complete contrast to modern Zulu practice, the primary enclosures at all these sites have distinctively cobbled entrances that face uphill and at Mgoduyanuka the houses are not concentrated in the uphill area of the homestead, which lacks a clear outer limit (Maggs et al. 1986). Hall and Maggs (1979) emphasise that these and other differences, along with radiocarbon determinations pointing to a date prior to the establishment of the Zulu state, require

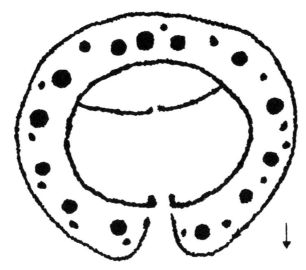

Figure 12.8   Rock engraving of a Zulu homestead, showing huts and granaries around the Central Cattle Pattern, with the entrance facing downhill, Muden area, KwaZulu-Natal, South Africa (after Maggs 1995: Fig 4; courtesy South African Archaeological Society).

that archaeologists do not base their interpretations solely on standardised ethnographic models. Important changes in settlement pattern clearly took place only a few generations before such models began to be generated.

One further feature of the Grassland Biome's archaeological record deserves mention, the occurrence of engravings showing detailed settlement plans (Fig. 12.8). The closeness of the association is reinforced by their proximity to actual settlements in KwaZulu-Natal or their presence on stone walls at Olifantspoort, North-West Province, and Boomplaas, Mpumalanga. Almost always alone, with only occasional human or animal figures, they emphasise the built environment and the importance of connections between settlement architecture and the worldview articulated in the CCP; the stress on cattle byres and the rarity of houses, granaries or fields suggest their production was a male activity (Maggs 1995).

Production and exchange

The lack of evidence for iron production by agropastoralists in the Free State serves as a useful introduction to considering the relations between production and exchange of a variety of materials and the connections between these processes and others promoting political centralisation. Though iron hoes, adzes, spear/knife-blades, awls, razors, sweat scrapers, bangles and beads have all been recovered, there is no sign of smelting and nothing conclusively to indicate local smithing, though copper was worked into jewellery, for example at

Makgwareng and Doornpoort 2826BD10 (Maggs 1976; Dreyer 1992a). Both metals must have been obtained from beyond the highveld itself. One source for iron was probably the upper Thukela Basin, where evidence of shaft mining of iron ore and a concentration of smelting sites at Mabhija date to 1690–1840 and are associated with pottery similar to that known from Mgoduyanuka (Maggs 1982b). With only poor-quality grazing and arable soils, oral traditions record the exchange of iron objects from this area for livestock and grain obtained from Sotho-speakers across the Drakensberg. Exchange between complementary areas was probably also how the Type B sites of the Babanango Plateau secured access to iron, though here lower-lying thornveld valleys may also have been used for grazing cattle in the winter part of an annual transhumant cycle (M. Hall and Mack 1983). Connections between highveld settlements and iron-producing communities in North-West Province remain to be investigated.

Considerable typological and technological variability exists among iron-smelting furnaces in southernmost Africa. Those from Mabhija are similar in size and shape to others from the Thukela Basin, i.e. bowl-shaped, elliptical in plan with openings at either end and little surviving superstructure. The same type occurs in Hluhluwe-Umfolozi National Park, where several may have been used simultaneously (M. Hall 1980b), but at Cato Manor near Durban much larger, oval furnaces indicate a different tradition (Whitelaw 1991). The availability of fuel to make charcoal was at least as important as access to iron, and at Itala ore was moved 7 km over broken terrain to the nearest suitable hardwoods (Maggs 1992b).

By the nineteenth century, if not long before, iron production in KwaZulu-Natal was concentrated in particular clans and lineages and generally carried out away from homesteads for fear of dark, mystical forces associated with death, witchcraft and pollution (Maggs 1992b). Often of high status, smiths generally worked under chiefly patronage, and there is evidence for an internal stratification between brassmakers, spearmakers and hoemakers. Hoards are known from many different contexts, in settlements, close to furnaces and away from smelting sites. Some may be family toolkits, others the caches of *Mfecane* refugees, but the apparently new spearheads from Rongpoort may have belonged to a trader (Maggs 1991). South of Durban comparatively few smelting sites are known (Whitelaw 1991), a trend even more apparent in Transkei, where ore sources are meagre and of poor quality (Feely 1987). As a result some people employed wooden spades, spears and weighted digging-sticks. Iron was avidly sought from shipwrecked Europeans, but longer-distance trade connections are poorly understood (Derricourt 1977).

Phalaborwa in Mpumalanga's arid lowveld was another important centre of metal production, encouraged by the possibilities of exchanging metal for food (Fig. 12.9). Ore is readily collectable on the surface, though in some cases it was still carried in quantity over distances of 20 km before being smelted (van der Merwe and Killick 1979). Reflecting Venda influence in this area, two furnace

Figure 12.9   Reconstructed Later Iron Age village at Masorini, Kruger National Park, Mpumalanga, South Africa.

types are reported, one of Venda type with a cylindrical plan, vertical section and three tuyère entrances confined to vertical slits running almost to the height of the wall. The other, Phalaborwa-type, sub-triangular in plan, narrower at the top and with a plaster floor, also occurs further east in Kruger National Park (Fig. 12.10). Both types were partly dug into the ground to retain heat (Evers 1982b); human bones found with forges or furnaces may have been used in ritual medicines to ensure success (Plug and Pistorius 1999).

Venda-associated furnaces with three tuyère inlets fall to the east of a line running south from Messina to Vereeniging. Further west, furnaces have two tuyère inlets and Sotho/Tswana affiliations, with both bowl and shaft furnace types known (Friede and Steel 1985). Evidence of iron-smelting seems particularly common in North-West Province, with furnaces commonly grouped together, perhaps for improving production flow (Friede and Steel 1981). Experimental reconstructions suggest that some furnaces were of limited efficiency and that both smelting and forging required considerable skill and experience (Küsel 1979; Friede and Steel 1986, 1988). The production (Binneman 1988) or recycling of much older stone tools (Binneman and van Niekerk 1986) for use in hide-working is therefore not as surprising as it might at first seem.

Other metals are much more restricted in occurrence. Copper was exploited in the Dwarsberg Mountains as early as the sixteenth century, with furnaces

Figure 12.10   Iron-smelting furnace at Kgopolwe, SPK-Vb, near Phalaborwa, Mpumalanga, South Africa (courtesy Nick van der Merwe).

known at both Ifafi and Uitkomst Cave (Mason 1962, 1982). As in the first millennium, Phalaborwa was another important source (Fig. 12.11), using both open and underground shafts and adits prior to refining and casting at village sites such as Harmony (van der Merwe and Scully 1971; Evers 1981). Copper from these sources and from Messina in the Limpopo Valley (Hanisch 1974) was widely traded, occurring not only at the highveld sites already mentioned, but beyond them at the Type R sites discussed below. As well as occurring as items of jewellery, a variety of ingots is known, the most common being *marale* (slender cylindrical shafts with a stubby head) and *metsuku* (squat blocks with studs adorning their bottoms; Killick 1991).

Tin ingots are rarer than those of copper and again occur in various shapes (Killick 1991). Trace element analysis suggests that all probably derive from sources in the Rooiberg Mountains, from which some 18,000 tonnes of ore were removed in precolonial times (Grant 1999). South of the Limpopo evidence of bronze production is restricted to the Waterberg (Wagner and Gordon 1929) and since very few tin or bronze artefacts have been recovered from southern Africa as a whole (Thompson 1949) almost all the metal was presumably exported overseas, first perhaps to India via the Great Zimbabwe polity and, after 1498, to European traders on the east coast. Rooiberg itself has produced only raw ingots and no cast pieces or glass beads, so something archaeologically invisible, perhaps cattle, probably formed the other part of the exchange

Figure 12.11   Cross-section of a copper-smelting furnace at Nagome, MN-1, near Phalaborwa, Mpumalanga, South Africa (courtesy Nick van der Merwe).

(Grant *et al.* 1994). Items of brass, for which there was a considerable demand, were apparently all made using imported metal as there is no sign of local zinc-smelting (Küsel 1974).

Metal may have been the most important and is certainly the most evident item traded between later farming communities in southernmost Africa. Of items less likely to survive archaeologically, salt was probably the most significant. In Mpumalanga, where some areas certainly lacked salt in the nineteenth century (Quin 1959), it continued to be made at the Eiland springs site, now using longer-lasting schist bowls rather than pottery for boiling the brine (Evers 1981). But essentials were far from the only thing exchanged. Sites in the Free State, for instance, have produced glass beads and Indian Ocean seashells, while siltstone pipes and the *dagga* and (later on) tobacco used in them were also traded (Maggs 1976). Nor should we forget the rôle here and elsewhere of forager groups in moving items across the landscape and supplying farmers with pigments, hides, feathers and ostrich eggshell beads among other items. The estimated 125,000 tonnes of rock removed from the Blinkklipkop and Doornfontein specularite mines in the Northern Cape, some of it using metal tools that suggest Tswana involvement along with that of Khoekhoen and Bushmen, concretely document the historically attested trade in this pigment across much of South Africa's western interior (Humphreys and Thackeray 1983).

Centralisation, incorporation and resistance

Control over trade played an important part in the development of more centralised polities, especially after the establishment of a European trading presence on the Mozambican coast. Emerging paramountcies had to devise new ways of controlling larger bodies of people and increasingly competed among themselves. More thorough-going assimilation of hunter-gatherers, on a scale greater than that seen during the first millennium, was another feature of later farming communities, though both they and others could also resist incorporation.

Tswana settlements in the western transVaal provide one of the best-documented instances of these processes. Here early Moloko populations probably took the form of low-density, dispersed settlement organised according to the Central Cattle Pattern. In the early seventeenth century the appearance of low stone walls defining homestead boundaries, demarcating byres and separating individual households suggests a more permanently settled and claimed landscape, accompanied by more restrictive reckoning of kin group membership (S. Hall 1995, 1998; Lane 1998b). Major site expansion followed in the early eighteenth century with some chiefdoms 'imploding' to produce agglomerated settlements of 10,000 people or more. Examples include Molokwane, capital of the Bakwena Bamodinosana Bammatau chiefdom (Pistorius 1994), and Kaditshwene, capital of a major section of the Hurutshe, whose population of 20,000 in 1820 made it the same size as contemporary Cape Town (Fig. 12.12; Boeyens 2000). Such sites were made up of multiple wards, each under its own headman, which served as administrative, legal and subsistence units of the larger whole. Moving every few years for ecological reasons and subject to fission during chiefly succession disputes, beyond them lay only temporary cattle posts and the fields to which many people decamped during the growing and harvest seasons.

Many of these larger sites lie on more broken, higher ground for defence; oral traditions confirm that the period after 1700 saw increased competition between chiefdoms for arable land and grazing, fuelled by population growth and the introduction of maize (see below). Cattle raiding was particularly important, since acquiring cattle for use as bridewealth allowed men to have more wives and thus more female labour for their fields. S. Hall (1995, 1998) suggests that changes in activity location within households reflect increasing gender differentiation and perhaps male anxieties over female agricultural production as women travelled longer distances away from home to their fields and to collect firewood. Male activities may also have altered, with metal-working and hide-working elaborated in discrete areas close to the chief and his court, as at Olifantspoort (Mason 1986) or Mabyanamatshwaana, where a young man buried in a cattle byre with an anvil and hammerstone suggests an association between iron-working and political power (Pistorius and Steyn 1995).

Figure 12.12   The large midden next to the central *kgotla* (court and men's
               assembly area), Kaditshwene, North-West Province, South Africa
               (courtesy Jan Boeyens).

Ceramics show related changes, becoming more standardised and blander after
1700 compared to earlier elaborate decoration that included red ochre and
graphite colouring. A partial explanation may again lie in increased time pressures on women, with pottery production sacrificed for other activities, though
the associated decline in bowl frequencies may reflect men asserting control
over food preparation by making their own wooden platters for eating. Together
these changes may relate to the need to find ways by which large numbers of
people could 'get along', e.g. by loosening the expression of ethnic differences
through material culture, while simultaneously strengthening gender boundaries as men exercised greater control and confinement over the potentially
polluting power of women (S. Hall 1998).

   The agglomeration of Tswana settlements in the western transVaal was
fuelled not only by population growth, but also by conflict over access to
elephant herds that produced ivory for long-distance trade to the east coast
(Manson 1995; Parsons 1995). Although the westernmost Tswana were also
coming under pressure from the advancing frontier of the Cape Colony
(chapter 13), chiefdoms such as the Hurutshe were trading almost wholly to
the east as late as 1820, when John Campbell (1822) recorded the presence of
Tsonga traders come to exchange glass beads for ivory. Northward expansion by
other Tswana groups into the eastern Kalahari may initially have been fuelled
by the trade opportunities presented by the Torwa state (van Waarden 1998), but

Figure 12.13   Stone walling at Modipe Hill, Botswana (courtesy Paul Lane).

by the late eighteenth century was certainly encouraged by the good elephant hunting to be had there. Competition between Tswana chiefdoms may have resulted in sites increasingly becoming located on hilltops, where they made use of stone walling as on the highveld (Fig. 12.13; Pearson 1995; van Waarden 1998). Earlier Kgalagadi groups, themselves hunters and herders of probable Eiland origin, were progressively incorporated (Okihiro 1976). The presence of both Eiland and Moloko ceramics at some southern Botswanan sites could, if it does not result from exchange, indicate the coexistence of both Kgalagadi and Tswana communities within the same settlements (Lane 1996).

Similar processes can be identified further north and east. Here considerable attention has been directed at the archaeology of Ndebele groups who settled in the transVaal centuries before the *Mfecane* and are *not* to be confused with the Ndebele of Mzilikazi who established themselves in western Zimbabwe in 1838. In the Waterberg sites attributable to the transVaal, Ndebele appear in the sixteenth century. Stonewalled and located on *kopjes*, they are accompanied by Nguni-type undecorated pottery and beehive houses (Huffman 1990b). Their presence probably encouraged local Sotho-Tswana to shift to higher, more defensible locations like Rooikrans (S. Hall 1995). Other Ndebele settled on the Pietersburg Plateau, but here their pottery belongs to the Letaba and Moloko Traditions (Loubser 1994). Letaba ceramics dominate at sites associated with more important rulers, reflecting lowveld connections and the importance of the early eighteenth-century Venda state. This ancestry was subsequently downplayed, perhaps under the influence of the *Mfecane*, to assert links with Nguni-speakers in KwaZulu-Natal. Despite an otherwise Sothoised material culture, however, the capping of ash layers in middens at Planknek so as to deny access to witches shows the survival of Nguni witchcraft beliefs; for Sotho/Tswana-speakers ash is good, rather than harmful (Huffman and Steel 1996).

Agricultural intensification and more direct involvement in trade with the east coast come together in the eastern transVaal. Here a second phase of the Moloko Tradition termed Marateng takes the form of ceramics with minimal decoration other than the application of graphite and red ochre. Post-dating 1600, it is identical to pottery still made by the region's North Sotho-speaking Pedi peoples. Aerial photography and ground survey have identified numerous stone ruins along the Drakensberg Escarpment, including villages, smaller enclosures for keeping caprines, areas of terracing, sometimes cross-cut by stone walls that may define land holdings, and trackways designed to prevent cattle from straying into terraced areas (Marker and Evers 1976; Collett 1982); rock engravings near Lydenburg illustrate many of these features (Maggs 1995; Fig. 12.14). Population levels seem to have been much higher than in the first

Figure 12.14   Sketch map drawn from air photograph of a settlement with circular homesteads and associated roads and terracing, Machadodorp area, Mpumalanga, South Africa (after Maggs 1995: Fig. 15; courtesy South African Archaeological Society).

millennium and demographic pressure probably helped drive the political centralisation that culminated in the pre-*Mfecane* Pedi paramountcy. Discussing this, Delius (1983) identifies control over growing numbers of cattle and the supply of iron implements for warfare, farming and bridewealth payments as key elements in the growing ascendancy of the Maroteng lineage. Raiding as far as the Soutpansberg and the Vaal may have been fuelled by increased competition for land, but more probably by the desire to control trade routes. Here a position as intermediaries between highveld and lowveld groups may have been key (Evers 1975), especially in accumulating sufficient ivory, copper and tin to trade with Europeans at Delagoa Bay. Pedi rulers sought to control ironworking and ivory (through tribute), while using **age-regiments** to hunt large game and restricting access to imported cloth and beads. Chiefly power was further strengthened through manipulating rôles in rain-making and dispute settlement, polygamy (to acquire more women for agricultural labour), and the accumulation of cattle via court fines and bridewealth payments obtained by 'giving' wives to other groups. Nevertheless, the Maroteng remained only *primus inter pares* within a congeries of chiefdoms over whom they were unable to establish permanent control (Delius 1983).

Until the early nineteenth century much the same seems to have been the case for emerging paramountcies in south-eastern southern Africa. In the eastern transVaal lowveld, indeed, the prevalence of malaria and trypanosomiasis probably made settlement by people and their cattle impossible at times, difficult and based principally on cultivation and hunting at others (Meyer 1984, 1988a); symbiotic exchange between metal-producing lowveld groups, like those living near Phalaborwa, and agricultural highveld ones is likely (Plug and Pistorius 1999). Tsonga groups may be among those represented in the lowveld, as well as in Swaziland, west of their present focus in southern Mozambique (Ohinata 2000). For much of the eighteenth/early nineteenth centuries they dominated Delagoa Bay and had primary access to European traders calling there, expanding at the expense of neighbours such as the Ngwane to their south (A.K. Smith 1973). However, a dispersed settlement pattern and the use of organic building materials mean that little is known from archaeological sources of developments here or in the lower-lying parts of KwaZulu-Natal prior to the 1820s.

In the Eastern Cape, surveys show later farming communities spread inland up valley systems, but little excavation has been carried out. At the same time hunter-gatherers persisted in the Drakensberg and its foothills and perhaps also along the coast (Feely 1987). Assimilation of both Khoekhoen and Bushmen into Xhosa society is documented in clan names and may have been much more effective than in the first millennium (Peires 1981). Because good year-round grazing is scarce, people moved cattle transhumantly between sweetveld and sourveld areas. How controlling such movements fed into the emergence of chiefdoms is unknown, as is the process by which the Tshawe lineage came to dominate other clans. Lineage fission, especially the split *c.* 1750 of the royal house into Gcaleka and Rharhabe divisions, propelled Xhosa communities westward where they encountered the expanding colonial frontier in the early eighteenth century. With little sign of ecological degradation (McKenzie 1984), trade with European settlers may have been more important than land scarcity in promoting centralisation in that it offered access to copper, iron, beads and cattle. However, the Xhosa remained only loosely integrated throughout the precolonial period and archaeologically focused studies of the consequences of trade with the Cape Colony remain very underdeveloped in contrast to the rich historical record (Peires 1981).

We have already touched on the rôle of hunter-gatherers in the exchange networks that tied later farming communities together. Sotho oral traditions are particularly good at showing the exchange of game, skins and ostrich feathers for grain and tobacco, and ostrich eggshell beads occur at some agropastoralist sites (Maggs 1976; Jolly 1996b). However, there is a danger in generalising to all interaction situations from the specific processes attested only in some: Bushmen making rain for farmers is, for example, only documented among the Mpondomise of the Eastern Cape, and there is no evidence for rain-making having been undertaken for Sotho/Tswana-speakers (Klatzow 1994). Sotho groups did, however, give cattle to Bushman clients and forge marriage alliances with them, strategies also pursued by at least some Nguni-speakers (Jolly 1996b). As previously remarked, such interactions demonstrably influenced farming communities in southern Africa. Along with genetics, language and ritual, rock art provides one important source of evidence for this: LSA engraving sites at Thaba Sione and Matsieng, for example, were taken over and used by Tswana chiefs in their own rain-making ceremonies, which have strong correspondences with Bushman beliefs (Ouzman 1995a; N. Walker 1997).

In broad terms we can distinguish between the assimilation of foragers well within the limits of farming settlement and their survival beyond. In the Magaliesberg, for example, second-millennium levels at Jubilee Shelter have few indicators of aggregation, and plant remains suggest episodic occupation throughout the year. Nearby stonewalled sites such as Olifantspoort have few ostrich eggshell beads or formal stone tools, suggesting little contact with hunter-gatherers (Wadley 1996b). Veld degradation brought about by overgrazing (D. Avery 1987b) may have made hunting more difficult and denser agropastoralist settlement may have hindered contact between forager groups. The effect may have been a progressive 'social strangulation' and fragmentation, recorded too by the proliferation of tiny rock-shelters ephemerally occupied across the southern transVaal at this time (Wadley 1987).

Further north in the agriculturally more marginal Waterberg, people of Bushman and mixed Bushman/black descent, the so-called 'Vaalpense', survived into the early twentieth century through foraging and providing client services, such as herding, hunting, tracking and supplying skins to agropastoralists (van der Ryst 1998). Coinciding with the local appearance of Eiland villages, LSA sites become much more visible around 1200. Goergap, for instance, has Eiland/Broadhurst pottery, while particularly after 1400 metal beads and earrings, glass beads and rare livestock bones also occur. Conversely, stone tools and ostrich eggshell beads are found at local agropastoralist sites which may increasingly have taken on an aggregation rôle for hunter-gatherers.

Data from the Thukela Basin, which has one of the richest records for farmer/forager interactions in the first millennium, are more intractable during the second. Forager occupation continued in central areas, as at Mbabane and eSinhlonhlweni (Mazel 1986), and also in the Drakensberg (Maggs and Ward 1980; Mazel 1984). Glass and iron beads, sorghum and Later Iron Age pottery indicate continued contacts with agropastoralists, perhaps in the form of exchange or client relationships. At other sites the rarity of stone and bone artefacts, coupled with more plentiful Iron Age ceramics, suggests their use by farmers; KwaThwaleyakhe (Mazel 1993) and Mzinyashana (Mazel 1997) exemplify this. Though more work is needed to try and establish firm criteria for distinguishing between the two kinds of occupation, we may surmise that hunter-gatherers were best able to maintain their independence furthest from areas occupied by farmers, such as in Lesotho's highlands and the northern Eastern Cape (Opperman 1987; Mitchell 1996e).

The Caledon Valley is probably the best-documented area of all for studying forager/farmer interactions during the second millennium. Agropastoralist settlement here was largely confined to the area north of Ladybrand, with a southern 'finger' extending downstream inside western Lesotho. In the north, LSA sites disappeared rapidly, with foragers pushed back towards the Maluti Mountains. Rose Cottage Cave, which had probably been a hunter-gatherer aggregation focus in the fourteenth/fifteenth centuries (Ouzman and Wadley 1997), went out of use, perhaps replaced by farming villages. Other large shelters register ephemeral use, but the primary focus of occupation shifted to much smaller sites (Mitchell *et al.* 1994; Wadley 1995). The rich rock art at sites like Tandjesberg, with its many trance-related images, may have helped substitute for the 'real' coming together of a now more dispersed population (Fig. 12.15; Wadley and McLaren 1998). The ceramics from these LSA sites exhibit an interesting sequence (Thorp 2000). Rare grit-tempered, Iron Age sherds at Rose Cottage reach back beyond 1300 and probably derive from KwaZulu-Natal, to which the data illustrated in Figs. 10.23–10.24 also point. Grass-tempered 'Smithfield' ceramics, on the other hand, indicate contacts with hunter-gatherers in the middle Gariep Valley and the Karoo. After 1400 these were increasingly replaced by Type V/Caledon Valley sherds, suggesting a refocusing of local forager ties onto newly arriving farming communities. Further south the same substitution occurred later. Iron Age sherds dominate

Figure 12.15   Trance-related images, Tandjesberg, Free State, South Africa. Those
illustrated belong to Cluster 5 of Panel 4 (Loubser 1993a) and
include seventeen monochrome figures, comprising an outer circle
of sitting, lying and standing figures, some of them clapping, who
surround two individuals who bend forwards. Each of these
individuals holds a stick, in one case (that of a woman) with a bored
stone weight attached. !Kung and /Xam ethnographies record bored
stones being used to communicate with the dead.

nineteenth-century levels at Tienfontein 2 (Brooker 1980), after an earlier period, represented at nearby Ventershoek (Sampson 1970), in which only iron
tools and iron and glass beads were obtained.

Ventershoek is one of many Caledon Valley sites at which cattle are depicted (Fig. 12.16). Elsewhere sheep and Sotho shields are shown, while horses
reflect nineteenth-century events. The frontier between foraging and farming
communities is neatly traced by the negative correlation between the distribution of these paintings and that of stonewalled agropastoralist villages (Thorp
2000). Loubser and Laurens (1994) note that these images and others associated with them differ from other Caledon Valley paintings in pigment choice,
a poster-like appearance that did not employ shading and motif spacing and
in overlying or being physically separated from clearly older, shaded images.
Their near-exclusive occurrence south of Ladybrand and a date from a fallen
slab at Glen Elliott (Sampson 1972) is consistent with a mostly eighteenth/
nineteenth-century age. Selected presumably as symbols of potency by
Bushman artists, they may only have been depicted after farming expansion

Figure 12.16   Polychrome cattle paintings, Tienfontein, Free State, South Africa.

ceased and a more 'closed' frontier was established. Within this foragers seem to have been dispossessed or assimilated, while along and beyond it they survived, in some cases accumulating cattle and developing more pronounced leadership structures because they were able to retreat, when pushed, into agriculturally marginal lands; isolated stone circles in the southern Free State reflect this (Loubser and Laurens 1994).

The best-documented instance of this kind of response comes from the Riet River Valley in the western Free State. Here numerous Type R stonewalled sites consist of a single very large enclosure surrounded by several smaller ones, sometimes, but not always, used for domestic activities (Humphreys 1988). Essentially, undecorated bowls and pots differ from both Iron Age ceramics and those found in LSA contexts in the Karoo. Within the same area and further west near Douglas (Humphreys 1982) are many cairn-covered burials of Khoisan individuals (Fig. 12.17; A. Morris 1992c). Grave goods indicate widespread exchange links, including not only copper earrings and bangles of Sotho/Tswana type, but also seashell ornaments from South Africa's western, southern and eastern seaboards and specularite from sources near Postmasburg (Humphreys 1970b; Humphreys and Maggs 1970; A. Morris 1981). Travelling through this area in 1811, Burchell (1967) encountered Bushmen pursuing a mixed subsistence strategy of herding and hunting, something reflected in the Pramberg fauna (J. Brink *et al.* 1992), though at OFD 1 cattle and caprines dominate (Maggs 1971); stable isotope analyses indicate a considerable animal food intake and reliance on wild plants, rather than cultivated cereals (Lee Thorp

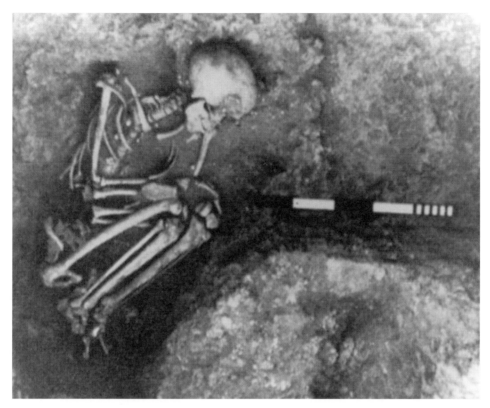

Figure 12.17   Burial MMK 329, Riet River Valley, Free State, South Africa (courtesy Alan Morris; see Humphreys and Maggs 1970).

et al. 1993). Radiocarbon dates place the Type R sites, of which Dithakong is the largest example (Fig. 12.18; D. Morris 1990c), *c.* 1500–1830, suggesting they began at approximately the same time as agropastoralist settlement spread into better-watered areas to the north and east. But though their livestock may have been acquired from this source, osteology indicates that intermarriage was one-way, i.e. into Tswana society (A. Morris 1992d), a pattern that in other parts of southern Africa may have helped bring about the encapsulation and cultural extinction of hunter-gatherer groups. Rock engravings on the Ghaap Plateau featuring Tswana shields, spears and house plans along with entoptic designs and rare animals hint at the complexity of these interactions, as does the preva-lence of watersnakes in Tswana, /Xam Bushman and Korana beliefs across the Northern Cape (D. Morris 1990d).

Archaeology and the *Mfecane*

The term *'Mfecane'* is traditionally used by historians to refer to the wars and population movements set in motion in early nineteenth-century KwaZulu-Natal which culminated in the establishment of the Zulu kingdom and came

Figure 12.18   Stone enclosures at Dithakong, a Type R site, Northern Cape, South
Africa.

to affect much of the interior, even beyond the Zambezi (Fig. 12.19). While ac-
knowledging the unfairly Zulu-centric nature of earlier interpretations, recent
debate centres on how far these processes resulted from internal African factors
or the activities of European slave-raiding (Hamilton 1995a). Articulating the
latter view, Cobbing (1988) emphasised the way in which the supposed genoci-
dal wars launched by the Zulu king Shaka kaSenzangakhona and the concomitant depopulation of much of KwaZulu-Natal, the Free State and the transVaal
were used to justify white minority rule and the land divisions of *apartheid*.
However, while arguing correctly that developments in south-eastern southern Africa cannot be looked at in isolation and that it is important to consider
interactions across the expanding colonial frontiers before 1820, the claim that
European slave-raiding played a pivotal rôle in bringing about the *Mfecane*
is misplaced. Eldredge (1995), Hamilton (1995b) and Peires (1995) all demonstrate that the supporting evidence is weak, particularly as regards the claim
for slave-trading centred on Delagoa Bay, just north of where the Zulu polity
formed. Since there was no reason to suppress information about what was,
before the early 1800s, a perfectly legal trade, eighteenth-century Dutch and
other European sources should be taken at face value in emphasising the export of ivory, some other goods and only minimal numbers of slaves (Eldredge
1995). Other explanations must be sought for the growth of more centralised,
aggressive polities.

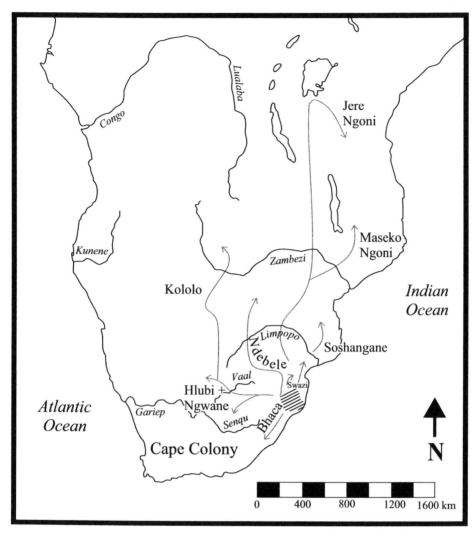

Figure 12.19 Location of areas affected by the *Mfecane*. The nucleus of the emerging Zulu kingdom is shaded diagonally.

If slaving was unimportant, the late eighteenth century *was* marked by rapidly intensifying demands for ivory on the part of European traders at Delagoa Bay: as many as 50 tonnes (perhaps from some 500 elephants; Estes 1992) were exported annually from 1750 to 1790 (A.K. Smith 1970). In return those in positions of authority in African societies obtained valued trade goods, notably glass beads, but also cloth and brass, which they could redistribute to juniors and also use to accumulate more cattle. As elephant populations declined, competition increased both for them and for the post-1790 supply of food to European and American whalers calling at Delagoa Bay (Hedges 1978). Conflicts between emerging paramountcies were further sustained and enhanced by cattle-raiding, conflicts over land and changes in climate and the subsistence base.

Most important here was the widespread adoption of maize, which may already have been growing in Transkei by 1635 (Derricourt 1977). With up to three times the yields of pearl millet or sorghum and demanding much less labour for its cultivation, maize-growing was encouraged by the higher rainfall evidenced in tree-rings for the second half of the eighteenth century (M. Hall 1976). Its consequences for population growth are demonstrated in KwaZulu-Natal by increased site numbers and greater use of more marginal land. Elsewhere, for example in the Manyikeni area of Mozambique, it encouraged a redistribution of population to the moister coastal belt where sorghum and pearl millet cultivation had previously been inhibited (Barker 1988). More concrete evidence comes from maize cobs from Mgoduyanuka (Maggs 1982a) and the proliferation of new larger, more deeply hollowed out grindstones that attest to its take-up both there and on the highveld (Huffman 1996b). However, both tree-rings and historical sources document several severe drought episodes in the early nineteenth century, some of them compounded by crop rust and cattle disease (e.g. Bonner 1983). Having made the shift to maize, which requires 25 per cent more rain than sorghum or pearl millet (Huffman 1996b), food shortages may have resulted. Competition for access to overseas trade had almost certainly already encouraged some leaders to replace locally organised circumcision schools and age-sets with more permanently maintained military regiments (amabutho) recruited from all young men of a given age. These were now used to gain access through warfare to land, cattle, stored food and the people to grow more. Though we should be wary of assuming fundamental changes in the mode of production, centralised control over the constituent units of the developing paramountcies went along with their geographical expansion (Wright 1995), and the power of lineage heads was, in some cases, increasingly subordinated to that of an emerging élite focused around a dominant royal lineage (e.g. Bonner 1983).

By the 1810s three groups, the Mthethwa, Ndwandwe and Ngwane, dominated northern KwaZulu-Natal. Conflicts between the first two of these paramountcies led to smaller chiefdoms moving away, among them the Dlamini-led abakwaNgwane who moved north of the Phongolo River to establish the nucleus of modern Swaziland (Bonner 1983). Not to be confused with them, one Ngwane section (the amaNgwane) eventually crossed the Drakensberg, pushing groups such as the Hlubi ahead of them. Fighting one another as well as resident Sotho, the result across both the transVaal and the highveld was several years of large-scale turmoil, made worse by the eastward expansion from the outer fringes of the Cape Colony of Griqua and Korana groups armed with guns and horses. Back in south-eastern southern Africa, the Mthethwa paramountcy was undermined by the killing of its head Dingiswayo c. 1818, leading to a brief period of Ndwandwe dominance. In consequence, one of Dingiswayo's former tributaries, the Zulu leader Shaka, established alliances with chiefdoms further south, sometimes (as in the Qwabe case) after defeating them militarily, and built up a Zulu-dominated coalition. This first resisted the Ndwandwe and then contributed, along with internal political tensions, to their downfall. Fissioning, some Ndwandwe moved north into Mozambique where they founded the Gaza kingdom. After a long and complex history of movements and interaction with other groups, including the Portuguese, other Ndwandwe offshoots (including those led by Jere and Maseko) founded a number of Ngoni chiefdoms as far afield as Zambia, Malawi and Tanzania. As the Zulu polity expanded through a combination of diplomacy and military aggression, consolidating its control over the areas between the Phongolo and Thukela rivers, many communities were incorporated into it. Others sought refuge from the continuing instability by moving south of the Thukela River, precipitating a further 'domino effect' as far as the Cape Colony's eastern border (Wright 1995). Along with Mzilikazi's Ndebele polity, itself centred around Nguni emigrants from KwaZulu-Natal who had formerly formed part of the Ndwandwe paramountcy, other larger, more stable nuclei that eventually developed out of all these conflicts included those of Moshoeshoe in the Caledon Valley, Sekonyela's Tlokwa, and a revived Pedi chiefdom under Sekwati (Omer-Cooper 1966).

Historians identify several means by which the leaders of these polities sought to strengthen their rule, often in the face of dissensions within the ruling lineage as well as continuing resistance from subordinate communities (Hamilton 1995b; Wright 1995). Drawing on the experience of the Mthethwa and others, these included in the Zulu case the institutionalisation of a permanent army based in purpose-built military homesteads (*amakhanda*) and the use of *amabutho* to tend royal cattle, hunt and work royal fields. Local chiefs lost power as initiation schools disappeared and women of royal lineage were placed in charge of the *amakhanda*, while the king attempted to control iron production and access to imported prestige goods (Guy 1978; Maggs 1992b). Precipitated by the *Mfecane*, one archaeological manifestation of these changes was the abandonment in some areas of earlier homestead styles, such as those of Type B, and the imposition instead of the lowland Zulu style that dominates today (M. Hall 1987). Related innovations marked other incipient states, as discussed by Eldredge (1993) for the Basotho and Bonner (1983) for the Swazi.

Archaeology's contribution to understanding these events has emphasised excavations at the royal centres of these new polities. In KwaZulu-Natal both Mgungundlovu, capital of the second Zulu king Dingane kaSenzangakhona, and Ondini, capital of the last independent monarch Cetshwayo kaMpande, have been examined in depth. Both exhibit the characteristic plan of Zulu *amakhanda* or regimental centres (Fig. 12.20), which in its essentials is a greatly expanded version of a normal homestead organised on the Central Cattle Pattern. Despite their size and administrative significance, however,

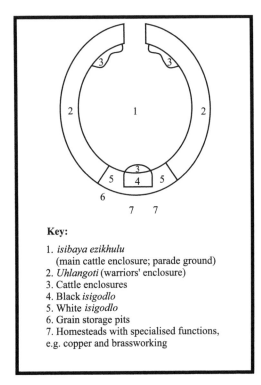

Key:

1. *isibaya ezikhulu*
   (main cattle enclosure; parade ground)
2. *Uhlangoti* (warriors' enclosure)
3. Cattle enclosures
4. Black *isigodlo*
5. White *isigodlo*
6. Grain storage pits
7. Homesteads with specialised functions,
   e.g. copper and brassworking

Figure 12.20   Generalised plan of Zulu royal capitals (*amakhanda*)
based on excavations at and historical accounts of
Mgungundlovu and Ondini.

the *amakhanda* remained provisioned largely from distant villages and do not seem to have been the focus of large-scale craft production.

Mgungundlovu, first built in 1829 and enlarged five years later, took the form of a central enclosure (*isibaya esikhulu*) for cattle, parades and dances, surrounded by barrack areas with evenly spaced, uniformly sized houses for warriors and scattered stilted storage huts for their shields. At the upper end of the *isibaya* and next to a smaller byre lay a royal enclosure (*isigodlo*) to which access was strictly controlled. Divided in two, this housed the king, his personal retinue and stores of meat, beer and milk. Behind this three smaller enclosures formed the *Bheje*, the central one occupied by the royal family. As Mgungundlovu was deliberately destroyed in 1838 after the Zulu defeat at Blood River, baked clay house bases have preserved well, helped by a prohibition on reusing former royal sites. Total population is estimated at 5000–7000 people living in some 1700 houses (Parkington and Cronin 1979). Excavation has identified Dingane's own house, with a 72 m² floor area, distinctive six-pointed central hearth and twenty-two postholes, each originally supporting a timber pole totally covered with glass beads; in this and other respects

Figure 12.21   Ondini, KwaZulu-Natal, South Africa, showing reconstructed houses and the fired clay floor of another house burnt during the site's destruction in the Anglo-Zulu War of 1879.

the archaeological data match surviving historical descriptions (Roodt 1992a). Excavations in and behind the *isigodlo* have demonstrated the existence of large grain storage pits, residues from brass-making using brass imported via Delagoa Bay and the location of girls' initiation rites (Roodt 1992b, 1993).

Prior to Dingane relocating the Zulu capital close to the graves of his ancestors in the Makosini Valley, Shaka had had his last capital (1827–28) at Dukuza, below the modern town of Stanger. Survey of Kwa-Bulawayo, his capital from 1819 to 1827, confirms that the general plan followed at Mgungundlovu was already in use, though on a significantly smaller scale (Whitelaw 1994b). It is displayed too at Ondini, just outside modern Ulundi, which was the last capital of an independent Zulu kingdom. Built in 1873, Ondini housed some 5000 people in 1500 houses. Destroyed by the British in 1879 during the Anglo-Zulu War, house floors were again baked and well preserved (Fig. 12.21). Excavations have identified Cetshwayo's private house and house of state, those of his female relatives and a three-roomed rectangular building the functions of which, to judge from its grindstones, pottery and glass bottles, included the preparation of ritual medicines and the entertainment of guests. Faunal assemblages from both Ondini and Mgungundlovu have been analysed (Plug and Roodt 1990; Watson and Watson 1990). They show an almost complete dependence on cattle, the vast majority mature, with the few young animals present only found in the *isigodlo*, suggesting preferential royal access to them. Butchery evidence confirms European accounts of a diet high in boiled, tough beef, though adult animals may also have been needed for skins with which to make shields. Rarer wild animals at Ondini may reflect their use in royal rituals or the making of regalia.

The Zulu kingdom remains by far the archaeologically best-investigated *Mfecane*-age polity. The Ndebele (Matebele) kingdom led by Mzilikazi derived its core from the KwaKhumalo chiefdom centred on the Type B settlements discussed above. Crossing the Drakensberg around 1822, it went through several relocations before ending up in what is now western Zimbabwe in 1838. The kingdom was based in the western/central transVaal until evicted by the Boers, and a village complex on its then western periphery shows the development from regimental base to homestead as its warriors married and had children (Pistorius 1997). Though some use was made of stone walls, houses were of grass and wood, and furnaces of Nguni, not Tswana, type. Further north in Zimbabwe many Ndebele settlements have been located (Summers and Pagden 1970) and work started on investigating Old Bulawayo, its last capital (Pikirayi 1997a). So-called 'Refuge Period' sites, typically with pottery and grainbins, in rock-shelters or hidden among granite boulders as at Zhizo Hill, reflect one local Shona response to the invasions of the Ndebele and their Ngoni predecessors (Fig. 12.22; K. Robinson 1966).

Other Nguni-derived polities are more poorly known, though Liesegang (1974) identified in western Mozambique the locations of two capitals of the Gaza polity founded by a Ndwandwe dissident, Soshangane, *c.* 1821. Perry's (1999) study of Swazi royal sites was on a similarly limited scale. In a more anthropologically orientated study, Collett (1987) considers what a study of historically known *Mfecane* migrations can add to archaeology's general theoretical understanding of migrations. Ngoni groups settling ultimately in Malawi and Zambia retained a Nguni arrangement of domestic space in their homesteads, perhaps linked to the importance of women in maintaining 'authentic' Nguni patterns of behaviour. Pottery styles, however, became those of the indigenous Luangwa Tradition. Sotho-speaking Kololo, however, who temporarily seized control of the Barotse kingdom in western Zambia, successfully introduced both their language and new ceramics, the Linyanti Tradition (D. Phillipson 1977). Though Collett implies that this may have been because the Kololo placed greater emphasis on pottery as a means of self-definition, concluding (*contra* Huffman 1989) that no precise correlation is discernible between ceramic style and ethnicity, his observations may also be explicable by the mixed ancestry of post-*Mfecane* Barotse.

Returning to southern Africa, on the highveld Moshoeshoe I, a Kwena chief, was able to establish a secure nucleus for what grew into the modern kingdom of Lesotho around the virtually impregnable mesa of Thaba Bosiu (Fig. 12.23). Attacked several times, it was never taken and remained occupied into the

Figure 12.22   Grain bin, refuge site, Matopo Hills, Zimbabwe.

1920s, continuing until today as Lesotho's national shrine and royal cemetery. The foundations of Moshoeshoe's European-style house and several middens have been located. Pottery, copper earrings and glass beads that parallel finds from seventeenth/eighteenth-century sites in the Free State also hint at a hitherto unknown pre-*Mfecane* occupation (Dreyer 1996). Beyond this, agropastoralist settlement in western Lesotho remains archaeologically unknown.

The impact of extended conflict in the early nineteenth century can be seen in both site abandonment and destruction in the Free State and transVaal (Maggs 1976). Oral traditions of cannibalism may be exaggerated, perhaps often metaphorical (Delius 1983), but it is clear that many communities were extensively disrupted. Schoeman (1998a, 1998b) illustrates this in the case

Figure 12.23   Thaba Bosiu, Lesotho, viewed from the south near Mahaheng.

of the Ndzundza Ndebele of the Steelpoort Valley, Mpumalanga. Though Nguni-speaking, building Nguni-style beehive grass houses and observing Nguni witchcraft beliefs as reflected in the capping of ash layers in middens, their ceramics resembled those of their Sotho-speaking Pedi neighbours. After their capital at KwaMaza was destroyed by Mzilikazi in the 1820s, royal occupation shifted to a defensible hilltop location at Esikhunjini (Fig. 12.24). Now in alliance with the Pedi, they continued to use similar ceramics, but more regularly and thoroughly capped middens than before, reflecting (not surprisingly) a greater preoccupation with the threat of witchcraft. Interestingly, too, their beehive houses now used *daga* for wall construction, perhaps to signal distance from invading Nguni-speaking raiders and links to the Pedi.

Another kind of disruption is shown by ephemeral cave occupations, such as near Ohrigstad and Sabie in Mpumalanga (Evers 1981). Lepalong near Potchefstroom is the most fully investigated such site. Two Kwena groups lived here while seeking refuge from Mzilikazi, both above ground and in a cavern below. Analysis of the spatial layout of the above-ground site shows that it lacks a central cattle byre, formally defined court area, perimeter walls or walls to define the front and back of individual houses, material demonstration of a loose, fragmented community whose worldview, at least as expressed architecturally, had been pruned to the minimum (S. Hall 1995). Spatial constraints make it impossible to expect the Central Cattle Pattern to be manifested in the cavern, but individual households seem more formally defined there than above. Byres and

Figure 12.24   Homestead 2 at Esikhunjini, Mpumalanga, South Africa (courtesy
Alex Schoeman). The central enclosure of this homestead is
identified as an assembly area on the basis of its location below the
senior homestead at the site and the absence of associated cattle
tracks. As well as pottery, an associated midden produced a few
glass beads and copper ornaments (Schoeman 1998b).

granaries in other transVaal cave systems indicate that underground protection
of livestock and grain was a widespread response to nineteenth-century insecurities. In the aftermath of the *Mfecane*, these insecurities were dramatically enhanced and eventually transformed as the nineteenth century witnessed
the eventual extension of colonial rule and European settlement across all of
southern Africa.

THE ARCHAEOLOGY OF COLONIALISM

In the early fifteenth century an impartial observer identifying outside powers with the potential to colonise southern Africa might have lighted upon China. In a series of voyages Admiral Zheng He and his subordinates impressed the power of its new Ming Dynasty rulers as far afield as Java, Sri Lanka and southern Arabia and called along the East African coast, collecting exotic animals *en route*. Yet nothing more concrete came of these expeditions, which terminated in 1434. Lacking competitors, faced with the imperative of guarding its northern land frontier and convinced of its own superiority at the centre of the known world, China did not pursue the opportunities for trade or colonisation in the Indian Ocean that these voyages opened up (Mote 1991).

Instead, first the Portuguese and then other Europeans, notably the Dutch and the British, sailed into southern African waters from the west, settling along the coast and ultimately expanding inland to wrest control of the sub-continent from its indigenous inhabitants. This penultimate chapter surveys the archaeological record of these events (Fig. 13.1). Most observations come from South Africa, where historical sources are plentiful and colonial archaeology best developed, but the interplay of written and archaeological materials for understanding the recent past is increasingly an important research theme across the sub-continent. As chapters 10–12 showed, textual sources, including oral histories, are important for understanding both early and later farming communities and their interaction with the world beyond southern Africa. What distinguishes this chapter, and historical archaeology as a sub-discipline, is an emphasis on tracking European colonial expansion and the associated processes of the growth of capitalism and a modern way of life, using archaeology to understand this from the standpoints of colonisers and colonised alike (Orser 1996).

The perspective of historical archaeology is thus very different from the long-standing emphasis of art and architectural historians on fine art objects and grand buildings at the expense of such non-élite concerns as vernacular architecture, food and everyday material culture (M. Hall 1993). Its slow development reflects the necessity of first challenging and then overcoming the dominance of these other disciplines in examining colonial material culture. This shift began in South Africa in the late 1970s, with the development of research programmes at several institutions in the Western Cape (Abrahams 1984).

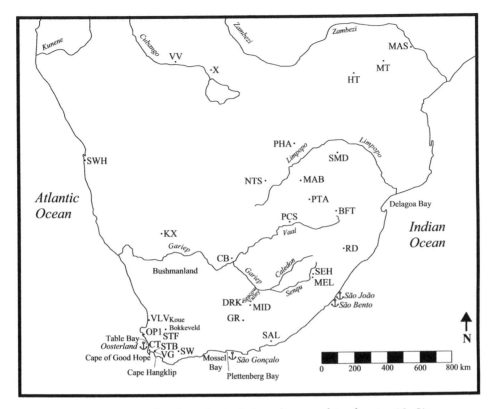

Figure 13.1   Location of archaeological sites discussed in chapter 13. Site
names abbreviated thus: BFT Bankfontein; CB Campbell; CT Cape
Town; DRK Driekoppen; GR Graaff-Reinet; HT Hartley; KX
//Khauxa!nas; MAB Mabotse; MAS Massangano; MEL Melikane;
MID Middelburg; MT Mtoko; NTS Ntsweng; OP1 Oudepost 1; PCS
Potchefstroom; PHA Phalatswe; PTA Pretoria; RD Rorke's Drift;
SAL Salem; SEH Sehonghong; SMD Schoemansdal; STB
Stellenbosch; STF Stompiesfontein; SW Swellendam; SWH
Sandwich Harbour; VG Vergelegen; VLV Verlorenvlei; VV Vungu
Vungu; X Xaro.

The subsequent establishment at the University of Cape Town of a Historical
Archaeology Research Group and of an office for conducting contract archaeology in the greater Cape Town area (chapter 14) were also vital in promoting
research on the colonial period. So too, fuelled by political change, has been the
increasingly widespread recognition across southern Africa of the importance
of understanding the past from a perspective that seeks to integrate, rather than
to divide, the histories of the sub-continent's various communities.

Though many areas remain to be researched and some projects have yet to
go beyond the archaeological documentation of what is already known from
historical sources, much has been achieved through the close engagement of

material culture and textual evidence. One important research theme considered below is the investigation of colonial frontiers, something with parallels not only to other parts of the world but also within southern Africa in the impact on hunter-gatherer populations of earlier pastoralist and agropastoralist expansions. A second involves exploring the archaeological record for evidence of the underclasses, including slaves, who go largely unrepresented in contemporary texts; one major theoretical concern here, again shared with other colonial situations, is the relationship between ethnicity and material culture. Researching the cognitive structures by which people, colonisers and colonised alike, organised their lives in new and challenging circumstances provides a third theme, explored, among others, by Gribble (1989) in the Western Cape and by Winer and Deetz (1990) in the Eastern Cape. As in Iron Age archaeology, while such cognitive-structural models help organise a mass of disparate information, they find explaining change more difficult (Behrens 1991; M. Hall 1993). Quite different in approach and emphasising close readings of particular situations, rather than the search for cognitive universals, what may be dubbed the 'archaeology of the text' (M. Hall 1993) forms a fourth theme in the archaeology of colonialism, illustrated by several studies of Cape colonial architecture, from the fortifications of Cape Town Castle (M. Hall *et al.* 1990a) through the design of gubernatorial estates (Y. Brink 1993) to the symbolism of gabled manor house roofs (M. Hall 1994).

Portuguese exploration and settlement

Portuguese maritime expansion began about the time of Zheng He's voyages, spurred by the desire to establish a searoute to the riches of the Far East. By 1485 Portugal's navigators had reached Cape Cross, where Diogo Cão set up a commemorative stone cross (*padrão*; Fig. 13.2). Three years later Bartolomeu Dias rounded the Cape of Good Hope, sailing as far as Mossel Bay. Less than a decade later Vasco da Gama called at several places along South Africa's coast, trading with Khoekhoen at Mossel Bay for livestock before reaching Mozambique and crossing the ocean to India. His voyage initiated a frantic few decades in which the Portuguese established bases from Iran to China (Boxer 1969). In building this empire, their African interests were limited to seizing important coastal trading towns to direct trade to themselves and gain access to the gold of the Zimbabwe Plateau. However, following a battle with Khoekhoen in Table Bay in 1510 in which the Viceroy of India was killed, their ships ceased to call along the South African coast (Elphick 1985).

Surviving *padrões* and other inscriptions document some of these early Portuguese voyages, but shipwrecks are potentially much more informative. One of the earliest is that of the *São João*, wrecked in June 1552 near Port Edward. Diving on the wreck site and collection of washed-up finds have

Figure 13.2   Reconstruction of the Portuguese *padrão*, Cape Cross, Namibia, erected by the German colonial authorities before the First World War.

produced a bronze cannon, carnelian beads and a range of Chinese porcelain and earthenwares mostly of mid-sixteenth-century date (Maggs 1984d). Similar material, along with gold jewellery, some of Indian manufacture, cowrie shells and peppercorns, comes from the *São Bento*, destroyed in 1554 off the Transkei coast (Auret and Maggs 1982). Survivors' accounts provide the first detailed historical information on south-eastern southern Africa's inhabitants, complemented by those of other shipwrecked crews through the late 1500s and 1600s. The campsite of one such group, survivors of the *São Gonçalo*, has been excavated at Plettenberg Bay. Dating to 1630, it included a probable iron-working area that used local laterite. Among other finds were a navigator's dividers, Indian carnelian beads, late Ming porcelain, and incense, used mixed with seal oil as a caulking material. During the ten months they spent here, the *São Gonçalo*'s crew traded with local Khoekhoen for cattle, hunted antelope, seals and penguins, fished and collected mussels, though they avoided the locally plentiful limpets which in Europe were only eaten in times of famine (A.B. Smith 1986).

On land Portuguese settlement of Mozambique began in 1505 with an attempt to gain control of Sofala and advanced swiftly. Small trading communities were established at strategic locations along the Zambezi by the 1540s and in the ensuing decades several others were constructed across northern Zimbabwe. Mtoko (known to the Portuguese as Luanze) and Hartley (in an area the Portuguese called Maramuca) are the best known, with sun-dried brick structures or pole-and-*daga* houses surrounded by earthen banks and, in the former case, ditches (Garlake 1967). Hartley's brick building, built on an artificial platform and subdivided into three long, narrow rooms, exactly parallels contemporary East African architecture, while Mtoko also had a church and a separate stonewalled enclosure containing further houses and a cemetery. With neither site intended for defence, historical sources confirm they were places for storing and selling merchandise. Finds include Chinese and European pottery, glass and gold beads, lead shot and traces of gold dust. Six similar earthwork enclosures tightly clustered north of Chinhoyi are of slightly later age, dating to either side of 1700 rather than the earlier seventeenth century (Garlake 1967).

The bulk of Portuguese trade with the African interior was soon controlled by *prazeros*, land-holders given royal grants to areas along the Zambezi Valley who began to use African symbols of chieftainship and to build up private slave armies to ensure tribute collection (M. Hall 1987). Little has been done archaeologically to explore the *prazo* system, though Newitt and Garlake (1967) describe the Massangano *prazo* downstream of Tete. It is thus documentary sources, rather than archaeology, that attest to the replacement of gold by ivory as the major commodity exported from the Portuguese coastal settlements in the seventeenth century, with slaves emerging as a principal export *c.* 1800. Full Portuguese control of Mozambique was established only in the early twentieth century.

Even before rounding the Cape of Good Hope, Portugal developed ties with the Kongo kingdom in what is now north-western Angola. Subsequent colonisation was largely directed at securing slaves for Portugal's Brazilian colony. Extraction of ivory and slaves from southern Angola was underway by the late 1700s and trade with the Herero and Owambo of northern Namibia developed quickly (Wilmsen 1989). This is represented by glass beads from sites such as Vungu Vungu (Sandelowsky 1979) and Xaro (Denbow and Wilmsen 1986), but the past of both the Owambo and the Herero remains archaeologically unknown. Nevertheless, a flourishing local trade network had certainly developed by the nineteenth century, one in which various Bushman groups were heavily involved (Gordon 1984; J. Kinahan 1986). By 1850 European interest in commodities such as ivory, cattle and ostrich feathers had brought them as far as the north-western Kalahari, something reflected in much higher numbers of glass beads (Wilmsen 1989). How far anthropologically observed Kalahari hunter-gatherers are merely impoverished remnants of the participants in these exchange systems continues to be debated and researched (A.B. Smith and Lee 1997; chapter 8).

Figure 13.3   View of Table Bay looking north from the summit of Table
Mountain, Western Cape, South Africa. The city centre of Cape
Town is visible in the centre of the photograph.

The Cape Colony: historical background

By the late 1500s other European nations threatened Portuguese supremacy in
the Indian Ocean. From 1591 numerous English and Dutch ships called at Table
Bay (Fig. 13.3), trading for livestock with local Khoekhoen. Initially the latter
demanded iron, but after 1610, perhaps because local demand had been satu-
rated, their preferences shifted to copper and tobacco, all items unavailable in
quantity locally (Elphick 1985; cf. D. Miller *et al.* 1998). Though never intend-
ing large-scale colonisation, the Dutch East India Company (VOC)[1] established
a permanent base in Table Bay in 1652 designed to provide fresh food and water
for VOC ships sailing between the Netherlands and Dutch colonial possessions
in south-east Asia. In an attempt to improve the supply of food, a few settlers
(freeburghers) were allowed to establish farms close to the main settlement in
1657. This demonstration of a permanent European presence precipitated the
First Dutch/Khoekhoe War, at the end of which Khoekhoen living on the Cape
Peninsula permanently lost access to pasture lands (Elphick 1985).

---

[1] *Generale Vereenigde Nederlanstche Geoctroyeerde Oostindische Compagnie*, or General United
Netherlands Chartered East India Company to give it its full title, hence the abbreviation 'VOC'.

Attempts to develop an intensive mixed farming economy rapidly failed because of shortages of capital and labour. Freeburghers turned instead to extensive wheat cultivation and livestock-raising. While the European population grew slowly, reaching 10,500 only as late as 1780 (Guelke 1989), the area of settlement expanded swiftly, with new administrative centres established at Stellenbosch (1679), Swellendam (1743) and Graaff-Reinet (1785; Elphick and Giliomee 1989). Already by the 1690s the Colony's frontier was too long to be effectively policed by VOC officials, allowing freeburghers to engage in illicit trade and pasture livestock beyond the settled areas.

With access to capital still limited and few alternatives to farming as a livelihood, many settlers expanded inland over the Cape Fold Mountain Belt from the early 1700s, leaving the areas closest to Cape Town to a plantation-owning landed gentry and a larger number of smaller farmers. These settlers, often termed *trekboeren*, were not simple subsistence farmers, whatever their dependence on stock-farming. Guns, gunpowder, wagons and other manufactured items, as well as tea, coffee, sugar and most clothes continued to be derived from Cape Town, while taxation, payment of rents on farms and the registration of baptisms and marriages maintained links with the VOC's power structures. The high costs of overland transport constrained their ability to sell livestock and other products, while settlement of the interior was increasingly restricted by military resistance from Khoisan groups (Guelke 1989). Strengthening European feelings of racial superiority and exclusiveness, this contributed, because of a lack of VOC military support, to growing opposition to Company authority along the frontier in the years before Britain conquered the Cape in 1795. Restored to Dutch control in 1803, the Cape's reconquest in 1806 initiated a century of British colonial expansion in southern Africa.

Up until 1820, when a major British settlement was implanted on its eastern frontier, the Cape Colony's European population remained almost wholly Dutch-speaking. Within twenty years a substantial fraction of this community had emigrated further into the interior, impelled by economic factors and dissatisfaction with British management of inter-racial relations, including the abolition of slavery (1838). First moving into southern KwaZulu-Natal and then, after Britain annexed Natal (1843), settling on the highveld and beyond the Vaal River, these Boers established several republics that rested on white domination of both politics and the economy. The disruptions of the *Mfecane* assisted their takeover of African lands, but the South African Republic, in particular, still faced strong military resistance into the 1890s. Only a few years later the Second South African War saw both it and the Orange Free State annexed by Britain, a move largely precipitated by British desire to control the goldfields of the Witwatersrand. With adjacent regions of the sub-continent (Botswana, Lesotho, Swaziland and Zimbabwe) also falling, directly or indirectly, under British rule, and Germany colonising Namibia, European control of the whole of southern Africa was firmly established prior to the First World War (Davenport and Saunders 2000).

Colonial archaeology at the Cape

As already indicated, the close interworking of material evidence and textual sources provides one of historical archaeology's key themes. The forts built by the VOC in what is now central Cape Town provide an illuminating illustration of this. Begun in 1652, the first, the Fort de Goede Hoop, remained in use until 1674. Excavations confirm that it followed a standard VOC design, quadrilateral with four corner bastions, encircled by a moat and breastwork. However, shortages of materials and skilled labour led to extensive use of local substitutes and construction of a moat with a V-shaped cross-section which needed far less manpower. From the beginning of colonial settlement, adaptations of European ideas to local circumstances were thus clearly required (Abrahams 1993), though not all VOC employees survived long enough to make them at the individual level (Fouché 1995). Faced with a badly deteriorating fort, the VOC ordered the building of a second, stronger structure with five bastions, the still-surviving Castle of Good Hope (Fig. 13.4). Several excavations

Figure 13.4   Excavations in the Granary, Cape Town Castle, Western Cape, South Africa (courtesy Tim Hart).

have taken place here (e.g. Abrahams 1984). They make clear that shortages of materials again hindered construction, which proceeded in fits and starts, handicapped by building on unstable foundations, until completion in 1679. Though a moat was built, its water content must have been highly variable and its size was greatly reduced. Far from being effective militarily, its primary significance was clearly symbolic, stamping a colonial presence on the landscape. No longer important in this respect, it became a rubbish dump under British rule (M. Hall *et al.* 1990a).

Moving beyond the Castle, Cape Town's city centre has witnessed several archaeological investigations (M. Hall 1993). The Barrack Street well (M. Hall *et al.* 1990b) is noteworthy for preserving many organic items, as well as iron tools, ceramics, glass and faunal remains from the eighteenth and nineteenth centuries. One important change is the shift from mostly Oriental porcelain in the 1700s to mostly European refined earthenwares in the 1800s. This reflects the replacement of primarily Asian suppliers in the Dutch East Indies by mass-produced British pottery after the British occupation (cf. Klose and Malan 2000), but survival of Oriental ceramics into the nineteenth century suggests a degree of resistance to the latest British fashions advocated by powerful wholesale merchants.

Probate inventories drawn up on a person's death to detail his or her possessions provide an important textual source for comparison with such archaeological evidence. They show, for example, how eighteenth-century Cape Town houses functioned simultaneously as stores, with retail businesses taking place in the living rooms of well-off, fashion-conscious households. This helps explain otherwise obscure phenomena, such as the extraordinarily high frequency of unmarked, unused porcelain recovered from a mid/late eighteenth-century dump at a house in Bree Street (Malan 1997). These domestically emplaced businesses seem to have been controlled by women, though public auctions were more a male domain. Only in the late eighteenth century, and then among the upper echelons of Cape Town society, is there evidence for the gradual separation of activities within houses and greater emphasis on domestic privacy (Malan 1990). Because probate inventories offer high resolution of time, place and person they also reveal how written sources can obscure gender and class distinctions. That of Philip Anhuyzer (died 1827), for example, is overwhelmingly masculine and bourgeois in emphasis, though finds from the Barrack Street well next door identify the local presence of women, children, soldiers and servants or slaves (M. Hall *et al.* 1990b).

Barrack Street was occupied by traders of middling status for most of its history. Excavations at the Castle and at Paradise, a timber-cutting station on Table Mountain's eastern flanks, are among those that suggest how material culture was used to uphold class differences. The Castle Grain Store, for example, which dates 1665–91, documents a diet of dried fish and poorer mutton cuts, while the ceramic assemblage is dominated by **provincial porcelain** and

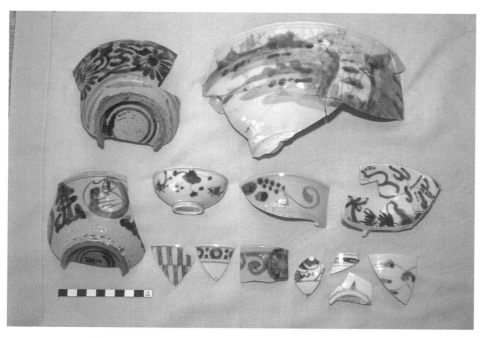

Figure 13.5   Chinese provincial porcelain (Asian market ware) from several
eighteenth-century colonial sites in and near Cape Town (courtesy
Jane Klose; Klose 1997).

everyday rough earthenwares; small quantities of high-quality porcelain were
probably scavenged. Though it is debatable if this signature is that of slaves, it
is clearly not that of the VOC élite who controlled the Colony (M. Hall 1993).
Founded in 1657, excavations at Paradise also produced ceramic assemblages
with high percentages of utilitarian provincial porcelains and coarse earthenwares that probably represent standard VOC issue to the lower echelons of its
staff (Fig. 13.5). Many of the earthenwares may have been made at the Cape,
initially perhaps by slaves (Abrahams 1994; Jourdan *et al.* 1999). Oriental porcelain, on the other hand, was in common use locally, in marked contrast to its
scarcity in Europe (Fig. 13.6). At Paradise, however, the occupant of the Main
House (the VOC Woodcutter) had better access to newer ceramic styles, passing
on less fashionable items to his subordinates in Outbuilding 1 (M. Hall *et al.*
1993).

Faunal analyses suggest that at least until 1750 the Main House at Paradise
also had preferential access to choicer mutton cuts, the dominant meat consumed in colonial Cape Town; even officers, despite their access to cut glass
drinking vessels and wine, monotonously ate mutton, only rarely consuming
poor cuts of beef or pork (Seeman 1992). Detailed archaeological studies of colonial foodways have only just begun, but eighteenth-century ceramics from the

Figure 13.6   Japanese export porcelain enamelled bowls from the
mid-eighteenth-century kitchen midden of the manor house at
Elsenburg, near Stellenbosch, Western Cape, South Africa (courtesy
Jane Klose). Three, possibly all four, of those shown are painted with
flowers and running hares. Unlikely to have formed part of an
official porcelain cargo, they may have been specially ordered
(Klose 1997).

site of the former Fort de Goede Hoop contribute to an understanding of how
food was stored, prepared and consumed (Abrahams-Willis 1998). Interestingly,
it seems that local drinking patterns remained more closely tied to Europe than
did what was eaten, where strong Malayo-Indonesian influences on ingredients
and techniques are apparent.

While some of the Oriental porcelain found at Paradise and the Fort de Goede
Hoop site arrived in official VOC consignments, other ceramics represent unof-
ficial trade by private individuals. Excavation of the *Oosterland*, which sank in
Table Bay in 1697, demonstrates this (Fig. 13.7). Both Chinese and Japanese
porcelains were found elsewhere than in the cargo holds and documentary
sources suggest that at this time the VOC itself was not trading porcelain
because of poor profits. Other finds from this, the first archaeological maritime salvage project undertaken in southern Africa, include spices, wicker
baskets that may contain indigo dye, tropical hardwoods, and cowries for sale
to the Dutch West India Company for buying slaves in West Africa. Along
with elements of the ship's armaments and more personal items, such as a

Figure 13.7   Excavating the wreck of the *Oosterland*, Table Bay, Western Cape,
South Africa. The photograph shows a diver measuring one of the
ship's timbers (courtesy Bruno Werz).

barber-surgeon's toolkit, the *Oosterland* provides a wealth of material dating
to a very specific moment in the colonial history of the Cape (Werz 1999).

Beyond Cape Town itself two major projects have examined different aspects
of the VOC Colony, one the small military outpost at Oudepost 1, the other the

country estate of an early Governor at Vergelegen. Oudepost 1, on the south-west shore of the Langebaan lagoon, was established in 1669 to ward off French interest, later becoming a provisioning station for ships and a trading post with local Khoekhoen. Abandoned after its garrison's partial massacre in 1673, it was later reoccupied until relocated nearby in 1732 (Schrire 1988). Excavations showed colonial debris scattered over some 2500 m², centred around a polyg-onal fort and two smaller buildings. All were constructed of local stone with reed roofs, plastered walls and, in the case of the fort, plastered floors. Neither stratigraphy nor artefacts distinguish pre- and post-massacre occupations, but clay pipe analysis (Schrire *et al.* 1990) and other finds provide a sequence span-ning the historically attested occupation.

Ceramics are, as expected, relatively plentiful, consisting mostly of the fine and provincial Chinese porcelain in common use on ships returning to Europe from the Far East; stonewares of mostly Rhineland origin probably used to store **arrack** or vinegar, and earthenwares, some perhaps of Cape manufac-ture, form the rest of the assemblage (Schrire *et al.* 1993). Rarer finds include coins, gaming counters and the seal from a cloth consignment (Schrire and Meltzer 1992), as well as gunflints, some made from local stone (Schrire and Deacon 1989). Excavations revealed a wide range of domesticates, but initially suggested most of the meat consumed was wild in origin (Cruz-Uribe and Schrire 1991). This is surprising, as documentary sources repeatedly state that sheep and some cattle were brought to Oudepost through trade with the Khoekhoen, or from VOC meat-provisioning stations and colonial farms further inland. Analysis of a dump dating to the earliest part of the site's occupation helps explain this. Consisting primarily of butchery residues thrown over the fort wall into the sea, rather than disposed of in rubbish pits on land, over half the bones belong to domesticates, almost wholly sheep and cattle (Schrire *et al.* 1993). Another historically documented activity, taking sealskins and seal oil, remains poorly represented in the surviving fauna, in this case because it was probably undertaken on offshore island rookeries (Cruz-Uribe and Schrire 1991).

Oudepost 1 figures heavily in recent discussions of the relations between herders and hunter-gatherers in the south-western Cape. Put simply, Schrire and Deacon (1989) argued that because documentary sources only refer to the presence of Khoekhoen, the LSA material culture found at Oudepost must be their product. Since it is no different from that found across the region, separate hunter-gatherer and herder populations cannot be recognised archae-ologically and probably did not exist (cf. Elphick 1985). No definite resolution has been obtained on whether the LSA and colonial residues at Oudepost 1 are unequivocally associated, or whether the former might have been left between 1673 and 1686 when the Dutch were absent (Yates and Smith 1993a, 1993b). However, in addition to confirming the original chronology of the Oudepost 1 site (Schrire 1993), several important points have arisen from this debate that need addressing when explaining LSA assemblage variability over the past 2000 years (Schrire 1992a; chapter 9).

A world away from Oudepost 1 in the social hierarchy of the Cape Colony was Vergelegen, the private estate of Willem Adriaan van der Stel, Governor of the Cape 1699–1707. Granted land by the VOC 50 km east of Cape Town, van der Stel attempted to use his estate to monopolise the supply of wheat, wine and livestock to the Company's ships. As its focus he constructed a set of buildings that included a house and overseer's dwelling on opposite sides of an octagonal, twin-walled garden, flanking which were a wine cellar, slave lodge, pigeon house and watermill-cum-stable (Markell 1993; Markell *et al.* 1995). Because of his dismissal and the eventual confiscation and sale of Vergelegen, much documentary evidence survives to assist interpretation of the excavations carried out here. These concentrated on the slave lodge (Fig. 13.8), mill/stable and wine cellar. All three are of a common North European vernacular type known as a *hallehuis*, long, rectangular and divided into three aisles, used in the Netherlands as farmhouses and for storing grain, keeping animals and craft activities. The Vergelegen outbuildings conform to this pattern, though probably replacing timber uprights with brick columns for the lodge and cellar roofs because of the local shortage of suitable wood (Markell 1993).

Excavation produced a diversity of finds. Most of the pottery from the mill and the lodge was Oriental porcelain, along with earthenware cooking pots and stoneware jugs and storage vessels. Each building also yielded one globular, flat-based earthenware cooking jar, formally similar to ceramics known from India and Indonesia; petrologically similar vessels come from an area of the Castle in Cape Town thought to have housed slaves (M. Hall *et al.* 1990a).

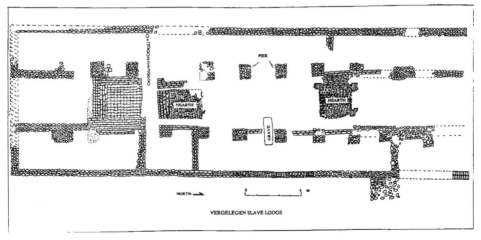

Figure 13.8   Plan of the slave lodge at Vergelegen (after Markell 1993: Fig. 6; courtesy South African Archaeological Society).

Iron tools relate to wood-working, farming and fishing, while personal items include clay tobacco pipes, buttons, buckles, thimbles and flint strike-a-lights; glass vessels were rare except in the cellar (Markell 1993). Faunal assemblages are overwhelmingly domestic, dominated by sheep and cattle, with minimal exploitation of wild resources.

Both Markell (1993) and Y. Brink (1993) argue that the very design of the Vergelegen estate makes a symbolic statement about van der Stel's aims and aspirations. They note its rigid symmetry and orderly north/south layout compared to most other Cape Colonial farms, as well as the effort expended to create the high-walled octagonal garden. Here we have the emulation of Renaissance architectural ideas in a colonial context, precisely as undertaken at the same time by the élite of Dutch society on their country estates. Though similar to walls used in Dutch forts in the Netherlands, at the Cape and in Brazil, as emphasised in van der Stel's own submissions to the VOC, the Vergelegen wall was merely a symbolic fortification, asserting control over the landscape and its inhabitants (Markell 1993). Provision of a specific and separate building to house slaves is also highly unusual for the early eighteenth-century Cape and again suggests van der Stel's desire to show off his power, wealth and status. This is further reflected in his use of an octagonal design in two other buildings built during his governorship (Y. Brink 1993).

The cultural construction of colonial landscapes at the Cape is an evolving subject of study. M. Hall (1991) and Y. Brink (1997) argue that while VOC maps supposedly aimed at scientific accuracy, they were produced as signs of control over territory. While emphasising the ordered grid system used to organise settlements, they omitted the untidy alleyways and sidestreets where the underclass lived. To maintain its supremacy over an expanding freeburgher population whom it still considered its servants, the VOC also employed language, enforcing strict censorship and emphasising the obedience owed it in exchange for its generosity. Architecture was one way in which rich freeburghers expressed dissent at this state of affairs, developing impressive, symmetrical manor houses and permanently installing them on the landscape in a manner impossible to deny (Fig. 13.9; Y. Brink 1990). Her research and other archaeologically orientated studies, including those of Paradise (M. Hall *et al.* 1993) and surviving buildings at Verlorenvlei on the Atlantic coast (Gribble 1989; Fig. 13.10), confirm Walton's (1965) view that Cape vernacular architecture evolved from linear three-roomed I-shaped houses into larger T-shaped and H-shaped forms.

Rural settlement in other areas of the Cape Colony is archaeologically less well investigated than at Vergelegen or Oudepost 1, though the socio-economically more marginal status of farmers in the late eighteenth- to early nineteenth-century western Overberg is reflected in smaller farm buildings and reduced emphasis on architectural elements signalling status relative to

Figure 13.9 The main building at Blaauwklippen, Western Cape, South Africa (courtesy John Hobart). Granted by Simon van der Stel in 1692, the present manor house dates to 1789 and was built by Dirk Wouter Hoffman. H-shaped with thatched roof, gables and a three-sided porch (*stoep*), it is now the focus of one of the Cape's most well-visited winefarms.

farms further west around Stellenbosch (Rademeyer-De Kock 1993). There excavations, architectural studies and historical sources have tracked changes in colonial domestic culture and the town's own development (Abrahams 1984; Klose 1997). Both Stellenbosch itself (Vos 1993) and Onrust, a farm just outside first granted in 1692 (M. Hall *et al.* 1988), again document the gradual development of local architectural styles from a North European building tradition constructed using local materials.

Other studies of nineteenth-century colonial settlement have focused on the Eastern Cape. At Salem (Fig. 13.11), a village founded in 1820, Winer and Deetz (1990) argue that its Methodist settlers marked out on the landscape an idealised cognitive map, their 'memory' of rural England. Their houses, however, show a contrast between an older 'hall-and-parlour' floor plan inside and fashionable, contemporary Georgian façades outside, something they see as reflecting the disruption experienced on relocating to the colonial frontier (Winer and Deetz 1990; Winer 1994). Pursuing research on this theme, Scott and Deetz (1990) trace the creation of a distinctively British South African

Figure 13.10   Vernacular architecture, Verlorenvlei, Western Cape, South Africa.

frontier culture that partly parallels earlier developments in colonial North America.

Slaves and freeblacks: what can archaeology say?

Until abolition in 1838 the Cape Colony was a slave society, with slaves accounting for just over half the population throughout much of the eighteenth century (Shell 1994). With a limited European population and initial difficulties in recruiting local Khoekhoen for work on farms, slaves were the answer to the Colony's labour shortage. Total arrivals probably numbered a few hundred a year at most, with Madagascar, India and Indonesia the main sources. Most Company-owned slaves were kept in a lodge in Cape Town and employed on VOC projects. Many of those owned privately were also concentrated in Cape Town, used as domestic servants, but also hired out as skilled and unskilled labour; most of the remainder formed the backbone of the agricultural labour force in the wheat- and wine-producing areas of Cape Town's hinterland. Severe punishments suppressed most resistance, but escaped slave communities were able to establish themselves on Table Mountain and at Cape Hangklip, where they survived by fishing and raiding farms; all remain archaeologically unexplored.

Figure 13.11   View of the centre of Salem, Eastern Cape, South Africa (courtesy
Margot Winer). The church (built in 1850) is at the rear, the
Methodist chapel (constructed in 1832 to replace the original 1822
building) at the far left and the village green in the foreground.

Worden (1985) predicted that the slave population's disparate origins and
its low number of women inhibited the development of a distinctive slave
material culture at the Cape. While few items found at the Vergelegen slave
lodge can unequivocally be attributed to slaves, things may not be quite so
simple. Markell *et al.* (1995) emphasise that many Cape slaves would already
have been familiar with porcelain and that the specific ceramic forms used
in the Colony were similar to those used in their traditional foodways. Other
items made and used by slaves, such as baskets and wooden boxes, may not
have been preserved (Markell 1993). On the other hand, the coins and counters
found may have formed part of a slave currency system (Shell 1994), while
several shallow brick-surrounded pit-hearths in the floor of one of the rooms
of the mill recall cooking places in other parts of Africa and Madagascar; they
are definitely not of Dutch origin (Markell *et al.* 1995). Finally, ostrich eggshell
may reflect the historically documented collection of eggs by slaves for sale to
visiting sailors, while the faunal assemblage's emphasis on mutton fits archival
evidence for slave rations. Recently initiated excavations at the slave lodge in
Cape Town, the only surviving VOC installation of its kind, are, however,
producing much richer and more comprehensive assemblages. Once analysed,

Figure 13.12   Excavations of the VOC slave lodge inside and below the South
                African Cultural History Museum, Cape Town, Western Cape,
                South Africa (courtesy South African Cultural History Museum,
                Gabeba Abrahams-Willis and Cecil Kortjie). Excavations in 2000
                produced a rich assemblage of artefacts and faunal remains and
                excited substantial community interest (Abrahams-Willis
                2000).

they should provide an unparalleled archaeological insight into the lives of
VOC slaves at the Cape (Fig. 13.12; Yutar 2000).

A unique find from the Vergelegen lodge that almost certainly does relate
to the presence of slaves on the estate is the burial of a mature woman in
a makeshift wooden coffin. Stable isotope analyses suggest that as a child
she lived in a well-watered environment, eating a diet rich in tropical grains
with little if any seafood. However, her adult diet changed radically to include
temperate grains and a significant seafood component, consistent with the
importance of fish in lower-class eighteenth-century Cape diets. Her burial
is the only one known from Vergelegen and in being east-facing in unconse-
crated ground follows neither Christian nor Muslim practice. Still a puzzle,
perhaps she was an important figure within the local slave community (Sealy
et al. 1993). Other slave burials include a mass grave on Cape Town's foreshore where stable isotope analyses again document a childhood diet rich in
tropical grains that later underwent a marked change. Patterns of tooth decoration point to an ultimate origin in northern Mozambique/Malawi, while

archival sources identify them as victims of a wrecked early nineteenth-century Portuguese slaver (Cox and Sealy 1997). Individuals showing comparable dental modification and again a tropical grain childhood diet from Cape Town's late eighteenth- to early nineteenth-century Cobern Street cemetery were probably first-generation African slaves (Cox 1999).

But the Cape Colony under the VOC did not merely consist of free white and slave populations. Along with increasingly incorporated and subordinated aboriginal Khoisan communities, there were also a substantial number of 'freeblacks', some of them freed slaves, others political exiles and ex-convicts from Dutch possessions in south-east Asia. Collectively they formed a significant part of the population of Cape Town and its immediate surroundings. Little studied archaeologically and difficult to recognise from other elements of the Colony's underclass, such as slaves, these individuals were, at least in the early eighteenth century, not clearly differentiated from the rest of the free population. However, one hint comes from probate inventories, which suggest that some 'freeblacks' owned only bowls and saucer dishes for an Asian-derived rice-and-relish based cookery, with no objects at all associated with European-style cooking (Malan 1998/99). Along with many elements of traditional Cape cuisine (Abrahams-Willis 1998) and influences on the development of Afrikaans from Dutch, 'freeblacks' and slaves had another long-lasting impact in the introduction of Islam. First arriving in the 1600s, Islam grew spectacularly, first by transplantation of people from Indonesia and later through active proselytisation (Elphick and Shell 1989). Surviving material evidence is rare before 1800, but the tombs of several prominent members of the early Muslim community remain important pilgrimage centres (Fig. 13.13). Several of the burials from Cobern Street are also probably of Muslims to judge from their orientation and lack of coffins or grave goods. Stable isotope analyses indicate a childhood origin in the Indian Ocean area, though they were buried along with slaves and people of local origin in an informally organised cemetery for colonial Cape Town's growing, racially mixed underclass (Cox 1999).

Resistance to European settlement

From the beginning of European contact with the Khoekhoen an image of them as uncouth savages dominated European accounts (A.B. Smith 1993b), even though more realistic records were sometimes made (A.B. Smith and Pheiffer 1992). Such views helped condition settler attitudes to the indigenous population, ultimately contributing to a rigidly hierarchical view of intergroup relations defined by 'race'. Following the VOC's victory in the First Dutch-Khoekhoe War, expeditions seeking livestock rapidly penetrated the interior of the Western Cape. A second war (1670–77) broke the power of one of the most powerful Khoekhoe groups, the Cochoqua, and soon thereafter illegal private livestock-trading becomes well attested alongside official VOC activity.

Figure 13.13   Tomb of Tuang Guru, a Muslim religious leader, Signal Hill, Cape Town, Western Cape, South Africa (courtesy John Hobart).

However, despite the loss of animals traded to the Dutch, this alone seems insufficient to account for the rapid collapse of independent Khoekhoe communities in the south-western and southern Cape. Elphick (1985) notes several interlinked processes: gradual expropriation of better pasture lands by Europeans; loss of manpower to the settler economy; and Dutch suppression of the intertribal conflicts that were among the traditional means of reaccumulating stock. That Khoekhoen working for Europeans were paid in tobacco and food, rather than with animals, further suppressed the possibilities of recouping lost livestock. Initial analyses of the Oudepost 1 fauna, which suggested an emphasis on wild game, also implied a direct colonial impact on the meat resources of local herders and foragers (Schrire 1990, 1991, 1992b; cf. Penn 1991). As a general principle this still seems plausible, even though the butchery dump from the earliest occupation at Oudepost indicates that domestic animals were much more important than originally believed (Schrire *et al.* 1993). The permanent loss to the indigenous cultural system of the people, land and animals that all these other processes entailed implies that early eighteenth-century small-pox epidemics, though destructive, may have had only a comparatively minor impact overall (A.B. Smith 1989).

By 1700 open resistance, cautious withdrawal and eager co-operation on the part of Khoekhoe leaders had all failed to stem Dutch advance (Elphick and Malherbe 1989). As well as demanding ever-increasing numbers of live-stock, the Company increasingly interfered in Khoekhoe politics. Though it insisted that the Khoekhoen were free, most of those within the areas of Dutch settlement were progressively subordinated and incorporated into the colonial economy as farm labourers. Traditional dress, *matjieshuise* and the Khoe language nevertheless survived well into the eighteenth century (Elphick 1985).

An alternative to incorporation was movement away from the Cape Colony, though from the standpoint of those already living further inland such move-ments undoubtedly represented the further expansion of the colonial frontier. Two main groups can be identified, along with the trekboers whom I dis-cuss below. Both moved predominantly northward parallel to the Atlantic. Oorlam groups were formed largely of Khoekhoen from within the Colony, while Bastaard communities were of mixed-race origin, Christianised, Dutch-speaking and generally held to be of higher socio-economic position (Legassick 1989). Raids across the Gariep from the Cape Colony were taking place by the 1730s and a generation later Namaqua groups long resident south of the river were moving into Namibia. Oorlam expansion eventually overtook them, their guns, wagons and horses giving them a military advantage over Nama and Herero pastoralists. Europeans calling along Namibia's coast from the late 1700s to whale and seal were able to trade for cattle, ivory, skins, dried fish and rare human captives with both indigenous and recently arrived communities (Gewald 1995). J.H.A. Kinahan (1991) illustrates how this trade dramatically increased the availability of glass beads, which may have been taken up along-side older copper and iron examples as the basis for social storage networks that could ease fluctuations in cattle numbers caused by drought, raiding and disease. However, as animals were lost to European traders such fluctuations could no longer be cushioned, precipitating a general impoverishment of local herders by the late 1800s. Near the coast people may have been forced back onto fish, shellfish and wild plants as subsistence mainstays, producing the subsistence pattern recorded a century later (Budack 1977).

J. Kinahan (1996) also describes an early nineteenth-century Oorlam base, //Khauxa!nas in south-eastern Namibia (Fig. 13.14). Close study shows that its perimeter walling was more for show and the control of livestock than for defence. Particular emphasis, for example, was placed on the south wall, fac-ing visitors from the Cape Colony. Both this and some of the houses were equipped with drains, despite their structural superfluity and the arid climate. Interestingly, only the larger rectangular houses had such drains, the majority of the inhabitants probably living in circular stone houses or *matjieshuise*. An analysis of intermovability within the site suggests restrictions existed on ac-cess to the larger houses, confirming the suspicion raised by the site's size that strongly unequal social relations were developing.

Figure 13.14   Perimeter wall at //Khauxa!nas, Namibia (courtesy John Kinahan).

Back along the Gariep it was the Korana and Griqua who spearheaded the expansion of the Khoekhoe (and colonial) frontiers. Already by the late 1700s the
Korana were intermarrying and trading with the Tswana-speaking Tlhaping.
Though retaining traditions of an origin near Cape Town, they were probably an amalgamation of disparate, displaced Khoekhoe communities who by
the early nineteenth century were raiding and settling as far as the Caledon
Valley (A. Morris 1992d). Finger paintings there and in the Northern Cape,
some showing horses or riders hunting elephant, may be their work (Dowson
et al. 1992; Ouzman 1996b; Fig. 13.15). Bastaard groups meanwhile had moved
into Namaqualand as early as the 1730s, but despite their similarity in lifestyle
to the trekboers few were accorded freeburgher status. Many leading families
thus shifted east to the Gariep *c.* 1800, where they combined stock-keeping with
cultivation, adopted the self-designation 'Griqua', came under the influence of
the London Missionary Society and created a series of short-lived, unstable
polities (Legassick 1989). Archaeological work is lacking to trace most of these
developments, but analysis of early nineteenth-century burials from Campbell
and other settlements indicates the use of Christian ritual, a diet rich in cultivated foods and a population of substantially Khoisan and Negroid, rather than
European, origin (A. Morris 1992d).

   The inland movement of Bastaard and Oorlam groups presaged and was
linked to the expansion of the trekboers, the surplus people of the Cape Colony's

Figure 13.15   Finger paintings in white of men on horseback, Free State, South Africa (courtesy Sven Ouzman).

political economy. Increasingly distinguishing themselves from Bastaard, Oorlam and similar mixed-race or Khoekhoe-derived groups, they sought to maintain an exclusivist, Christian and European lifeway (Elphick and Shell 1989). Trekboer settlement of the Cape Colony's interior focused on areas with sufficient resources (water, grazing) to support a seasonally transhumant pastoralist economy. Not surprisingly, these were also those most favoured by indigenous herders and hunter-gatherers, with the most intense armed resistance developing along the boundary between summer and winter rainfall régimes (Penn 1986, 1987). From 1774 onward aboriginal resistance was met by co-ordinated attacks that killed well over 3000 Bushmen in the period to 1795 (Penn 1986). Captured women and children were 'apprenticed' in a system little different from slavery (Newton-King 1999). Despite attempts at settling Bushmen on mission stations during the early 1800s, the same processes of genocide, land expropriation and enforced assimilation into the European economy played themselves out along the Cape frontier and beyond through the nineteenth century.

One area where archaeology has successfully tracked these processes is the Seacow Valley, where the first European stockposts were established in 1770. However, resistance by local Swy èi Bushmen stalled European advance until the early 1800s; even then the threat of raids led to farms clustering more than environmental factors would suggest (Sampson *et al.* 1994). Work co-ordinated by Garth Sampson has traced the gradual appearance in local rock-shelter sequences of the glass beads, European ceramics and other artefacts and the progressive disappearance of traditional stone and bone tools and indigenous pottery. Interestingly, despite historical evidence for goods, including tobacco and *dagga*, being given or traded to Bushmen, beads are virtually the only exotic finds before 1840 (Saitowitz and Sampson 1992; Sampson 1993; Sampson and Plug 1993). European destruction of local game herds, which accelerated rapidly after 1810, helped bring about changes in subsistence, as surviving Bushmen were forced increasingly to settle on farms, working as herdsmen, acquiring domestic stock and gaining access to cultivated grains, fruits and vegetables (Sampson 1994). Bushmen themselves may have become active participants in herd destruction as game was shot for them and they acquired muskets of their own. One consequence may have been to allow some sites to be occupied for longer, with Driekoppen, in particular, becoming a ritual centre (Fig. 13.16; Plug and Sampson 1996).

In the Northern Cape British annexation of Bushmanland (1847) precipitated a war of attrition for control of water sources, culminating in an 1868–69 campaign against Korana pastoralists along the Gariep and the /Xam Bushmen of its hinterland. Among the /Xam sent to Cape Town as convict labour were some

Figure 13.16   Driekoppen Shelter, Eastern Cape, South Africa (courtesy Garth Sampson).

who later worked with Wilhelm Bleek and Lucy Lloyd in the 1870s and 1880s (J. Deacon 1996a). Archaeological investigations of early nineteenth-century sites confirm several of these informants' statements regarding differences in the material culture signatures of different /Xam groups and suggest a gendered differentiation of campsites into areas for food-preparation and raw material processing. Visible connections with the colonial economy are limited to a few glass beads and, possibly, a few sheep in an otherwise wild fauna (J. Deacon 1986, 1996b).

The /Xam no longer produced rock engravings in the mid-nineteenth century, but rock art dating to the colonial period is plentiful in many parts of southern Africa. In the Western Cape identifiable colonial images are almost entirely concentrated in the area known as the Koue Bokkeveld. Paintings are crude and largely done using fingers, compared to the fine, realistic detail of earlier naturalistic art. All may postdate 1750 since at Stompiesfontein horses, not oxen, are shown pulling wagons (Fig. 13.17). Connections to earlier shamanistic art in exaggerated male genitalia, the use of finger dots around images and various 'unreal', possibly hallucinated, features implicate Khoisan people in the production of these paintings, but probably after their subordination to the European farmers who colonised the area in the early 1700s. This art may thus be part of the overall process of the disappearance and transformation

Figure 13.17   Trekboer wagon, apparently being drawn by horses or mules, Stompiesfontein, Western Cape, South Africa (courtesy Tony Manhire).

Figure 13.18   Paintings of four part horse (rear half), part eland (front half)
creatures, Melikane, Lesotho. The conflation of species and
the presence of an additional rear leg in the eland at the far
right indicate that these are hallucinatory animals and also
attest to the incorporation of horses into Bushman beliefs
in mid-nineteenth-century Lesotho.

(resistance?) of Khoisan culture through the later eighteenth century (Yates
et al. 1993).

By far the greatest concentration of nineteenth-century rock art lies in
the Drakensberg and Maluti Mountains. Only the foothills of these ranges
had been settled by Iron Age farmers, leaving the mountains to Bushman
hunter-gatherers, who also survived in the interstices of farming communities. Documentary sources show that some were participating in the ivory
trade with Europeans in the Eastern Cape and KwaZulu-Natal in the 1820s
(Jolly 1996b); paintings of elephant-hunting may relate to this (Dowson 1995).
But scenes which, from the presence of Europeans, horses or other imagery,
must be of nineteenth-century date cannot merely be taken as records of real
events (C. Campbell 1987; Fig. 13.18). Rather, they must be interpreted within
the broader context of Bushman rock art as a whole, which shows that they
frequently include 'non-real' images of shamanistic origin (C. Campbell 1986).
Faced with increasing Sotho, Nguni and then European settlement in areas previously inhabited largely, if not exclusively, by themselves, the destruction of
game herds and Boer raids that aimed at both genocide and the acquisition of

captive labourers, Bushmen responded by flight into the mountains, attaching themselves as clients to Bantu-speaking farmers and military resistance. Wright (1971) and Vinnicombe (1976) detail the raids launched into KwaZulu-Natal in the mid-1800s, while Jolly (1996b) provides an overview of events there and in the Free State and northern Eastern Cape.

Ivory trading, raiding, making rain for black farmers and working for them as herdsmen and hunters were all strategies that helped precipitate changes in the social relations of hunter-gatherer communities, perhaps accelerating processes already underway as a result of centuries of earlier, if less intense, interaction with agropastoralists. Some shamans probably used their abilities to protect their communities from enemies, obtain cattle in exchange for rain-making, and co-ordinate raids and trade to establish positions of dominance and leadership (C. Campbell 1987). Undated paintings in the northern Eastern Cape may show such an evolution from an egalitarian background (Dowson 1994). Such developments are also attested from archival sources (Macquarrie 1962), but they were insufficient to secure the survival of independent hunter-gatherer communities. Boer and Sotho raids destroyed the last of these in the Free State in the 1860s, with many survivors assimilating into the Sotho-speaking Phuthi people of southern Lesotho (Jolly 1996b). The latter's conquest by British troops in 1879 and the Sotho settlement of the Lesotho Highlands that began in earnest after their 1866 defeat by the Orange Free State marked the end of an era. By the time Orpen (1874) travelled along the upper Senqu Valley, groups such as that led by Soai, which had been based at Sehonghong rock-shelter, were being killed, captured or dispersed (Vinnicombe 1976). Individuals survived, sometimes retaining ritual rôles for the black farmers among whom they lived (Prins 1990), but their communities, some of the last Bushmen to survive south of the Kalahari, were comprehensively destroyed.

Archaeology of the late nineteenth and twentieth centuries

Despite, or perhaps because of, the depth and breadth of historical research, archaeology has so far made little contribution to our understanding of more recent southern African history. Excavations at Cape Town's Waterfront provide a range of cultural material of later nineteenth-century date (Saitowitz *et al.* 1993; Abrahams-Willis 1997) and its industrial development is also now under study (Wirth 2000). Limited investigations have also taken place of collieries at Bankfontein, Mpumalanga (Loubser *et al.* 1991), a Cape Town glass factory (Saitowitz *et al.* 1985), early twentieth-century town dumps at Middelburg, Eastern Cape (Sampson 1992) and the Boer settlement at Schoemansdal, Northern Province, a major mid-nineteenth-century ivory-procurement centre (Meyer 1988b). Beyond South Africa, J.H.A. Kinahan's (1991) study of late nineteenth-century commercial fisheries at Sandwich Harbour, Namibia, is one of the fullest projects undertaken to date, integrating investigations of both colonial and indigenous communities. Southern Africa's military past has attracted greater attention than its industrialisation. Studies include those of the fortifications built to defend Pretoria between 1880 and 1902 (van Vollenhoven 1994, 1996), the British fort at Potchefstroom (Mason 1975), the Anglo-Zulu War battlefield at Rorke's Drift (Webley 1993; Fig. 13.19), the 1904 German-Herero War (Haacke 1992) and rock art produced during the Second South African War of 1899–1902 (Ouzman 1999). Much more could be done to investigate such military sites and the cultural changes experienced by formerly rural (white as well as black) communities as they became increasingly urbanised and incorporated into the capitalist, industrial economy. The same holds for the ways in which increasingly formalised and legislatively enforced structures of racial discrimination were expressed, imposed and resisted through the medium of material culture. Archaeologically informed analyses of the monumental architecture erected by the Afrikaner nationalist movement and the later *apartheid* state, for example, remain to be undertaken (Fig. 13.20)

Work in two areas has begun to document the impact of some of these changes on indigenous African communities. At Mabotse, Northern Province, the Tswana-speaking community of Chief Makapan selected from a range of European influences during the period 1872–80 as they sought to escape the South African Republic's demands for taxes and labour (S. Hall 1997). New commercial and subsistence opportunities for women may have led to increasing gender tensions and attempts at re-establishing male control. Thus, byres, courtyards and the chief's court area are rectangular and houses circular in plan, but this recalls traditional associations for these designs rather than superficial mimicry of European architectural practice. Ceramic assemblages, on the other hand, show patterned substitution of European items for indigenous wares. The latter's technological superiority saw them retained for storing liquids, but cast iron vessels came to be used for cooking, while annular wares and hand-painted ceramics replaced traditional bowls for serving food. Once again, gender relations may be at work as men used trading and employment opportunities to gain such items to compensate for the collapse of the traditional (male-controlled) iron-working industry.

Work at two Tswana capitals in Botswana also shows Africans actively incorporating European influences of relevance to their own societies (Reid *et al.* 1997). At Ntsweng (headquarters of the Bakwena) rectangular houses are rare and seem to reflect their owners' wealth, but at Phalatswe (headquarters of the Bangwato), where none is known outside the European area, their construction was strictly controlled by Chief Khama III. Attitudes to chiefly power are also revealed in the positions accorded missionary churches. At Phalatswe the church physically dominated the town (Fig. 13.21), fitting Khama III's Christian commitment and his harnessing of Christianity and its missionaries to his own chiefly office in building up his power against traditionalists. At Ntsweng,

Figure 13.19   The British fort at KwaMondi, Eshowe, KwaZulu-Natal, South Africa (courtesy Tony Pollard, University of Glasgow, Director of the Anglo-Zulu War Archaeological Project). The photograph shows the excavation of the Norwegian Mission Church established in the 1860s and used by British forces as a field hospital during the Zulu siege of the fort in 1879. The fort's defensive bank is visible in the background.

Figure 13.20   Voortrekker Monument, Winburg, Free State, South Africa.

however, the church is several kilometres from the settlement, reflecting the more ambiguous stance of Sechele, the Bakwena ruler; though he expressed interest in the new religion and attempted to absorb Christian spiritual powers, his simultaneous maintenance of polygamy and the rain-making rituals that also supported his authority resulted in him being refused church membership.

While the inhabitants of Mabotse, Ntsweng and Phalatswe sought to carve out for themselves the best-possible lives in rapidly changing circumstances,

Figure 13.21   The London Missionary Society church, Phalatswe, Botswana
(courtesy Andrew Reid).

around them Europeans, or southern Africans of European descent, had begun the process of developing archaeology as a discipline that could inform on
their past. A. Anderson (1887), for example, collected Middle Stone Age artefacts in the territories ruled by both Khama III and Sechele. For over a century

archaeological research, as detailed in chapter 2, proceeded largely independently of any concern for its impact on, or connection with, the descendants of those studied. With minority régimes having finally lost power across the sub-continent and archaeology as a whole entering into new relationships with indigenous peoples, the next and final chapter examines the contemporary practice of archaeology within southern Africa.

CHAPTER 14

SOUTHERN AFRICAN ARCHAEOLOGY TODAY

In September 1985 the meeting of the Southern African Association of Archaeologists (SA3) in Grahamstown, South Africa, learned of the intention of the Southampton-based organisers of a forthcoming major international conference to prohibit attendance by South African and Namibian scholars. Two years after Mozambican and Zimbabwean archaeologists had quit SA3 because of its reluctance openly to condemn *apartheid*, and weeks after the National Party government's declaration of a state of emergency to quell growing resistance to its rule, this was a pointed reminder of the difficulties of keeping politics and academic activity as separate as many wished. As it turned out, the ban had little impact on South African archaeology and none at all on the South African government. However, the 1986 Southampton World Archaeological Congress (WAC) and its successors did succeed in contributing to a more profound engagement with issues of concern to developing countries and the indigenous populations descended from those frequently studied by archaeologists. With Namibian independence in 1990 and rapid political change following in South Africa, South African scholars were admitted to full membership of WAC in 1994. Its subsequent, highly successful 1999 meeting in Cape Town saw the closing of the circle opened up fourteen years before (M. Hall 1998; Malone and Stoddart 1999), but still left archaeology across the sub-continent confronting many problems. This final chapter attempts to outline what these are and how they are being met by focusing on three themes: the alienation of southern Africa's archaeological heritage from its inhabitants; the threats currently posed to it; and the challenges that this heritage poses for future study.

The alienated past

One of the saddest legacies of colonial and minority rule was the alienation of southern Africa's people from their past and the denigration or denial of its richness and value, coupled to widespread indifference to the results of archaeological research (Shepherd 1998). Right up until independence, for example, the Rhodesia Front régime insisted that there was no proof that Great Zimbabwe was the work of ancestral Shona. The continued popularity of such ideas, in the face of all evidence to the contrary, can be gauged from sales of popular books attributing the site to Indian miners or other exotic groups

(Hromnik 1981; Mallows 1984), or from the totally fictitious creation of a 'Lost City' to serve as the core of an international holiday resort in South Africa's North-West Province (M. Hall 1995). Across the sub-continent, prior to independence or liberation, archaeology was a white and, in some countries, totally amateur activity, largely unconcerned with the descendants of those whom it studied. Particularly in South Africa, where the *apartheid* government's educational system (Christian National Education, CNE) openly aimed at maintaining white supremacy, school curricula and official publications systematically ignored the results of archaeological research (Esterhuysen 2000). Textbooks denied the antiquity of black, agropastoralist presence south of the Limpopo and stressed the primitiveness, physical distinctiveness and inevitable decline after European colonisation of South Africa's Khoisan communities (A.B. Smith 1983; Mazel and Stewart 1987). Human evolution was a third casualty of CNE, banned from school syllabi to placate the prejudices of the Dutch Reformed Churches (Esterhuysen and Smith 1998). The dominance of South African historiography in neighbouring countries meant that these biases continued to impact beyond South Africa's own borders even after independence (A. Campbell 1998).

Independence, liberation and the establishment of democratic systems of government all precipitated changes in this situation (cf. Morais 1984). Staying with South Africa, the 'outcomes-based' National Qualifications Framework originally scheduled for full implementation in 2005, though now subject to amendment, positively includes archaeology in the school curriculum; archaeologists and historians have also been invited to advise Government on how best to strengthen history teaching. Initial attempts at introducing archaeology into schools, which began on a small scale in the late 1980s, have been highly successful. Though a lack of resources, especially suitably qualified and informed teachers, may constrain their long-term effectiveness, archaeology is well placed to challenge the racial and gender stereotypes promoted by *apartheid* and reach a wider audience than ever before (Esterhuysen 1999, 2000).

Museums provide another means by which archaeologists communicate their work to the public. Though existing in all seven southern African countries, their extent and capacities vary tremendously. At the time of writing, for example, Lesotho still lacks a national museum, while that in Swaziland has no archaeologists on its permanent staff. Nor are national museums, located in capital cities remote from much of the population, sufficient by themselves. Macamo (1996) provides an indication of the regional network envisaged for Mozambique, which involves the re-establishment of local museums, such as that at the Manyikeni *zimbabwe*, destroyed during that country's civil war. Only Botswana, South Africa and perhaps Zimbabwe have reasonably extensive networks of regional museums, some of them important local centres for archaeological research and, in Botswana, frequently community based (Phaladi 1998). Access, however, both physical and intellectual, can still be difficult. To address this problem, Botswana's National Museum offers an innovative solution, a travelling museum, complete with artefacts, that visits every primary school in the country once every three years (Metz 1994).

That museum displays in southern Africa required change and modernisation as the sub-continent's politics altered goes without saying: witness the establishment during the 1990s in institutions such as the National Museum, Bloemfontein, or Pretoria's Transvaal Museum of displays that for the first time dealt with human evolution. But Ndoro (1994) makes the powerful point that archaeological sites and museum displays are too often geared to foreign tourists or people of European descent. At Great Zimbabwe, for instance, displays and guidebooks were previously pitched (solely in English) at a reading level significantly higher than that of most Zimbabwean university students and without even the pretence of engaging with traditional beliefs or knowledge. Similar criticisms could be made of other institutions, by no means only in southern Africa. Much more is required, but post-liberation South Africa has seen considerable effort made to address them, for example by providing multilingual sources of information and involving representatives from historically disadvantaged communities in exhibition planning and design (e.g. J. Brink *et al.* 1996).

Zimbabwe provides one of the clearest instances of another problem provoked by the alienation of people from their past. On the one hand, land reapportionment during the colonial era saw many local communities deprived of access to spiritually significant sites (Pwiti and Ndoro 1999). Indeed, the very designation of a site as a protected national monument sometimes had the same effect. The much visited Domboshava rock art site, for example, near Harare is also a sacred rain-making location for the local population, producing a conflict of interests between tourist access and the shelter's religious significance that has proven difficult to resolve (Pwiti and Mvenge 1996). On the other hand, where communities' ties to monuments or sites remain intact, traditional custodians may themselves prove some of the best guardians of (their) archaeological heritage, a situation described by Pwiti (1996b) for Mutapa-associated sites in the Dande communal lands of northern Zimbabwe.

Working with such communities, as at Thulamela (Steyn *et al.* 1998) or in north-eastern Namibia (A.B. Smith and Lee 1997; Lee and Hitchcock 1998), is clearly the way forward. Where such collaboration is most imperative is probably in the analysis of human remains. This does not yet pose challenges to archaeologists on an Australian or North American scale, but the emergence on the South African political scene of groups highlighting Khoisan descent has already precipitated calls for the reburial of all human skeletons in existing museum collections, encouraged by previous scientific bad practice in their collection and display (A. Morris 1996; Jordan 1999). How far such moves will go is unclear, though South Africa's National Heritage Resources Act (1999) allows excavation of human remains only after a concerted effort has been made to consult communities and individuals having a traditional interest in the grave or burial ground and after agreement has been reached with them on their future. The same Act also provides for restitution to such communities of 'heritage objects' from national collections. Reburial of individuals of perceived importance to local communities has already taken place at their request, with the old slave woman from Vergelegen (Sealy *et al.* 1993) and the royal burials from Thulamela (Steyn *et al.* 1998) two of the best-known examples.

The threatened past

Protection of archaeological sites and the integration of local communities into this process is clearly of major importance in their conservation and management. The threats posed to such sites are numerous and widely shared across southern Africa, as are the solutions being developed for them. As examples I focus on tourism, rock art, the 'salvage' of shipwrecks and large-scale dam-building projects before turning to more general issues of cultural heritage management and the growth of contract archaeology.

Though increased public access to archaeological sites can promote awareness of the past, increase support for the discipline and be a significant source of income for local communities (e.g. through curio sales), tourism is not without problems of its own. As well as the issues of presentation discussed above, there are the effects of bringing large numbers of people to sites that lack proper provision for them, or which may, however inadvertently, be damaged in the process (see Ndoro (1994) for a discussion of these points as they affect Great Zimbabwe). Zimbabwe's national conservation strategy bears these issues in mind in planning future tourist development as part of an integrated heritage management programme (Collett 1991). Botswana too has thought through such issues at a national level (Phaladi 1998), while in South Africa this has been done in a more *ad hoc* manner, with one particular focus major sites such as Thulamela (in Kruger National Park) and Mapungubwe (in Vhembe National Park) that are located in areas already geared to wildlife tourism. Wholly different, but with perhaps even greater scope for attracting visitors as well as filling a major lacuna in South African history, is ongoing research into slavery at the Cape, including excavations of the VOC slave lodge in Cape Town and another project at Elim, Western Cape, where several hundred slaves settled after emancipation (Jensen 2000).

Despite tourism being seen as a major vehicle for economic growth and development by all southern African countries, other, less monumental archaeological sites remain a largely unexploited resource. Rock paintings and engravings are certainly one category of site with widespread appeal, not least in offering a view of history that articulates indigenous rather than European concerns (Ouzman 1996c). Unfortunately, they are also eminently susceptible not only to natural processes of deterioration, but also to vandalism,

Figure 14.1   Graffiti on rock paintings, Elands Bay Cave, Western Cape, South
Africa. This particular photograph was taken in 1990, months after
the unbanning in South Africa of the African National Congress and
other liberation movements.

whether in the form of graffiti (Fig. 14.1), the deliberate wetting of paintings to
'improve' their photogenic qualities or, in the worst cases, attempts at removal
(Loubser 1991b). Where they occur in national parks, controls may be comparatively easy to establish, but sites on privately owned land are at much greater
risk, despite success stories such as at Tandjesberg, Free State (Loubser 1993a).
This site, along with several unpainted rock-shelters recently developed along
South Africa's Cape coast (Fig. 14.2; J. Deacon and Brett 1993), shows what
can be achieved in making archaeological sites accessible and informative at
relatively little cost, while integrating them into regional tourism initiatives
(http://www.africandream.org). They set targets for the presentation of others,
such as the early hominin sites of the Sterkfontein Valley and its environs, one
of the few archaeological complexes in southern Africa currently to hold World
Heritage status.

Thankfully, southern Africa has so far largely escaped the treasure-hunting
that afflicts so many parts of the world. Perhaps reflecting the dissociation between its European-derived populations and the archaeology of its indigenous
inhabitants' ancestors, it is nineteenth- and twentieth-century objects that are
most at risk, whether from the illegal export of military artefacts taken from
battlefields of the Anglo-Zulu War (J. Deacon 1991) or from the looting of more

Figure 14.2   Display panel showing an impression of the lifestyle of the late
Pleistocene Robberg occupants of Nelson Bay Cave, Western Cape,
South Africa.

recent town dumps (HARG 1993). While true of land-based archaeology, these
generalisations do not hold for the shipwrecks scattered along southern Africa's
coasts. Intensive surveys have been undertaken only for Table Bay (Werz 1999)
and the area surrounding Mozambique Island (Morais 1984), but it is clear that
wrecks of pre-twentieth-century age number in the hundreds. In the past, their
investigation has been undertaken mostly for profit, with few, if any, archaeological controls. Happily, the establishment of a maritime museum and a
(regrettably discontinued) academic presence in maritime archaeology at the
University of Cape Town have gone hand-in-hand with more rigorously enforced legislation and a more productive relationship between archaeologists
and salvors, as reflected in the excavation of the *Oosterland* (Werz 1999) and
ongoing work on the *Brederode* and the *Grosvenor*.

If unregulated 'salvage' activities and looting pose the main threat to underwater archaeological resources, then the principal one confronting southern
Africa's terrestrial archaeological heritage has to be various forms of 'economic
development'. In a part of the world where the majority of the population is
still desperately poor and lacks access to such basic resources as clean water,
sanitation or electricity, let alone stable employment opportunities, tackling
these problems by promoting economic growth is clearly a national priority.
The difficulty for archaeologists, no less than elsewhere, is that this inevitably

impacts on the archaeological environment. Though many of these impacts are the result of fairly small-scale activities, others have the potential for much more massive effects. While the future of the Batoka Gorge Project in the mid-Zambezi Valley is uncertain, damming the river would undoubtedly have disastrous consequences for the area's archaeology and wildlife, let alone its human inhabitants. The Lesotho Highlands Water Project, on the other hand, is already well into the second phase of a scheme that will, if completed, create six, perhaps seven, reservoirs and linking tunnels in the Maluti Mountains, the whole designed to impound water for sale and transfer to South Africa. Though the relevant Lesotho government body (the Lesotho Highlands Development Authority) employs one archaeologist and has commissioned surveys and excavations more-or-less commensurate with the level of impact thus far, it (and the project's international donors, such as the World Bank) have totally failed to act on successive recommendations to initiate a comprehensive impact assessment of the Senqu Valley, where hundreds of sites, some of international significance like Sehonghong, are known to exist (Fig. 14.3).

Practice does, indeed, differ between the various countries of southern Africa in how the archaeological consequences of development projects are assessed

Figure 14.3   Looking downstream along the Senqu Valley, Lesotho Highlands, Lesotho, a few kilometres north of Likoaeng. Many of the archaeological sites along this stretch of the Senqu River will be destroyed should Phase III of the Lesotho Highlands Water Project be undertaken.

or mitigated and cultural resources protected and managed. However, as a generalisation archaeological remains cannot be disturbed without authorisation, while environmental impact assessments (EIAs) are widely undertaken, if not legally mandated, in all seven states. In Botswana, for example, all archaeological sites are protected by law, a line of argument that supports the case for EIAs even where these are not otherwise required (van Waarden 1996). EIAs are principally conducted by archaeologists based in regional museums or at the University of Botswana, with licensing and monitoring of these projects and all other archaeological research undertaken by the National Museum (Phaladi 1998). Though much information has been recovered through such studies, several problems are identifiable, among them a lack of awareness of relevant protective legislation on the part of national and local government, shortages of trained staff to monitor and inspect projects, and insufficient financial penalties coupled with an unwillingness to prosecute those responsible for wilfully destroying archaeological sites (Phaladi 1998).

Much the same could be said of South Africa's experience (J. Deacon 1996c). Though the first legislation protecting archaeological remains was enacted in 1911, successive amendments exempted destruction (except of rock-shelters, coastal shell middens and specifically proclaimed national monuments) during the normal course of mining, engineering or agricultural activity. Nor was provision made for archaeological surveys in advance of development, while ownership of finds rested with the landowner. Given the then National Monuments Council's disinclination to prosecute those contravening even this level of legislative protection, the law remained a toothless tiger, honoured by archaeologists, but by few others. Specific protection of the cultural as well as the natural environment came with the 1989 Environmental Conservation Act, but the regulations enforcing this took another decade to be promulgated. EIAs are now compulsory in advance of any development activity, though many large corporations and government departments have routinely undertaken them for some time (Fig. 14.4).

South Africa's post-*apartheid* constitution makes the country's cultural heritage a primarily provincial responsibility. This and new national legislation have substantially altered the framework within which the protection of archaeological remains is undertaken. The National Monuments Council has been transformed into the South African Heritage Resources Agency, which maintains a national policy on the country's cultural heritage, controls shipwrecks and exports, and monitors the behaviour of other organisations. Mining, agriculture and engineering no longer constitute exemptions from the laws protecting archaeological sites, all archaeological objects are the property of the state, and active involvement in heritage management by non-governmental organisations is encouraged. Within this framework protection of South Africa's cultural heritage has devolved to the nine provinces and, below them, to

Figure 14.4   Contract archaeology excavations in progress at the Waterfront,
Cape Town, Western Cape, South Africa (courtesy Dave Halkett and
Tom Hart). Below a former fish factory, the excavations are exposing
remains of the Chavonnes Battery, a VOC military installation built
between 1714 and 1725 to defend Table Bay.

local authorities. KwaZulu-Natal paved the way in 1997 by creating its own
heritage body, Amafa KwaZulu-Natal, which employs its own archaeologists
for research and for contract work arising from EIAs (A. Hall 1995); 1997
also saw the creation of a Cultural Resource Management Section within the
Southern African Association of Archaeologists, bringing together those archaeologists specifically interested in pursuing contract archaeology. A code

of ethics provides agreed minimum standards for fieldwork, analysis and curation, while SA3 has also identified those kinds of site particularly worthy of mitigation efforts. The practical impact of both efforts and their integration with the new structure for managing South Africa's cultural heritage remain to be worked out.

In countering the threats just outlined and in protecting and interpreting southern Africa's archaeological heritage the availability of adequate resources is critical. Nowhere can these be considered sufficient, whether this is because of the redirection of government expenditure to other sectors, a genuinely limited economic base or mismanagement of national economies. Museums and universities across the sub-continent face a funding crisis. South Africa illustrates this well with the consolidation of national museums into fewer 'flagship institutions', the handing over of others to the relevant provinces and the possibility that some institutions could even close. Nor is the story better if one looks at the universities. Stellenbosch University closed its archaeology department in 1998, that at Pretoria merged with anthropology several years before, while archaeology at the University of the Witwatersrand is being amalgamated with geography. Elsewhere archaeologists are much fewer on the ground than in South Africa. Though Botswana, Mozambique and Zimbabwe all have several full-time professionally qualified individuals and university teaching departments, Lesotho, for example, has only one and Swaziland none at all. The widely predicted growth of contract-based archaeology as environmental impact assessments become widespread, if not mandatory, has yet to create the posts and opportunities to transform this depressing situation. Everywhere this holds out little promise for the employment of new archaeology graduates or the professional advancement of women (Solomon and Smith 1994), while in South Africa it also bodes ill for the professional involvement of the non-white majority. Despite the wishes of the archaeological community itself and a Wenner-Gren Foundation-funded bursary scheme at the University of Cape Town, poor job prospects and salaries, especially in museums, make it hard to recruit good students.

The challenge of the past

The present situation is certainly one of uncertainty and under-resourcing, but all is far from gloom. Compared even to the early 1980s, archaeology has come a long way. This is especially so when considered on a sub-continental scale, with a real expansion of posts in countries such as Botswana and Zimbabwe, enactment of much stronger laws governing cultural heritage management and major transformations in our understanding of the southern African past. Indeed, even if the number of university departments is falling substantially in percentage terms, changes in how undergraduate degrees are delivered may mean that more students encounter *some* archaeology during their university career (Maggs 1998). Institutional success stories can also be found, for example in the growth

of the Rock Art Research Institute at the University of the Witwatersrand, formerly directed by David Lewis-Williams and now led by Ben Smith. The Historical Archaeology Research Group at the University of Cape Town provides
another example of such success, all the more striking for the relative late-
ness with which this part of the discipline developed and the small number of
historical archaeologists within southern African archaeology as a whole.

Another significant development, and one directly linked to changes in the
sub-continent's politics, is the expansion of collaborative ties between southern
African researchers and those from overseas. Particularly significant has been
the involvement of Sweden, pioneered through a three-year research grant to
Mozambican scholars from the Swedish Agency for Research Co-operation, followed in 1982 by direct co-operation with the Swedish Board of Antiquities.
Morais (1984) and Sinclair *et al.* (1993a) record the success of these initiatives,
extended to embrace Botswana, Zimbabwe and Namibia, as well as several
East African and Indian Ocean states, through the Urban Origins in East Africa
Project and its successors. The post-independence revitalisation of archaeology in Zimbabwe and Mozambique, including training of indigenous archaeologists, is proof of their impact. International contacts with South Africa and
Namibia, though never severed under *apartheid*, have certainly flourished since
1990. The flurry of recent international conferences held there (Dual Congress
of the International Association of Human Biologists and the International
Association for the Study of Human Palaeontology 1998; International Union
for Quaternary Sciences 1998; World Archaeological Congress 1999) demonstrates this, as does the wide range of projects, by no means fully comprehensive, included in Table 14.1. Given the many key research questions to which
southern African archaeology is in a position to contribute and the relative
strengths of local and foreign currencies, such international links are likely to
grow further. With due regard for proper and equitable collaboration with local
scholars, including, wherever feasible, commitments to building the capacities of local archaeological infrastructures, this can only be to the benefit of
southern African archaeology as a whole.

Bringing the results of all this research into the light of day through prompt
and appropriate publication is both a clear ethical responsibility of the archaeologist and a necessity in increasing public awareness and thus the constituency
that can support archaeological work. On the one hand, far too much remains
difficult, if not impossible, to locate in university dissertations and the proliferation of almost wholly unpublished contract archaeology reports. Journals,
such as the *South African Archaeological Bulletin, Southern African Field
Archaeology, Botswana Notes and Records* and *Zimbabwean Prehistory*, offer
some scope for countering this explosion in 'grey literature'. So too do more
informal newsletters, like *Crossmend* (produced by the University of Cape
Town's Historical Archaeology Group) and *Die Rooi Olifant*,[1] which records

---

[1] Afrikaans for 'The Red Elephant'.

Table 14.1 *External individuals and institutions active in archaeological research in southern Africa 1991–2000*

Individual	Nationality	Institution	Project
C. Bollong	American	Arizona State University	Ceramics of the Seacow Valley, Eastern Cape
B. Bousman	American	Southern Methodist University	Palaeoenvironments and LSA archaeology, Blydefontein Basin, Eastern Cape
F. Bugarin	American	University of Florida	Nineteenth-century colonial frontier interactions, Fort Wilshire, Eastern Cape
N. Conard *et al.*	German	University of Tübingen	Stone Age landscapes of the Geelbek Dunes, Western Cape
T. Dowson	South African	University of Southampton	Rock art recording and analysis, Namibia
K. Fouché	American	University of Kansas	Physical anthropology of early colonial skeletons, Western Cape
H. Greenfeld	American	University of Winnipeg	Excavation of Ndondonwane Early Iron Age site, KwaZulu-Natal
F. Grine *et al.*	American	State University of New York	Excavation of LSA/MSA site at Die Kelders, Western Cape
G. Haynes and J. Klimowicz	American	University of Nevada	Palaeoenvironments and archaeology of Hwange National Park, Zimbabwe
J. Hobart	British	University of Oxford	Hunter-gatherer/farmer interaction, Lesotho and Natal Drakensberg
R. Klein *et al.*	American	Stanford University	Excavation of Duinefontein, Acheulean open-air site, Western Cape
L. Larsson	Swedish	University of Lund	MSA of Zimbabwe
T. Lenssen-Erz	German	University of Cologne	Rock art recording and analysis, Brandberg, Namibia
A. Lindahl	Swedish	University of Lund	Ceramic ethnoarchaeology and excavation of Zimbabwe Tradition sites, Zimbabwe

J. McNabb	British	University of Southampton	Investigation of Acheulean sites, Northern Cape
R. Milo	American	Chicago State University	Faunal analysis, MSA and LSA sites
P. Mitchell	British	University of Oxford	LSA archaeology of the Lesotho Highlands
F. Ohinata	Japanese	University of Oxford	Survey and excavation of Iron Age sites, Swaziland
S. Pfeiffer	American	University of Guelph	Physical anthropology of LSA and MSA humans, South Africa
A. Pollard	British	University of Glasgow	Isandhlwana battlefield survey, KwaZulu-Natal
L. Robbins *et al.*	American	Michigan State University	Excavation of LSA/MSA sites, Tsodilo Hills, Botswana
T. Saetersdal	Norwegian	University of Bergen	Rock art analysis and recording, Manicaland, Zimbabwe
G. Sampson *et al.*	South African	Southern Methodist University	Survey and excavation of sites relating to the impact of the colonial frontier on the Bushmen of the Seacow Valley, Eastern Cape
A. Sinclair *et al.*	British	University of Liverpool	MSA landscapes, Cave of Hearths, Northern Province
P. Sinclair	Swedish	University of Uppsala	Excavation and survey of Manyikeni *zimbabwe*, Mozambique
R. Soper	Zimbabwean	British Institute in Eastern Africa	Survey and excavation, Nyanga Highlands, Zimbabwe
R. Vogelsang	German	University of Cologne	MSA of south-western Namibia; survey and excavation of LSA sites, northern Namibia
A. Watchman	Australian	James Cook University	Radiocarbon accelerator dating of rock paintings, KwaZulu-Natal

the work of local rock art researchers in South Africa's Northern Province. Electronic media too may eventually play an important rôle in disseminating the results of fieldwork and other research, though so far they have been little developed (cf. http://www.geocities.com/athens/6398/thulamel.html; http://www.wits.ac.za/archaeology/acacia/acacia.htm).

But this is still archaeologists talking to archaeologists, even if it includes a commitment to provide access to the results of commercially funded contract archaeology. Publication has also increasingly to be literally that, *public*ation. Popularisation of archaeology through printed and visual media, a concern for informing local communities, especially schools, and production of guides and other non-specialist literature in the vernacular, as well as in English, Afrikaans or Portuguese, are also needed. So too, perhaps, is exploring new and alternative ways of writing, as exemplified by Schrire's (1995) highly successful *Digging through darkness* or the collected papers in Skotnes (1996). Electronic resources will, no doubt, also increasingly become important here, as indicated by the Archaeology Africa website developed by historical archaeologists from the University of Cape Town in association with local schools (http://www.archafrica.uct.ac.za). Bringing to wider public attention the results of the many archaeological projects in southern Africa can surely only help meet the challenges that the discipline faces, simultaneously ensuring that archaeologists and the broader public in other parts of the world are also made aware of its significance.

Though only a personal selection, Table 14.2 attempts to identify some of the key research questions for the near future of southern African archaeology, with the first and arguably most important, if still insufficiently grasped, the contribution that archaeology can make to managing the impact of global climatic change. Beyond this, one safe prediction, perhaps, is that much more concern will be shown for examining phenomena such as the spread of herding, the expansion of agropastoralist economies and state formation within a broader comparative spatio-temporal context. Simultaneously, one can anticipate the redirection of ethnoarchaeological and archaeological research to emphasise the long-term historical context from which recent anthropological observations spring (Lane 1998a), the investigation of variability within that ethnography and the consequences of both for understanding the archaeological record (S. Hall 1990; Lane 1994/95). A third and final area, as yet little investigated outside the fields of colonial archaeology and rock art research (but see S. Hall 1997, 1998), is the post-processualist concern with the active part played by material culture in the building of society and the pursuit of individuals' social, political and economic agendas. The links between these last two themes are obvious, if as yet little examined.

Strengthening archaeology's infrastructure, ensuring appropriate cultural resource management, publishing better, faster and more widely, improving

Table 14.2 *Key research questions for the near future of southern African archaeology: a personal selection*

1. Establishing more detailed knowledge of past climatic and ecological parameters to assist modelling of the effects of global climatic change on southern African biomes
2. Continuing excavation of known early hominin sites and identifying new ones
3. Locating and investigating Acheulean sites with preserved organics
4. Determining the behavioural significance of the Middle Pleistocene initial appearance of MSA technology
5. Locating and excavating MSA sites with preserved organics and establishing a firm chronology for the MSA
6. Determining the behavioural significance of the appearance of bone tools, changes in subsistence practice and evidence of symbolic activity in MSA contexts
7. Establishing the spatio-temporal integrity and significance of Howieson's Poort assemblages
8. Exploring the effects of radiocarbon calibration on our understanding of LSA archaeology
9. Tracing changes in population demography through the late Pleistocene and Holocene, including relating archaeological evidence to linguistic and ethnographic data on Bushman populations (cf. N. Walker 1995b)
10. Establishing a sounder chronology for rock paintings and engravings and integrating rock art evidence more closely with other components of the archaeological record
11. Investigating spatio-temporal variability in the production and content of rock art
12. Expanding the range of ethnographic data used in the study of LSA populations and establishing theoretically and empirically sound connections between social theory and archaeological data
13. Determining the circumstances in which sheep were initially acquired and then spread by/among LSA communities *c.* 2000 BP
14. Determining the significance and associations of Bambata ware
15. Investigating in detail the subsistence base of agropastoralist communities and spatio-temporal variation in their economies
16. Investigating commoner sites and living areas of the Zimbabwe Tradition
17. Investigating the political structure and processes of Zimbabwe Tradition communities
18. Locating sites in southern and eastern Africa at which to investigate in detail Huffman's (1989) model for Sotho-Tswana and Nguni origins
19. Investigating rural settlement patterns in the Cape Colony and the historical archaeology of Portuguese settlement in Mozambique
20. Exploring southern Africa's recent past using archaeology, especially processes of industrialisation, urbanisation and resistance to minority domination

Figure 14.5   Educational archaeology in action, Thulamela, Northern Province, South Africa (courtesy Mandy Esterhuysen).

overall public awareness and developing international co-operative links, particularly those with other parts of Africa, are some of the key challenges for southern African archaeology in the twenty-first century. But archaeology itself poses challenges by its very nature, not least in building and rebuilding local, national and regional identities, processes reflected in the naming of Zimbabwe after one of that country's most impressive archaeological sites and the incorporation of Bushman rock art imagery into South Africa's coat-of-arms (B. Smith *et al.* 2000). Beyond identity-building, archaeology can and should question and critique received ideas, emphasising innovative and socially concerned research about a past made accessible to all (Lewis-Williams 1993; Esterhuysen 1999; Fig. 14.5). Viewed in these terms, southern African archaeology is as much about building an informed, democratic future for the sub-continent as it is about demonstrating its relevance to the whole human story over the past 3 million years and more.

GLOSSARY

Adze Stone tool with straight or concave working edges retouched by characteristic step-flaking that is partly deliberate and partly the result of use; principally employed in wood-working.

Age-regiment Group of individuals (generally male) of roughly the same age, recruited at the same time into a military or quasi-military formation and employed in warfare and/or public works among some southern African Bantu-speaking societies.

Agonistic behaviour Aggressive/competitive behaviour within species.

Alcelaphine Tribe of antelope, including blesbok, bontebok, hartebeest and wildebeest.

Annealing Heating a metal object and then cooling it slowly to obtain a desired microstructure.

Arrack Grain-based spirit of Asian origin.

Backed Blunting of a stone tool's edge by abrupt vertical retouch to alter its shape or facilitate hafting.

Backed microliths Formally designed microlithic tools with maximum dimension of 25 mm, the shape of which is defined by their backing.

Bipolar core Core (often small and/or of quartz) flaked using a hammer and anvil technique such that flakes are detached from both ends simultaneously when it is struck. Those that can be flaked no further are termed *pièces esquillées*, *outils écaillés* or core-reduced pieces.

Bladelet Parallel-sided flake, at least twice as long as it is wide, with one or more dorsal ridges and ≤25 mm long. **Blades** have the same properties, but are >25 mm long.

Bored stone Spherical stone the centre of which has been hollowed out for use as a digging-stick weight.

Buchu Sweet-smelling aromatic herbs.

Caprine General term for sheep and goats where these cannot or need not otherwise be distinguished (after Gifford-Gonzalez 2000).

Celadon High-quality, green-glazed Chinese stoneware.

Chaîne opératoire Sequence of actions in reducing toolstone from its initial selection to discard of exhausted tools.

Cichlid Family of fresh and brackish water fish, including tilapia and largemouth breams.

Daga (Sometimes spelt *dhaka*, the Shona form of the word) building material of puddled clay binding together a fine gravel aggregate.

Dagga Cannabis (*Cannabis sativa*).

Dassie Rock hyrax (*Procavia capensis*).

Denticulate MSA retouched artefact with a multiply notched edge.

Encephalisation Brain expansion relative to body size.

Faceted   Describes the series of very small flakes removed at right angles to a core to provide a striking platform, part of which then comes away with the flake. Common in many MSA assemblages as an additional means of predetermining flake size and shape.

Farwestern Cape   That part of the Western Cape focused around Verlorenvlei and its interior inland into the Cedarberg Mountains, principally investigated by J. Parkington and colleagues. Often referred to in the literature as 'western' or 'south-western Cape'.

Flake-blade   Flake at least twice as long as it is wide, with at least one dorsal ridge, but not necessarily strictly parallel sides. Commonly employed in analysing MSA assemblages where it includes blades *sensu stricto*.

Geophyte   Plant with underground storage organs, such as roots, tubers or rhizomes. Many species were important staple foods for indigenous peoples.

Glottochronology   Estimation of the age at which two languages diverged by comparing the degree to which their core vocabularies share cognate words and assuming a constant rate of vocabulary change.

Haematite   Iron ore-containing mineral that yields a red pigment.

Highveld   Highland grasslands in South Africa's interior, especially the Grassland Biome areas of the Free State and Gauteng.

Holocene   The geological epoch spanning the last 10,000 years.

Hominid   Traditionally describes human-like primates ancestral, or closely related, to modern humans, but now often extended to embrace gorillas and chimpanzees.

Hominin   In the light of the previous point, this term is now used to describe modern humans, their immediate bipedal fossil ancestors and relatives.

Hxaro   System of delayed, reciprocal exchange for all goods save food among the Ju/'hoansi Bushmen.

Kasouga flake   Distinctive wood-working tools made from silcrete blades.

Knife   MSA retouched artefact, retouched along a straight edge.

Kopje   Isolated hill or mesa.

Levallois technique   Stoneworking technique in which a roughly circular prepared core is first trimmed to permit detachment of a single flake of predetermined size and shape. One surface of the core is covered with preparation scars truncated by removal of the Levallois flake.

Linkshaft   Bone component of ethnographically described Bushman arrows connecting the mainshaft and the point and designed to allow the latter to separate on impact so the point stays in the wound.

Lowveld   Low-lying areas of South Africa east of the Great Escarpment and of Zimbabwe south of the Plateau.

Mastic   Plant-derived gum or resin for hafting stone tools.

N!ao   Ju/'hoan Bushman term for a series of beliefs relating human and animal behaviour to weather pattern.

Naturally backed knife   Large sidestruck flake with natural cortex backing, the opposite edge retouched with overlapping step-flaking to a gently convex shape.

Opaline   Fine-grained rocks frequently employed to make stone tools. Also known as crypto-crystalline silicas, they include chalcedony, jasper and agate.

Osteodontokeratic   Term invented by Dart (1957), meaning 'bone-tooth-horn', to describe the use of organic materials by australopithecines prior to the first stone tools and thought (wrongly in the light of subsequent research) to be represented by the faunal assemblage from Makapansgat.

Oxygen isotope stage (OIS)   Climatic stage defined by changes in the relative frequency of ^{18}O to ^{16}O and thus largely reflecting growth and decline of icesheets.

Palette   Thin piece of ground stone of uncertain function found in some LSA assemblages.

Phytolith   Silica body in plant cell walls identifiable to genus or species.

Pleistocene   Geological period from some 1.7 million years ago to 10,000 BP.

Pliocene   Geological period from 5.2–1.7 million years ago.

Plio-Pleistocene   The period spanning the boundary between the Pliocene and Pleistocene.

Point   MSA flake or flake-blade retouched on two converging edges to form a point.

Provincial porcelain   Coarse Chinese porcelain unsaleable in Europe, but widely used for domestic purposes in the Cape Colony in food preparation and cooking (Klose 1992/93).

Quaternary   The Pleistocene and Holocene periods together.

Sagittal crest   Bony ridge along the midline of the skull for attaching the temporalis (jaw) muscles.

'Schlepp effect'   The patterning in a faunal assemblage at a living site where only selected cuts of meat are returned from the kill site.

Scraper   Formally designed stone tool with a convexly retouched working edge, principally used to work hides.

Segment   Formally designed stone tool with a straight, sharp edge opposite to a curved arc backed by abrupt retouch.

Sexual dimorphism   Systematic size differences within a species between males and females.

Skeuomorph   Copy of an object in another material.

Specularite   A crystalline form of haematite, a glistening, black pigment.

Spokeshave   Variant of the adze, with deeply retouched concave working edges, common in Lesotho and KwaZulu-Natal.

Therianthropic   Describes part-human, part-animal figures represented in rock art.

Toolstone   Raw materials used to make stone tools.

transVaal   Those parts of South Africa lying north of the Vaal River (after Hamilton 1995). Identical to the former Transvaal Province, now divided between Gauteng, Mpumalanga, North-West Province and Northern Province.

Tuyère   Nozzled pipe through which air is forced into a furnace or forge.

Ungulate   Hoofed mammal, including antelope, zebra, giraffe and rhinoceros.

Zygomatic arch   Cheekbone.

REFERENCES

Abrahams, G. 1984 The development of historical archaeology at the Cape, *Bulletin of the South African Cultural History Museum* 5: 20–3.

1993 The Grand Parade, Cape Town: archaeological excavations of the seventeenth century Fort de Goede Hoop, *South African Archaeological Bulletin* 48: 3–15.

1994 Coarse earthenwares of the V.O.C. period: 18th century pottery excavated from the Grand Parade at the Cape, *Annals of the South African Cultural History Museum* 6: 1–52.

Abrahams-Willis, G. 1997 Report on finds at the Victoria and Albert Waterfront, Cape Town, between 1990–1993, *Southern African Field Archaeology* 6: 50–6.

1998 Archaeology and local cuisine: signatures of the Cape around 1750, *Annals of the South African Cultural History Museum* 10: 1–66.

2000 Slave Lodge to become a major tourism magnet: preliminary report on year 2000 excavations, *Quarterly Bulletin of the National Library of South Africa* 54 (4): 134–43.

Aiello, L. and Wheeler, P. 1995 The expensive-tissue hypothesis: the brain and the digestive system in human and primate evolution, *Current Anthropology* 36: 199–221.

Aitken, M.J., Stringer, C.B. and Mellars, P.A. (eds.) 1993 *The origin of modern humans and the impact of chronometric dating*, Princeton: Princeton University Press.

Alexander, J.E. 1967 *An expedition of discovery into the interior of Africa*, Cape Town: Van Riebeeck Society.

Alley, R.B., Meese, D.A., Shuman, C.A., Gow, A.J., Taylor, K.C., Grootes, P.M., White, J.W.C., Ram, M., Waddington, E.D., Mayewski, P.A. and Zieginski, G.A. 1993 Abrupt increase in Greenland snow accumulation at the end of the Younger Dryas event, *Nature* 362: 527–9.

Ambrose, S.H. 1998a Late Pleistocene human population bottleneck, volcanic winter, and differentiation of modern humans, *Journal of Human Evolution* 34: 623–51.

1998b Chronology of the Later Stone Age and food production in East Africa, *Journal of Archaeological Science* 25: 377–92.

Ambrose, S.H. and Lorenz, K. 1990 Social and ecological models for the Middle Stone Age of southern Africa, in P.A. Mellars (ed.), pp. 3–33.

Ancieux de Faveaux, E. and de Maret, P. 1984 Premières datations pour la fonte du cuivre du Shaba (Zaire), *Bullétin de la Société Royale Belge d'Archéologie et de la Préhistoire* 95: 5–20.

Anderson, A.A. 1887 *Twenty-five years in a waggon in the gold regions of Africa*, London: Chapman and Hall.

Anderson, G. 1996 The social and gender identity of gatherer-hunters and herders in the south-western Cape, MPhil thesis, University of Cape Town.

1997 Fingers and finelines: paintings and gender identity in the south-western Cape, in L. Wadley (ed.), pp. 13–70.

Andersson, C.J. 1968 *The Okavango River: a narrative of travel, exploration and adventure*, Cape Town: C. Struik.

Arbousset, T. and Daumas, F. 1968 *Narrative of an exploratory tour to the northeast of the Cape of Good Hope*, Cape Town: C. Struik.

Argyle, J. 1994/95 Khoisan–Southern Bantu livestock exchanges: reinterpreting the linguistic evidence, *Azania* 29/30: 199.

Armstrong, A.L. 1931 Rhodesian archaeological expedition (1929): excavations in Bambata Cave and researches on prehistoric sites in Southern Rhodesia, *Journal of the Royal Anthropological Institute* 61: 239–76.

Asfaw, B., Berhane, Y., Suwa, G., Walter, R.C., White, T.D., WoldeGabriel, G. and Yemane, T. 1992 The earliest Acheulean from Konso-Gardula, *Nature* 360: 732–4.

Asfaw, B., White, T., Lovejoy, O., Latimer, B., Simpson, S. and Suwa, G. 1999 *Australopithecus garhi*: a new species of early hominid from Ethiopia, *Science* 284: 629–35.

Ashton, H. 1952 *The Basuto*, Oxford: Oxford University Press.

Aukema, J. 1989 Rain-making: a thousand year-old ritual? *South African Archaeological Bulletin* 44: 70–2.

Auret, C. and Maggs, T.M.O'C. 1982 The Great Ship *São Bento*: remains from a mid-sixteenth century Portuguese wreck on the Pondoland coast, *Annals of the Natal Museum* 25: 1–39.

Avery, D.M. 1982 Micromammals as palaeoenvironmental indicators and an interpretation of the late Quaternary in the southern Cape Province, South Africa, *Annals of the South African Museum* 85: 183–374.

1987a Late Pleistocene coastal environment of the southern Cape Province of South Africa: micromammals from Klasies River Mouth, *Journal of Archaeological Science* 14: 405–21.

1987b Micromammalian evidence for natural vegetation and the introduction of farming during the Holocene in the Magaliesberg, Transvaal, *South African Journal of Science* 83: 221–5.

1992 Micromammals and the environment of early pastoralists at Spoeg River, Western Cape Province, South Africa, *South African Archaeological Bulletin* 47: 116–21.

2000 Micromammals, in T.C. Partridge and R.R. Maud (eds.), pp. 305–38.

Avery, G. 1975 Discussion on the age and use of tidal fish-traps (*visvywers*), *South African Archaeological Bulletin* 30: 105–13.

1987 Coastal birds and prehistory in the Western Cape, in J.E. Parkington and M. Hall (eds.), pp. 164–91.

Avery, G., Cruz-Uribe, K., Goldberg, P., Grine, F.E., Klein, R.G., Lenardi, M.J., Marean, C.W., Rink, W.J., Schwarcz, H.P., Thackeray, A.I. and Wilson, M.L. 1997 The 1992–1993 excavations at the Die Kelders Middle and Later Stone Age cave site, South Africa, *Journal of Field Archaeology* 24: 263–91.

Backwell, L.R. and d'Errico, F. 2000 A new functional interpretation of the Swartkrans early hominid bone tools, Abstract for the Paleoanthropology Society Meeting, *Journal of Human Evolution* 38 (3): A4–A5.

Bada, J.L. and Deems, L. 1975 Accuracy of dates beyond the 14-C dating limit using the aspartic acid racemization reaction, *Nature* 255: 218–19.

Bailey, G.N. 1983 Concepts of time in Quaternary prehistory, *Annual Review of Anthropology* 12: 165–92.

Bamford, M. 1999 Pliocene fossil woods from an early hominid cave deposit, Sterkfontein, South Africa, *South African Journal of Science* 95: 231–7.

Bar-Yosef, O. 1994 The contributions of south-west Asia to the study of origin of modern humans, in M.H. Nitecki and V. Nitecki (eds.), pp. 23–66.

Bar-Yosef, P., Arnold, M., Belfer-Cohen, A., Goldberg, P., Houseley, R., Laville, H., Meignen, L., Mercier, N., Vogel, J.C. and Vandermeersch, B. 1996 The dating of the Upper Palaeolithic layers in Kebara Cave, Mt. Carmel, *Journal of Archaeological Science* 23: 297–306.

Bard, E., Hamlin, B., Fairbanks, R.G. and Zindler, A. 1991 Calibration of the ^{14}C timescale over the past 30,000 years using mass spectrometric U-Th ages from Barbados corals, *Nature* 345: 405–10.

Barham, L.S. 1989a The Later Stone Age of Swaziland, PhD thesis, University of Pennsylvania.

1989b A preliminary report on the Later Stone Age artefacts from Siphiso shelter in Swaziland, *South African Archaeological Bulletin* 44: 33–43.

1989c Radiocarbon dates from Nyonyane Shelter, Swaziland, *South African Archaeological Bulletin* 44: 117–18.

1992 Let's walk before we run: an appraisal of historical materialist approaches to the Later Stone Age, *South African Archaeological Bulletin* 47: 44–51.

1996 The Middle Stone Age at Mumbwa Caves, central Zambia, in G. Pwiti and R. Soper (eds.), pp. 191–200.

Barker, G. 1978 Economic models for the Manekweni Zimbabwe, Mozambique, *Azania* 13: 71–100.

1988 Cows and kings: models for zimbabwes, *Proceedings of the Prehistoric Society* 54: 223–39.

Barnard, A. 1992 *Hunters and herders of southern Africa: a comparative ethnography of the Khoisan peoples*, Cambridge: Cambridge University Press.

Barnett, W.K. 1995 Putting the pot before the horse: earliest ceramics and the Neolithic transition in the western Mediterranean, in W.K. Barnett and J.W. Hodges (eds.), *The emergence of pottery: technology and innovation in ancient societies*, Washington DC: Smithsonian Institution, pp. 79–88.

Barrow, J. 1801 *An account of travels into the interior of southern Africa in the years 1797 and 1798*, London: Cadell and Davies.

Bartram, L.E. and Marean, C.W. 1999 Explaining the 'Klasies Pattern': Kua ethnoarchaeology, the Die Kelders Middle Stone Age archaeofauna, long bone fragmentation and carnivore ravaging, *Journal of Archaeological Science* 26: 9–29.

Barut Kusimba, S. 1999 Hunter-gatherer land use patterns in Later Stone Age East Africa, *Journal of Anthropological Archaeology* 18: 165–200.

Beach, D.N. 1980 *The Shona and Zimbabwe 900–1850*, London: Heinemann.

1994 *The Shona and their neighbours*, Oxford: Blackwells.

1996 Archaeology and history in Nyanga, Zimbabwe: an overview, in G. Pwiti and R. Soper (eds.), pp. 715–18.

1998 Cognitive archaeology and imaginary history at Great Zimbabwe, *Current Anthropology* 30: 47–73.

Beach, D.N., Boudrillon, M.F.C., Denbow, J., Hall, M., Lane, P., Pikirayi, I. and Pwiti, G. 1997 Reviews of T.N. Huffman, Snakes and crocodiles: power and symbolism in ancient Zimbabwe, *South African Archaeological Bulletin* 52: 125–38.

Beaumont, P.B. 1973 The ancient pigment mines of southern Africa, *South African Journal of Science* 69: 41–6.

1978 Border Cave, MA thesis, University of Cape Town.

1981 The Heuningneskrans Shelter, in E. Voigt (ed.), pp. 133–45.

1986 Where did all the young men go during O-18 stage 2? *Palaeoecology of Africa* 17: 79–86.

1990a Kathu, in P.B. Beaumont and D. Morris (eds.), pp. 75–100.

1990b Wonderwerk Cave, in P.B. Beaumont and D. Morris (eds.), pp. 101–34.

1990c Nooitgedacht 2 and Roseberry Plain 1, in P.B. Beaumont and D. Morris (eds.), pp. 4–6.

Beaumont, P.B. and Boshier, A.K. 1974 Report on test excavation at a pigment mine near Postmasburg, Northern Cape, *South African Archaeological Bulletin* 29: 41–51.

Beaumont, P.B., De Villiers, H. and Vogel, J.C. 1978 Modern man in sub-Saharan Africa prior to 49000 years BP: a review and evaluation with particular reference to Border Cave, *South African Journal of Science* 74: 409–19.

Beaumont, P.B. and Morris, D. (eds.) 1990 *Guide to archaeological sites in the Northern Cape*, Kimberley: McGregor Museum.

Beaumont, P.B., Smith, A.B. and Vogel, J.C. 1995 Before the Einiqua: the archaeology of the Frontier Zone, in A.B. Smith (ed.), pp. 236–64.

Beaumont, P.B. and Vogel, J.C. 1972 On a new radiocarbon chronology for Africa south of the equator. Part 2, *African Studies* 31: 155–81.

1989 Patterns in the age and context of rock art in the Northern Cape, *South African Archaeological Bulletin* 44: 73–81.

Behrens, J. 1991 Bo Kaap architecture: a critique of structuralist theory, BA thesis, University of Cape Town.

Bent, T. 1892 *The sacred city of the Ethiopians*, London: Longman.

Berger, L.R. and Clarke, R.J. 1995 Eagle involvement in accumulation of the Taung child fauna, *Journal of Human Evolution* 29: 275–99.

Berger, L.R., Keyser, A.W. and Tobias, P.V. 1993 Gladysvale: first early hominid site discovered in South Africa since 1948, *American Journal of Physical Anthropology* 92: 107–11.

Berger, L.R. and Parkington, J.E. 1995 A new Pleistocene hominid-bearing locality at Hoedjiespunt, South Africa, *American Journal of Physical Anthropology* 98: 601–9.

Bickerton, D. 1981 *The roots of language*, Ann Arbor: Karoma.

Biesele, M. 1975 Folklore and ritual of !Kung Bushmen, *Natural History* 76: 31–7.

1993 *Women like meat: the folklore and foraging ideology of the Kalahari Ju/'hoan*, Johannesburg: Witwatersrand University Press.

Binford, L.R. 1980 Willow smoke and dogs' tails: hunter-gatherer settlement systems and archaeological site formation, *American Antiquity* 45: 4–20.

1984 *Faunal remains from Klasies River Mouth*, New York: Academic Press.

Binneman, J.N.F. 1982 Mikrogebruikstekens op steenwerktuie: eksperimentele waarnemings en 'n studie van werktuie afkomstig van Boomplaasgrot, MA thesis, University of Stellenbosch.

1988 Edgewear analysis of stone tools from Kruger Cave and Olifantspoort, in R.J. Mason (ed.), pp. 279–310.

1994a Note on a digging stick from Augussie Shelter, eastern Cape, *Southern African Field Archaeology* 3: 112–13.

1994b A unique stone tipped arrowhead from Adam's Kranz Cave, Eastern Cape, *Southern African Field Archaeology* 3: 58–60.

1996a Symbolic construction of communities during the Holocene Later Stone Age in the south-eastern Cape, DPhil thesis, University of the Witwatersrand.

1996b Preliminary results from investigations at Kulubele, an Early Iron Age farming settlement in the Great Kei River valley, Eastern Cape, *Southern African Field Archaeology* 5: 28–35.

1997a Usewear traces on Robberg bladelets from Rose Cottage Cave, *South African Journal of Science* 93: 479–81.

1997b Results from a test excavation at The Havens Cave, Cambria valley, south-eastern Cape, *Southern African Field Archaeology* 6: 93–105.

1999 Mummified human remains from the Kouga Mountains, Eastern Cape, *The Digging Stick* 16 (2): 1–3.

Binneman, J.N.F. and Beaumont, P.B. 1992 Use-wear analysis of two Acheulean handaxes from Wonderwerk Cave, Northern Cape, *Southern African Field Archaeology* 1: 92–7.

Binneman, J.N.F. and Deacon, J. 1986 Experimental determination of usewear on stone adzes from Boomplaas Cave, South Africa, *Journal of Archaeological Science* 13: 219–28.

Binneman, J.N.F. and Hall, S.L. 1993 The context of four painted stones from the Eastern Cape, *Southern African Field Archaeology* 2: 89–95.

Binneman, J.N.F. and Mitchell, P.J. 1997 Microwear analysis of Robberg bladelets from Sehonghong Shelter, Lesotho, *Southern African Field Archaeology* 6: 42–9.

Binneman, J.N.F. and van Niekerk, J.C. 1986 Polished stone implements from the Barberton District, eastern Transvaal, *South African Archaeological Bulletin* 41: 87–9.

Bishop, W.W. and Clark, J.D. (eds.) 1967 *Background to evolution in Africa*, Chicago: University of Chicago Press.

Blacking, J. 1985 The Great Enclosure and domba, *Man* 20: 542–5.

Blanton, R.E., Feinman, G.M., Kowalewski, S.A. and Peregrine, P.N. 1996 A dual-processual theory for the evolution of Mesoamerican civilization, *Current Anthropology* 37: 1–14.

Bleed, P. 1986 The optimal design of hunting weapons: maintainability and reliability, *American Antiquity* 51: 737–47.

Bleek, D.F. 1928 *The Naron: a Bushman tribe of the central Kalahari*, Cambridge: Cambridge University Press.

1931 Customs and beliefs of the /Xam Bushmen. Part I: baboons, *Bantu Studies* 5: 167–9.

1932a Customs and beliefs of the /Xam Bushmen. Part II: the lion, *Bantu Studies* 6: 47–63.

1932b Customs and beliefs of the /Xam Bushmen. Part III: game animals, *Bantu Studies* 6: 233–49.

1932c Customs and beliefs of the /Xam Bushmen. Part IV: omens, wind-making, clouds, *Bantu Studies* 6: 323–42.

1933a Beliefs and customs of the /Xam Bushmen. Part V: the rain, *Bantu Studies* 7: 297–312.

1933b Beliefs and customs of the /Xam Bushmen. Part VI: rain-making, *Bantu Studies* 7: 375–92.

1935 Beliefs and customs of the /Xam Bushmen. Part VII: sorcerers, *Bantu Studies* 9: 1–47.

1936a Beliefs and customs of the /Xam Bushmen. Part VIII: more about sorcerers and charms, *Bantu Studies* 10: 131–62.

1936b Special speech of animals and the moon used by the /Xam Bushmen, *Bantu Studies* 10: 163–99.

1956 *A Bushman dictionary*, New Haven: American Oriental Society.

Bleek, W.H.I. 1873 *Report of Dr Bleek concerning his researches into the Bushman language and customs presented to the Honourable House of Assembly by command of His Excellency the Governor*, Cape Town: House of Assembly.

1875 *A brief account of Bushman folklore and other texts. Second report concerning Bushman researches presented to both Houses of Parliament of the Cape of Good Hope*, Cape Town: Juta.

Bleek, W.H.I. and Lloyd, L. 1911 *Specimens of Bushman folklore*, London: Allen.

Boeyens, J.C.A. 2000 In search of Kaditshwene, *South African Archaeological Bulletin* 55: 3–17.

Bogucki, P. 1995 The Linear Pottery culture of central Europe: conservative colonists?, in W.K. Barnett and J.W. Hodges (eds.), *The emergence of pottery: technology and innovation in ancient societies*, Washington, DC: Smithsonian Institution, pp. 89–97.

Bollong, C.A., Jacobson, L., Peisach, M., Pineda, C.A. and Sampson, C.G. 1997 Ordination versus clustering of elemental data from PIXE analysis of herder-hunter pottery: a comparison, *Journal of Archaeological Science* 21: 319–27.

Bollong, C.A. and Sampson, C.G. 1996 Later Stone Age ceramic stratigraphy and direct dates on pottery: a comparison, *Southern African Field Archaeology* 5: 3–16.

Bollong, C.A., Vogel, J.C., Jacobson, L., van der Westhuizen, W.A. and Sampson, C.G. 1993 Direct dating and identity of fibre temper in pre-contact Bushman (Basarwa) pottery, *Journal of Archaeological Science* 20: 41–55.

Bonner, P. 1983 *Kings, commoners and concessionaires: the evolution and dissolution of the nineteenth century Swazi state*, Johannesburg: Ravan Press.

Boonzaier, E., Malherbe, C., Berens, P. and Smith, A.B. 1996 *The Cape herders: a history of the Khoikhoi of southern Africa*, Cape Town: David Philip.

Borland, C.H. 1986 The linguistic reconstruction of prehistoric pastoralist vocabulary, *South African Archaeological Society Goodwin Series* 5: 31–5.

Bousman, C.B. 1988 Prehistoric settlement patterns in the Senqunyane valley, Lesotho, *South African Archaeological Bulletin* 43: 33–7.

1989 Implications of dating the Lockshoek Industry from the interior plateau of southern Africa, *Nyame Akuma* 32: 30–4.

1991 Holocene palaeoecology and Later Stone Age hunter-gatherer adaptations in the South African interior plateau, PhD thesis, Southern Methodist University.

Bower, J. 1991 The Pastoral Neolithic of East Africa, *Journal of World Prehistory* 5: 49–82.

Boxer, C.R. 1969 *The Portuguese seaborne empire*, London: Hutchinson.

Brain, C.K. 1974 Human food remains from the Iron Age at Zimbabwe, *South African Journal of Science* 70: 303–9.

1975 An interpretation of the bone assemblage from the Kromdraai australopithecine site, South Africa, in R.H. Tuttle (ed.), *Palaeoanthropology, morphology and palaeoecology*, The Hague: Mouton, pp. 225–43.

1981 *The hunters or the hunted? An introduction to African cave taphonomy*, Chicago: University of Chicago Press.

1985 Cultural and taphonomic comparisons of hominids from Swartkrans and Sterkfontein, in E. Delson (ed.), *Ancestors: the hard evidence*, New York: Alan Liss, pp. 72–5.

(ed.) 1993 *Swartkrans: a cave's chronicle of early man*, Pretoria: Transvaal Museum.

Brain, C.K. and Brain, V. 1977 Microfaunal remains from Mirabib: some evidence of palaeoecological changes in the Namib, *Madoqua* 10: 285–93.

Brain, C.K. and Sillen, A. 1988 Evidence from the Swartkrans cave for the earliest use of fire, *Nature* 336: 464–6.

Bräuer, G. 1982 Early anatomically modern man in Africa and the replacement of the Mediterranean and European Neandertals, in H. de Lumley (ed.), *L'Homo erectus et la place de l'homme de Tautavel parmi les hominidés fossiles*, Nice: Centre National de la Recherche Scientifique, p. 112.

1989 The evolution of modern humans, in P.A. Mellars and C.B. Stringer (eds.), pp. 123–54.

1992 Africa's place in the evolution of *Homo sapiens*, in G. Bräuer and F.H. Smith (eds.), pp. 83–98.

Bräuer, G., Deacon, H.J. and Zipfel, F. 1992 Comment on the new maxillary finds from Klasies River, South Africa, *Journal of Human Evolution* 23: 419–22.

Bräuer, G. and Mbua, E. 1992 *Homo erectus* features used in cladistics and their validity in Asian and African hominids, *Journal of Human Evolution* 22: 79–108.

Bräuer, G. and Smith, F.H. (eds.) 1992 *Continuity or replacement: controversies in* Homo sapiens *evolution*, Rotterdam: Balkema.

Bräuer, G., Yokoyama, Y., Falguères, C. and Mbua, E. 1997 Modern human origins backdated, *Nature* 386: 337–8.

Breuil, H. 1948 The White Lady of the Brandberg, South West Africa, her companions and her guards, *South African Archaeological Bulletin* 3: 2–11.

Brink, J.S. 1987 The archaeozoology of Florisbad, Orange Free State, *Memoirs van die Nasionale Museum, Bloemfontein* 24: 1–155.

Brink, J.S. and Deacon, H.J. 1982 A study of a last interglacial shell midden and bone accumulation at Herolds Bay, Cape Province, South Africa, *Palaeoecology of Africa* 15: 31–9.

Brink, J.S., Dreyer, J.J.B. and Loubser, J.N.H. 1992 Rescue excavations at Pramberg, Jacobsdal, south-western Orange Free State, *Southern African Field Archaeology* 1: 54–60.

Brink, J.S. and Henderson, Z.L. 2001 A high-resolution Last Interglacial MSA horizon at Florisbad in the context of other open-air occurrences in the central interior of southern Africa: an interim statement, in N.J. Conard (ed.), *Settlement dynamics of the Middle Palaeolithic and Middle Stone Age*, Tübingen: Kerns Verlag, pp. 1–20.

Brink, J.S., Henderson, Z.L. and Rossouw, L. 1996 Guide to the Florisbad Quaternary site, in J.J.B. Dreyer *et al.* (eds.), pp. 70–6.

Brink, J.S. and Webley, L. 1996 Faunal evidence for pastoralist settlement at Jakkalsberg, Richtersveld, Northern Cape Province, *Southern African Field Archaeology* 5: 70–8.

Brink, Y. 1990 The *voorhuis* as a central element in early Cape houses, *Social Dynamics* 16: 38–54.

1993 The octagon: an icon of Willem Adriaan van der Stel's aspirations? *South African Archaeological Society Goodwin Series* 7: 92–7.

1997 Figuring the landscape: land, identity and material culture at the Cape in the eighteenth century, *South African Archaeological Bulletin* 52: 105–12.

Broecker, W.S. and Denton, G.H. 1990. What drives glacial cycles?, *Scientific American* January: 43–50.

Bromage, T.G. and Dean, M.C. 1985 Re-evaluation of the age at death of immature fossil hominids, *Nature* 317: 525–7.

Brook, G.A., Haberyan, K.A. and De Filippis, S. 1992 Evidence of a shallow lake at Tsodilo Hills, Botswana, 17 500 to 15 000 yr BP: further confirmation of a widespread Late Pleistocene humid period in the Kalahari Desert, *Palaeoecology of Africa* 23: 165–75.

Brooker, M. 1980 Rescue excavations at the Welbedacht Dam site, *Humanitas* 6: 35–42.

Brooks, A.S., Hare, P.E., Kokis, J.E., Miller, G.H., Ernst, R.D. and Wendorf, F. 1990 Dating Pleistocene archaeological sites by protein diagenesis in ostrich eggshell, *Science* 248: 60–4.

Brooks, A.S., Helgren, D.M., Cramer, J.S., Franklin, A., Hornyak, W., Keating, J.M., Klein, R.G., Rink, W.J., Schwarcz, H., Leith Smith, J.N., Stewart, K., Todd, N.E., Verniers, J. and Yellen, J.E. 1995 Dating and context of three Middle Stone Age sites with bone points in the Upper Semliki Valley, Zaire, *Science* 268: 548–53.

Brooks, A.S. and Robertshaw, P.T. 1990 The Glacial Maximum in tropical Africa: 22,000–12,000 BP, in C.S. Gamble and O. Soffer (eds.), pp. 121–69.

Broom, R. 1936 A new fossil anthropoid skull from South Africa, *Nature* 138: 486–8.

1937 Discovery of a lower molar of *Australopithecus*, *Nature* 140: 681–2.

Brown, A.J.V. and Verhagen, B.T. 1985 Two *Antidorcas bondi* individuals from the Late Stone Age site of Kruger Cave 35/83, Olifantsnek, Rustenburg District, South Africa, *South African Journal of Science* 81: 102.

Brown, P. 1993 Recent human evolution in East Asia and Australasia, in M.J. Aitken *et al.* (eds.), pp. 217–33.

Brunet, M., Beauvillon, A., Coppens, Y., Henitz, E., Moutaye, H.E. and Pilbeam, D. 1996 *Australopithecus bahrelghazali*, une nouvelle espèce d'hominidé ancien de la région de Koro Toro (Tchad), *Comptes Rendus des Séances de l'Academie des Sciences* 322: 907–13.

Budack, K.F.R. 1977 The _Aonin or Topnaar of the lower !Khuiseb valley and the sea, *Khoisan Linguistic Studies* 3: 1–42.

Burchell, W.J. 1967 *Travels in the interior of southern Africa*, Cape Town: C. Struik.

Burkitt, M.C. 1928 *South Africa's past in stone and paint*, Cambridge: Cambridge University Press.

Butchart, D. 1995 Biomes of southern Africa, in J. Ledger (ed.), *Vision of wildlife, ecotourism and the environment in southern Africa*, Johannesburg: Endangered Wildlife Trust, pp. 6–7.

Butzer, K.W. 1984a Archaeogeology and Quaternary environment in the interior of southern Africa, in R.G. Klein (ed.), pp. 1–64.

1984b Late Quaternary environments in South Africa, in J.C. Vogel (ed.), *Late Cenozoic palaeoclimates of the Southern Hemisphere*, Rotterdam: Balkema, pp. 235–64.

Butzer, K.W., Fock, G.J., Scott, L. and Stuckenrath, R. 1979 Dating and context of rock engravings in southern Africa, *Science* 203: 1201–14.

Cable, J.H.C. 1984 *Late Stone Age economy and technology in southern Natal.* Oxford: British Archaeological Reports.

Cable, J.H.C., Scott, K. and Carter, P.L. 1980 Excavations at Good Hope Shelter, Underberg District, Natal, *Annals of the Natal Museum* 24: 1–34.

Campbell, A.C. 1991 The riddle of the stone walls, *Botswana Notes and Records* 23: 243–9.

1998 Archaeology in Botswana: origins and growth, in P. Lane *et al.* (eds.), pp. 24–49.

Campbell, A.C., Denbow, J.R. and Wilmsen, E.N. 1994 Paintings like engravings: rock art at Tsodilo, in T.A. Dowson and J.D. Lewis-Williams (eds.), pp. 131–58.

Campbell, A.C., Holmberg, G. and van Waarden, C. 1991 A note on recent archaeological research around Gaborone, *Botswana Notes and Records* 23: 288–90.

Campbell, A.C., van Waarden, C. and Holmberg, G. 1996 Variation in the Early Iron Age of south-eastern Botswana, *Botswana Notes and Records* 28: 1–22.

Campbell, C. 1986 Images of war: a problem in San rock art research, *World Archaeology* 18: 255–68.

1987 Art in crisis: contact period rock art in the south-eastern mountains of southern Africa, MSc thesis, University of the Witwatersrand.

Campbell, J. 1822 *Travels in South Africa*, London: Westley.

Cann, R.L., Rickards, O. and Lum, J.K. 1994 Mitochondrial DNA and human evolution: our one Lucky Mother, in M.H. Nitecki and D.V. Nitecki (eds.), pp. 135–48.

Cann, R.L., Stoneking, M. and Wilson, A.C. 1987 Mitochondrial DNA and human evolution, *Nature* 325: 31–6.

Carr, M.J., Carr, A.C. and Jacobson, L. 1978 Hut remains and related features from the Zerrissene Mountain area: their distribution, typology and ecology, *Cimbebasia (B)* 2: 235–58.

Carter, P.L. 1969 Moshebi's Shelter: excavation and exploitation in eastern Lesotho, *Lesotho Notes and Records* 8: 1–11.

1970 Late Stone Age exploitation patterns in southern Natal, *South African Archaeological Bulletin* 25: 55–8.

1978 The prehistory of eastern Lesotho, PhD thesis, University of Cambridge.

Carter, P.L., Mitchell, P.J. and Vinnicombe, P. 1988 *Sehonghong: the Middle and Later Stone Age industrial sequence at a Lesotho rock-shelter*, Oxford: British Archaeological Reports.

Carter, P.L. and Vogel, J.C. 1974 The dating of industrial assemblages from stratified sites in eastern Lesotho, *Man* 9: 557–70.

Cartwright, C. and Parkington, J.E. 1997 The wood charcoal assemblages from Elands Bay Cave, south-western Cape: principles, procedures and preliminary interpretation, *South African Archaeological Bulletin* 52: 59–72.

Cashdan, E.A. 1987 Trade and its origins on the Botletli River, Botswana, *Journal of Anthropological Research* 43: 121–38.

Caton-Thompson, G. 1931 *The Zimbabwe Culture, ruins and reactions*, Oxford: Clarendon Press.

Champion, T.C. (ed.) 1989 *Centre and periphery: comparative studies in archaeology*, London: Unwin Hyman.

Chapman, J. 1971 *Travels in the interior of South Africa 1849–1863*, Cape Town: Balkema.

Chase, P. and Dibble, H.L. 1987 Middle Palaeolithic symbolism: a review of current evidence and interpretations, *Journal of Anthropological Archaeology* 6: 263–96.

Chavaillon, J. 1976 Evidence for the technical practices of Early Pleistocene hominids, Shungura Formations, Lower Omo Valley, Ethiopia, in Y. Coppens, F.C. Howell, G.Ll. Isaac and R.E.F. Leakey (eds.), *Earliest man and environments in the Lake Rudolf Basin*, Chicago: University of Chicago Press, pp. 565–73.

Chipunza, K.T. 1997 A diachronic analysis of the standing structures of the Hill Complex at Great Zimbabwe, in G. Pwiti (ed.), pp. 125–42.

Churcher, C.S. and Richardson, M.L. 1978 Equidae, in V.J. Maglio and H.B.S. Cooke (eds.), *Evolution of African mammals*, Cambridge, MA: Harvard University Press, pp. 379–422.

Churchill, S.E., Brink, J.S., Berger, L.R., Hutchison, R.A., Rossouw, L., Stynder, D., Hancox, P.J., Brandt, D., Woodborne, S., Loock, J.C., Scott, L. and Ungar, P. 2000 Erfkroon: a new Florisian fossil locality from fluvial contexts in the western Free State, South Africa, *South African Journal of Science* 96: 161–3.

Churchill, S.E., Pearson, O.M., Grine, F.E., Trinkaus, E. and Holliday, T.W. 1996 Morphological affinities of the proximal ulna from Klasies River main site: archaic or modern? *Journal of Human Evolution* 31: 213–37.

Clark, A.M.B. 1997a The MSA/LSA transition in southern Africa: new technological evidence from Rose Cottage Cave, *South African Archaeological Bulletin* 52: 113–21.

1997b The final Middle Stone Age at Rose Cottage Cave: a distinct industry in the basutolian ecozone, *South African Journal of Science* 93: 449–58.

Clark, J.D. 1955 Note on a wooden implement from the level of Peat I at Florisbad, Orange Free State, *Researches of the National Museum (Bloemfontein)* 1: 135–40.

1959 *The prehistory of southern Africa*, Harmondsworth: Penguin.

1964 Stone vessels from Northern Rhodesia, *Man* 64: 70–2.

1969 *Kalambo Falls prehistoric site*, vol. I, Cambridge: Cambridge University Press.

1974 Africa in prehistory: peripheral or paramount? *Man* 10: 175–98.

1982 Cultures of the Middle Palaeolithic/Middle Stone Age, in J.D. Clark (ed.), *Cambridge history of Africa*, vol. I, *From the earliest times to c. 500 B.C.*, Cambridge: Cambridge University Press, pp. 248–341.

1988 The Middle Stone Age of East Africa and the beginnings of regional identity, *Journal of World Prehistory* 2: 235–303.

1993a Stone artefact assemblages from members 1–3, Swartkrans Cave, in C.K. Brain (ed.), pp. 167–94.

1993b African and Asian perspectives on the origins of modern humans, in M.J. Aitken, C.B. Stringer and P.A. Mellars (eds.), *The origin of modern humans and the impact of chronometric dating*, Princeton: Princeton University Press, pp. 148–78.

1996 Decision-making and variability in the Acheulean, in G. Pwiti and R. Soper (eds.), pp. 93–8.

2001 *Kalambo Falls prehistoric site*, vol. III, Cambridge: Cambridge University Press.

Clark, J.D., de Heinzelin, J., Schick, K.D., Hart, W.K., White, T.D., Woldegabriel, G., Walter, R.C., Suwa, G., Asfaw, B., Vrba, E. and Haile-Selassie, Y. 1994 African *Homo erectus*: old radiometric ages and young Oldowan assemblages in the Middle Awash Valley, Ethiopia, *Science* 264: 1907–9.

Clark, J.D. and Haynes, C.V. 1970 An elephant butchery site at Mwanganda's Village, Karonga, Malawi, and its relevance for Palaeolithic archaeology, *World Archaeology* 1: 390–411.

Clark, J.D., Oakley, K.P., Wells, L.H. and McClelland, J.A.C. 1950 New studies on Rhodesian man, *Journal of the Royal Anthropological Institute* 77: 7–32.

Clark, J.G.D. 1975 *The earlier Stone Age settlement of Scandinavia*, Cambridge: Cambridge University Press.

Clarke, D.L. 1976 Mesolithic Europe: the economic basis, in G. Sieveking, I.H. Longworth and K. Wilson (eds.), *Problems in economic and social archaeology*, Cambridge: Cambridge University Press, pp. 449–81.

Clarke, R.J. 1985 A new reconstruction of the Florisbad cranium, with notes on the site, in E. Delson (ed.), *Ancestors: the hard evidence*, New York: Alan Liss, pp. 301–5.

1994 On some new interpretations of Sterkfontein stratigraphy, *South African Journal of Science* 90: 211–14.

1998 First ever discovery of a well-preserved skull and associated skeleton of *Australopithecus*, *South African Journal of Science* 94: 460–3.

1999a Discovery of complete arm and hand of the 3.3 million-year-old *Australopithecus* skeleton from Sterkfontein, *South African Journal of Science* 95: 477–80.

1999b Mr, Mrs and Miss-conceptions in studies of human ancestry, in J. Gibert (ed.), *The hominids and their environments during the Lower and Middle Pleistocene of Eurasia, Proceedings of the International Conference of Human Palaeontology, Orce, Spain*, Orce: Museo de Prehistoria, pp. 327–9.

Clarke, R.J., Howell, F.C. and Brain, C.K. 1970 More evidence of an advanced hominid at Swartkrans, *Nature* 225: 1219–22.

Clarke, R.J. and Tobias, P.V. 1995 Sterkfontein Member 2 foot bones of the oldest South African hominid, *Science* 269: 521–4.

Close, A.E. 1995 Few and far between: early ceramics in North Africa, in W.K. Barnett and J.W. Hodges (eds.), *The emergence of pottery: technology and innovation in ancient societies*, Washington DC: Smithsonian Institution, pp. 23–37.

Close, A.E. and Sampson, C.G. 1998 Did the Seacow River Bushmen make backed microliths? *Southern African Field Archaeology* 7: 3–11.

Cobbing, J. 1988 The Mfecane as alibi: thoughts on Dithakong and Mbolompo, *Journal of African History* 29: 487–519.

Coetzee, J. 1967 Pollen analytical studies in east and southern Africa, *Palaeoecology of Africa* 3: 1–146.

Cohen, A. 1999 Mary Elizabeth Barber, the Bowkers and South African prehistory, *South African Archaeological Bulletin* 54: 120–7.

Cohen, A.L., Parkington, J.E., Brundrit, G.B. and van der Merwe, N.J. 1992 A Holocene marine climatic record in mollusc shells from the south-west African coast, *Quaternary Research* 38: 379–85.

Collett, D.P. 1982 Excavations of stone-walled ruins in the Badfontein valley, eastern Transvaal, South Africa, *South African Archaeological Bulletin* 37: 34–43.

1987 A contribution to the study of migrations in the archaeological record: the Ngoni and Kololo migrations as a case study, in I. Hodder (ed.), *Archaeology as long term history*, Cambridge: Cambridge University Press, pp. 105–16.

1988 The spread of early ironproducing communities in eastern and southern Africa, PhD thesis, University of Cambridge.

1991 *The archaeological heritage of Zimbabwe: a masterplan for resource conservation and development*, Harare: National Museums and Monuments of Zimbabwe.

Collett, D.P., Vines, A.E. and Hughes, G. 1992 The chronology of the Valley Enclosures: implications for the interpretation of Great Zimbabwe, *African Archaeological Review* 10: 139–62.

Cooke, C.K. 1963 Report on excavations at Pomongwe and Tshangula Caves, Matopos Hills, Southern Rhodesia, *South African Archaeological Bulletin* 18: 73–151.

1964 Iron Age influences in the rock art of Southern Rhodesia, *South African Archaeological Bulletin* 18: 172–5.

1965 Evidence of human migrations from the rock art of Southern Rhodesia, *Africa* 35: 263–85.

1966 Reappraisal of the industry hitherto named the Proto-Stillbay, *Arnoldia (Rhodesia)* 2 (22): 1–14.

1971 Excavations in Zombepata Cave, Sipolilo district, Mashonaland, Rhodesia, *South African Archaeological Bulletin* 26: 104–26.

1978a The Redcliff Stone Age site, Rhodesia, *Occasional Papers of the National Museum of Rhodesia A* 1: 45–73.

1978b Nyazongo rock shelter: a detailed re-examination of the cultural material, *Arnoldia (Rhodesia)* 20: 1–20.

1979 Excavations at Diana's Vow Rock Shelter, Maroni District, Zimbabwe, Rhodesia, *Occasional Papers of the National Museum of Rhodesia A* 4: 115–48.

1984 The industries of the Upper Pleistocene in Zimbabwe, *Zimbabwea* 1: 23–7.

Cooke, C.K. and Simons, H. 1969 Mpato Shelter: Sentinel Ranch, Beitbridge, Rhodesia: excavation results, *Arnoldia (Rhodesia)* 4 (18): 1–9.

Cowling, R.M. and Richardson, D. 1995 *Fynbos: South Africa's unique floral kingdom*, Vlaeberg: Fernwood Press.

Cox, G. 1999 Cobern Street burial ground: investigating the identity and life histories of the underclass of eighteenth century Cape Town, MA thesis, University of Cape Town.

Cox, G. and Sealy, J.C. 1997 Investigating identity and life histories: isotopic analysis and historical documentation of slave skeletons found on the Cape Town foreshore, South Africa, *International Journal of Historical Archaeology* 1: 207–24.

Crawford, J. 1967 The Monk's Kop Ossuary, *Journal of African History* 8: 373–82.

Cronin, M. 1982 Radiocarbon dates for the Early Iron Age in Transkei, *South African Journal of Science* 78: 38–9.

Cruz-Uribe, K. and Klein, R.G. 1983 Faunal remains from some Middle and Late Stone Age archaeological sites in South West Africa, *Journal of the South West African Scientific Society* 36/37: 91–114.

1994 Chew marks and cut marks on animal bones from Kasteelberg B and Dune Field Midden Later Stone Age sites, Western Cape Province, South Africa, *Journal of Archaeological Science* 21: 35–49.

Cruz-Uribe, K. and Schrire, C. 1991 Analysis of faunal remains from Oudepost 1, an early outpost of the Dutch East India Company, *South African Archaeological Bulletin* 46: 92–106.

Cunliffe, B. 1997 *The ancient Celts*, Oxford: Oxford University Press.

Dalby, D. 1975 The prehistorical implications of Guthrie's Comparative Bantu: problems of internal relationship, *Journal of African History* 16: 481–501.

Dale, L. 1870 Stone implements in South Africa, *Cape Monthly Magazine* 1: 236–9.

Dart, R.A. 1925 *Australopithecus africanus*: the man-ape of South Africa, *Nature* 115: 195–9.

1957 The osteodontokeratic culture of *Australopithecus africanus*, *Memoirs of the Transvaal Museum* 10: 1–105.

Darwin, C. 1871 *The descent of man, and selection in relation to sex*, London: John Murray.

Davenport, T.R.H. and Saunders, C. 2000 *South Africa: a modern history*, London: Macmillan.

Davies, O. 1971 Excavations at Blackburn, *South African Archaeological Bulletin* 26: 165–78.

1974 Excavations at the walled early Iron Age site in Moor Park near Estcourt, *Annals of the Natal Museum* 22: 289–323.

1975 Excavations at Shongweni South Cave, *Annals of the Natal Museum* 22: 627–62.

Davison, C.C. and Clark, J.D. 1976 Transvaal heirloom beads and Rhodesian archaeological sites, *African Studies* 35: 123–37.

Davison, P. 1988 The social use of domestic space in a Mpondo homestead, *South African Archaeological Bulletin* 43: 100–8.

de Heinzelin, J., Clark, J.D., White, T., Hart, W., Renne, P., WoldeGabriel, G., Beyene, Y. and Vrba, E. 1999 Environment and behaviour of 2.5-million-year-old Bouri hominids, *Science* 284: 625–9.

de Maret, P. 1986 The Ngovo Group: an industry with polished stone tools and pottery in Lower Zaire, *African Archaeological Review* 4: 103–33.

De Villiers, H. 1970 Die Skelettreste der Ziwa-kultur und die Frage des frühesten Auftretens von Negriden in Südafrika, *Homo* 21 (1): 17–28.

de Vos, A. 1975 *Africa, the devastated continent?*, The Hague: W. Junk.

de Wet-Bronner, E. 1995a The faunal remains from four Late Iron Age sites in the Soutpansberg region: Part II: Tshitheme and Dzata, *Southern African Field Archaeology* 4: 18–29.

1995b The faunal remains from four Late Iron Age sites in the Soutpansberg region: Part III: Tshirululuni, *Southern African Field Archaeology* 4: 109–19.

Deacon, H.J. 1966 Dating of the Nahoon footprints, *South African Journal of Science* 62: 111–13.

1970 The Acheulian occupation at Amanzi Springs, Uitenhage District, Cape Province, *Annals of the Cape Provincial Museums* 8: 89–189.

1972 A review of the post-Pleistocene in South Africa, *South African Archaeological Society Goodwin Series* 1: 26–45.

1975 Demography, subsistence and culture during the Acheulean in southern Africa, in K.W. Butzer and G.Ll. Isaac (eds.), *After the australopithecines*, The Hague: Mouton, pp. 543–69.

1976 *Where hunters gathered: a study of Holocene Stone Age people in the Eastern Cape*, Claremont: South African Archaeological Society.

1979 Excavations at Boomplaas Cave: a sequence through the Upper Pleistocene and Holocene in South Africa, *World Archaeology* 10: 241–57.

1983 The peopling of the Fynbos region, in H.J. Deacon *et al.* (eds.), 183–204.

1985 Review of: L.R. Binford, Faunal remains from Klasies River Mouth, *South African Archaeological Bulletin* 40: 59–60.

1989 Late Pleistocene palaeoecology and archaeology in the southern Cape, in P.A. Mellars and C.B. Stringer (eds.), pp. 547–64.

1993 Planting an idea: an archaeology of Stone Age gatherers in South Africa, *South African Archaeological Bulletin* 48: 86–93.

1995 Two late Pleistocene–Holocene archaeological depositories from the southern Cape, South Africa, *South African Archaeological Bulletin* 50: 121–31.

Deacon, H.J. and Brooker, M. 1976 The Holocene and Upper Pleistocene sequence in the southern Cape, *Annals of the South African Museum* 71: 203–14.

Deacon, H.J. and Deacon, J. 1980 The hafting, function and distribution of small convex scrapers with an example from Boomplaas Cave, *South African Archaeological Bulletin* 35: 31–7.

1999 *Human beginnings in South Africa*, Cape Town: David Philip.

Deacon, H.J., Deacon, J. and Brooker, M. 1976 Four painted stones from Boomplaas Cave, Oudtshoorn District, *South African Archaeological Bulletin* 31: 141–5.

Deacon, H.J., Deacon, J., Brooker, M. and Wilson, M.L. 1978 The evidence for herding at Boomplaas Cave in the southern Cape, South Africa, *South African Archaeological Bulletin* 33: 39–65.

Deacon, H.J., Deacon, J., Scholtz, A., Thackeray, J.F., Brink, J.S. and Vogel, J.C. 1984 Correlation of palaeoenvironmental data from the Late Pleistocene and Holocene deposits at Boomplaas Cave, southern Cape, in J.C. Vogel (ed.), *Late Cainozoic palaeoclimates of the Southern Hemisphere*, Rotterdam: Balkema, pp. 339–52.

Deacon, H.J. and Geleijnse, V.B. 1988 The stratigraphy and sedimentology of the main site sequence, Klasies River, South Africa, *South African Archaeological Bulletin* 43: 5–14.

Deacon, H.J., Hendey, Q.B. and Lambrechts, J.N. (eds.) 1983a *Fynbos palaeoecology: a preliminary synthesis*, Pretoria: Council for Scientific and Industrial Research.

Deacon, H.J., Scholtz, A. and Daitz, D. 1983b Fossil charcoals as a source of palaeoecological information in the fynbos region, in H.J. Deacon *et al.* (eds.), pp. 174–82.

Deacon, H.J. and Schuurman, R. 1992 The origins of modern people: the evidence from Klasies River, in G. Bräuer and F.H. Smith (eds.), pp. 121–9.

Deacon, H.J., Talma, A.S. and Vogel, J.C. 1988 Biological and cultural development of Pleistocene people in an Old World southern subcontinent, in J.R. Prescott (ed.), *Early man in the southern hemisphere*, Adelaide: University of Adelaide.

Deacon, H.J. and Thackeray, J.F. 1984 Late Pleistocene environmental changes and implications for the archaeological record in southern Africa, in J.C. Vogel (ed.), *Late Cainozoic palaeoclimates of the Southern Hemisphere*, Rotterdam: Balkema, pp. 375–90.

Deacon, J. 1972 Wilton: an assessment after 50 years, *South African Archaeological Bulletin* 27: 10–45.

1974 Patterning in the radiocarbon dates for the Wilton/Smithfield complex in southern Africa, *South African Archaeological Bulletin* 29: 3–18.

1984a *The Later Stone Age of southernmost Africa*, Oxford: British Archaeological Reports.

1984b Later Stone Age people and their descendants in southern Africa, in R.G. Klein (ed.), pp. 221–328.

1986 'My place is the Bitterputs': the home territory of Bleek and Lloyd's /Xam San informants, *African Studies* 45: 135–56.

1988 The power of a place in understanding southern San rock engravings, *World Archaeology* 20: 129–40.

1990a Weaving the fabric of Stone Age research in southern Africa, in P.T. Robertshaw (ed.), *A history of African archaeology*, London: James Currey, pp. 39–58.

1990b Changes in the archaeological record in South Africa at 18,000 BP, in C.S. Gamble and O. Soffer (eds.), pp. 170–88.

1991 Editorial, *South African Archaeological Bulletin* 46: 1.

1992 *Arrows as agents of belief amongst the /Xam Bushmen*, Cape Town: South African Museum.

1994 Rock engravings and the folklore of Bleek and Lloyd's /Xam San informants, in T.A. Dowson and J.D. Lewis-Williams (eds.), pp. 237–56.

1995 An unsolved mystery at the Howieson's Poort name site, *South African Archaeological Bulletin* 50: 110–20.

1996a The /Xam informants, in J. Deacon and T.A. Dowson (eds.), pp. 11–39.

1996b Archaeology of the Flat and Grass Bushmen, in J. Deacon and T.A. Dowson (eds.), pp. 245–70.

1996c Cultural resources management in the new South Africa, in G. Pwiti and R. Soper (eds.), pp. 839–48.

1997 'My heart stands in the hill': rock engravings in the Northern Cape, *Kronos* 24: 18–29.

Deacon, J. and Brett, M. 1993 Peeling away the past: the display of excavations at Nelson Bay Cave, *South African Archaeological Bulletin* 48: 98–104.

Deacon, J. and Dowson, T.A. (eds.) 1996 *Voices from the past: /Xam Bushmen and the Bleek and Lloyd collection*, Johannesburg: Witwatersrand University Press.

Deacon, J. and Lancaster, I.N. 1988 *Late Quaternary palaeoenvironments of southern Africa*, Oxford: Clarendon Press.

Deetz, J. 1977 *In small things forgotten: the archaeology of early American life*, New York: Doubleday.

Delius, P. 1983 *The land belongs to us: the Pedi polity, the Boers and the British in the nineteenth century Transvaal*, Johannesburg: Ravan Press.

Delson, E. 1987 Evolution and paleobiology of robust *Australopithecus*, *Nature* 327: 654–5.

Denbow, J.R. 1981 Broadhurst – a 14th century expression of the Early Iron Age in south-eastern Botswana, *South African Archaeological Bulletin* 36: 66–74.

1984 Cows and kings: a spatial and economic analysis of a hierarchical Early Iron Age settlement system in eastern Botswana, in M. Hall *et al.* (eds.), pp. 24–39.

1986 A new look at the later prehistory of the Kalahari, *Journal of African History* 27: 3–28.

1990 Congo to Kalahari: data and hypotheses about the political economy of the western stream of the Early Iron Age, *African Archaeological Review* 8: 139–75.

1999 Material culture and the dialectics of identity in the Kalahari: AD 700–1700, in S.K. McIntosh (ed.), *Beyond chiefdoms: pathways to complexity in Africa*, Cambridge: Cambridge University Press, pp. 110–23.

Denbow, J.R. and Wilmsen, E.N. 1986 Advent and the course of pastoralism in the Kalahari, *Science* 234: 1509–15.

Dennell, R. 1997 The world's oldest spears, *Nature* 385: 787–8.

Denninger, E. 1971 The use of paper chromatography to determine the age of albuminous binders and its application to rock paintings, *South African Journal of Science Special Publication* 2: 80–4.

Derricourt, R.M. 1977 *Prehistoric man in the Ciskei and Transkei*, Cape Town: C. Struik.

Dewey, W.J. 1991 Pleasing the ancestors: the traditional art of the Shona people of Zimbabwe, PhD thesis, Indiana University.

Diamond, J. 1997 *Guns, germs and steel*, London: Jonathan Cape.

Dickinson, R.W. 1975 The archaeology of the Sofala coast, *South African Archaeological Bulletin* 30: 84–105.

Dobkin de Rios, M. 1986 Enigma of drug-induced altered states of consciousness among the !Kung Bushmen of the Kalahari Desert, *Journal of Ethnopharmacology* 15: 297–304.

Döckel, W. 1998 Re-investigation of the Matjes River Rock Shelter, MA thesis, University of Stellenbosch.

Dos Santos, J. and Ervedosa, C.M.N. 1970 A estacao arqueologica de Benfica (Luanda-Angola), *Ciencias Biologicas (Luanda)* 1: 31–51.

Dowson, T.A. 1988a Shifting vegetation zones in the Holocene and Later Pleistocene: preliminary charcoal evidence from Jubilee Shelter, Magaliesberg, southern Transvaal, *Palaeoecology of Africa* 19: 233–9.

1988b Revelations of religious reality: the individual in San rock art, *World Archaeology* 20: 116–28.

1992 *Rock engravings of southern Africa*, Johannesburg: Witwatersrand University Press.

1994 Reading art, writing history: rock art and social change in southern Africa, *World Archaeology* 25: 332–44.

1995 Hunter-gatherers, traders and slaves: The 'Mfecane' impact on Bushmen, their ritual and their art, in C. Hamilton (ed.), pp. 51–70.

1999 Rain in Bushman belief, politics and history: the rock-art of rain-making in the south-eastern mountains, southern Africa, in C. Chippindale and P. Taçon (eds.), *Archaeology of rock art*, Cambridge: Cambridge University Press, pp. 73–89.

Dowson, T.A., Blundell, G. and Hall, S.L. 1992 Finger paintings in the Harts River valley, Northern Cape Province, South Africa, *Southern African Field Archaeology* 1: 27–32.

Dowson, T.A. and Lewis-Williams, J.D. (eds.) 1994 *Contested images: diversity in southern African rock art research*, Johannesburg: Witwatersrand University Press.

Drennan, M.R. 1953 The Saldanha Skull and its associations, *Nature* 172: 791.

Dreyer, J.J.B. 1992a The Iron Age archaeology of Doornpoort, Winburg, Orange Free State, *Navorsinge van die Nasionale Museum, Bloemfontein* 8: 261–390.

1992b A report on the archaeology of the QwaQwa Museum site, *Southern African Field Archaeology* 1: 78–87.

1996 Thaba-Bosiu, mountain fortress of Lesotho, in J.J.B. Dreyer *et al.* (eds.), pp. 37–46.

1999 Tlokwa history: report on an archaeological survey of stone-walled sites in the north-eastern Free State, *Southern African Field Archaeology* 8: 46–55.

Dreyer, J., Brink, J.S., Henderson, Z.L. and Ouzman, S. (eds.) 1996 *Guide to archaeological sites in the Free State and Lesotho*, Bloemfontein: National Museum.

Duarte, R.T. 1976 Three iron age sites in Massangir area, Gaza Province, Moçambique and their importance in the southern Moçambique Bantu settlement, in M.L.T. Duarte, T. Cruz e Silva, J.C. Semma Martinez, J.M.M. Morais and R.T. Duarte (eds.), *Iron Age research in Moçambique: collected preliminary reports*, Maputo: Mozambique Institute for Scientific Investigation, pp. 1–29.

1993 *Northern Mozambique in the Swahili world: an archaeological perspective*, Uppsala: Societas Archaeologica Upsaliensis.

Duarte, R.T. and Meneses, M.P. 1996 The archaeology of Mozambique Island, in G. Pwiti and R. Soper (eds.), 555–9.

Dunn, E.J. 1930 *The Bushman*, London: Griffin.

Dunwiddie, P.W. and LaMarche, V.C. 1980 A climatically-responsive tree-ring record from *Widdringtonia cedarbergensis*, Cape Province, South Africa, *Nature* 286: 796–7.

Earthy, E. 1933 *Valenge women: the social and economic life of the Valenge women of Portuguese East Africa*, Oxford: Oxford University Press.

Eastwood, E.B. and Blundell, G. 1999 Re-discovering the rock art of the Limpopo–Shashi confluence area, southern Africa, *Southern African Field Archaeology* 8: 17–27.

Eastwood, E. and Fish, W. 1996 Sheep in the rock paintings of the Soutpansberg and Limpopo River valley, *Southern African Field Archaeology* 5: 59–69.

Eggert, M.K.H. 1994/95 Pots, farming and analogy: early ceramics in the equatorial rainforest, *Azania* 29/30: 332–8.

Ehret, C. 1973 Patterns of Bantu and Central Sudanic settlement in central and southern Africa (ca. 1000 B.C.–500 A.D.), *Transafrican Journal of History* 3: 1–71.

1982 The first spread of food production to southern Africa, in C. Ehret and M. Posnansky (ed.), *The archaeological and linguistic reconstruction of African History*, Berkeley: University of California Press, pp. 158–81.

1998 *An African classical age: eastern and southern Africa in world history, 1000 B.C. to A.D. 400*, Oxford: James Currey.

Eldredge, E.A. 1993 *A South African kingdom: the pursuit of security in nineteenth-century Lesotho*, Cambridge: Cambridge University Press.

1995 Sources of conflict in southern Africa *c.* 1800–1830, the Mfecane reconsidered, in C. Hamilton (ed.), pp. 123–61.

Eliade, M. 1964 *Shamanism: archaic techniques of ecstacy*, Princeton: Routledge and Kegan Paul.

Ellenberger, V. 1953 *La fin tragique des Bushmen*, Paris: Amiot Dumont.

Eloff, J.F. and Meyer, A. 1981 The Greefswald sites, in E.A. Voigt (ed.), pp. 7–22.

Elphick, R. 1985 *Khoikhoi and the founding of white South Africa*, Johannesburg: Ravan Press.

Elphick, R. and Giliomee, H. (eds.) 1989 *The shaping of South African society, 1652–1840*, Cape Town: Maskew Miller Longman.

Elphick, R. and Malherbe, V.C. 1989 The Khoisan to 1828, in R. Elphick and H. Giliomee (eds.), pp. 3–65.

Elphick, R. and Shell, R.C.-H. 1989 Intergroup relations: Khoikhoi, settlers, slaves and free blacks, in R. Elphick and H. Giliomee (eds.), pp. 184–239.

Engela, R. 1995 Space, material culture and meaning in the late Pleistocene and early Holocene at Rose Cottage Cave, MA thesis, University of the Witwatersrand.

Engelbrecht, J.A. 1936 *The Korana*, Cape Town: Maskew Miller.

Erlich, H., Bergström, T.F., Stoneking, M. and Gyllensten, U. 1995 HLA sequence polymorphism and the origin of modern humans, *Science* 274: 1552–4.

Esterhuysen, A.B. 1996 Palaeoenvironmental reconstruction from Pleistocene to present: an outline of charcoal from the eastern Free State and Lesotho, MA thesis, University of the Witwatersrand.

1999 Archaeology, time and space in the human and social sciences: curriculum 2005, *Perspectives in Education* 18: 83–9.

2000 The birth of educational archaeology in South Africa, *Antiquity* 74: 159–65.

Esterhuysen, A.B., Behrens, J. and Harper, P. 1994 Leliehoek Shelter: a Holocene sequence from the eastern Orange Free State, *South African Archaeological Bulletin* 49: 73–8.

Esterhuysen, A.B. and Mitchell, P.J. 1997 Palaeoenvironmental and archaeological implications of charcoal assemblages from Holocene sites in western Lesotho, southern Africa, *Palaeoecology of Africa* 24: 203–32.

Esterhuysen, A.B. and Smith, J. 1998 Evolution: 'the forbidden word'? *South African Archaeological Bulletin* 53: 135–7.

Estes, R.D. 1992 *The behavior guide to African mammals*, Berkeley: University of California Press.

Evans, U. 1994 Hollow Rock Shelter: a Middle Stone Age site in the Cederberg, *Southern African Field Archaeology* 3: 63–73.

Evers, T.M. 1975 Recent Iron Age research in the eastern Transvaal, South Africa, *South African Archaeological Bulletin* 30: 71–83.

1977 Plaston Early Iron Age site, White River district, eastern Transvaal, South Africa, *South African Archaeological Bulletin* 32: 170–8.

1980 Klingbeil Early Iron Age sites, Lydenburg, eastern Transvaal, South Africa, *South African Archaeological Bulletin* 35: 46–57.

1981 The Iron Age in eastern Transvaal, South Africa, in E.A. Voigt (ed.), pp. 64–109.

1982a Excavations at the Lydenburg Heads site, eastern Transvaal, South Africa, *South African Archaeological Bulletin* 37: 16–23.

1982b Two Later Iron Age sites on Mabete, Hans Merensky Nature Reserve, Letaba District, north-eastern Transvaal, *South African Archaeological Bulletin* 37: 63–7.

1983 Mr Evers replies, *South African Journal of Science* 79: 261–4.

1984 Sotho-Tswana and Moloko settlement patterns and the Bantu cattle pattern, in M. Hall *et al.* (eds.), pp. 236–47.

1988 The recognition of groups in the Iron Age of southern Africa, PhD thesis, University of the Witwatersrand.

Evers, T.M., Huffman, T.N. and Wadley, L. (eds.) 1988 *Guide to archaeological sites in the Transvaal*, Johannesburg: University of the Witwatersrand.

Evers, T.M. and van der Merwe, N.J. 1987 Iron Age ceramics from Phalaborwa, north-eastern Transvaal Lowveld, South Africa, *South African Archaeological Bulletin* 42: 87–106.

Fagan, B.M. 1969 Excavations at Ingombe Ilede, 1960–62, in B.M. Fagan, D.W. Phillipson and S.G. Daniels (eds.), *Iron Age cultures in Zambia*, vol. II, London: Chatto and Windus, pp. 55–161.

Fagan, B.M. and van Noten, F. 1971 *The hunter-gatherers of Gwisho*, Tervuren: Musée Royale de l'Afrique Centrale.

Feathers, J.K. 1996 Luminescence dating and modern human origins, *Evolutionary Anthropology* 5: 25–36.

Feathers, J.K. and Bush, D.A. 2000 Luminescence dating of Middle Stone Age deposits at Die Kelders, *Journal of Human Evolution* 38: 91–119.

Feely, J.M. 1987 *The early farmers of Transkei, southern Africa, before AD 1870*. Oxford: British Archaeological Reports.

Field, A. 1999 An analytic and comparative study of the Earlier Stone Age archaeology of the Sterkfontein Valley, MSc thesis, University of the Witwatersrand.

Fielden, G. 1905 The Stone Age in the Zambezi Valley and its relation in time, *Nature* 63: 77–8.

Fock, G.J. 1954 Stone balls in the Windhoek Museum, *South African Archaeological Bulletin* 9: 108–9.

1960 Another stone bowl from southern Africa, *South African Archaeological Bulletin* 15: 114.

1968 Rooidam: a sealed site of the First Intermediate, *South African Journal of Science* 64: 153–9.

1979 *Felsbilder in Südafrika I, Die Graiverungen auf Klipfontein, Kaapprovinz,* Cologne: Böhlau.

Foley, R.A. 1989 The ecology of speciation: comparative perspectives on the origins of modern humans, in P.A. Mellars and C.B. Stringer (eds.), pp. 298–320.

1991a How many species of hominid should there be?, *Journal of Human Evolution* 20: 413–29.

1991b Hominids, humans and hunter-gatherers: an evolutionary perspective, in T. Ingold, D. Riches and J. Woodburn (eds.), *Hunters and gatherers: history, evolution and social change*, Oxford: Berg, pp. 207–21.

1992 Evolutionary ecology of fossil hominids, in E.A. Smith and B. Winterhalder (eds.), *Evolutionary ecology and human behaviour*, Chicago: Aldine, pp. 131–64.

1994 Speciation, extinction and climate change in hominid evolution, *Journal of Human Evolution* 26: 275–89.

1995 *Humans before humanity: an evolutionary perspective*, Oxford: Blackwells.

Foley, R.A. and Lahr, M.M. 1997 Mode 3 technologies and the evolution of modern humans, *Cambridge Archaeological Journal* 7: 3–36.

Fouché, K. 1995 Two seventeenth century coffin burials at the Cape, *Southern African Field Archaeology* 4: 103–8.

Fouché, L. 1937 *Mapungubwe: ancient Bantu civilization on the Limpopo*, Cambridge: Cambridge University Press.

Fox, F.W. and Norwood Young, M.E. 1982 *Food from the veld*, Johannesburg: Delta Books.

Frankenstein, S. and Rowlands, M.J. 1978 The internal structure and regional context of Early Iron Age society in south-west Germany, *Bulletin of the Institute of Archaeology, London University*, 15: 73–112.

Frayer, D.W., Wolpoff, M.H., Thorne, A.S., Smith, F.H. and Pope, G.G. 1994 Getting it straight, *American Anthropologist* 96: 424–38.

Freeman-Grenville, G.P.S. 1962 *The East African coast: select documents from the first to the earlier nineteenth century*, Oxford: Clarendon Press.

Freundlich, J.C., Schwabedissen, H. and Wendt, W.E. 1980 Köln radiocarbon measurements II, *Radiocarbon* 22: 68–81.

Friede, H.M. 1977 Iron Age metalworking in the Magaliesberg area, *Journal of the South African Institute of Mining and Metallurgy*, 77: 224–32.

Friede, H.M. and Steel, R. 1981 Schietkraal, an iron-smelting site near Zeerust, *South African Archaeological Bulletin* 36: 88–91.

1985 Iron Age iron smelting furnaces of the western/central Transvaal – their structure, typology and affinities, *South African Archaeological Bulletin* 40: 45–9.

1986 Traditional smithing and forging of South African bloomery iron, *South African Archaeological Bulletin* 41: 81–6.

1988 Notes on an iron smelting pit furnace found at Bultfontein Iron Age site 41/85 (Central Transvaal) and on general features of pit furnaces, *South African Archaeological Bulletin* 43: 38–42.

Friedman, J. and Rowlands, M.J. 1978 Notes towards an epigenetic model of the evolution of 'civilization', in J. Friedman and M.J. Rowlands (eds.), *The evolution of social systems*, London: Duckworth, pp. 201–76.

Gabunia, L., Vekua, A., Lordkipanidze, D., Swisher, C.C., Ferring, R., Justus, A., Nioradze, M., Tvalchrelidze, M., Antón, S.C., Bosinski, G., Jöris, O., de Lumley, M.-A., Majsuradze, G. and Mouskhelishvili, A. 2000 Earliest Pleistocene hominid cranial remains from Dmanisi, Republic of Georgia: taxonomy, geological setting and age, *Science* 288: 1019–25.

Gamble, C.S. 1982 Interaction and alliance in palaeolithic society, *Man* 17: 92–107.

1986 *The Palaeolithic settlement of Europe*, Cambridge: Cambridge University Press.

1993 *Timewalkers: the prehistory of global colonization*, Stroud: Alan Sutton.

Gamble, C.S. and O. Soffer (eds.) 1990 *The World at 18 000 BP*, vol. II, *Low latitudes*, London: Unwin Hyman.

Gardner, G.A. 1963 *Mapungubwe*, Pretoria: J.L. van Schaik.

Garlake, P.S. 1967 Seventeenth century Portuguese earthworks in Rhodesia, *South African Archaeological Bulletin* 21: 157–70.

1968 Test excavations at Mapela Hill, near the Shashi River, Rhodesia, *Arnoldia* 3 (34): 1–29.

1970 Iron Age sites in the Urungwe District of Rhodesia, *South African Archaeological Bulletin* 25: 25–44.

1973a *Great Zimbabwe*, London: Thames and Hudson.

1973b Excavations at the Nhunguza and Ruanga Ruins in northern Mashonaland, *South African Archaeological Bulletin* 27: 107–43.

1976 An investigation of Manekweni, Mozambique, *Azania* 11: 25–47.

1978 Pastoralism and *zimbabwe*, *Journal of African History* 19: 479–94.

1982 *Great Zimbabwe: described and explained*, Harare: Zimbabwe Publishing House.

1990 Symbols of potency in the paintings of Zimbabwe, *South African Archaeological Bulletin* 45: 17–27.

1995 *The hunter's vision: the prehistoric art of Zimbabwe*, London: British Museum Press.

Gewald, J.-B. 1995 Untapped sources: slave exports from southern and central Namibia up to *c.* 1850, in C. Hamilton (ed.), 417–35.

Gibbons, A. 1995 The mystery of humanity's missing mutations. *Science* 267: 35–6.

Gibbs, H.A.R. 1962 *Travels of Ibn Battuta*, Cambridge: Cambridge University Press.

Gifford-Gonzalez, D. 2000 Animal disease challenges to the emergence of pastoralism in sub-Saharan Africa, *African Archaeological Review* 17: 95–139.

Goldstein, D.B., Ruiz Linares, A.R., Cavalli-Sforza, L.L. and Feldman, M.W. 1995 Genetic absolute dating based on microsatellites and the origin of modern humans, *Proceedings of the National Academy of Sciences (USA)* 92: 6723–7.

Gooch, W.D. 1881 The Stone Age of South Africa, *Journal of the Anthropological Institute* 11: 124–82.

Goodman, M. 1996 A personal account of the origins of a new paradigm, *Molecular Phylogenetic Evolution* 5: 269–85.

Goodwin, A.J.H. 1926 *A handbook to the collections of stone implements*, Cape Town: South African Museum.

1938 Archaeology of the Oakhurst Shelter, George, *Transactions of the Royal Society of South Africa* 25: 229–324.

1956 Metal working among the early Hottentots, *South African Archaeological Bulletin* 11: 46–51.

Goodwin, A.J.H. and van Riet Lowe, C. 1929 The Stone Age cultures of South Africa, *Annals of the South African Museum* 27: 1–289.

Gordon, R.J. 1984 The !Kung in the Kalahari exchange: an ethnohistorical perspective, in C. Schrire (ed.), *Past and present in hunter-gatherer studies*, Orlando: Academic Press, pp. 195–224.

Gowlett, J.A.J. 1990 Archaeological studies of human origins and early prehistory in Africa, in P.T. Robertshaw (ed.), pp. 13–38.

Grab, S. 2000 Periglacial features, in T.C. Partridge and R.R. Maud (eds.), pp. 207–16.

Grant, M.R. 1999 The sourcing of southern African tin artefacts, *Journal of Archaeological Science* 26: 1111–17.

Grant, M.R., Huffman, T.N. and Watterson, J.I.W. 1994 The role of copper smelting in the precolonial exploitation of the Rooiberg tin field, *South African Journal of Science* 90: 85–90.

Gribble, J. 1989 Verlorenvlei vernacular: a structuralist analysis of sandveld folk architecture, MA thesis, University of Cape Town.

Grine, F.E. 1981 Trophic level differences between 'gracile' and 'robust' australopithecines: a scanning electron microscope analysis of occlusal events, *South African Journal of Science* 77: 203–30.

1998 Additional human fossils from the Middle Stone Age of Die Kelders Cave 1, South Africa: 1995 excavation, *South African Journal of Science* 94: 229–35.

Grine, F.E., Henshilwood, C.S. and Sealy, J.C. 2000 Human remains from Blombos Cave, South Africa: (1997–1998 excavations), *Journal of Human Evolution* 38: 755–65.

Grine, F.E., Jungers, W.L., Tobias, P.V. and Pearson, O.M. 1995 Fossil *Homo* femur from Berg Aukas, northern Namibia, *American Journal of Physical Anthropology* 97: 151–85.

Grine, F.E. and Kay, R.F. 1988 Early hominid diets from quantitative image analysis of dental microwear, *Nature* 333: 765–8.

Grine, F.E. and Klein, R.G. 1985 Pleistocene and Holocene human remains from Equus Cave, South Africa, *Anthropology* 8: 55–98.

1993 Late Pleistocene human remains from the Sea Harvest site, Saldanha Bay, South Africa, *South African Journal of Science* 89: 145–52.

Grine, F.E., Klein, R.G. and Volman, T.P. 1991 Dating, archaeology and human fossils from the Middle Stone Age levels of Die Kelders, South Africa, *Journal of Human Evolution* 21: 363–95.

Grine, F.E. and Martin, L.B. 1988 Enamel thickness and development in *Australopithecus* and *Paranthropus*, in F.E. Grine (ed.), *Evolutionary history of the 'Robust' australopithecines*, New York: Aldine, pp. 223–43.

Groves, C. 1989 A regional approach to the problem of the origin of modern humans in Australasia, in P.A. Mellars and C.B. Stringer (eds.), pp. 274–85.

Grün, R., Beaumont, P.B. and Stringer, C.B. 1990a ESR dating evidence for early modern humans at Border Cave in South Africa, *Nature* 344: 537–9.

Grün, R., Brink, J.S., Spooner, N.A., Taylor, L., Stringer, C.B., Francicus, R.G. and Murray, A.S. 1996 Direct dating of the Florisbad hominid, *Nature* 382: 500–1.

Grün, R., Shackleton, N.J. and Deacon, H.J. 1990b Electron spin resonance dating of tooth enamel from Klasies River Mouth Cave, *Current Anthropology* 31: 427–32.

Grün, R. and Stringer, C.B. 1991 Electron spin resonance dating and the evolution of modern humans, *Archaeometry* 33: 153–99.

Guelke, L. 1989 Freehold farmers and frontier settlers, 1657–1780, in R. Elphick and H. Giliomee (eds.), pp. 66–108.

Guenther, M.G. 1991 Animals in Bushman thought, myth and art, in T. Ingold, D. Riches and J. Woodburn (eds.), *Hunters and gatherers: property, power and ideology*, Oxford: Berg, pp. 192–202.

1994 The relationship of Bushman art to ritual and folklore, in T.A. Dowson and J.D. Lewis-Williams (eds.), pp. 257–74.

1996 Diversity and flexibility: the case of the Bushmen of southern Africa, in S. Kent (ed.), pp. 65–86.

Guy, J. 1978 Production and exchange in the Zulu kingdom, *Mohlomi* 2: 96–106.

Haacke, W.D. 1992 The Kalahari expedition March 1908: the forgotten story of the final battle of the Nama War, *Botswana Notes and Records* 24: 1–28.

Haddon, A.C. 1905 Presidential Address, Section H, *Reports of the British Association for the Advancement of Science (South Africa)* 1905: 511–27.

Hahn, T. 1879 Felzeichnungen der Buschmänner, *Verhalen Berlin Geschichtes Anthropologie*: 307–8.

Hall, A. 1995 Opinions: provincialisation of measures for control of heritage resources, *Southern African Field Archaeology* 4: 65–7.

Hall, M. 1976 Dendroclimatology, rainfall and human adaptation in the later Iron Age of Natal and Zululand, *Annals of the Natal Museum* 22: 693–703.

1980a Enkwazini, an Iron Age site on the Zululand coast, *Annals of the Natal Museum* 24: 97–109.

1980b An iron-smelting site in the Hluhluwe Game Reserve, Zululand, *Annals of the Natal Museum* 24: 165–75.

1981 *Settlement patterns in the Iron Age of Zululand*, Oxford: British Archaeological Reports.

1983 Tribes, traditions and numbers: the American model in southern African Iron Age studies, *South African Archaeological Bulletin* 38: 51–61.

1984 The myth of the Zulu homestead: archaeology and ethnography, *Africa* 54: 65–79.

1986 The role of cattle in southern African agropastoral societies: more than bones alone can tell, *South African Archaeological Society Goodwin Series* 5: 83–7.

1987 *The changing past: farmers, kings and traders in southern Africa, 200–1860*, Cape Town: David Philip.

1988 At the frontier: some arguments against hunter-gathering and farming modes of production in southern Africa, in T. Ingold, D. Riches and I. Woodburn (eds.), *Hunters and gatherers: history, evolution and social change*, Oxford: Berg, pp. 137–47.

1990 'Hidden history': Iron Age archaeology in southern Africa, in P.T. Robertshaw (ed.), pp. 59–77.

1991 High and low in the townscapes of Dutch South America and South Africa: the dialectics of material culture, *Social Dynamics* 17: 41–75.

1993 The archaeology of colonial settlement in southern Africa *Annual Review of Anthropology* 22: 177–200.

1994 The secret lives of houses: women and gables in the eighteenth century Cape, *Social Dynamics* 20: 1–48.

1995 The Legend of the Lost City; or, the man with golden balls, *Journal of Southern African Studies* 21: 179–99.

1996 *Archaeology Africa*, Cape Town: David Philip.

1998 Guest editorial: South African archaeology and the World Archaeological Congress, *South African Archaeological Bulletin* 53: 1–2.

Hall, M., Avery, G., Avery, D.M., Wilson, M.L. and Humphreys, A.J.B. (eds.) 1984 *Frontiers: Southern African archaeology today*, Oxford: British Archaeological Reports.

Hall, M., Brink, Y. and Malan, A. 1988 Onrust 87/1: an early colonial farm complex in the Western Cape, *South African Archaeological Bulletin* 43: 91–9.

Hall, M., Halkett, D., Huigen van Beek, P. and Klose, J. 1990a 'A stone wall out of the earth that thundering cannon cannot destroy'? Bastion and moat at the Castle, Cape Town, *Social Dynamics* 16: 22–37.

Hall, M., Halkett, D., Klose, J. and Ritchie, G. 1990b The Barrack Street well: images of a Cape Town household in the nineteenth century, *South African Archaeological Bulletin* 45: 73–92.

Hall, M. and Mack, K. 1983 The outline of an eighteenth century economic system in south-east Africa, *Annals of the South African Museum* 91: 163–94.

Hall, M. and Maggs, T.M.O'C. 1979 Nqabeni: a Later Iron Age site in Zululand, *South African Archaeological Society Goodwin Series* 3: 159–76.

Hall, M., Malan, A., Amann, S., Honeyman, L., Kiser, T. and Ritchie, G. 1993 The archaeology of Paradise, *South African Archaeological Society Goodwin Series* 7: 40–58.

Hall, M. and Vogel, J.C. 1980 Some recent radiocarbon dates from southern Africa, *Journal of African History* 21: 431–55.

Hall, R.N. 1905 *Great Zimbabwe*, London: Methuen.

Hall, S.L. 1986 Pastoral adaptations and forager reactions in the Eastern Cape, *South African Archaeological Society Goodwin Series* 5: 42–9.

1988 Settlement and subsistence developments during the Later Stone Age in the lower Fish River Basin, Eastern Cape, *Palaeoecology of Africa* 19: 221–32.

1990 Hunter-gatherer-fishers of the Fish River Basin: a contribution to the Holocene prehistory of the Eastern Cape, DPhil thesis, University of Stellenbosch.

1994 Images of interaction: rock art and sequence in the Eastern Cape, in T.A. Dowson and J.D. Lewis-Williams (eds.), pp. 61–82.

1995 Archaeological indicators for stress in the Western Transvaal Region between the seventeenth and nineteenth centuries, in C. Hamilton (ed.), pp. 307–21.

1997 Material culture and gender correlations: the view from Mabotse in the late nineteenth century, in L. Wadley (ed.), pp. 209–19.

1998 A consideration of gender relations in the Late Iron Age 'Sotho' sequence of the western highveld, South Africa, in S. Kent (ed.), pp. 235–58.

Hall, S.L. and Binneman, J.N.F. 1987 Later Stone Age burial variability in the Cape: a social interpretation, *South African Archaeological Bulletin* 42: 140–52.

Hamilton, C. (ed.) 1995a *The Mfecane aftermath: reconstructive debates in southern African history*, Johannesburg: Witwatersrand University Press.

1995b 'The character and objects of Chaka': a reconsideration of the making of Shaka as Mfecane motor, in C. Hamilton (ed.), pp. 183–211.

Hammer, M.F. 1995. A recent common ancestry for human Y chromosomes, *Nature* 378: 376–8.

Hammond-Tooke, W.D. 1993 *The roots of Black South Africa*, Johannesburg: Jonathan Ball.

1998 Selective borrowing? The possibility of San shamanistic influence on Southern Bantu divination and healing practices, *South African Archaeological Bulletin* 53: 9–15.

Hanisch, E. 1974 Copper working in the Messina District, *Journal of the South African Institute of Mining and Metallurgy* 74: 250–3.

1979 Excavations at Icon, northern Transvaal, *South African Archaeological Society Goodwin Series* 3: 72–9.

1981 Schroda: a Zhizo site in the northern Transvaal, in E.A. Voigt (ed.), pp. 37–53.

HARG (Historical Archaeology Research Group, University of Cape Town) 1993 Opinions: rubbish or treasure? *Southern African Field Archaeology* 2: 1–2.

Harpending, H.C., Sherry, S.T., Rogers, A.R. and Stoneking, M. 1993 The genetic structure of ancient human populations, *Current Anthropology* 34: 483–96.

Harper, P.T.N. 1997 The Middle Stone Age sequences at Rose Cottage Cave: a search for continuity and discontinuity, *South African Journal of Science* 93: 470–5.

Hart, T.J.G. 1987 Porterville survey, in J.E. Parkington and M. Hall (eds.), pp. 403–23.

Hay, R.L. 1987 Geology of the Laetoli area, in M.D. Leakey and J.M. Harris (eds.), *Laetoli: a Pliocene site in northern Tanzania*, Oxford: Oxford University Press, pp. 23–47.

Hay, R.L. and Leakey, M.D. 1982 The fossil footprints of Laetoli, *Scientific American* 246 (2): 50–7.

Hayden, B. 1989 From chopper to celt: the evolution of resharpening techniques, in R. Torrence (ed.), *Time, energy and stone tools*, Cambridge: Cambridge University Press, pp. 7–15.

1990 Nimrods, piscators, pluckers and planters: the emergence of food production, *Journal of Anthropological Archaeology* 9: 31–69.

Hedenström, A. 1995 Lifting the Taung child, *Nature* 378: 670.

Hedges, D.W. 1978 Trade and politics in southern Mozambique and Zululand in the eighteenth and early nineteenth centuries, PhD thesis, University of London.

Hedges, S.B., Kumar, S., Tamura, K. and Stoneking, M. 1992 Human origins and analysis of mitochondrial DNA sequences, *Science* 255: 737–9.

Helgren, D.M. and Brooks, A.S. 1983 Geoarchaeology at Gi, a Middle Stone Age and Later Stone Age site in the north-west Kalahari, *Journal of Archaeological Science* 10: 181–97.

Henderson, Z.L. 1992 The context of some Middle Stone Age hearths at Klasies River Shelter 1B: implications for understanding human behaviour, *Southern African Field Archaeology* 1: 14–26.

Henderson, Z L. and Binneman, J.N.F. 1997 Changes in the significance of a site: the Klasies Cave Complex in the Middle and Later Stone Ages, in C. Bonsall and C. Tolan-Smith (eds.), *The human use of caves*, Oxford: British Archaeological Reports, pp. 175–84.

Henshilwood, C. 1996 A revised chronology for pastoralism in southernmost Africa: new evidence of sheep at *c.* 2000 b.p. from Blombos Cave, South Africa, *Antiquity* 70: 945–9.

Henshilwood, C., Nilssen, P. and Parkington, J.E. 1994 Mussel drying and food storage in the late Holocene, south-west Cape, South Africa, *Journal of Field Archaeology* 21: 103–9.

Henshilwood, C. and Sealy, J.C. 1997 Bone artefacts from the Middle Stone Age at Blombos Cave, southern Cape, South Africa, *Current Anthropology* 38: 890–5.

Herbert, E.W. 1996 Metals and power at Great Zimbabwe, in G. Pwiti and R. Soper (eds.), pp. 641–7.

Hewitt, J. 1921 On several implements and ornaments from Strandloper sites in the Eastern Province, *South African Journal of Science* 18: 454–67.

Hewitt, R.L. 1986 *Structure, meaning and ritual in the narratives of the southern San*, Hamburg: Helmut Buske Verlag.

Higgs, E.S. (ed.) 1972 *Papers in economic prehistory*, Cambridge: Cambridge University Press.

Hill, A., Ward, S., Delno, A., Curtis, G. and Drake, R. 1992 Earliest *Homo* from Baringo, Kenya, *Nature* 355: 719–22.

Hodder, I. (ed.) 1978 *The spatial organization of culture*, London: Duckworth.

Hoff, A. 1997 The Water Snake of the Khoekhoen and /Xam, *South African Archaeological Bulletin* 52: 21–38.

1998 The Water Bull of the /Xam, *South African Archaeological Bulletin* 53: 109–24.

Holleman, J.F. 1952 *Shona customary law*, Oxford: Oxford University Press.

Holloway, R.L. 1983 Human brain evolution: a search for units, models and synthesis, *Canadian Journal of Anthropology* 3: 215–30.

Horai, M., Hayasaka, K., Kondo, R., Tsugane, K. and Takahata, N. 1995 Recent African origin of modern humans revealed by complete sequences of hominoid mitochondrial DNAs, *Proceedings of the National Academy of Sciences, USA* 92: 532–6.

Horowitz, A., Sampson, C.G., Scott, L. and Vogel, J.C. 1978 Analysis of the Voigtspost site, O.F.S., South Africa, *South African Archaeological Bulletin* 33: 152–9.

Horwitz, L., Maggs, T.M.O'C. and Ward, V. 1991 Two shell middens as indicators of shellfish exploitation patterns during the first millennium AD on the Natal North Coast, *Natal Museum Journal of Humanities* 3: 1–28.

How, M. W. 1962 *The Mountain Bushmen of Basutoland*, Pretoria: Van Schaik.

Howell, F.C., Washburn, S.L. and Ciochon, R.L. 1978 Relationships of *Australopithecus* and *Homo*, *Journal of Human Evolution* 7: 127–31.

Hromnik, C. 1981 *Indo-Africa: towards a new understanding of the history of sub-Saharan Africa*, Cape Town: Juta.

Hudelson, J.E. 1995 One hundred years among the San: a social history of San research, in A.J.G.M. Sanders (ed.), *Speaking for the Bushmen*, Gaborone: The Botswana Society, pp. 3–35.

Huffman, T.N. 1970 The Early Iron Age and the spread of the Bantu, *South African Archaeological Bulletin* 25: 3–21.

1971a Cloth from the Iron Age in Rhodesia, *Arnoldia* 5 (14): 1–19.

1971b Excavations at Leopard's Kopje main kraal: a preliminary report, *South African Archaeological Bulletin* 26: 85–9.

1972 The rise and fall of Zimbabwe, *Journal of African History* 13: 353–66.

1974 The Leopard's Kopje tradition, *Memoirs of the National Museum of Rhodesia* 6: 1–150.

1977 Zimbabwe: southern Africa's first town, *Rhodesian Prehistory* 7 (15): 9–14.

1978a The Iron Age of the Buhwa district, Rhodesia, *Occasional Papers of the National Museums and Monuments of Rhodesia, Series A, Human Sciences* 4: 81–100.

1978b The origins of Leopard's Kopje: an 11th century Difaquane, *Arnoldia* 8 (23): 1–23.

1979 Test excavations at NaBa and Lanlory, northern Mashonaland, *South African Archaeological Society Goodwin Series* 3: 14–46.

1980 Ceramics, classification and Iron Age entities, *African Studies* 39: 123–74.

1983 The trance hypothesis and the rock art of Zimbabwe, *South African Archaeological Society Goodwin Series* 4: 49–53.

1984a Leopard's kopje and the nature of the Iron Age in Bantu Africa, *Zimbabwea* 1: 28–35.

1984b Expressive space in the Zimbabwe culture, *Man* 19: 593–612.

1984c Where you are the girls gather to play: the Great Enclosure at Great Zimbabwe, in M. Hall *et al.* (eds.), pp. 252–65.

1986 Iron Age settlement patterns and the origins of class distinction in southern Africa, *Advances in World Archaeology* 5: 291–338.

1988 Ngwenani ya Themeli, in T.M. Evers *et al.* (eds.), pp. 52–5.

1989 Ceramics, settlements and late Iron Age migrations, *African Archaeological Review* 7: 155–82.

1990a Broederstroom and the origins of cattle-keeping in southern Africa, *African Studies* 49 (2): 1–12.

1990b The Waterberg research of Jan Aukema, *South African Archaeological Bulletin* 45: 117–19.

1993 Broederstroom and the Central Cattle Pattern, *South African Journal of Science* 89: 220–6.

1994 Toteng pottery and the origins of Bambata, *Southern African Field Archaeology* 3: 3–9.

1996a Archaeological evidence for climatic change during the last 2000 years in southern Africa, *Quaternary International* 33: 55–60.

1996b *Snakes and crocodiles: power and symbolism in ancient Zimbabwe*, Johannesburg: Witwatersrand University Press.

1997a Architecture and settlement patterns, in J.O. Vogel (ed.), *Encyclopedia of precolonial Africa*, Walnut Creek: Altamira Press, pp. 149–55.

1997b Zambezian states, in J.O. Vogel (ed.), *Encyclopedia of precolonial Africa*, Walnut Creek: Altamira Press, pp. 513–20.

1997c Reply to reviews of T.N. Huffman, Snakes and crocodiles: power and symbolism in ancient Zimbabwe, *South African Archaeological Bulletin* 52: 138–43.

1998 The antiquity of *lobola*, *South African Archaeological Bulletin* 53: 57–62.

2000 Mapungubwe and the origins of the Zimbabwe culture, *South African Archaeological Society Goodwin Series* 8: 14–29.

Huffman, T.N. and Hanisch, E.O.M. 1987 Settlement hierarchies in the northern Transvaal: Zimbabwe ruins and Venda history, *African Studies* 46: 79–116.

Huffman, T.N. and Herbert, R.K. 1994/95 New perspectives on Eastern Bantu, *Azania* 29/30: 27–36.

Huffman, T.N. and Steel, R. 1996 Salvage excavations at Planknek, Potgietersrus, Northern Province, *Southern African Field Archaeology* 5: 45–56.

Huffman, T.N., van der Merwe, N.J., Grant, M.R. and Kruger, G.S. 1995 Early copper mining at Thakadu, Botswana, *Journal of the South African Institute of Mining and Metallurgy* 2: 53–61.

Huffman, T.N. and Vogel, J.C. 1991 The chronology of Great Zimbabwe, *South African Archaeological Bulletin* 46: 61–70.

Humphreys, A.J.B. 1970a The role of raw material and the concept of the Fauresmith, *South African Archaeological Bulletin* 25: 139–44.

1970b The remains from Koffiefontein burials excavated by W. Fowler and preserved in the McGregor Museum, Kimberley, *South African Archaeological Bulletin* 25: 104–15.

1974 Comments on the occurrence of core-axe-like artifacts in the Northern Cape, *Annals of the Cape Provincial Museums* 9: 249–59.

1979 The Holocene sequence in the Northern Cape and its position in the prehistory of South Africa, PhD thesis, University of Cape Town.

1982 Cultural material from burials on the farm St Clair, Douglas area, Northern Cape, *South African Archaeological Bulletin* 37: 68–70.

1984. Sociable arrows, *The Digging Stick* 1: 2–3.

1987 Prehistoric seasonal mobility: what are we really achieving?, *South African Archaeological Bulletin* 42: 34–8.

1988 A prehistoric frontier in the Northern Cape and western Orange Free State: archaeological evidence in interaction and ideological change, *Kronos* 3: 3–13.

1991 On the distribution and dating of bifacial barbed and tanged arrowheads in the interior of South Africa, *South African Archaeological Bulletin* 46: 41–3.

Humphreys, A.J.B. and Maggs, T.M.O'C. 1970 Further graves and cultural material from the banks of the Riet River, *South African Archaeological Bulletin* 25: 116–26.

Humphreys, A.J.B. and Thackeray, A.I. 1983 *Ghaap and Gariep: Later Stone Age studies in the Northern Cape*, Cape Town, South African Archaeological Society.

Hylander, W.L. 1988 Implications of *in vivo* experiments for interpreting the functional significance of 'Robust' australopithecine jaws, in F.E. Grine (ed.), *Evolutionary history of the 'Robust' australopithecines*, New York: Aldine, pp. 55–83.

Ikeya, K. 1993 Goat-raising among the San in the central Kalahari, *African Study Monographs* 14 (1): 39–52.

Illenberger, W.K. and Verhagen, B. 1990 Environmental history and dating of coastal dunefields, *South African Journal of Science* 86: 311–14.

Imbrie, J. and Imbrie, K.P. 1979 *Ice Ages: solving the mystery*, London: Macmillan.

Inskeep, R.R. 1967 The Late Stone Age, in W.W. Bishop and J.D. Clark (eds.), pp. 557–82.

1978 *The peopling of southern Africa*, Cape Town: David Philip.

1986 A preliminary survey of burial practices in the Later Stone Age, from the Orange River to the Cape coast, in R. Singer and K. Lundy (eds.), *Variation, culture and evolution in African populations*, Johannesburg: Witwatersrand University Press, pp. 221–40.

1987 *Nelson Bay Cave, Cape Province, South Africa: the Holocene levels*, Oxford: British Archaeological Reports.

Inskeep, R.R. and Maggs, T.M.O'C. 1975 Unique art objects in the Iron Age of the Transvaal, *South African Archaeological Bulletin* 30: 114–38.

Irish, J.D. 1998 Ancestral dental traits in recent sub-Saharan Africans and the origins of modern humans, *Journal of Human Evolution* 34: 81–98.

Isaac, G.Ll. 1980 Comment on time and place, *South African Archaeological Bulletin* 35: 96–8.

1984 The archaeology of human origins: studies of the Lower Pleistocene in East Africa: 1971–1981, *Advances in World Archaeology* 3: 1–87.

Jacobson, L. 1984 Hunting versus gathering in an arid ecosystem: the evidence from the Namib Desert, in M. Hall *et al.* (eds.), pp. 75–79.

1987 The size variability of ostrich eggshell beads from central Namibia and its relevance as a stylistic and temporal marker, *South African Archaeological Bulletin* 42: 55–8.

1989 Some comments on the origins of the Khoikhoi, *The Digging Stick* 6 (3): 5–6.

1997 Lost Valley of the Hungorob, *South African Archaeological Bulletin* 52: 73–5.

Jacobson, L., Loubser, J.N.H., Peisach, M., Pineda, C.A. and van der Westhuizen, W. 1991 PIXE analysis of pre-European pottery from the northern Transvaal and its relevance to the distribution of ceramic styles and social interaction, *South African Archaeological Bulletin* 46: 19–24.

Jacobson, L. and Vogel, J.C. 1975 Recent radiocarbon dates from the Brandberg, *South African Journal of Science* 71: 349.

1977 Radiocarbon dates for a shell midden complex from Wortel, Walvis Bay, *Madoqua* 10 (1): 85–6.

Jensen, R. 2000 Cape Town's ignored past, *Cape Business News* May: 6–7.

Jerardino, A. 1995 The problem with density values in archaeological analysis: a case study from Tortoise Cave, Western Cape, South Africa, *South African Archaeological Bulletin* 50: 21–7.

1996 Changing social landscapes of the Western Cape coast of southern Africa over the last 4500 years, PhD thesis, University of Cape Town.

1998 Excavations at Pancho's Kitchen Midden, Western Cape coast, South Africa: further observations into the megamidden period, *South African Archaeological Bulletin* 53: 16–25.

1999 A first account of fat-tailed sheep in the rock paintings of the Western Cape coast, *South African Archaeological Bulletin* 54: 64–6.

Jerardino, A. and Parkington, J.E. 1993 New evidence for whales on archaeological sites in the south-western Cape, *South African Journal of Science* 89: 6–7.

Jerardino, A. and Swanepoel, N. 1999 Painted slabs from Steenbokfontein Cave: the oldest known parietal art in southern Africa, *Current Anthropology* 40: 542–8.

Jerardino, A. and Yates, R. 1996 Preliminary results from excavations at Steenbokfontein Cave: implications for past and future research, *South African Archaeological Bulletin* 51: 7–16.

1997 Excavations at Mike Taylor's Midden: a summary report and implications for a re-characterisation of megamiddens, *South African Archaeological Bulletin* 52: 43–51.

Jerardino, A., Yates. R., Morris, A.G. and Sealy, J.C. 1992 A dated human burial from the Namaqualand coast: observations on culture, biology and diet, *South African Archaeological Bulletin* 47: 75–81.

Johanson, D.C. and Edey, M.A. 1981 *Lucy: the beginnings of humankind*, New York: Simon and Schuster.

Johanson, D.C. and White, T.D. 1979 A systematic assessment of early African hominids, *Science* 202: 321–30.

Jolly, P. 1986 A first generation descendant of the Transkei San, *South African Archaeological Bulletin* 41: 6–9.

1995 Melikane and Upper Mangolong revisited: the possible effects on San art of symbiotic contact between south-eastern San and southern Sotho and Nguni communities, *South African Archaeological Bulletin* 50: 68–80.

1996a Symbiotic interactions between Black farmers and south-eastern San: implications for southern African rock art studies, ethnographic analogy and hunter-gatherer cultural identity, *Cultural Anthropology* 37: 277–306.

1996b Interaction between south-eastern San and southern Nguni and Sotho communities, *c.* 1400 – *c.* 1880, *South African Historical Journal* 35: 30–61.

Jolly, P. and Prins, F.E. 1994 M – a further assessment, *South African Archaeological Bulletin* 49: 16–23.

Jones, D., Brock, A. and McFadden, P.L. 1986 Palaeomagnetic results from the Kromdraai and Sterkfontein hominid sites, *South African Journal of Science* 82: 160–3.

Jones, N. 1920 On the implement-bearing deposits of Taungs and Tiger Kloof in the Cape Province of South Africa, *Journal of the Royal Anthropological Institute* 50: 412–24.

Jones, P. 1984 Mobility and migration in traditional African farming and Iron Age models, in M. Hall *et al.* (eds.), pp. 289–96.

Jones, P.R. 1979 Effects of raw materials on biface manufacture, *Science* 204: 835–6.

1980 Experimental butchery with modern stone tools and its relevance for Palaeolithic archaeology, *World Archaeology* 12: 153–75.

Jones, R. 1990 From Kakadu to Kutikina: the southern continent at 18,000 years ago, in C.S. Gamble and O. Soffer (eds.), pp. 264–95.

Jonsson, J. 1998 *Early plant economy in Zimbabwe*, Uppsala: Uppsala University Press.

Jordan, B. 1999 Row erupts as Khoisan call for return of old bones, *Sunday Times* (South Africa) 17 January.

Jourdan, S.C., Schrire, C. and Miller, D. 1999 Petrography of locally produced pottery from the Dutch Colonial Cape of Good Hope, South Africa, *Journal of Archaeological Science* 26: 1327–38.

Kannemeyer, D.R. 1890 Stone implements: with a description of Bushman stone implements and relics: their names, uses, modes of manufacture and occurrence, *Cape Illustrated Magazine* 1: 120–30.

Kaplan, J. 1987 Settlement and subsistence at Renbaan Cave, in J.E. Parkington and M. Hall (eds.), pp. 350–76.

1990 The Umhlatuzana Rock Shelter sequence: 100 000 years of Stone Age history, *Natal Museum Journal of Humanities* 2: 1–94.

Katz, R. 1982 *Boiling energy: community healing among the Kalahari !Kung*, Cambridge, MA: Harvard University Press.

Keeley, L.H. and Toth, N. 1981 Microwear polishes on early stone tools from Koobi Fora, Kenya, *Nature* 293: 464–5.

Keller, C.M. 1973 Montagu Cave in prehistory, *University of California Anthropological Records* 28: 1–150.

Kelly, R.L. 1995 *The foraging spectrum: diversity in hunter-gatherer lifeways*, Washington: Smithsonian Institution.

Kent, S. 1992 The current forager controversy: real versus ideal views of hunter-gatherers, *Man* 27: 45–70.

(ed.) 1996 *Cultural diversity among twentieth century foragers: an African perspective*, Cambridge: Cambridge University Press.

(ed.) 1998 *Gender in African prehistory*, Walnut Creek: Altamira Press.

Keyser, A., Menter, C.G., Moggi-Cecchi, J., Pickering, T.R. and Berger, L.R. 2000 Drimolen: a new hominid-bearing site in Gauteng, South Africa, *South African Journal of Science* 96: 193–7.

Killick, D. 1991 A tin *lerale* from the Soutpansberg, northern Transvaal, South Africa, *South African Archaeological Bulletin* 46: 137–41.

Kimbel, W.H., Walter, R.C., Johanson, D.C., Aronson, J.L., Assefa, Z., Eck, G.G., Hovers, E., Marean, C.W., Bobe-Quinteros, R., Rak, Y., Reed, K.E., Vondra, C., Yemane, T., York, D., Chen, Y., Evensen, N.M. and Smith, P.E. 1996 Late Pliocene *Homo* and Oldowan tools from the Hadar Formation (Kada Hadar Member), Ethiopia, *Journal of Human Evolution* 31: 549–61.

Kinahan, J. 1986 Settlement patterns and regional exchange: evidence from recent Iron Age sites on the Kavango River, north-eastern Namibia, *Cimbebasia (B)* 3: 109–16.

1991 *Pastoral nomads of the central Namib Desert: the people history forgot*, Windhoek: New Namibia Books.

1994/95 A new archaeological perspective on nomadic pastoralist expansion in south-western Africa, *Azania* 24/25: 211–26.

1995 Much ado about herding at Geduld: a response to Smith and Jacobson, *South African Archaeological Bulletin* 50: 176–7.

1996a Alternative views on the acquisition of livestock by hunter-gatherers in southern Africa: a rejoinder to Smith, Yates and Jacobson, *South African Archaeological Bulletin* 51: 106–8.

1996b The archaeology of social rank among eighteenth-century nomadic pastoralists in southern Namibia, *African Archaeological Review* 13: 225–46.

1999 Towards an archaeology of mimesis and rain-making in Namibian rock art, in P.J. Ucko and R. Layton (eds.), *The archaeology and anthropology of landscape*, London: Routledge, pp. 336–57.

2000 Traumland Südwest: two moments in the history of German archaeological enquiry in Namibia, in H. Härke (ed.), *Archaeology, ideology and society: the German experience*, Frankfurt am Main: Peter Lang, pp. 353–74.

Kinahan, J. and Kinahan, J.H.A. 1998 The archaeology and symbolic dimensions of a thirteenth century village in eastern Botswana, *Southern African Field Archaeology* 7: 63–71.

Kinahan, J. and Vogel, J.C. 1982 Recent copper working sites in the Khuiseb drainage, Namibia, *South African Archaeological Bulletin* 37: 44–5.

Kinahan, J.H.A. 1991 The historical archaeology of nineteenth century fisheries at Sandwich Harbour on the Namib coast, *Cimbebasia* 13: 1–27.

Kitagawa, H. and van der Plicht, J. 1998 Atmospheric radiocarbon calibration to 45,000 yr BP: late glacial fluctuations and cosmogenic isotope production, *Science* 279: 1187–90.

Kiyaga-Mulindwa, D. 1993 The Iron Age peoples of east-central Botswana, in T. Shaw, P.J.J. Sinclair, B.W. Andah and A. Okpoko (eds.), *The archaeology of Africa: foods, metals and towns*, London: Routledge, pp. 386–90.

Klapwijk, M. 1974 A preliminary report on pottery from the north-eastern Transvaal, South Africa, *South African Archaeological Bulletin* 29: 19–23.

Klapwijk, M. and Evers, T. M. 1987 A twelfth century Eiland facies site in the north-eastern Transvaal, *South African Archaeological Bulletin* 42: 39–44.

Klapwijk, M. and Huffman, T.N. 1996 Excavations at Silver Leaves: a final report, *South African Archaeological Bulletin* 51: 84–93.

Klatzow, S. 1994 Roosfontein: a contact site in the eastern Orange Free State, *South African Archaeological Bulletin* 49: 9–15.

Klein, R.G. 1972 The Late Quaternary mammalian fauna of Nelson Bay Cave (Cape Province, South Africa): its implications for megafaunal extinctions and environmental and cultural change, *Quaternary Research* 2: 135–42.

1973 Geological antiquity of Rhodesian man, *Nature* 244: 311–12.

1974 Environment and subsistence of prehistoric man in the southern Cape Province, South Africa, *World Archaeology* 5: 249–84.

1975 Middle Stone Age man–animal relationships in southern Africa: evidence from Die Kelders and Klasies River Mouth, *Science* 190: 265–7.

1976 The mammalian fauna of the Klasies River Mouth site, southern Cape Province, South Africa, *South African Archaeological Bulletin* 31: 75–99.

1977 The mammalian fauna from the Middle and Later Stone Age (Later Pleistocene) levels at Border Cave, Natal Province, South Africa, *South African Archaeological Bulletin* 32: 14–28.

1978a A preliminary report on the larger mammals from Boomplaas Stone Age cave site, Cango Valley, Oudtshoorn District, South Africa, *South African Archaeological Bulletin* 33: 66–75.

1978b The fauna and overall interpretation of the 'Cutting 10' Acheulean site at Elandsfontein (Hopefield), south-western Cape Province, South Africa, *Quaternary Research* 10: 69–83.

1978c Stone Age predation on large African bovids, *Journal of Archaeological Science* 5: 195–217.

1980 Environmental and ecological implications of large mammals from Upper Pleistocene and Holocene sites in southern Africa, *Annals of the South African Museum* 81: 223–83.

1981 Stone Age predation on small African bovids, *South African Archaeological Bulletin* 36: 55–65.

(ed.) 1984a *Southern African prehistory and palaeoenvironments*, Rotterdam: Balkema.

1984b The large mammals of southern Africa: Late Pliocene to Recent, in R.G. Klein (ed.), pp. 107–46.

1984c Later Stone Age faunal samples from Heuningneskrans Shelter, Transvaal, and Leopard's Hill Cave, Zambia, *South African Archaeological Bulletin* 39: 109–16.

1984d Mammalian extinctions and Stone Age people in Africa, in P.S. Martin and R.G. Klein (eds.), *Quaternary extinctions: a prehistoric revolution*, Tuscon: Arizona University Press, pp. 553–73.

1986a Carnivore size and Quaternary climatic change in southern Africa, *Quaternary Research* 26: 153–70.

1986b The prehistory of Stone Age herders in the Cape Province of South Africa, *South African Archaeological Society Goodwin Series* 5: 5–12.

1988 The archaeological significance of animal bones from Acheulean sites in southern Africa, *African Archaeological Review* 6: 3–26.

1989 Why does skeletal part representation differ between smaller and larger bovids at Klasies River Mouth and other archaeological sites?, *Journal of Archaeological Science* 16: 363–81.

1991 Size variations in the Cape dune molerat (*Bathyergus suillus*) and late Quaternary climatic change in the south-western Cape Province, South Africa, *Quaternary Research* 36: 243–56.

1995 Anatomy, behavior and modern human origins, *Journal of World Prehistory* 9: 167–98.

1999 *The human career: human biological and cultural origins*, Chicago: University of Chicago Press.

Klein, R.G., Avery, G., Cruz-Uribe, K., Halkett, D., Hart, T., Milo, R.G. and Volman, T.P. 1999 Duinefontein 2: an Acheulean site in the Western Cape Province of South Africa, *Journal of Human Evolution* 37: 153–90.

Klein, R.G. and Cruz-Uribe, K. 1983 Stone Age population numbers and average tortoise size at Byneskranskop Cave 1 and Die Kelders Cave 1, southern Cape Province, South Africa, *South African Archaeological Bulletin* 38: 26–30.

1987 Large mammal and tortoise bones from Elands Bay Cave and nearby sites, Western Cape Province, South Africa, in J.E. Parkington and M. Hall (eds.), pp. 132–63.

1989 Faunal evidence for prehistoric herder-forager activities at Kasteelberg, Western Cape Province, South Africa, *South African Archaeological Bulletin* 44: 82–97.

1996 Exploitation of large bovids and seals at Middle and Later Stone Age sites in South Africa, *Journal of Human Evolution* 31: 315–34.

Klimowicz, J. and Haynes, G. 1996 The Stone Age archaeology of Hwange National Park, Zimbabwe, in G. Pwiti and R. Soper (eds.), pp. 121–8.

Klose, J. 1992/93 Excavated oriental ceramics from the Cape of Good Hope: 1630–1830, *Transactions of the Oriental Ceramic Society* 57: 69–81.

1997 Analysis of ceramic assemblages from four Cape historical sites dating from the late seventeenth century to the mid-nineteenth century, MA thesis, University of Cape Town.

Klose, J. and Malan, A. 2000 The ceramic signature of the Cape in the nineteenth century, with particular reference to the Tennant Street site, Cape Town, *South African Archaeological Bulletin* 55: 49–59.

Knapp, B. (ed.) 1992 *Archaeology, annales and ethnohistory*, Cambridge: Cambridge University Press.

Knight, C.D., Power, C. and Watts, I. 1995 The human symbolic revolution: a Darwinian account, *Cambridge Archaeological Journal* 5: 75–114.

Korsman, S. and Plug, I. 1994 Two Later Stone Age sites on the farm Honingklip in the eastern Transvaal, *South African Archaeological Bulletin* 49: 24–32.

Krige, E.J. and Krige, J.D. 1943 *The realm of a rain queen*, Oxford: Oxford University Press.

Krings, M., Stone, A., Schmitz, R., Krainitzki, H., Stoneking, M. and Pääbo, S. 1997 Neandertal DNA sequences and the origin of modern humans, *Cell* 90: 19–30.

Kuman, K.A. 1994a The archaeology of Sterkfontein – past and present, *Journal of Human Evolution* 27: 471–95.

1994b The archaeology of Sterkfontein: preliminary findings on site formation and cultural change, *South African Journal of Science* 90: 215–19.

1996 The Oldowan Industry from Sterkfontein: raw materials and core forms, in G. Pwiti and R. Soper (eds.), pp. 139–46.

1998 The earliest South African industries, in M.D. Petraglia and R. Karisettar (eds.), *Early human behaviour in global context*, London: Routledge, pp. 151–86.

Kuman, K.A. and Clarke, R.J. 1986 Florisbad – new investigations at a Middle Stone Age site in South Africa, *Geoarchaeology* 1: 103–25.

2000 Stratigraphy, artefact industries and hominid associations for Sterkfontein Member 5, *Journal of Human Evolution* 38: 827–47.

Kuman, K., Field, A.S. and Thackeray, J.F. 1997 Discovery of new artefacts at Kromdraai, *South African Journal of Science* 93: 187–93.

Kuman, K., Inbar, M. and Clarke, R.J. 1999 Palaeoenvironments and cultural sequence of the Florisbad Middle Stone Age hominid site, South Africa, *Journal of Archaeological Science* 26: 1409–25.

Kuper, A. 1980 Symbolic dimensions of the southern Bantu homestead, *Africa* 1: 8–23.

Küsel, U.S. 1974 Extractive metallurgy in Iron Age South Africa, *Journal of the South African Institute of Mining and Metallurgy* 74: 246–9.

1979 'n Argeologiese studie van vroeë ystersmelting in Transvaal, MA thesis, University of Pretoria.

1992 A preliminary report on settlement layout and gold smelting at Thulamela, a Late Iron Age site in the Kruger National Park, *Koedoe* 35: 53–64.

Lahr, M. 1994 The multiregional model of modern human origins, *Journal of Human Evolution* 26: 33–56.

Lahr, M. and Foley, R. 1994 Multiple dispersals and modern human origins, *Evolutionary Anthropology* 3: 48–60.

Laidler, P.W. 1931 South African native ceramics: their characteristics and classification, *Transactions of the Royal Society of South Africa* 26: 93–172.

1934 The archaeological sequence in the Transkei and Ciskei, *South African Journal of Science* 31: 535–46.

1936 A Late Stone Age cave deposit in the Transkei, *South African Journal of Science* 33: 888–92.

Lancaster, I.N. 2000 Eolian deposits, in T.C. Partridge and R.R. Maud (eds.), pp. 73–87.

Lane, P. 1994/95 The use and abuse of ethnography in Iron Age studies of southern Africa, *Azania* 29/30: 51–64.

1996 Archaeological survey and excavation in south-east Botswana, 1992, *Nyame Akuma* 45: 11–23.

1998a Ethnoarchaeological research – past, present and future, in P. Lane *et al.* (eds.), pp. 177–205.

1998b Engendered spaces, bodily practices in the Iron Age of southern Africa, in S. Kent (ed.), pp. 179–204.

Lane, P., Reid, A. and Segobye, A.K. (eds.) 1998 *Ditswa Mmung: the archaeology of Botswana*, Gaborone: The Botswana Society.

Lanfranchi, R. and Clist, B. (eds.) 1991 *Aux origines de l'Afrique centrale*, Libreville: Centres Culturels Français d'Afrique Centrale.

Larsson, L. 1996 The Middle Stone Age of Zimbabwe: some aspects of former research and future aims, in G. Pwiti and R. Soper (eds.), pp. 201–6.

Leakey, M.G., Feibel, C.S., McDougall, I. and Walker, A.C. 1995 New four-million-year-old hominid species from Kanapoi and Allia Bay, Kenya, *Nature* 376: 565–71.

Lee, R.B. 1979 *The !Kung San: men, women and work in a foraging society*, Cambridge: Cambridge University Press.

Lee, R.B. and Guenther, M. 1991 Oxen or onions? The search for trade (and truth) in the Kalahari, *Current Anthropology* 32: 592–601.

Lee, R.B. and Hitchcock, R.K. 1998 African hunter-gatherers: history and the politics of ethnicity, in G. Connah (ed.), *Transformations in Africa: essays on Africa's later past*, Leicester: Leicester University Press, pp. 14–45.

Lee Thorp, J.A., Sealy, J.C. and Morris, A.G. 1993 Isotopic evidence for diets of prehistoric farmers in South Africa, in J.B. Lambert and G. Grupe (eds.), *Prehistoric human bone: archaeology at the molecular level*, Berlin: Springer Verlag, pp. 99–120.

Lee Thorp, J.A., Sealy, J.C. and van der Merwe, N.J. 1989 Stable carbon isotope ratio differences between bone collagen and bone apatite, and their relationship to diet, *Journal of Archaeological Science* 16: 585–99.

Lee Thorp, J.A. and Talma, A.S. 2000 Stable light isotopes and environments in the southern African Quaternary and Late Pliocene, in T.C. Partridge and R.R. Maud (eds.), pp. 236–51.

Lee Thorp, J.A., van der Merwe, N.J. and Brain, C.K. 1994 Diet of *Australopithecus robustus* at Swartkrans from stable carbon isotopic analysis, *Journal of Human Evolution* 27: 361–72.

Legassick, M. 1989 The Northern Frontier to *c.* 1840: the rise and decline of the Griqua people, in R. Elphick and H. Giliomee (eds.), pp. 358–420.

Lenssen-Erz, T. 1997 Gemeinschaft–Gleichhart–Mobilitaet. Felsbilder im Brandberg, Namibia, und ihre Bedeutung. Grundlagen einer textuellen Felsbilderarchaeologie. PhD thesis, University of Cologne.

Leslie, M. 1989 The Holocene sequence from Uniondale rock shelter in the Eastern Cape, *South African Archaeological Society Goodwin Series* 6: 17–32.

Lewis-Williams, J.D. 1972 The syntax and function of the Giant's Castle rock paintings, *South African Archaeological Bulletin* 27: 49–65.

1974 Rethinking the southern African rock paintings, *Origini* 8: 229–57.

1981a *Believing and seeing: symbolic meanings in southern San rock paintings*, Cambridge: Cambridge University Press.

1981b The thin red line: southern San notions and rock paintings of supernatural potency, *South African Archaeological Bulletin* 36: 5–13.

1982 The economic and social context of southern San rock art, *Current Anthropology* 23: 429–49.

1984 Ideological continuities in prehistoric southern Africa: the evidence of rock art, in C. Schrire (ed.), *Past and present in hunter-gatherer studies*, New York: Academic Press, pp. 225–52.

1985 Testing the trance explanation of southern African rock art: depictions of felines, *Bolletino del Centro Camuno di Studi Preistorici* 22: 47–62.

1986a The last testament of the southern San, *South African Archaeological Bulletin* 41: 10–11.

1986b Beyond style and portrait: a comparison of Tanzanian and southern African rock art, in R. Vossen and K. Keuthmann (eds.), *Contemporary studies on Khoisan 2*, Hamburg: Helmut Buske Verlag.

1987 A dream of eland: an unexplored component of San shamanism and rock art, *World Archaeology* 19: 165–77.

1990 Documentation, analysis and interpretation: dilemmas in rock art research, *South African Archaeological Bulletin* 45: 126–36.

1992 Ethnographic evidence relating to 'trance' and 'shamans' among Northern and Southern Bushmen, *South African Archaeological Bulletin* 47: 56–60.

1993 Southern African archaeology in the 1990s, *South African Archaeological Bulletin* 48: 45–50.

1995 Modelling the production and consumption of rock art, *South African Archaeological Bulletin* 50: 143–54.

1996 'A visit to the Lion's house': the structure, metaphors and sociopolitical significance of a nineteenth century Bushman myth, in J. Deacon and T.A. Dowson (eds.), pp. 122–41.

1998 *Quanto?*: the issue of many meanings in southern African San rock art research, *South African Archaeological Bulletin* 53: 86–97.

Lewis-Williams, J.D. and Biesele, M. 1978 Eland hunting rituals among northern and southern San groups: striking similarities, *Africa* 48: 117–34.

Lewis-Williams, J.D. and Dowson, T.A. 1988 The signs of all times: entoptic phenomena in Upper Palaeolithic art, *Current Anthropology* 29: 201–45.

1990 Through the veil: San rock paintings and the rock face, *South African Archaeological Bulletin* 45: 5–16.

1993 On vision and power in the Neolithic: evidence from the decorated monuments, *Current Anthropology* 34: 55–65.

1994 Aspects of rock art research: a critical retrospective, in T.A. Dowson and J.D. Lewis-Williams (eds.), pp. 201–21.

1999 *Images of power: understanding Bushman rock art*, Johannesburg: Southern Books.

Lewis-Williams, J.D. and Loubser, J.N.H. 1986 Deceptive appearances: a critique of southern African rock art studies, *Advances in World Archaeology* 5: 253–89.

Lewthwaite, J. 1986 The transition to food production: a Mediterranean perspective, in M. Zvelebil (ed.), *Hunters in transition: Mesolithic societies of*

Temperate Eurasia and the transition to farming, Cambridge: Cambridge University Press, pp. 53–66.

Liengme, C. 1987 Botanical remains from archaeological sites in the Western Cape, in J.E. Parkington and M. Hall (eds.), pp. 237–61.

Liesegang, G.J. 1974 Historic continuity and ceramic change: a note on the wares used by the Gaza Nguni in the nineteenth century, *South African Archaeological Bulletin* 29: 60–4.

Lim, I. 1992 A site-oriented approach to rock art: a study from Usandawe, PhD thesis, Brown University.

Lloyd, L.C. 1889 *A short account of further Bushman material collected, third report concerning Bushman researches, presented to both Houses of Parliament of the Cape of Good Hope.* London: David Nutt.

Loubser, J.N.H. 1985 Buffelshoek: an ethnoarchaeological consideration of a Late Iron Age settlement in the southern Transvaal, *South African Archaeological Bulletin* 40: 81–7.

1989 Archaeology and early Venda history, *South African Archaeological Society Goodwin Series* 6: 54–61.

1990 Oral traditions, archaeology and the history of Venda *Mitupo*, *African Studies* 49: 13–42.

1991a The ethnoarchaeology of Venda-speakers in South Africa, *Navorsinge van die Nasionale Museum (Bloemfontein)* 7: 146–464.

1991b The conservation of rock paintings in Australia and its applicability to South Africa, *Navorsinge van die Nasionale Museum (Bloemfontein)* 7: 111–43.

1993a A guide to the rock paintings of Tandjesberg, *Navorsinge van die Nasionale Museum (Bloemfontein)* 9: 345–84.

1993b Ndondonwane: the significance of features and finds from a ninth-century site on the lower Thukela River, Natal, *Natal Museum Journal of Humanities* 5: 109–51.

1994 Ndebele archaeology of the Pietersburg area, *Navorsinge van die Nasionale Museum (Bloemfontein)* 10: 61–147.

1998 Comment on D.N. Beach, Cognitive archaeology and imaginary history at Great Zimbabwe, *Current Anthropology* 30: 63–4.

Loubser, J.N.H. and Brink, J.S. 1992 Unusual paintings of wildebeest and a zebra-like animal from north-western Lesotho, *Southern African Field Archaeology* 1: 103–7.

Loubser, J.N.H. and Dowson, T.A. 1987 Tombo-la-ndou: the Venda perception of San rock art, *South African Archaeological Bulletin* 42: 51–5.

Loubser, J.N.H. and Laurens, G. 1994 Depictions of domestic ungulates and shields: hunter/gatherers and agro-pastoralists in the Caledon River Valley area, in T.A. Dowson and J.D. Lewis-Williams (eds.), pp. 83–118.

Loubser, J.N.H., Loubser, S. and Lipschitz, N. 1991 Digging for roots: material reminders of life at Bankfontein Collieries (Breyten), eastern Transvaal highveld, *The Digging Stick* 8 (1): 2–4.

Lowe, J.J. and Walker, M.J.C. 1994 *Reconstructing Quaternary environments*, London: Longman.

Loy, T.H. 1998 Organic residues on Oldowan stone tools from Sterkfontein Cave, South Africa, in M.D. Raath, H. Soodyall, D. Barkhan, K.L. Kuykendall and P.V. Tobias (eds.), *Abstracts of contributions to the Dual Congress of the International Association for the Study of Human Palaeontology and the*

International Association of Human Biologists, Johannesburg: University of the Witwatersrand, p. 74.

Macamo, S.L. 1996 The problems of conservation of archaeological sites in Mozambique, in G. Pwiti and R. Soper (eds.), pp. 813–16.

Macamo, S.L. and Duarte, R.T. 1996 Oral tradition and the Songo Ruins, in G. Pwiti and R.C. Soper (eds.), pp. 561–3.

McBrearty, S. 1992 Sangoan technology and habitat at Simbi, *Nyame Akuma* 38: 34–9.

McCall, D. F. 1970 *Wolf courts girl: the equivalence of hunting and mating in Bushman thought*, Ames: Ohio University Papers in International Studies, Africa Series 7.

MacCalman, H.R. 1962 A further stone bowl from South West Africa, *South African Archaeological Bulletin* 17: 237.

1965 Carbon 14 dates from South West Africa, *South African Archaeological Bulletin* 20: 215.

MacCalman, H.R. and Viereck, A. 1967 Peperkorrel: a factory site of Lupemban affinities from central South West Africa, *South African Archaeological Bulletin* 22: 41–50.

McFadden, P.L. and Brock, A. 1984 Magnetostratigraphy at Makapansgat, *South African Journal of Science* 80: 482–3.

McHenry, H.M. 1992 Body size and proportions in early hominids, *American Journal of Physical Anthropology* 87: 407–31.

McHenry, H.M. and Berger, L. 1996 Apelike body proportions in *Australopithecus africanus* and their implications for the origin of *Homo, American Journal of Physical Anthropology* 22 (supplement): 163–4.

MacIver, D.R. 1906 *Medieval Rhodesia,* London: Macmillan.

McKee, J.K. 1993 Faunal dating of the Taung hominid fossil deposit, *Journal of Human Evolution* 25: 363–76.

McKenzie, B. 1984 Utilization of the Transkeian landscape: an ecological interpretation, *Annals of the Natal Museum* 26: 165–72.

Macquarrie, J.W. (ed.) 1962 *The reminiscences of Sir Walter Stanford*, Cape Town: Van Riebeeck Society.

Maggs, T.M.O'C. 1967 A quantitative analysis of the rock art from a sample area in the Western Cape, *South African Journal of Science* 63: 100–4.

1971 Pastoral settlements along the Riet River, *South African Archaeological Bulletin* 26: 37–63.

1975 Iron Age patterns and Sotho history on the southern highveld, South Africa, *World Archaeology* 7: 318–32.

1976 *Iron Age communities of the southern highveld*, Pietermaritzburg: Natal Museum.

1980a Msuluzi Confluence: a seventh century Early Iron Age site on the Tugela River, *Annals of the Natal Museum* 24: 111–45.

1980b Mzonjani and the beginning of the Iron Age in Natal, *Annals of the Natal Museum* 24: 71–96.

1982a Mgoduyanuka: Terminal Iron Age settlement in the Natal grasslands, *Annals of the Natal Museum* 25: 85–113.

1982b Mabhija: pre-colonial industrial development in the Tugela Basin, *Annals of the Natal Museum* 25: 123–41.

1984a The Iron Age south of the Zambezi, in R.G. Klein (ed.), pp. 329–60.

1984b Ndondonwane: a preliminary report on an Early Iron Age site on the lower Tugela River, *Annals of the Natal Museum* 26: 71–94.

1984c Iron Age settlement and subsistence strategies in the Tugela River Basin, Natal, in M. Hall *et al.* (eds.), pp. 194–206.

1984d The Great Galleon *São João*: remains from a mid-sixteenth century wreck on the Natal South Coast, *Annals of the Natal Museum* 26: 173–86.

1991 Metalwork from Iron Age hoards as a record of metal production in the Natal region, *South African Archaeological Bulletin* 46: 131–6.

1992a Name calling in the Iron Age, *South African Archaeological Bulletin* 47: 131.

1992b 'My father's hammer never ceased its song day and night': the Zulu ferrous metalworking industry, *Natal Museum Journal of Humanities* 4: 65–87.

1993 Sliding doors at Mokgatle's, a nineteenth century Tswana town in the central Transvaal, *South African Archaeological Bulletin* 48: 32–6.

1994/95 The Early Iron Age in the extreme south: some patterns and problems, *Azania* 29/30: 171–8.

1995 Neglected rock art: the rock engravings of agriculturist communities in South Africa, *South African Archaeological Bulletin* 50: 132–42.

1998 Guest editorial: archaeology at South African universities: the future?, *South African Archaeological Bulletin* 53: 55–6.

Maggs, T.M.O'C. and Michael, M.A. 1976 Ntshekane: an Early Iron Age site in the Tugela Basin, Natal, *Annals of the Natal Museum* 22: 705–40.

Maggs, T.M.O'C., Oswald, D., Hall, M. and Rüther, T. 1986 Spatial parameters of Late Iron Age settlements in the upper Thukela Valley, *Annals of the Natal Museum* 27: 455–80.

Maggs, T.M.O'C. and Sealy, J.C. 1983 Elephants in boxes, *South African Archaeological Society Goodwin Series* 4: 44–8.

Maggs, T.M.O'C. and Speed, V. 1967 Bonteberg Shelter, *South African Archaeological Bulletin* 22: 80–93.

Maggs, T.M.O'C. and Ward, V. 1980 Driel Shelter: rescue at a Late Stone Age site on the Tugela River, *Annals of the Natal Museum* 24: 35–70.

1984 Early Iron Age sites in the Muden area of Natal, *Annals of the Natal Museum* 26: 105–40.

Maggs, T.M.O'C. and Whitelaw, G. 1991 A review of recent archaeological research on food producing communities in southern Africa, *Journal of African History* 21: 3–24.

Maguire, J.M. 1985 Recent geological, stratigraphic and palaeontological studies at Makapansgat Limeworks, in P.V. Tobias (ed.), *Hominid evolution: past and present*, New York: Alan Liss, pp. 151–64.

Maguire, J.M., Pemberton, D. and Collett, M.H. 1980 The Makapansgat Limeworks grey breccia: hominids, hyaenas, hystricids or hillwash?, *Palaeontologia Africana* 23: 75–98.

Mahachi, G. and Ndoro, W. 1997 The socio-political context of southern African Iron Age studies with special reference to Great Zimbabwe, in G. Pwiti (ed.), pp. 69–88.

Maingard, L.F. 1937 Notes on health and disease among the Bushmen of the southern Kalahari, *Bantu Studies* 11: 285–94.

Malan, A. 1990 The archaeology of probate inventories, *Social Dynamics* 16: 1–10.

1997 The material world of family and household: the Van Sitterts in eighteenth century Cape Town, 1748–1796, in L. Wadley (ed.), pp. 273–301.

1998/99 Chattels or colonists? 'Freeblack' women and their households, *Kronos* 25: 50–71.

Mallows, W. 1984 *The mystery of the Great Zimbabwe*, New York: Norton.

Malone, C. and Stoddart, S. 1999 Editorial, *Antiquity* 73: 1–12.

Manhire, A.H. 1987 *Later Stone Age settlement patterns in the sandveld of the south-western Cape Province*, Oxford: British Archaeological Reports.

1993 A report on the excavations at Faraoskop Rock Shelter in the Graafwater District of the south-western Cape, *Southern African Field Archaeology* 2: 3–23.

1998 The role of handprints in the rock art of the south-western Cape, *South African Archaeological Bulletin* 53: 98–108.

Manhire, A.H., Parkington, J.E., Mazel, A.D. and Maggs, T.M.O'C. 1986 Cattle, sheep and horses: a review of domestic animals in the rock art of southern Africa, *South African Archaeological Society Goodwin Series* 5: 22–30.

Manhire, A.H., Parkington, J.E. and Yates, R. 1985 Nets and fully recurved bows: rock paintings and hunting methods in the Western Cape, South Africa, *World Archaeology* 17: 161–74.

Mann, A. and Weiss, M. 1996 Hominoid phylogeny and taxonomy: a consideration of the molecular and fossil evidence in a historical perspective, *Molecular Phylogenetic Evolution* 5: 169–81.

Manson, A. 1995 Conflict in the western highveld/southern Kalahari c. 1750–1820, in C. Hamilton (ed.), pp. 351–61.

Markell, A.B. 1993 Building on the past: the architecture and archaeology of Vergelegen, *South African Archaeological Society Goodwin Series* 7: 71–83.

Markell, A.B., Hall, M and Schrire, C. 1995 The historical archaeology of Vergelegen, an early farmstead at the Cape of Good Hope, *Historical Archaeology* 29: 10–34.

Marker, M. and Evers, T.M. 1976 Iron Age settlement and soil erosion in the eastern Transvaal, South Africa, *South African Archaeological Bulletin* 31: 153–65.

Marshall, L. 1976 *The !Kung of Nyae-Nyae*, Cambridge, MA: Harvard University Press.

Martin, C. 1938 A rock shelter on Nyazongo Mountain, Penhalonga District, Southern Rhodesia, *Queen Victoria Memorial Library Occasional Paper* 1: 1–18.

Martin, P.S. and Klein, R.G. 1984 *Quaternary extinctions: a prehistoric revolution*, Tucson: University of Arizona Press.

Marzke, M.W. 1997 Precision grips, hand morphology and tools, *American Journal of Physical Anthropology* 102: 91–110.

Mason, R.J. 1962 *Prehistory of the Transvaal*, Johannesburg: Witwatersrand University Press.

1972 Locational trends of Transvaal Iron Age settlements, in D.L. Clarke (ed.), *Models in archaeology*, London: Methuen, pp. 871–85.

1975 Archaeology of the 1880–1881 Fort, Potchefstroom, *South African Military History Journal* 3: 132–7.

1981 Early Iron Age settlement at Broederstroom 24/73, Transvaal, South Africa, *South African Journal of Science* 77: 401–16.

1982 Prehistoric mining in South Africa and Iron Age copper mines in the Dwarsberg, Transvaal, *Journal of the South African Institute of Mining and Metallurgy* 82: 135–42.

1983 'Oori' or 'Moloko'? The origins of the Sotho-Tswana on the evidence of the Iron Age of the Transvaal, *South African Journal of Science* 79: 261.

1986 *Origins of the Black People of Johannesburg and the southern, western and central Transvaal AD 350–1880*, Johannesburg: University of the Witwatersrand Archaeological Research Unit Occasional Paper 16.

(ed.) 1988 *Kruger Cave*, Johannesburg: University of the Witwatersrand Archaeological Research Unit Occasional Paper 17.

Mason, R.J., Klapwijk, M., Welbourne, R.G., Sandelowsky, B.H. and Maggs, T.M.O'C. 1973 Early Iron Age settlement of southern Africa, *South African Journal of Science* 69: 324–6.

Matenga, E. 1993 The Budiriro burial excavations, Harare, May/June 1990, *Nyame Akuma* 39: 60–8.

1994 A report on a cairn burial at Nyakambiri Dam, Marondera, Zimbabwe, *Zimbabwean Prehistory* 21: 38–43.

Mauch, C. 1969 *The journals of Carl Mauch* (ed. E.E. Burke), Salisbury: National Archives of Rhodesia.

Mauss, M. and Beuchat, H. 1906 Essai sur les variations saisonnières des sociétés Eskimos, *L'Année Sociologique* 9: 39–132.

Mazel, A.D. 1984 Diamond 1 and Clarke's Shelter: report on excavations in the northern Drakensberg, *Annals of the Natal Museum* 26: 25–70.

1986 Mbabane Shelter and eSinhlonhlweni Shelter: the last two thousand years of hunter-gatherer settlement in the central Thukela Basin, Natal, South Africa, *Annals of the Natal Museum* 27: 389–453.

1988 Nkupe Shelter: report on excavations in the eastern Biggarsberg, Thukela Basin, Natal, South Africa, *Annals of the Natal Museum* 29: 321–78.

1989 People making history: the last ten thousand years of hunter-gatherer communities in the Thukela Basin, *Natal Museum Journal of Humanities* 1: 1–168.

1990 Mhlwazini Cave: the excavation of late Holocene deposits in the northern Natal Drakensberg, Natal, South Africa, *Natal Museum Journal of Humanities* 2: 95–133.

1992a Early pottery from the eastern part of southern Africa, *South African Archaeological Bulletin* 47: 3–7.

1992b Collingham Shelter: the excavation of late Holocene deposits, Natal, South Africa, *Natal Museum Journal of Humanities* 4: 1–51.

1993 kwaThwaleyakhe Shelter: the excavation of mid and late Holocene deposits in the central Thukela Basin, Natal, South Africa, *Natal Museum Journal of Humanities* 5: 1–36.

1996 Maqonqo Shelter: the excavation of early and mid Holocene deposits in the eastern Biggarsberg, Thukela Basin, KwaZulu-Natal, South Africa, *Natal Museum Journal of Humanities* 8: 1–39.

1997 Mzinyashana Shelters 1 and 2: excavation of mid and late Holocene deposits in the eastern Biggarsberg, Thukela Basin, South Africa, *Natal Museum Journal of Humanities* 9: 1–35.

Mazel, A.D. and Stewart, P.M. 1987 Meddling with the mind: the treatment of San hunter-gatherers and the origins of South Africa's Black population in recent South African school history textbooks, *South African Archaeological Bulletin* 42: 166–70.

Mazel, A.D. and Watchman, A.L. 1997 Accelerator radiocarbon dating of Natal Drakensberg paintings: results and implications, *Antiquity* 71: 445–9.

Mehlman, M. 1991 Context for the emergence of modern man in eastern Africa: some new Tanzanian evidence, in J.D. Clark (ed.), *Cultural beginnings:*

approaches to understanding early hominid lifeways in the African savanna, Mainz: Römisch-Germanisches Zentralmuseum, pp. 177–96.

Mellars, P.A. 1989 Major issues in the emergence of modern humans. *Current Anthropology* 30: 349–85.

(ed.) 1990 *The emergence of modern humans*, Edinburgh: Edinburgh University Press.

1996 *The Neanderthal legacy: an archaeological perspective from western Europe*, Princeton: Princeton University Press.

Mellars, P.A. and Stringer, C.B. (eds.) 1989 *The human revolution: behavioural and biological perspectives on the origins of modern humans*, Edinburgh: Edinburgh University Press.

Meneses, P. 1996 Some aspects regarding the Acheulean in southern Mozambique, in G. Pwiti and R. Soper (eds.), pp. 129–38.

Merrick, H.V. and Brown, F.H. 1984 Obsidian sources and patterns of source utilization in Kenya and northern Tanzania: some initial findings, *African Archaeological Review* 2: 129–52.

Merriweather, D.A., Clark, A.G., Ballinger, S.W., Schurr, T.G., Soodyall, H., Jenkins, T., Sherry, S.T. and Wallace, D.W. 1991 The structure of human mitochondrial DNA variation, *Journal of Molecular Evolution* 33: 543–55.

Metz, G. 1994 Working with comunities in Botswana, in B. Krafchik (ed.), *The South African Museum and its public: negotiating partnerships*, Cape Town: South African Museum, pp. 11–14.

Meyer, A. 1984 A profile of the Iron Age in the Kruger National Park, South Africa, in M. Hall *et al.* (eds.), pp. 215–27.

1988a 'n Kultuurhistoriese interpretasie van die Ystertydperk in die Nasionale Krugerwildtuin, PhD thesis, University of Pretoria.

1988b Schoemansdal, nineteenth century pioneer settlement in the northern Transvaal, in T.M. Evers *et al.* (eds.), pp. 56–9.

1998 *The archaeological sites of Greefswald*, Pretoria: University of Pretoria Press.

Meyer, A. and Esterhuizen, V. 1994 Skerwe uit die verlede: handel tussen Mapungubwe en China, *South African Journal of Ethnology* 17: 103–8.

Midgley, G., Ashwell, A., Rutherford, M., Bond, W. & Hannah, L. 2000 Beyond boundaries: climate change in southern Africa, *Africa Environment & Wildlife* 8 (8): 26–9.

Miller, D.E. 1996 *The Tsodilo jewellery: metal work from northern Botswana*, Cape Town: University of Cape Town Press.

Miller, D.E., Manhire, A., Yates, R., Jerardino, A. and Parkington, J.E. 1998 Metalwork found in Late Stone Age contexts in the Western and southern Cape, *Southern African Field Archaeology* 7: 106–10.

Miller, D.E. and Sandelowsky, B. 1999 Smelting without ceramics: the Drierivier copper smelting site near Rehoboth, Namibia, *South African Archaeological Bulletin* 54: 28–37.

Miller, D.E. and van der Merwe, N.J. 1994 Early metal working in sub-Saharan Africa: a review of recent research, *Journal of African History* 35: 1–36.

Miller, D.E. and Webley, L. 1994 The metallurgical analysis of artefacts from Jakkalsberg, Richtersveld, Northern Cape, *Southern African Field Archaeology* 3: 82–93.

Miller, D.E. and Whitelaw, G. 1994 Early Iron Age metal working from the site of KwaGandaganda, Natal, South Africa, *South African Archaeological Bulletin* 49: 79–89.

Miller, G.H., Beaumont, P.B., Jull, A.J.T. and Johnson, B. 1993 Pleistocene geochronology and palaeothermometry from protein diagenesis in ostrich eggshells: implications for the evolution of modern humans, in M.J. Aitken *et al.* (eds.), pp. 49–68.

Miller, S.F. 1969 The Nachikufan industries of the Zambian Later Stone Age, PhD thesis, University of California, Berkeley.

Milo, R.G. 1998 Evidence for hominid predation at Klasies River Mouth, South Africa, and its implications for the behaviour of early modern humans, *Journal of Archaeological Science* 25: 99–133.

Mitchell, P.J. 1988 *The early microlithic assemblages of southern Africa*, Oxford: British Archaeological Reports.

1990 A palaeoecological model for archaeological site distribution in southern Africa during the Upper Pleniglacial and Late Glacial, in C.S. Gamble and O. Soffer (eds.), pp. 189–205.

1993a The archaeology of Tloutle rock-shelter, Maseru District, Lesotho, *Navorsinge van die Nasionale Museum (Bloemfontein)* 9: 77–132.

1993b Archaeological investigations at two Lesotho rock-shelters: the terminal Pleistocene/early Holocene assemblages from Ha Makotoko and Ntloana Tsoana, *Proceedings of the Prehistoric Society* 59: 39–60.

1994 Understanding the MSA/LSA transition: the pre-20,000 BP assemblages from new excavations at Sehonghong Rock Shelter, Lesotho, *Southern African Field Archaeology* 3: 15–25.

1995 Revisiting the Robberg: new results and a revision of old ideas at Sehonghong Rock Shelter, Lesotho, *South African Archaeological Bulletin* 50: 28–38.

1996a The late Quaternary landscape at Sehonghong in the Lesotho highlands, southern Africa, *Antiquity* 70: 623–38.

1996b The late Quaternary of the Lesotho highlands, southern Africa: preliminary results and future potential of ongoing research at Sehonghong Shelter, *Quaternary International* 33: 35–44.

1996c Marine shells and ostrich eggshell as indicators of prehistoric exchange and interaction in the Lesotho highlands, *African Archaeological Review* 13: 35–76.

1996d Filling the gap: the early and middle Holocene assemblages from new excavations at Sehonghong Rock Shelter, Lesotho, *Southern African Field Archaeology* 5: 17–27.

1996e Sehonghong: the late Holocene assemblages with pottery, *South African Archaeological Bulletin* 51: 17–25.

1997 The Holocene Later Stone Age south of the Limpopo River, 10,000–2000 B.P., *Journal of World Prehistory* 11: 359–424.

1998 The South African Stone Age in the collections of the British Museum: content, history and significance, *South African Archaeological Bulletin* 53: 26–36.

1999 Pressure-flaked points in Lesotho: dating, distribution and diversity, *South African Archaeological Bulletin* 54: 90–6.

2000 The organization of Later Stone Age lithic technology in the Caledon Valley, southern Africa, *African Archaeological Review* 17: 141–76.

Mitchell, P.J. and Charles, R.L.C. 2000 Later Stone Age hunter-gatherer adaptations in Lesotho, in G.N. Bailey, R.L.C. Charles and N. Winder (eds.), *Human ecodynamics: proceedings of the conference of the Association of Environmental Archaeology*, Oxford: Oxbow Press, pp. 90–9.

Mitchell, P.J., Parkington, J.E. and Yates, R. 1994 Recent Holocene archaeology in western Lesotho, *South African Archaeological Bulletin* 49: 33–52.

Mitchell, P.J. and Steinberg, J.M. 1992 Ntloana Tsoana: a Middle Stone Age sequence from western Lesotho, *South African Archaeological Bulletin* 47: 26–33.

Moll, E. 1987 Review of some new concepts in 'Fynbos' ecology, in J.E. Parkington and M. Hall (eds.), pp. 120–31.

Monro, D.F. and Spies, C.W. 1975 Excavations at Musimbira, Bikita district, Rhodesia, *Arnoldia* 7 (22): 1–11.

Moon, B.P. and Dardis, G.F. (eds.) 1988 *The geomorphology of southern Africa*, Johannesburg: Southern Books.

Morais, J. 1984 Mozambican archaeology: past and present, *African Archaeological Review* 2: 113–28.

1988 *The early farming communities of southern Mozambique*, Stockholm: Central Board of National Antiquities.

Morris, A.G. 1981 Copper discolouration of bone and the incidence of copper artefacts with human burials in South Africa, *South African Archaeological Bulletin* 36: 36–42.

1992a Biological relationships between Upper Pleistocene and Holocene populations in southern Africa, in G. Bräuer and F. H. Smith (eds.), pp. 131–43.

1992b *Master catalogue of Holocene human skeletons in southern Africa*, Johannesburg: Witwatersrand University Press.

1992c Holocene human skeletons from the Saldanha and Elands Bay regions of the Western Cape Province: with notes on certain specimens, in A.B. Smith and B. Mütti (eds.), pp. 55–9.

1992d *The skeletons of contact*, Johannesburg: Witwatersrand University Press.

1993 Human remains from the Early Iron Age sites of Nanda and kwaGandaganda, Mngeni Valley, Natal, South Africa, *Natal Museum Journal of Humanities* 5: 83–98.

1996 Trophy skulls, museums and the San, in P. Skotnes (ed.), pp. 67–80.

Morris, D. 1988 Engraved in place and time: a review of variability in the rock art of the Northern Cape and Karoo, *South African Archaeological Bulletin* 43: 109–20.

1990a Powerhouse Cave, in P.B. Beaumont and D. Morris (eds.), pp. 160–165.

1990b Nauga ochre mine, in P.B. Beaumont and D. Morris (eds.), pp. 59–61.

1990c Dithakong: 'The place of ruins', in P.B. Beaumont and D. Morris (eds.), pp. 148–54.

1990d Water-snakes and waggons: rock engravings of the Ghaap Plateau and Kuruman River Valley, in P.B. Beaumont and D. Morris (eds.), pp. 135–42.

1991 Stone bowls in the Northern Cape: a new find and its possible context, *South African Archaeological Bulletin* 46: 38–40.

Morris, D. and Beaumont, P.B. 1991 !Nawabdanas: archaeological sites at Renosterkop, Kakamas District, Northern Cape, *South African Archaeological Bulletin* 46: 115–24.

1994 Portable rock engravings at Springbokoog and the archaeological contexts of rock art in the Upper Karoo, in T.A. Dowson and J.D. Lewis-Williams (eds.), pp. 11–28.

Morse, K.M. 1993 New radiocarbon dates from North West Cape, Western Australia: a preliminary report, in M.A. Smith, M. Spriggs and B. Fankhauser (eds.), *Sahul in review: Pleistocene archaeology in Australia, New Guinea and Island Micronesia*, Canberra: Australian National University, pp. 153–63.

Mossop, E.E. (ed.) 1935 *The journal of Hendrik Jacob Wikar (1779)*, Cape Town: Van Riebeeck Society.

Mote, F.W. 1991 China in the age of Columbus, in J.A. Levenson (ed.), *Circa 1492: art in the Age of Exploration*, New Haven: Yale University Press, pp. 337–50.

Mountain, J.L., Lin, A.A., Bowcock, A.M. and Cavalli-Sforza, L.L. 1993 Evolution of modern humans: evidence from nuclear DNA polymorphisms, in M.J. Aitken *et al.* (eds.), pp. 69–83.

Mudenge, S.I.G. 1988 *A political history of Munhumutapa c. 1400–1902*, Harare: Zimbabwe Publishing House.

Mulvaney, D.J. 1969 *The prehistory of Australia*, Harmondsworth: Penguin.

Musonda, F.B. 1984 Late Pleistocene and Holocene microlithic industries from the Lusemfwa Basin, Zambia, *South African Archaeological Bulletin* 39: 24–36.

Nackerdien, R. 1989 Klipfonteinrand 2: a sign of the times, BA thesis, University of Cape Town.

Ndoro, W. 1994 The preservation and presentation of Great Zimbabwe, *Antiquity* 68: 616–23.

Nei, M. and Roychoudhury, A.K. 1974 Genic variation within and between the three major races of Man, Caucasoids, Negroids and Mongoloids, *American Journal of Human Genetics* 26: 421–43.

Newitt, M.D.D. 1978 The southern Swahili coast in the first century of European expansion, *Azania* 13: 111–26.

Newitt, M.D.D. and Garlake, P.S. 1967 The 'aringa' at Massangano, *Journal of African History* 8: 133–56.

Newton-King, S. 1999 *Masters and servants on the Eastern Cape Frontier*, Cambridge: Cambridge University Press.

Nitecki, M.H. and Nitecki, D.V. (eds.) 1994 *Origins of anatomically modern humans*, New York: Plenum.

Noble, W. and Davidson, I. 1996 *Human evolution, language and mind: a psychological and archaeological inquiry*, Cambridge: Cambridge University Press.

Nogwaza, T. 1994 Early Iron Age pottery from Canasta Place, East London district, *Southern African Field Archaeology* 3: 103–6.

Noli, D. and Avery, G. 1987 Stone circles in the Cape Fria area, northern Namibia, *South African Archaeological Bulletin* 42: 59–63.

1988 Protein poisoning and coastal subsistence, *Journal of Archaeological Science* 15: 395–401.

Nurse, D. 1994/95 Historical classifications of the Bantu languages, *Azania* 29/30: 65–81.

Nurse, G.T., Weiner, J.S. and Jenkins, T. 1985 *The peoples of southern Africa and their affinities*, Oxford: Oxford University Press.

Oakley, K. 1954 Evidence of fire in South African cave deposits, *Nature* 174: 261–2.

O'Brien, E.M. and Peters, C.R. 1999 Landforms, climate, ecogeographic mosaics and the potential for hominid diversity in Pliocene Africa, in T.R. Bromage and F. Schrenk (eds.), *African biogeography, climate change and human evolution*, Oxford: Oxford University Press, pp. 115–37.

Oddy, A. 1984 Gold in the southern African Iron Age: a technological investigation of Mapungubwe and other finds, *Gold Bulletin* 17 (2): 70–8.

Official Year Book of the Republic of South Africa 1974 Pretoria: Department of Information.

Ohinata, F. 2000 Preliminary results of the 1998 field survey of farming community sites in Swaziland, *Nyame Akuma* 53: 42–9.

Okihiro, G.Y. 1976 Hunters, herders, cultivators and traders: interaction and change in the Kgalagadi, nineteenth century, PhD thesis, University of California, Los Angeles.

Oliver, R. 1966 The problem of the Bantu expansion, *Journal of African History* 7: 361–76.

Omer-Cooper, J.D. 1966 *The Zulu aftermath: a nineteenth century revolution in Bantu Africa*, London: Longman.

Opperman, H. 1978 Excavations in the Buffelskloof rock shelter near Calitzdorp, southern Cape, *South African Archaeological Bulletin* 33: 18–38.

1987 *The Later Stone Age of the Drakensberg Range and its foothills*, Oxford: British Archaeological Reports.

1989 An excavation of a Middle Stone Age deposit in Grassridge Rockshelter, Sterkstroom District, Cape Province, *University of Fort Hare Papers* 9: 51–62.

1992 A report on the results of a test pit in Strathalan Cave B, Maclear District, north-eastern Cape, *Southern African Field Archaeology* 1: 98–102.

1996a Strathalan Cave B, north-eastern Cape Province, South Africa: evidence for human behaviour 29,000–26,000 years ago, *Quaternary International* 33: 45–54.

1996b Excavation of a Later Stone Age deposit in Strathalan Cave A, Maclear District, Northeastern Cape, South Africa, in G. Pwiti and R. Soper (eds.), pp. 335–42.

Opperman, H. and Heydenrych, B. 1990 A 22,000 year old Middle Stone Age camp site with plant food remains from the north-eastern Cape, *South African Archaeological Bulletin* 45: 93–9.

Orpen, J.M. 1874 A glimpse into the mythology of the Maluti Bushmen, *Cape Monthly Magazine* 9: 1–13.

Orser, C.E. 1996 *A historical archaeology of the modern world*, New York: Plenum.

Ouzman, S. 1995a Spiritual and political uses of a rock engraving site and its imagery by San and Tswana-speakers, *South African Archaeological Bulletin* 50: 55–67.

1995b The fish, the shaman and the peregrination: San rock art paintings of mormyrid fish as religious and social metaphors, *Southern African Field Archaeology* 4: 3–17.

1996a Thaba Sione: place of rhinoceroses and rock art, *African Studies* 55: 31–59.

1996b A brief history of rock art research in the eastern Free State, South Africa, in J.J.B. Dreyer *et al.* (eds.), pp. 28–36.

1996c Archaeo-tourism and images of Africa, *Southern African Field Archaeology* 5: 57–8.

1997a Hidden in the common gaze: collective and idiosyncratic rock paintings at Rose Cottage Cave, South Africa, *Navorsinge van die Nasionale Museum (Bloemfontein)* 13: 225–56.

1997b Between margin and centre: the archaeology of southern African bored stones, in L. Wadley (ed.), pp. 71–106.

1999 'Koeka ka kie, hents op bokkor of ik schiet!' Introducing the rock art of the South African Anglo-Boer War, 1899–1902, *The Digging Stick* 16 (3): 1–5.

Ouzman, S. and Wadley, L. 1997 A history in paint and stone from Rose Cottage Cave, South Africa, *Antiquity* 71: 386–404.

Ownby, C. 1985 Early Nguni history: the linguistic evidence and its correlation with archaeology and oral tradition, PhD thesis, University of California, Los Angeles.

Pager, H. 1971 *Ndedema Gorge*, Graz: Akademische Druck- und Verlaganstalt.

1975 *Stone Age myth and magic*, Graz: Akademische Druck.

1989 *The rock paintings of the upper Brandberg. Part I: Amis Gorge*, Cologne: Heinrich Barth Institute.

1993 *The rock paintings of the upper Brandberg. Part II: Hungorob Gorge*, Cologne: Heinrich Barth Institute.

1995 *The rock paintings of the upper Brandberg. Part III: Southern Gorges* Cologne: Heinrich Barth Institute.

Parkington, J.E. 1972 Seasonal mobility in the Late Stone Age, *African Studies* 31: 223–43.

1977 Follow the San, PhD thesis, University of Cambridge.

1980a The Elands Bay cave sequence: cultural stratigraphy and subsistence strategies, in R.A. Leakey and B.A. Ogot (eds.), *Proceedings of the Eighth Pan-African Congress of Prehistory and Quaternary Studies*, Nairobi: Tillmiap, pp. 315–20.

1980b Time and place: some observations on spatial and temporal patterning in the Later Stone Age sequence in southern Africa, *South African Archaeological Bulletin* 35: 75–83.

1984a Changing views of the Later Stone Age of South Africa, *Advances in World Archaeology* 3: 89–142.

1984b Soaqua and Bushmen: hunters and robbers, in C. Schrire (ed.), *Past and present in hunter-gatherer studies*, Orlando: Academic Press, pp. 151–74.

1986 Landscape and subsistence changes since the Last Glacial Maximum along the Western Cape coast, in L.G. Straus (ed.), *The end of the Palaeolithic in the Old World*, Oxford: British Archaeological Reports, pp. 201–27.

1987 Prehistory and palaeoenvironments at the Pleistocene–Holocene boundary in the Western Cape, in O. Soffer (ed.), *The Pleistocene in the Old World*, New York: Plenum, pp. 349–63.

1988 The Pleistocene/Holocene transition in the Western Cape, South Africa: observations from Verlorenvlei, in J. Bower and D. Lubell (eds.), *Prehistoric cultures and environments in the late Quaternary of Africa*, Oxford: British Archaeological Reports, pp. 349–63.

1989 Interpreting paintings without a commentary, *Antiquity* 63: 13–26.

1990a A critique of the consensus view on the age of Howieson's Poort assemblages in South Africa, in P.A. Mellars (ed.), pp. 34–55.

1990b A view from the south: southern Africa before, during and after the Last Glacial Maximum, in C.S. Gamble and O. Soffer (eds.), pp. 214–28.

1991 Approaches to dietary reconstruction in the Western Cape: are you what you have eaten?, *Journal of Archaeological Science* 18: 331–42.

1992 Making sense of sequence at the Elands Bay Cave, Western Cape, South Africa, in A.B. Smith and B. Mütti (eds.), pp. 6–12.

1993 The neglected alternative: historical narrative rather than cultural labelling, *South African Archaeological Bulletin* 48: 94–7.

1996 What is an eland? *N!ao* and the politics of age and sex in the paintings of the Western Cape, in P. Skotnes (ed.), pp. 281–90.

1998 Resolving the past: gender in the Stone Age archaeological record of the Western Cape, in S. Kent (ed.), pp. 25–38.

1999 Western Cape landscapes, *Proceedings of the British Academy* 99: 25–35.

Parkington, J.E. and Cronin, M. 1979 The size and layout of Mgungundlovu 1829–1838, *South African Archaeological Society Goodwin Series* 4: 133–48.

Parkington, J.E. and Hall, M. (eds.) 1987a *Papers in the prehistory of the Western Cape, South Africa*, Oxford: British Archaeological Reports.

1987b Patterning in recent radiocarbon dates from southern Africa as a reflection of prehistoric settlement and interaction, *Journal of African History* 28: 1–25.

Parkington, J.E., Manhire, A.H. and Yates, R. 1996 Reading San images, in J. Deacon and T.A. Dowson (eds.), pp. 212–33.

Parkington, J.E., Nilssen, P., Reeler, C. and Henshilwood, C. 1992 Making sense of space at Dunefield Midden campsite, Western Cape, South Africa, *Southern African Field Archaeology* 1: 63–70.

Parkington, J.E. and Poggenpoel, C.A. 1971 Excavations at De Hangen 1968, *South African Archaeological Bulletin* 26: 3–36.

1987 Diepkloof Rockshelter, in J.E. Parkington and M. Hall (eds.), pp. 269–93.

Parkington, J.E., Poggenpoel, C.A., Buchanan, W., Robey, T., Manhire, A.H. and Sealy, J.C. 1987 Holocene coastal settlement patterns in the Western Cape, in G.N. Bailey and J.E. Parkington (eds.) *The archaeology of prehistoric coastlines*, Cambridge: Cambridge University Press, pp. 22–41.

Parkington, J.E., Yates, R., Manhire, A.H. and Halkett, D. 1986 The social impact of pastoralism in the south-western Cape, *Journal of Anthropological Archaeology* 5: 313–29.

Parsons, N. 1995 Prelude to *Difaqane* in the interior of southern Africa *c.* 1600 – *c.* 1822, in C. Hamilton (ed.), pp. 323–49.

Partridge, T.C. 1997 Cainozoic environmental change in southern Africa, with special emphasis on the last 200 000 years, *Progress in Physical Geography* 21: 3–22.

(ed.) 1999 *Tswaing: investigations into the origin, age and palaeoenvironments of the Pretoria Saltpan*, Pretoria: South African Council for Geoscience.

2000 Hominid-bearing cave and tufa deposits, in T.C. Partridge and R.R. Maud (eds.), pp. 100–30.

Partridge, T.C., Avery, D.M., Botha, G.A., Brink, J.S., Deacon, J., Herbert, R.S., Maud, R.R., Scholtz, A., Scott, L., Talma, A.S. and Vogel, J.C. 1990 Late Pleistocene and Holocene climatic change in southern Africa, *South African Journal of Science* 86: 302–6.

Partridge, T.C. and Brink, A.B.A. 1967 Gravels and terraces of the Lower Vaal River, *South African Geographical Journal* 49: 21–38.

Partridge, T.C. and Maud, R.R. 1987 Geomorphic evolution of southern Africa since the Mesozoic, *South African Journal of Geology* 90: 179–208.

(eds.) 2000 *The Cenozoic of southern Africa*, Oxford: Oxford University Press.

Partridge, T.C., Shaw, J., Heslop, D. and Clarke, R.J. 1999 The new hominid skeleton from Sterkfontein, South Africa: age and preliminary assessment, *Journal of Quaternary Science* 14: 293–8.

Patrick, M., Smith, A.B. and de Koning, A.J. 1985 Gas-liquid chromatographic analysis of fatty acids in food residues from ceramics found in the south-western Cape, South Africa, *Archaeometry* 27: 231–46.

Patterson, W. 1790 *A narrative of four journeys into the country of the Hottentots and Caffraria in the years 1777, 1778, 1779*, second edition, London: J. Johnson.

Pauketat, T.R. and Emerson, T.E. (eds.) 1997 *Cahokia: domination and ideology in the Mississippian world*, Lincoln: University of Nebraska Press.

Pearson, N. 1995 Archaeological research at Modipe Hill, Kgatleng District: survey and excavations, 1992 to 1995, *Botswana Notes and Records* 27: 21–40.

Peires, J.B. 1981 *The House of Phalo: a history of the Xhosa People in the days of the independence*, Johannesburg: Ravan Press.

1995 Matiwane's road to Mbolompo: a reprieve for the Mfecane?, in C. Hamilton (ed.), pp. 213–39.

Penn, N. 1986 Pastoralists and pastoralism in the Northern Cape frontier zone during the eighteenth century, *South African Archaeological Society Goodwin Series* 5: 62–8.

1987 The frontier in the Western Cape, 1700–1740, in J.E. Parkington and M. Hall (eds.), pp. 462–503.

1991 'Excavating archives at Oudepost': a riposte, *Social Dynamics* 17: 101–5.

1995 The Orange River Frontier Zone, *c.* 1700–1805, in A.B. Smith (ed.), pp. 21–109.

Péringuey, L. 1911 The Stone Ages of South Africa, *Annals of the South African Museum* 8: 1–218.

Péringuey, L. and Corstophine, G.S. 1900 Stone implements from Bosman's Crossing, Stellenbosch, *Memoirs of the Proceedings of the South African Philosophical Society* 11: xxiv.

Perry, W.R. 1999 *Landscape transformations and the archaeology of impact: social disruption and state formation in Southern Africa*, New York: Kluwer Academic/Plenum Publishers.

Peters, J., Gautier, A. and Brink, J.S. 1994 Late Quaternary extinction of ungulates in sub-Saharan Africa: a reductionist's approach, *Journal of Archaeological Science* 21: 17–28.

Pfeiffer, J.E. 1982 *The creative explosion*, New York: Harper and Row.

Phaladi, S. 1998 The organisation of archaeology, in P. Lane *et al.* (eds.), pp. 233–9.

Phillipson, D.W. 1976 *The prehistory of eastern Zambia*, Nairobi: British Institute in Eastern Africa.

1977 *The later prehistory of eastern and southern Africa*, London: Heinemann.

1989 The first South African pastoralists and the Early Iron Age, *Nsi* 6: 127–34.

1993 *African archaeology*, Cambridge: Cambridge University Press.

1999 Review of: C. Ehret, An African classical age: eastern and southern Africa in world history 1000 BC to AD 400, *South African Archaeological Bulletin* 54: 68–9.

Phillipson, L. and Phillipson, D.W. 1970 Patterns of edge damage on the Late Stone Age industry from Chiwemupula, Zambia, *Zambia Museums Journal* 1: 40–75.

Phimister, I.R. 1976 Pre-colonial gold mining in southern Zambezia: a reassessment, *African Social Research* 21: 1–30.

Pickering, T.R. 1999 Taphonomic interpretations of the Sterkfontein early hominid site (Gauteng, South Africa) reconsidered in the light of recent evidence, PhD thesis, University of Wisconsin, Madison.

Pickford, M. 1990 Some fossiliferous Plio-Pleistocene cave systems of Ngamiland, Botswana, *Botswana Notes and Records* 22: 1–15.

Pikirayi, I. 1993 *The archaeological identity of the Mutapa state: towards an historical archaeology of northern Zimbabwe*, Uppsala: Societas Archaeologica Upsaliensis.

1996 Ceramics and culture change in northern Zimbabwe: on the origins of the Musengezi tradition, in G. Pwiti and R. Soper (eds.), pp. 629–39.

1997a Research trends in historical archaeology on the Zimbabwe Plateau and adjacent margins, in G. Pwiti (ed.), pp. 143–56.

1997b Pots, people and culture: an overview of ceramic studies in Zimbabwe, in G. Pwiti (ed.), pp. 69–87.

Pistorius, J.C. 1994 Molokwane, a seventeenth century Tswana village, *South African Journal of Ethnology* 17: 38–54.

1997 The Matabele village which eluded history, *South African Journal of Ethnology* 20: 43–55.

Pistorius, J.C. and Steyn, M. 1995 Iron working and burial practices amongst the Kgatla-Kwena of the Mabyanamatshwaana complex, *Southern African Field Archaeology* 4: 68–77.

Plug, I. 1981a Some research results on the late Pleistocene and Holocene deposits of Bushman Rock Shelter, eastern Transvaal, *South African Archaeological Bulletin* 36: 14–21.

1981b Upper Zambezi Iron Age projects. Specialist reports, *Archaeologica Zambiana* 20: 17–22.

1982 Bone tools and shell, bone and ostrich eggshell beads from Bushman Rock Shelter (BRS), eastern Transvaal, *South African Archaeological Bulletin* 37: 57–62.

1989 Aspects of life in the Kruger National Park during the Early Iron Age, *South African Archaeological Society Goodwin Series* 6: 62–8.

1990 The macrofaunal remains from Mhlwazini Cave, a Holocene site in the Natal Drakensberg, *Natal Museum Journal of Humanities* 2: 135–42.

1992 The macrofaunal remains from Collingham Shelter, a Late Stone Age site in Natal, *Natal Museum Journal of Humanities* 4: 53–9.

1993a The macrofaunal and molluscan remains from Tloutle, a Later Stone Age site in Lesotho, *Southern African Field Archaeology* 2: 44–8.

1993b The macrofaunal remains of wild animals from Abbot's Cave and Lame Sheep Shelter, Seacow Valley, *Koedoe* 36: 15–26.

1993c The faunal remains from Nanda, an Early Iron Age site in Natal, *Natal Museum Journal of Humanities* 5: 99–107.

1993d KwaThwaleyakhe Shelter: the faunal remains from a Holocene site in the Thukela Basin, Natal, *Natal Museum Journal of Humanities* 5: 37–45.

1996a Domestic animals during the Early Iron Age in southern Africa, in G. Pwiti and R. Soper (eds.), pp. 515–20.

1996b Seven centuries of Iron Age traditions at Bosutswe, Botswana: a faunal perspective, *South African Journal of Science* 92: 91–7.

1997 Early Iron Age buffalo hunters on the Kadzi River, Zimbabwe, *African Archaeological Review* 14: 85–106.

1999 The fauna from Later Stone Age and contact sites in the Karoo, South Africa, in C. Becker, H. Manhart, J. Peters and J. Schibler (eds.), *Historia animalium ex ossibus*, Rahden: Maria Leidorf, pp. 343–53.

Plug, I., Bollong, C.A., Hart, T.J.G. and Sampson, C.G. 1994 Context and direct dating of pre-European livestock in the upper Seacow River valley, *Annals of the South African Museum* 104: 31–48.

Plug, I. and Engela, R. 1992 The macrofaunal remains from recent excavations at Rose Cottage Cave, Orange Free State, *South African Archaeological Bulletin* 47: 16–25.

Plug, I. and Keyser, A.W. 1994 A preliminary report on the bovid species from recent excavations at Gladysvale, South Africa, *South African Journal of Science* 90: 357–9.

Plug, I. and Pistorius, J.C.C. 1999 Animal remains from industrial Iron Age communities in Phalaborwa, South Africa, *African Archaeological Review* 16: 155–84.

Plug, I. and Roodt, F. 1990 The faunal remains from recent excavation at uMgungundlovu, *South African Archaeological Bulletin* 45: 47–52.

Plug, I. and Sampson, C.G. 1996 European and Bushman impacts on Karoo fauna in the nineteenth century: an archaeological perspective, *South African Archaeological Bulletin* 51: 26–31.

Plug, I., Soper, R.C. and Chirawu, S. 1997 Pits, tunnels and cattle in Nyanga, Zimbabwe: new light on an old problem, *South African Archaeological Bulletin* 52: 89–94.

Plug, I. and Voigt, E. 1985 Archaeozoological studies of Iron Age communities in southern Africa, *Advances in World Archaeology* 4: 189–238.

Poggenpoel, C.A. 1987 The implications of fish bone assemblages from Eland's Bay Cave, Tortoise Cave and Diepkloof for changes in the Holocene history of the Verlorenvlei, in J.E. Parkington and M. Hall (eds.), pp. 212–36.

Poggenpoel, C.A. and Robertshaw, P.T. 1981 The excavation of Smitswinkelbaai Cave, Cape peninsula, *South African Archaeological Bulletin* 36: 29–35.

Potgieter, E.F. 1955 *The disappearing Bushmen of Lake Chrissie: a preliminary survey*, Pretoria: J.L. van Schaik.

Power, C. and Watts, I. 1996 Female strategies and collective behaviour: the archaeology of earliest *Homo sapiens sapiens*, in J. Steele and S. Shennan (eds.), *The archaeology of human ancestry: power, sex and tradition*, London: Routledge, pp. 306–30.

Prendergast, M.D. 1975 A new furnace type from the Darwendale dam basin, *Journal of the Prehistoric Society of Rhodesia* 7: 16–20.

Price, T.D. and Brown, J.A. (eds.) 1985 *Complex hunter-gatherers*, New York: Academic Press.

Price-Williams, D. 1980 Archaeology in Swaziland, *South African Archaeological Bulletin* 35: 13–18.

1981 A preliminary report on recent excavations of Middle and Late Stone Age levels at Sibebe Shelter, north-west Swaziland, *South African Archaeological Bulletin* 36: 22–8.

Price-Williams, D. and Barham, L.S. 1982 Swaziland Archaeological Research Association, *Nyame Akuma* 21: 43.

Price-Williams, D. and Watson, A. 1982 New observations on prehistory and palaeo-climate of the late Pleistocene of southern Africa, *World Archaeology* 13: 372–81.

Prins, F.E. 1990 Southern Bushman descendants in the Transkei – rock art and rainmaking, *South African Journal of Ethnology* 13: 110–16.

1994/95 Climate, vegetation and early agriculturist communities in Transkei and KwaZulu-Natal, *Azania* 29/30: 179–86.

1996 Praise to the Bushman ancestors of the water: the integration of San-related concepts in the beliefs and rituals of a diviners' training school in Tsolo, Eastern Cape, in P. Skotnes (ed.), pp. 211–23.

Prins, F.E. and Grainger, J.E. 1993 Early farming communities in northern Transkei: the evidence from Ntsitsana and adjacent areas, *Natal Museum Journal of Humanities* 5: 153–74.

Prins, F.E. and Hall, S. 1994 Expressions of fertility in the rock art of Bantu-speaking agriculturists, *African Archaeological Review* 12: 177–203.

Prins, F.E. and Rousseau, L. 1992 Magico-religious interactions, dreams and ritual transformations: towards a better understanding of trance experiences among the Khoi, *Southern African Field Archaeology* 1: 33–9.

Prinsloo, H.P. 1974 Early Iron Age site at Klein Afrika near Wyliespoort, Soutpansberg Mountains, South Africa, *South African Journal of Science* 70: 271–73.

Prinsloo, H. 1989 Vroeë Ystertydperk terreine in die Soutpansberg, MA thesis, University of Pretoria.

Prior, J. and Price-Williams, D. 1985 An investigation of climatic change in the Holocene Epoch using archaeological charcoal from Swaziland, southern Africa, *Journal of Archaeological Science* 12: 457–75.

Protsch, R. 1975 The absolute dating of Upper Pleistocene sub-Saharan fossil hominids and their place in human evolution, *Journal of Human Evolution* 4: 297–322.

Pwiti, G. 1996a Settlement and subsistence of prehistoric farming communities in the mid-Zambezi Valley, northern Zimbabwe, *South African Archaeological Bulletin* 51: 3–6.

1996b Let the ancestors rest in peace? New challenges for heritage management in Zimbabwe, *Conservation and Management of Archaeological Sites* 1: 151–60.

(ed.) 1997a *Caves, monuments and texts: Zimbabwean archaeology today*, Uppsala: Societas Archaeologica Upsaliensis.

1997b Aspects of spatial studies in Zimbabwean archaeology, in G. Pwiti (ed.), pp. 55–68.

Pwiti, G. and Mvenge, G. 1996 Archaeologists, tourists and rainmakers: problems in the management of rock art sites in Zimbabwe: a case study of Domboshava national monument, in G. Pwiti and R. Soper (eds.), pp. 817–24.

Pwiti, G. and Ndoro, W. 1999 The legacy of colonialism: perceptions of the cultural heritage in southern Africa, with special reference to Zimbabwe, *African Archaeological Review* 16: 143–54.

Pwiti, G. and Soper, R. (eds.) 1996 *Aspects of African archaeology*, Harare: University of Zimbabwe Press.

Quin, P.J. 1959 *Food and feeding habits of the Pedi*, Johannesburg: Witwatersrand University Press.

Rademeyer-De Kock, C. 1993 'n Argeologiese ondersoek van historiese nedersettings-patrone in die westelike Overberg, MA thesis, University of Stellenbosch.

Rak, Y. 1983 *The australopithecine face*, New York: Academic Press.

Raper, P.E. and Boucher, M. (eds.) 1988 *Robert Jacob Gordon: Cape travels, 1777 to 1786*, Johannesburg: Brenthurst Press.

Rayner, R.J., Moon, B.P. and Masters, J.C. 1993 The Makapansgat australopithecine environment, *Journal of Human Evolution* 24: 219–31.

Reed, K.E. 1997 Early hominid evolution and ecological change through the African Plio-Pleistocene, *Journal of Human Evolution* 32: 289–322.

Reid, A. 1994/95 Early settlement and social organisation in the Interlacustrine region, *Azania* 29/30: 303–13.

1996 Cattle herds and the redistribution of cattle resources, *World Archaeology* 28: 43–57.

Reid, A., Lane, P., Segobye, A.K., Borjeson, L., Mathibidi, N. and Sekgarametso, P. 1997 Tswana architecture and responses to colonialism, *World Archaeology* 28: 370–92.

Reid, A., Sadr, K. and Hanson-James, N. 1998 Herding traditions, in P. Lane *et al.* (eds.), pp. 81–100.

Reid, A. and Segobye, A.K. 2000 An ivory cache from Botswana, *Antiquity* 74: 326–31.

Relethford, J.H. and Harpending, H.C. 1995 Ancient differences in population size can mimic a recent African origin of modern humans, *Current Anthropology* 36: 667–74.

Renfrew, A.C. and Cherry, J.F. (eds.) 1986 *Peer polity interaction and socio-political change*, Cambridge: Cambridge University Press.

Richardson, N. 1992 Conjoin sets and stratigraphic integrity in a sandstone shelter: Kenniff Cave (Queensland, Australia), *Antiquity* 66: 408–19.

Richmond, B.G. and Jungers, W.L. 1995 Size variation and sexual dimorphism in *Australopithecus afarensis* and living hominoids, *Journal of Human Evolution* 29: 229–45.

Rickard, J. 1881a Notes on four series of Palaeolithic implements from South Africa, *Proceedings of the Cambridgeshire Antiquaries Society* 5: 57–66.

1881b Notes on some Neolithic implements from South Africa, *Proceedings of the Cambridgeshire Antiquaries Society* 5: 67–74.

Rightmire, G.P. 1976 Relationships of Middle and Upper Pleistocene hominids from sub-Saharan Africa, *Nature* 260: 238–40.

1984 The fossil evidence for hominid evolution, in R.G. Klein (ed.), pp. 147–68.

1987 L'évolution des premiers hominidés en Asie du Sud-Est, *L'Anthropologie* 91: 455–66.

1996 The human cranium from Bodo, Ethiopia: evidence for speciation in the Middle Pleistocene, *Journal of Human Evolution* 31: 21–39.

Rightmire, G.P. and Deacon, H.J. 1991 Comparative studies of Late Pleistocene human remains from Klasies River Mouth, South Africa, *Journal of Human Evolution* 20: 131–56.

Robbins, L.H. 1986 Recent archaeological research in south-eastern Botswana: the Thamaga site, *Botswana Notes and Records* 18: 1–13.

1990 The Depression site: a Stone Age sequence in the north-west Kalahari Desert, Botswana, *National Geographic Research* 6: 329–38.

1999 Direct dating of worked ostrich eggshell in the Kalahari, *Nyame Akuma* 52: 11–16.

Robbins, L.H., Campbell, A.C., Murphy, M.L. and Ferone, T. 1993 Prehistoric mining and new discoveries of rock art at the Tsodilo Hills, *Nyame Akuma* 40: 2–5.

Robbins, L.H. and Murphy, M.L. 1998 The Early and Middle Stone Age, in P. Lane *et al.* (eds.), pp. 50–64.

Robbins, L.H., Murphy, M.L., Campbell, A.C. and Brook, G.A. 1996a Excavations at the Tsodilo Hills Rhino Cave, *Botswana Notes and Records* 28: 23–45.

Robbins, L.H., Murphy, M.L., Campbell, A.C., Brook, G.A., Reid D.M., Haberyan, K.H. and Downey, W.S. 1998 Test excavation and reconnaissance palaeoenvironmental work at Toteng, Botswana, *South African Archaeological Bulletin* 53: 125–32.

Robbins, L.H., Murphy, M.L., Stevens, N.J., Brook, G.A., Ivester, A.H., Haberyan, K.A., Klein, R.G., Milo, R., Stewart, K.M., Matthiesen, D.G. and Winkler, A.J. 1996b Paleoenvironment and archaeology of Drotsky's Cave: western Kalahari Desert, Botswana, *Journal of Archaeological Science* 23: 7–22.

Robbins, L.H., Murphy, M.L., Stewart, K.M., Campbell, A.C. and Brooks, G.A. 1994 Barbed bone points, paleoenvironment and the antiquity of fish exploitation in the Kalahari Desert, Botswana, *Journal of Field Archaeology* 21: 257–64.

Roberts, D.L. and Berger, L. 1997 Last interglacial (*c.* 117 kyr) human footprints in South Africa, *South African Journal of Science* 93: 349–50.

Roberts, R.G., Jones, R. and Smith, M.A. 1994 Beyond the radiocarbon barrier in Australian prehistory: a critique of Allen's commentary, *Antiquity* 68: 611–16.

Robertshaw, P.T. 1977 Excavations at Paternoster, south-western Cape, *South African Archaeological Bulletin* 32: 63–73.

1979 Coastal settlement, freshwater fishing and pastoralism in the later prehistory of the Western Cape, South Africa, PhD thesis, University of Cambridge.

1984 Excavations at Fairview rock shelter – a contribution to the prehistory of the eastern Cape Province of South Africa, *Annals of the Cape Provincial Museums (Human Sciences)* 1: 55–92.

1988 Environment and culture in the Late Quaternary of Eastern Africa: a critique of some correlations, in J. Bower and D. Lubell (eds.), *Prehistoric cultures and environments in the late Quaternary of Africa*, Oxford: British Archaeological Reports, pp. 115–26.

(ed.) 1990 *A history of African archaeology*, London: James Currey.

Robey, T.S. 1980 Mpambanyoni, a Late Iron Age site on the Natal South Coast, *Annals of the Natal Museum* 24: 147–64.

1987 The stratigraphic and cultural sequence at Tortoise Cave, Verlorenvlei, in J.E. Parkington and M. Hall (eds.), pp. 294–325.

Robinson, J. 1954 Prehominid dentition and hominid evolution, *Evolution* 8: 324–34.

Robinson, K.R. 1952 Excavations in two rock shelters near the Rusawi river, central Mashonaland, *South African Archaeological Bulletin* 7: 108–29.

1958 Some Stone Age sites in Inyanga District, in R. Summers (ed.), pp. 270–309.

1959 *Khami ruins*, Cambridge: Cambridge University Press.

1961 Excavations on the Acropolis Hill, *Occasional Papers of the National Museums of Southern Rhodesia* 23a: 159–92.

1966 The Leopard's Kopje Culture: its position in the Iron Age of Southern Rhodesia, *South African Archaeological Bulletin* 21: 5–51.

Roodt, F. 1992a Koning Dingane se woonhut by Mgungundlovu, *South African Journal of Ethnology* 15: 95–101.

1992b Evidence for girls' initiation rites in the Bheje umuzi at Mgungundlovu, *South African Journal of Ethnology* 15: 9–14.

1993 'n Rekonstrusie van geelkoperbewerking by Mgungundlovu, MA thesis, University of Pretoria.

Rosa, L. and Marshall, F. 1996 Meat eating, hominid sociality and home bases revisited, *Current Anthropology* 37: 307–38.

Rowley-Conwy, P. 1986 Between cave painters and crop planters: aspects of the Temperate European Mesolithic, in M. Zvelebil (ed.), *Hunters in transition: Mesolithic societies of Temperate Eurasia and the transition to farming*, Cambridge: Cambridge University Press, pp. 17–32.

Rudd, S. 1984 Excavations at Lekkerwater ruins, Tsindi Hill, Theydon, Zimbabwe, *South African Archaeological Bulletin* 39: 83–105.

Rudner, J. 1968 Strandloper pottery from South and South West Africa, *Annals of the South African Museum* 49: 441–663.

  1979 The use of stone artefacts and pottery among the Khoisan peoples in historic and protohistoric times, *South African Archaeological Bulletin* 34: 3–17.

Ruff, C.B. 1991 Climate and body shape in hominid evolution, *Journal of Human Evolution* 21: 81–105.

Russell, T. 2000 The application of the Harris Matrix to San rock art at Main Caves North, KwaZulu-Natal, *South African Archaeological Bulletin* 55: 60–70.

Rutherford, M.C. and Westfall, R.H. 1986 Biomes of southern Africa – an objective categorization, *Memoirs of the Botanical Survey of South Africa* 54: 1–98.

Ruvolo, M. 1995 Seeing the forest and the trees, *American Journal of Physical Anthropology* 98: 218–32.

  1996 A new approach to studying modern human origins *Molecular Phylogenetic Evolution* 5: 202–19.

Sadr, K. 1998 Kalahari archaeology and the Bushman debate, *Current Anthropology* 38: 104–12.

Sadr, K. and Sampson, C.G. 1999 Khoekhoe ceramics of the upper Seacow River valley, *South African Archaeological Bulletin* 54: 3–15.

Sadr, K. and Smith, A.B. 1991 On ceramic variation in the south-western Cape, South Africa, *South African Archaeological Bulletin* 46: 107–15.

Saitowitz, S.J. 1996 Glass beads as indicators of contact and trade in southern Africa *ca.* AD 900 – AD 1250, PhD thesis, University of Cape Town.

Saitowitz, S.J., Heckroodt, R.O. and Lastovica, E. 1985 The Cape Glass Company, Glencairn: archaeology of an historical site, *South African Archaeological Bulletin* 40: 88–93.

Saitowitz, S.J., Reid, D.L. and van der Merwe, N.J. 1995 Glass bead trade from Islamic Egypt to South Africa *ca* AD 900–1250, *South African Journal of Science* 91: 101–4.

Saitowitz, S.J. and Sampson, C.G. 1992 Glass trade beads from rock shelters in the Upper Karoo, *South African Archaeological Bulletin* 47: 94–103.

Saitowitz, S.J., Seemann, U.A. and Hall, M. 1993 The development of Cape Town's waterfront in the earlier nineteenth century: history and archaeology of the North Wharf, *South African Archaeological Society Goodwin Series* 7: 98–103.

Sampson, C.G. 1970 The Smithfield Industrial Complex: further field results, *Memoirs of the National Museum (Bloemfontein)* 5: 1–172.

  1972 The Stone Age industries of the Orange River Scheme Area and South Africa, *Memoirs of the National Museum (Bloemfontein)* 6: 1–288.

  1974 *The Stone Age archaeology of southern Africa*, New York: Academic Press.

  1985a Atlas of Stone Age settlement in the Seacow Valley, *Memoirs of the National Museum (Bloemfontein)* 20: 1–116.

1985b Review of: Janette Deacon The Later Stone Age of southernmost Africa, *South African Archaeological Bulletin* 40: 56–8.

1988 *Stylistic boundaries among mobile hunter-foragers*, Washington, DC: Smithsonian Institution.

1992 A different way of recovery, *The Digging Stick* 9 (1): 10–11.

1993 'Zeer grote liefhebbers van tobak': nicotine and cannabis dependency of the Seacow River Bushmen, *The Digging Stick* 9 (3): 2–6.

1994 Ostrich eggs and Bushman survival on the north-east frontier of the Cape Colony, South Africa, *Journal of Arid Environments* 26: 383–99.

1995 Acquisition of European livestock by the Seacow River Bushmen between AD 1770–1890, *Southern African Field Archaeology* 4: 30–6.

1996 Spatial organization of Later Stone Age herders in the upper Karoo, in G. Pwiti and R. Soper (eds.), pp. 317–26.

Sampson, C.G., Bailiff, I. and Barnett, S. 1997 Thermoluminescence dates from Later Stone Age pottery on surface sites in the Upper Karoo, *South African Archaeological Bulletin* 52: 38–42.

Sampson, C.G., Hart, T.J.G., Wallsmith, D. and Blagg, J.D. 1989 The ceramic sequence in the upper Seacow valley: problems and implications, *South African Archaeological Bulletin* 44: 3–16.

Sampson, C.G. and Plug, I. 1993 Late Holocene and historical bone midden density in rock shelters of the upper Seacow River valley, *Southern African Field Archaeology* 2: 59–66.

Sampson, C.G. and Sadr, K. 1999 On the size and shape of Later Stone Age fibre-tempered vessels from the upper Seacow River valley, *Southern African Field Archaeology* 8: 3–16.

Sampson, C.G., Sampson, B.E. and Neville, D. 1994 An early Dutch settlement pattern on the north east frontier of the Cape Colony, *Southern African Field Archaeology* 3: 74–81.

Sampson, C.G. and Vogel, J.C. 1995 Radiocarbon chronology of Later Stone Age pottery decorations in the upper Seacow valley, *Southern African Field Archaeology* 4: 84–94.

Sandelowsky, B.H. 1977 Mirabib – an archaeological study in the Namib, *Madoqua* 10: 221–83.

1979 Kapako and Vungu Vungu: Iron Age sites on the Kavango River, *South African Archaeological Society Goodwin Series* 3: 52–61.

Sandelowsky, B.H., van Rooyen, J.H. and Vogel, J.C. 1979 Early evidence for herders in the Namib, *South African Archaeological Bulletin* 34: 50–1.

Sarich, V.M. and Wilson, A.C. 1967 Immunological time scale for hominid evolution, *Science* 158: 1200–3.

Schapera, I. 1930 *The Khoisan peoples of South Africa: Bushmen and Hottentots*, London: George Routledge and Sons.

1971 *Rainmaking rites of Tswana tribes*, Leiden: Afrika-Studiecentrum.

Schmidt, S. 1979 The rain bull of the South African Bushmen, *African Studies* 38: 201–24.

Schoeman, M.H. 1998a Excavating Ndzundza Ndebele identity at KwaMaza, *Southern African Field Archaeology* 7: 42–52.

1998b Material culture 'under the animal skin': excavations at Esikhunjuni, a mfecane period Ndzundza Ndebele site, *Southern African Field Archaeology* 7: 72–81.

Schoenbrun, D.L. 1998 *A green place, a good place: a social history of the Great Lakes Region, earliest times to the fifteenth century*, London: Heinemann.

Schofield, J.F. 1948 *Primitive pottery: an introduction to South African ceramics, prehistoric and protohistoric*, Cape Town: South African Archaeological Society.

Scholtz, A. 1986 Palynological and palaeobotanical studies in the southern Cape, MA thesis, University of Stellenbosch.

Schrenk, F., Bromage, T.G., Betzler, C.G., Ring, U. and Juyawewi, Y.M. 1993 Oldest *Homo* and Pliocene biogeography of the Malawi Rift, *Nature* 365: 833–5.

Schrire, C. 1962 Oakhurst: a re-examination and vindication, *South African Archaeological Bulletin* 17: 181–95.

1980 An inquiry into the evolutionary status and apparent identity of San hunter-gatherers, *Human Ecology* 8: 9–29.

1988 The historical archaeology of the impact of colonialism in 17th-century South Africa, *Antiquity* 62: 214–25.

1990 Excavating archives at Oudepost 1, Cape, *Social Dynamics* 16: 11–21.

1991 Is the Penn mightier than the shovel? A sally to a riposte, *Social Dynamics* 17: 106–9.

1992a The archaeological identity of hunters and herders at the Cape over the last 2000 years: a critique, *South African Archaeological Bulletin* 47: 62–4.

1992b Digging archives at Oudepost 1, Cape, South Africa, in A.E. Yentsch and M.C. Beaudry (eds.), *The art and mystery of historical archaeology: essays in honor of James Deetz*, Boca Raton: CRC Press, pp. 361–72.

1993 Assessing Oudepost 1: reply to Yates and Smith, *Southern African Field Archaeology* 2: 105–6.

1995 *Digging through darkness: chronicles of an archaeologist*, Richmond: University of Virginia Press.

Schrire, C., Cruz-Uribe, K. and Klose, J. 1993 The site history of the historical site at Oudepost 1, Cape, *Souh African Archaeological Society Goodwin Series* 7: 21–32.

Schrire, C. and Deacon, J. 1989 The indigenous artefacts from Oudepost 1, a colonial outpost of the VOC at Saldanha Bay, Cape, *South African Archaeological Bulletin* 44: 105–13.

Schrire, C., Deetz, J., Lubinsky, D. and Poggenpoel, C.A. 1990. The chronology of Oudepost 1, Cape, as inferred from an analysis of clay pipes, *Journal of Archaeological Science* 17: 269–300.

Schrire, C. and Meltzer, L. 1992 Coins, gaming counters and a bale seal from Oudepost, Cape, *South African Archaeological Bulletin* 47: 104–7.

Schultze, L. 1928 Zur Kenntnis des Körpers der Hottentotten und Büschmanner, *Zoologische und anthropologische Ergebnisse einer Forschungsreise im westlischen und zentralen Südafrika* 5 (3): 147–227.

Schwarcz, H.P., Grün, R. and Tobias, P.V. 1994 ESR dating studies of the australopithecine site of Sterkfontein, South Africa, *Journal of Human Evolution* 26: 175–81.

Schwarcz, H.P. and Rink, J. 2000 ESR dating of the Die Kelders Cave 1 site, South Africa, *Journal of Human Evolution* 38: 121–8.

Schweitzer, F.R. 1979 Excavations at Die Kelders, Cape Province, South Africa: the Holocene deposits, *Annals of the South African Museum* 78: 101–232.

Schweitzer, F.R. and Wilson, M.L. 1982 Byneskranskop 1: a late Quaternary living site in the southern Cape Province, South Africa, *Annals of the South African Museum* 88: 1–203.

Scott, L. 1982 A late Quaternary pollen record from the Transvaal Bushveld, South Africa, *Quaternary Research* 17: 339–70.

1989 Late Quaternary vegetation history and climatic change in the eastern Orange Free State, South Africa, *South African Journal of Botany* 55: 107–16.

1996 Palynology of hyrax middens: 2000 years of palaeoenvironmental history in Namibia, *Quaternary International* 33: 73–9.

Scott, L. and Bousman, C.B. 1990 Palynological studies of hyrax middens from southern Africa, *Palaeogeography, Palaeoclimatology and Palaeoecology* 76: 367–79.

Scott, P.E. and Deetz, J. 1990 Building, furnishings and social change in early Victorian Grahamstown, *Social Dynamics* 16: 76–89.

Scudder, T. 1962 *The ecology of the Gwembe Tonga*, Manchester: Manchester University Press.

Sealy, J.C. 1989 The use of chemical studies for reconstructing prehistoric diets: a case study in the south-western Cape, *South African Archaeological Society Goodwin Series* 6: 69–76.

Sealy, J.C., Morris, A.G., Armstrong, R., Markell, A.B. and Schrire, C. 1993 An historic skeleton from the slave lodge at Vergelegen, *South African Archaeological Society Goodwin Series* 7: 84–91.

Sealy, J.C., Patrick, M.K., Morris, A.G. and Alder, D. 1992 Diet and dental caries among Later Stone Age inhabitants of the Cape Province, South Africa, *American Journal of Physical Anthropology* 88: 123–34.

Sealy, J.C. and Pfeiffer, S. 2000 Diet, body size and landscape use among Holocene people in the southern Cape, South Africa, *Current Anthropology* 71: 642–55.

Sealy, J.C., Pfeiffer, S., Yates, R., Willmore, K., Manhire, A., Maggs, T.M.O'C. and Lanham, J. 2000 Hunter-gatherer child burials from the Pakhuis Mountains, Western Cape: growth, diet and burial practices in the late Holocene, *South African Archaeological Bulletin* 55: 32–43.

Sealy, J.C. and van der Merwe, N.J. 1986 Isotope assessment and the seasonal mobility hypothesis in the south-western Cape of South Africa, *Current Anthropology* 27: 135–50.

1988 Social, spatial and chronological patterning in marine food use as determined by ∂^{13}C measurements of Holocene human skeletal remains from the south-western Cape, South Africa, *World Archaeology* 20: 87–102.

1992 On 'Approaches to dietary reconstruction in the Western Cape: are you what you have eaten?' – a reply to Parkington, *Journal of Archaeological Science* 19: 459–66.

Sealy, J.C. and Yates, R. 1994 The chronology of the introduction of pastoralism to the Cape, South Africa, *Antiquity* 68: 58–67.

1996 Direct radiocarbon dating of early sheep bones: two further results, *South African Archaeological Bulletin* 51: 109–10.

Seeman, U.A. 1992 The Amsterdam Battery: a late 18th century Dutch military installation in Table Bay, *Southern African Field Archaeology* 1: 71–8.

Segobye, A.K. 1994 Farming communities in Botswana: an archaeological study of land use and settlement in the Mokgware Hills *c.* 10th–15th centuries AD, PhD thesis, University of Cambridge.

Shackleton, C.M. and Prins, F.E. 1992 Charcoal analysis and 'the principle of least effort' – a conceptual model, *Journal of Archaeological Science* 19: 631–7.

Shackleton, N.J. 1982 Stratigraphy and chronology of the KRM deposits: oxygen isotope evidence, in R. Singer and J. Wymer, pp. 194–9.

Shackley, M.L. 1984 ≠Hing-≠hais: an early Holocene stoneworking site in central Namibia, *Madoqua* 13: 271–9.
　1985 Palaeolithic archaeology of the central Namib Desert, *Cimbebasia Memoir* 6: 1–84.
Shaw, E.M. and van Warmelo, N.J. 1974 The material culture of the Cape Nguni. Part 2: technology, *Annals of the South African Museum* 58: 103–214.
Shell, R.C.-H. 1994 *Children of bondage: a social history of the slave society at the Cape of Good Hope, 1652–1838*, Johannesburg: Witwatersrand University Press.
Shepherd, N. 1998 Archaeology and post-modernism in South Africa, PhD thesis, University of Cape Town.
Shott, M.J. 1992 On recent trends in the anthropology of foragers: Kalahari revisionism and its archaeological implications, *Man* 27: 843–71.
Sibley, C.G. and Ahlquist, J.E. 1984 The phylogeny of the hominoid primates as indicated by DNA–DNA hybridization, *Journal of Molecular Evolution* 20: 2–15.
Silberbauer, F. 1979 Stable carbon isotopes and prehistoric diets in the eastern Cape Province, South Africa, MA thesis, University of Cape Town.
Silberbauer, G.B. 1981 *Hunter and habitat in the central Kalahari Desert*, Cambridge: Cambridge University Press.
　1991 Morbid reflexivity and overgeneralisation in Mosarwa studies, *Current Anthropology* 32: 96–9.
Sillen, A. 1992 Strontium–calcium ratios (Sr/Ca) of *Australopithecus robustus* and associated fauna from Swartkrans, *Journal of Human Evolution* 23: 495–516.
Sillen, A., Hall, G. and Armstrong, R. 1995 Strontium calcium ratios (Sr/Ca) and strontium isotope ratios (^{87}Sr/^{86}Sr) of *Australopithecus robustus* and *Homo* sp. from Swartkrans, *Journal of Human Evolution* 28: 277–85.
Sillen, A. and Morris, A.G. 1996 Diagenesis of bone from Border Cave: implications for the age of the Border Cave hominids, *Journal of Human Evolution* 31: 499–506.
Sinclair, P.J.J. 1984 Some aspects of the economic level of the Zimbabwe state, *Zimbabwea* 1: 48–53.
　1987 *Space, time and social formation: a territorial approach to the archaeology and anthropology of Zimbabwe and Mozambique, c. 0–1700 AD*. Uppsala: Societas Archaeologica Upsaliensis.
Sinclair, P.J.J., Morais, J.M.F., Adamowicz, L. and Duarte, R.T. 1993a A perspective on archaeological research in Mozambique, in T. Shaw, P.J.J. Sinclair, B. Andah and A. Okpoko (eds.), *The archaeology of Africa: food, metals and towns*, London: Routledge, pp. 409–31.
Sinclair, P.J.J., Pikirayi, I., Pwiti, G. and Soper, R. 1993b Urban trajectories on the Zimbabwean plateau, in T. Shaw, P.J.J. Sinclair, B. Andah and A. Okpoko (eds.), *The archaeology of Africa: food, metals and towns*, London: Routledge, pp. 705–31.
Singer, R. and Wymer, J. 1982 *The Middle Stone Age at Klasies River Mouth in South Africa*, Chicago: University of Chicago Press.
Skotnes, P. 1994 The visual as a site of meaning: San parietal painting and the experience of modern art, in T.A. Dowson and J.D. Lewis-Williams (eds.), pp. 315–30.
　(ed.) 1996 *Miscast: negotiating the presence of the Bushmen*, Cape Town: University of Cape Town Press.

Smith, A.B. 1981 An archaeological investigation of Holocene deposits at Rooiels
    Cave, south-western Cape, *South African Archaeological Bulletin* 36: 75–83.
    1983 The hotnot syndrome: myth-making in South African school textbooks,
    Social Dynamics 9 (2): 37–49.
    1986 Excavations at Plettenberg Bay, South Africa, of the camp-site of the
    survivors of the wreck of the *São Gonçalo*, 1630, *The International Journal of
    Nautical Archaeology and Underwater Exploration* 15: 53–63.
    1987 Seasonal exploitation of resources on the Vredenburg peninsula after 2000
    B.P., in J.E. Parkington and M. Hall (eds.), pp. 393–402.
    1989 Khoikhoi susceptibility to virgin soil epidemics in the 18th century,
    South African Medical Journal 75: 25–6.
    1990 On becoming herders: Khoikhoi and San ethnicity in southern Africa,
    African Studies 49: 50–73.
    1992a *Pastoralism in Africa: origins and developmental ecology*, London: Hurst
    and Co.
    1992b Kasteelberg, in A.B. Smith and B. Mütti (eds.), pp. 28–30.
    1993a Different facets of the crystal: early European images of the Khoikhoi at
    the Cape, South Africa, *South African Archaeological Society Goodwin
    Series* 7: 8–20.
    1993b Exploitation of marine mammals by prehistoric Cape herders, *South
    African Journal of Science* 89: 162–5.
    (ed.) 1995a *Einiqualand: studies of the Orange River frontier*, Cape Town:
    University of Cape Town Press.
    1995b Archaeological observations along the Orange River and its hinterland, in
    A.B. Smith (ed.), pp. 265–300.
    1998 Khoesaan orthography, *South African Archaeological Bulletin* 53: 37–8.
Smith, A.B. and Jacobson, L. 1995 Excavations at Geduld and the appearance of
    early domestic stock in Namibia, *South African Archaeological Bulletin*
    50: 3–14.
Smith, A.B. and Lee, R.B. 1997 Cho/ana: archaeological and ethnohistorical
    evidence for recent hunter-gatherer/agropastoralist contact in northern
    Bushmanland, Namibia, *South African Archaeological Bulletin* 52: 52–8.
Smith, A.B. and Mütti, B. (eds.), 1992 *Guide to archaeological sites in the
    south-western Cape*, Cape Town: Southern African Association of
    Archaeologists.
Smith, A.B. and Pheiffer, R.H. 1992 Col. Robert Jacob Gordon's notes on the
    Khoikhoi 1779–80, *Annals of the South African Cultural History Museum* 5
    (1): 1–54.
Smith, A.B. and Poggenpoel, C.A. 1988 The technology of bone tool fabrication in
    the south-western Cape, South Africa, *World Archaeology* 20: 103–15.
Smith, A.B. and Ripp, M.R. 1978 An archaeological reconnaissance of the
    Doorn/Tanqua Karoo, *South African Archaeological Bulletin* 33: 118–33.
Smith, A.B., Sadr, K., Gribble, J. and Yates, R. 1991 Excavations in the
    south-western Cape, South Africa, and the archaeological identity of
    prehistoric hunter-gatherers within the last 2000 years, *South African
    Archaeological Bulletin* 46: 71–90.
Smith, A.B., Woodborne, S., Lamprecht, E.C. and Riley, F.R. 1992 Marine mammal
    storage: analysis of buried seal meat at the Cape, South Africa, *Journal of
    Archaeological Science* 19: 171–80.

Smith, A.B., Yates, R. and Jacobson, L. 1996 Geduld *contra* Kinahan, *South African Archaeological Bulletin* 51: 36–9.

Smith, A.K. 1970 The struggle for the control of southern Mozambique, 1720–1835, PhD thesis, University of California, Los Angeles.

1973 The peoples of southern Mozambique: an historical survey, *Journal of African History* 14: 568–80.

Smith, B., Lewis-Williams, J.D., Blundell, G. and Chippindale, C. 2000 Archaeology and symbolism in the new South African coat of arms, *Antiquity* 74: 467–8.

Smith, H. 1989 Growth and development and its significance for early hominid behaviour, *Ossa* 14: 63–96.

Smith, J. 1997 Stable isotope analysis of fauna and soils from sites in the eastern Free State and western Lesotho, southern Africa: a palaeoenvironmental interpretation, MA thesis, University of Cape Town.

Smith, P., Horowitz, L.K. and Kaplan, E. 1992 Skeletal evidence for population changes in the late Holocene of the south-western Cape: a radiological study, *South African Archaeological Bulletin* 47: 82–8.

Solomon, A.C. 1989 Division of the earth: gender, symbolism and the archaeology of the southern San, MA thesis, University of Cape Town.

1992 Gender, representation, and power in San ethnography and rock art, *Journal of Anthropological Archaeology* 11: 291–329.

1994 'Mythic women': a study in variability in San rock art and narrative, in T.A. Dowson and J.D. Lewis-Williams (eds.), pp. 331–72.

1996 Some questions about style and authorship in later San paintings, in P. Skotnes (ed.), pp. 291–5.

1997 The myth of ritual origins? Ethnography, mythology and interpretation of San rock art, *South African Archaeological Bulletin* 52: 3–13.

1999 Meaning, models and minds: a reply to Lewis-Williams, *South African Archaeological Bulletin* 54: 51–60.

2000 On different approaches to San rock art, *South African Archaeological Bulletin* 55: 77–8.

Solomon, A.C. and Smith, J. 1994 Opinions, *Southern African Field Archaeology* 3: 61–2.

Solway, J.S. and Lee, R.B. 1990 Foragers, genuine or spurious? Situating the Kalahari San in history, *Current Anthropology* 31: 109–46.

Soper, R. 1994 Stone enclosures on Mount Fura, northern Zimbabwe, *Zimbabwean Prehistory* 21: 23–8.

1996 The Nyanga terrace complex of eastern Zimbabwe: new investigations, *Azania* 31: 1–36.

1997 Review of: T.N. Huffman Snakes and crocodiles: power and symbolism in ancient Zimbabwe, *Azania* 32: 123–7.

Soper, R. and Pwiti, G. 1988 Preliminary report on excavations at Wazi Hill, Centenary, northern Zimbabwe, *Zimbabwean Prehistory* 20: 16–20.

Sparrman, A. 1786 *A voyage to the Cape of Good Hope towards the Antarctic Polar Circle and around the World, but chiefly into the country of the Hottentots and Caffres, from the year 1772 to 1776*, London: Robinson.

Speth, J.D. 1987 Early hominid subsistence strategies in seasonal habitats, *Journal of Archaeological Science* 14: 13–29.

Stayt, H. 1931 *The Bavenda*, Oxford: Oxford University Press.

Stevenson, J. 1995 Man-the-shaman: is it the whole story? A feminist perspective on the San rock art of southern Africa, MA thesis, University of the Witwatersrand.

Steyn, M. 1997 A reassessment of the human skeletons from K2 and Mapungubwe (South Africa), *South African Archaeological Bulletin* 52: 14–20.

Steyn, M., Loots, M. and Prinsloo, H. 1994 An Early Iron Age human skeleton from the Soutpansberg district, South Africa, *South African Journal of Science* 90: 552–5.

Steyn, M., Miller, S., Nienaber, W.C. and Loots, M. 1998 Late Iron Age gold burials from Thulamela (Pafuri region, Kruger National Park), *South African Archaeological Bulletin* 53: 73–85.

Steyn, M., Neinaber, W.C., Loots, M., Meiring, J.H. and Meyer, A. 1999 An infant grave from K2 (Greefswald), *South African Archaeological Bulletin* 54: 102–6.

Stiles, D., Hay, R. and O'Neil, J. 1974 The MNK Chert Factory Site, Olduvai Gorge, Tanzania, *World Archaeology* 5: 285–308.

Stoneking, M., Sherry, S.T., Redd, A.J. and Vigilant, L. 1993 New approaches to dating suggest a recent age for the human mtDNA ancestor, in M.J. Aitken *et al.* (eds.), pp. 84–103.

Stow, G.W. 1905 *The native races of South Africa*, London: Swan Sonnenschein and Co.

1930 (D.F. Bleek ed.) *Rock paintings in South Africa*, London: Macmillan.

Straus, L.G., Eriksen, B.V., Erlandson, J.M. and Yesner, D.R. (eds.) 1996 *Humans at the end of the Ice Age: the archaeology of the Pleistocene–Holocene transition*, New York: Plenum.

Stringer, C.B. 1985 Middle Pleistocene hominid variability and the origin of Late Pleistocene humans, in E. Delson (ed.), *Ancestors: the hard evidence*, New York: Alan Liss, pp. 289–95.

1999 Has Australia backdated the human revolution? *Antiquity* 73: 876–9.

Stringer, C.B. and Bräuer, G. 1994 Methods, misreading and bias, *American Anthropologist* 96: 416–24.

Stringer, C.B. and Gamble, C.S. 1993 *In search of the Neanderthals*, London: Thames and Hudson.

Stuiver, M. 1969 Yale natural radiocarbon measurements IX, *Radiocarbon* 11: 545–658.

Stuiver, M., Reimer, P.J., Bard, E., Beck, J.W., Burr, G.S., Hughen, K.A., Kromer, B., McCormac, G., van der Plicht, J. and Spurk, M. 1998 INTCAL98 radiocarbon age calibration, 24,000–0 cal BP, *Radiocarbon* 40: 1041–84.

Summers, R. 1950 Iron Age cultures in Southern Rhodesia, *South African Journal of Science* 47: 95–107.

(ed.) 1958 *Inyanga: prehistoric settlements in Southern Rhodesia*, Cambridge: Cambridge University Press.

1961 Excavations in the Great Enclosure, *Occasional Papers of the National Museums of Southern Rhodesia* 23a: 236–88.

1969 *Ancient mines of Rhodesia and adjacent areas*, Salisbury: National Museums of Rhodesia.

1971 *Ancient ruins and vanished civilizations of southern Africa*, Cape Town: Bulpin.

Summers, R. and Pagden, C.W. 1970 *The warriors*, Cape Town: Books of Africa.

Summers, R., Robinson, K.R. and Whitty, A. 1961 Zimbabwe excavations, *Occasional Papers of the National Museums of Rhodesia* 3: 15–332.

Susman, R.L. 1988 Hand of *Paranthropus robustus* from Member 1, Swartkrans: fossil evidence for tool behavior, *Science* 240: 781–4.

Sutton, J. 1994/95 Editor's introduction, *Azania* 29/30: 1–14.

1998 Kilwa: a history of the ancient Swahili town with a guide to the monuments of Kilwa Kisiwani and adjacent islands, *Azania* 33: 113–69.

Swan, L. 1994 *Early gold mining on the Zimbabwean Plateau*. Uppsala: Societas Archaeologica Upsaliensis.

Swisher, C.C., Curtis, G.H., Jacob, T., Getty, A.G., Suprijo, A. and Widiasmoro 1994 Age of the earliest known hominids in Java, Indonesia, *Science* 263: 1118–21.

Swisher, C.C., Rink, W., Antón, S.C., Schwarcz, H.P., Curtis, G.H., Suprijo, A. and Widiasmoro 1996 Latest *Homo erectus* of Java: potential contemporaneity with *Homo sapiens* in South East Asia, *Science* 274: 1870–4.

Szabo, B.J. and Butzer, K.W. 1979 Uranium-series dating of lacustrine limestones from pan deposits with Final Acheulian assemblages at Rooidam, Kimberley district, South Africa, *Quaternary Research* 11: 257–60.

Talma, A.S. and Vogel, J.C. 1992 Late Quaternary palaeotemperatures derived from a speleothem from Cango Caves, Cape Province, South Africa, *Quaternary Research* 37: 203–13.

1993 A simplified approach to calibrating ^{14}C dates, *Radiocarbon* 35: 317–22.

Taylor, M.O.V. 1979 Late Iron Age settlements on the northern edge of the Vredefort Dome, MA thesis, University of the Witwatersrand.

Templeton, A.R. 1993 The 'Eve' hypothesis: a genetic critique and reanalysis, *American Anthropologist* 95: 51–72.

Tesele, F.T. 1994 Symbols of power: beads and flywhisks in traditional healing in Lesotho, BA thesis, University of Cape Town.

Thackeray, A.I. 1977 Stone artefacts from Klipfonteinrand, BA thesis, University of Cape Town.

1983 Dating the rock art of southern Africa, *South African Archaeological Society Goodwin Series* 4: 21–6.

1989 Changing fashions in the Middle Stone Age: the stone artefact sequence from Klasies River Mouth main site, South Africa, *African Archaeological Review* 7: 33–57.

1992 The Middle Stone Age south of the Limpopo River, *Journal of World Prehistory* 6: 385–440.

2000 Middle Stone Age artefacts from the 1993 and 1995 excavations of Die Kelders Cave 1, South Africa, *Journal of Human Evolution* 38: 147–68.

Thackeray, A.I., Thackeray, J.F. and Beaumont, P.B. 1983 Excavations at the Blinkklipkop specularite mine near Postmasburg, Northern Cape, *South African Archaeological Bulletin* 38: 17–25.

Thackeray, A.I., Thackeray, J.F., Beaumont, P.B. and Vogel, J.C. 1981 Dated rock engravings from Wonderwerk Cave, South Africa, *Science* 214: 64–7.

Thackeray, J.F. 1979 An analysis of faunal remains from archaeological sites in southern South West Africa (Namibia), *South African Archaeological Bulletin* 34: 18–33.

1984 Climatic change and mammalian fauna from Holocene deposits in Wonderwerk cave, Northern Cape, in J.C. Vogel (ed.), *Late Cainozoic palaeoclimates of the Southern Hemisphere*, Rotterdam: Balkema, pp. 371–4.

1987 Late Quaternary environmental changes inferred from small mammalian fauna, southern Africa, *Climatic Change* 10: 285–305.

1988a Quantification of climatic change during the Late Quaternary in southern Africa, *Palaeoecology of Africa* 19: 317–24.

1988b Molluscan fauna from Klasies River, South Africa, *South African Archaeological Bulletin* 43: 27–32.

1990a Temperature indices from Late Quaternary sequences in South Africa: comparisons with the Vostok core, *South African Geographical Journal* 72: 47–9.

1990b Carnivore activity at Klasies River Mouth: a response to Binford, *Palaeontologia Africana* 27: 101–9.

1994 Animals, conceptual associations and southern African rock art: a multidisciplinary, exploratory approach, in T.A. Dowson and J.D. Lewis-Williams (eds.), pp. 223–36.

Thom, H.B. 1952–58 *Journal of Jan Van Riebeeck*, 3 vols., Cape Town: A.A. Balkema.

Thomas, D.S.G. and Shaw, P.A. 1991 *The Kalahari environment*, Cambridge: Cambridge University Press.

Thompson, L.C. 1949 Ingots of native manufacture, *South African Native Affairs Department Annual* 26: 7–22.

Thorp, C.R. 1984 A cultural interpretation of the faunal assemblage from Khami Hill Ruin, in M. Hall *et al.* (eds.), pp. 266–76.

1995 Kings, commoners and cattle at Zimbabwe Tradition sites. *National Museums and Monuments of Zimbabwe Memoir New Series* 1: 1–130.

2000 *Hunter-gatherers and farmers: an enduring frontier in the Caledon Valley, South Africa*, Oxford: British Archaeological Reports.

Tishkoff, S.A., Dietrich, E., Speed, W., Pakstis, A.J., Kidd, J.R., Cheung, K., Bonné-Tamir, B., Santachiara-Benerecetti, A.S., Moral, P., Krings, M., Pääbo, S., Watson, E., Risch, N., Jenkins, T. and Kidd, K.K. 1996 Global patterns of linkage disequilibrium at the CD4 locus and modern human origins, *Science* 271: 1380–7.

Tobias, P.V. 1971 Human skeletal remains from the Cave of Hearths, Makapansgat, northern Transvaal, *American Journal of Physical Anthropology* 34: 355–68.

2000 The fossil hominids, in T.C. Partridge and R.R. Maud (eds.), pp. 252–76.

Torrence, R. 1989 Retooling: towards a behavioral theory of stone tools, in R. Torrence (ed.), *Time, energy and stone tools*, Cambridge: Cambridge University Press, pp. 57–66.

Toth, N.J. 1985 The Oldowan reassessed: a close look at early stone artefacts, *Journal of Archaeological Science* 12: 101–20.

Toth, N. and Schick, K. 1986 The first million years: the archaeology of protohuman culture, *Advances in Archaeological Method and Theory* 9: 1–96.

Toth, N., Schick, K., Savage-Rumbaugh, E.S., Sevcik, R.A. and Rumbaugh, D. 1993 *Pan the tool-maker, Journal of Archaeological Science* 20: 81–91.

Traill, A. 1996 !Khwa-Ka Hhouiten Hhouiten 'The rush of the storm': the linguistic death of /Xam, in P. Skotnes (ed.), pp. 161–83.

Trigger, B. 1989 *A history of archaeological thought*, Cambridge: Cambridge University Press.

Turner, A. 1989 Sample selection, schlepp effects and scavenging: the implications of partial recovery for the interpretations of the terrestrial mammal assemblage from Klasies River Mouth, *Journal of Archaeological Science* 16: 1–11.

Turner, G. 1987 Herders and hunters of the Okavango Delta, Northern Botswana, *Botswana Notes and Records* 19: 25–40.

Tusenius, M.L. 1989 Charcoal analytical studies in the north-eastern Cape, South Africa, *South African Archaeological Society Goodwin Series* 6: 77–83.

Tyson, P.D. 1986 *Climatic change and variability in southern Africa*, Cape Town: Oxford University Press.

Tyson, P.D. and Lindesay, J.A. 1992 The climate of the last 2000 years in southern Africa, *The Holocene* 2: 271–8.

Van Andel, T.H. 1989 Late Pleistocene sea levels and the human exploitation of the shore and shelf of southern South Africa, *Journal of Field Archaeology* 16: 133–55.

  1998 Middle and Upper Palaeolithic environments and the calibration of ^{14}C dates beyond 10,000 BP, *Antiquity* 72: 26–33.

van der Merwe, N.J. and Killick, D. 1979 Square: an iron smelting site near Phalaborwa, *South African Archaeological Society Goodwin Series* 3: 86–93.

van der Merwe, N.J. and Scully, R. 1971 The Phalaborwa story: archaeological and ethnographic investigation of a South African Iron Age group, *World Archaeology* 3: 178–96.

van der Merwe, N.J., Sealy, J.C. and Yates, R. 1987 First accelerator carbon-14 date for pigment from a rock painting, *South African Journal of Science* 33: 56–7.

van der Plicht, J. 1999 Radiocarbon calibration for the Middle/Upper Palaeolithic: a comment, *Antiquity* 73: 119–23.

van der Ryst, M. 1998 *The Waterberg Plateau in the Northern Province, Republic of South Africa, in the Later Stone Age*, Oxford: British Archaeological Reports.

van Ewyk, J.F. 1987 The prehistory of an Iron Age site on Skutwater, PhD thesis, University of Pretoria.

van Noten, F. 1974 Excavations at the Gordons Bay shell midden, south-western Cape, *South African Archaeological Bulletin* 29: 122–42.

van Reenen, J.F. 1987 Tooth mutilating and extraction practices amongst the peoples of South West Africa (Namibia), in R. Singer and J.K. Lundy (eds.), *Variation, culture and evolution in African populations*, Johannesburg: Witwatersrand University Press, pp. 159–70.

van Rijssen, W.J. 1984 Rock art: the question of authorship, in T.A. Dowson and J.D. Lewis-Williams (eds.), pp. 159–76.

van Schalkwyk, J.A. 1998 Archaeological investigations of the Beauley Early Iron Age site in the Blouberg, Northern Province, *Southern African Field Archaeology* 7: 35–41.

van Schalkwyk, L.O. 1994a Mamba confluence: a preliminary report on an Early Iron Age industrial centre in the lower Thukela Basin, Natal, *Natal Museum Journal of Humanities* 6: 119–52.

  1994b Wosi: an Early Iron Age village in the lower Thukela Basin, Natal, *Natal Museum Journal of Humanities* 6: 65–117.

  1994/95 Settlement shifts and socio-economic transformations in early agriculturist communities in the lower Thukela Basin, *Azania* 29/30: 187–98.

van Schalkwyk, L.O., Greenfield, H. and Jongsma, T. 1997 The Early Iron Age site of Ndondonwane, KwaZulu-Natal, South Africa: preliminary report on the 1995 excavations, *Southern African Field Archaeology* 6: 61–77.

van Vollenhoven, A.C. 1994 An historical archaeological investigation of Fort
    Daspoortrand, Pretoria, *Southern African Field Archaeology* 3: 49–54.
    1996 Historical-archaeological research in the Pretoria area, in G. Pwiti and
    R. Soper (eds.), pp. 719–24.
van Waarden, C. 1987 Matanga, a late Zimbabwe cattle post, *South African
    Archaeological Bulletin* 42: 107–24.
    1991 The granaries of Vumba: structural interpretation of a Khami commoner
    site, *Journal of Anthropological Archaeology* 8: 131–57.
    1996 The pre-development archaeology programme of Botswana, in G. Pwiti
    and R. Soper (eds.), pp. 829–36.
    1998 The Later Iron Age, in P. Lane *et al.* (eds.), pp. 115–60.
van Wyk, E.B. 1969 Die indeling van die Sotho-taalgroep, in Government
    Ethnologists (eds.), *Ethnological and linguistic studies in honour of N.J. van
    Warmelo*, Pretoria: Government Printer, pp. 169–79.
Vansina, J. 1984 Western Bantu expansion, *Journal of African History* 25: 129–46.
    1994/95 A slow revolution: farming in subequatorial Africa, *Azania* 29/30:
    1–14.
    1995 New linguistic evidence and 'the Bantu expansion', *Journal of African
    History* 36: 173–95.
Vermeersch, P.M., Paulissen, E., Stokes, S., Charlier, C., van Peer, P., Stringer,
    C.B. and Lindsay, W. 1998 A Middle Palaeolithic burial of a modern human at
    Taramsa Hill, Egypt, *Antiquity* 72: 475–84.
Vierich, H. and Hitchcock, R. 1996 Kua: farmer/foragers of the eastern Kalahari,
    Botswana, in S. Kent (ed.), pp. 108–24.
Vigilant, L., Stoneking, M., Harpending, H., Hawkes, K. and Wilson, A.C. 1991
    African populations and the evolution of human mitochondrial DNA, *Science*
    253: 1503–7.
Vinnicombe, P. 1972 Myth, motive and selection in southern African rock art,
    Africa 42: 192–204.
    1976 *People of the eland*, Pietermaritzburg: University of Natal Press.
Vogel, J.C. 1983 Isotopic evidence for past climates and vegetation of South Africa,
    Bothalia 14: 391–4.
    1995 The temporal distribution of radiocarbon dates for the Iron Age in
    southern Africa, *South African Archaeological Bulletin* 50: 106–9.
Vogel, J.C. and Beaumont, P.B. 1972 Revised radiocarbon chronology for the Stone
    Age in South Africa, *Nature* 237: 50–1.
Vogel, J.C. and Fuls, A. 1999 Spatial distribution of radiocarbon dates for the Iron
    Age in southern Africa, *South African Archaeological Bulletin* 54: 97–101.
Vogel, J.C., Fuls, A. and Visser, E. 1986 Pretoria radiocarbon dates III, *Radiocarbon*
    28: 1133–72.
Vogel, J.C. and Kronfeld, J. 1997 Calibration of radiocarbon dates for the late
    Pleistocene using U/Th dates on stalagmites, *Radiocarbon* 39: 27–32.
Vogel, J.C. and Marais, M. 1971 Pretoria radiocarbon dates, *Radiocarbon*
    13: 378–94.
Vogel, J.C. and Partridge, T.C. 1984 Preliminary radiometric ages of the Taung
    tufas, in J.C. Vogel (ed.), *Late Cainozoic palaeoclimates of the Southern
    Hemisphere*, Rotterdam: Balkema, pp. 507–14.
Vogel, J.C., Plug, I. and Webley, L. 1997 New dates for the introduction of sheep
    into South Africa: the evidence from Spoegrivier Cave in Namaqualand,
    South African Journal of Science 93: 246–8.

Vogel, J.C. and Visser, E. 1981 Pretoria radiocarbon dates II, *Radiocarbon* 23: 43–80.

Vogel, J.C., Wintle, A. and Woodborne, S. 1999 Luminescence dating of coastal sands: overcoming changes in environmental dose rate, *Journal of Archaeological Science* 26: 729–33.

Vogel, J.O. 1978 The Gokomere tradition, *South African Archaeological Bulletin* 33: 12–17.

1984 An Early Iron Age settlement system in southern Zambia, *Azania* 19: 61–78.

Vogelsang, R. 1996 The Middle Stone Age in south-western Namibia, in G. Pwiti and R. Soper (eds.), pp. 207–12.

1998 Archaeological survey in the Kaokoveld, Namibia, *Nyame Akuma* 50: 22–4.

Voigt, E.A. 1980 The faunal sample from Msuluzi Confluence, *Annals of the Natal Museum* 24: 140–5.

(ed.) 1981 *Guide to archaeological sites in the northern and eastern Transvaal*, Pretoria: Southern African Association of Archaeologists.

1983 *Mapungubwe: an archaeozoological interpretation of an Iron Age community*, Pretoria: Transvaal Museum.

1986 Iron Age herding: archaeological and ethnoarchaeological approaches to pastoral problems, *South African Archaeological Society Goodwin Series* 5: 13–21.

Voigt, E.A. and Peters, J. 1994 The faunal assemblage from the Early Iron Age site of Mamba I in the Thukela Valley, Natal, *Natal Museum Journal of Humanities* 6: 145–52.

Voigt, E.A. and Von den Driesch, A. 1984 Preliminary report on the faunal assemblage from Ndondonwane, Natal, *Annals of the Natal Museum* 26: 141–63.

Volman, T.P. 1978 Early archaeological evidence for shellfish collecting, *Science* 201: 911–13.

1981 The Middle Stone Age in the southern Cape, PhD thesis, University of Chicago.

1984 Early prehistory of southern Africa, in R.G. Klein (ed.), pp. 169–220.

von den Driesch, A. and Deacon, H.J. 1985 Sheep remains from Boomplaas Cave, South Africa, *South African Archaeological Bulletin* 40: 39–44.

Vos, H. 1993 An historical and archaeological perspective of colonial Stellenbosch 1680–1860, MA thesis, University of Stellenbosch.

Vossen, R. 1998 Historical classification of Khoe (Central Khoisan) languages of southern Africa, *African Studies* 57: 93–106.

Vrba, E.S. 1982 Biostratigraphy and chronology, based particularly on Bovidae, of southern hominid-associated assemblages: Makapansgat, Sterkfontein, Taung, Kromdraai, Swartkrans; also Elandsfontein (Saldanha), Broken Hill (now Kabwe) and Cave of Hearths, in M.A. de Lumley (ed.), *L'Homo erectus et la place de l'homme de Tautavel parmi les hominidés fossiles*, Nice: Centre National de la Recherche Scientifique, pp. 707–52.

1992 Mammals as a key to evolutionary theory, *Journal of Mammology* 73: 1–28.

Vrba, E.S., Denton, G.H., Partridge, T.C. and Burckle, L.H. (eds.) 1995 *Palaeoclimate and evolution with emphasis on human origins*, New Haven: Yale University Press.

Wadley, L. 1979 Big Elephant Shelter: its role in the Holocene prehistory of central South West Africa, *Cimbebasia (B)* 3: 1–76.

1984a Subsistence strategies in the Transvaal Stone Age: a preliminary model, in M. Hall *et al.* (eds.), pp. 207–14.

1984b On the move: a look at prehistoric food scheduling in central Namibia, *Cimbebasia (B)* 4 (4): 41–50.

1987 *Later Stone Age hunters and gatherers of the southern Transvaal: social and ecological interpretations*, Oxford: British Archaeological Reports.

1988 Stone Age sites in the Magaliesberg, in T.M. Evers *et al.* (eds.), pp. 9–39.

1989 Gender relations in the Thukela Basin, *South African Archaeological Bulletin* 44: 122–6.

1991 Rose Cottage Cave: background and a preliminary report on the recent excavations, *South African Archaeological Bulletin* 46: 125–30.

1992 Reply to Barham: aggregation and dispersal phase sites in the Later Stone Age, *South African Archaeological Bulletin* 47: 52–5.

1993 The Pleistocene Later Stone Age south of the Limpopo, *Journal of World Prehistory* 7: 243–96.

1995 Review of dated Stone Age sites recently excavated in the eastern Free State, South Africa, *South African Journal of Science* 91: 574–9.

1996a The Robberg levels of Rose Cottage Cave: technology, environments and spatial analysis, *South African Archaeological Bulletin* 51: 64–76.

1996b Changes in the social relations of precolonial hunter-gatherers after agropastoral contact: an example from the Magaliesberg, South Africa, *Journal of Anthropological Archaeology* 15: 205–17.

1997a Rose Cottage Cave: archaeological work 1987 to 1997, *South African Journal of Science* 93: 439–44.

(ed.) 1997b *Our gendered past: archaeological studies of gender in southern Africa*, Johannesburg: Witwatersrand University Press.

1997c Where have all the dead men gone? Stone Age burial practices in South Africa, in L. Wadley (ed.), pp. 107–34.

1998 The invisible meat providers: women in the Stone Age of South Africa, in S. Kent (ed.), pp. 69–82.

2000 The early Holocene layers of Rose Cottage Cave, eastern Free State: technology, spatial patterns and environment, *South African Archaeological Bulletin* 55: 18–31.

Wadley, L. and Binneman, J.N.F. 1995 Arrowheads or pen knives? A microwear analysis of mid-Holocene stone segments from Jubilee Shelter, Transvaal, *South African Journal of Science* 91: 153–5.

Wadley, L. and Harper, P. 1989 Rose Cottage Cave revisited: Malan's Middle Stone Age collection, *South African Archaeological Bulletin* 44: 23–32.

Wadley, L. and McLaren, G. 1998 Tandjesberg Shelter, eastern Free State, South Africa, *Natal Museum Journal of Humanities* 10: 19–32.

Wadley, L. and Turner, G. 1987 Hope Hill Shelter: a Later Stone Age site in the southern Transvaal, *South African Journal of Science* 83: 98–105.

Wagner, P.A. and Gordon, H.S. 1929 Further notes on ancient bronze smelters in the Waterberg District, Transvaal, *South African Journal of Science* 26: 563–74.

Wainscoat. J.S., Hill, A.V.S., Thein, S.L., Flint, J., Chapman, J.C., Weatherall, D.J., Clegg, J.B. and Higgs, D.R. 1989 Geographic distribution of Alpha- and Beta-globin gene cluster polymorphisms, in P.A. Mellars and C.B. Stringer (eds.), pp. 31–8.

Walker, A.C. and Leakey, R.E.F. (eds.) 1993 *The Nariokotome* Homo erectus *skeleton*, Cambridge, MA: Harvard University Press.

Walker, A.C., Zimmerman, M.R. and Leakey, R.E.F. 1982 A possible case of hypervitaminosis A in *Homo erectus, Nature* 296: 248–50.

Walker, N.J. 1980 The ground stone axes of Zimbabwe (Rhodesia), *South African Archaeological Bulletin* 35: 113–20.

1983 The significance of an early date for pottery and sheep in Zimbabwe, *South African Archaeological Bulletin* 38: 88–92.

1987 The dating of Zimbabwean rock art, *Rock Art Research* 4: 137–49.

1990 Zimbabwe at 18,000 BP, in C.S. Gamble and O. Soffer (eds.), pp. 206–13.

1991 Report on a burial at Castle Kopje, Wedza, *South African Archaeological Bulletin* 46: 142–8.

1993 Excavations at Gokomere Eastern Cave, Zimbabwe, *Transactions of the Zimbabwean Scientific Association* 67: 13–23.

1994a Later Stone Age funerary practice in the Matopos, Zimbabwe: a contribution to understanding prehistoric death rites in southern Africa, *Southern African Field Archaeology* 3: 94–102.

1994b The Late Stone Age of Botswana: some recent excavations, *Botswana Notes and Records* 26: 1–36.

1995a *Late Pleistocene and Holocene hunter-gatherers of the Matopos*, Uppsala: Societas Archaeologica Upsaliensis.

1995b The archaeology of the San: the Late Stone Age of Botswana, in A.J.G.M. Sanders (ed.), *Speaking for the Bushmen*, Gaborone: The Botswana Society, pp. 54–87.

1997 In the footsteps of the ancestors: the Matsieng creation site in Botswana, *South African Archaeological Bulletin* 52: 95–104.

Walker, N.J. and Thorp, C. 1997 Stone Age archaeology in Zimbabwe, in G. Pwiti (ed.), pp. 9–32.

Walker, N.J. and Wadley, L. 1984 Evidence for an early microlithic industry at Duncombe Farm in Zimbabwe, *Cookeia* 1: 4–13.

Walker, P.J. 1993 The architectural development of Great Zimbabwe, *Azania* 28: 87–102.

Wallerstein, I. 1974 *The modern world system*, New York: Academic Press.

Wallsmith, D. 1990 Driekoppen: a Middle Stone Age rockshelter, *Nyame Akuma* 33: 13–16.

Walton, J. 1965 *Homesteads and villages of South Africa*, Pretoria: Van Schaik.

Ward, V. 1997 A century of change: rock art deterioration in the Natal Drakensberg, South Africa, *Natal Museum Journal of Humanities* 9: 75–97.

Ward, V. and Maggs, T.M.O'C. 1988 The slipped disc: a guide to the identification of shell disc-beads, *Annals of the Natal Museum* 29: 407–16.

1994 Changing appearances: a comparison between early copies and the present state of rock paintings from the Natal Drakensberg as an indication of rock art deterioration, *Natal Museum Journal of Humanities* 6: 153–78.

Watson, E.J. and Watson, V. 1990 'Of commoners and kings': faunal remains from Ondini, *South African Archaeological Bulletin* 45: 33–46.

Watts, I. 1998 The origin of symbolic culture: the Middle Stone Age of southern Africa and Khoisan ethnography, PhD thesis, University of London.

Webley, L. 1986 Pastoralist ethnoarchaeology in Namaqualand, *South African Archaeological Society Goodwin Series* 5: 57–61.

1990 The use of stone 'scrapers' by semi-sedentary pastoralist groups in Namaqualand, South Africa, *South African Archaeological Bulletin* 45: 28–32.

1992a The history and ethnoarchaeology of pastoralist and hunter-gatherer settlement in the north-western Cape, South Africa, PhD thesis, University of Cape Town.

1992b Early evidence for sheep from Spoeg River Cave, Namaqualand, *Southern African Field Archaeology* 1: 3–13.

1993 Archaeological investigations at the battlefield of Rorke's Drift, northern Natal, *Southern African Field Archaeology* 2: 24–34.

1997a Jakkalsberg A and B: the cultural material from two pastoralist sites in the Richtersveld, Northern Cape, *Southern African Field Archaeology* 6: 3–19.

1997b Wives and sisters: changing gender relations among Khoe pastoralists in Namaqualand, in L. Wadley (ed.), pp. 167–208.

Webley, L., Archer, F. and Brink, J.S. 1993 Die Toon: a Late Holocene site in the Richtersveld National Park, Northern Cape, *Koedoe* 36 (2): 1–9.

Wellington, J.H. 1955 *Southern Africa: a geographical study*, Cambridge: Cambridge University Press.

Wells, P.S. 1981 *Culture contact and culture change*, Cambridge: Cambridge University Press.

Wendt, W.E. 1972 Preliminary report on an archaeological research programme in South West Africa, *Cimbebasia B* 2: 1–61.

1975 Ein Rekonstruktionsversuch der Besiedlungsgeschichte des westlischen Gross-Namalandes seit dem 15 Jahrhundert, *Journal of the South West Africa Scientific Society* 29: 23–56.

1976 'Art mobilier' from the Apollo 11 Cave, South West Africa: Africa's oldest dated works of art, *South African Archaeological Bulletin* 31: 5–11.

Werger, M.J.A. 1978 The Karoo–Namib region, in M.J.A. Werger (ed.), *Biogeography and ecology of southern Africa*, The Hague: Junk, pp. 301–462.

Werz, B.E.J.S. 1999 *Diving up the human past: perspectives on maritime archaeology, with special reference to developments in South Africa until 1996*, Oxford: British Archaeological Reports.

West, F. 1981 *The archaeology of Beringia*, New York: Columbia University Press.

Westphal, E.O.J. 1963 The linguistic prehistory of southern Africa: Bush, Kwadi, Hottentot and Bantu linguistic relationships, *Africa* 33: 237–65.

White, D.A. 1977 The excavation of an Iron Age site at Palmietfontein near Klerksdorp, *South African Archaeological Bulletin* 32: 89–92.

White, T.D. 1987 Cannibals at Klasies? *Sagittarius* 2 (2): 6–9.

White, T.D., Suwa, G. and Asfaw, B. 1994 *Australopithecus ramidus*: a new species of early hominid from Aramis, Ethiopia, *Nature* 371: 306–12.

Whitelaw, G. 1991 Precolonial iron production around Durban and in southern Natal, *Natal Museum Journal of Humanities* 3: 29–39.

1993 Customs and settlement patterns in the first millennium AD: evidence from Nanda, an Early Iron Age site in the Mngeni Valley, Natal, *Natal Museum Journal of Humanities* 5: 47–81.

1994a KwaGandaganda: settlement patterns in the Natal Early Iron Age, *Natal Museum Journal of Humanities* 6: 1–64.

1994b Preliminary results of a survey of Bulawayo, Shaka kaSenzangankhona's capital from about 1820 to 1827, *Southern African Field Archaeology* 3: 107–9.

1994/95 Towards an Early Iron Age worldview: some ideas from KwaZulu-Natal, *Azania* 29/30: 37–50.

1996 Lydenburg revisited: another look at the Mpumalanga Early Iron Age sequence, *South African Archaeological Bulletin* 51: 75–83.

Whitelaw, G. and Moon, M. 1996 The distribution and ceramics of pioneer agriculturists in KwaZulu-Natal, *Natal Museum Journal of Humanities* 8: 53–79.

Whitfield, L.S., Sulston, J.E. and Goodfellow, P.N. 1995. Sequence variation of the human Y chromosome, *Nature* 378: 379–80.

Whitley, D.S. 1992 Shamanism and rock art in far western North America, *Cambridge Archaeological Journal* 2: 89–113.

Whitley, D.S. and Annegarn, H.J. 1994 Cation-ratio dating of rock engravings from Klipfontein, Northern Cape, in T.A. Dowson and J.D. Lewis-Williams (eds.), pp. 189–97.

Wiessner, P. 1977 *Hxaro*: a regional system of reciprocity for reducing risk among the !Kung San, PhD thesis, University of Michigan.

1982 Risk, reciprocity and social influence on !Kung San economics, in E. Leacock and R.B. Lee (eds.), *Politics and history in band societies*, Cambridge: Cambridge University Press, pp. 61–84.

1983 Style and social information in Kalahari San projectile points, *American Antiquity* 48: 253–76.

Williamson, B.S. 1996 Preliminary stone tool residue analysis from Rose Cottage Cave, *Southern African Field Archaeology* 5: 36–44.

1997 Down the microscope and beyond: microscopy and molecular studies of stone tool residues and bone samples from Rose Cottage Cave, *South African Journal of Science* 93: 458–64.

Wilmsen, E.N. 1989 *Land filled with flies: a political economy of the Kalahari*, Chicago: University of Chicago Press.

Wilmsen, E.N. and Denbow, J.R. 1990 Paradigmatic history of San-speaking peoples and current attempts at revision, *Current Anthropology* 31: 489–524.

Wilson, M.L. 1986 Notes on the nomenclature of the Khoisan, *Annals of the South African Museum* 97: 251–66.

1989 The problem of the origins of the Khoikhoi, *The Digging Stick* 6 (1): 2–4.

1996 The late Holocene occupants of Die Kelders: hunter-gatherers or herders? *Southern African Field Archaeology* 5: 79–83.

Wilson, M.L. and Lundy, J.K. 1994 Estimated living statures of dated Khoisan skeletons from the south-western coastal region of South Africa, *South African Archaeological Bulletin* 49: 2–8.

Wilson, M. and Thompson, L. (eds.) 1969 *Oxford History of South Africa*, Oxford: Oxford University Press

Winer, M. 1994 Landscapes of power: British material culture of the Eastern Cape Frontier, South Africa: 1820–1860, PhD thesis, University of California, Berkeley.

Winer, M. and Deetz, J. 1990 The transformation of British culture in the Eastern Cape, 1820–1860, *Social Dynamics* 16: 55–75.

Wingfield, C. 2000 Interpreting iron in Zimbabwe, BA thesis, University of Oxford.

Wirth, D. 2000 A smoke belching congestion of factories: Cape Town's neglected industrial heritage, *Industrial Patrimony* 2: 65–72

Wobst, M.H. 1990 Afterword: minitime and megaspace in the Palaeolithic at 18K and otherwise, in C.S. Gamble and O. Soffer (eds.), pp. 322–34.

Wolf, E.R. 1982 *Europe and the people without history*, Berkeley: University of California Press.

Wolpoff, M.H., Thorne, A.G., Smith, F.H., Frayer, D.W. and Pope, G.G. 1994 Multiregional evolution: a world-wide source for modern human populations, in M.H. Nitecki and D.V. Nitecki (eds.), pp. 175–99.

Wood, B. 1992 Origin and evolution of the genus *Homo, Nature* 355: 783–90.

Wood, B. and Collard, M. 1999 The human genus, *Science* 284: 65–71.

Wood, M. 2000 Making connections: relationships between international trade and glass beads from the Shashe–Limpopo area, *South African Archaeological Goodwin Society Series* 8: 78–90.

Woodburn, J. 1982 Egalitarian societies, *Man* 17: 431–51.

1988 African hunter-gatherer social organization: is it best understood as a product of encapsulation? in T. Ingold, D. Riches and J. Woodburn (eds.), *Hunters and gatherers*, vol. I, *History, evolution and social change*, Oxford: Berg, pp. 31–64.

Worden, N. 1985 *Slavery in Dutch South Africa*, Cambridge: Cambridge University Press.

Wright, J.B. 1971 *Bushman raiders of the Drakensberg 1840–1870*, Pietermaritzburg: University of Natal Press.

1995 Political transformations in the Thukela-Mzimkhulu region in the late eighteenth and early nineteenth centuries, in C. Hamilton (ed.), pp. 163–81.

Wurz, S. 1999 The Howiesons Poort backed artefacts from Klasies River: an argument for symbolic behaviour, *South African Archaeological Bulletin* 54: 38–50.

Wynn, T. 1991 Tools, grammar and the archaeology of cognition, *Cambridge Archaeological Journal* 1: 191–206.

Wynn, T. and McGrew, W.C. 1989 An ape's view of the Oldowan, *Man* 24: 383–98.

Yates, R., Golson, J. and Hall, M. 1985 Trance performance: the art of Boontjieskloof and Sevilla, *South African Archaeological Bulletin* 40: 70–80.

Yates, R. and Manhire, A.H. 1991 Shamanism and rock paintings: aspects of the use of rock art in the south-western Cape, South Africa, *South African Archaeological Bulletin* 46: 3–11.

Yates, R., Manhire, A.H. and Parkington, J.E. 1993 Colonial era paintings in the rock art of the south-western Cape: some preliminary observations, *South African Archaeological Society Goodwin Series* 7: 59–70.

1994 Rock painting and history in the south-western Cape, in T.A. Dowson and J.D. Lewis-Williams (eds.), pp. 29–60.

Yates, R. and Smith, A.B. 1993a Ideology and hunter/herder archaeology in the south-western Cape, *Southern African Field Archaeology* 2: 96–104.

1993b A reevaluation of the chronology of Oudepost: a reply in part to Schrire, *South African Archaeological Bulletin* 48: 52–3.

Yellen, J.E. 1977 *Archaeological approaches to the present*, New York: Academic Press.

1984 The integration of herding into prehistoric hunting and gathering economies, in M. Hall *et al.* (eds.), pp. 53–64.

1998 Barbed bone points: tradition and continuity in Saharan and sub-Saharan Africa, *African Archaeological Review* 15: 173–98.

Yellen, J.E. and Brooks, A.S. 1989 The Late Stone Age archaeology of the !Kangwa–/Xai/Xai valleys, Ngamiland, *Botswana Notes and Records* 20: 5–27.

Yellen, J.E., Brooks, A.S., Cornelissen, E., Mehlman, M.J. and Stewart, K. 1995 A Middle Stone Age worked bone industry from Katanda, Upper Semliki Valley, Zaire, *Science* 268: 553–6.

Yutar, D. 2000 Testimony of the spade reveals our slave history, *Cape Argus* 2 March: 11.

Zawada, P.K. 2000 Slackwater sediments and paleofloods, in T.C. Partridge and R.R. Maud (eds.), pp. 198–206.

Zvelebil, M. (ed.) 1986 *Hunters in transition: Mesolithic societies of Temperate Eurasia and the transition to farming*, Cambridge: Cambridge University Press.

Internet references cited in the text

http://www.africandream.org
http://www.geocities.com/athens/6398/thulamel.html
http://www.uct.ac.za/depts/age/
http://www.wits.ac.za/archaeology/acacia/acacia.htm

INDEX

Numbers in **bold** refer to illustrations.